# Old English and
# Middle English Poetry

# The Routledge History of English Poetry

General Editor

R. A. Foakes

*Professor of English,*
*The University of Kent at Canterbury*

The Routledge History of English Poetry

Volume 1

# Old English and Middle English Poetry

Derek Pearsall

*Centre for Medieval Studies*
*University of York*

Routledge & Kegan Paul
London, Henley and Boston

*First published in 1977*
*by Routledge & Kegan Paul Ltd*
*39 Store Street,*
*London WC1E 7DD,*
*Broadway House,*
*Newtown Road,*
*Henley-on-Thames,*
*Oxon RG9 1EN and*
*9 Park Street,*
*Boston, Mass. 02108, USA*
*Photosetting by Thomson Press (India) Limited*
*New Delhi*
*and printed in Great Britain by*
*Unwin Bros. Ltd*

*ISBN 0 7100 8396 3*

# Contents

# General editor's preface

The last major history of English poetry was that published in six volumes by W. J. Courthope between 1895 and 1910. In this century there have been some discoveries, some major shifts of critical opinion, and many revaluations of particular authors or periods. Twentieth-century poets have both added an exciting new chapter to the story and in doing so altered perspectives on the nineteenth and earlier centuries. In addition, there has been a massive growth in the publication of works of criticism and scholarship, many of which have helped to provide a better context for understanding what poets at various periods were trying to do, and for appreciating their achievement. Courthope's principal interest was in poetry as an aspect of intellectual history, as related to ideas, culture and political institutions. It is time for a fresh appraisal, and one of a rather different kind.

This new critical history of English poetry is planned to extend through six volumes, each written by a different author. Each author, a specialist in his period, has been encouraged to develop his own argument about the poetry he deals with, and to select his own historical emphases. The volumes will be uniform in appearance, but each will reflect in style, presentation, critical perspectives, and historical emphases, one person's viewpoint, and, no doubt, his own intellectual background; for, as is appropriate at a time when so much of the best criticism of English literature is being produced outside England, the authors are drawn from the USA and Canada, as well as Britain. The aim of the volumes is not to provide merely another account of the major figures, but to reassess the development of English poetry. The authors have been asked to take into account poetry that seemed important when it was published, and to set what now seems important in the context of the views held at the time it was written. The volumes are not necessarily separated in terms of a strict chronological division, and some poets may figure in different aspects in more than one of them, for a degree of overlapping has been encouraged where it seems appropriate.

Above all, each volume represents its author's personal testimony about a range of poets and poetry in the light of current knowledge, and taking into account, so far as this is helpful, current modes of criticism. In the present volume, which deals with English poetry from the earliest emergence of Anglo-Saxon alliterative verse to the decline of the medieval tradition in the fifteenth century, the author is chiefly concerned with poetry written before the introduction of printing into England in the 1470s. He is especially interested in reviving for the modern reader a sense of what it meant to know and transmit poetry through manuscript books and collections. An important feature of the book is the provision of two appendices, designed to supplement the main text and to be used in conjunction with it; one provides an explanation of technical terms, and the other sets out in a chronological table the dates of poets, major poems, and manuscripts in relation to the most important historical events of the period.

R. A. F.

# Introduction

The particular feature of this history of early English poetry is that it pays attention throughout to matters of provenance and audience, so as to provide as much information as possible on poetry as a social phenomenon as well as an artistic one. The questions that are asked, in addition to the more familiar questions of genre, form, style, literary descent and artistic value, are questions of function: what was poetry understood to be for? What were the circumstances in which it was produced? By whom and for whom was it written? Many of these questions are difficult to answer, especially in the early centuries, when essential information on authorship, audience and readership is apt to be lacking. There is in consequence inevitably a speculative element in some of the reconstruction of social circumstance attempted here for these early poems. One source of information, however, has been thought to be of particular value, and has been given consistent emphasis throughout (with an attempt at systematic presentation in Appendix 2), and that is the evidence provided by manuscript books as to the nature and function of the poetry they contain. To return poems from the antiseptic conditions of the modern critical edition to their original context in the manuscript books is to become aware of some significant differences in attitudes towards poetry, and perhaps goes some way also towards explaining and understanding those differences.

The assumption behind this approach is that the conditions out of which poetry grew and the functions it was assigned were an important part of its nature, and are to be understood historically, and that this historical understanding is as necessary to an informed appreciation of the poetry as is a proper reading of the language. Such, in fact, seems to be the only justification for a 'history' of early poetry. It is true that the work of an individual poet can sometimes defy and transcend the order of history, but the ways in which this happens are too complex to be grasped without the historical understanding that precedes a sensible and sensitive response.

Nevertheless, it is important to stress that this attention to social and historical circumstance, for which Appendix 2 provides further data, is only a mode of approach to the poetry, the essential nature and meaning of which is the final object of study. The preoccupation of a history of poetry, in this concern with its intrinsic nature, is the attempt to relate poems to the intellectual and formal

xi

traditions by which they are shaped and given their being. As to the former, it is assumed here that poetry, in any significant sense of the word, does not exist except in relation to intellectual traditions, to learning, to books, and to a sense of the past. If in some poems these traditions may be attenuated or decayed, then such poems are likely to be less interesting. It may be thought that these assumptions are merely dictated by circumstances, since what survives is likely, given the conditions of manuscript survival, to be 'bookish'; and it may be thought also that it is dangerous to neglect poetry not of literate and learned provenance in an age of predominantly oral culture. In a sense these criticisms are unanswerable, for one can only write a history of the poetry that exists in written copies. Nevertheless, the fragments of 'popular' poetry that survive from this oral culture give little cause to regret the nature of the historical circumstances by which we are constrained. The point may be made, and is frequently made in this study, that it is much more important to understand the international affiliations of English poetry during this period than to invoke native traditions. The intellectual environment is a European one and English poetry is unintelligible except in relation to Latin and French poetic tradition. Indeed, there is a long period after the Conquest when English poetry is so closely dependent upon and interconnected with the Latin and Anglo-Norman poetry being written in England that it can hardly be said to have an independent existence.

The exception to these remarks concerns the formal rather than the intellectual traditions of English poetry, for it is readily apparent that English poetry during this period is sustained and recurrently re-invigorated through the native traditions of alliterative verse. Although not an exclusively English phenomenon, alliterative verse as a form is independent of the dominant French and Latin traditions, and it can be regarded as the most powerful formal influence at work in the period. The Middle English period, however, is infiltrated by formal influences from French, Latin and other sources, preparing for the total exoticism of form in Chaucer. The co-existence or blending of different poetic forms, and indeed of completely independent principles of versification, creates some problems of description, especially on those occasions when a history of poetry finds itself forced to be a history of prose as well, and one of the painful discoveries of the historian of poetry is that there is no agreed technical language of poetic form, and in many cases no agreed principles of interpretation. This study attempts to be systematic in its interpretation but is nevertheless eclectic in its descriptive terminology, since the invention of a new language seemed impractical. The definitions of formal, especially metrical terms included in Appendix 1 will, it is hoped, make clear the consistency of usage.

It remains for me to thank my colleagues and students at the University of York, who have had the attitudes and ideas of this book tried out on them over a good many years, and whose criticism has helped to give them whatever validity they may have. I owe a particular debt to Professor Norman Blake of the University of Sheffield who read the whole book in typescript and made many valuable suggestions for correction and improvement. Professor Reg Foakes, the general editor of the present *History of English Poetry*, has also read the book, and kept a shrewd eye on its progress from the beginning.

# Abbreviations

| | |
|---|---|
| Add. | Additional (collection of MSS in B. M.) |
| AN | Anglo-Norman |
| *Archiv* | *Archiv für das Studium der neueren Sprachen und Literaturen* |
| *ASPR* | *The Anglo-Saxon Poetic Records*, 6 vols, ed. G. P. Krapp and E. V. K. Dobbie (New York, 1931–53) |
| *BJRL* | *Bulletin of the John Rylands Library* (Manchester) |
| B. M. | British Museum |
| c. | circa (about) |
| cap. | capitulum (chapter) |
| CFMA | Classiques français du Moyen Âge |
| *CL* | *Comparative Literature* |
| col. | column |
| *CT* | *Canterbury Tales* |
| C.U.L. | Cambridge University Library |
| *E & S* | *Essays and Studies by Members of the English Association* |
| *EC* | *Essays in Criticism* |
| EETS | Early English Text Society (OS, Original Series; ES, Extra Series; Supp., Supplementary Series) |
| *EHR* | *English Historical Review* |
| *ELH* | *English Literary History* |
| *EPS* | *English Philological Studies* |
| ex | explicit ('ends') |
| Fr. | French |
| Gk. | Greek |
| Gm. | German |
| in | incipit ('begins') |
| It. | Italian |
| *JEGP* | *Journal of English and Germanic Philology* |
| Lat. | Latin |
| m. | metrum (in Boethius) |
| *MÆ* | *Medium Ævum* |
| MLA | Modern Language Association of America |

| | |
|---|---|
| *MLN* | *Modern Language Notes* |
| *MLQ* | *Modern Language Quarterly* |
| *MLR* | *Modern Language Review* |
| *MP* | *Modern Philology* |
| *MS* | *Mediaeval Studies* |
| MS | manuscript |
| *Neoph.* | *Neophilologus* |
| *NM* | *Neuphilologische Mitteilungen* |
| *NQ* | *Notes and Queries* |
| n.s. | new series |
| NWM | North-West Midlands |
| OE | Old English |
| OF | Old French |
| *Pat. Lat.* | *Patrologia Latina* |
| *PBA* | *Proceedings of the British Academy* |
| *PMLA* | *Publications of the Modern Language Association of America* |
| *PQ* | *Philological Quarterly* |
| *RES* | *Review of English Studies* |
| s.a. | sub anno ('under the year ...') |
| SATF | Société des Anciens Textes Français |
| SC | Summary Catalogue of Western Manuscripts in the Bodleian Library at Oxford, ed. F. Madan, etc. |
| *SP* | *Studies in Philology* |
| STS | Scottish Text Society |
| s.v. | sub verbo ('under the word ...') |
| *TPS* | *Transactions of the Philological Society* |
| *TRHS* | *Transactions of the Royal Historical Society* |
| U.P. | University Press |
| *UTQ* | *University of Toronto Quarterly* |
| *YES* | *Yearbook of English Studies* |

N. B.  In bibliographical detail of published books, London is omitted when it is the place of publication.

# 1 *Beowulf* and the Anglo-Saxon poetic tradition

A history of English poetry might begin with Tacitus, and his report of the traditional hymns sung by the tribes of Germania in the first century AD;[1] or it might begin with the landing of St Augustine in Kent in 597 and the Christian mission to the Anglo-Saxons. Tacitus would serve to remind us that the sources of a nation's poetry are to be found in the deepest recesses of its history; that the Anglo-Saxons brought with them from the continent, and held in common with other Germanic peoples, certain materials, notably heroic legends, and certain habits of verse-making, hymnic, encomiastic and mnemonic, which lie obscure yet potent behind some of the extant written remains; that they brought with them, above all, a form of verse, the alliterative four-stress line, also part of a common Germanic heritage, which held universal sway throughout the Anglo-Saxon period, survived vigorously in various metamorphoses thereafter, and which can lay claim to being the dominant pattern in English versification, fairly ingrained in the language, the secret power and anvil of the pentameter. English verse, on this reading, would go back to the earliest recorded Germanic alliterative line, the runic inscription on the horn of Gallehus, dug up in 1734 on the German-Danish border, and dated about 400 AD:

> Ek Hlewagastir Holtijar    horna tawido.[2]
>
> (I, Hlewagastir a Holting, made this horn.)

What scraps and fantasies these may seem, though, when set beside the consequence of the Gregorian mission, the integration of Anglo-Saxon England into the world of Latin Christendom. For if by poetry we mean extant poetic literature, *litterae*, letters, and not unrecorded oral verse-making, then England has no poetry but that of the Christian tradition—'In England there has never been any literacy other than Christian literacy'[3]—and the Germanic heritage, when it emerges in Anglo-Saxon poetry, emerges re-shaped, absorbed, chastened, in a form quite distinct from survivals elsewhere of the pagan, heroic, Germanic past. There is no pagan mythology in Anglo-Saxon poetry as there is in the *Elder Edda*, no weird cosmogony such as we find in the *Volospá*, nothing alien or unfamiliar: the way back is smoothed by the common inheritance of Latin

1

Christianity, even to Grendel and his descent from Cain. Beowulf is understandable in a way that Grettir—or Achilles, or Cuchulain—is not.[4] From this point of view, English poetry begins with Caedmon's *Hymn of Creation*, composed, according to Bede, during the abbacy of Hild at Whitby (657–80), and copied, in the Northumbrian dialect, into the earliest manuscript of the Latin *Ecclesiastical History* (737).[5]

The interpretation of Old English poetry might sway for ever between these two poles. In the past the poetry has been ransacked, especially by German scholars, for Germanic remains: poems have been fragmented and broken open to reveal the essential pagan kernel, and the links sought have been with history, archaeology and Old Norse analogues. Even Klaeber, in his monumental edition of *Beowulf*, speaks of the 'Christian coloring' of the poem, as if it were something that could be washed out again in an easy operation. The present mood is to stress the position of Anglo-Saxon poetry as 'part of the literature of Western Christendom and not as part of the common Germanic literary heritage marred in preservation.'[6] The very existence of the poetry is due to the Church, for of the 30,000 lines remaining (it is less than the output of a single poet like Chaucer) the great bulk, apart from specialised productions like the verse translations of the Psalter and of the *Metra* of Boethius, is extant in four codices, all of them the product of the monastic revival of the late tenth century: MS Junius XI in the Bodleian (the 'Caedmon manuscript'), containing the 'scriptural' poems, *Genesis*, *Exodus*, *Daniel*, and *Christ and Satan*; MS Cotton Vitellius A XV in the British Museum, containing *Beowulf* and *Judith*, with some vernacular prose; the Vercelli MS, still in the cathedral library of Vercelli in northern Italy, where it was deposited by some early eleventh-century traveller to Rome,[7] and containing homiletic, devotional and hagiographical writing in prose and verse, including *Andreas*, *The Fates of the Apostles*, *The Dream of the Rood* and *Elene*; and the Exeter Book, donated to Exeter cathedral library, where it remains, before 1072, and containing a rich miscellany of verse, including *Christ*, *Guthlac*, *Juliana*, *The Phoenix*, *Widsith*, *Deor*, the 'elegies', and the riddles. All of these books survive by singular chance, two of them probably because they had pictures, and none of them is likely to have been much read.[8] With such a comparatively small corpus of poetry surviving, and with so few poets known by name (apart from Caedmon, only Cynewulf, of whom we know nothing more than his name, spelt out in runic 'signatures' to four poems), it is not surprising that Old English poetry may appear comparatively unimportant beside the central Latin tradition of Bede, Aldhelm, Alcuin,[9] or beside the tradition of vernacular prose, of Alfred, Ælfric and Wulfstan, in which far more of the intellectual impetus of the Anglo-Saxon is engaged. Against this it might be said that the circumstances of preservation are not the circumstances of composition (*Beowulf* was copied into a book which seems to have catered for an interest in monsters,[10] but this is not why the poem was written); that intellectual history is not the history of poetry; and that for Anglo-Saxon poetry to become a series of addenda to the *Patrologia Latina* would be as sad a distortion as for it to be treated on a level with runic scrapings.

*Germanic traditions*

Evidence of the Germanic inheritance is unquestionably present in the extant poetry, in a whole range of allusion in *Widsith, Deor*, and *Beowulf* to the legends of the *Völkerwanderung*, the great tribal migrations of the fourth to the sixth centuries, and to early Germanic history. Figures like Sigemund, Heremod, Ingeld, Eormenric, Weland, appear, their 'history' hammered out into authentic heroic shapes of loyalty and revenge, in allusions so cryptic and casual that they argue the presence of a body of well-known heroic 'lays' behind the extant remains. These lays would have been short recitations, celebrating a hero, or some exploit in which heroic values were crucially tested, and would have been sung to the harp by the minstrel, or *scop*, in the mead-hall before the king and his warriors. The classic model would be the fight to the death in a narrow place, and the classic literary allusion in Old English poetry is in *Beowulf*, where the lay of Finnesburh is sung at the feast following Beowulf's victory over Grendel:

> Þær wæs sang ond sweg    samod ætgædere
> fore Healfdenes    hildewisan,
> gomenwudu greted,    gid oft wrecen,
> ðonne healgamen    Hroþgares scop
> æfter medobence    mænan scolde,
> be Finnes eaferum.... [11]

(There was both song and music together before Healfdene's battle-leader, the harp plucked, many a lay recited, when Hrothgar's *scop* was to regale the mead-benches with the story of Finn's retainers.)

It is likely that such an allusion represents, in idealised and elevated form, the actual practice at Anglo-Saxon courts during the sixth to eighth centuries: the society, even long after the conversion, was essentially a warrior-society, heroically violent, such as would nurture heroic lays. The history of the times is full of kings, such as Edwin of Northumbria or Cædwalla of Wessex, whose lives and actions seem an epitome of the heroic warrior-ethic, and full of themes and motives, often explicitly recognised, which reflect those prevalent in heroic poetry—loyalty to the death, blood revenge, treachery and exile.[12] The laws of Anglo-Saxon England record the painful progress towards containment of this violence, the substitution of *wergild* ('payment for a man', i.e. payment of legal compensation for injury or death), for instance, for the blood-feud. It is possible that heroic episodes in historical narrative, such as that of Cynewulf and Cyneheard in the *Anglo-Saxon Chronicle* (s.a. 755), may be adapted from lays celebrating contemporary events.[13]

This is all hypothesis, of course, and has to be: the literary culture was that established by Latin Christianity, which means that heroic lays had little chance of being written down in their 'pure' form, and even less of being preserved. Literacy, education, books, libraries, were the exclusive preserve of the Church, and above all of monasteries, and only those aspects of heroic tradition which could be construed in some way as consonant with Christian teaching were likely to survive in written form. Such a construction might be easier to make in the tenth century, where two battle-poems, *Brunanburh* and *Maldon*, full of heroic gesture, embody a concept of the theocratic nation-state embattled against a heathen enemy, but the resistance of earlier monastic tradition to poems about contemporary events seems to have been extraordinarily rigorous; a poem like *Beowulf* has an almost antiquarian air, as if the materials must be remote before they can be 'safe'. It should be stressed that this is a peculiarly English phenomenon: literacy as it was introduced into Ireland and Iceland was equally a Christian literacy, yet in both countries a substantial pagan and heroic literature, in both prose and verse, survives. Various explanations of this difference might be offered. One concerns the depth and tenacity of the native secular culture, and another the circumstances under which Christianity, and literacy, were introduced. The Icelanders received Christianity in AD 1000, only a hundred years after colonisation, but they had already established a settled community, a national identity, and a saga-culture, which conversion, accepted with a respectful pragmatism, barely disturbed,[14] though the new literacy did make it possible for the sagas and the Eddic poetry to be written down. In Ireland a much longer-established pagan culture had its own secular learning, represented by the *filid*, a close corporation of official savants and *litterateurs*, with schools, an elaborate system of training, a cryptic language, great prestige, and an established responsibility to preserve and pass on, orally, the national inheritance of saga and history, and to compose panegyric, satire and lament.[15] The Patrician conversion of the fifth century struck deep root, but in independent monastic communities, largely isolated from the secular state, rather than in an organised pastoral system. As a result, secular literature, when it began to assume written form in the early seventh century, underwent Latinist influence, as in metrics, but remained secular in subject-matter. In England, by contrast, the Anglo-Saxons, though not newcomers, were only recently settled in recognisable communities. The first settlements were made soon after 449, but there was a good deal of re-migration to the continent after the battle of Mons Badonicus (c. 500), and a British army was fighting near Dunstable, at the battle of Bedcan Ford, as late as 571. We know little of the social and economic history of the period, but for a long time the Anglo-Saxons must have been like squatters among the ruins of an imperial civilisation;[16] whatever secular culture may have had a chance to develop was easily overwhelmed and absorbed by Latin Christianity. Gregory's timing was perfect, and his organisation thorough—for this was a Roman conversion, directed from Rome with Roman resources and efficiency, an episcopal annexation in a country already Romanised and among peoples already in contact with Christianity through the British Church and through Frankish influence.[17] When there was a temporary setback, as with the reversion of Northumbria to paganism after the mission of Paulinus in 627, the Irish monks in Iona were waiting to attack from the rear. Anglo-Saxon paganism hardly had a chance. Within 60 years of Augustine's arrival, the last heathen king of the Anglo-Saxons, Penda of Mercia, had been killed in battle and the flowering of Northumbrian culture was begun.

4

*The 'heroic' poems*

The important conclusion of all this for the history of poetry is that writing was entirely in the hands of clerics: what they would record of pagan heroic tradition would be what their creed sanctioned or what appealed to them in some way. *Widsith* and *Deor*, both in the Exeter Book, are examples. In *Widsith*, the poet is an imaginary *scop*, the 'far-wanderer', who speaks at length of his journeyings among the Germanic—and other—peoples: the journeyings are, of course, a metaphor for the world of heroic song.[18] The poem consists largely of lists of tribes and kings: two of these lists are of great antiquity, while another, which mentions people like the Israelites and the Assyrians, looks like an inept and bookish addition. The poem contains embedded some of the oldest lines of poetry, in the form of mnemonics, in the English language; it was presumably worked up and preserved because of its encyclopaedic interest—monks could never resist a good catalogue. The other poem, *Deor*, is also spoken in the first person, by the *scop* of that name, who laments his supplantation at the court of the Heodeningas by a rival minstrel, but consoles himself that his time of adversity may soon pass—

Þæs ofereode,  þisses swa mæg

(That passed away, so may this)—

as it did for others: he gives five instances from heroic legend, followed by a vaguely Christianised consolation—all things are mutable, so things may take a turn for the better. The poem is cryptic and has been variously interpreted, but seems to owe its survival partly to its allusions, which would have attracted the monastic compiler and persuaded him to ensure the poem's respectability by incorporating an apparently Christian reference—a strangely incongruous one, too, since improvement in worldly fortune can never be the theme of Christian consolation.

Of the other remains of 'heroic' poetry, *Waldere* would be important if it survived in any fuller form than the two extant fragments, discovered by chance in 1860 among some loose papers in the Royal Library at Copenhagen. The fragments refer to an episode in the story of Walter of Aquitaine where he defends his mountain retreat in the Vosges against the Burgundian Gunther; they consist almost entirely of speeches. The leisurely treatment suggests a literary epic constructed on a generous scale, and the blending of heroic and Christian attitudes is similarly reminiscent of *Beowulf*. The fragments, which, like most Anglo-Saxon poetry, are a late tenth-century copy of a presumably eighth-century original, are most interesting as evidence that *Beowulf* is not an oddity. The 48-line fragment of *The Battle of Finnesburh* is, by contrast, of supreme and unique importance, for it is an indubitable example of what we have been denying the possibility of in Anglo-Saxon poetry, the 'pure' heroic lay, untouched by Christianity or indeed by any humane or civilising impulse whatever. The circumstances of its survival are more than usually fortuitous: it was published

5

by George Hickes in 1705 from his transcription of a leaf which he said he found in a Lambeth collection of late Old English homilies. The leaf has never come to light, and all evidence of the poem's provenance and date is lost. If we had more of it, we might have to revise our notion of 'Christian literacy', but as it stands it is hard even to be certain that it is authentic survival and not brilliant pastiche. The choice of subject—the defence of the hall by a small band of warriors—is almost suspiciously predictable, and there are touches of imagery which suggest leisured composition:

>                              Swurdleoma stod,
> Swylce eal Finnsburuh    fyrenu wære.[19]

(There was gleaming of swords, as if all Finnesburh were in flames.)

But the obscurity and abruptness of the narrative movement (it is impossible to understand what is going on except by reference to the larger context of the Finn episode in *Beowulf*) is authentic to the heroic lay, as is the total lack of moral commentary. One would judge the poem to be a genuine survival, somewhat polished in the record, and preserved (at who knows what spiritual cost) by a monk of antiquarian tastes. It is a document of great historical importance, comparable with the Old High German *Hildebrandslied* and the Eddic poems, recording the certain presence of Germanic heroic lays among the Anglo-Saxons, and recording too, perhaps, a 'primitive' stage in the development of Anglo-Saxon verse technique. In contrast to the developed 'classical' style in which nearly all Anglo-Saxon poetry is written, there is here very little enjambement or syntactical 'variation'[20] (the name given to a form of appositional construction elaborately employed in the classical style): the lines are mostly end-stopped, the syntax direct and simple, characterised by repetition of form and the use of *ða* as connective:

> Ða aras mænig goldhladen ðegn,    gyrde hine his swurde.
> Ða to dura eodon    drihtlice cempan,
> Sigeferð and Eaha,    hyra sword getugon.
> and æt oþrum durum    Ordlaf and Guþlaf,
> and Hengest sylf    hwearf him on laste.                    (13–17)

(Then rose up many a gold-decked thane, belted on his sword.
Then to the door went the noble warriors, Sigeferth and Eaha, drew their swords, and at the other door Ordlaf and Guthlaf, and Hengest himself came behind them.)

This end-stopped line and simple syntax may be presumed to be characteristic of early Germanic verse-form: as features of style they appear also in primitive remnants embedded elsewhere in the catalogues of *Widsith*, in royal genealogies,[21] in the metrical charms and gnomic poems.[22] *Deor*, with its vestigial strophic form and refrain, may bear marks of a similarly ancient ancestry. It should be stressed, however, that the presence in these poems of 'primitive' features does not mean that the poems themselves are necessarily of early date. It will be argued later (p. 74 below) that such features persist throughout the 'classical' period of Old English poetry and reappear in strength with the decline of the classical *ars poetica*.

Beowulf: *heroic and Christian traditions*

To move from the *Battle of Finnesburh* to the Finn episode in *Beowulf*, and from there to the larger context of the poem as a whole, is to become aware not only of a more sophisticated poetic medium but of a wholly different poetic world. *Finnesburh* glories in battle, and is content to see the crisis of existence in the here and now of violent action; its heroes neither think nor feel, only make ready, fight and die. In the Finn episode—and it is supposed to be a celebratory recitation at a pagan court—the emphasis is on character and sentiment: there is very little of battle, but much of its consequence—grief, suffering, loss and exile, an infinite sadness. It is so throughout the poem; action is related to a larger and more meaningful world, it has, in Auerbach's phrase, more 'pendulation';[23] the crisis has been shifted from action to cause, will, intention, to concepts of good and evil both more crude and more subtle than any provided by the heroic ethic. *Finnesburh*, like the horrors of the *Volundarkviða* or the *Atlakviða*, is essentially incomprehensible, but Beowulf, though nominally a pagan, inhabits our world, and we have to remind ourselves to be surprised when he attributes the dragon's ravaging his country to some moral defect in himself (2330), or scans his life for cause of blame as he dies (2730), or when the poet concludes his praise of the dead hero in these, the last words of the poem:

Swa begnornodon     Geata leode
hlafordes hryre,     heorðgeneatas;
cwædon þæt he wære     wyruldcyninga
manna mildust     ond monðwærust,
leodum liðost     ond lofgeornost.

(So the men of the Geats, his personal retainers, mourned their lord's
death; they said that he was, of all the world's kings, the mildest of men
and the gentlest, the most generous to his people and the most eager
for fame.)

A radical change has taken place in the function of heroism. In the *Battle of Finnesburh* there is no sense that Hengest and his Danes are more 'right' than Finn and his Frisians, though the Danes may have the audience's sympathy; both sides are equally part of the heroic order. Beowulf, however, undertakes a cleansing of society, and fights against monsters—Grendel, Grendel's dam, and the dragon—not against men; and in Grendel's case with forces hostile to God (he is *Godes andsaca*, 'God's enemy'), the evil progeny of Cain. Faced with the moral intractability or complexity or even total moral inconsequence of much heroic action, the poet has chosen a subject in which the moral issues are clearly polarised. The poem, in fact, is on the edge of allegory, as any poem might be which portrayed its hero setting out for his last battle *twelfa sum*, 'one of twelve' (2401). In this it offends the purists, for whom it violates every canon of the heroic ethic: 'Bards avoid ... not merely moralising comments and descriptions of things and places for description's sake, but anything that smacks of ulterior or symbolical intentions'.[24] Ker's censure of the poem for placing its genuinely heroic historical material at the edges, in the allusions, and a simple folk-tale at the centre is based on a sense of its betrayal of the heroic ethic.[25] And likewise the poem's 'ulterior intentions' make it easy prey for the pan-allegorists, since it is not difficult to find fairly full patristic backing for the moral platitudes which lie at the heart of the poem,[26] which are indeed exposed in Hrothgar's sermon, nor to find theoretical justification for the procedure: 'The poetic art gives moral or natural teaching by means of imaginary fictions and allegorical analogies in order to exercise the human spirit: this is the proper function of heroic poets who praise figuratively the deeds and customs of heroes'.[27]

The poem deserves to be rescued from such over-simplifications: its glory is to be impure. It is certainly, in its existing form, the work of a Christian poet: the prevailing moral vision, habits of thought, attitudes, everything down to casual and unthought linguistic usages[28] (*Godes leoht geceas*, 'chose God's light', 2469, for the death of a pagan), all bespeak a mind that has no other way to think significantly about men and their actions. Yet there is no evangelising, and no mention of Christ. It is nonsense to argue that this suggests an imperfect understanding of Christianity, or an early stage of conversion; the Gospels are simply not relevant to the poem's subject. No doubt the poet could have dragged them in if he had been trying to preach, but his attempt, clearly, is to write a poem about the admirableness of Beowulf, not about the admirableness of the Christian religion. As a Christian, the poet is rarely embarrassed in this attempt, since the qualities he approves in his hero—bravery, generosity, loyalty, fortitude, wisdom—are Christian virtues, and since he does not display his hero in situations where he would need to call on other heroic qualities such as ruthlessness and cunning, less compatible with Christian values.

Yet he is sometimes embarrassed, and for this reason one might doubt that there is a systematic contrast, in the central story of Beowulf and the more authentically heroic world of the allusions, 'between noble, disinterested deeds for the good of the human race and actions of violence and passion, arising from divided loyalties, or, worse still, from ambition and treachery'.[29] The embarrassment, the impurity, is present in the last lines of the poem, already quoted, and it is present in the whole poem. The poet has not 'invented' the monster-slayings as a vehicle for a symbolic contest of good and evil: he has chosen them as his central story because they make most sense to him in terms of what he admires. As events they are as historical and real as any other events alluded to in the poem—it is indeed one function of the allusions to give them a fully historical context—and if we baulk at this, it is worth recalling that 'fiery dragons were seen flying in the air' in Northumbria in 793, according to the *Anglo-Saxon Chronicle*; and that a division of the poem into 'historical' and 'fabulous' elements is a modern one, based on a simplified assumption about 'what people really believe'—one that we can hardly make even about the materials of our own experience, in a sceptical and empirical age. It follows from this that the monster-slayings, being authentic to Germanic tradition, occasionally carry with them an intractable *sens*, and present the poet who uses them with some confusing moral issues. Grendel is clearly evil, his mother slightly less so; but the real problem is the dragon. The dragon is the guardian of the treasure, and the cause of his depredations in Geatland is the disturbance of the treasure; it seems to be in the nature of things that he should act in this way, just as it seems appropriate that Beowulf should determine on a single combat to save his people. The intrusive element is Beowulf's desire to gain the treasure:

>                       Ic mid elne sceall
> gold gegangan,     oððe guð nimeð,
> feorhbealu frecne     frean eowerne.                    (2535–7)

(I will win the gold by my valour, or else the fearful peril of battle will carry off your lord.)

This seems irrelevant both as a motive and in its consequence, since the treasure is all either burnt with the body or left in the ground. The motif of gold-lust is repeated again and again, coming to a singular climax in Beowulf's dying speech of thanks to God that he has been able to see the treasure-hoard and win it for his people:

> Nu ic on maðma hord     mine bebohte
> frode feorhlege. . . .                                 (2799–800)

(Now I have sold my old life for a hoard of treasure.)

He seems to have forgotten the whole point of the fight against the dragon (2312 ff). It could be argued that the poet intends some criticism of Beowulf for seeking the treasure, that it is this hitherto hidden flaw of avarice which brings about his downfall: if so, the introduction of the motive is belated, inconsistent and inept. Or it could be argued that the dragon which guards the treasure 'stands for' (*id est*, in the language of exegesis) the evil which is always waiting to be released and activated by men's desire for worldly wealth—and away goes the poem in a puff of allegory. Such a dehistoricising process is quite at odds with the poem, which persistently refuses allegorisation, and is shaped to resist it through its allusions. The explanation of Beowulf's desire for treasure must recognise that it is geologically intrusive in the poem's structure: the story of the accursed dragon-guarded treasure carries with it motifs and associations too powerful to be suppressed, and one of them is the unquestioned assumption that it is the hero's proper function to desire to win the treasure. No blame attaches to him for this, and the *Beowulf*-poet is never crass enough to suggest any, but his mode of treating his hero has created in us expectations as to the nature of his heroism which are offended by the exercise of this obsolete function. We may be over-sensitive.

There are other impurities in the poem, other collisions between the traditional materials and the poet's interpretation of them. One of them concerns the function of *Wyrd*. The poet is reluctant to abandon altogether the gloomily poetic notion of pagan doom, yet he knows that it makes no sense under the Christian dispensation, and so he wavers uneasily between the two: God (or Fate) will protect the warrior if he is brave (in a good cause, presumably) and undoomed—and if his armour holds.[30] The most notorious inconsistency, however, is the passage in which the poet reminds us that the Danes were pagans, and made sacrifice in heathen fanes to rid Heorot of Grendel—

> Swylc wæs þeaw hyra,
> hæþenra hyht; helle gemundon
> in modsefan, Metod hie ne cuþon.... (178–80)

(Such was their custom, their hope as heathens; they had mind of hell in their hearts, they knew not the Lord.)

less than a hundred lines after describing the Song of Creation sung by the *scop* in Heorot (89–98). It has sometimes been suggested that the poet is alluding to recent or even contemporary events in England, where apostasy and relapse into heathendom were common in times of peril,[31] and there is some support in the poem for this interpretation:

> Wa bið þæm ðe sceal
> þurh sliðne nið sawle bescufan
> in fyres fæþm, frofre ne wenan,
> wihte gewendan.... (183–6)

(It is a sad fate for him who must consign his soul in dire affliction to the fire's embrace, and can look for no comfort nor any kind of change.)

Yet what he describes among the Danes is a condition not a relapse. Perhaps it is sufficient to say that the poet knows, as a matter of fact, that the society he describes is a pagan one, just as Chaucer knew that the Troy of *Troilus and Criseyde* and the Athens of *The Knight's Tale* were pagan, and is obliged to remind us explicitly, at least once, of this fact; but for the rest he has to entrench a Christian or quasi-Christian frame of mind in those whom he admires, particularly Beowulf and Hrothgar, in order to make them admirable or even intelligible. Fortunately a noble pagan monotheism has much in common with Christianity, and the distinction, once observed, can be forgotten.

The poet's generous interpretation of what he admits to be a pagan society is chiefly motivated by his unconcealed admiration for the heroic age: he portrays it as a quasi-Christian society because he wants to, and needs to. Our sense of incongruity is perhaps partly misplaced, and the consequence of a later hardening of attitudes. Certainly the Roman Church took a hard line on the damnation of the heathen after the suppression of Pelagianism, but the Irish Church, which exerted a profound influence on English Christianity, especially in the north in the seventh to eighth centuries, retained a deep respect for its pre-Christian past, and this may have offered poets a licence in their interpretation of the Germanic past.[32] It is noticeable, too, that Bede reserves his fiercest condemnation for apostates and heretics, and not for pagans; for him the British Church is the real enemy of the true faith, and he lavishes fulsome praise on the pagan Ethelfrid, King of Northumbria, 'a very brave King, and most eager of glory', for his slaughter of the British, including the monks of Bangor, at Chester in 603.[33] Pagans, in a sense, have a special claim on the sympathy and admiration of Christians, and, for a poet writing in the eighth-century, the idea of the noble pagan must have been powerfully renewed by contacts with Germanic heathendom during the Anglo-Saxon missions to Germany: a letter from Boniface to Ethelbald of Mercia in 746/7 reproaches him for his loose life, holding up the pagan Germans as an example of virtue.[34] It is quite possible, too, that the detailed knowledge of and interest in heathen customs such as obsequies (Scyld's ship-burial and Beowulf's funeral pyre) is partly attributable to continental contacts,[35] though the discovery of the Sutton Hoo ship-burial (c. 625) has made it clear that the poet would not need to go very far back in the history of his own people for similar evidences. There is material to suggest that the world of *Beowulf*, in so far as it can be archaeologically attested—weapons, armour, ornaments, buildings—is rooted in the not-far-distant past.[36] The poem comes out of a Christian world, therefore, but one which has grown out of a long contact and coexistence with a pagan world,[37] and in which the frontiers are still capable of being blurred. We might cut a simple swathe through the undergrowth of the preceding paragraphs by saying that the homiletic and scriptural poems are 'Christian' in a way that *Beowulf* is not, while *Beowulf* is 'Christian' in a way the Eddic poems are not.[38]

Beowulf: *methods, style and form*

The poet's admiration for the heroic world, whether it is touched by nostalgia or not, is undoubted. He is moved by its ethic, and impressed by its ceremonies: some of the noblest passages in the poem report the grandeur of those ceremonies—the obsequies of Scyld and Beowulf, Beowulf's arrival in Denmark and his reception at Hrothgar's court, the feast of celebration after the defeat of Grendel. In its construction and expression the poem seeks a grandeur which

11

will match the world it describes—formal, artificial, ceremonial, and elaborately decorated. The basic narrative is very simple—three successive fights, each more dangerous than the last—but the method of narration is very elaborate. The poem is constructed as a series of set pieces—for instance descriptions and formal speeches—which embody and suggest the story rather than tell it, so that the effect is one of monumental 'composition' rather than linear narration,[39] with every form of narrative movement, even the sea-voyage (210–24), slowed to a stately ceremony. Through and around these set pieces is woven a network of allusion, offering, behind the main scenes, a rich perspective of antiquity. The narrative is continually interrupted by digressions, prophecies, anticipations, parenthetic comment, backward and forward reference, so that we often know of effects before causes, of the consequences of events before the events themselves. Within the allusions an equally complex mode of exposition is used: we have to reconstruct Hygelac's Frankish raid out of four separate, fragmentary and non-chronological references, and similarly with the Geatish wars against the Swedes, which provide the ominous historical background to Beowulf's death-fight. Klaeber explained this 'lack of a steady flow in the narrative' as one of the 'reminders of a primitive or, perhaps, "natural" method of expression, suggesting the manner of conversational talk or of recitation before a crowd of listeners.'[40] This is a strange view, of the poem as well as of the nature of recitation (Statius, it might be remembered, wrote the *Thebaid* for public recitation), and a poor reward for the poet's deliberate skill in *ordo artificialis*, which he cultivates, from hints in the lays but at least partly under the influence of Latin poetic, as an aspect of the grand style.

Any suggestion of the 'primitive' would be similarly out of place in a discussion of the poem's style, which, like that of nearly all Anglo-Saxon poetry, is heavily ornamented, self-consciously 'poetic', manneristic, inflexible, a provincial epitome of Silver Age poetic. Two features may be selected for special emphasis, compounding and variation, since they dominate one's impression of the style of the poetry, and also seem to have been consciously recognised by Anglo-Saxon poets, in their rare comments on poetic expression, as professional devices. Compounding is the basis of the elaborate poetic diction of Anglo-Saxon poetry: the image that poets use is of 'unlocking the word-hoard',[41] and a poet's skill is measured by the richness of his coinage. Hence the endless synonymy, especially with referents frequently needed, such as warrior, battle, sword, sea, ship. Often it is a mechanical procedure, dominated by the exigencies of alliteration, and it is a gross indecorum in modern criticism to detect ironies in synonyms for the Danes like *Sige-Scyldinga* ('victory-Danes'), *Gar-Denum* ('spear-Danes'), in a speech by Beowulf commenting on the failure of the Danes to cope with Grendel (597–601). With many of the compounds, therefore, especially those based on commonplace elements like *guð*, 'war', and *þegn*, 'thane', the effect is one of copiousness rather than richness. But there is a form of compound called the kenning (a term derived from Icelandic poetic, which should strictly be reserved for compounds where one element is metaphorical),[42] where the imaginative potential is greater. Expressions like *yða ful*, 'the cup of the waves', and *hron-rad*, 'whale-road', for the sea, and *woruld-candel*, 'world-candle', for the sun,[43] have an undeniable poetic effectiveness in the way they shift the angle of perception. But the nature of the imagination at work needs defining, for it is not a romantic imagination, as is often assumed by those who seek, for instance, nature-feeling in Anglo-Saxon poetry: the kennings quoted above, though they refer to nature, are neither concrete nor evocative. Their function is not to create an imaginative correlative, but to identify a point of intersection where two referents meet and create a third. There is nothing in Old English poetry quite as extravagant as the skaldic kennings of Icelandic poetry—such as *hverlögr Óðins*, 'Odin's kettle-liquor', for poetry, or *Amlóða kvern*, 'Hamlet's handmill', for the sea,[44] where each term needs tracing back through three or four displacements to recognise the significance of the intersection—but the underlying poetic is clearly similar. It is the notion of poetry as a form of advanced enigma, a cultivation of obscure, extravagant and ostentatiously poetic language. This concept of style is dominant in late Latin poetic and in the medieval academic rhetoric which was largely derived from it, and is represented in extreme form during the Anglo-Saxon period in the Irish-Latin *Hisperica Famina*.[45] This production, which seems an outgrowth of the influence of late Latin grammars and rhetorics on Irish scholars, is a rhetorical text-book, using a variety of pedagogic situations, including colloquy, as poetic 'occasions' to display and teach a hermetic style of fantastic extravagance and desperate obscurity. In various modified forms, the 'Hisperican' style had a good deal of vogue with Anglo-Latin writers in both verse and prose, especially Aldhelm, and, partly through him, even in such documents as charters.[46] It would be very surprising if there were no contact at all between Anglo-Latin and vernacular writers and they clearly share a taste for other forms of poetry as enigma: Cynewulf's runic signatures reflect Boniface's interest in cryptograms,[47] and the Anglo-Saxon riddles are a counterpart, indeed sometimes a translation, of the Latin *ænigmata* of Aldhelm and others.

The other dominant technique of Anglo-Saxon poetry, variation, is presumably what the *Beowulf*-poet refers to when he describes the poetic method of the 'cyninges þegn' who celebrates Beowulf's victory in song on the journey back from Grendel's mere:

> word oþer fand
> soðe gebunden;    secg eft ongan
> sið Beowulfes    snyttrum styrian,
> ond on sped wrecan    spel gerade,
> wordum wrixlan....    (870–4)

(He sought out other words, properly linked together [i.e. with alliteration]; then the man proceeded to frame a skilful narrative of Beowulf's exploit, reciting the story in an expert manner, varying the words.)

*Word oþer fand* and *wordum wrixlan* could well describe the practice of constructing

13

elaborate sentences by interlacing variations on the components of simple ones,
for example:

> Ða wæs gylden hilt  gamelum rince,
> harum hildfruman  on hand gyfen,
> enta ærgeweorc;  hit on æht gehwearf
> æfter deofla hryre  Denigea frean,
> wundorsmiþa geweorc....         (1677–81)

(Then was the golden hilt, the ancient work of giants, handed to the
aged warrior, the grey-haired war-chief; it passed, the work of
marvellously skilful smiths, into the possession of the lord of the Danes,
after the death of the devils.)

The skeleton of this sentence is in the first, second, fourth and seventh half-lines.
Characteristic forms of variation are displayed in these lines,

> Swylce oft bemearn  ærran mælum
> swiðferhþes sið  snotor ceorl monig,
> se þe him bealwa to  bote gelyfde,
> þæt þæt ðeodnes bearn  geþeon scolde,
> fæderæþelum onfon,  folc gehealdan,
> hord ond hleoburh,  hæleþa rice,
> eþel Scyldinga.         (907–13)

(So in earlier times many a wise man had lamented the brave man's
journey [into exile], for they had thought of him as a remedy for all
their afflictions, that he would prosper as a prince, inherit his father's
qualities, rule over the people, the treasure and stronghold, the
warrior-kingdom, land of the Scyldings.)

where variation tails out the sentence to a dying period; or in these,

>     No þæt læsest wæs
> hondgemota,  þær mon Hygelac sloh,
> syððan Geata cyning  guðe ræsum,
> freawine folca  Freslondum on,
> Hreðles eafora  hiorodryncum swealt,
> bille gebeaten.         (2354–9)

(Nor was that the least of battles, where Hygelac was slain, when the
king of the Geats, beloved lord of his people, son of Hrethel, died 'by
sword-drinks' in Friesland in the thick of the fight, hacked down by
swords.)

where the bones of the sentence are first exposed and then fleshed out with variation. Many closer kinds of analysis can be made, but the technique is familiar enough, possibly over-familiar to the beginner in Anglo-Saxon. Like the mode of narration referred to above, it is essentially an elaborate superstructure laid on a simple foundation, a loaded simple syntax rather than a complex one, and like that mode of narration its origin is in an attempt to achieve high style by imitating the complex articulation of syntax in Latin poetry. Such a style, as I have said (p. 6, above), is not characteristic of 'primitive' poetry.

As a technique of style, variation is closely related to, and dependent on, the formal device of enjambement, which characterises the stichic structure of classical Anglo-Saxon poetry. Briefly stated, Anglo-Saxon versification is based on a two-stress half-line with a variable number of syllables; half-lines are bound into full lines by alliteration, which is borne always by the first stress of the second half-line and by either or both of the stresses of the first half-line. Alliteration thus holds one formal unit, the long line, in tension against another formal unit, the verse-paragraph composed of an indefinite number of half-lines freely run on. It is a favourite device of Anglo-Saxon poetry to heighten this tension by placing major syntactical breaks at the medial caesura. It has long been the practice to analyse the stress-patterns of the half-line according to five types, a system first evolved by the German scholar Sievers, thus:[48]

| A | / × / × |
|---|---|
| B | × / × / |
| C | × / / × |
| D | / / \ × |
| E | / \ × / |

The types may occur in any combination or sequence. The following lines from *Beowulf* exemplify all five:

| | | | |
|---|---|---|---|
| he þæs frofre gebad, | | | B |
| weox under wolcnum | weorðmyndum þah, | A | E |
| oð þæt him æghwylc | ymbsittendra | A | D |
| ofer hronrade | hyran scolde. (7–10) | C | A |

(He lived to see better days, led a prosperous and successful life, loaded with honours, and brought to submission all the neighbouring peoples over the ocean.)

It will be clear that Sievers does not offer a metrical system, if by that we mean, as we normally do in English prosody, a regular line, or regularly repeated pattern of lines, with a fixed number of stresses regularly disposed. Such a *metrical* system lies beneath all forms of English verse, whether *accentual* (Coleridge's 'new' principle, as propounded in his preface to *Christabel*) or *syllabic* (i.e. with regular disposition of unstressed as well as stressed syllables), and whatever local variations may be worked, in the interests of *rhythm*, by rhetorical and syntactical

15

patterning. Sievers's omission has not gone unnoticed, nor unsupplied. Various types of scansion have been suggested to bring Old English verse into line with what is normally expected of metre: the five types have been regarded as an arbitrary schematisation, *alla tedesca*, of the manifold variations possible in a basic two-stress line, either A or B; a four-stress half-line has been proposed; and a full musical scansion has been offered, with extra-metrical anacrusis, pause-beats, and other sophistications.[49] The truth is, though, that Sievers's analysis is a perfectly accurate description of the linguistic facts of Old English verse, and cannot be shuffled aside. His type C, which certainly exists in precisely the form he says, is alone sufficient to defy all attempts at orthodox metrical scansion. At the most basic level, what we can say is that Old English verse represents a tightening up, a heightened and formalised version, of a basic natural rhythm of the language, the two-stress group.[50] The most careful account of its techniques is that provided by A. J. Bliss:

> Whereas in most types of verse the metrical patterns are arbitrary, in Old English verse they are not: the metrical patterns are selected from among the rhythms which occur most commonly in natural speech. Thus there can be no question of accommodating the speech-rhythm to the metrical pattern ... variety and flexibility are achieved in another way. It is the metrical patterns themselves which are varied and flexible.... What is characteristic of Old English verse is that the divergencies from the norm are to be found, not in the more or less exact accommodation of the speech-material to the metrical pattern, but in the variation of the metrical pattern itself.[51]

One might demur from Bliss's use of the word 'metrical', since it obscures the precise meaning (if the meaning outlined above is accepted) of a useful word, but his analysis seems very satisfactory. What we have in Old English is something different from what we are used to and what our ears (and eyes) are conditioned to expect: to analyse it in our own terms is like trying to scan Latin verse in ignorance of quantity. All that remains is the trivial matter of finding a name for the form. It is not metre, and it would be misleading to call it prose, since it is so obviously 'poetic' in style; maybe we can be content to call it 'alliterative verse' for the time being, though there will be further problems when alliteration is discarded.

The approach to Old English versification suggested above may seem unnecessarily cautious, but the plain fact is that we are lacking all kinds of evidence needed for more elaborate theorising. For instance, we have no idea how this poetry was delivered, and cannot assume that the mode of recitation described in *Beowulf*, in an idealised portrayal of the heroic age, is the mode of recitation of the poem itself. And even if we do assume that *Beowulf* was recited to the harp, we have no idea how the harp was used, whether to provide rhythmic background, melodic accompaniment, free arabesques, or to supply intermittent speech-rests.[52] Nor does it seem possible to associate the use of the harp with some of the scriptural and devotional poetry (or the riddles!), yet this poetry is written in the same form as *Beowulf*. There was a harp (or lyre) at Sutton Hoo, and another in Bede's Caedmon story, but the use of the harp in oral verse-making at secular courts and secular gatherings cannot simply be transferred to lettered poetry.

Some kind of mannered recitative would seem appropriate for such poetry on the occasions when it was read aloud, but a temperate consideration of the question of delivery has been made difficult by the proliferating fantasy of 'oral-formulaic' theory, which assumes that Old English poetry, even as we have it, was orally improvised. The basis of the theory, first applied to Old English poetry by F.P. Magoun,[53] is in the work of Milman Parry and Lord among unlettered Yugoslav epic singers:

> Oral epic song is narrative poetry composed in a manner evolved over many generations by singers of tales who did not know how to write; it consists of the building of metrical lines and half-lines by means of formulas and formulaic expressions and of the building of songs by the use of themes.... By formula I mean 'a group of words which is regularly employed under the same metrical conditions to express a given essential idea'. This definition is Parry's.[54]

Many things can be admitted as true: that oral-formulaic verse-making is described with complete accuracy by Lord; that his conclusions may be extended to verse-making among all unlettered peoples, including Germanic peoples; that the heroic lays which we have presumed to exist down into Anglo-Saxon times were composed in this way; that the extant written poetry is formulaic in technique—

| Beowulf maþelode, | bearn Ecgþeowes |
|---|---|
| Hroðgar maþelode, | helm Scyldinga |
| Wiglaf maðelode, | Weohstanes sunu—[55] |

(*maþelode* : spoke, *helm* : lord)

and that some of these formulae may be derived from a formulaic stockpile accumulated in oral tradition. The further proposition, that Old English poetry, in its existing written form, was composed extempore, is untenable. Lord himself points out that literacy is the death-blow to oral tradition, and that the writing down of orally composed verse is impossible (before the invention of the phonograph) or at least artistically disastrous, as with the method of 'oral dictation'; yet this, it is presumed, is how all existing Old English poetry came to be written down. Furthermore, much Old English poetry consists of quite close translation from Latin—the Paris Psalter, the *Metra* of Boethius, the Kentish Psalm, parts of *The Phoenix* (including a macaronic)—and could not possibly

17

have been composed extempore;[56] yet this poetry employs exactly the same techniques, including formulaic usage, as all the other poetry. If it be argued that the technique in such poems is vestigial, then the sole ground for assuming that the technique in the other poems is anything other than vestigial, namely formulaic usage, is removed. Finally, another quotation from Lord:

> The absence of necessary enjambement is a characteristic of oral composition and is one of the easiest touchstones to apply in testing the orality of a poem ... periodic enjambement is characteristic of 'literary' style.[57]

It is difficult to know how Lord could have regarded it as proved 'that *Beowulf* was composed orally', that it 'belongs to the category of oral dictated texts',[58] when, as we have seen, enjambement is an essential formal characteristic of Old English poetry.

Oral-formulaic theory has not been a complete waste of time. Its methods of analysis, though masquerading as a theory of poetic genesis, and though often dominated by naïve notions of what is important in the 'making' of a poem ('The singer has got Beowulf out of Geatland ... will get Grendel to Heorot ... will get Wælhþeow to her seat ... '),[59] have produced some quite useful practical criticism of Old English poetry, at a grammarian's level. But the theory is irrelevant to most of the important questions about the poetry, and, by substituting the crude notion of improvisation for the many more varied and subtle kinds of *composition*, has distracted attention from the quality of Anglo-Saxon poetry that most needs stressing, its learned and lettered provenance.

With religious poetry, the case for such a provenance is clear. With *Beowulf*, it is slightly more complicated, because of the 'primitive' nature of the story-materials. Yet some suggestions have already been made about the influence of Latin models in the re-casting of these materials, and it is now necessary to enquire further into the relationships between Latin and vernacular literature and into the kind of cultural context which might encourage such relationships.

Beowulf: *Latin and monastic background*

*Beowulf*, we have said, seems to be indebted to classical models in certain aspects of narrative and stylistic technique. One might go further and say that the very idea of a long narrative poem, as opposed to the short heroic lay, is derived from Virgilian epic; and that particular episodes in *Beowulf*, such as the song of creation at a court celebration and the hero's extended narrative of past events, may be imitations of similar passages in the *Æneid*.[60] None of this evidence is proof of a direct knowledge of Latin literature, and it must be admitted that the Virgilian echoes in *Beowulf* are shadowy compared with the universal, unmistakable and persistent presence of Virgil in all Anglo-Latin writing, and, more pertinently, in *Waltharius*, the only Latin epic based on a Germanic heroic subject.[61] Yet when this evidence is combined with the evidence of Christian Latinity in the poem, in particular the use of words and compounds derived from Latin sources,[62] it seems that some kind of Latin background must be postulated for *Beowulf*.

It is perhaps our mistake to make too distinct a separation between Latin and vernacular traditions. Latin was, of course, confined to the literate, far more useful to them than the vernacular, and admired for its greater elegance,[63] but the vernacular was not held in contempt. As in Irish literature,[64] there seems to have been easy interchange between the two traditions. A famous story in the twelfth-century *Gesta Pontificum* of William of Malmesbury tells how Aldhelm, the most abstruse of Anglo-Latin poets, had mastered the art of vernacular poetry, and was able to compose a lay *(cantum)* and chant or recite it in the proper manner: he would take up his stand as a minstrel on the only bridge out of town and draw the people to more edifying matter when he had won their attention.[65] Bede knew the vernacular poetry well, as he shows in the Caedmon story and in the reference to *carmina vulgarium poetarum* (which he associates with Latin rhythmical verse) in the *De re metrica*,[66] and he is credited with a five-line 'Death Song' in the *Epistola Cuthberti de obitu Bedae*:[67] the poem is regular in form though extraordinarily plain and 'unpoetic' in manner. Elsewhere, an Anglo-Saxon verse proverb is quoted in an anonymous letter in the Latin correspondence of Winfrid (Boniface) and Lullus,[68] and, at a later date, Alfred did not think his Christian Latin learning to be at all incompatible with a love of 'Saxon poetry'.[69] Examples could be multiplied, of Latin influence on vernacular poetry, of the influence of alliteration in Latin poetry, of the fluid exchange between the two in macaronic,[70] without at all trespassing into the more complex territory of the tenth-century monastic revival.

If Latin and vernacular literacy, Latin and vernacular poetic tradition, could be associated in this way, the question remains, where, and by whom? The *scop* and the mead-hall seem increasingly unlikely to provide the answer, though clearly the former provides some of the materials and traditions of Anglo-Saxon poetry and the latter a possible place of 'publication', at least for a poem like *Beowulf*. The only plausible answer seems to be that Anglo-Saxon poetry, in its existing written form, is the product of monastic culture, and if our sense of the secular and heroic content of *Beowulf* is so strong as to make us wish to resist such a conclusion, then probably what needs revising is not our sense of the poem but our concept of monastic culture.

In the first place, Anglo-Saxon monasticism, during the period in which the poetry was written, is unreformed Benedictine monasticism, different from the severer monasticism of the tenth-century revival, and radically different from the ascetic forms introduced by the Carthusian, Cistercian and other orders in the eleventh and twelfth centuries. Its interpretation of the role of learning in the monastery was a generous one, and it would not be any the less generous for being touched by the influence of the Celtic Church.[71] Attitudes to secular literature varied in the early Christian centuries, but on the whole patristic writers accepted it as inevitable that the learning of Latin involved some contact with classical poets, especially since the standard grammars, Donatus and Priscian, relied on extensive quotation from them. Augustine of Hippo accommodated pagan literature to Christian doctrine through an interpretation of the biblical story that the Israelites left behind pagan idols in Egypt but took with them a small treasure of silver and gold: the former are identified as lying and superstitious fictions, the latter 'whatever human learning is useful and is gathered in human books'.[72] Augustine's own writing is deeply pervaded by his knowledge of secular literature, as is that of Jerome, who uses a similar technique to justify it.[73] Gregory himself, the instigator of the English mission, was much sterner in his opposition to classical literature, claiming that all forms of eloquence were exemplified in the Scriptures (though his own Latin is classical), and it is likely that the books Augustine brought with him were strictly professional ones, biblical, liturgical and patristic texts. However, the arrival of Archbishop Theodore of Tarsus and Abbot Hadrian to consolidate the mission in 669 heralded a new kind of learning. Bede tells us that Theodore was well read in both sacred and secular literature and had knowledge of Greek, and that he established a broad monastic curriculum, with instruction in the liberal arts and in the arts of ecclesiastical poetry.[74] Within a few years Aldhelm, whose own education had been at the hands of the Irish scholar Maeldubh in Wiltshire, could compare Canterbury favourably with Irish centres of learning.[75] Meanwhile, Benedict Biscop had begun a series of journeys to the continent, collecting the books with which he endowed his double foundation at Wearmouth and Jarrow (674, 685): the library there, Bede's library, was one of the richest in the West, and it was soon matched by other monastic libraries at Lindisfarne and York. These libraries are the sources of the Northumbrian renaissance of the age of Bede, and of England's intellectual hegemony in the West during the eighth century. They consisted principally, of course, of biblical, patristic and hagiographical writings, but contained also much secular Latin literature. Alcuin's celebration of the library at York, where he received his own education before joining the court of Charlemagne, mentions Virgil, Statius, Lucan, Pliny and Cicero, as well as the grammarians Donatus, Priscian and Servius, and Christian poets such as Sedulius, Juvencus, Alcimus (Avitus), Arator, Fortunatus and Lactantius.[76] Bede himself, like Aldhelm, echoes Virgil constantly, and uses classical poets for illustration in the *De re metrica*—though not in the *De Schematibus*, which is designed to show that all the arts of rhetorical style can be illustrated from the Bible. Other kinds of evidence of secular learning, in addition to library-lists and allusions, include the Latin–Old English glossaries, which clearly show that Virgil and Cicero were being read,[77] though the overwhelming preponderance is of glosses to Christian writers. It is easy to distort the evidence, and give to secular literature a greater importance than it actually had in monastic learning: Bede's citations of secular writers, for instance, in the *De re metrica* are nearly all derived from grammarians or from Isidore's *Etymologies*.[78] But there is no denying the ubiquity of Virgil, and the argument for a more broadly-based concept of monastic culture hardly needs more.

There would be further support for such an argument in the nature of the

Anglo-Saxon monastery during the seventh and eighth centuries, for it was by no means a closed nor entirely a spiritual community. Lay scholars were admitted into the monastic schools, particularly youths of noble family,[79] and it is clear that some monasteries were 'secular' foundations, 'founded less to realise ascetic conceptions than to settle members of the founder's family'.[80] The intake for most monasteries was largely aristocratic, and the anonymous *Life of Ceolfrith*, Abbot of Jarrow, records the difficulty the abbot had in persuading these nobles to submit to a regular discipline.[81] Monks were not always in orders, and many of them had no Latin. Add to this the common practice among Anglo-Saxon kings, such as Ceolwulf of Northumbria in 737 and his successor Eadberht in 758, of retiring into monastic life at the end of their active career, or simply to unburden themselves of kingship,[82] and it could seem that the Anglo-Saxon monastic community was much less monolithic than we might assume, or than such as Bede might have hoped, and a likelier soil, therefore, for the growth of the blended tradition we have suggested.

A final argument for the cloistered provenance of *Beowulf* might be seen in Alcuin's letter to the bishop of Lindisfarne in 797:

> Let the Word of God be heard at the meals of the brethren. There it is proper to hear a reader, not a harper, the sermons of the Fathers, not the songs of the pagans. What has Ingeld to do with Christ? (*Quid Hinieldus cum Christo?*) The house is narrow; it cannot hold both of them.[83]

Ingeld makes a significant appearance in *Beowulf* (2064), of course, but one would not presume this to be a direct reference to the poem, nor would one deny that Alcuin is speaking generally and rhetorically, consciously echoing famous earlier condemnations of the study of classical poets by clerics, such as Jerome's 'What has Horace to do with the Psalter? or Virgil with the Gospels? or Cicero with the Apostle?' and ultimately derived from St Paul's 'What concord hath Christ with Belial?'[84] But Alcuin's adaptation of the convention to refer to the practice of singing songs about Germanic heroes in the monastic refectory-hall is surely important evidence of precisely the kind we seek, as to the provenance of *Beowulf*. It is not the sort of thing one would expect clerical writers to make much mention of, normally, and Alcuin's condemnation is connected, significantly, with the Carolingian movement towards monastic reform. But Alcuin's evidence is not unsupported. Cuthbert, Abbot of Wearmouth, writes to Archbishop Lullus of Mainz in 764 asking him to send a glass-maker and a harpist.

> It would delight me also to have a harpist who could play on the harp which we call 'rottae', for I have a harp and am without a player.... I beg that you will not scorn my request nor think it laughable.[85]

Ecclesiastical opposition to such practice suggests that the harping was not merely for spiritual relaxation. As early as 679 a council at Rome declared that

English bishops should not keep harpers or musicians, and the decrees of the Council of 'Clovesho' in 747 require bishops to see that monasteries are not places of amusement and the resort of poets and harpers.[86] Proscription proves the practice, as it does in the Carolingian empire, where frequent attempts are made to prevent the clergy singing secular songs, or nuns composing *winileodas* (love-songs). Once the harp was allowed in, it seems, the barriers were down—

> Whenever a monastery or bishop's court . . . had any pretensions to musical culture, it admitted to a greater or lesser extent songs intended for entertainment and not for cult, songs performed in hall rather than in church or oratory—[87]

though it might be the effort of conscientious reformers to put them back up again (as Bede does in the Caedmon story), an effort attended with remarkable success, judging by the extant remains of monastic verse-making. If it be argued that monks might listen to and enjoy secular songs being sung and secular poems being recited but that they would hardly go to the trouble of copying them down, then it could be pointed out that the earliest surviving musical manuscript (late ninth century), from the monastery of Saint-Martial at Limoges, contains secular battle-lays as well as penitential and biblical lyrics.[88] And of course, to bring the argument full circle, the very poetry we are talking about survives in monastic copies of monastic copies.[89]

## Beowulf: *date and provenance*

If we have established, in the monasteries, a likely home for *Beowulf*, there is no need to make the monastic claim an exclusive one. The poem may have been composed and written down there, but the easy interplay, at certain times, between court and monastic circles suggests that it may have reached a court audience too. A likely occasion is the reign of Aldfrith of Northumbria (685–705), 'one of the most brilliant periods in the history of the North', when literature, scholarship, manuscript painting, sculpture and building all flourished, and perhaps vernacular literature too.[90] Aldfrith was himself a scholar and spent several years in Iona, as Bede tells us in the *Life of St Cuthbert* (Chap. XXV), pursuing the study of literature and the arts. He may have studied in Ireland too, since he is famous in tradition as an Irish poet.[91] Bede, Aldhelm and Alcuin all speak of him as a man of learning. A later candidate for the 'patron' of *Beowulf* might be Eadberht of Northumbria (737–58), who retired eventually as a monk of York, and whose reign was looked on as a golden age by Alcuin.

Yet such speculations are besieged by doubt. Even though we may conclude fairly firmly that a poem like *Beowulf* comes out of a monastic cultural background, the same background in fact that produces virtually all, if not all, Anglo-Saxon poetry, we know nothing of actual provenance, date and place of composition and can prove little. Linguistic evidence is dubious: Sisam has shown that the convenient assumption, based on the presence of Anglian forms, that Anglo-Saxon poetry is Northumbrian, or at least Anglian, in origin, but transmitted in West-Saxon texts, is not tenable, and concludes that the extant poetry is written in 'a general Old English poetic dialect' and could come from any of the Kingdoms.[92] Other kinds of evidence, external and internal, produce a multitude of sometimes conflicting theories, though there is a general consensus that most of the poetry, including *Beowulf*, was written in the eighth century. It is dangerous to make too close an association between political stability and literary productivity, but certainly not much would be possible until well after the defeat of the heathen Penda at Winwæd in 654, while the sack of Lindisfarne by Norwegian raiders in 793 looks like the beginning of the end of things—'It partly seems that the happiness of the English is nearly at an end', says Alcuin.[93] For *Beowulf*, 793 has maybe a special significance, since it is a human enough assumption that a poem glorifying Scandinavian heroes would not be popular when their descendants were plundering the country.

It would be hard to go much beyond this. Eighth-century Northumbria retains most of one's favour as a speculative home for Anglo-Saxon poetry, but it may be partly because the culture of the kingdom in this period is so richly documented. If we knew more of Offa's Mercia, it might provide an equally attractive cultural context for vernacular poetry in the late eighth century: the only conceivable compliment in Beowulf is to Offa, in the reference (1931–62) to his legendary predecessor and namesake, king of the continental Angles, and it was to surviving Mercian scholarship that Alfred turned when he began to rebuild.[94] It may not be fanciful, however, in discussing provenance, to suggest that *Beowulf* has something in common with the great surviving monuments of Northumbrian art of the period, such as the carved crosses of Ruthwell and Bewcastle, and the Lindisfarne Gospels. The blending of Christian, classical and 'barbaric' elements in the poem may be compared with similar blending in the Lindisfarne St Matthew.[95] The picture, whether it is imitated from the Ezra portrait in the Codex Amiatinus or from some common model, derives its design and figure-posture and the whole idea of a picture that 'tells a story' from sixth-century Italian art and ultimately classical sources, just as the poem derives its concept and some of its methods of narrative from Virgilian epic. But the effect of the picture is quite different from the rather placid representationalism of the Ezra portrait: colour is used purely decoratively, there is no relief, and the handling of line has been invaded by a vigour, authority and freedom derived from barbaric art. It is a marvellous picture, humane and moving in a way that the purely barbaric 'carpet-page' in the same manuscript is not, and its strength is in its blending of traditions. Tentatively, one might suggest that the 'barbaric' elements in *Beowulf*, such as the Germanic story-materials (represented in 'pure' form in *Finnesburh*) and the formulaic technique, contribute similarly to its strength. Likewise, the Ruthwell and Bewcastle crosses derive many of their sculptural characteristics—developed plastic sense, use of narrative, the vine scroll ornament—from Mediterranean models, perhaps even local Romano-British remains, but their essential character is in the blending of

23

these motifs with the native taste for repetitive ornament, interlace and zoomorphs.[96] The form is created out of impurity. One of the disappointing things about the Franks casket in the British Museum, which might be thought to supply the very mixture of Germanic, classical and Christian motifs we are speaking of, is that no creative fusion has taken place: the scenes of Weland and Sigurd, of Romulus and Remus, of the Magi and the Capture of Jerusalem, are juxtaposed in the same bare style, without any kind of lively interpenetration. We may lack some basic allegorical programme which would unite the themes didactically, if not artistically, but the effect is remarkably like that sometimes produced by the Germanic admixture in the scriptural poetry.

Such a comparison between *Beowulf* and Northumbrian art is really, of course, trying to say more about the nature of the poem than about its provenance, and can say it only in riddles. Its strength, I have suggested, is in its rich compounding of diverse traditions into a monumental whole. It is a full and complete and marvellously well-*composed* poem, the very opposite of the noble fragments that are all we are entitled to expect. Its handling of language has an assurance that seems to argue a long ancestry of literary experimentation and stabilisation. In the end, though, its solidity betrays a certain intransigence of both thought and style. The heroic and Christian elements are blended, but only by arresting their development and blurring their consequence; the effect is impressive but confused. The elaborately formulaic technique of the poem, likewise, brilliantly and variously displayed in the first 1200 lines of the poem, stiffens to a hieratic formality in the latter half, a level eloquence that acts as a narcotic on those very faculties that should be attentive, so that scholars are desperately put to it to find subtleties in the poem's language. The effect of solemn celebration seems not at all hard won. Perhaps this inflexibility is a characteristic of heroic poetry; it is no less a limitation.

# 2    Anglo-Saxon religious poems

The great bulk of Anglo-Saxon poetry is explicitly religious and didactic in character, its purpose being to glorify God and draw man to praise him. *Beowulf*, though infused with Christian thinking, is not explicitly religious in this way, but apart from *Beowulf* there are only the few pagan remains that have been mentioned. The religious poetry can be loosely divided into five categories: scriptural (*Genesis, Exodus, Daniel, Christ and Satan*, i.e. the poems of MS Junius XI); hagiographical (*Andreas* and *Elene* in the Vercelli Book, *Guthlac* and *Juliana* in the Exeter Book); devotional (*The Dream of the Rood*, Vercelli, and *Christ I*, Exeter); homiletic (*Christ II* and *III* and a large number of shorter poems in both MSS), and reflective (the 'elegies' in the Exeter Book), though there is a residue of miscellaneous material in the gnomic poetry, riddles and bestiary fragments of the Exeter Book. There need be no hesitancy about the provenance of this poetry, for it is monastic in its every aspect, the work of bookish and devout men, self-conscious professional artists, who maintain a level of high competence such as we do not often find in the arid wastes of Middle English religious verse. The poetry has the air of libraries about it, of men who know their way about books, who know how to shape materials to specific and limited purposes, and who have at their command a powerful if inflexible organ of style. With some glorious exceptions, it achieves respectability rather than excellence, and maintains an extraordinary uniformity: there seem to be no poems in which we can discern preliminary stages of stylistic development, and few signs of fading.

The poems, apart from some clearly intended for private reading and instruction, can readily be assigned a monastic function as lectionary material. The readings for Holy Saturday, for instance, included the biblical stories of Creation, the Deluge, Isaac, the Crossing of the Red Sea, and the children in the Fiery Furnace,[1] and one can well imagine that the poems of Junius XI would provide supplementary *lectiones* in the vernacular on such occasions. The divisions of many of the poems into sections or 'fitts' would suggest that they were put to such a use. There is a *Praefatio* associated with the *Heliand*, the Old Saxon poem directly imitated from Anglo-Saxon scriptural poetry, which relates how a certain Old Saxon poet paraphrased biblical materials into 'the Teutonic language' (*theudisca lingua*) and, after the manner of that poetry, divided the whole work into 'fitts, which we call lections or chapters' *(per vitteas distinxit, quas lectiones vel sententias possumus appellare).*[2] A more informal mode of recitation may also be envisaged. Alcuin complained (see above, p. 21) of secular songs being sung in the refectory hall: these poems, however, in their various ways, would provide unexceptionable reading-matter on such comparatively relaxed occasions, at the same time satisfying some of the taste for poetic pleasure and excitement. Perhaps the 'cantos' of *Beowulf* can also be related to such a practice.[3] There is no need to assume, however, that the heroic style, as it pervades much of this religious poetry, satisfied in a covert way some kind of hankering for heroic poetry. It is simply that the heroic style, with its characteristic vocabulary and mannerisms, was the dominant poetic tradition.

There is a well-established sequence in Christian Latin poetry whereby the practice of biblical paraphrase seems to precede other kinds of religious poem, and it has long been customary to regard the poems of Junius XI as the earliest of the Anglo-Saxon religious poems, and to date them in the early eighth century. Such dating is necessarily tentative, in view of the late date of the MS and the palimpsest-like quality of the linguistic evidence, but certain relative datings seem possible. It may be assumed, for instance, that the pervasively Christian quality of the language of *Beowulf*, and the fact that many of its compounds are derived from Christian-Latin sources, argue for a pre-existing Christian poetry, since they would hardly be introduced for the first time in a poem not itself explicitly Christian. This pre-existing Christian poetry may all have been lost, but it is simpler to assume, and there is evidence for the assumption, that it is represented in the *Genesis*, and perhaps in other scriptural poems, though not in *Exodus*, which is directly indebted to *Beowulf*. Other poems, such as *Andreas*, are more deeply indebted to *Beowulf*, and we can construct therefore a tentative sequence and float it somewhere in the eighth and early ninth centuries. Four poems *(Juliana, Elene, Christ II, The Fates of the Apostles)* are 'signed' by Cynewulf, though this is not very helpful, since we do not know who he was, or when and where he lived. There is some suggestion that he was of Mercian origin, since the form of his name that he gives did not become current in Northumbria until the middle of the ninth century.[4] On the other hand, there is nothing to prove that he did not write in the ninth century, which saw a recession in Anglo-Saxon culture but not a paralysis of it.

We are to imagine, therefore, that the first adaptation of the traditional heroic style to Christian poetry is in scriptural paraphrase, though we cannot assume that all the stages of this adaptation are preserved for us. Bede's story of Caedmon provides a miracle to bridge the gap: Caedmon is a layman, a farm-hand on one of the abbatial estates at Whitby, and he is accustomed to festive gatherings at which the harp is passed round and songs sung (or lays recited), though he himself knows no songs and takes no part. On one such occasion, he leaves the feast and, in the cattle-byre, has a dream in which he is told to sing 'about the beginning of created things'. Bede gives a Latin prose translation of this song, but the scribe of the earliest MS of the *Historia* appends the vernacular 'original', in the Northumbrian dialect, and the same text is preserved in many

other MSS of both Latin and Alfredian versions of the *Historia*, in both Northumbrian and West-Saxon. Here is the West-Saxon version:

Nu sculon herigean     heofonrices weard,
meotodes meahte     and his modgeþanc,
weorc wuldorfæder,     swa he wundra gehwæs,
ece drihten,     or onstealde.
He ærest sceop     eorðan bearnum
heofon to hrofe,     halig scyppend;
Þa middangeard     moncynnes weard,
ece drihten,     æfter teode
firum foldan,     frea ælmihtig.[5]

(Now we must praise the ruler of the heavenly kingdom for his divine
power and wisdom, the work of the father of glory, the eternal lord, who
first established the beginning of all wondrous things. He, the holy
creator, first shaped the firmament as a roof for the sons of earth; then
the ruler of mankind, the eternal lord, almighty god, afterwards made
middle-earth as a place for men.)

Caedmon remembers his song when he awakes, and recites it to the Abbess
Hild, who encourages him to take monastic vows. He is given instruction in
sacred history, which he proceeds to turn 'into the most melodious verse':

He sang about the creation of the world, the origin of the human race,
and the whole history of Genesis, of the departure of Israel from Egypt
and the entry into the promised land and of many other of the stories
taken from the sacred Scriptures: of the incarnation, passion and
resurrection of the Lord, of His ascension into heaven, of the coming of
the Holy Spirit and the teaching of the apostles. He also made songs
about the terrors of future judgment, the horrors of the pains of hell, and
the joys of the heavenly kingdom.[6]

This covers the subjects of all the existing scriptural poems, and others as well,
which is not surprising, since it is a more or less complete prospectus of biblical
history; the poems of Junius XI can hardly be attributed to Caedmon on the
strength of it. There is no need to disbelieve Bede's story of a man who discovers
he has a gift for poetry, and it is easy to see how the story could be turned into a
miracle, and how 'Caedmon's Hymn' could be tailored to fit the legend.[7] But
the myth is less important than the reality for which it is a metaphor, for what
Bede is describing and 'explaining' is the growth of religious poetry on the basis
of secular verse-making, the first development of this poetry in scriptural paraphrase, and the widespread existence of such poetry in the early eighth century.
    The adaptation of traditional verse-form, style and vocabulary to religious
purposes involved the transfer of a good deal of military terminology, since most

heroic poetry dealt with battles. It is for this reason that Abraham and Moses appear in Old English poetry as Germanic chieftains, or the Apostles as a kind of *comitatus*, or body of armed retainers:

> þæt wæron mære     men ofer eorðan,
> frome folctogan     ond fyrdhwate,
> rofe rincas,     þonne rond ond hand
> on herefelda     helm ealgodon,
> on meotudwange.               (*Andreas*, 7–11)

(They were men famous throughout the earth, bold and resolute chieftains, tough warriors, when shield and hand guarded helm on the field of battle.)

Clearly, such language would often be appropriate, when the poet was speaking of battles, even of metaphorical battles against the forces of darkness: even Bede can speak of Cuthbert as 'the soldier of Christ'.[8] Often, however, it seems, on the surface, inappropriate, and we are not to suppose, in such instances, that the Scriptures are being invaded by Germanic ethic. There is, as I have said, no 'hankering'. But there is a strong residual heroic quality in the vocabulary and in the handling of certain themes: poets may have been unable to excise it, or, as seems more likely, did not want to do so. In other words, Old English religious poetry had to live through a heroic phase in order to take over the heritage. What the religious poets are doing—and it implies no contempt for heroic poetry as such—is to fulfil the potential of the heroic style by diverting it from useless fictions to profitable truths.

We may find, and perhaps Old English poets found, apt precedent for this practice in Christian-Latin poetry. Here, too, educated and devout men found themselves confronted with a secular literary tradition, that of Virgilian epic, of overwhelming prestige and universal currency. It was the tradition in which they themselves had been instructed in the Latin language. Not all of them went as far as the fourth-century poetess Proba, who narrates selected episodes from the Old and New Testaments in a *cento* entirely composed of lines and half-lines drawn from Virgil.[9] But all of them are consciously adapting Virgilian diction and techniques to Christian narrative, giving to the biblical story the elegance of classical style, and redirecting the love of good poetry from false gods to the true one. It is in these terms that Juvencus, one of the earliest of these biblical poets, prefaces his epic of the life of Christ, the *Historia Evangelica* (AD 329):

> Quod si tam longam meruerunt carmina famam,
> Quae veterum gestis hominum mendacia nectunt,
> Nobis certa fides aeternae in saecula laudis
> Immortale decus tribuet, meritumque rependet.
> Nam mihi carmen erit Christi vitalia gesta,
> Divinum in populis falsi sine crimine donum.[10]

(And if poems that weave lying fables into the deeds of the ancients have deserved such long-lived fame, then our sure faith must deserve the reward of an immortality of fame throughout eternity. For the theme of my poem shall be the life-giving deeds of Christ, the blameless sacrifice made by God for his people.)

The fifth-century Sedulius shows a similar consciousness of secular poetic tradition in the *Carmen Paschale*, another Gospel epic, well-known in Anglo-Saxon England,[11]

Cum sua gentiles studeant figmenta poetae
Grandisonis pompare modis, tragicoque boatu...
Cur ego...
Clara salutiferi taceam miracula Christi?[12]

(When pagan poets are so zealous to deck out their fictions in high-sounding and bombastic phrases, ... why should I ... be silent on the glorious miracles of our Saviour Christ?)

Like the Old English poets, the Christian Latin poets echo the secular poetic language constantly and take over its mythological and cultural background. The fourth-century *Liber in Genesin*, a paraphrase of the first book of the Bible, formerly attributed to Juvencus, borrows from Ovid as well as Virgil, mixes classical and Christian freely, referring commonly to God as *Tonans* ('the Thunderer'),[13] while a poem on the Harrowing of Hell, *Triumphus Christus Heroicus*, also attributed to Juvencus, introduces Charon, Cerberus, Gorgons, Harpies, Megaera, Tisiphone, Alecto, the Parcae, beside Abraham, Isaac and Jacob.[14] In the *Hamartigenia*, a poem on the origins of evil, Prudentius (d. 413) portrays Sodom in Roman style, with its *forum*, *balnea* (baths), *templa*, *theatra*, and *madidae popinae* (taverns).[15] The development of this Latin poetry, also, seems to parallel quite closely that of Old English scriptural poetry: the earliest poems, those of Juvencus and Cyprian of Gaul (the *Heptateuchos*), consist of fairly close paraphrase of biblical material, as in the Old English *Genesis*; later, in the *Carmen de Deo* (*De laudibus Dei*) of Dracontius (late fifth century) and the paraphrase of Genesis and Exodus by Avitus (d. 518), there is much more freedom and a much richer embroidery of biblical narrative, as in the Old English *Exodus* or *Genesis B*. Eventually, in Venantius Fortunatus, as in *The Dream of the Rood* or *Christ*, biblical narrative is superseded by new varieties of poetic structure.

All these poets were well-known in Anglo-Saxon England, some of them, such as Juvencus, Sedulius and Prudentius, very well-known,[16] and some particular resemblances will be mentioned later. Meanwhile, it might be observed that a further usefulness of the comparison between Old English and Latin scriptural poetry is that it provides a more proper context of appreciation. Literary historians often give a false picture of this kind of poetry, regarding it as uninteresting in subject-matter and decadent in style, hostile, indeed, with its didactic preoccupations, to 'real' poetry. Praise of its technical skills is grudging, since they are judged to be misapplied. De Labriolle's criticisms of Avitus seem to be touched by the same prejudices as W. P. Ker's strictures on *Beowulf*:

> Once we admit the principle of his poetry which treats subjects specifically Christian by means of the methods inherited from the classics ... we must acknowledge that brilliant and happily-conceived pieces are not wanting.... His style, refined and artificial, precious and dainty, also furnishes an excellent choice of examples whereby to illustrate the history of literary decadence.[17]

Such judgments are not borne out by the spirit and enterprise and verbal felicity of much of the Latin poetry. We must not assume that Christian poets felt themselves constrained to lesser tasks by their faith: their theme was a greater one, and they knew it. The history of art can provide us—as it often does, with its more objective controls and comparative freedom from dogmatic prejudice— with a more accurate perspective; for no art-historian would claim that the adoption of classical illusionism by Christian artists in the late Roman period was a form of 'decadence'.

Another point can lead us directly into a discussion of the Old English scriptural poems, and that is that these poems, like the Latin biblical epics, are learned works, designed for the delight and edification of a learned (i.e. monastic) audience. There is no question of such poetry reaching an unlettered public, and any tendency to associate it with biblical and other religious poetry in Middle English as a form of vernacularisation for lay consumption should be dispelled. These poets move freely in the world of Christian Latin learning, incorporating it in their poetry, sometimes developing it.[18] The very term 'biblical paraphrase' may sometimes mislead, suggesting as it does an early attempt to get the Scriptures into the vernacular, so as to convey them to the laity, as if the extant poems were fragments of an instructional programme like that of Ælfric or Wycliff. They are, on the contrary, learned poetic structures, and their authors assume a respect for the vernacular, in relation to Latin, which is lost within two centuries and which Milton is still labouring to recover.

*Scriptural poems*

These arguments for a vigorous intellectual context are not necessarily arguments for intrinsic poetic merit, and such a qualification may seem particularly apposite in the case of the Old English *Genesis*. The poem is certainly no mere paraphrase: a theme is announced, echoing the words of the Preface to the Mass (*Vere dignum et justum est* ...) and, incidentally, of Caedmon's *Hymn*:

> Us is riht micel    ðæt we rodera weard,

wereda wuldorcining,    wordum herigen,
modum lufien....                                          (1–3)

(It is very right and proper for us to give praise in words to the ruler of the heavens, the glorious Lord of Hosts, and to love him in our hearts.)

and this theme, the praise of God through the demonstration of his justice and mercy in his dealings with man (Milton phrases it somewhat more arrogantly), dominates the poem. Details are constantly added or emphasised to elucidate the theme, and there is a constant awareness, derived from patristic traditions, of the typological implications of the narrative.[19] It is no accident that the poem ends, as does Bede's commentary on *Genesis*, with the story of Isaac: Abraham gives thanks for all God's gifts and in so doing both completes the theme of praise and concludes the narrative of Fall in the promise of Redemption (Isaac being a significant prefiguration of Christ). But a good theme does not make a good poem, and *Genesis* is monotonous in stylistic technique, predictable in both its vocabulary and its methods of variation. It is the sort of poem that by its length, regularity and good taste could easily establish a pattern of style, one which showed how the emphatic rhetoric of heroic verse could be levelled to a consistent narrative and expository tone, and in which the heroic overtones of words like *hæleð* for Noah could be unobtrusively absorbed. There is no opposition to the heroic style, however, and the poet allows it full rein in the one episode where it is manifestly appropriate, the war of the Elamites against the kings of Sodom and Gomorrah, and Abraham's rescue of Lot from the Elamite army. The theme of battle is announced in the traditional epic formula, *Da ic gefrægn* (1960), and the description of battle is full of heroic motifs (*Sang se wanna fugel ... deawigfeþera*, 1983), sentiments and turns of phrase:

                Abraham sealde
wig to wedde,    nalles wunden gold,
for his suhtrigan....                           (2069–71)

(Abraham gave battle in payment of his nephew's ransom, not gold rings.)

The episode ends, as suddenly and deliberately as it began, with a curt summary of characteristically heroic values:

                Næfre mon ealra
lifigendra her    lytle werede
þon wurðlicor    wigsið ateah,
þara þe wið swa miclum    mægne geræsde.     (2092–5)

(No one ever attacked so great an army with so small a band of men and won a greater victory.)

The handling of the episode is perfectly decorous, but it does demonstrate the poet's recognition of the special kind of poetic excitement that the full heroic style can generate, and his respect for it.

Lines 235–850 of the *Genesis* are quite different in style and treatment from the rest of the poem, and it was recognised that they represented an interpolation long before Sievers's famous deduction in 1875 that they were based on an Old Saxon original, a deduction confirmed by the discovery in the Vatican library in 1894 of three fragments of an Old Saxon *Genesis*, one of which corresponds word for word to lines 791–817 of the English poem. The interpolation, usually known as *Genesis B*, is clearly a close translation from an Old Saxon original, and as such represents a kind of return on England's investment in Germany in the eighth century. Boniface and his successors presumably took the English Christian poetry with them on their missions, and there would have been further contacts through the visits to England of such men as the Frisian Liudger, who was taught at York by Alcuin and there consecrated Bishop to the Old Saxons in 767.[20] Whatever the mode of transmission, the Old Saxon epic of the Life of Christ, the *Heliand* (cf. O.E. *hælend*, 'saviour'), is a direct imitation of Old English poetic style. The Emperor Lewis (814–40) commanded further poetic versions of the Old and New Testaments to be made and the Old Saxon *Genesis* is perhaps one of the consequences. It is likely to have become known in England as a result of Alfred's importation of Saxon monks (c. 885) to help in his revival of learning, though the German contacts were stronger in the reign of Athelstan.[21] Some slightly peculiar usages in the English version suggest that the translator was himself a Saxon.[22] Presumably the translation was known in part or whole to the copyist of Junius XI or its exemplar, and he inserted a passage from it to fill a lacuna in his copy-text, or perhaps because he recognised that it was so good.

*Genesis B* is thus a good deal later in date than the rest of the poem, and it may appear something of a paradox that Old English poetry had to wait on continental inspiration for the production of its masterpiece. Perhaps the Old English poets grew too comfortable too early. At any rate, here is a poet who can concentrate his imagination on the events and actors of the great drama of the Fall, who can respond and *think*, whose language is pliant and free, rich rather than copious, and who can give powerful dramatic realisation to Satan's flashy heroics—

> Wa la, ahte ic minra handa geweald
> and moste ane tid    ute weorðan,
> wesan ane winterstunde,    þonne ic mid þys werode—
> Ac licgað me ymbe    irenbenda,
> rideð racentan sal.    Ic eom rices leas....     (368–72)

(Ah, if only I had the use of my hands, and could escape this place for a while, just a short while, then I, with this band of warriors—But iron shackles lie upon me, a fetter of chain that chafes cruelly. I have lost my kingdom....)

as well as to the realities of the Fall. Satan is marvellously and subtly fitted to the heroic pattern, releasing yet perverting all its energies: his relationship to God is that of *þegnscipe* (326), which he betrays, and for that is doomed to exile in hell, where he himself acts out a parody of lordship, but as *morþres brytta* ('death-giver'), not *sinces brytta* ('treasure-giver').[23] The scenes in hell have been much admired, and they are good enough to endure the comparison with *Paradise Lost*,[24] but the narrative of the Fall that follows is an equal revelation of the poet's art. In the simple nobility of Adam's first reply to Satan's emissary (522–46), the poet's imagination seems to penetrate to the very heart of unfallen innocence—naturally credulous yet naturally obedient, puzzled yet instinctively saying and doing the right thing. Adam's mild repudiation of the envoy is the very instrument of the envoy's power over Eve, for he persuades her that Adam needs rescuing from a disastrous error of judgment, and, pathetically, she urges Adam to eat *þurh holdne hyge* ('out of loyalty to him') (708). But it is hell and death that they eat:

> He æt þam wife onfeng
> helle and hinnsið            (717–18)

(From the woman he received hell and death.)

In imagination, they not only see hell open up greedily to receive them, but hear it roaring (793–4). Such passages have a 'pendulation' which makes even *Beowulf* seem empty, ceremonial. This may be simply to say that Christianity has a superior mythology, but at least the poet can be given the credit for recognising it.

There are tantalising echoes throughout *Genesis B* of Book II, 'De originali peccato', of the Old Testament epic *De Mosaicae Historiae Gestis* of Avitus.[25] The treatment of Satan shows many resemblances, and the lines that follow those just quoted—

> hit wæs þeah deaðes swefn     and deafles gespon,
> hell and hinnsið     and hæleða forlor,
> menniscra morð,     þæt hie to mete dædon,
> ofet unfæle—           (720–3)

(But it was the sleep of death and the lure of the devil, hell and death
and man's destruction, the slaughter of mankind, that they took for
food in that unholy fruit.)

are reminiscent of Avitus' glossier and more epigrammatic

> Dulce subit virus, capitur mors horrida pastu.      (ii.224)[26]

(The delicious poison enters, the horror of death is given admission with
that morsel.)

33

Yet the poet has made profound changes in the story of the Fall, as it appears in Avitus, or in traditional hexameral commentary.[27] His Satanic emissary goes first to Adam, not Eve, and uses his refusal as a source for the temptation of Eve; and when they realise they are deceived they repent immediately and ask for forgiveness. Eve's reply to Adam's rebuke has a touching simplicity,

> Þu meaht hit me witan,     wine min Adam,
> wordum þinum;     hit þe þeah wyrs ne mæg
> on þinum hyge hreowan     þonne hit me æt heortan deð.          (824–6)

(You may well reproach me with your words, dear my lord; but you cannot have deeper cause for sorrow in your heart than I have in mine.)

as has Adam's lament for the loss of *þegnscipe*:

> Nis me on worulde niod
> æniges þegnscipes,     nu ic mines þeodnes hafa
> hyldo forworhte,     þæt ic hie habban ne mæg.          (835–7)

(I have no desire for any service on earth, now that I have forfeited the favour of my lord, and may possess it no more.)

All the poet's changes have the effect of presenting man in a more favourable light, as the victim of deception not temptation, and though the poet is well aware of the nature and consequences of the Fall, the design seems to be to explore dramatic situation and motive in a more credibly human and humane way. It seems doubtful that he took the line for these interests from Germanic epic; the Carolingian renaissance may have more to do with it. Certainly there is a very marked Latinate influence at work in the style, as in the control exerted over genuinely complex sentences (e.g. 409–21) and the use of sophisticated devices like aposiopesis (370, quoted above). In other ways, too, the poet shows divergences from 'classical' Old English style: he uses the expanded or hyper-metric line far more often than any Old English poet, distributes unstressed syllables more freely, subdues variation and compounding, and thus suggests the first movement towards that more discursive, articulated, expansive narrative style which we associate with the best Middle English alliterative poetry.

With *Exodus* we are back at the heart of the classical style. Again the title is misleading, since it is not a paraphrase of a book of the bible but a development of the theme of obedience, of God's ways with his chosen servants, based on the single episode of the Crossing of the Red Sea. It is to underline this theme that the poet introduces allusions, which are otherwise gratuitous, to the stories of the Flood and Abraham and Isaac at the moment of the Crossing (362).[28] The poem is thus, like *Genesis A*, perfectly coherent didactically, but it lacks totally the sobriety of that poem, for it is a consistently exuberant heroicised treatment of the story, deploying the full epic paraphernalia. The opening, quite different from the opening of *Genesis*, with its echoes of the liturgy, is the epic call for attention:

> Hwæt! we feor and neah     gefrigen habað
> ofer middangeard     Moyses domas....

(Lo, we have heard far and near over all the earth of Moses' laws.)

The promise of battle (though it's all promise) evokes traditional associations,

> Hreopon herefugolas,     hilde grædige,
> deawigfeðere ...     Wulfas sungon
> atol æfenleoð—                                    (162–5)

(Birds of prey shrieked out, greedy for battle, dewy-feathered ...
wolves sang a terrible evening-song.)

and Pharaoh's host is invested with all the traditional heroic attributes of the *comitatus*:

> Ymb hine wægon     wigend unforhte,
> hare heorowulfas     hilde gretton,
> þurstige þræcwiges,     þeodenholde.                (180–2)

(Around him paced fierce warriors, grey-haired veterans of war eagerly awaiting battle, thirsting for action, loyal to their lord.)

The Israelites too are drawn up for battle with all the usual panoply, but with rather less point, since the plan is to flee across the Red Sea anyway (*Ofest is selost/þæt ge of feonda fæðme weorðen*, 'Haste is best, so that you may escape from your enemies' grasp', 293–4), and the account of the fierce-hearted readiness for battle-play of the Israelite *sæwicingas*, 'sea-rovers' (333), as they cross the Red Sea seems a little inappropriate. There is perhaps a warning for the unwary reader here, if he assumes that the poet has simply been 'carried away', for the deliberate resistance that the poem sets up to a literal reading may be a way of drawing attention to an allegorical meaning, of referring, for instance, to the 'battle of life' which follows baptism (a familiar typological interpretation of the Red Sea crossing).[29] This would not, however, affect radically the comments on style made here.

  The poem, throughout, exploits to the full the resources of the Old English poetic style: there are many new and original compounds, and some extraordinarily contorted patterns of variation (e.g. 389–96).[30] The richly decorative language, which certainly suggests the influence of Book V, 'De transitu Maris Rubri', of Avitus, has sometimes a startling power, though often it is inadequately adapted to the matter. There is a kind of imagination at work in the image of

35

the cloud that shelters the Israelites as a sail (81) with invisible sailyard, but it is an imagination that takes its eye fatally from the object, something more like Coleridge's fancy. The description of the parting of the seas and the sea-bed exposed, *ealde staðolas* (285), to trampling feet has some Ovidian touches, but in the *tour de force* of the poem, the overwhelming of Pharaoh's host in the return-ing waters, rhetorical elaboration runs loose into hectic extravagance, dissolving into desperate, lurid, empty, isolated gestures:

> Flod famgode,      fæge crungon,
> lagu land gefeol,   lyft wæs onhrered,
> wicon weallfæsten,   wægas burston....                    (482–4)

(The sea foamed, doomed men fell, water flooded the land, the air was in tumult, the water-walls gave way, the waves burst through.)

*Daniel*, the next poem in Junius XI, is linked with the *Exodus*, explicitly, through an introduction which moralises the course of Jewish history from Moses' deliverance to the time of Nebuchadnezzar, and implicitly, through the common theme of God's protection of his chosen servants—a theme which may have had particular attractions for a monastic community in its earlier years or in a time of danger. The handling of the narrative is straightforward and economical, except for the elaborate and expansive treatment given to the central section, the prayer of Azarias and the song of the three children in the Fiery Furnace, both of them rhapsodic hymns of praise to the Creator. These form the centre-piece of the poem, and are perhaps its original nucleus: the two songs had an independent existence as canticles of the Church, and played a large part in the liturgy, especially of Holy Week. They carry the typological message of the poem, of God's deliverance of man from hell-fire and the devil, and are evidence, with Caedmon's *Hymn* and *Christ I*, of a developed Old English tradition of rhapsodic, psalmic poetry, with perhaps some influence from the Irish *retorics*.[31] The two songs, with their narrative link, exist separately in the *Azarias* of the Exeter Book, in a text related probably by oral transmission.[32] The most famous lines in *Daniel* describe the fire as no more to the three Israelites than a mild shower on a summer's day, *windig and wynsum* (346). The poet rather spoils the effect by repeating it.[33]

The poem, or series of poems, called *Christ and Satan* completes the book, and looks as though it was deliberately designed to, as an afterthought: the other three poems in the MS are in one hand, but this is by three successive copyists, and there is no illustration in this part of the MS. The poem, which could be of any date but is probably quite late, deals with three episodes: first, the Fall of the Angels, with an imperfect transition to, second, the Harrowing of Hell, followed by an exposition, very homiletic in tone, of Redemption, Resurrection and Ascension, leading to, third, an account of the Temptation. The old title is not a bad one since the poem, in a tripartite structure reminiscent of the *De laudibus Dei* of Dracontius, provides successive and climactic proofs of God's

(Christ's) power over the devil, culminating in the God-like fortitude of the incarnate Christ in the Temptation.[34] It thus completes the development of a dominant theme in the Junius XI series, but reverses the technique: the other three poems provide narrative with typological implication, while this provides the typological fulfilment, with narrative allusion.[35] It may have been the work of a scrupulous ecclesiastic, who wished to see the doctrinal themes more severely and explicitly underlined, and who wanted, in particular, a version of the Fall of the Angels with more orthodox commentary. The lectionary character of the poem is more marked than ever, and it is on the whole the product of a fairly pedestrian, routine competence.

*Christ and Satan* begins with a reference to Creation as the primary demonstration of God's power:

> Þæt wearð underne     eorðbuendum,
> þæt meotod hæfde     miht and strengðo
> ða he gefestnade     foldan sceatas.

(God's power was made manifest to men in the creation of the earth in all its parts.)

Power, as a theme of praise and source of faith, is a persistent preoccupation of these scriptural poems, and its relevance to monastic communities has already been suggested. It perhaps had a more general relevance to the beleaguered role of Christian faith in a warrior-society, and to the constant need of that faith to demonstrate, in warrior-like terms, its power and efficacy. In Bede's story of the conversion of Northumbria by Paulinus, what the heathen high priest Coifi asks for is a demonstration of the power of the new religion, evidence of some tangible reward for service, for, as he confesses, he has gained neither virtue nor profit from the old one: 'If the gods had any power they would have helped me more readily, seeing that I have always served them with greater zeal.'[36] Histories and saints' lives are full of examples of victories in battle preceded or followed by dramatic conversions or gestures of faith: the best-known is Bede's account of Oswald's victory over Cadwalla at Rowley Burn in 633, with an army 'small in numbers but strengthened by their faith in Christ'.[37] The most consistent and overt exposition, however, of this doctrine of power, of the temporal rewards of faith, is in the *Life of Bishop Wilfrid* of Eddius Stephanus. As Eddius says, 'when King Ecgfrith lived in peace with our bishop, the kingdom, as many bear witness, was increased on every hand by his glorious victories; but when the agreement between them was destroyed ... the King's triumph came to an end during his own lifetime'.[38] Perhaps Eddius was affected by the well-developed power-consciousness of his subject. He returns to the theme when describing the massiveness of the churches that Wilfrid founded at Ripon and at Hexham (cap. XVII, XXII): they are declarations of God's power, and Boniface also speaks in similar terms of the influence of majestic illuminated books on the heathen.[39]

If, combined with this imperative need to demonstrate the temporal power of the faith, one recalls the pervasively militaristic language of the heroic poetic tradition, which would tend to translate all action, even running away, into victorious battle, then the theme of *meotodes meahte* ('God's power') would seem a historical and poetic as well as doctrinal necessity, and we need not be surprised at its dominance in Anglo-Saxon religious poetry. A late and splendid expression of the theme, which we may relate to the scriptural poetry already discussed, is the poem *Judith*. This poem occurs, in fragmentary form (the beginning is lost), in the *Beowulf*-manuscript, and is generally presumed to be of late date, perhaps tenth century, because of certain licences in alliteration and a tendency to rhyme. It has also been generally assumed that the fragment represents only the concluding sections of a full-scale treatment of the apocryphal book of Judith, but Huppe makes a convincing case that the poem as it stands is virtually complete,[40] and that the author uses a technique similar to that of *Exodus* and *Daniel* (that is, the elaboration of a central major episode in the biblical story, in this case the slaying of Holofernes, rather than a systematic paraphrase) to exemplify a similar theme, namely God's power to protect his faithful servants:

> Him feng dryhten god
> fægre on fultum, frea ælmihtig. (299–300)

(The lord god almighty gave them precious help.)

The place of *Judith* in the *Beowulf*-MS is perhaps due to the scribe's feeling, in the dark days of the late tenth century, that she was a good example of resistance to a heathen invader: Ælfric, who himself did a 'metrical' version of the book of Judith for homiletic purposes, certainly refers to the poem as an example of this kind in his introduction to his translation of the Old Testament,[41] though any specific connection with Æthelflæd, the 'Lady of the Mercians', and her wars against the Danes, seems doubtful.

The poet's methods are perhaps simpler than those of his predecessors, for he tends to strip the story of its theological and typological associations in patristic commentary,[42] and to isolate it as a more purely exemplary piece of hagiography, in which the daughter of the faith, the exemplar of Christian virtue and chastity, triumphs over the monstrous prince of darkness. But if his conception of the story is simple, his dramatic and stylistic techniques are impressively rich and complex. Like the poet of *Beowulf*, he uses a persistent contrastive imagery of light and darkness, depicting a lurid world of drunken orgies, lustful desires, decadently rich ornament (like Holofernes' *fleohnet*, 47), violence and fear, against which Judith shines radiant. As in *Beowulf*, too, there is constant commentary, and a grim relish in the anticipation of the destruction of the godless Assyrian,

> Gewat ða se deofulcunda,
> galferhð gumena ðreate,

bealofull his beddes neosan,    þær he sceolde his blæd forleosan
ædre binnan anre nihte.                                     (61–4)

(Then the devil-born, evil-hearted lecher went, with his troop of men, to seek his bed, where he was to yield up all his glory in one short night.)

or in the triumphant tirade which accompanies his soul to hell:

> Læg se fula leap
> gesne beæftan,    gæst ellor hwearf
> under neowelne næs    and ðær genyðerad wæs,
> susle gesæled    syððan æfre,
> wyrmum bewunden,    witum gebunden,
> hearde gehæfted    in hellebryne
> æfter hinsiðe.    Ne ðearf he hopian no,
> þystrum forðylmed,    þæt he ðonan mote
> of ðam wyrmsele,    ac ðær wunian sceal
> awa to aldre    butan ende forð
> in ðam heolstran ham,    hyhtwynna leas.       (111–21)

(The foul carcass lay destitute of life, the soul departed elsewhere into the bottomless pit, and there laid low, bound in pain for ever, wound about with serpents, confined in torment, cruelly fettered after death. Nor has he any cause for hope, in that overwhelming darkness, that he may escape from that serpent-hall, but he shall dwell there for ever without end in that dark home, lost to all hope of happiness.)

Such a passage illustrates the poem's use of loosely accumulative patterns of variation and characteristically late use of rhyme, and illustrates too the still-persistent influence of classical compounding technique in a coinage like *wyrmsele* for hell. Consciousness of heroic tradition is strong in this poem: the hero's vaunting-speech (*gylpspræc*) before battle appears metamorphosed in Judith's prayer for forgiveness and blessing for what she is about to do, while the final battle of the Hebrews against the leaderless Assyrians is fully enriched with heroic motifs. But the special quality of the poem, one it shares with *Genesis B*, is its dramatic power, particularly its evocation of the sinister, corrupt, doom-ridden atmosphere of the Assyrian camp on the night before Holofernes' death, or the grim ironies of the morning after, where the Assyrians, with defeat at hand, are fearful to wake Holofernes from his night of love:

> Næs ðeah eorla nan
> þe ðone wiggend    aweccan dorste
> oððe gecunnian    hu ðone cumbolwigan
> wið ða halgan mægð    hæfde geworden,

39

metodes meowlan....                                                                    (257–61)
                  Hogedon þa eorlas aweccan
hyra winedryhten:      him wiht ne speow.                                 (273–4)

(There was not one of the men that dared wake the warrior, to find out
how the battle-leader had fared with the holy maiden, the lady of God.
. . . The men thought to wake their lord: they did not succeed.)

### Saints' lives

*Judith* draws close at times, in its simple placings of emphasis, to saint's life, a
genre of writing widespread in England during the Anglo-Saxon period, in
Latin and the vernacular, in both verse and prose. Saints' lives made a powerful
appeal to the emotions and offered rich sustenance to faith: they gave examples
of how fortitude in suffering wins access to divine sources of power:

                ahte bega geweald,
lifes ond deaðes,      þa he lustum dreag
eaðmod on eorðan      ehtendra nið.
Forþon is nu arlic      þæt we æfæstra
dæde demen,      secgen dryhtne lof.               (*Guthlac*, 523–7)

(He had power over both life and death when he suffered on earth the
persecutions of his enemies with glad humility. Wherefore it is proper
that we should celebrate the deeds of the faithful, give praise to the Lord.)

They give praise to God and hope to man. Unfortunately, their simplicity of
design allows little scope for interesting literary development, whatever language
they are written in. Nevertheless, they are a major form of narrative for many
centuries, absorbing the cult of the hero, in England as in Ireland, to simpler
and more purely spiritual goals. This process of absorption may seem only
partially complete in the poem *Andreas*, though the effect is more the product of a
lavishly inappropriate use of heroic diction than of a blending of values. The
poet, treating of St Andrew's sea-journey to Mermedonia to rescue Matthew
from cannibals and of his own subsequent sufferings, follows fairly closely a Latin
translation of a Greek original, recounting the apocryphal acts of the Apostles.
The original narrative already displays the love of sensational incident made
popular by the progenitor of the form, the life of St Antony by Athanasius (c. 360),
with its borrowings from Greek romances, but the English poet is clearly determined to improve on his original. His method is to portray Andrew as a Beowulf-
like warrior, setting out to rescue another Hrothgar from another tribe of cannibals. Occasionally, the vocabulary of heroism is successfully transferred: the
evocation of the theme of loyalty and loss of *þegnscipe* in the refusal of St Andrew's
followers to leave him is a minor triumph:

Hwider hweorfað we     hlafordlease,
geomormode,     gode orfeorme,
synnum wunde,     gif we swicað þe?           (405–7)

(Where shall we go, bereft of our Lord, sad at heart, lost to all good,
stricken with sins, if we desert you?)

(The elegies, as we shall see, exploit much more purposefully a similar potential
in the language of exile and lordlessness.) But the more explicitly militaristic
vocabulary is hopelessly inappropriate and seems so from the beginning of the
poem, where the apostles, going out to suffer and to preach, are portrayed as
warrior-thanes going forth into battle:

Þæt wæron mære     men ofer eorðan,
frome folctogan     ond fyrdhwate,
rofe rincas,     þonne rond ond hand
on herefelda     helm ealgodon,
on meotudwange.           (7–11)

(They were men famous throughout the earth, bold and resolute
chieftains, tough warriors, when shield and hand guarded helm on the
field of battle.)

This, in the light of Christ's injunction to the Apostles to be 'as sheep in the midst
of wolves' (Matthew 10: 16), is ridiculous, and the treatment of Andrew throughout the poem often compounds the absurdity. He approaches the gates of the
prison in the Mermedonian city, *beorn beaduwe heard* ('the battle-hardened
warrior'), bristling with heroic epithets—but to little or no purpose, since he is
invisible anyway and the guards fall down dead without word or blow, *þurh
handhrine haliges gastes* (1000).

    The stylistic bravado is associated with a generally uneasy imaginative
control. The poet has clearly been swept off his feet by *Beowulf*, and substitutes
its sonorous language for any real engagement with his subject: he imitates a
famous *Beowulf* kenning, *ealuscerwen* ('serving of bitter drink', i.e. disaster, panic)
in his *meoduscerwen*, describing the disaster of the flood which overwhelms the
city, but ruins the metaphor by replacing *ealu*, 'a bitter drink', with *meodu*, 'a
sweet drink', for the sake of alliteration.[43] A winter-scene which in *Beowulf*
balances a real function in the narrative against its symbolic power as an image
of Hengest's state of mind (1131–3) is elaborated in independent bravura style
to the point where the context is overburdened and a crude allegorical motive
naïvely exposed (1255–62). There is an endearing vigour and enthusiasm with
all this occasional ineptitude, and beneath the exuberance of style an unthought
simplicity of theme in which the function of the narrative as a demonstration of
God's power is consistently reiterated. Power is the subject of the divine Helms-
man's discourse on Christ's miracles, of frequent interpolated asides and affir-

mations, and it is power (the flooding of the city) that manifests to the heathen the necessity of obedience.[44] In this, *Andreas* is close kin to the scriptural poems.

*Andreas* is followed in the Vercelli Book by *The Fates of the Apostles*, a short verse martyrology and typical routine product of monastic verse-making. Its interest is that it is one of the four poems with the Cynewulfian runic 'signature', and the length of the signature in relation to the poem has led to speculation that the *Fates* is an epilogue to *Andreas*, and that both poems are to be attributed to Cynewulf. The attribution of *Andreas* cannot be sustained on any grounds. The *Fates* is written in a subdued heroic style and has the characteristic nerveless orthodoxy of treatment which prompts one to think of each of Cynewulf's poems in turn as the final product of a declining old age. Cynewulf is the monastic craftsman *par excellence*, a poet who could satisfy any occasion, and he has much in common with another good monastic journeyman, John Lydgate. He writes fluently and amply, with decorum but without excitement, smoothing the cluttered syntax of the heroic style and the extravagance of the heroic vocabulary to a more consistent propriety of tone. His subjects are suggested by the calendar and services of the Church,[45] and he treats all with a level competence.

*Elene*, which is also in the Vercelli Book, is certainly his best poem. It deals with the conversion of Constantine and the journey of his mother, St Helena, to Palestine to find the True Cross, and was presumably written for lectionary use on the feast-day of the Invention of the Holy Cross, 3 May. The early part of the poem offers, in Constantine's battle against the Huns and in the sea-voyage to Palestine, opportunities for descriptive elaboration in the traditional manner which Cynewulf manages extremely well; the rest involves much argument and exposition, in Helena's confrontations with Judas, the spokesman of the Jewish community, and is less interesting. The possibilities of a dialogue between Jew and Christian are inhibited by the dogmatic cast of the genre, which must assume and demonstrate the inevitability of the saint's triumph, and by the inflexibly smooth and well-amplified manner, which turns every speech into a rhetorical set-piece. The best passages are those in the elevated hymnic style, such as Judas's invocation and prayer for divine guidance in discovering the Cross (725–801). An extended personal epilogue precedes the signature and should be of interest as the first autobiographical statement by an English poet, but its postures are as unrewardingly conventional as those of Lydgate. The poem ends with a vision of the Last Judgment, a favourite topic in Anglo-Saxon religious poetry.

There is little of specific interest in Cynewulf's other two signed poems. *Juliana* is a conventional saint's life, quite lacking the passion and vitality of the Middle English prose version. The only striking departure from the Latin original is in the portrayal of the Virgin's suitor Heliseus (Eleusius), who in the Latin is quite prepared to be 'converted' as a realistic compromise, but who in Cynewulf's poem becomes an exceptionally zealous defender of heathenism. This makes the conflict of good and evil even more stark, as with Judith and Holofernes, and simplifies an already simple situation. In style, the poem is comparatively plain and spiritless, looking forward perhaps to the more natural and flexible manner of late Old English prose, though the residual strength of the heroic style produces a moment of unexpected extravagance at Heliseus' death:

Ne þorftan þa þegnas     in þam þystran ham,
seo geneatscolu     in þam neolan scræfe,
to þam frumgare     feohgestealda
witedra wenan,     þæt hy in winsele
ofer beorsetle     beagas þegon,
æpplede gold.                           (683–8)

(Nor need the men of his retinue in that dark home, that dark cave, look for any share of treasures from their chief, that they would receive rings or 'appled' gold as they sat at drink in the hall.)

The style also still resists the intrusion of alien classical names, such as Apollo and Diana, from the Latin original. This is partly because well-established metrical and alliterative patterns make alien names difficult to absorb (even repetitions of names of characters, like Heliseus, are kept to a minimum),[46] but it is also a matter of stylistic decorum. In other words, the poetry will accept one kind of cultural transfer, from Germanic to Christian, but not another as well, and proper names are a good index to this resistance.

Cynewulf's other signed poem is not a saint's life, but it may be mentioned here. It is a poem on the Ascension, a free paraphrase of a sermon by St Gregory, and forms the second of a cycle of three poems traditionally called *Christ*. This cycle stands at the beginning of the Exeter Book, and the three sections have the manuscript indications of separate poems (there are, of course, no titles in the manuscript). However, a thoughtful compiler recognised that the three poems, on Advent, Ascension and Doomsday, relate to three stages in the fulfilment of Christ's promise to mankind, and has presumably placed them deliberately in the present sequence. There are no explicit links and no patchwork, though *Christ II* alludes to the Nativity in its first few lines and the signature, as in *Elene* and *Juliana*, includes a reference to the Last Judgment. The relationships within the cycle are, however, quite different from those in *Christ and Satan*, and it is probably most helpful for the modern reader to think of *Christ I, II* and *III* as separate poems. *Christ II* is a skilful professional piece of work, and if it seems unremarkable this may in itself be a tribute to the ease with which Cynewulf moves in the sermon's world of scriptural allusion and the total mastery with which he has absorbed the traditional poetic style, without loss of grandeur, to non-heroic themes.

The poem that follows *Christ* in the Exeter Book, *Guthlac*, is the last of the hagiographical group. There are, in fact, two poems, independently and very freely related to the Latin prose life of Guthlac of Crowland (d. 714) written about 730 by Felix of Crowland for Ælfwald, King of East Anglia. The two poems, *Guthlac A* and *B*, are dated about 800; there is also a later prose version in the Vercelli Book. *Guthlac A* concentrates on the saint's debate and conflict with the devils who daily besiege him in his island fastness in the fen; it shows some of the limitations of the adapted heroic style in constantly substituting physical for spiritual confrontation. Inward analysis of the allegorically heroic temper of martyrdom seems imprisoned within the inflexibilities of the inherited style, and the exchange of patently empty threats and predictably stalwart declarations of faith is monotonous. *Guthlac B*, which deals only with the last days and death of the saint, is quite different. The dialogue here is with the saint's faithful companion and servant, who acts as an agent of lay understanding, receiving and giving insight into the suffering and joy of a death worthy of a saint's passion. The language of lordship is powerfully evoked: to the sorrowing servant it is the death of his master as well as a saint, and the memorable close portrays a grief unassuaged by the enclosing sanctity:

> Ellen biþ selast      þam þe oftost sceal
> dreogan dryhtenbealu,      deope behycgan
> þroht þeodengedal,      þonne seo þrag cymeð,
> wefen wyrdstafum....
>
>                   Ic sceal sarigferð,
> heanmod hweorfan,      hyge drusendne.      (1348–51, 1378–9)

(Courage is best for him who has to endure great affliction, reconcile himself deep in his heart to the grievous loss of his lord, when the bitter moment comes decreed by fate.... I must go forth, wretched and sorrowful at heart, cast down in spirit.)

It has something of the effect of Ector's lament at the end of Malory's *Morte d'Arthur*.

### Devotional poems

These saints' lives are usually reworkings of Latin prose originals. They are written in poetry because the prevailing literary mode is poetic—later, in the tenth century, they will be in prose—and as poems they can display only infrequently, accidentally or perversely the characteristic excellences of the Old English poetic style. Two poems which embody more of its richness are *Christ I* and *The Dream of the Rood*: 'devotional' is only a label for these poems, and would be clearly misleading if it implied anything of the affective spirit of post-Bernardine devotional writing. But they are different from other Old English poems, partly because they both draw their inspiration from the most lyrical parts of the liturgy. *Christ I* is an Advent cantata, a sequence of twelve poems woven freely and rhapsodically from and around the O's of Advent, a series of antiphons used in Vespers in the week before Christmas. The poems celebrate the coming of Christ, the Virgin Birth, Mary as the gateway to Salvation, the Trinity, the prophecies and types of Advent; one poem (VII), quite independent of the antiphons, presents a dialogue of Joseph and Mary. The poet moves about freely in the liturgy, the Scriptures and Church Fathers, drawing on a rich repertory of scriptural forms and meanings.[47] Thus the opening lines,

> Ðu eart se weallstan     þe ða wyrhtan iu
> wiðwurpon to weorce.

(You are the wall-stone that the workers of old rejected from their work.)

are no 'poetic' metaphor, but an allusion to an elaborate scheme of typological reference, beginning in the antiphon, '*O Rex gentium et desideratus earum, lapisque angularis qui facis utraque unum: veni, et salva hominem quem de limo formasti*' and stretching out into the Bible (e.g. Psalm 117: 22; Matthew 21: 42; 1 Peter 2:7) and biblical commentary. It is clearly a poem by a man used to hearing the divine office and chanting the hours day after day:[48] its function is both worship and instruction, to celebrate and also to provide that sub-structure of understanding and meditation which makes the liturgy meaningful. A precise parallel is provided by Lydgate, who, as a monk writing for his fellow-monks, works similar vernacular rhapsodies out of the Marian antiphons and the sequence *Letabundus*.[49] There is a big difference in poetic vitality, though, and *Christ I* gains added strength from its sequence-form. Though the poems are separate, they relate to an invisible but ever-present narrative of momentous significance, running from *Wæs seo fæmne geong*, 'The maiden was young' (35) to *Nu we on þæt bearn foran breostum stariað*, 'Now we look upon the child at your breast' (341). The exploration of the typological themes of the antiphons is thus constantly pressed upon by the anticipation and need of the historical acts which began with Christ's coming and which now at Advent are re-enacted:

> Us is ðinra arna þearf!
> Hafað se awyrgda     wulf tostenced,
> deor dædscua,     dryhten, þin eowde,
> wide towrecene.     Þæt ðu, waldend, ær
> blode gebohtes,     þæt se bealofulla
> hyneð heardlice,     ond him on hæft nimeð
> ofer usse nioda lust.
>
> (255–61)

(We have need of your grace! The accursed wolf, the beast of darkness, has scattered wide your flock, O Lord. What you, Lord, bought with your blood the evil one harasses cruelly, and seizes into his power all against our will.)

The sense of crisis, both historical and personal, and the mood of hope certain to be fulfilled are both powerfully evoked, in a manner which may be compared with works of considerably greater dramatic sophistication, Langland's *Piers Plowman* (C. XIX. 118 ff) and Auden's *For the Time Being*. The poem ends with

45

exhortation to praise God (430), a restatement of the theme of *Vere dignum et justum est.*

*The Dream of the Rood* is perhaps the best of all Old English religious poems, or at least the most perfectly achieved. This in itself may be surprising, since it seems to be of composite origin. Fragments of the poem, closely related to the text in the Vercelli Book, are found inscribed in runic letters on the Ruthwell Cross, which dates from the early eighth century. This seems unexpectedly early for a poem like *The Dream of the Rood*, and the conclusion might be that the poem in its present form is a reworking of earlier pieces, some of them specifically written to be inscribed on a monumental cross, as if the cross were speaking. If this is the origin of the central prosopopeia of the poem, then it has been turned to brilliant literary effect. The poem begins with the dreamer's vision of the cross, *syllicre treow*, a cross of victory *(sigebeam)* covered with gold and set with jewels. It is the idea of the Cross that the Anglo-Saxons were used to, and a sign of victory in a very literal sense, since faith in it brought victory in battle: Constantine's victory over the Huns, retold in *Elene*, followed his vision of the Cross, a token of which he had carried before him into battle, and Oswald prepares for battle against Cadwalla by planting a cross before his army.[50] But as the dreamer watches, he sees that the Cross, through its gold, bears marks of suffering, a wound on the right side:

> Geseah ic þæt fuse beacen  
> wendan wædum ond bleom;   hwilum hit wæs mid wætan bestemed,  
> beswyled mid swates gange,   hwilum mid since gegyrwed.   (21–23)

(I saw that shining symbol change in appearance and hue; sometimes it was wet with moisture, streaming with blood, sometimes adorned with jewels.)

This dazzling enigma is developed in the Cross's own narrative of the Crucifixion. It is the enigma of divine strength which openly embraces suffering and humiliation, of the *geong hæleð, Christ,* who 'mounted' *(gestah)* the Cross, 'embraced' it *(ymbclypte)* willingly. The key to the poem's success is the way the Cross is made to bridge the gulf between Christ incarnate and fallen sinful man, and by so doing to act as agent of the dreamer's understanding.[51] The tree torn from the forest shares Christ's strength and man's weakness: it might strike down its foes, yet it suffers; it trembles and is appalled, yet stands firm.

> Ealle ic mihte  
> feondas gefyllan,   hwæðre ic fæste stod....   (37–8)

> Sare ic wæs mid sorgum gedrefed,   hnag ic hwæðre þam secgum to handa,  
> eaðmod   elne mycle.   (59–60)

(I could have laid low the enemies, but I stood firm.... I was troubled

with grief, yet I submitted to the hands of those men with brave
humility.)

'Weakness' gives strength, suffering joy, death life—

> On me bearn godes
> þrowode hwile.　　Forþan ic þrymfæst nu
> hlifige under heofenum,　　ond ic hælan mæg
> æghwylcne anra,　　þara þe him biþ egesa to me.　　　　(83–6)

(Upon me the Son of God suffered for a while. Wherefore I now tower
high under the heavens, full of glory, and may heal any man who stands
in awe of me.)

and out of this divine paradox the dreamer's faith is made strong.

There is nothing new in these ideas. Many of them find a close parallel in the
well-known hymns of the sixth-century Venantius Fortunatus, *Vexilla regis
prodeunt*, where the Cross is a banner of triumph and throne of victory, and
*Pange lingua gloriosi*, where the Tree is endowed with human feeling:

> Flecte ramos arbor alta,
> Tensa laxa viscera,
> Et rigor lentescat ille,
> Quem dedit nativitas;
> Et superni membra Regis
> Tende miti stipite

> (Bend, proud tree, thy spreading branches,
> Loosen thy rigidity,
> All that ruggedness begotten
> Of thy stern heredity:
> Thine to throne the King of heaven;
> Hold his body tenderly.)[52]

The very heart of the paradox, the co-existence in Christ of the unapproachable
Godhead and a full capacity for human suffering, is the orthodox dogma of the
Incarnation, insisted upon by the Church 'with a vehemence and rigidity deriving from more than two centuries of heretical Christological dispute.'[53] Nor
is a detail like that of the *geong hæleð* anything new, since it draws on the well-
established iconography of *Christus miles*: certainly it has nothing to do with
Germanic heroic tradition. What is new about *The Dream of the Rood* is the poetic
mode and structure: the envelope of dream and prosopopeia, with their power
of multiplying awareness, and above all the use of the Cross as a dramatic,
enigmatic, shifting, developing symbol, a referent for the dreamer's own growth
in understanding and an agent in it. Within the poem the Cross fulfils something

47

of the function of the pearl in the Middle English *Pearl*-poem, or of Piers in Langland's poem.

## Homiletic poetry

These two poems have 'occasions', but they transcend those occasions. The much larger body of straightforward homiletic poetry has a more routine quality, as one might expect. These are craftsmanlike, unspectacular productions within a well-established monastic tradition, and they probably played a fairly small part in that tradition. There are two homiletic poems in the Vercelli Book, for instance, one a debate of the body and soul, the other a free version of Psalm 28, and these exist side by side with other religious poems, *Andreas*, *The Fates*, *Elene* and *The Dream of the Rood*; but all are overshadowed by the twenty-two prose homilies which occupy the bulk of the volume and which seem to have been regarded as intrinsically more important, if we are to judge by the fact that they have titles and more elaborate initials.

Nevertheless, the vernacular poetic tradition is recognised as a perfectly respectable one, and the dozen or so homiletic poems scattered through the Exeter Book include some learned and serious pieces, as well as themselves providing a didactic continuum in which the more miscellaneous material of the collection is embedded. The poem called *Vainglory*, for instance, is very conscious of heroic tradition: it begins with what appears to be an echo of *Beowulf*,

> Hwæt, me frod wita  on fyrndagum
> sægde, snottor ar,  sundorwundra fela!

(Lo, a wise old man, a wise messenger, told me in days long ago of many wonders.)

and its warnings against pride and arrogance are directed specifically against the traditional vaunting-speeches of the mead-hall. Such boastfulness is associated with the example of the rebellious angels, and the alternative offered is Christian humility and peaceableness and love of one's enemies. What the poem does, in fact, is to offer a schematic doctrinal commentary on what elsewhere, in *Beowulf* or *Maldon*, is more complexly registered as deplorable or suspect as a pattern of human behaviour not essentially Christian: it has the same sort of relation to the narrative poems as Chaucer's *Parson's Tale* to the rest of the *Canterbury Tales*. The attempt to absorb and transcend heroic values seems quite deliberate, and can be seen too in the opening, where the poem's wisdom is declared to be derived, not from traditional lore, but from a man learned in books, *beorn boca gleaw*, that is, a biblical commentator.[54] This wise man is introduced as expositor towards the end of the poem, so that what we seem to have is a fairly simple model for the dramatic techniques of poems like *The Wanderer* and *The Seafarer* (which it follows in the Exeter Book), poems with an essentially

similar homiletic purpose but with a far richer notion of the way poetry functions. The poem called *The Order of the World* has an embryonically dramatic
structure rather like that of *Vainglory*, with a first-person narrator (the preacher)
who introduces a *wisne woðboran* as a bringer of wisdom (the exegete) and gives
an account of the Creation as an example of the mysteries he opens to the *fus
hæle*, 'the man ready for a journey', the pilgrim on life's way.[55] Again, it is essentially an envelope to a plain homily, and clearly derives from an extension of
sermon-techniques, but the potential for a richer poetic development is nevertheless there.

Two longer poems in the Exeter Book are more orthodox in approach, though
they have their splendours. *Christ III* is a vision of the Last Judgment, eclectically
constructed and powerfully written, like *Christ I*. Its theme is a favourite one
with Anglo-Saxon poets, and is recurred to in another short poem in the Exeter
Book, in several of Cynewulf's epilogues, and in an excellent late translation of
Bede's *De die judicii*. It is not hard, perhaps, to understand why the subject
should be so favoured: theologically, it is simple, graphic and effective; poetically,
it gives endless opportunities for apocalyptic thunder, and Anglo-Saxon poetry
is good at this. Parts of *Christ III* have an irresistible cumulative power; as a
whole, it goes the way of most attempts at the 'cosmic sublime', into a thunderous
monotony.

*The Phoenix*, on the other hand, is one of the most unusual and interesting of
Anglo-Saxon poems. The first part is a free version of the *De Ave Phoenice* of
Lactantius, a Latin poet of the fourth century who became a Christian in mature
life. His poem is pervasively classical in image and diction, with a particular
debt to Ovid, and one of the striking things about the English poem is the ease,
confidence and totality with which the poem is transferred to a new idiom.
Here, for instance, is the way the two poets write of the Phoenix's dedication to
the Sun:

> Paret et obsequitur Phoebo memoranda satelles:
> Hoc Natura parens munus habere dedit.[56]

> (It yields homage and submission to Phoebus, as his honourable
> attendant: to this service it is dedicated by its parent Nature.)

> Se sceal þære sunnan     sið behealdan
> ond ongean cuman     godes condelle,
> glædum gimme,     georne bewitigan,
> hwonne up cyme     æþelast tungla
> ofer yðmere     estan lixan,
> fæder fyrngeweorc     frætwum blican,
> torht tacen godes.                    (90–6)

> (There it is accustomed to turn its face to watch the journey of the sun,
>  God's candle, the precious jewel, eagerly observe when that noblest of

49

stars comes up over the sea-waves, shining from the east, the ancient work of the father, the bright token of God, radiant in its adornments.)

It is not merely that the language has been purged of classical allusion: the notion of 'service', of relation, has been changed, and the significance of the sun has been transformed. In the lines that follow, the painted mythological allusions of a Virgilian dawn,

> Lutea cum primum surgens Aurora rubescit,
> cum primum rosea sidera luce fugat.... (35–6)

(When first the rising saffron dawn grows red, and puts to flight the stars with its rosy light....)

are translated into a totally native idiom—

> Tungol beoþ ahyded,
> gewiten under waþeman  westdælas on,
> bideglad on dægred,  ond seo deorce niht
> won gewiteð. (96–9)

(The stars are hidden, slipped under the waves in the west at daybreak, and the dark night passes away.)

So complete is the transference that it is often difficult to trace the precise relationship between Latin original and English paraphrase; the extraordinary uniformity of impression in the English poem, the slightness of the response to particular stylistic influences from its source, is a potent reminder of the highly developed poetic tradition to which it was heir, and of the associated difficulty of disentangling individual voices. The other striking thing about *The Phoenix* is the thoroughness with which the Latin poem has been absorbed and adapted to a stricter didactic purpose. Certainly, Lactantius is a Christian poet, his language bathed in that of the Scriptures and constantly echoing, in a cultured and witty way, the paradoxes of Christian resurrection:

> Mors illi Venus est, sola est in morte voluptas:
> Ut possit nasci, appetit ante mori ...
> Ipsa quidem, sed non eadem est, eademque nec ipsa est,
> Aeternam vitam mortis adepta bono. (165–6, 169–70)

(Death is its beloved, its only delight is in death: to be able to be born, it yearns first to die ... its very self, but not the same self, wins eternal life through the blessed gift of death.)

The English poet changes all this: for him the Latin poem is an invaluable source of 'historical' knowledge, albeit with hints of possible allegorical treatment, and he uses it as the basis of a thoroughgoing and complex homiletic allegory.[57] His sense of its allegorical significance presses constantly upon his account of the Phoenix, eventually absorbing it altogether into a rapturous celebration of redemption and resurrection. The poem illustrates very clearly the parity of intellectual exchange between Latin and the vernacular, and the respected position of Old English poetry in the monastic tradition, at least during the eighth and early ninth centuries.

There are a number of other short homiletic poems of a fairly commonplace kind in the Exeter Book, as well as some miscellaneous poems, which may be mentioned here briefly. Whatever the motives of the compiler of the Exeter Book (or its original) he clearly had a less rigorous sense of his mission than the executors of the Vercelli and Junius MSS. He includes material which can only be regarded as the débris or spoil-heaps of the monastic tradition—catalogues of attributes (*The Gifts of Men, The Fortunes of Men*), collections of *Precepts*, gnomic poems, fragments of a bestiary, sets of riddles. It is the raw material of poetry rather than poetry itself, though sometimes there are the first crude indications of some attempt at shaping, as in the first-person introduction to *Maxims*. The sources of such verse-making are in the monastic educational system: though they may incorporate some native material, they are mostly school-exercises on Latin models such as Cato's *Distichs*. What preserves them is the appeal they make to the inexhaustible appetite for encyclopaedias which is one of the most enduring characteristics of the monastic tradition. They correspond, on a small scale, to the miscellaneous output of John Lydgate—and if the resemblances to Lydgate may seem to have been pressed rather hard in this chapter, the justification would be that Lydgate is the first monastic poet to give back to English poetry, in the fifteenth century, the status in the cloisters that it possessed freely in the eighth and ninth centuries. Thus *The Gifts of Men* is closely analogous to Lydgate's *Everything to his Semblable*, having a common source and a common appeal. The *Riddles* are a perverse encyclopaedia, a kind of 'everything to its nature' in reverse, where the pleasure is in restoring the order of nature out of its artificially disordered data. Some are quite lengthy and serious poems, like Riddle 40, translated from Aldhelm's *Creatura*, but others are light-hearted, or even obscene, with room for comic verse-effects, double-entendre and cryptograms, and show that the monastic curriculum had its moments of relaxation.

*Meditative poems: the 'elegies'*

None of these poems would have met any resistance in a monastic environment, or would have been at all difficult to include in a monastic commonplace-book or miscellany. This fact should make us wary of detaching the remaining six poems in the Exeter Book from their monastic context, even if we are tempted to do so on the basis of secular allusions or apparently secular themes. The six poems are scattered through the Exeter Book but are habitually grouped by modern scholars as the 'elegiac' poems, because of a common strain of melancholy sentiment. In fact, three of them, *The Wanderer, The Seafarer* and *The Ruin*, are straightforward meditative poems on the transience of the world, and are among the most enduringly beautiful poems in English; while the other three, known as *The Wife's Lament, The Husband's Message*, and *Wulf and Eadwacer*, are so fragmentary and enigmatic that it is difficult to know what to say of them.

What *The Wanderer* and *The Seafarer* do is to embody the predicament of mortality in the imagery of secular and heroic life and then out of loss and destitution to generate the need for the Christian consolation, which is stated in the closing lines. The poetic success of both is essentially in the process of generation: the imagery of mortality is not invented or produced to demonstrate the need, nor is it allegorical, but it is made to embody an experience that seems to have been felt, and through which the speaker comes to his own understanding of the Christian consolation. It is the process of *Piers Plowman* in miniature, and depends similarly on the creation within the poem of an apt *persona*. In *The Wanderer* it is the *anhaga*, the solitary, whose memories of his lost lord contrast with his present wintry exile:

> Þinceð him on mode       þæt he his mondryhten
> clyppe ond cysse,       ond on cneo lecge
> honda ond heafod,       swa he hwilum ær
> in geardagum       giefstolas breac.
> Donne onwæcneð eft       wineleas guma,
> gesihð him biforan       fealwe wegas,
> baþian brimfuglas,       brædan feþra,
> hreosan hrim ond snaw,       hagle gemenged.                    (41–8)

(It seems to him in his mind that he embraces and kisses his Lord, lays hands and head on his knee, where he once was ruler. Then he reawakens, the friendless man, to the reality of dark waves before him, sea birds bathing and spreading their feathers, frost and snow falling, mingled with hail.)

Happiness in life is expressed as the relation of *þegnscipe*, and all human misery in its loss. As the *eardstapa*, the wanderer, goes on to generalise his condition (58), his own destitution is echoed in the decayed evidences that man sees all around:

> Ongietan sceal gleaw hæle       hu gæstlic bið,
> Þonne ealre þisse worulde wela       weste stondeð,
> swa nu missenlice       geond þisne middangeard
> winde biwaune       weallas stondaþ,
> hrime bihrorene,       hryðge þa ederas.
> Woriað þa winsalo,       waldend licgað
> dreame bidrorene,       duguþ eal gecrong,
> wlonc bi wealle.                    (73–80)

(A wise man will realise how fearful it will be when all the glories of our worldly state stand waste, as even now here and there throughout the world there are walls standing, buffeted by the wind, hung with rime, storm-beaten ruined dwellings. The wine-halls fall into ruin, their lords lie bereft of joy, the pick of their men struck down in their pride at the wall.)

The image of the empty, roofless, windswept hall, so potent in reality to the Anglo-Saxons in the ruined Roman cities of England, is added to those of exile and lordlessness to produce a sadness so overwhelming that it can only find issue in the final vision of the world wasted,

> Her bið feoh læne,    her bið freond læne,
> her bið mon læne,    her bið mæg læne,
> eal þis eorþan gesteal    idel weorþeð          (108–10)

(Here all things are transitory—wealth, friends, man and woman alike—the whole foundation of earth will become void.)

where in pressing his thought to its relentless completion, the speaker has 'annihilated the very ground that breeds these vanishing satisfactions'.[58]

The materials that go to the making of *The Wanderer* are all fairly commonplace. The theme of lordlessness is exploited as an image of ultimate human loss in *Andreas*, *Guthlac* and *Genesis B* ; the deserted hall is a favourite elegiac topos in *Beowulf* (2247–66, 2444–62) and elsewhere; the reproach to vainglory (65–72) reminds one of the poem of that name, and the list of ways of meeting death reminds one of the necrology in *The Fortunes of Men* ;[59] the Latin topos of *Ubi Sunt* is alluded to (92–3), and the final lines are as conventional as any preachment. But some poetic alchemy has been at work on these ingredients, essentially the creation of a poetic *persona* who can be shown, dramatically, going through the process of acquiring wisdom. It is this that gives to the images of exile, loss and suffering, of mutability and decay, their particular forcefulness, and makes it impossible for those images to be dissolved, though they may be transcended, in the final consolation. Out of this comes an added strength, for the value of what is lost is somehow realised in the poem, even the value of suffering and feeling loss, and the invocation of Christian consolation is made to seem a painful and sad necessity, inevitable indeed but without the meretricious ease of *contemptus mundi*. It is a Christian poem, but one that gives full recognition to the nature of human experience in a heroic society.

The dramatic development of *The Seafarer* is more rugged, the conflict between different phases of the speaker's response to experience more acute, so much so that some interpretations postulate, quite without support from the text, two speakers. The sea-journey, briefly alluded to in *The Wanderer*, is here the central theme, first for its misery, cold and solitude.

>                   þæt se mon ne wat
> þe him on foldan    fægrost limpeð,
> hu ic earmcearig    iscealdne sæ
> winter wunade    wræccan lastum,
> winemægum bidroren,
> bihongen hrimgicelum;    hægl scurum fleag.

> Þær ic ne gehyrde      butan hlimman sæ,
> iscaldne wæg.                            (12–19)

(The man who enjoys a fortunate life on land can know nothing of my misery as a winter-exile on the ice-cold sea, cast out from my beloved kinsmen, hung with icicles; hailstorms swept down. I heard nothing there but the boom of the sea's icy billows.)

and then, by a startling reversal, as a challenge to the man who seeks something more than an easy life on land, where beauty is the harbinger to decay and the cuckoo's song, to a wise man, only a sad prelude in the mortal cycle.

> Bearwas blostmum nimað,      byrig fægriað,
> wongas wlitigiað,      woruld onetteð;
> ealle þa gemoniað      modes fusne
> sefan to siþe,      þam þe swa þenceð
> on flodwegas      feor gewitan.
> Swylce geac monað      geomran reorde,
> singeð sumeres weard,      sorge beodeð
> bitter in breosthord.                    (48–55)

(The woods are in blossom, the townships look gay, the meadows are bright, the world hastens on; all these things remind a thoughtful man of the journey to be made far over the sea. So when the cuckoo sings its sad song as summer's herald, it only pierces the heart deeper with sorrow.)

*Woruld onetteð*, the world hastens to its end, and the seafarer longs to throw off its distractions:

>                    Forþon me hatran sind
> dryhtnes dreamas      þonne þis deade lif,
> læne on londe.                       (64–6)

(So the joys of the lord are a more passionate concern for me than the transience of mortal life on earth.)

Thus the sea-journey, at first evoked with compelling authenticity, then touched with other-worldly aspirations, develops as a symbol of the renunciation of worldly life and the acceptance of the sufferings involved in the quest for God, and the poem closes, like *The Wanderer*, with homiletic commonplaces.

Yet the sea-journey is not allegorised out of existence: its images are too real for that, and in each phase of its development the poem throws down deep roots into the intractable paradoxes of experience. Indeed the very 'symbol' of renunciation is itself a reality, for many an Irish *peregrinus* put to sea in an oarless boat for the love of God.[60] The difficulty of the poem is that, instead of moving steadily from the particular to the general to the transcendental as in *The Wanderer*, it juxtaposes two moods which strive for supremacy. Interpretations which smooth out this conflict may be over-fastidious. Perhaps we should be content not always to explain 'difficulties' away, but to accept that a poem does its work if it exposes without expounding, juxtaposes without dialectic, opens the mind and the senses (for instance, to the possibility that there may be more than one kind of 'seafaring'—'Fare forward, voyagers...') without springing an allegorical trap on them. Systematic allegorisation may well devalue the imaginative quality of the first half of the poem,[61] though it must be admitted that little could be done to devalue that of the second half, where moral platitudes of extreme banality are strung loosely together.

The striking innovation in both these poems is the creation of a dramatic *persona* to carry the poem forward on a flood of supposed reminiscence. The freedom that this nameless and timeless personage gives the poet may be estimated by comparing the stereotyped complaints of mutability and mortality, such as Cynewulf's epilogues, made in the author's name and derived from Latin models. It may be that the idea for the innovation owes some initial debt to the Old Welsh elegies associated with Llywarch Hên: the cuckoo boding sorrow seems to be a specific borrowing.[62] *The Ruin*, however, seems to be based exclusively on Latin models: the literature of late Rome and Roman Gaul is full of lamentations on the fall of ancient cities. But here, as in *The Wanderer*, the lamentation has a depth of feeling far removed from such rhetorical exercises, coming as it does from the very heart of Anglo-Saxon experience. For a people living amidst the decaying ruins of a once great, now dead, civilisation, these wondrous walls, *enta geweorc*, now grey with lichen and stained with red *(ræghar ond readfah)*, were potent reminders of glory and mortality. The city is Bath, judging from the frequent mention of bathhouses and hot springs, but many Roman cities could have evoked the same sentiments: the Lindisfarne *Life of St Cuthbert* describes how the reeve of Carlisle showed the bishop over the remains of the Roman city, 'the city wall and the well formerly built in a wonderful manner by the Romans'.[63] The poem is unfinished, and no doubt concluded with some apt moralisation, but its mood is one of admiration not contempt, a comprehensive vision, like that of *The Wanderer*, in which decay affirms the tragic splendour of what once was as well as the vanity of all things.[64]

The presence of such poems in the Exeter Book needs no explanation. It may be that for the three others, which seem to be exclusively secular in theme and allusion, we should invoke the more generous interpretation of monastic culture put forward in discussing the background of *Beowulf*.[65] It was not unknown for monastic manuscripts at this date to contain secular poems, even love-poems, and *The Wife's Lament* and *Wulf and Eadwacer*, on this basis, may be seen as examples of *Frauenlied*, the woman's lament of love, which seems to be a widespread early form of love-lyric.[66] It is possible that *Wulf and Eadwacer*, with its irregular alliteration, semi-strophic form, end-stopped lines and simple repetitive syntax, represents a relic of a genuine popular form;[67] beyond this, with such a fragment, it is hard to go. *The Wife's Lament*, however, seems to be deliberately obscure; though the poem is complete, the speaker's dramatic situation is not made at all clear, and her dwelling-place in exile,

under actreo      in þam eorðscræfe      (28)

(under the oak-tree in the earth-cave)

seems fantastic. Only a couple of inflexions serve to identify the speaker as a woman at all (the title is modern, of course) and nothing in the language implies a sexual relationship. It could be that the context is lost, or that a clever scribe has supplied a false one, and that what we have is the lament of a mad exile in the wilderness, rather like the Irish *Suibhne's Lament*.[68] On the other hand, similar lays of complaint by women in the Icelandic *Edda* show a similar taste for cryptic allusion. Whatever the case, some kind of deliberate riddling is part of the poetic motive, and in this at least *The Wife's Lament* is akin to *The Husband's Message*, though any narrative connection is most improbable. The latter poem is spoken by a rune-stave (the bark of a tree) which carries a message from a husband in exile bidding his wife join him. The poem is in three parts, each marked as a separate poem in the manuscript; it follows Riddle 60, uses a technique of prosopopeia commonplace in the riddles, and has often been thought to be, in part or whole, a riddle. With such manifold problems and peculiarities of structure and style, the two poems are ripe for the allegorist. One scholar sees the speaker of *The Husband's Message* as the Cross, bringing the message of Christ the lover to his lady, the Soul or Church,[69] others see *The Wife's Lament* as the Church's yearning for Christ and *The Husband's Message* as Christ's reply in the person of a *peregrinus*,[70] the two poems being 'a vernacular paraphrase of the Song of Songs'.[71] All the difficulties disappear, as they usually do when such allegorical panaceas are applied: the poems disappear too, more footnotes to the *Patrologia Latina*.

To reject such explanations as unhistorical, unprofitable and unlikely is not necessarily to saddle oneself with the task of providing a different one, but one or two tentative observations might be made. In the first place, *Wulf and Eadwacer* seems to be an authentic fragment of inexplicable passion, quite unworked: its presence in the Exeter Book is mere chance. *The Husband's Message* is a structurally complex piece of riddling, but its dramatic situation is fairly simple and not much particularised: Kaske's explanation is perhaps an over-explicit version of what the poet was working towards. *The Wife's Lament* is the real puzzle: it is so particular, in parts so physically circumstantial, so haunting, that no simple explanation will do. One might suspect that the text is corrupt, or has been subjected only to a preliminary working-over. In other words the present existence of these two poems may be foetus-like: the monastic compiler would take over scraps of lays and other secular material and copy them down to provide challenging opportunities, or simple fodder, for subsequent moralistic interpretation. These three poems would represent different stages in that process.

# 3    Late Old English poetry and the transition

It has been the assumption of the previous two chapters that the corpus of Old English poetry, as it is preserved in the four great codices, was mostly composed in the eighth and early ninth centuries, even though the copies that survive are of the later tenth century. There are strong grounds, both internal and external, for this assumption, and no one would seriously question it, though clearly the codices were not closed to contemporary work: *Genesis B* and *Judith* are major examples of tenth-century composition, and a few other poems, such as *Christ and Satan* and perhaps some of the minor homiletic pieces in the Exeter Book, may be of comparatively late date. Yet they are few, and it is not difficult to understand why the extant copies should be so late, nor why there should have been such a marked decline in the practice of poetry after about 850. The Danish invasions, the destruction of the monasteries and their books, the decline of the primarily monastic learning of the earlier centuries, are reason enough. Alfred's lament over the decayed state of learning in England, even before the Danes came, is well-known:

> Swæ clæne hio wæs oðfeallenu on Angelcynne ðæt swiðe
> feawa wæron behionan Humbre ðe hiora ðeninga cuðen
> understondan on Englisc oððe furðum an ærendgewrit of
> Lædene on Englisc areccean; ond ic wene ðætte noht
> monige begiondan Humbre næren. Swæ feawa hiora
> wæron ðæt ic furðum anne anlepne ne mæg geðencean
> be suðan Temese ða ða ic to rice feng.[1]

> (So complete was the decline [of learning] in England that there were
> very few on this side of the Humber who could understand their service-
> books in English or even translate a letter from Latin into English; and I
> think there were not many beyond Humber. There were so few that I
> cannot remember a single one south of the Thames, when I became
> king.)

It may be exaggerated: certainly there were pockets of monastic culture that remained untouched by the Danish incursions, such as West Mercia, whence Alfred drew scholars like Plegmund and Werferth to assist in his revival of learning. But the spirit of Alfred's remarks is true to the trauma of the ninth century, and is reflected in many particular and tangible ways—the almost complete cessation of building, for instance, or the decline of Latinity in charters and other legal documents, or the chance recovery of the Stockholm *Codex Aureus* of the Gospels from Danish plunderers,[2] or the pathetic contrast between the scratchily drawn and crudely coloured initials of Alfred's translation of Gregory's *Pastoral Care* (Bodleian MS Hatton 20)—the very work in which he ponders the state of England—and the majestic illuminated manuscripts from Lindisfarne in the eighth or Winchester in the tenth centuries.[3] Many monasteries were physically obliterated; others survived as buildings, but organised monastic life had practically died out, except perhaps at St Augustine's, Canterbury, and the inmates were little more than secular estate-holders who had to be bodily removed at the time of the revival before monks could be re-established.[4]

The monastic revival of the tenth century, when it came, produced a decisive transformation in all aspects of English culture. It begins with Edmund's establishment of Dunstan as Abbot of Glastonbury in 940, and is consolidated in the reign of Edgar (959–75), with Dunstan appointed Archbishop of Canterbury in 960 and Oswald and Æthelwold made Bishops of Worcester and Winchester respectively in 963. It was a revival made possible by the continental contacts promoted by Athelstan, and firmly rooted in the continental movement towards monastic reform. It was organised by powerful leaders, received royal support during the reign of Edgar, and proved strong enough to withstand and absorb the Danish invasions which began again in 980. It is monasticism with a new face, an organ of education and government rather than spirituality and learning. Rules abound: there is a proliferation of English versions of the Rule of St Benedict and of documents of Carolingian reform like the Rule of Chrodegang and the Capitula of Theodulf. The Council of Winchester of 975 established a *Regularis Concordia* and an orthodox consistency of monastic life and practice which the abortive and optimistic councils of earlier centuries could not seriously hope for. That such a movement should have given no powerful new incentive for the writing of vernacular poetry is not surprising: in such an impressively determined and single-minded programme there is little room for poetry. The copying of the poetic codices may seem to contradict this, but they are essentially an offshoot of the revival: they have little significance in it, little consequence or issue, and were little if at all read.[5] They were acts of homage to the past. The real authority and impetus of the revival is in prose, where Ælfric and Wulfstan forge a magnificent instrument of instruction, persuasion and organisation. While the poetic codices mouldered unread, the works of Ælfric were copied and re-copied, glossed and annotated, right up to the middle of the thirteenth century.

The change of outlook, the strengthening and narrowing of intellectual foundation, is well illustrated in Ælfric. Ælfric addresses himself to laymen and uneducated clerics; his aim is to provide for them a systematic course of instruction in the teachings of the Church. He is aware of the errors hitherto prevalent in English books, and aware too, as he explains in the Preface to his translation of Genesis, of the dangers of presenting the literal text of the Bible to the unlearned:

> Ic ondræde, gif sum dysig man þas boc ræt oððe rædan gehyrþ, þæt
> he wille wenan, þæt he mote lybban nu on þære niwan æ, swa swa þa
> ealdan fæderas leofodon þa on þære tide.... We secgað eac foran to þæt
> seo boc is swiþe deop gastlice to understandenne, and we ne writaþ
> na mare buton þa nacedan gerecednisse. Þonne þincþ þam ungelæredum
> þæt eall þæt andgit beo belocen on þære anfealdan gerecednisse, ac hit
> ys swiþe feor þam.[6]

> (I fear that some foolish man, reading this book or hearing it read, will
> think that he can live in the new age as our forefathers lived in that
> time.... We must make it clear, here and now, that the book is very
> difficult to understand spiritually, and we set down no more than the bare
> narrative. An unlearned man may think that the whole meaning is
> contained in that simple literal narrative, but that is far from true.)

His favourite mode therefore is homily and homiletic narrative, where he can present the material with the proper doctrinal interpretation carefully explained. His care extends to the copy: his frequently reiterated concern for the accurate transmission of his text demonstrates a newly cautious and self-conscious orthodoxy. The contrast with the old poetry is striking: there, a rich variety of treatment and address, here a pragmatic single-mindedness; there, a vigorous confidence in vernacular poetry and a free interchange with and within the Latin tradition, here a definite and necessary reaching down to a more ignorant audience. Ælfric's concern that doctrine should not be perverted by allowing lay access to the Scriptures is an aspect of a new and restrictive, though not yet repressive, orthodoxy which seems much more characteristic of the Middle Ages than the comparative freedom of the earlier poetry. The poets of the eighth and ninth centuries write at least partly from within a tradition of Latin and Christian-Latin poetry, and for an audience which is, like themselves, monastic and learned, an audience of equals; Ælfric writes exclusively from within the tradition of biblical exegesis, patristic commentary, and homily, and his audience is an unlearned one, whether lay or clerical, which needs instruction. The great growth of English prose, which was directly due to the decline of Latin learning in the ninth century and to Alfred's attempt to supply the deficiency by using the vernacular, was accompanied by a steady devaluation of the native poetic tradition. Its bleak future is to take up some of the more menial didactic functions of Ælfrician prose, so that not for five centuries after 850 does any established tradition of English poetry have a reputable literary status. As for intellectual tradition, the change of quality and temper is perhaps indicated by comparing the scientific treatises of Bede, which have a part in the intellectual history of Europe, with Ælfric's *De Temporibus Anni*, a simplified digest of Bede's treatises on the subject, or with Byrhtferth's *Manual*, an astronomical primer addressed to 'clericum and uplendiscum preostum' and 'iunge mynstermen',[7] with the more difficult Latin passages translated and explained in English. If Bede had lived in the tenth century he would probably have emigrated.

Such stark contrasts are not likely to pass unchallenged, and it will be the business of some pages now to introduce the necessary qualifications. But the contrast is worth some preliminary over-emphasis, if only to indicate the insignificance of the tumultuous political events of the eleventh century in the history of English poetry beside the long-term consequences of the collapse of learning in the ninth century. The Conquest contributed to the decline of a poetry already moribund, deprived of both status and function. When we talk of Old English poetry, therefore, we talk of a literature produced, apart from some isolated fragments and erratics, between 700 and 850. There is little to renew those former glories until the fourteenth century.

## 'Classical' poetry in late Old English

Of those 'fragments' and of the poetic tradition they represent it is now time to speak more generously. *Genesis B* and *Judith* have already been mentioned.[8] The vigour and dramatic power of the former is all attributable to the Old Saxon original: it is one of the ironies of literary history that England should receive such a splendid return on its investment in Saxon Germany at the very time that its own vernacular culture is being constrained to the same rigidity as that of those German nations uninfluenced by the Anglo-Saxon missions. Another poem which may owe a debt to continental influences is *Judgment Day II*, a translation of Bede's *De die judicii*, in which a number of verbal borrowings suggest a knowledge of Old High German *Mariendichtung*.[9] The poem is of the late tenth century and demonstrates certain stylistic developments characteristic of the later verse, such as more regular end-stopping, occasional rhyme and a comparatively restricted use of compounding and variation: it is, however, extremely accomplished and may well be a product of the surviving schools of religious poetry at St Augustine's, Canterbury,[10] or Worcester.

As for *Judith*, if the poem has its origin in some sort of response to the new wave of Danish invasions, then it can be associated with that other miraculous resurrection of Old English poetic energy, *The Battle of Maldon*. In itself, the skirmish at Maldon in 991 between the Essex levies led by ealdorman Byrhtnoth and a Danish raiding party was of little historical importance, and it receives only a passing mention in the *Chronicle*. Something, however, prompted a stirring of the old heroic pulse and this splendid battle-fragment is the result. Of the provenance of the poem little can now be known: the original MS, Cotton A.xii, was destroyed in the Cottonian fire of 1731 and the surviving text is based on Thomas Hearne's print of 1726. A simple view might be that it was still the custom to have a *scop* attached to the household of a provincial noble, that the practice was stimulated by the example of the *skald* in Danish England, and that this poem is a chance survival, influenced by skaldic verse, of a long and continued tradition of eulogy and battle-poem.[11] But this interpretation misses the significance of the known facts about the poem as well as the peculiar quality of the poem itself. One of the known facts is that Byrhtnoth, as well as being of royal birth, was a great monastic benefactor, celebrated almost to the point of sanctification in monastic histories and in a Latin *Life of St Oswald*;[12] his fall was portrayed as a kind of martyrdom. It is to these circumstances, surely, that we owe the present poem, with its merging of heroism and hagiography, and it would be impossible to ascribe it to any but a clerical author. In form the poem is elaborate and leisurely in the epic Beowulfian manner, with formalised single combat and long set speeches, and has little in common with the heroic lay.[13] The setting and actual incidents of the battle are briefly and somewhat vaguely indicated, not at all in the manner of an eye-witness, and all the poetic emphasis is reserved for the careful unfolding of a composed tragic narrative, in which Byrhtnoth's arrogant confidence *(ofermod)* in allowing the Vikings to cross to shore brings about his destruction. After his death, his followers, who are so different in rank and origin that they seem to have been chosen (or invented) to make a microcosm of all England,[14] speak in deliberate periods of their intention to fight now to the death beside the body of their lord. Byrhtwold, an old retainer speaks last:

> Hige sceal þe heardra,     heorte þe cenre,
> mod sceal þe mare,     þe ure mægen lytlað.
> Her lið ure ealdor     eall forheawen,
> god on greote.     A mæg gnornian
> se ðe nu fram þis wigplegan     wendan þenceð.
> Ic eom frod feores;     fram ic ne wille,
> ac ic me be healfe     minum hlaforde,
> be swa leofan men,     licgan þence.         (312–19)

(The mind must be more resolute, courage keener, spirit greater, as our strength grows less. Here lies our good lord on the ground, all cut to pieces. May he who thinks to turn from this battle now regret it for ever. I am old; I will not turn my back, but mean to lay my bones beside my beloved lord.)

This great speech has to be set beside Byrhtnoth's first taunting answer to the Vikings,

> Gehyrst þu, sælida,     hwæt þis folc segeð?
> Hi willað eow to gafole     garas syllan,
> ættryne ord     ond ealde swurd,
> þa heregeatu     þe eow æt hilde ne deah.
> Brimmanna boda,     abeod eft ongean,

sege þinum leodum      miccle laþre spell,
þæt her stynt unforcuð      eorl mid his werode,
þe wile gealgean      eþel þysne,
Æþelredes eard,      ealdres mines,
folc and foldan.      Feallan sceolon
hæþene æt hilde.      To heanlic me þinceð
þæt ge mid urum sceattum      to scype gangon
unbefohtene,      nu ge þus feor hider
on urne eard      in becomon.
Ne sceole ge swa softe      sinc gegangan;
us sceal ord and ecg      ær geseman,
grim guðplega,      ær we gofol syllon.      (45–61)

(Do you hear, pirate, what this people says? The 'tribute' they offer you is spears, deadly spear-points and well-tempered swords, weapons that bring you little comfort in battle. Go back, you messenger of the sea-rovers, and give your people this unpleasing message—that here stands a noble earl with his army, who will fight to the end for this land, kingdom of Ethelred my liege lord, the fatherland and its people. Heathens must be put to the sword. It seems shameful to me that you should take our treasure back to your ships without a fight now that you have come so far into our land. And you will not obtain treasure so easily; spear-point and sword-blade must first make us at one in grim battle-play before we give tribute.)

and then beside his pious death-speech,

Geþancie þe,      ðeoda waldend,
ealra þæra wynna      þe ic on worulde gebad.
Nu ic ah, milde metod,      mæste þearfe
þæt þu minum gaste      godes geunne,
þæt min sawul to ðe      siðian mote
on þin geweald,      þeoden engla,
mid friþe ferian.      (173–9)

(I thank you, O lord of nations, for all the joys I have had in this world. Now, gentle lord, I have most need that you should endow my spirit with grace, so that my soul may pass peacefully, prince of angels, into your keeping.)

to suggest the rich blend of heroic and Christian impulse in the poem. For now, in this late age, personal heroism can receive perfect sanction in the celebration of a saintly national hero of blameless reputation (or near-blameless, for *ofermod* is not a virtue). It looks more like a triumphant collusion of circumstance than a chance survival.

There is nothing of quality in the late Old English period to set beside these few poems, though there are a number of routine productions which show that the skills of classical Old English verse were not forgotten. Alfred himself may be responsible for the metrical translations of the Metres of Boethius which were adapted from his earlier prose version. They are not really translations, but free expansions, much simplified in thought and rather wordy, evidence that Alfred had learnt his 'Saxon poetry' well and knew his synonyms and variation. They have no distinction[15] and are on the whole less interesting than Alfred's vigorous handling of the general argument in the Proses, where his individuality, his desire for truth, his faith, come through with an immediacy that transcends time—quite different from Chaucer's laboured crib. Alfred probably also wrote the metrical Preface and Epilogue to his translation of Gregory's *Pastoral Care* : the latter is an unusually abstruse *allegoria*, while the former is spoken in the riddle-like *persona* of 'the book' like one or two later scraps of verse.[16] At about the same time, maybe during Alfred's reign, a metrical version of the last hundred Psalms was made, and survives in a handsome Psalter which once belonged to the Duc de Berry. The translation is mechanical and colourless, and shows how close Old English verse could come to the prosaic without becoming prose. It continues a process, which we have already seen beginning in poems like Cyne-wulf's *Juliana*, by which poetry, being deprived of its traditional diction and stylistic techniques and fitted to simpler didactic functions, is gradually emptied of its traditional character, a process to which the monastic revival of the tenth century gives a final impetus.

One of the few poems outside the codices to preserve the traditional poetic style and with it something of the generosity of temper and range of interests of the older poetry is *Solomon and Saturn*. There are in fact two poetical 'dialogues' in which these two representatives of Christian and pagan learning confront each other with difficult questions: both dialogues appear in one MS of the late tenth century and a fragment of the first is copied in the margins of a late eleventh century copy of the Alfredian Bede. The first poem has little of a dialogue about it, being chiefly a demonstration of the power of the Paternoster, each runic letter of the prayer and also the Paternoster itself being personified as a warrior. The idea of the Paternoster as a magical formula or incantation (it is put to a similar use in the *Charms*) is here a Christianised version of the magical power assigned to Solomon in Hebrew tradition and cabbalistic writings, while the use of runes to embody this power is another example of Germanic cultural transfer. The use of personification is reminiscent of some of the more extra-vagant Irish *loricae* (protective incantations), and the channel for oriental tradition may well have been Celtic, just as the general eccentricity of the whole poem may echo Hisperican tradition. The emphasis on the importance of the Paternoster anticipates, though it does not at all resemble, the emphasis given to the basic articles of the faith in the tenth century revival. The capitulary of Theodulf declares that unless a man commits to memory the Paternoster and the Creed, 'catholicus esse non poterit': Ælfric and Wulfstan repeat this,[17] but they would hardly have countenanced the strange mixture of oriental, Germanic and Christian elements in this poem.

63

The second poem is more like a true dialogue, with Saturn asking Solomon serious riddle-like questions. It is partly didactic, partly a contest of wit like some of the Eddic poems, especially the *Vafþrúðnismál*. Most of the questions are about death, doomsday and *Wyrd*, and here the Germanic inheritance comes through strongly, blended with Christian belief in a manner somewhat reminiscent of *Beowulf—Wyrd bið wended hearde*, 'Fate is hard to avoid' (437). The contrast with Ælfric, for whom *Wyrd* is simply a false belief, is as striking as the comparison with Alfred, grappling equally with the problems of the powerful *Wyrd* that he substitutes for Boethius' more manageable (because illusory) Fortuna.[18] The Dialogues thus reflect the blending of Germanic and Christian elements and also many of the preoccupations, gnomic, enigmatic, didactic and philosophic, of the Exeter Book, and though these preoccupations there produce better and less eccentric poems they are here not unworthily represented.

As one moves into the later tenth century the decline of poetic production and the hardening of function is readily perceptible. Most of the poems appear as brief interludes in MSS dedicated to the narrower homiletic and liturgical purposes of the Anglo-Saxon Church. Corpus Christi (Cambridge) MS 201, for instance, probably written at Worcester, contains vernacular homilies, laws, and other documents; in the middle is a group of poems, including *Judgment Day II*, a severely purposeful *Exhortation to Christian Living* ('Ceapa þe mid æhtum/ eces leohtes'), a macaronic *Summons to Prayer*, and free rhapsodic paraphrases of the *Lord's Prayer* and the *Gloria*. MS Junius 121 is another Worcester manuscript, a collection of canons and constitutions in the vernacular, with a version of the Benedictine Office which includes some poems, all based on the Office—a variant text of the *Gloria*, a shorter version of the *Lord's Prayer*, a *Creed*, and various fragments of Psalms derived from the same original as the Paris Psalter. MS Cotton Vespasian D.vi is a Kentish manuscript containing a miscellany of Latin texts, but including two vernacular poems, the *Kentish Hymn*, which recalls similar hymnodic compositions in *Daniel* and *Azarias* in theme if not in vigour, and a very expansive paraphrase of Psalm 50; these may be the work of the St Augustine's school. Elsewhere we find a *Menologium*, or calendar of Saints' days and festivals, and another set of gnomic poems, *Maxims II*, written down as prefatory matter to the manuscript of the Chronicle known as the Abingdon Chronicle; and a hortatory poem called *Seasons for Fasting*, known from a transcript made in 1562 by Laurence Nowell from a manuscript later burnt in the Cottonian fire. It shares with the *Creed* in Junius 121 a peculiarity of grouping the alliterative lines in 8-line stanzas and has been assigned to a common author on these grounds,[19] probably a Worcester monk.

These poems do not of course represent new monastic preoccupations or new uses for vernacular poetry. There are parallels for many of these productions in the poetic codices, though not for those of a more narrowly functional cast. What is different is that this monastic hack-work now appears in bleak isolation, without the supporting variety of themes, materials and methods of the poetic codices, and in a fragmentary and sporadic way which suggests approaching sterility. At the same time, there is no sign of a breakdown in the traditional *ars poetica* : these poems are necessarily more limited in vocabulary but the poets clearly know the traditional techniques of versification and syntax.

The same is true of the five poems in the 'classical' style embedded in the *Anglo-Saxon Chronicle*, which are, of course, also by monastic authors, and which represent another feeble line of descent for the stricter Anglo-Saxon poetic tradition. The first of them, *The Battle of Brunanburh* (937), even has a certain notoriety as a *rifacimento* of traditional motifs and phrases. Different from Maldon, Brunanburh was a battle of real national importance, and Athelstan's victory over the allied northern forces is greeted by the chronicler with a paean of triumphant celebration. The poet understands very clearly the political significance of the battle and has a grasp of history which is quite lacking in *Maldon*; but when it comes to poetry he has more enthusiasm than judgment, and strings together 'poetic' compounds with a wild abandon, as if the needs of poetry cancel all discrimination. It is what an inverately prosaic mind thinks of as poetry. His allusion to the 'beasts of battle' motif produces the most extensive menagerie in Anglo-Saxon poetry,

Letan him behindan  hræw bryttian
saluwigpadan,  þone sweartan hræfn,
hyrnednebban,  and þane hasewanpadan
earn æftan hwit,  æses brucan,
grædigne guðhafoc  and þæt græge deor,
wulf on wealde.            (60–5)

(They left behind to share the carnage the dark-coated, horn-billed raven and the dark-coated eagle with the white-tipped tail, to enjoy the carrion-feast with the greedy war-hawk and the grey beast, the forest-wolf.)

at the same time missing the whole point of the motif, which is ominously to foreshadow the coming slaughter, not to indicate how the battlefield is cleared up afterwards. In technique the poem is very strict, with a wide range of compounds and some elaborate variation (e.g. 10–17, 47–52).

The poems that follow show a decline in everything but correctness. The second, on the capture of the Five Boroughs (942), is a mechanical piece, preoccupied with place-names, and the third, on the coronation of Edgar (973), spends much of its little energy on a periphrastic indication of date. Monastic pedantry is much to the fore, as it is in the poem on the death of Edgar (975), a gloomy survey of the world running to ruin. The poet still has some inkling of what poetry is supposed to be like,

And þa wearð eac adræfed  deormod hæleð,
Oslac, of earde  ofer yða gewealc,
ofer ganotes bæð,  gamolfeax hæleð,
wis and wordsnotor,  ofer wætera geðring,

ofer hwæles eðel     hama bereafod.                    (24–8)

(Then too the bold Oslac was driven from his land over the tossing waves, the gannet's bath, the grey-haired warrior, wise and prudent in counsel, over the tumult of waters, the whale's home, into exile.)

but his imitation is lame and repetitive. The last classical poem appears on the eve of the Conquest, in the Abingdon and Worcester Chronicles only,[20] and is on the death of Edward (1065). The poetic form is still very regular, as if the traditional *ars poetica*, having lasted for four centuries, will last for ever, but the sonorousness is empty. The poignancy of

And se froda swa þeah     befæste þæt rice
heahþungenum menn,     Harolde sylfum,
æþelum eorle. . . .                     (29–31)

(But the wise king entrusted the kingdom to a high-born man, Harold himself, the noble earl.)

is in history, not in the poetry. And even this is not the end, for there was written soon after 1104 (the date of the translation of the remains of St Cuthbert to Durham) an encomium of Durham and its relics which is perfectly regular in form and betrays its date only in some minor linguistic changes.

When all this is added up, it still provides only a pathetic argument for the continuity of the stricter Anglo-Saxon poetic tradition after the reign of Alfred. The limited quantity—at a time when manuscripts, even of vernacular poetry, might expect a better chance of survival—the narrowness of range, the monotony of technique, all suggest that the tradition was bankrupt, and that its preservation in attenuated form was due to nothing more than the natural conservatism of monasteries—or at least of certain monasteries. For there was of course nothing bankrupt about the state of England nor its monastic culture at this time, despite the hard contrasts that were made at the beginning of this chapter. Dorothy Whitelock remarks at one point, of the Chronicle poem on the death of Edgar, that it is 'of a quality to make one glad that the Chroniclers mainly used prose'.[21] This is the paradox, for the lame verses of the Chronicle are surrounded by a prose of wonderful variety, versatility and power. The paradox here is real enough, for there is no relation between the verse and the prose, but it would be premature to suggest that the prose of Ælfric and Wulfstan implies a similar paradox, for in fact their prose absorbs much of the energy and some of the techniques of verse and, what is more significant, perhaps hands them back, transformed, at a later date.

## Poetry and prose

The close relation in the late Old English period between prose and verse has been the subject of a good deal of comment, as well as some arid terminological controversy. That there should be such a relation is not at all surprising when one recalls that the rhythmical organisation of Old English verse[22] is based on a systematisation of certain two-stress patterns inherent in the language, or inherent at least in all heightened and self-consciously eloquent forms of the language. The strict refinement of these patterns in Old English verse, the partial observance of quantity, the use of alliteration, the elaborate apparatus of compounding and variation, do not disguise this fundamental relation. But poetry of the traditional kind would have seemed to Ælfric, with his professionally pedagogic cast of mind, an uneconomical and unnecessarily elaborate instrument. Yet he was unwilling to dispense altogether with the persuasive possibilities of its rhythms and alliteration, and he devised therefore a kind of rhythmical prose as a compromise. In so doing he was pressing to a conclusion a tendency that had long been present in Old English verse, a certain impatience with the more leisurely and ornamental rituals of the traditional *ars poetica*. Perhaps Bede's *Death-Song* is one example of an attempt at simplification; certainly Cynewulf's *Juliana* shows many signs of reaching towards a plainer style, and by the time of Alfred such a style is well established in the Paris Psalter. This is not to suggest that such works provided Ælfric with models, though it is likely that their plainer methods appealed to him, just as it is likely that he was influenced by the mildly rhythmical qualities of some earlier homiletic prose writing.[23]

Ælfric developed his technique gradually. Rhythmical prose appears first, intermittently, in the second series of *Catholic Homilies*, becomes regular in the third series (on *Lives of the Saints*) and habitual in his later writing for all purposes.[24] It is possible to see how certain tendencies towards rhythmical heightening and alliteration in the 'ordinary' prose of his earlier period are developed into regular formal controls. In its developed form, Ælfric's prose is based on two-stress phrasal units, more extended and less tightly patterned than those of poetry, linked in pairs by fairly regular alliteration, usually *ax/ax* or *xa/ax*, sometimes *aa/ax*. There is no poetic ornament, no compounding or syntactical variation, and the weaker vocalic alliteration is very common. Skeat's collection of the homilies on the *Lives of the Saints*[25] is probably the best place to study Ælfric's rhythmical prose, since it is here mixed with 'ordinary' prose, and the contrast helps to define the form. The first sermon, for instance, on the Nativity, is plain prose, technical and expository, dealing with difficult and important matters of dogma; the second, on St Eugenia, is quite different:

> Eugenia hæfde.     ær þan asteald
> mynecena mynster.     mid mycelre gehealdsumnysse.
> and seo modor Claudia.     hit micclum gegodode.
> and hi þær be-byrgdon     þone bisceop Philippum.     (310–13, i. 42)

> (Eugenia had already founded a convent of nuns, with great devotion, and her mother Claudia endowed it liberally; and there they buried bishop Philip.)

The manuscript punctuation, as transmitted by Skeat, is obviously an important indication of the form of this prose. The 'rhythmical' punctuation of some Ælfric MSS reflects contemporary practice in liturgical MSS and suggests how Ælfric was additionally drawn to the development of a structured rhythmical prose by the traditional cadence-groupings or *positurae* of the liturgy.[26] A similar punctuation system is used in early Middle English, in both verse and prose, one of its effects being to blur the dividing line between the two.

Pope is cautious about printing Ælfric as verse, but reaches a pragmatic conclusion: 'The form is too insistently regular to be disregarded and yet not quite clear enough to make its structure apparent at a glance without further guidance.'[27] As one reads, every so often the rhythms tighten to a perfect verse-line:

> Hi wurdon þa ealle.    þurh þa wundra onbryrde.
> and on godes herungum    hi sylfe gebysgodon.
> and gearcodon heora mod.    to ðam martyr-dome.
> caflice to campienne.    for cristes geleafan.[28]

(They were all encouraged by these miracles, and fell to praising God eagerly, and prepared their minds for martyrdom, boldly to fight for Christ's faith.)

Sometimes a whole sequence of lines recalls the regularity of verse:

> We andettað mid muðe.    and on mode gelyfað
> on þa halgan ðrynnysse.    þe is heofonlic god.
> þæt is fæder and sunu.    and se frefrigende gast.
> and we bodiað mannum    middan-eardes alysednysse
> þurh ðone halgan sunu    þe se heofonlica fæder
> sylf-willes asende    to slege for us.[29]

(We acknowledge in words our belief in the holy Trinity which is heavenly God, that is the father and son and comforting spirit, and we preach to men the redemption of the world through the holy son that the heavenly father of his own will sent to be slain for us.)

But alliterative and rhythmic patterning, and the occasional use of Latin rhetorical devices that Ælfric allows himself, such as word-play and repetition, are never allowed to upset the smooth flow of sense. Cynewulf was always compromising in his attempt to articulate fuller speech-patterns: for Ælfric, sense, and an absolutely fluent syntactical line, are all-important. It is not difficult to demonstrate this, but maybe a quotation from Ælfric's homily on the Book of Judith, set beside the corresponding passage from the Old English poem[30] will suggest how far his prose, even if it is thought of as verse, is from poetry:

> Iudith geseah þa,    þa þa he on slæpe wæs,
> þæt hire wæs gerymed    to hire ræde wel forð,

and het hire þinene      healdan þa duru
and gelæhte his agen swurd      and sloh to his hneccan
and mid twam slegum      forsloh him þone swuran
and bewand þæt bodig      mid ðam beddclaðum.[31]

(Judith saw then, as he was asleep, a ready way to the accomplishment of
her mission; she told her handmaid to guard the door, seized his own
sword and struck at his neck, severing it with two blows, and then
wrapped the body in the bedclothes.)

Ælfric's rhythmical prose is his own invention. He took hints from elsewhere,
and passed on a large and frequently copied body of writing which had great
influence, particularly in tending to diminish the distinction between prose
and verse, but no one else wrote in precisely his style. Wulfstan, the other
great prose-writer of the late Old English period, writes in a distinctly
different style,[32] though the needs and concerns that produced it are much the
same as those that operated on Ælfric. Wulfstan uses the two-stress phrase as
his basic rhythmical unit, like Old English verse and Ælfric's prose, but his
range of rhythmical patterns is wider than the former, narrower than the latter.
His phrases are shorter, more abrupt, more emphatically separate than those of
Ælfric, and are marked by the recurring use of certain tags (e.g. *swutol & gesene,
oft & gelome*) and formulae, by occasional rhyme, and by a powerfully dominant
falling rhythm. The major distinguishing structural feature of Wulfstan's prose,
however, is that alliteration, though it is often used within the two-stress phrase,
is not used to bind the phrases in pairs into long lines. The whole effect is one of
irresistible onrush, as opposed to Ælfric's steady flow. Wulfstan's most famous
piece of writing is his vehement denunciation of the corruption of the English
nation at the height of the Danish attacks (1014), a quotation from which will
serve to demonstrate his techniques at their most forceful:

Ne dohte hit nu lange      swyðe gedrehtan,
inne ne ute,      & us unwedera foroft
ac wæs here & hunger,      weoldan unwæstma;
bryne & blodgyte      forþam on þysan earde wæs,
on gewelhwylcan ende      swa hit þincan mæg,
oft & gelome;      nu fela geara
& us stalu & cwalu,      unrihta fela
stric & steorfa,      & tealte getrywða
orfcwealm & uncoþu,      æghwær mid mannum.[33]
hol & hete
& rypera reaflac
derede swyþe þearle,
& [us] ungylda

(Things have been bad for a long time everywhere, with war and famine,

burning and slaying throughout the land always; we have been
afflicted with theft and murder, pestilence and disease, murrain and
plague, hatred and persecution, and plundering by robbers; we have been
oppressed by taxation, our crops ruined by bad weather; so it seems that
evil has stalked abroad in this land for many years now, and truth has
lost its hold on men.)

Wulfstan is usually printed as prose, but this 'Hudibrastic' lay-out brings out
best the nature and power of his rhythms. His homilies were widely known and
frequently copied until late in the twelfth century, and there can be no doubt
that his style exercised a powerful influence on the concept of vernacular eloquence, in both prose and verse, during these confused centuries.

### 'Popular' poetry

There is, however, in addition to 'classical' verse and the rhythmical prose of
Ælfric and Wulfstan, another poetic tradition at work in these centuries, and
one which brings us for the first time to the full realisation that what we are dealing
with here is not simply the breakdown of a poetic form but the creation, in the
wake of the recession of classical verse, of a state of flux in which some of the
dominant forms and rhythms of Middle English verse are held as if suspended.

Five Chronicle poems, in the classical style, have already been described;
there are twelve others. One is on the accession of Edgar (959), another on the
death of Edgar (975), and both are so much in Wulfstan's style that they are now
attributed to him. But there is another poem on the death of Edgar in a different
style altogether: it appears in the Worcester and Peterborough Chronicles where
the other three MSS have the classical poem on Edgar's death,[34] so that for the
one event the Chronicle has examples of three different poetic modes. It is a
puzzling poem:

Her Eadgar gefor      bugon to cyninge
Angla reccent      swa wæs him gecynde.
West Seaxena wine      Næs se flota swa rang.
& Myrcene mundbora.      ne se here swa strang.
Cuð wæs þet wide      þe on Angelcynne
geond feola þeoda      æs him gefetede.
Þe aferan Eadmund[es]      þa hwile þe se æþela cyning
ofer ganetes bað      cynestol gerehte.[35]
Cyningas hine wide
wurðodon side.

(In this year Edgar died, ruler of the English, friend of the West Saxons,
protector of the Mercians. It was well known to many peoples that
Edmund's son commanded the allegiance of kings far and wide over the
ocean, as was his birthright. No fleet or army was so strong that it could

win plunder for itself in England while this noble king possessed the throne.)

It has the character of both relic and embryo. Two-stress phases dominate, two with independent internal alliteration and some traditional-sounding formulas and one authentic kenning *(ganetes bað)*. But the emergent principle is rhyme. Lines 13–14 have a ring altogether different from classical verse, and suggest, even at this stage, how the whole weight of the half-line is shifted by the addition of end-rhyme. Two further 'poems', of a nature very difficult to analyse, follow, in the Peterborough Chronicle only, one on the murder of Edward (979), the other on the capture of Ælfeah (1011): no clear pattern of rhythm, alliteration or rhyme emerges, though the authors seem obsessed with a heavy kind of anti-thesis, perhaps learnt from liturgical prose. In 1036, however, there is a poem on the persecution of Alfred the Ætheling in the Abingdon and Worcester Chronic-les which establishes a non-classical style for the first time decisively:

Ac Godwine hine þa gelette,
& hine on hæft sette;
& his geferan he to-draf;
& sume mislice ofsloh,
sume hi man wið feo sealde,
sume hreowlice acwealde,
sume hi man bende,
sume hi man blende.
sume hamelode.
sume hættode;
Ne wearð dreorlicre dæd gedon
on þison earde;
syþþan Dene comon
& her frið namon.[36]

(But Godwine prevented him, and made him captive. He dispersed his
followers and killed off some in various ways: he had some sold into
slavery, some cruelly murdered, or put in chains, or blinded, mutilated
or scalped. Never was such a horrible deed done in this country since the
Danes came and made peace.)

The influence of Wulfstan on these emphatic phrases is obvious. Alliteration is still present, but seems now superfluous beside the dominating presence of rhyme, which is used forcefully but clumsily.

A number of shorter poems follow, most of them, like the 1036 outburst, inspired by a faithful if faintly petulant adherence to the old West Saxon dynasty on the part of the monastic chroniclers or their sources. They appear in the Worcester and/or Peterborough Chronicles only. One, on the death of Edward the Ætheling (1057), is impossible to analyse, having no discernible pattern of rhythm, alliteration or rhyme, and may have been corrupted in transmission or through partial adaptation into prose; two (1067, 1075) are very short, with rhyme clearly evident; two (1075, 1104) are simply rhymed couplets. The poem on the death of William the Conqueror (1086) is more extended: it shows alliteration almost completely decayed, rhyme regularly used if irregularly placed, and rhythm suffering from this irregular placing, since the poet does not seem to be very certain whether he is working in lines or half-lines:

Castelas he let wyrcean.
& earme men swiðe swencean.
Se cyng wæs swa swiðe stearc.
& benam of his underþeoddan.        manig marc
goldes.        & ma hundred punda seolfres.
Ðet he nam be wihte.        & mid mycelan unrihte
of his land-leode, for littelre neode.
he wæs on gitsunge befeallan.
& grædinæsse he lufode mid ealle.[37]

(He had castles built by forced labour. He was a harsh king and took from his subjects many marks in gold and more hundreds of pounds in silver; these he took by weight from his people, quite unjustly and needlessly. He was sunk in greed and all given up to avarice.)

From one point of view this poem looks like the last staggering steps towards dissolution; from another, it seems to contain the seeds of Laȝamon and the short rhymed couplet of Middle English.

The repeated appearance of this kind of verse in the last century and a half of the Chronicle raises a crucial question: is it a debased form of classical verse or an early written form of the popular verse which may be supposed to have pre-existed or co-existed with the classical verse and come to the surface after its decline? The question is impossible to answer decisively, because of the fragmentary nature of the evidence, but one or two tentative conclusions can be drawn. The first concerns the presence of rhyme. It is often assumed that rhyme *caused* the breakdown of classical verse, and was introduced in the tenth century as an innovation, perhaps from skaldic verse. It would be a more reasonable assumption that rhyme was always known in Anglo-Saxon times, since the rhymed Latin accentual hymns were very familiar from the sixth century onwards: rhyming phrases appear in the charms and in some of the laws,[38] that is, in places where the traditional rules of eloquence, of the high style, do not apply, as well as sporadically in all Anglo-Saxon poetry.[39] On this interpretation, it was the normal concern of Anglo-Saxon poets to *avoid* rhyme, perhaps because they considered it popular, perhaps because they considered it rhythmically subversive, and the more frequent appearance of rhyme in the later poems and especially in tenth century poems like *Judith* and *Maldon* is due to the gradual relaxation of the rules of the traditional *ars poetica*. In other words, rhyme is the product and not the cause of the decline of classical verse.

One piece of evidence may seem enigmatic: in the Exeter Book there is a poem called the *Riming Poem*, which may seem a desperate title but which is the only one apt to such a lunatic exercise. Rhyme is everywhere in this poem, regularly on four consecutive half-lines, sometimes more extended, with internal rhyme as well:

> Wercyn gewiteð,    wælgar sliteð,
> flahmah fliteþ,    flan mon hwiteð,
> borgsorg biteð,    bald ald þwiteþ,
> wræcfæc wriþað,    wraþ að smiteþ,
> singryn sidað,    searofearo glideþ....        (61–5)

> (Men pass away, the spear kills, evil flourishes, an arrow wipes out a crime, sorrow of debt bites deep, brashness cuts down age, exile is cruel bondage, an oath in anger is a defilement, the snare lies ever open [sorrow always lies in wait?], the path of secret evil is smooth.)[40]

In theme the poem is a travesty of the 'elegies'—vague joys are cut off by even vaguer calamities, leading to a lugubrious contemplation of the world's transience.[41] It is obviously a monastic exercise, showing the same taste for the eccentric as the runes and cryptograms, and there is no reason at all to date it after the central period of Anglo-Saxon verse-production, the eighth century, except the dubious assumption that rhyme was introduced late under Scandinavian influence. With the plethora of rhyme, alliteration is preserved with insistent regularity, *aa/ax*, but the poem demonstrates the effect of rhyme on alliterative verse, how it immediately makes alliteration superfluous and therefore decorative and heavier, and how it demands a metrical pattern of much-increased regularity:

> Secgas mec segon,    symbel ne alegon,
> feohgiefe gefegon;    frætwed wægon
> wicg ofer wongum    wennan gongum,
> lisse mid longum    leoma gehongum.        (5–8)

> (Men sought me out, there were feasts and the delight of treasure-giving; gaily caparisoned horses galloped over the plain, joyfully along the length of paths, brushed by overhanging boughs.)

The *Riming Poem* is clear evidence of the knowledge of rhyme amongst the monastic poets, and evidence too of their habitual good sense in avoiding it.

There is a parallel for this deliberate policy towards rhyme in the attitude of the classical Latin poets towards the earlier accentual metres of so-called Saturnian verse: that too disappeared, or was submerged, when quantitative verse began to be cultivated as a mark of the high style, and re-emerged when the classical rigours were relaxed, having survived, as Ker puts it, 'in country places'.[42] There would be a strong supposition that Anglo-Saxon England had its 'country places' too: it is impossible that there should have been no tradition of popular verse-making—indeed the Caedmon story is clear evidence that there was—and equally impossible that it should have taken the sophisticated and manneristic form of classical poetry. It would be a natural step to go on from this to the supposition that the Chronicle verses of 975, 1036 and 1086 are the first written examples of this popular verse, taken over and adapted, or imitated, by monastic chroniclers as they sensed the weakening of the monolithic classical tradition.

Such an interpretation would be impossible to prove and might be thought to carry some dangerously 'populist' implications. Certainly, it is possible that the 975 poem is a debased form of classical verse, though the further mutations of the form are difficult to explain without adducing the intrusion of another tradition. But there is one other line of evidence that needs to be recalled: in the two previous chapters there was allusion[43] to the existence in Anglo-Saxon times of a kind of poetry which differed from the classical norms in having looser alliteration, stronger end-stopping, simpler and more repetitive syntax and, occasionally, relics of strophic form and refrain. When one puts these poems together—*Finnesburh*, parts of *Widsith*, *Deor*, some of the gnomic poetry, the charms, *Wulf and Eadwacer*—there seems to be sufficient evidence of a tradition which might well be called popular, an archaic protoplasmic form from which the classical style was derived by a process of refinement, which cropped out persistently in its unprocessed state in accidental or eccentric survivals and to which, with the addition of rhyme, English poetry returned with the decline of the classical style. If this hypothetical history is true, it provides a remarkable parallel to the process through which alliterative verse again went during and after the 'classical' period of the fourteenth century.

One important reservation needs to be made: the argument for the existence of a non-classical tradition does not necessarily suppose that any extant poetry is itself 'popular' in origin. Since it has been written down and survives, it will always be the product of or have passed through the modifying processes of a literate mind and an intellectual tradition, however, debased and diluted. All the argument supposes is the existence of a rhythmical 'bank', a repertory of simple forms and procedures, upon which literate verse-makers could draw. A crude analogy might be provided by the persistent pressure of 'common metre', an unarguably poetic form, behind English poetry from the fifteenth century to the present day.

*Transitional verse and prose*

The decline of classical verse left English poetry in a state of flux, with a number of bastard inheritors—simplified or debased forms of classical verse, forms influenced by popular verse, rhythmical prose in the style of Ælfric or Wulfstan—

contending for domination. Out of this state of flux it is possible to trace a number of developing forms, with and without rhyme, in poems of the early Middle English period—in Laȝamon and in early didactic and religious literature. A consideration of these poems in their general cultural context will be reserved for the next chapter: what remains here is to explore, in them, the more particular fate of alliterative writing, and the way flux is stabilised into continuum.

Old English learning was kept up at a number of monasteries well into the twelfth century, principally through the copying of homiletic prose. Six major Ælfric MSS date from the twelfth century[44] and the quality of the copy, though it often reflects a degree of linguistic change, shows that the language was generally well understood. Rochester and Canterbury were particularly strong centres, and at places such as these composition as well as copying went on,[45] as it did at Peterborough, where the *Anglo-Saxon Chronicle* was kept up until 1154, though the last entry, a composite one for the reign of Stephen, shows signs of breakdown. The most famous centre for the preservation of Old English learning, however, was Worcester, where St Wulfstan's [46] episcopacy (1062–95) spanned and long survived the Conquest. His life was written in the vernacular by his secretary Coleman (d. 1113), and the Worcester scriptorium continued to turn out copies of liturgical and homiletic texts in Old English long after the Conquest. Many other Old English MSS found their way to the Worcester library, and perhaps the most striking demonstration of the continuity of tradition is the way Old English homiletic prose continues to be read and glossed at Worcester until well into the thirteenth century. The work of a particular glossator, working about 1225–50, and readily recognisable from his 'tremulous' hand,[47] is clear evidence that Old English prose was known, understood and valued at this date, and that someone, perhaps a teacher in the monastic school, was trying to make it more readily available, through Latin glosses, to his contemporaries. At the same time, his efforts suggest that the language was inevitably passing into obscurity[48] and, though one can point here to a continuing interest in Old English writing, some of it in the alliterative homiletic style, it would be most unwise to associate such narrowly cloistered traditions at all directly with the revival of alliterative poetry in the West in the fourteenth century.[49] Some even later glosses, as in Bodley 343, of the fifteenth century, are of curiosity value only.

Some of the twelfth-century copies of Old English prose writing naturally contain fragments of verse, just as we found with eleventh-century MSS (see above, p. 64). Some of these verses are quite regular, in the simplified classical form, others show increasing licence: it may be that the former are copies, the latter new compositions, but possible too that the more regular pieces are from the centres where Old English learning was stronger. They include a short charm in B.M. MS Royal 4.A.xiv, a Latin commentary on the Psalms, and a short poem on *The Grave* in Bodley MS 343,[50] whilst in Cambridge University Library MS Ii.1.33, an anthology of readings of saints' lives and passions drawn from Ælfric, there is a collection of versified apothegms now called *Instructions for Christians*.[51] The copy is mid-twelfth-century, the text not much earlier, yet in form the poem is still recognisably an Anglo-Saxon poem, with little more licence in alliteration

75

or in the occasional use of rhyme than *Maldon*.[52] It is in passing from this poem to the *Worcester Fragments* which were probably in fact written earlier, that one might record, for form's sake, the beginning of Middle English poetry. There are two fragments, occupying the end pages of a MS containing Ælfric's *Grammar*, in the hand of the 'tremulous' glossator: the MS was later broken up to make covers for another book, and the surviving leaves, now reassembled, most of them imperfect, form MS 174 in Worcester Cathedral library. *Fragment A* is a short celebration of Anglo-Saxon learning and a lament on its decline with the introduction of foreign teachers:

> Þeos lærden ure leodan on englisc.
> næs deorc heore liht.     ac hit fæire glod.
> nu is þeo leore forleten.     & þet folc is forloren.
> nu beoþ oþre leoden.     þeo læreþ ure folc.
> & feole of þen lorþeines losiæþ.     & þet folc forþ mid.[53]

(These taught our people in English; their light shone bright, not dark. Now those teachings are all forgotten, the people lost and helpless; now our people are taught in other languages, and many of the teachers are damned, and the people with them.)

The poem dates from about 1100, when the monasteries had been flooded with Norman monks, and was written and refers to experiences at a place like Winchester rather than Worcester, where there would have been no such cause for complaint. The poem is both symptom and witness of decline, since it confuses Ælfric with Alcuin and twice dissolves into prose lists despite its attempt to ape the elevated style of Old English verse. Rhythm and alliteration are alike irregular, and demonstrate the shaking-loose of the tight structure of Old English verse even when it is not under pressure from other forms. The second fragment is a much longer poem, *The Soul's Address to the Body*, in the stern homiletic vein of two Old English poems on the same subject as well as a sermon by Wulfstan, perhaps with more of the stridency of the latter. Alliteration is fairly regular, but the rhythmical patterns of the half-line are looser and there is a good deal of sporadic rhyme and assonance. Statistical analyses of such features[54] are not much help in identifying the character of the form: comparison with the Old English poems on the same subject (which are not directly related) suggests, however, the total change in the shape of the line which has taken place. It is now longer, more fluent, more prosaic, with little or none of the traditional poetic language or the traditional forms of syntactical patterning such as inversion or variation. The most this verse affords itself in the way of rhetorical elaboration is simple antithesis and cumulative repetition in the manner of Wulfstan. Generally speaking, it is a compromise, in which the late plain style of Old English verse, with rhyme hovering as an uneasy intruder from the non-classical tradition, is partly stabilised within the powerful orbit of rhythmical homiletic prose.

There is a well-established theory which explains the further development of the alliterative line in the following terms: the addition of rhyme at half-line and line-end, which had always threatened the internal rhythmical structure of the half-line, eventually broke the line into a couplet, of wavering rhythm and two or three stresses, which subsequently fell in with the four-stress couplet derived from French octosyllabic. Meanwhile, in another and more legitimate line of descent, the alliterative long line, having 'shaken off' the tendency to rhyme, established itself with renewed strength as an integral unit, end-stopped, with the first half-line rhythmically and rhetorically dominant over the second. This is a fair description of the end results of the process, but whether the process itself can be described in such (or similar) evolutionary terms is more doubtful. The texts on which the weight of argument falls are of indeterminate date and mostly in an advanced state of textual corruption, so that the temptation to make them fit the argument is strong. It may be that we should abandon evolutionary language and think instead of a 'continuum' of alliterative writing of wide currency and varied function, a set of flexible and unformulated procedures within which individual writers could work according to their knowledge and inclinations.[55]

### Transitional verse

*The Proverbs of Alfred* (c. 1180) is one of the most confusing of these transitional texts. It is a compilation of moralistic sayings, arranged in short sections (headed 'Þus queþ Alured'), more homely and expansive than the Old English gnomic poetry but echoing the same taste for apothegm and touched by the same sense of the transience of the world. There is a grained and seasoned toughness in the language, and occasional moments of vividness—

> If þu hauest seorewe.
> ne seye þu hit nouht þan arewe.
> seye hit þine sadelbowe.      and ryd þe singinde forþ.[56]

> (*þan arewe*: to the enemy)

but the whole is eclectic and shapeless, and obviously vulnerable to scribal interference. The fullest text that comes down to us is in Trinity College, Cambridge, MS 323 (B.14.39), a miscellany of Latin, Anglo-Norman and English, the scribe of which seems ignorant of the English language; the best-known text, in Jesus College, Oxford, MS 29, another miscellany, with more English material, is from a scribe who understands English only too well, for he meddles constantly with language and metre; there are two other MSS, one fragmentary. The attribution to Alfred is a fabrication made plausible by the astute use of some tantalisingly authentic scraps of history: the opening lines describe a *witenagemot* addressed by Alfred at *Seuorde*, presumably Seaford, in Sussex, near to the royal manor of Dene which Asser describes as the place of his first meeting with Alfred;

and the opening sections, on the duties of king and noble, bear some striking resemblances to a homiletic discourse supposed to have been addressed to the king and *witan* at a national assembly, and found amongst Wulfstan's works.[57] Later sections, however, are more practical and domestic and relate most closely to the *Distichs of Cato*, a widely used school-book. The last sections, in the Trinity MS only, are more homely still: they incorporate, rather clumsily, an address to *sone min swo leue* ('my dear son') along with the attribution to Alfred, and are evidently drawn from the literature of parental instruction. The *Proverbs* are a by-product of learned tradition, not at all incompatible with the vernacular interests of a monk or clerical schoolmaster: what little can be ascertained of the provenance of the MSS suggests that they are associated with small religious houses.[58]

Technically, it is difficult to know what to make of the poem. Part is in the alliterative line without rhyme, and part in two- or three-stress couplets, often with alliteration: there are a good many lines with neither alliteration nor rhyme. There seems to be some tendency to compose individual sections in one form or the other, but it is not consistently maintained. Sometimes an alliterative section will end, sensibly enough, with a rhymed couplet:

> Þus queþ Alured.
> Wyþ-vte wysdome    is weole wel vnwurþ
> for þey o mon ahte.    huntseuenti Acres.
> and he hi hadde isowen.    alle myd reade golde.
> And þat gold greowe.    so gres doþ on eorþe.
> nere he for his weole.    neuer þe furþer.
> Bute he him of frumþe.    freond iwrche.
> for.    hwat is gold.    bute ston.
> bute if hit haueþ wismon.          (77–85)

(*weole*: wealth, *hi*: them, *of frumþe*: from the start)

The difficulty of coming to any conclusion is exacerbated by the corruption of the texts through scribal ignorance, error and interference (in the sixth line above, for instance, the Trinity MS reads *wrþer* for *furþer*, which restores the alliteration), and particularly by what seems to be, on the part of the Jesus scribe, 'a conscious effort to replace the archaic alliterative line with a more up to date poetical form'.[59] If the alliterative lines seem feebler, therefore, and the rhyming couplets more positive, it may be the process of transmission which is accountable. What it does seem possible to say is that the original author was well aware of the difference between the two forms of verse, and kept them more or less distinct, though history and scribes proved not to be on his side; and that his reason for using two metres was not that he was hopelessly confused and found the one dissolving into the other at the very touch, as might appear from the present texts, but that he was acquainted with Latin verse-compilations (like the *Physiologus*) in which the use of different metres was regular practice. As the same time, it cannot be denied that the alliterative lines, even in their uncorrupted form, are fragile, and their vulnerability to linguistic change and scribal error seems a mark of their narrow inheritance from the non-classical verse tradition un-strengthened by the broader rhythms of prose.

This interpretation of the *Proverbs* might seem to be confirmed by the *Bestiary*, a free adaptation, from the early thirteenth century, of parts of the Latin *Physiologus* of the eleventh-century Thetbaldus. The single MS (B. M. Arundel 292) is another multilingual miscellany, the scribe again probably Anglo-Norman, with little knowledge of English language or metre, and the provenance East Midland, which suggests that the West, though it was the home of most alliterative writing, did not have a monopoly of it. The work takes the traditional form: various animals are described as possessing particular, often perfectly fanciful attributes which are then allegorised. A monastic or pedagoguic background seems certain. In form, the English poem quite consciously imitates the Latin in using several distinct metres—the alliterative long line, occasionally with medial rhyme added, a four-stress couplet derived from French octosyllabic, a three-stress couplet and, more occasionally, septenary and 'common metre' ($a^4b^3a^4b^3$, i.e. septenary with medial rhyme). Particular sections usually fall into one or other of these metres, though there is some mixing, and the same apparently deliberate practice as in the *Proverbs* of ending an alliterative section with rhymed couplets:

> *(Natura araneé)*
> ... ðanne renneð ge rapelike.    for ge is ai redi.
> nimeð anon to ðe net.    & nimeð hem ðere.
> bitterlike ge hem bit.    & here bane wurðeð.
> drepeð & drinkeð here blod.
> doð ge hire non oðer god.
> bute fret hire fille
> & dareð siðen stille.[60]

> (*ge*: she, *rapelike*: quickly, *nimeð*: seizes, *bane*: killer, *drepeð*: kills, *fret*: eats, *dareð*: lurks)

The mixing of forms in the *Bestiary* is often described in dynamic and patriotic terms: the alliterative line is 'shaking off' rhyme and 'resisting' syllabic rhythm. It is true that the sections in couplet are more stable than those in the alliterative line, but the transitional appearance of the latter is due rather to the fact that the alliterative lines are in a worse textual state than the rest of the poem, and this in turn is because they have been misunderstood and perhaps partly worked over by a scribe ignorant of the technique. Again, with such a conscious metrist, it is difficult to see the three-stress couplets as relics of the alliterative half-line when there is a perfectly regular model in the hexasyllabic couplets of Anglo-Norman (and Latin), which are in fact used, beside octosyllabics, in the slightly earlier *Bestiaire* of Philippe de Thaon.[61] What one might stress is the element of

79

choice in the use of alliterative verse-form, and the need to discuss such a process of choice in the context of the individual poem, rather than to dissolve the poems into a general and impersonal myth of internal conflict and struggle for survival. The evidence is too sparse to make such a procedure anything more than highly speculative and, when it is linked with the myth of 'nationalistic' revival, highly tendentious. About the poet's choice in this case, though, one might say that it suggests limited access to the most durable kinds of alliterative writing.

Laȝamon's[62] *Brut*, far from clarifying the situation, which one might expect from its great length, only sets the same problems over again, with the added complication that the poet seems to have some knowledge of classical alliterative verse. The poem, of over 16,000 long lines, was written by the parish priest of Areley Kings in Worcestershire in the early thirteenth century: it has come down in two MSS, the second of which, Cotton Otho C. xiii, probably only slightly later in date (c. 1275) than the first, Cotton Caligula A.ix, tends to modernise the language, though not systematically, and with no apparent metrical bias. The verse is more regular than in other transitional poems, partly because the text is better, and despite the usual licences in rhythm, alliteration, and the use of rhyme. At times, the regularity is very marked, and there are echoes of compounding, poetic vocabulary, formulaic phrasing, even variation, which recall, for the first time since *Maldon*, the character of classical alliterative verse:

> Þer com Arður him aȝein, ȝaru mid his fehte,
> In ane brade forde þa ferden heom imetten;
> Fastliche onsloȝen [snelle heore kempen];
> Feollen þa uæie [uolden to grunde].
> Þer wes muchel blod-gute; balu þer wes riue;
> [Brustlede scæftes; beornes þer ueollen]....
> Þus seide Arður, aðelest kingen ...
> 'Ah nu is þe dæi icumen þe Drihten haueð idemed,
> Þat he scal þat lif leosen, and leosien his freonden,
> Oðer we sculle dæde beon; ne muȝe we hine quic iseon.
> Scullen Sæxisce men sorȝen ibiden,
> [And we wreken wurhliche ure wine-maies].'[63]

(There Arthur met him, ready with his army. The armies joined battle at a wide ford. Brave men smote fiercely at their champions, doomed men fell, struck to the ground. There was much bloodshed, danger was everywhere, spears bristled, men fell.... Thus said Arthur, noblest of kings ... 'Now is the day come that God has decreed that he [Colgrim] must depart from life and friends alike, or else we must die—we cannot live and see him alive. The Saxons must suffer sorrow if we are to avenge our friends and kinsmen worthily.')

It is, of course, in battle-poetry that these resemblances are most striking, but that is a matter of choice on the poet's part, not coincidence, and does not affect the deduction that he had access to the tradition of classical verse. Whether it was a living tradition is doubtful: Laȝamon's lines read like imitation, and have an archaic flavour, which the Otho scribe, as in the passage quoted above, tries to minimise. It seems a very deliberate choice on Laȝamon's part, and it is not his only choice: elsewhere there are syllabic couplets of three or four stresses which are very far from being debased relics of the alliterative half-line with rhyme.[64] They are scattered rather than bunched and, like the alexandrines in Dryden, seem to be part of a conscious pattern of metrical variation. They are not associated with particular subject-matter and do not increase in proportion as the poem goes on, so that it cannot be said that Laȝamon came more and more under the influence of the octosyllabics of his Anglo-Norman original: indeed, the practice of variation may itself be derived from Anglo-Norman models.[65] It is not a pattern of variation that it is easy to get used to, any more than Dryden's alexandrines, but it is clearly deliberate. Laȝamon also quite often uses rhyme or assonance as an additional ornament within predominantly alliterative lines: there seems to be a distinct difference of quality between these assonantal rhymes and the rhymes of the syllabic couplets. There is still something puzzling about Laȝamon's versification: at times it seems that, if he has made a choice, it was not a very good one. But the principle of choice seems an important one to set against the usual 'dynamic' theory, which has Laȝamon floundering along disconsolately for 16,000 lines amidst the wreckage of the alliterative line without discovering any systematic principle of versification.

## Transitional 'prose'

The strength of alliterative verse is vigorously asserted by Laȝamon; nevertheless the *Brut* seems rather an isolated phenomenon, something created out of a 'continuum' by an individual will and consciousness rather than a chance survival floating on a powerful submerged tradition. It is instructive to turn to developments in alliterative prose, where the situation is rather different. The continuity of copying in the twelfth century has already been mentioned, but even from the thirteenth century there are MSS of homiletic prose which include copies of works by Ælfric. A comparison of the thirteenth-century copy of the homily *De Duodecim Abusiuis* ('The Twelve Abuses') in Lambeth MS 487, which is to all intents and purposes in Middle English, with the Old English original tells us something rather unexpected:

Ure Hælend on his jugoðe    wæs gehyrsum his magen,
& his Heofonlice Fæder    he gehyrsumode oð deað.
Swa swa þan ealden gedafonigeð    dugende ðeawes
& geripode syfernysse,    swa gerist þan jungan
Þæt he habbe gehyrsumnysse    & underðeodnysse.
Godes æ beot eac    þæt mann arwurðige symle
his fæder & moder    mid mycelre underðeodnysse,
& gyf he heo weregað,    he byð wurðe deaðes.

(Our Saviour in his youth was obedient to his parents, and obeyed his Heavenly Father unto death. As it is right for the old to have virtuous habits and true faith, so it is right for the young to be obedient and submissive. God's law decrees also that a man should ever honour his father and mother with great respect, and is worthy of death if he curses them.)

> Vre helend on his ȝuheðe wes ihersum his cunne.
> and his heouenlich federe he hersumede to ða deðe.
> Swa swa þan alden bihouað duȝende þewas
> and triwe treofestnesse; swa birised þan ȝungan
> Þet he abbe ihersumnesse. and ibuhsumnesse.
> Godes laȝe bit ec mon wurðie efre
> his feder and his moder mid muchelere wurþunge.
> and ȝif he heom werieð; he bid deðes wurðe.[66]

It appears that Ælfric's rhythmical alliterative prose had a capacity far more enduring than alliterative verse to survive 'translation' and modernisation. It has the flexibility to contain the impact of the accelerated linguistic changes of the twelfth century (accelerated, because the strength of the traditional West Saxon literary language had hitherto acted as a preservative of older written forms), where the more rigid patterns of verse prove frangible. Changes of words to make them intelligible often ruin the alliteration, but the framework is loose enough to accommodate such change without destroying the general rhythm, and the rhythm strong enough to sustain the increase and redistribution of unstressed syllables.

In the same MS, Lambeth 487, there is an incomplete fragment of a prose lyric, *On Ureisun of Oure Louerde* ('An Orison of Our Lord'), one of a group of four associated with the longer prose texts of the *Katherine*-group in a cluster of MSS of Western provenance.[67] All these works are written for women-recluses or nuns: this is why they are written in English, since men would presumably have been expected to understand Latin,[68] and it is also why they concentrate so intensely on the person of Christ and his relation of love and suffering with the contemplative virgin-Bride. The prose-lyrics of the *Wooing*-group, particularly, are heady with suppressed eroticism, and written in an extravagantly heightened form of alliterative prose:

> Iesu swete Iesu. mi druð. mi derling. mi drihtin. mi healend. mi huniter.
> mi haliwei. Swetter is munegunge of þe þen mildeu o muðe. Hwa ne
> mei luue þi luueli leor? Hwat herte is swa hard þet ne mei to-melte i þe
> munegunge of þe? Ah hwa ne mej luue þe luueliche iesu?[69]

(*druð*: darling, *drihtin*: lord, *huniter*: honey-drop, *haliwei*: balm, *munegunge*: memory, *mildeu*: honey, *leor*: face)

One is often reminded of Wulfstan in these cumulative sequences of emphatic two-stress phrases, but clearly another and subtler influence is at work in addition to what the writers draw from native tradition. The interweaving of phrases, sometimes symmetrical, sometimes varied, into elaborately composed sentences, the use of alliteration as a source of enrichment and emphasis, the extension of alliteration in crossed and echoing patterns over a series of phrases—all these are vernacular imitations of the rhetorical Latin prose of the Bernardine tradition, affected, rhapsodic, cadenced and figured. A sentence like this has a rhythm and structure new to English prose:

> Bringen forð longis wið þet brade scharpe spere. he þurles his side
> cleues tat herte. & cumes flowinde ut of þet wide wunde. Þe blod þet
> bohte. Þe water þet te world wesch of sake & of sunne.[70]

(*þurles* : pierces, *sake* : strife)

The traditions of this prose are continued in the fourteenth century in *A Talkyng of the Love of God*,[71] another example of the persistence of alliterative writing, in its various manifestations and metamorphoses.

A work like the *Wohunge* makes it hard to draw clear lines between 'prose' and 'verse'. It could easily be printed as verse, and so could the three saints' lives of the *Katherine*-group. These too are influenced by Latin prose, but their functions are simpler (they are intended for public reading in church on the saint's day rather than for private meditation)[72] and the native tradition emerges more strongly. *Juliana*, for instance, sets up from the start a regular expectation of rhythmical two-stress phrases, with alliteration to identify and emphasise the rhythmical unit and also often to string two or more phrases together in sequence. *Katherine* is similar, rather plainer in style, the most elaborate of the three being *Margaret*, perhaps because its Latin original is in a more elevated style. Here, particularly in the prayers and invocations of the saint, emphatic rhythm and heavy alliteration, often exuberantly prolonged on a single letter, are combined with controlling rhetorical devices of balance, repetition and repetition-with-variation in a prose of extraordinary vigour and variety:

> Brihtest bleo of alle þat euer iboren weren, blosme iblowen & iboren o
> meidenes bodi; Iesu, godd & godes bern, iblescet beo þu euer. Ich am
> gomeful & gled, lauerd, of þi godlec; keiser of kinges, drihtin undedlich.
> Þu haldest & heuest up treowe bileaue. Þu art walle of wisdom, & euch
> wunne wakeneð & waxeð of þe. Þu art englene weole, þat weldest &
> witest ham wið-uten wonunge.[73]

(*bleo* : face, *gomeful* : joyful, *godlec* : goodness, *undedlich* : immortal, *wunne* : joy, *weole* : joy, *witest* : guard, *wonunge* : ceasing)

A history of English poetry cannot ignore this writing, nor is there any incentive to, since it is part of the best established literary tradition between the ninth century and the fourteenth. Poetry cannot annex its greatest achievement, the

*Ancrene Wisse*, which is prose without question and almost without fault. But it could be said of the saints' lives that those who wrote them, whether they thought they were writing 'prose' or not, had a better grasp of the essential rhythms of alliterative 'verse' than others who recognised themselves as poets.

There is a natural tendency to seek an explanation for this West Midland writing of the early thirteenth century in terms of some direct link with authentic traditions of the past. The connection with rhythmical homiletic prose is an obvious one,[74] and the distinctly developed literary character of the language suggests a tradition of composition going back perhaps to West Mercian originals.[75] But none of this can 'explain' the *Katherine*-group, which is better seen as the product of some subtle alchemy involving native and Latin traditions. What is important is the confirmation of the intrinsic strength of the alliterative form, its tenacious hold on some of the central areas of English writing, and its potential to manifest itself vigorously in a variety of metamorphoses. It does not matter that we cannot trace direct lines of descent from the saints' lives of the *Katherine*-group: we shall find instead, at the beginning of the fourteenth century[76] new varieties of alliterative writing, not confined to the West, which bear continued witness to the inherent strength of the alliterative 'continuum'. On this interpretation, therefore, the alliterative revival of the fourteenth century would not be an inexplicable reversion to the past but a prolonged and particularly splendid episode in the history of a long, unbroken and powerful tradition.

# 4    Poetry in the early Middle English period

The last chapter, in its attempt to trace the fortunes of alliterative writing after the Conquest, had its eye frankly to the future, and the flowering of alliterative poetry in the fourteenth century. The stress was on the continued availability of the alliterative form, to a variety of writers and needs, rather than on the continuity of the Anglo-Saxon poetic tradition, which was, in its classical form, moribund by the time the extant poetry was written down and dead by the eleventh century. Laȝamon is obviously archaistic. Classical poetry, conceived and brought to perfection in the generous atmosphere of early Anglo-Saxon monastic culture, gave way to looser forms of alliterative writing, which accommodated the more didactic and practical needs of the late tenth and eleventh centuries. These looser forms, constituting what I have grown accustomed to calling a 'continuum', were available to writers after the Conquest, occasionally being wrought up, by an archaist like Laȝamon, or under the influence of other stylistic traditions such as that of Latin prose, into something memorable. It is not a part of this argument that the choice of such forms was in any way an act of patriotic self-assertion.

Alliterative verse is now, in the twelfth and thirteenth centuries, available as one of a number of possible forms, with a wider currency in the West, but by no means confined to a particular region. This variety of choice is part of the new cultural pattern of post-Conquest England. The dominance of the classical tradition in Old English verse is almost monolithic, and one searches painfully for scraps and evidences of other influences; it seems to have no tentative beginnings and it dies choking on its own magnificence; its resistance to alien forms such as rhyme is remarkable. Early Middle English verse, by contrast, is amorphous:[1] not the product of a single coherent tradition with a systematic style and diction and a standardised language, but a series of fragmentary and imperfect responses to a multitude of European influences, in a language thrown open to the winds of change. Anglo-Saxon England had its contacts with the continent, but England is now part of the continent, and not a very important part.

*English and Anglo-Norman*

England's loss of independence is a loss of status. There are times, as during the reign of Henry II, when England is merely a province of the Angevin Kingdom.

Above all, and more far-reaching in its consequences for poetry than anything else, is the decline in the status of the English language. Anglo-Saxon had achieved, by the eleventh century, an importance in relation to Latin which no other vernacular was to match for centuries. This was partly due to the prestige won for it by poetry within the monastic tradition, but more particularly to the reforms instituted by Alfred and the translations put in hand by him, made necessary by the decline of Latin learning during the Danish invasions. Though it never replaced Latin as the language of higher learning, Old English came to be used for a wide variety of purposes in law, church, education and administration as well as history and literature. The Conquest ended this state of affairs, which was anomalous in Western Europe, and Latin resumed its normal role as the language of all learning and officialdom. This did not happen suddenly, nor by decree, but by an inevitable process of change. William kept the Old English Chancery going for a year or two—even tried to learn the language himself—before government reverted to Latin; the *Anglo-Saxon Chronicle* was continued for a few years after the Conquest—longer at Peterborough—but soon gave way to Latin in the great flowering of Anglo-Latin historiography of the twelfth century; Old English learning was kept up in some monasteries well into the twelfth century, but they gradually became more and more isolated.

There was no deliberate attempt to suppress the English language: in fact, it would be a mistake to relate national consciousness or patriotism at all closely with linguistic consciousness in these early medieval centuries.[2] Laʒamon is full of a fiery patriotism, but it is mostly inherited from the Latin of Geoffrey of Monmouth through the Anglo-Norman of the Jerseyman Wace; and a poem in Anglo-Norman on the crusading fortunes of William Longespée can be just as virulently anti-French as the English romance of *Richard Coeur de Lion*.[3] It is remarkable how quickly the Chronicle itself swallows its indignation at the imposition of Norman customs in the monasteries, and represents the defeat of Robert of Normandy's invading forces, after the accession of William II (1087), as a victory for 'Englishmen' and not a futile intervention in foreign dynastic squabbles.[4] Nevertheless, the Conquest and William's subsequent actions produced an erosion of the status of the English language just as effective as any suppression. The systematic destruction of the English nobility, the plantation of a Norman land-holding aristocracy throughout England, and the vigorous activity of Lanfranc, Archbishop of Canterbury, in flooding monasteries with Norman monks and the church with Norman appointees meant that English was deprived of most of the sources of status. Latin surged back, and for a time in the twelfth century acquired a universality and importance that was itself exceptional: Giraldus Cambrensis and Walter Map are court writers in the late twelfth century, but have no thought of writing in any other language but Latin. Then, as the vernacular begins to creep back into the legal system, into the lower functions of government, education and business, into the monasteries, into history and literature, it is the Anglo-Norman vernacular that holds sway, not English.

Thus, during the thirteenth century, the prestige vernacular in England is Anglo-Norman.[5] In form, Anglo-Norman is a development of the Norman dialect of French spoken by the invaders; it remained perfectly intelligible to French speakers but gradually acquired a provincial character which distinguished it further from metropolitan French. It is often stigmatised as an 'artificial' language by English scholars, but it was clearly a lively and widely spoken vernacular: the only artificiality is its historical situation. During the period of its dominance it penetrated deep into the middle and lower layers of English society, and was by no means confined to the upper classes: certainly no one with any pretensions to education or literacy would be without it. There are a number of references to the wide currency of Anglo-Norman: Marie de France, for instance, addresses her *Espurgatoire S. Patrice* to 'la simple gent'[6] and Denis Piramus, monk of Bury, speaks of 'franceis' as the language which all are able to understand,

Li grant, li mien e li mendre.[7]

As late as the early fourteenth century, a monk of Canterbury writes in French, as he says, 'pur ces ke comunement la gent cel langage entendent'.[8] These references to 'simple' people and 'common' understanding do not of course mean that the rural peasantry were bilingual, but they imply a wide knowledge of Anglo-Norman amongst the literate and semi-literate outside the courts and cloisters.

It is one of the ironies of history that just as Anglo-Norman entered its ascendancy its roots should have been cut by the loss of Normandy, in 1204, and the division of the Anglo-French kingdom. England remained thoroughly Anglo-Norman in culture throughout the thirteenth century—even the attack on the foreignness of Henry III's French favourites was mounted by a French-speaking immigrant—but the language was already doomed, and signs of decay appear in the form of grammars and glossaries towards the end of the century. French was becoming a useful acquisition rather than a native language, and the regulations being introduced at the same time to encourage the speaking of French in monasteries and colleges tell the same story. The fourteenth century sees a rapid decline in Anglo-Norman, though it retains its hold in some fields, such as official and business records and correspondence, well into the fifteenth century, and in law of course until the seventeenth century. The last major English writer to use Anglo-Norman is John Gower (d. 1408) and he disguises what is fast becoming a narrowly provincial and backward language by writing in a much closer approximation to continental French. He uses English for his major poem, however, and Chaucer uses nothing else. Circumstances conspired to create a vacuum, and English rolled back into the lusher pastures of royal and aristocratic patronage. Richard II's is the first English-speaking court since that of Harold Godwinson.

It is against this background that English poetry has to be set, and it must be admitted that the task is a complex one. Poetry depends not only on the existence of a literary language but also on the use of the language as a vernacular, and therefore all kinds of evidence as to the currency and status of the English language has to be considered. This evidence is scattered and not always easy to interpret: it is also very vulnerable to tendentious interpretation, and can often be used to prove what one wants to prove. For one scholar, the presence of Frenchmen at Edward the Confessor's court is a sign that he is 'coquetting with France'; for another, it is a matter for surprise that there are so few.[9] On the whole, English scholars such as Chambers and Wilson,[10] whilst gleaning every scrap of evidence for the continuity of English, have tended to neglect Anglo-Norman, and Miss Legge is right to reprove them so sharply; Miss Legge, on the other hand, with a mass of evidence to deploy, sometimes overplays her hand. The hypothesis of an Anglo-Norman original for the *Ancrene Wisse*, which she flirts with more than once,[11] has long since been exploded; and when she comments on the letter of Walter Map to Giraldus Cambrensis in 1209 (regretting that he wrote only in Latin and not in French) that he wouldn't have dreamt of suggesting English,[12] it ought to be mentioned that a contemporary English poem, *The Owl and the Nightingale*, is quite as sophisticated as anything in Walter Map.

A general conclusion might be that English naturally remained the sole language of the peasantry; that elsewhere it was never completely displaced as a spoken language by French except among a very restricted court and aristocratic circle—admittedly an important milieu for literature—and that there was necessarily a good deal of bilingualism in the middle and upper strata of society. Probably French had always a greater social prestige even in bilingual situations: an interesting sidelight on this is provided by the Holkham Bible Picture Book, about 1326, where the writer of the captions, who normally uses French, drops into English for the shepherds' speech.[13] One can perhaps argue that there can be no true parity of esteem in a bilingual situation, and that one language or the other is bound to be dominant, if not generally, at least in particular sets of circumstances. The difficulty of pronouncing with certainty about English and French is that high court and manorial court, street and shop, great hall, kitchen and nursery, all had their different patterns of speech-behaviour, and that the two languages existed side by side with an extraordinary lack of resentment until propagandist remarks about 'English for Englishmen' start to be made about 1300. A further complication is introduced by regional differences: the authors of the *Katherine*-group use English where writers in other parts of the country, addressing the same audience of nuns and women-recluses, use French. And finally, there is the dimension of time, to which this shifting pattern of dominance is also related. Tentatively, one might argue for a period in the thirteenth century, roughly the reign of Henry III, when Anglo-Norman had a definite pre-eminence; before and after this, for different reasons and with much local variation, there is a more equal interchange.

Among the clergy, who are of course the actual writers of literature in nearly every case, the linguistic situation is even more complicated. For one thing, learning is still the prerogative of the Church, and Latin the universal acquisition and distinguishing mark of the learned man and cleric; on the other hand, the church needs the vernacular for its pastoral role. One would expect the clergy, therefore, to be trilingual, and probably they were, except at the bottom of the scale, where French would be a luxury, and at the top, where foreign-trained and imported clerics might not bother to learn English. During the Anglo-Norman ascendancy, even a man like Robert Grosseteste, a low-born and country-bred Englishman before his elevation to the see of Lincoln, might use little English: certainly, French is his primary vernacular. Somewhat earlier, at the end of the twelfth century, Abbot Samson of Bury recommends the verna-cular, whether French or English, to his preachers: he himself preached in English but his Norfolk accent is said to have caused difficulty to a Suffolk audience. This illustrates one enormous advantage of Anglo-Norman—that it was a true *lingua franca*, perfectly intelligible throughout the country (and France too) where the English dialects, after the break-up of the West-Saxon *Schriftsprache*, were growing further and further apart and had no common literary standard.

*Clerical tradition: poetry of the 'schools'*

Out of this complex and quite fascinating linguistic and cultural situation it is now possible to draw one or two strands which relate specifically to the history of poetry. There are some poems, as we have seen, which can be counted an afterbirth of Anglo-Saxon monasticism.[14] But twelfth-century poetry begins already to reflect a wider variety of traditions, not exclusively monastic, and certainly not exclusively Anglo-Saxon. For a time, that is, in the clerical tradition at least, English poetry matches Anglo-Norman poetry step for step. *The Proverbs of Alfred* can be set beside the *Proverbs of Solomon* of Sanson de Nantuil, written for the son of the patroness:[15] the English poem is both more homely and more learned than the French one. It also reflects a shared interest in Alfred: the Anglo-Normans made much of the descent of Edward the Confessor from Alfred, and Marie de France ascribes to Alfred the English *Fables* which she professes to be translating.[16] Likewise, the English *Bestiary* is drawn from the same sources as the somewhat earlier *Bestiaire* of Philippe de Thaon. The fact that the two English poems are partly in alliterative verse has prejudiced inter-pretation, so that they have come to be regarded as relics, when in fact they are the first fruits of a new bilingual cultural tradition. If they come from monasteries, it is not from the great houses, where Latin is now firmly re-established, with Anglo-Norman for lighter occasions, but from smaller foundations; or they may come from the grammar schools, which were often under the jurisdiction of monasteries, and where the *Proverbs of Alfred* would have provided a useful supplement to the construing of Cato's *Distichs* in the curriculum, or the *Bestiary* to Æsop's *Fables*—both are standard basic text-books in the Middle Ages.

Another poem from the same background is the *Poema Morale*, a verse-sermon which begins as a confession in old age and develops its call to penitence and salvation through meditation on the transience of life, the imminence of Judgment, the pains of hell and the joys of heaven. A ruthlessly direct and personal address is maintained throughout, supported by a style full of gritty proverbs and abrupt antitheses:

> Þe wel ne doð þe hwile he mai ne sal he þan he wolde ...
> Wo wurðe soreʒe seue ʒier for seue nihte blisse.[17]

The poem comes down in six MSS, a surprisingly large number, of which two are collections of Old English homiletic material, partly Ælfrician (Lambeth 487 and Trinity B.14.52)[18] and the others multilingual (Egerton 613, Digby A.4, Jesus 29 and Fitzwilliam McClean 123). It thus stands at the junction of two traditions: it is completely untouched by the new devotional feeling of the twelfth century (only fear is invoked, never love) and is quite at home in an Anglo-Saxon homiletic collection; on the other hand it is written in an accomplished imitation of the Latin septenary, with rich rhyme and no trace of alliteration or Old English poetic diction. In its use of a non-native metre it can be associated with another more commonplace piece in Lambeth 487, a verse exposition of the Paternoster in fairly regular four-stress couplets. But the most interesting literary relationship for the *Poema Morale* is with the *Sermon en Vers* or *Romaunz de Temtacioun de Secle* of Guischard de Beaulieu, written slightly later, towards the end of the twelfth century.[19] This poem, addressed by a monk of a small Bedfordshire priory to a great lady of the neighbourhood, resembles the English poem closely in its choice and development of themes, and uses English words here and there, just as the *Poema Morale* uses French ones (e.g. 365–6). Such a resemblance is not remarkable, since both poems deal in homiletic commonplaces, but it does demonstrate, along with the other parallels mentioned above, that English and Anglo-Norman verse tradition had much in common in the twelfth century and that English was not immediately, if ever, cast out into the Western darkness. If most of the great monastic houses, such as Bury and St Alban's, prime targets for Norman infiltration, soon went over to Anglo-Norman as the alternative to Latin for 'literary' work, yet still in the smaller houses—and we have already seen that this is where some of the MSS are found—[20] a greater variety of practice prevailed, depending on individual members and local traditions.

Thus English poetry had the same opportunities as Anglo-Norman in the clerical didactic tradition, though much less frequently, to judge by the relative bulk of poetry surviving. But in one important area, English poetry could not approach Anglo-Norman: there is nothing in English, and could not conceivably be anything, to correspond to the noble *Tristan*-fragments of Thomas, the *Tristan* of Beroul, or the *Lais* of Marie de France. These are courtly poems, reflecting the tastes and interests of the exclusively French court of Henry II and his queen, Eleanor of Aquitaine. There will be no such grace, passion and subtlety in English until the late fourteenth century. Furthermore, there is for the Anglo-Norman poems in general a network of names of authors, patrons and aristocratic families, a suggestion of a literary milieu, which is quite lacking for the English poems. English is totally deprived, as one might expect, of all aristocratic patronage, and this is its severest limitation in the centuries before Chaucer.

The existence of *The Owl and the Nightingale*, for all that it is a marvel in its own right, does not contradict this argument. This witty and sophisticated and altogether delightful poem presents a debate between the two birds in which each puts forward his own claims to superiority. Some of these claims are sufficiently bird-like—their appearance, their song, their usefulness to mankind—others are frankly anthropomorphic, and it soon becomes clear that two views of life are being light-heartedly canvassed, one earnest and serious and concerned with duty, the other gay and frivolous and concerned with pleasure. In the process a number of serious issues are touched on, but never seriously debated, and the poem ends with the birds flying off to ask Master Nicholas of Guildford, who has a living at Portisham in Dorset, for a judgment. We can assume that these topical intellectual issues, which the poet airs, were much in the minds of his circle—the new vogue for astrology and prognostication, the contrast between the old hellfire preaching and the new gospel of sweetness and song,[21] the fashionable cult of adulterous love. In the treatment of love and sexuality there are faint echoes of Alain de Lille and the school of Chartres as well as hints of goliardic irreverence. What learning there is is worn very lightly, and everything bespeaks a sophisticated late twelfth-century milieu not much different from that of Walter Map, who wrote in Latin, or Hue de Rotelande, who wrote in Anglo-Norman. The covertness of all its allusions suggests a clique, perhaps the household of some church dignitary or a school of more than usually secular canons. Nicholas of Guildford has himself, of course, been proposed as the author, since he is at least named, and the poem has been regarded as his testimonial for promotion, but the closing eulogy of his virtues, in which Owl and Nightingale at last join in chorus, is comically fulsome, and the accusations of nepotism against his bishops would be hardly likely to help him win the preferment he is supposed to seek. The assumption is rather futile anyway, since Nicholas cannot be identified. The vast amount of speculation as to his identity, however, does give some support to the idea that the poet, whoever he was and whether or not he was an archdeacon's chaplain or a member of a bishop's household, like Master Nicholas in two of his numerous manifestations, was at least a member of that same great army of clerics who had completed their training in the schools but who were yet on the fringes of ecclesiastical advancement.

The poem is indebted to the Latin tradition of debate-poetry, long established as a form of rhetorical exercise, and recently stimulated by the growth of dialectic and the use of disputation as practice in fictitious litigation. Like the Latin poems,[22] and co-derivatives in the Anglo-Norman tradition such as *Le Petit Plet* of Chardri,[23] which occurs in both MSS of the English poem, *The Owl and the Nightingale* is a form of intellectual play, not a didactic exercise, and like them it concludes inconclusively, with a deferral of judgment. But in every aspect of treatment it is superior—more lively, varied, inventive and dramatic. In place of the stilted set speeches of unvarying length of the Latin tradition, there is here a wealth of narrative and comment, evasions, interruptions, ploy and counter-ploy, and a constant tracing in the dialogue of the feelings, whether of anger, anxiety, elation or frustration, of the combatants.

The Nightingale begins by describing the filthy habits of the Owl and its young in their nest,

> Vel wostu þat hi doþ þarinne:
> Hi fuleþ hit up to þe chinne.[24]

The Owl is furious,

> & sat tosvolle & ibolwe
> Also ho hadde one frogge isuolȝe                                    (145–6)

(*tosvolle & ibolwe*: puffed up and swollen with anger)

but the Nightingale returns to the attack with the accusation that the Owl is unnatural since she prefers darkness to light and her song is mournful and miserable. The Owl replies with patient logic that it is her nature to hunt by night, and as for her song,

> Mi stefne is bold & noȝt unorne;
> Ho is ilich one grete horne,
> & þin is ilich one pipe
> Of one smale wode unripe.
> Ich singe bet þan þu dest;
> Þu chaterest so doþ on Irish prost.                             (317–22)

(*stefne*: voice, *unorne*: thin and scratchy, *wode*: weed)

The Nightingale, somewhat put out, grows reckless, and accuses the Owl of singing only in winter, when men are miserable, and says it is because she hates the idea of men enjoying themselves; the Nightingale, however, comes in spring when the earth is awakening and men are joyful. The Owl answers that men know their friends by what they are in times of need; the songs of spring, any-way, are only incentives to lechery, and the Owl spends rather longer than necessary on the rankness of animal and human lust. Somewhat over-heated, she descends to less substantial charges:

> Among þe wode, among þe netle
> Þu sittest & singst bihinde þe setle.
> Þar me mai þe ilomest finde
> Þar men worpeþ hore bihinde.                                    (593–6)

(*setle*: privy-seat, *ilomest*: most often, *worpeþ*: stick out)

The Nightingale, in a difficult situation, for it is difficult to fight 'aȝen soþ & aȝen riȝte' (668), tells the Owl, with patent sophistry, that her song is joyful to remind men of the joys of heaven. The Owl's reply has something of the frustrated and impotent anger of one who knows he is in the right but sees himself being beaten in argument. Worse is to come, when the Nightingale associates her song with the noble and beautiful things of life: why should she forego her nature,

> Þat ich ne singe bi þe bedde
> Þar louerd haueþ his loue ibedde?
> Hit is mi riȝt, hit is mi laȝe
> Þat to þe hexst ich me draȝe. (967–70)

The Owl explains how her song, foreboding evils and misery to come, is a direct help to men: it is all for their good, even though they do not realise it, and are not grateful (one detects a certain envy of the entertainer's easy popularity). The Nightingale condemns such prognostication as witchcraft, and turns to her own defence: her song encourages love, not wantonness, and she affirms that the love of man and wife far surpasses any other; nevertheless love is always a good thing, unless it be stolen,

> . . . for heo beoþ wode
> Þe bute nest goþ to brode (1385–6)

(*wode* : mad, *bute* : without)

Lechery in any case is not a mortal sin, being far less serious than pride, and finally, says the Nightingale, raking together the last stray arguments, however contradictory, in her armoury, her song is a useful reminder to maidens of the nature of carnal love—pleasant but brief. The Owl desperately claims a special virtue in that she is useful to man as a scarecrow even after she is dead:

> An for heom ich chadde mi blod.
> Ich do heom god mid mine deaþe. (1616–17)

The Nightingale seizes on this as an admission of disgrace, a *stultiloquium*,

> Þu seist þat gromes þe ifoð
> An heie on rodde þe anhoð (1645–6)

(*ifoð* : catch, *anhoð* : hang)

hops on to a higher branch in her excitement and declares the case conceded. The Owl threatens to summon the birds of prey and declare war but the wren intervenes and recommends them to Nicholas as arbitrator.

It may seem extravagant to paraphrase the poem at such length, but it is the only way of conveying something of its unique flavour. It would be crass to talk about the subject of the debate, or its point, or to 'explain' the allusions, because the intellectual content of the poem has been totally absorbed into its form and structure. The Owl is obviously 'right', but truth and falsehood dissolve into each other unattainably in the intoxication of argument. The constant flicker of allusion to human affairs is never systematically allegorical, never free from irony, burlesque or exaggeration, but the birds take themselves seriously —their philosophies of life are at stake, after all—and moments of passionate conviction alternate with high comedy. It is both frothy and substantial, flippant and warmly human, a poem very like Chaucer's *Nun's Priest's Tale*, and not at all inferior; and if one had to isolate its unique quality one would describe it in terms of a Chaucerian subtlety and irony, a delicious and disconcerting awareness that the poet is cleverer than we are, that each joke is part of a larger joke and that if only we have the wit to follow it will all add up....

Technically, the poet's skills are no less remarkable: he handles a wide range of source-materials with deceptive ease, introducing proverbs (ascribed to Alfred, again) and exemplary stories as if spontaneously, and lacing the debate with technical terms to give it the air of a lawsuit; the language, a blend of the homely and the sophisticated, would itself argue against any sort of depressed status for English; and the octosyllabic couplet is given a variety and richness which no other medieval poet, not even Chaucer, can match, with crisp rhymes tightening the structure and skewering the wandering mind as rhymes should. *The Owl and the Nightingale* is often treated by English scholars as if it were some kind of freak, and perhaps no poem demonstrates more sharply how inexplicable early Middle English poetry is if it is not related to its multilingual background. The true context of the poem is a Latin one, and only in Latin, in the best of the goliardic poets, shall we find anything to match its artful ease. Nor need it be a matter for surprise, in view of what has been said above about the clerical tradition, to find such a poem in English.

### The friars' miscellanies

*The Owl and the Nightingale* appears in two MSS, Cotton Caligula A.ix and Jesus 29. These collections have already been mentioned on a number of occasions (the former contains the *Brut*, the latter the *Poema Morale* and the *Proverbs of Alfred*) and have great importance as illustrations of the early clerical tradition. Yet Jesus 29 is in fact a friars' miscellany of the third quarter of the thirteenth century, and the survival of poetry from the earlier tradition is thus partly due to the diligence of the friars. This, added to the fact that they were themselves the main inheritors of the clerical tradition of vernacular poetry and were responsible for the production and preservation of most English poetry of a learned cast in the thirteenth century,[25] is an indication of the importance of the friars in the history of poetry during this century as well as the first part of the next.

Two important dates can introduce a discussion of the friars' miscellanies.

The first is 1215, the date of the Fourth Lateran Council, one of the decrees of which made annual confession to the parish priest compulsory for all Christians. The decree was put into force by the Council of Oxford, 1222, and implemented with particular rigour, it seems, in England. Its consequences were profound: the practice of confession is an art and the receiving of it a greater one, and the laity and parish clergy of England were often trained in neither. A great flood of manuals of confession, treatises on the Seven Deadly Sins, and encyclopaedias of the vices and virtues followed, designed partly for the parish priest and partly for the educated layman; and a great stimulus was given to preaching in the vernacular and to the production of vernacular literature, particularly of an affective and penitential kind. In all these movements the friars were the spearhead. The black monks were settling back in their fat abbeys; the tide of Cistercian spirituality had ebbed, its energies now absorbed in the great sheep-ranches of the Welsh Marches and the Yorkshire Dales; but in 1221 the Dominicans arrived and in 1224, the second of our important dates, the Franciscans. They were greeted with gloom and resentment by the old orders—'Eodem anno [1224] O dolor! O plus quam dolor! O pestis truculenta! Fratres minores venerunt in Angliam', says a Peterborough chronicler[26]—but their effect elsewhere was electrifying. They had behind them a great dedication to learning (the Franciscan school at Oxford in the thirteenth century was one of the most prominent in Western Europe) and the unstinted support of the Papacy, yet they spoke to the people in their own language, preached with fervour, sang new songs to the old tunes and, for a time, lived the life of Christ they professed. Their power and influence was unbounded: from the first they were licensed to preach and hear confession, and in 1250 the bull *Cum a nobis petitur* gave them permission to bury in their own churches anyone who so desired, which brought rich families into their fief, lucrative chantries, and a growing alienation from the parish clergy, who thereby lost a major source of revenue. Within a hundred years, or less, the spiritual impetus of the friars was dead, and the way clear for the endless satirical diatribes of the fourteenth century, but for this period the friars were the centre of intellectual life in the country.

The friars' miscellanies are their literary stock-in-trade: they sometimes include Latin material, of a useful rather than a learned kind, but mostly consist of English and Anglo-Norman poems of a religious and didactic nature. There is no clear distinction of kind or class between the two languages, though rubrics are usually in French (if not Latin) and the English poems cover a wider spectrum and include pieces with a more popular appeal: clearly the friars equipped themselves to deal with every audience. Equally clearly, they did not restrict themselves, in either the miscellanies or commonplace-books (in which copies are entered by a number of hands), to material of a strictly useful or edifying kind—the more fortunately for us. We can assume that they gathered together in these volumes songs to sing, stories and treatises to read aloud, verse-sermons, exempla and proverbs to incorporate in sermons, as well as a great store of other useful things, but that they sometimes copied in poems interesting for their own sake.

Jesus 29—to which Caligula A.ix is a sister-volume[27]—is one of the more serious collections. It is in one hand, and dated after 1256,[28] but incorporates *The Owl and the Nightingale*, the *Poema Morale* and the *Proverbs of Alfred*, all from before 1200. The Anglo-Norman poems of Chardri, whose *Petit Plet* has been mentioned as a product of the same cultural milieu and literary traditions as *The Owl and the Nightingale*, are also included, probably from the early thirteenth century. For the rest, it is difficult to say: one group of poems, on death and doomsday, could be directly from the earlier homiletic tradition, though such themes are never out of place in the Middle Ages. Two of them, *Doomsday* and *The Latemest Day*,[29] appear in other friars' miscellanies, Digby 86 and Trinity 323, and the second seems to have echoes of the Worcester *Body and Soul* poem as well as the *Poema Morale*.[30] A stanza will suggest its grim strength and imaginative limitation:

> Þenne þe latemeste day.  deþ haueþ ibrouht.
> Bi-nymeþ ure speche.  ure syhte. and þouht.
> And in uyche lyme.  deþ us haueþ þureh-souht.
> Þenne beoþ ure blisse.  al i-turnd to nouht.[31]

(*Bi-nymeþ* : takes away)

Two other shorter poems, *The Signs of Death*, and *Three Sorrowful Tidings*,[32] could well be from the older native tradition; both are widespread in a variety of forms, and the latter is translated into Latin in one MS as a fragment of proverbial lore.[33]

The dominant metrical form in this collection is a loose long line composed of mixed septenaries and alexandrines, rhyming in couplets or quatrains, and sometimes with internal rhyme added to produce the equivalent of ballad-metre ($a^4b^3a^4b^3$) or an 8-line stanza on the same pattern. Printing in short lines, however, disguises the real nature of this form, which is indebted to both Latin and Anglo-Norman models, particularly to the latter in its admission of lines of varied length.[34] This will not make sense to the metrical purist, but it is what the texts clearly demonstrate, and if the verses are read aloud with emphatic delivery—which is what they were intended for—there is no confusion, and some gain over the monotony of continuous septenaries. The stanza quoted above will demonstrate further that there is no metrical barrier against the invasion of the native four-stress line, whose powerful cadences seem to lie behind every borrowed form, even though that form may be announced initially with unequivocal clarity:

> Hwenne ich þenche of domes-day.  ful sore ich may adrede.[35]

In one poem, *Hwon holy chireche is under uote*, an attack on corruption within the church,[36] the invasion is well advanced, and in another, *On Serving Christ*, it is complete,[37] for this poem is in an irregular long alliterative line, rhyming in *laisses* of varied length in imitation of Anglo-Norman.

Native themes and forms, however, merge and coexist happily with borrowed traditions. A poem on *The XI Pains of Hell*, in octosyllabic couplet, expertly handled, begins in French with the narrator setting the scene, and passes into English for the speech of Satan and the risen soul who has seen hell; French and English again stand side by side in the epilogue. A doomsday poem, *Sinners Beware*, repeats the familiar homiletic warnings, but is written in tail-rhyme (³*aabaab*) derived from Latin models; another poem on death, *Long Life* ('Mon may longe lyves wene/Ac ofte him lyeþ þe wrench'), is in a complex 10-line stanza and is clearly designed for singing.[38] This development of vernacular religious song is one of the friars' characteristic contributions, and is illustrated further, along with an equally characteristic form of devotion, in two Marian lyrics. The more homely side of the friars' work is represented in two pieces, one a straightforward popular narrative of *The Passion of Our Lord*, offered as an alternative to tales of 'Karlemeyne' and the 'Duzeper', the other *A Lutel Soth Sermun*, which adopts a very homely tone of address ('Herkneþ alle gode men/And stylle sitteþ adun') and develops its theme of penitence on a frankly popular level: among those who will go to hell are bakers and brewers who give bad measure and priests' wives (one imagines cheers), but also those who bill and coo in church, Wilkin and Watkin and Malkin.[39] The gem of the collection, however, the *Luue-Ron*, composed by the Franciscan Thomas of Hales at the request of a maiden vowed to God, is in a completely different class. The dedicatee is a lady of education and sensibility, one of the women religious who are so important in the development of vernacular writing; the poet is a man of learning, author also of saints' lives in Latin and a sermon in French; the poem, after some typically Franciscan play with the theme of 'love-song', turns to a gentle meditation on the transience of the world, its joys, its love and lovers:

> Hwer is Paris and Heleyne
> Þat weren so bryht and feyre on bleo,
> Amadas and Ideyne,
> Tristram, Yseude and alle þeo,
> Ector, wiþ his scharpe meyne,
> And Cesar, riche of wordes feo?
> Heo beoþ iglyden ut of þe reyne
> So þe schef is of þe cleo.[40]

(*bleo* : face, *þeo* : those, *wordes feo* : worldly wealth, *schef* : sheaf, *cleo* : clay?)

and concludes that Christ is the only 'soþ leofmon'. The theme of Christ the lover is muted, compared with the lyrics of the *Wohunge*-group, more sentimental than erotic, and the texture of the writing is altogether thinner and less strenuous, but the poet is sensible of sadness, and develops the familiar themes of *Ubi sunt* and the *contemptus mundi* with a rare note of regret; the sweetness is fresh and does not cloy.

Digby 86 is a Dominican miscellany (c. 1275) from Worcestershire of a rather different character, trilingual where Jesus 29 is almost entirely bilingual, with the items in different languages more freely mixed, and with a generally more up-to-date and fashionable look. There is more French than English, a larger proportion of secular material, and none of the older poems represented in Jesus 29. Indeed, there seems to be some evidence of a deliberate attempt to up-date older traditions. Instead of the *Proverbs of Alfred* there are the *Proverbs of Hendyng*, a more carefully composed collection, shaped under the influence of Anglo-Norman models, and written in regular tail-rhyme ($aa^4b^3cc^4b^3$). It is, in the event, a lesser work, as is *The Thrush and the Nightingale* compared with *The Owl and the Nightingale*: the poem in Digby 86 returns to the strict formal tradition of debate, with the subject (the worth of women) announced in advance, mechanical allocation of speeches, and no characterisation of the participants. The standard of debate is not high—

Þis world nere nout ȝif wimen nere[41]

and the poem is monotonous despite its comparative brevity, perhaps because the poet is only really interested in the *volte-face* at the end, where the Thrush admits defeat after the Nightingale has invoked Mary in defence of womanhood. This piece is also in tail-rhyme, which, with the octosyllabic couplet, is the dominant metrical form in the collection, though there is one poem, *What Love is Like*, in the long alliterative line, rhymed in quatrains:

Loue had his stiuart bi sti and bi strete.
Loue makeþ moni mai hire wonges to wete.
Loue is hap, wo hit haueþ, hon for to hete.
Loue is wis, loue is war and wilfful an sete.[42]

The poem is secular in content, but its place in the collection would not have been difficult to justify: such poems provided material for quotation and illustration, and models for religious 'parody' (as in the Rolle poem quoted in the note), as well as being interesting, surreptitiously or not, in themselves.

The Latin pieces in Digby 86 are religious and practical (e.g. familiar prayers and hymns, a Calendar of Saints, medical notes, the Pseudo-Daniel on dream-interpretation),[43] but the French is much more varied, and includes everything from basic confessional material and Guischard's *Sermon* to the *Lai du Cor* and a treatise on courtesy. The English pieces are equally varied: there are verse-sermons on the Fifteen Signs before Judgment and the Eleven Pains of Hell (friars found such numerical techniques particularly useful), a poem on the theme of 'Ubi sount qui ante nos fuerount', as well as a sweet song to 'Swete Ihesu King of blisse' and a version of the dialogue *Stabat iuxta Christe crucem* which appears elsewhere as vernacular quotation in a Latin sermon[44]—interesting evidence of the use to which such work was put. Many of these are well-known anthology-pieces, and are to be found in such famous early fourteenth-century collections as Harley 2253 and the Auchinleck MS, which will be dealt with in the next chapter. Not all are pious in nature: a free paraphrase of Maximian's first elegy, *Le Regret de Maximian*, shares some themes, naturally enough, with the familiar penitential lament in old age, but there is nothing penitential about the development of the themes, for instance, of declining sexual power, nor about the ending:

> Were ich mon so ich was ...
> And ich hire heuede bi þe trasce
> In a derne place.... [45]

*Maximian* appears in Harley 2253 too, but Digby 86 is the unique MS for the only surviving examples of early fabliau, *The Fox and the Wolf* and *Dame Sirith*. The former is a rare representative in England of the continental beast-epic, the *Roman de Renart*, though its immediate source is likely to be some version of the story known in England, such as item XXIII in the *Disciplina Clericalis* of Petrus Alphonsus,[46] a well-known manual of school-instruction based on exemplary stories. The fable, the familiar one of the fox in the well and the trick he plays on the wolf, is told in a lively way, abruptly economical and abbreviated in accordance with rhetorical precept for the 'low' style (e.g. omission of connectives, 27, 113). Dialogue is particularly crisp:

> 'Gossip', quod þe wolf, 'wat nou?
> Wat hauest þou imunt—weder wolt þou?'
> 'Weder Ich wille?' þe vox sede,
> 'Ich wille oup, so God me rede!'[47]

There are some nice touches which cannot be traced in the analogues, such as the Fox's impudent claim to Chauntecler that he has been letting his hens' blood for their own good (40) or the mock-confession to which he subjects the wolf before allowing him into 'paradise' (at the bottom of the well): the prize moment here is the wolf's apology for having thought ill of the Fox after finding him in bed with his wife (214). Clerical satire is never far below the surface in such medieval fables, of course, and is explicit in such a parody of the confessional, but it would be missing the point of the comedy to labour such allegorical 'meanings'.[48]

*Dame Sirith* is presumably proof against any allegorisation: the lover, repulsed by the wife, goes for help to the old dame, skilled in the crafts of love (though not witchcraft, she asserts indignantly), and she persuades the wife that the clerk has power to turn her into a bitch if she refuses him again. The treatment is not very skilful, but what is interesting about the piece is that it is cast in quasi-dramatic form, with speakers indicated by initials in the margin and at least one transition (279) completely unmarked in the text. What lies behind the poem it is hard to say—there is a tradition of secular farce in France if not in England—but the presence of a narrator as one 'part' suggests that in its present form it is a kind of dramatic monologue, with one speaker using mime and impersonation to take all the parts.[49] There are French analogues, and the Latin models, the 'elegiac comedies' of the twelfth century, include two by Vitalis of Blois, whose epitaph describes him as a monologuist and mimer. The fragmentary *Interludium de Clerico et Puella* in B.M. MS Add. 23986 (a small roll) may be derived from *Dame Sirith*, with Mome Elwis (Mother Heloise) taking the part of the go-between. Only the first two 'scenes' survive. The incorporation in the text of full speech-prefixes and the absence of a narrator make the dramatic structure more explicit, but it is most likely still designed as a monologue, performed, as the title indicates, between courses at a feast. Quite honestly, the only amusement to be derived from such pieces would be in their delivery by a virtuoso impersonator.

It is unnecessary to describe the other friars' miscellanies in detail. Trinity College, Cambridge, MS 323 (B.14.39) is a genuine scrapbook, in a variety of hands: it includes one or two now familiar items (*Doomsday*, *The Latemest Day*) and a fragmentary text of the *Proverbs of Alfred*, but many items seem to have been composed *ad hoc*: an Epiphany poem follows an epitome of biblical history, from which it is derived through a first draft written in the margins;[50] often Latin original and English translation, freshly minted, stand side by side. Languages intermingle freely: in *Gaude Virgo Mater Christi* the Latin text alternates, stanza by stanza, with the English; Anglo-Norman and English alternate similarly in *A Prayer to the Redeemer*; and there are two Latin-English macaronics, one of them the lovely song 'For on þat is so feir ant brist/*uelud maris stella*'.[51] Two pieces may allude to popular tradition: 'Say me, viit in þe brom' reports a visit to a rural Mome Elwis for advice on how to win a husband's love—though the answer has a clerical and Catonian ring ('Hold þine tunke stille/& hawe al þine wille'); while *The Bargain of Judas*, in the septenary/alexandrine couplets which are the origin of ballad-metre, has many claims, with its laconic style, abrupt and intensely dramatic dialogue, and use of incremental repetition, to be considered the first English ballad.[52] Another miscellany, Digby 2, probably from a Franciscan house at Oxford, has a few short English poems, including one in praise of the friars' life ('Frer menur i wil me make/and lecherie i wil asake'),[53] among Latin treatises on grammar, logic and astronomy, while Harley 913, a multilingual Franciscan collection from Kildare, in Ireland, includes the charming *Land of Cokaygne*. In this goliardic Utopia, abbeys are built of puddings and pies, and the geese fly up ready roasted on the spit crying 'Gees, al hote, al hot!'[54] When the monks will not leave hawking to return for evensong, the abbot flourishes a girl's bottom and beats the tabors and they all hurry back,

> And goþ þe wench al abute,
> And þakkeþ al hir white toute,
> And siþ aftir her swinke
> Wendiþ meklich hom to drink,
> And goþ to har collacione
> A wel fair processione. (141–6)

(þakkeþ : pat, *swinke* : exertions)

Their adventures with the local nuns are similarly touched with gentle erotic fantasy. The English poem is more skilful and comic than its Latin and French analogues: it is only here that it is made a paradise specifically of monks, and the comic parody of the earthly paradise is developed with some neat touches. The point about Cokaygne is that it is *better*:

> What is þer in Paradis
> Bot grasse and flure and grene ris? (7–8)

> (*ris*: leafy twig)

Some of the same goliardic comic skills are displayed in other poems in the same MS, a *Satire on the people of Kildare*, a complaint against tyranny in the form of beast-fable, a satire on chop-logic, and a Latin song on the venality of judges.[55]

Outside the friars' collections the clerical tradition of 'occasional' vernacular poetry is only thinly represented in the thirteenth century, though it did not die out altogether. The earliest scraps of lyric are incorporated in Latin sermons and treatises—which is how we know of them—and are probably from popular tradition, but Brown's No. 1, that most beautiful and precisely evocative of all medieval lyrics—

> Nou goth sonne under wod
> me reweth, Marie, þi faire rode.
> Nou goþ sonne under tre
> me reweþ, marie, þi sone and þe.

> (*rode*: face, complexion—an allusion to the Song of Solomon, 1 : 6)

is found in the *Merure de Seinte Eglise*, the Anglo-Norman translation (c. 1275) of a treatise for religious by St Edmund of Abingdon, the *Speculum Religiosorum* (c. 1230). Two secular songs, 'Mirie it is while sumer ilast' and 'Foweles in þe frith,'[56] are similarly compressed in their allusion to the nature-introductions of Latin love-lyric and are certainly of learned authorship. We might suppose that the best-known of thirteenth-century songs, 'Sumer is icumen in', was of popular origin if we did not know that it comes from Reading Abbey, is found in a MS (Harley 978) containing other musical pieces in Latin and Anglo-Norman, and that the English words have clearly been composed to fit a complicated part-song (and then provided with a pious Latin alternative). Again, one of the best and most passionate of the spring-songs on the Passion,

> Nu yh she blostme sprynge,
> hic herde a fuheles song.
> a swete longinge
> myn herte þureþhut sprong....[57]

is found in a MS which originally belonged to St Alban's Abbey, while three more sober pieces are found in a collection which is presumed to have belonged to and perhaps been written by a chaplain of Llanthony Priory (on the Welsh border) who was also master of the local grammar school.[58]

## Poetry of popular instruction

The bulk of clerical verse-production, however, outside the friars' miscellanies, is directed in both English and Anglo-Norman towards more practical objectives, especially after the Lateran Council decree of 1215. The provision of instructional and edifying material in English for parish priests and laity involved all classes of the clergy, except the monks, who had no immediate pastoral role and who seem to have cultivated Anglo-Norman primarily. It has already been suggested that the spectrum of English is wider than that of Anglo-Norman: it includes an expression of Bernardine and Franciscan devotion as sophisticated as anything in Anglo-Norman; but it also includes works with a more directly popular appeal, or addressed more obviously to an uneducated laity. Such a qualification is necessary for the pioneer among these popularisers, Orrm, for his work, the *Orrmulum*, has no appeal of any kind. His ambition, as he describes it in his Dedication, is to provide English verse-translations of the Gospels in the mass-book for the whole year, with appropriate homiletic interpretation,[59] and a table of contents in the unique autograph MS lists 242 homilies. Of these, 32 are complete, and occupy over 10,000 septenary lines of inexorable 15-syllable regularity. The first line will speak for all:

þiss boc iss nemmnedd Orrmulum forrþi þatt Orrm itt wrohhte.[60]

Orrm uses neither rhyme nor alliteration, and his poetic principles are amply stated in his Dedication, where he explains that he may sometimes use words not in the Gospel or commentaries 'þe rime swa to fillenn', but he never adds anything of significance. This is true, and his methods of filling out his verses, combined with a propensity to explain and repeat everything several times over, make for infinite tedium. By profession, Orrm was an Augustinian canon, member of an order which practised a modified version of the communal monastic life but retained certain pastoral responsibilities, often being attached to the secular (i.e. non-monastic) cathedral churches. He himself, writing about 1200 in the North-East Midlands,[61] clearly takes his preaching function very seriously, since his work is intended to be read to the laity. His scrupulous care to ensure that it is properly read aloud and understood extends to the invention of an elaborate spelling-system, of extraordinary phonetic consistency, as a key to pronunciation. Presumably, those whom he expected to deliver his verses were more used to Latin than English, perhaps like himself. Indeed, the whole thing 'reads rather like the composition of a diligent and ingenious missionary in foreign parts struggling to put scripture for the first time into a barbarous tongue.'[62] Yet, in his modest way, Orrm anticipates the whole thirteenth-century movement towards a codification in verse, for the laity, of the central programme of Christian teaching.

Before this movement is fully under way, two Old Testament verse-narratives appear (c. 1225–50) which hark back to older traditions. *Genesis and Exodus* is a paraphrase of the first two books of the Bible, with some material from later books to round off the story of Moses, and explicitly addressed to the uneducated laity:

> Man og to luuen ðat rimes-ren
> ðe wisseð wel ðe logede men
> hu man may him wel loken
> ðog he ne be lered on no boken.[63]

> (*og* : ought, *ren* : course, *logede* : lay, *ðog* : though)

The loss sustained in this adaptation to the needs of an unlearned audience, compared with the Old English biblical poems, is painful to witness. We are at the beginning of a drab age for poetry, when verse will be used not to move or to heighten interest but as the routine instrument of routine didactic purposes. The paraphrase, in octosyllabic couplets, is based less on the Vulgate than on the digest of biblical history provided by Peter Comestor in his *Historia Scholastica* (1169–75). It may seem strange that the poet should go to a secondary source, but it is usual: the Church was reluctant to make the Scriptures directly available to the laity, since they needed, especially the Old Testament, so much explanation and exegesis to make them intelligible and doctrinally profitable.

*Jacob and Joseph* is a shorter poem, dealing with episodes from the same part of the Bible in a still more popular vein. The opening adopts the minstrel's tone of address,

> Wolle ȝe nou ihere wordes swiþe gode
> of one patriarke after Noees flode?[64]

and continues with the characteristic minstrel's complaint that people are too preoccupied with their bellies to listen to a good story,

> While men loueden meri song, gamen and feire tale;
> Nou hem is wel leuere gon to þe nale.　　　　　　　　　　(5–6)

> (*While* : once, *leuere* : preferable, *nale* : alehouse [ = þen ale])

The treatment is cheap, but lively and inventive, and transfers the story into a contemporary setting, just as do the Old English poets, or at least a setting similar to that of contemporary popular romance, complete with castles, minstrels and porters. The story rattles along briskly in the familiar septenary/alexandrine couplets, with some laconic use of dialogue reminiscent of *Judas* : comparison

103

of parallel passages with *Genesis and Exodus* makes the poet seem an effective populariser.

The full impact of the movement towards the popularisation of religious teaching is made evident in the collection of saints' lives known as the *South English Legendary*. A few saints' lives in English survive independently from the thirteenth century, including a *St Margaret* in Trinity 323 and *St Eustace* in Digby 86, but the *Legendary* seems to have absorbed most English writing of the kind. It exists in a variety of versions in over 50 MSS, ranging in date from the late thirteenth to the early fifteenth century. The earliest MS, Laud 108, is disordered,[65] but later MSS evolve a systematic calendar of saints *(sanctorale)*, with the saints' lives arranged according to the order of the saints' days and interspersed at the appropriate points with accounts and interpretations of the major festivals of the liturgical year *(temporale)*, in which the chief events of Old and New Testaments and the central truths of dogmatic religion are all somewhere expounded. The collection seems to have been begun about the same time (c. 1280) as the great continental legendary, the *Legenda Aurea* of the Dominican Jacobus de Voragine, and, though it is more popular in tone, it has been associated similarly with the friars.[66] Analysis of the early MSS suggests that the first approaches to a systematic collection were made in the central West Midland area, but that versions spread and multiplied rapidly, expanding to include more and more material in both *sanctorale* and *temporale*, and with the former being adapted to local needs. There is thus no single 'text' of the *Legendary*, only variable compilations growing by accretion, though all arise from the same need to provide a comprehensive code of instruction and inspiring example.[67]

Materials for the *Legendary* were drawn from a variety of hagiographical traditions, English, Latin and Anglo-Norman, and the *Legendary* absorbed also a great variety of other material: legends and folk-lore, in the accounts of purgatory (St Patrick) and the blessed isles (St Brendan); medieval natural science, in the account of hell in St Michael; recent English history, in St Thomas and St Edmund Rich; even romantic adventures, in the story of St Thomas's parents. It is as well to draw attention to this variety, for the staple diet is a dreary one, endless tortures—Vincent 'yscourged so. Þat me miȝte iseo ech bon/And euerich ioint and synueu', or Lawrence, 'Platen of ire al bernynge.        in is wonden hi pulte sore'[68]—miraculous conversions, fantastic proofs of sainthood. Even a legend like that of St Kenelm, which has much to interest us in its range of local allusion and obvious indebtedness to a local tradition so old that it has preserved two lines of Old English alliterative verse fossilised within it,[69] in the end strains one's patience with its surfeit of petty miracles—the cow sitting idle near the boy-martyr's grave and giving twice as much milk as her sisters chewing the cud all day, or the wicked queen whose eyes drop out as she tries to curse the corpse out of existence with Psalm 109.[70]

Accumulation is the whole principle of such a work: if one saint's life is good, three score are better, and the same with tortures and miracles. It is the same habit of mind that governs the popular romances, where giants and dragons are correspondingly multiplied. Of shape or design there is no trace, except for that which is provided by the liturgical year, and the fact that the whole thing is in verse (the usual septenary/alexandrine couplet, with a considerable four-stress element) reflects only professional calculation as to popular success. We may presume that individual compilers took what material was already collected and added whatever else was needed or to hand, throwing it roughly into the usual verse-form, often only a degree away from plain prose.[71] Yet the fact remains that the *Legendary* was enormously successful, as appears from the number of MSS: perhaps we should make allowance for the dimension added by an effective delivery, something catered for by the provision of constant asides and exhortations to the audience:

Wy sitte ȝe so stille.    wi ne segge ȝe amen.[72]

Also, it would be a mistake to attribute the deficiencies of the *Legendary*, in our eyes, to incompetence or ignorance. A great edifice of learning is being ransacked for the *temporale*, and the Prologue which is prefixed to some versions develops the military imagery of Christian warfare with some care and a shrewd eye to the romances:

Men wilneþ muche to hure telle.    of bataille of kynge
And of kniȝtes þat hardy were.    þat muchedel is lesynge
Wo so wilneþ muche to hure.    tales of such þinge
Hardi batailles he may hure.    here þat nis no lesinge
Of apostles & martirs.    þat hardy kniȝtes were
Þat studeuast were in bataille.    & ne fleide noȝt for fere.    (59–64)

The authors, whether friars or not, were well aware of the needs, desires and intellectual limitations of their audience, and tailored their product to cater for them with great efficiency and success.

One long poem, composed for inclusion among the *temporale*, stands out. This is the *Southern Passion*,[73] offered as a continuous narrative of events from the Entry into Jerusalem to Pentecost. Its quality, perhaps, is that it is the product of an individual mind rapt in its purpose, not a professional compiler. It is a disciplined and scrupulously didactic treatment, carefully pointing out how contemporary liturgical practice symbolises the events of Passion week, offering elaborate and pointed expositions of Christ's parables in relation to daily life, and making a constant outspoken criticism of present-day corruption and of the priests who ought to be like Christ. The author is a thinking man: a passage on women and their defamation at the hands of men (1923–90) is honest and compassionate and worth a dozen formal debates. When he comes to the Crucifixion he offers a very restrained narrative, with nothing from the usual apocryphal sources, not even a *Planctus Mariae*:

We ne ffyndeþ nouȝt ywrite.    þat oure lady in al hure sore
Spak ouȝt bote made deol ynow.    ne miȝte no womman more.

    (1515–16)

He knows the *Meditationes Vitae Christi*, the enormously influential Franciscan meditation on the humanity of Christ and his suffering, and evolves for himself a simplified version of its dramatic and deictic methods, with interjection ('O. Ihesus muchel was þe schame.     þat þo gyewes þe wrouȝte'), rhetorical question ('O. Ihesus. to al þin oþer wo.     whuch drinke þe was ybrouȝt') and exhortation to feeling ('O. Ihesu. who may þis yhure.     wiþoute wop of heorte?')[74] His laconic technique and purposeful didacticism have much to recommend them, and the effectiveness of his selective treatment of the *Meditationes* can be measured by comparing a close paraphrase of the same work, the *Meditations on the Supper of Our Lord and the Hours of the Passion*,[75] where the appeal to popular sentimentality (it is addressed to 'þys congregacyun') is rarely resisted.

At the end of the century there appeared in the north of England—the first major piece of writing from that area since the decline of Northumbrian culture—another comprehensive work of popular religious instruction, this time on a straightforward historical basis, the *Cursor Mundi*, so called because it 'courses' through the whole history of the world, from Creation to Judgment:

> Cursur o werld man aght it call,
> For almast it ouer-rennes all.[76]

The poet, a parish priest, as he tells us in his final exhortation (23,881), deals at length, in just under 24,000 lines, with all the principal events of the Old and New Testaments, drawing mainly on Comestor, and weaving into the narrative a mass of material from apocryphal and legendary sources—on the nature of Paradise, the person of Christ, the debate of the Four Daughters of God, the Castle of Love, the infancy of Jesus, the Harrowing of Hell, Antichrist, the Fifteen Signs before Judgment—so that the whole offers a programme of instruction as complete, on its own level, as the *Summae* which were the preoccupation of scholars in the thirteenth century. The poet makes an attempt at architectural shaping, dividing the history of the world, according to well-established practice, into seven ages, weaving into the narrative recurrent reference to the legends of the Cross, and framing the whole work in the context of Marian devotion. The larger didactic context of the work is well indicated by a series of accretions to the main MSS which include a long poem on the Sorrows of Mary, an exposition of the Creed and Paternoster, and a book of Penance with elaborate detail on the practice of confession.

Yet the author aims to make his work attractive to a lay audience. He sets himself up deliberately as a rival to the romances, whose stories he catalogues in detail in his prologue,

> Man yhernes rimes for to here,
> And romans red on maneres sere                                    (1–2)

associating them generally with folly and lechery. The address is that of minstrel-recitation, frequently suggestive of a listening audience,

> Sittes stell now mar and lesse,
> And hers now þis mirines, (20509–10)

as are the many explicitly pointed transitions:

> Siþen sal yee here quat wise
> Ihesu did lazar to rise,
> Bot ar þat i sua ferr sal ga,
> I sal spek of his sisters tua. (13962–5)

Some MSS introduce more of these allusions,[77] as if the poem were being 'punctuated' for delivery. For all its length, the poem maintains a lively sense of detail, and the narrative is often quite racy: it certainly compares very favourably with popular romances. The sense of an individual mind at work is strong, both in the architectonics and in such things as the character of the comment which introduces the account of the Passion, where the poet explains a change of metre, from octosyllabic to septenary couplets, in terms of aesthetic decorum:

> Es resun þat wee ur rime rume,
> And set fra nu langer bastune. (14922–3)

> (*bastune* : verse-form)

Such an exercise of choice is a mark of some sophistication.

The poet of the *Cursor Mundi* is unexpectedly assertive about his use of English:

> Þis ilk bok is es translate
> In to Inglis tong to rede
> For the loue of Inglis lede,
> Inglis lede of Ingland,
> For the commun at understand.
> Frankis rimes here I redd,
> Comunlik in ilka sted,
> Mast es it wroght for frankis man:
> Quat is for him na frankis can? (232–40)

Such comments begin to multiply towards the end of the century, as we shall see in the romances, and are to be associated with a number of factors, such as the decline and growing artificiality of Anglo-Norman, and the spread of literature to an audience which had probably never had much French anyway. But a note of propagandist fervour is detected too, an appeal to a sense of social and parochial if not national identity. There may be local reasons. It is noteworthy that one group of MSS omits lines 237–40, as if the conditions there described no longer pertained—a change similar to that later made by Trevisa when translating Higden's comment on the use of French in schools.[78]

107

The tradition of popular religious instruction in verse continues unabated after 1300, beyond the bounds of this chapter, but there is a temptation to trespass a little so as to make mention of one of its most notable products, begun in 1303, Robert Mannyng's *Handlyng Synne*, a free expanded version of the Anglo-Norman *Manuel des Pechiez* (c. 1260). Robert Mannyng of Brunne (Bourne in Lincolnshire) was a canon of the Gilbertine order at Sempringham Priory, probably master of the novices,[79] and he prepared the book for himself to read to both lay brothers and novitiate canons at the priory:

> Nat to lered onely, but eke to lewed.[80]

At the beginning, however, he stresses that he writes in English primarily for the sake of those who cannot read:

> Of þys clerkys wyl y nouȝt seye ...
> For þey wote þat ys to wetyn,
> And se hyt wel before hem wrytyn ...
> For lewde men y undyr-toke
> On englyssh tunge to make þys boke. (37–44)

Like the *Manuel*, *Handlyng Synne*, whose characteristically homely title Mannyng explains at length (77–140), is 'a confessional manual for laymen embellished with *exempla* and supported by passages of theological exposition'.[81] It is constructed around a series of numerical themes, the Ten Commandments, the Seven Deadly Sins, the Seven Sacraments, and the Points and Graces of Confession, but its attraction for the modern reader is likely to be its wealth of casual social realism—a necessity, as Robertson points out, in the Confessional manual—and its lively inset narratives. Mannyng loves a good story, adds many of his own, and always embarks on them with the relish of a born story-teller:

> Þyr was a man beȝunde þe see,
> A mynour, woned yn a cyte,—
> Mynurs, þey make yn hyllys holes,
> As yn þe west cuntre men seke coles.—
> Þys mynur soȝte stones undyr þe molde.... (10729–33)

Like the author of the *Cursor Mundi*, Mannyng displays plenty of vigour, though his professional role allows little sophistication.

## Laȝamon

Not all the energies of the clergy were absorbed into religious writing, however: secular poems, as we have seen, were composed as well as preserved by the friars, and the greatest secular poem of the thirteenth century, Laȝamon's

*Brut* (c. 1225), is by a parish priest.[82] Laȝamon seems little concerned for the spiritual welfare of his audience, but thinks rather to instil in them, by writing a chronicle, an admiration for England and its noble antiquity:

> Hit com him on mode.  & on his mern þonke.
> Þet he wolde of Engle.  þa æðelæn tellen.[83]

(*mode* : mind, *mern* : lofty, *æðelæn* : noble deeds)

He speaks of himself, in the Prologue, in the third person, as if he were a public orator speaking to posterity on behalf of England, and any personal note, or relaxation of this oracular role, is rare. His sense of England and its history is nourished by his knowledge of Old English verse, whose language and forms he echoes in a vigorous yet strangely stereotyped manner;[84] and it is emphasised by his claim to have used English sources of venerable antiquity, such as Bede— when in fact his only substantial source, apart from his own rich invention, is Wace's French chronicle, the *Roman de Brut*. This may seem an odd pedigree for a national epic, but the tone of the Prologue (which was probably written last) should not necessarily be applied to the work at its first inception: Laȝamon's initial ambition was simply to write an English verse-chronicle to match those of Wace and Gaimar.

The *Brut* (the MS title is *Hystoria Brutonum*—the short title is taken from later popular histories) begins with Brutus, the eponymous founder of Britain, leaving Troy, and ends with the death of Cadwallader, the last 'British' king with serious claims to dominion in England. The basis for the story[85] is Geoffrey of Monmouth's *Historia Regum Britanniae* (1130–8), one of the most influential books ever written, since it is the primary source for Arthurian legend, as well as the only source for such stories as those of Lear and Cymbeline. Geoffrey took something from traditional legend, oral and written, but invented far more, his purpose being to supply England with the history it lacked, to claim descent, as did Rome and other nations of Western Europe, from Troy, and to create a great national hero in Arthur. Geoffrey's inventions are dressed up as sober, plausible history, full of names (Geoffrey has a special fondness for 'explaining' the derivation of place-names) and statistics, and treated in a serious and coolly rationalistic manner. He favours the Bretons throughout, perhaps because of his own origin, as the true inheritors of 'British' tradition, and shows contempt for the Anglo-Saxons. Geoffrey was an ambitious cleric, and these were the people his masters, and potential patrons, had recently subdued. Geoffrey's *Historia* is in Latin prose, in 190 MSS; Wace's translation into French octosyllabics, finished in 1155, exists in 26. Wace is a sensible professional poet, writing probably for Henry II.[86] He adds little, but reinterprets the whole story in a manner more fitting to courtly taste, with detail from court life and customs, up-to-date terms from warfaring and siegecraft, and a few allusions to love: Arthur is a king more in accord with the ethos of chivalric romance, more courtly, less stern and barbarous. Wace also dramatises the narrative more vividly, incorporating much direct speech and commentary. Laȝamon (extant in two MSS) intensifies the dramatic treatment, but otherwise works against Wace in creating a heroic and martial rather than a courtly atmosphere and in portraying Arthur as a fierce warrior-king: yet he never works back in the direction of Geoffrey, whose Latin he did not know. The difference in tone between Wace and Laȝamon is sharply epitomised in a scene at Arthur's coronation where Gawain argues for peace, in Wace as an opportunity for gallantry and social courtesy—

> Bone est la pais emprés la guerre,
> Plus bele e mieldre en est la terre;
> Mult sunt bones les gaberies
> E bones sunt les drueries.
> Pur amistié e pur amies
> Funt chevaliers chevaleries

> (*emprés* : after, *gaberies* : songs, *drueries* : love-affairs)

but in Laȝamon in severely religious and ethical terms:

> For god is grið and god is frið.    þe freoliche þer halдеð wið.
> and godd sulf hit makede.    þurh his godd-cunde.
> for grið makeð godne mon.    gode workes wurchen.[87]

> (*grið, frið* : peace)

On the other hand, Laȝamon is not incompetent in dealing with matters of love when they are necessary to the story.[88]

Laȝamon is an archaist: how much so is suggested by the omissions of the Otho MS,[89] where archaic and 'poetic' language is excised, along with emotive and rhetorical passages, so that the narrative line is pared down to that of more sober chronicle. He is also a patriot—his archaism is part of that—and a poet of passionate convictions. One has a sense that Wace was a poor choice for such a man, and there is no doubt that Laȝamon is at odds with himself for half the poem, confused to know where to place his sympathies[90] and labouring respectfully, king by confected king, after a far inferior poet when he might be ransacking him as a store of materials for truly imaginative purposes. He is too good a poet not to make a tolerable job of it, and certain episodes are treated with real dramatic power, such as Corineus' scornful address to Locrine, who has taken another wife and scorned his daughter, or the handling of the conversation of Maglaunus (Albany) and Gornoille or Lear's lament in the Lear-story.[91] But only those who have laboured through the first 18,000 lines will remember the note of mounting excitement as Uther's battles prepare for Arthur (e.g. 18,096) and the hush of anticipation when his name and coming are first announced:

> Þe time com þe wes icoren.    þa wes Arður iboren.        (19,252–3)

Arthur is a focus for all Laȝamon's imaginative energies, a figure in whom he can confidently invest all his patriotic passions and with whom he can exploit all his love of heroic battle-poetry. The splendours of the *Brut* are concentrated in the 2000 lines or so which tell of Arthur's battles against the Saxon invaders (Laȝamon is much less interested in the continental wars of aggression which follow), and here he uses Wace only as a springboard, expanding and elaborating with unprecedented freedom.

Wace's first introduction of Arthur in person is cool, measured, generalised and abstract, proposing to tell without exaggeration the faults and virtues of one who surmounted all

> De curteisie et de noblesce
> E de vertu e de largesce. (9031–2)

Laȝamon excises all comment on love and courtesy, and concentrates on particular detail to build up a portrait of extravagant heroism and kingliness, steeped in religious awe. The battle with Colgrim that follows is described briefly by Wace, but Laȝamon brings to it for the first time the full panoply of heroic poetry, with detailed combat, vaunting-speeches, and the first of the famous similes:

> Up bræid Arður his sceld foren to his breosten,
> and he gon to rusien swa þe rimie wulf,
> þenne he cumeð of holte, bihonged mid snawe.[92]

Victory here is followed by news of Childric's landing in the north, which causes Arthur to retreat south towards London; in Laȝamon Arthur holds a council, and the advice manages to suggest that marching south is an aggressive act, not a tactical withdrawal. The subsequent attack on Childric at Lincoln is rapidly narrated by Wace, with less battle-description than detail of the plan to starve the survivors into submission in Calidon forest. Laȝamon handles the episode with brilliant panache, expanding and particularising on every hint, constantly adding speeches of vaunting hyperbole and exhortation, taunting irony,

> Iþonked wurðe Drihtene, þe alle domes waldeð,
> Þat Childric þe stronge is sad of mine londe!
> (2678–9, Madden 20,827–30)

culminating in the extended comparison of Childric trapped in the forest with the fox driven to ground (2684–99). The Saxons now, after vowing allegiance, sail along the south coast and make a treacherous raid in the south-west. The account in Wace is generalised, well-articulated, with the sequence and geography of events in clear perspective; Laȝamon is full of graphic, violent, often inessential detail, poured out pell-mell as if the verse can hardly contain the fury and indignation and bitter foreshadowing irony. The Battle of Bath is the climax

111

of this sequence: Wace prepares for it with a careful description of Arthur's coming, and an elaborate and solemn speech of exhortation, before describing the battle quite briefly (more briefly than Geoffrey, who, as always, gives a precise and circumstantial account of battlefield and general strategy). These careful preparations are almost swept aside in the onrush of Laȝamon's martial fervour, with vigorous scenes of individual combat and mêlée punctuated with vows of vengeance, boastings, denunciation, execration, scorn and triumph, ending in Arthur's paean over the fleeing Saxons drowned in the Avon:

> Ȝurstendæi wes Baldulf cnihten alre baldest;
> nu he stant on hulle and Auene bihaldeð;
> hu ligeð i þan stræme stelene fisces,
> mid sweorde bigeorede.    Heore sund is awemmed;
> heore scalen wleoteð swulc gold-faȝe sceldes.. . .

(2924–8, Madden 21,319–28)

Throughout Wace is calm, practical, rational, with an eye for the realities of war and strategy; Laȝamon is aggressive, violent, heroic, ceremonial and ritualistic.

If battles are the essence of heroic poetry, Laȝamon is our greatest heroic poet, inexhaustibly energetic and inventive, sustained by a great surge of patriotic feeling. It is not what we should expect of a parish priest, not even one encouraged by the patronage of 'þan gode cniþte',[93] and we can hardly relate it to a listening audience, for there is no trace in the poem of adaptation to oral delivery. Laȝamon's violence is all bookish,[94] and there is a temptation to trace his heroic style back to Old English tradition: his language and verse-forms certainly show knowledge of the classical verse, and his home was only ten miles from the great centre of Old English learning at Worcester. But the more one examines Laȝamon's battle-poetry, the more apparent it becomes that it is quite different in character from Old English: compounding and variation exist only as traces, enjambement is rare,[95] typical themes like the beasts of battle are totally absent.[96] On the other hand, similes, never conspicuous in Old English, have emerged as a distinctive characteristic of style, and when we find that the simile stands at the head of an authoritative classification of the characteristic devices of the Old French epic style, followed by ironic metaphor, innuendo, foreshadowing, hyperbole, understatement, taunt, and other features well illustrated in the analysis above,[97] it seems unnecessary to go for a model to Virgil, or Welsh poetry, or homiletic tradition, all of which have been suggested. There were *chansons de geste* in the epic style in Anglo-Norman as well as French, including a version of Geoffrey in *laisses*,[98] and Laȝamon is more or less certain to have known such work. Wace could hardly be the only French poet he had read.

Laȝamon is a massive erratic in the history of English poetry. He proves nothing about the continuity of the alliterative tradition but his own obstinacy: his sources and models lay outside the tradition, his language was archaic in its own day and survives for us only because of a scribal fidelity in Caligula

A.ix verging on the eccentric, and his metrical compromise had no influence. His relation to Anglo-Norman tradition, on the other hand, points the way for succeeding poets, or at least establishes the context in which we should consider them.

## Thirteenth-century romance and chronicle

No doubt a great deal of popular narrative poetry, dealing with the exploits of heroes such as Edmund Ironside and Hereward the Wake, has been lost from the twelfth and thirteenth centuries.[99] By its nature it would achieve written form only ephemerally, if at all, or else in a totally different guise, as the story of Hereward, for instance, is known only in Latin chronicles, or as the Anglo-Norman *Waldef* claims to be based on an English source.[100] Laʒamon, of course, with his claims to learning and his character as a chronicler-historian, would be in a different category. It would therefore be dangerous to apply an evolutionary scheme to the extant remains of early 'romance'—difficult, even, to be sure that we should allow that term a generic existence. For if we agree that 'the romance genre is the creation of Renaissance critics who designed it as an escape route for Ariosto',[101] then a good deal of the work that has been done on the formal definition of the genre would seem to have been misplaced. Certainly, attempts to classify the existing body of 'romances' according to subject-matter[102] are continually frustrated by the blurring of the form into history, chronicle, saint's life, exemplum, fable and biography. More will be said on this subject in the next chapter, but meanwhile perhaps it is possible to suggest that there is a recognisable body of writing, which we may call 'romance', which consists of secular narratives, with a hero, designed for entertainment. This is vague enough, but necessarily so, and one would be equally reluctant to make any general assumptions about authors and audiences. The most one could say, before speaking of individual poems, is that professional minstrels are unlikely to have played any part in their composition or copying, though they may have had some influence as distributors,[103] and that the poems as they exist in the extant written copies are likely to have had a wide audience, not confined to any class of society, though of course excluded from court and aristocratic circles.

The first evidences of the form are not primitive in an evolutionary sense, but rather random outcroppings, survivals of what must have been a variety of efforts at translation and adaptation, or at 'literary' versions of popular heroic stories. The earliest romances are the two that appear in C.U.L. MS Gg. iv. 27 (c. 1250), *King Horn* and *Floris and Blauncheflur*. Both are fairly sophisticated, and the MS collection, which includes also a poem on the Assumption, might be the sort of thing that a favoured cleric would gather together for reading among the ladies of a well-to-do but not aristocratic household.[104]

*King Horn*, which appears also, in widely differing copies, in MS Laud 108 of the *Legendary* and in Harley 2253 (it is the only romance in this distinctly 'highbrow' collection), is one of the best of the English romances, a brilliantly concise retelling of the story that appears also in the Anglo-Norman *Horn* (c. 1170) of 'mestre Thomas'. Thomas's poem is itself a fine one, a leisurely and well-amplified working of the story, drawing on both *chanson de geste* and chivalric romance, with much precise and detailed portrayal of courtly life and a well-developed interest in character and motive. It is difficult to see the English poem as either a source or abridgment of the Anglo-Norman one, and both probably draw on a common original. *King Horn* eschews all courtly decoration and psycho-logising, stripping the narrative down to its bare essentials, and its setting of all precision and circumstance, so as to expose more starkly its themes of love and truth. Nothing is misunderstood: when the poet wishes to allude to courtly sentiments or habits of mind he can do so with perfect ease, and his handling of thematic repetition shows how subtly he is aware of echoing and foreshadowing techniques.[105] Everything about the poem—the sparse narrative, abrupt transitions, cryptic allusiveness, repetitive phrasing—is reminiscent of ballad-technique, and *King Horn* may be a representative of the wrought form of sung lay which preceded both ballad and romance.[106] It is written in an unusual three-stress couplet (so unusual that the later MSS try to adapt it as four-stress couplet) which has frequently been explained as a degenerate form of alliterative half-line: it is true that there are two-stress lines here and there, but this is endemic in English verse of the period and, since alliteration is hardly noticeable, the obvious model seems to be the hexasyllabic couplet of Anglo-Norman poems like the *Lai du Cor*.[107]

*Floris and Blauncheflur* is an idyllic story of young lovers and their not-too-perilous adventures in an eastern emir's palace. Disguises, mistakes and a saucy maidservant provide continual gentle comedy, and the turtledove-truth of the lovers finally, as each attempts to press on the other a magic ring which has power to preserve life, softens the heart of the emir: even Saracens are treated as human beings in this poem. *Floris* is written in the same metre, octosyllabic couplet, as its French (not Anglo-Norman) original, which it abbreviates and simplifies, though without losing any of its charm, sophistication or sensibility.

The remaining romances of this period come from towards the end of the century, are all in four-stress couplet, and are on the whole less sophisticated. *Havelok* is again ambiguously related to Anglo-Norman analogues, the *Lai d'Haveloc* and a summary of the story interpolated in Gaimar's *Estoire des Engleis*, but the relationship is indirect, through a common source, rather than direct. All the versions are associated with Lincolnshire, which is the story's principal location, and Robert Mannyng, also a Lincolnshire man, inserts a summary of the story in his *Chronicle*. The only complete copy of the English poem is in Laud 108 (c. 1290), where it stands beside *Horn* in a separate fascicule associated at an early date with a MS of the *Legendary*.[108] *Havelok* seems very much at home here, since it is aggressively pious, but the grafting of the story into chronicles is perhaps better evidence of how a medieval audience would have regarded it. It is a plain and vigorous telling of a story which in its general exile-and-return pattern resembles that of *Horn*, though in all other respects the two poems are very different. *Havelok* is ostentatiously uncourtly, with much detail of common life, including episodes in Havelok's career when he works as a fisherman and a kitchen-scullion. There is much appeal to practical good sense and practical piety, as well as to a bourgeois political realism which is interested in the well-governed land and the rule of law, in rights, duties and fit punishments, rather than in deeds of derring-do.[109] On the other hand, the skilful handling of the narrative, certain passages of description, and such 'literary' features as the imitation of the Anglo-Norman *laisse* on identical rhymes (87–105), indicate an accomplished professional writer. He may be a cleric with a taste for local history: certainly he is involved with the narrative, concerned to embody in it serious moral and political values, in a way quite different from the usual professional entertainers.

The work of the latter is well illustrated in two late thirteenth-century English redactions of Anglo-Norman 'ancestral romance', *Guy of Warwick* and *Beves of Hamtoun*. The originals were designed to glorify the putative ancestors of the newly raised Anglo-Norman aristocracy, but they became popular in translation as miscellaneous pot-pourris of adventure, with an English background and an overlay of piety. Both exist in a number of MSS, mostly standard romance-collections, and *Guy* in no less than three independent versions. They are the fashionable popular novels of their day, competently told, fast-moving, brimming with incident, and quite devoid of any other motive than to pass the time entertainingly. There is some vulgarisation in transition from Anglo-Norman to English—in *Guy*, for instance, there seems to be a need for more explanation of the fashionable code of love, few technical terms of hunting, more patriotism and simple piety, more oral material, and some catchpenny repetition of successful 'effects'[110] but it would be wrong to exaggerate the difference between the two prospective audiences. Both English and Anglo-Norman versions have a wide appeal and provide something for everyone. *Guy* has some spurious history (the narrative of the fight against the Danish champion Colbrond was incorporated into a good many chronicles) and an equally spurious appeal to patriotism, as well as some pious sentiment, which prompts Guy, halfway through the story, to leave his bride of a fortnight and go back adventuring on the continent as a crusading knight—the only difference apparent being that he now fights in disguise. *Beves* is a freer version of its Anglo-Norman original (which only survives as a fragment), and is full of extravagant and sensational incident, lurid and ludicrous by turns. It gives the impression of having been written to a successful recipe, and we should not underestimate the professional skill of these English compilers. The switch from couplet to tail-rhyme, a more lyrical metre, in the Auchinleck text of *Guy* to introduce a note of romantic piety at his 'conversion' is a deft touch, and the authors are keen in their judgment of fashionable popular taste. Who they were it is hard to say—clerics of lost vocation, presumably, attached to some large household or perhaps marketing their skills commercially among the growing London bourgeoisie.

Three other romances from the end of the century, *Richard Coeur de Lion*, *Arthour and Merlin* and *Kyng Alisaunder*, are similar. All three appear, in part or whole, in the Auchinleck MS (like *Guy* and *Beves*), as well as in other standard

115

anthologies of romance, and all three are ascribed to a single Kentish author, which seems convenient if not particularly significant.[111] *Richard*, based on a lost Anglo-Norman original, again deals with an English hero, and is distinguished by its brutal and obscene relish in Richard's feats of arms and his occasional cannibalism. Its historical content is slight, though it found its way into at least one handsomely illuminated historical MS (College of Arms HDN 58) containing Robert of Gloucester's Chronicle. *Arthour and Merlin* is the first representative in English of the French Arthurian cycle: it deals with Arthur's early battles in a stereotyped style by now tediously familiar, and is preoccupied with Merlin's tricks. *Kyng Alisaunder* is a great deal better: based on the Anglo-Norman *Roman de Toute Chevalerie*, it enhances its original with stylistic devices drawn from an extensive knowledge of the Old French *chansons de geste*, including short seasonal transition-passages which are a particular delight of, and in, this poet,[112] and shows throughout both education and taste—the love-scenes, for instance, are generously handled. Most of the poem is still battles and marvels, of course, but the sophistication of the handling would argue that the fourteenth century inherited rather more than vigour from the thirteenth. If it is by the same author as the other two, then he is presumably writing for a different audience. It is interesting that both *Richard* and *Arthour* are prefaced by rather aggressive statements about the English language. In *Richard* it is the usual explanation for writing in English:

> In Frenssche bookys þis rym is wrouȝt
> Lewede men ne knowe it nouȝt
> Lewede men cune Frensch non
> Among an hondryd unneþis on.[113]

In *Arthour*, matters have advanced:

> Of Freynsch no Latin nil y tel more
> Ac on Inglisch ichil tel þer-fore;
> Riȝt is þat Inglische understond,
> Þat was born in Inglond;
> Freynsche use þis gentilman
> Ac euerich Inglische Inglische can;
> Mani noble ich haue yseiȝe
> Þat no Freynsche couþe seye.[114]

The poet, with an eye to his public, detects, or purports to detect, a growing disinclination, even amongst the nobility (different from those who need to be thought gentlemen, 'þis gentilman'), to struggle with an obsolete language. In doing so, he advances his claim for his own poem, in English. In *Kyng Alisaunder* he simply makes good his claim, and annexes the gentler audience. His statements are, of course, personal propaganda of different kinds for his own poems, but are nevertheless significant of change.

Two verse-chronicles from the end of the century and after offer further evidence that English is taking over from Anglo-Norman. Robert of Gloucester's *Chronicle* (c. 1300), in septenary/alexandrine couplets, draws for its first 9000 lines on the Anglo-Latin historians of the twelfth century, including Geoffrey of Monmouth; the remaining 3000 lines, the only part ascribed to Robert himself, is from contemporary tradition and personal experience, and has many vivid touches in the relation of local events, as well as a general honesty and seriousness of purpose. The chronicle as a whole is of monastic origin, which is a striking return to Old English practice. One recalls Miss Legge's comment that the Western houses are only thinly represented as centres of Anglo-Norman:[115] there seems very little doubt that English was kept up much more vigorously in the West and always retained a higher status there. It is interesting that the Gloucester Chronicle draws freely on the *Legendary* for its account of Becket, and that some later recensions insert passages borrowed directly from the un-revised text of Laȝamon:[116] both sources are of Western origin. The comment of the first anonymous chronicler on the arrival of the Normans and the adoption of their language is very revealing:

> Vor bote a man conne frenss.    me telþ of him lute.
> Ac lowe men holdeþ to engliss.    & to hor owe speche ȝute.
> Ich wene þer ne beþ in al þe world.    contreyes none.
> Þat ne holdeþ to hor owe speche.    bot engelond one.
> Ac wel me wot uor to conne.    boþe wel it is.
> Vor þe more þat a mon can.    þe more wurþe he is.[117]

( *telþ lute* : esteem little, *ȝute* : still, *one* : alone)

The compromise of the last two lines is a sensible one, and probably what was practised by most educated men, but the monk clearly regards it as an unnatural situation, and thinks of English as the national language ('hor owe speche').

Robert Mannyng's *Chronicle*, however, completed in 1338, takes us nearly up to the birth-date of Chaucer without any sign, from him at least, that the relative status of the two languages has changed. He writes in English, he says, 'not for þe lerid bot for þe lewed'[118] and he speaks humbly of his inability to match the eloquence of his Anglo-Norman original, the Chronicle of Peter of Langtoft, canon of Bridlington.[119] Quite apart from the fact that in making a direct translation of an Anglo-Norman work he is suggesting that the two audiences cannot be so very different, Mannyng is perhaps not the best guide to general practice, for he has a provincial narrowness of outlook and a provincial ignorance (he knows, for instance, no Arthurian material in English, 10,605–8), and he makes something of a profession of rough simplicity, declaring that he will not write for professional recitation,

> I mad noght for no disours,
> ne for no seggers, no harpours

(75–6)

nor use 'strange Inglis' (78) nor have any truck with complex stanza forms, 'in ryme couwee/Or in strangere or enterlace' (85–6), such as are used in the romances of Erceldoune and Kendale: such poems, he says, are bound to suffer in transmission, are not easily understood, are only written to show off, and anyway are beyond him. Mannyng seems to regard poetic elaboration and the attempt to extend the poetic vocabulary of English as almost immoral, but his comments are the best evidence that it was going on.[120]

Robert Mannyng embodies much of the vigour of English poetry in the thirteenth century and at the same time much of its restricted professional outlook. There is a period, early on, around 1200, when English is a genuine alternative to Anglo-Norman, when the best writing of the early Middle English period is produced (in prose), and when two notable attempts (*The Owl and the Nightingale* and Laȝamon) are made to extend the range of poetry and poetic language. These attempts bore little fruit, and the potential of English, though it is exploited on a small scale, remains undeveloped. The language of even the best poems, in the friars' miscellanies, is simple and unambitious, and if it were not for the work of the friars in collecting and composing, the century would be dominated by a narrow, sometimes drab professionalism, in both secular and religious writing, with versifiers catering, in a deliberate way, for an audience rather than developing their own purposes. The application of verse to these routine tasks is a characteristic development of the thirteenth century, one of the less fortunate consequences of Anglo-Norman influence: it is noteworthy that Anglo-Norman, like French, strives in this century to develop an effective prose for such purposes, partly under the influence of that very same English prose[121] which is being superseded—an ironic reversal, and a sad one.

# 5   Some fourteenth-century books and writers

A history of English poetry for any other period would by now have produced a fair assembly of named poets, and would no doubt have organised its discussion, partly at any rate, around what was known of their lives and careers. So far we have produced only a handful. The reasons for this are obvious: there was no cult of the individual poet in the clerical tradition—as distinct from the secular poetic tradition of, say, Provençal poetry—and all the poetry we have dealt with has been from this tradition. Furthermore, English poetry, at a time when it might have been expected to emerge from the anonymity of the monastic tradition, lost the kind of aristocratic patronage which preserves for Anglo-Norman such an elaborate network of names and families. Even for those writers who did have an inclination to make themselves known to posterity, circumstances are not favourable, since the parts of a work where they might name themselves, the beginning and the end, are the most likely to be lost or mutilated or altered by scribes in the passage of time. And finally, even when we do know the names and something of the lives of these early poets, it is of little significance in our reading of their poetry, since they do little to exploit their individuality as persons: the first important canon is the Chaucer canon.

Although the fourteenth century sees the beginnings of court and aristocratic patronage for English poetry, and the appearance of the first poets whose lives are known to us and whose individuality is important to our discussion of their poetry, the older traditions are still generally dominant, still provide the background against which the new poetry is to be understood. For this reason, the fourteenth century, one of the great ages of English poetry, is introduced in this chapter with a consideration of this general traditional background. The discussion is largely organised around particular manuscript-books, some of them unique of their kind, some of them representative of types of book, since only in this way can we keep constantly in mind what the poetry was intended for and how it was used. One is much more familiar with organisation according to genres, but it must be admitted that genre-study often distorts the nature or skims the realities of medieval verse-production. 'Romance' has already been mentioned as a genre classification which produces more debate as to its theoretical nature and whether certain poems belong to it than illuminating insights

119

about the poems themselves. It could be argued that there is an ideological core to the concept of romance in the notion of the knight setting forth to prove the values of his class in otherwise unmotivated adventures,[1] but discussion of the English romances from this point of view only proves that few of them are romances.[2] 'Lyric' is another term which began to be used in the sixteenth century and which has acquired a more and more precise and esoteric range of associations:[3] the attempt to analyse the shorter poems of the Middle Ages in terms of these definitions only leads to special pleading or calamitous distortion, or to explanations as to why such definitions are irrelevant. If therefore such terms are used in the following pages, it is as a convenient form of reference only: 'romance' means no more than was suggested above (p. 113) and 'lyric' means a short poem.

It might be added that while modern critical works distort the realities of medieval poems in one way, by imposing on them categories of form derived from post-Renaissance theory, the nature of modern critical editions distorts them in another. The very concept of the critical edition is alien to the nature of much Middle English poetry, since the scribe as much as the poet is the 'author' of what we have in extant copies. Only in the fourteenth century does there begin to appear that self-consciousness about the text and the possibility of textual corruption[4] that makes critical editions viable. Even there, and certainly for earlier periods, modern editions offer sterilised and anaesthetised versions of Middle English poems, hypothetical texts of poems that never actually succeeded in getting written, divorced from their proper context and arranged according to modern habits of mind. A return to the old nineteenth-century editions of Wright, Morris and Furnivall, with their habit of associating poems together because they appear in the same MS, is sometimes a useful reminder of the actual conditions under which poetry was produced, disseminated and read.

## MS Harley 2253

MS Harley 2253 is one MS which needs no such preamble, which demands consideration in its own right, as a unique record of the state of English poetry during the early years of the fourteenth century. With Cotton Nero A.x, it is the most important single MS of Middle English poetry. It contains unique copies of poems and groups of poems whose loss would wipe out our knowledge of whole areas of English poetry, some of it the very best of its kind, in a critical time of change. Such a MS is another reminder of the perilous conditions of survival for any but the most obviously useful didactic and religious verse; for one Harley 2253 there are over fifty MSS of the contemporary *South English Legendary* and over a hundred of *The Prick of Conscience*. Furthermore, of the English religious pieces within the MS itself all but five appear elsewhere, whereas there is no other MS of any of the secular love-poems or political poems.[5] The MS is dated about 1330–40,[6] and is essentially a miscellany, not at all dissimilar from the friars' miscellanies of the thirteenth century,[7] though with a wider and more sophisticated range of English verse, reflecting the changing status of the language in relation to Anglo-Norman as well as its long-established eminence in the West. The MS is from Herefordshire and has associations both with the aristocratic Mortimer family and with Adam de Orleton, Bishop of Hereford. In addition to English verse (there is no English prose, except for a few recipes, added later), it includes an approximately equal number of items in French, both verse and prose (the prose is predominantly religious), and a smaller number of Latin prose pieces, some of them of a definitely specialised ecclesiastical nature. One might speculate that the compiler was a cleric in the bishop's household, with well-developed literary tastes, who was or had been attached to the Mortimer household, perhaps in an administrative capacity. This fairly summarises the level of sophistication expected in the audience of the English poems, though it tells us less than we might hope of their authorship, since they were composed over a period of fifty years or more, and do not all originate in the West.

The earliest poem, one of a number of political and satirical pieces scattered through the MS, is the *Song of Lewes*, a vigorous celebration of Simon de Montfort's victory (1264) over the king's party and particularly over the hated Richard of Cornwall, the king's brother:

> Richard, þah þou be euer trichard,
> tricchen shalt þou neuermore![8]

(*þah* : though, *trichard* : traitor)

It is in a 7-line stanza, basically a monorhymed quatrain with a two-stress 'bob' (short linking line) and 'wheel' (sequence of short regular rhyming lines) of two four-stress lines. The bob and wheel come to be used very frequently in association with the alliterative long line: here the quatrain is in the native four-stress line (different from the more regularly syllabic four-stress line of the wheel) with irregular alliteration, and is clearly an attempt, which we shall find repeated in septenary, alexandrine and the full alliterative long line, to imitate the septenary monorhymed quatrain of Latin political verse and similar alexandrine quatrains of French.[9] The tone is popular, coarse and raucous, with minstrel-opening ('Sitteþ alle stille & herkneþ to me'), ballad-like repetition (30, 35) and unvaried refrain. One would not associate such a 'popular' tone with an exclusively popular audience, since it is rhetorically appropriate to the genre of political song, and there is little temptation to attribute the poem to a professional minstrel, since what we know of the class suggests that they were low performers,[10] who might have mangled a poem in recitation but not composed one such as we have here. It is worth emphasising the distinction between 'popular by origin' and 'popular by destination',[11] because it seems unlikely that any poetry in the former category will survive independently in written copies while the clergy has a monopoly of education. There are fragments of soldiers' songs, of perhaps genuinely popular origin, preserved as fossils in alien contexts,[12] and the English political songs included by Langtoft in his Anglo-Norman account of contemporary events[13] may be of this kind. They are curt, abusive, colloquial, they sum up episodes in the manner of popular tags, and they use a version of the alliterative half-line:

> Thair kinges sette of Scone/Es driven over done,
>     To Lunden i-ledde;
> In toune herd I telle,/Thair baghel and thair belle
>     Ben filched and fledde.[14]

(*done* : downs, *baghel* : jewels)

On the other hand, the short-line tail-rhyme arrangement has a literary model in the Anglo-Norman *Lament for Simon de Montfort* of 1267.[15] The relationship of the *Song of Lewes* to the Anglo-Norman *Song of the Barons* is similarly ambiguous. The two languages draw close together in social range in Harley 2253, and these two poems are not widely different in appeal: both are probably addressed to a general audience, the Anglo-Norman to townsmen, the English to countrymen.[16] Both poems, as well as a learned Latin poem on the same event, taking the same point of view, are possibly by Franciscan friars, who were warm admirers of Simon de Montfort,[17] and who would have had cause, occasion and means to popularise his cause among all classes of society.

Two later poems on contemporary events in Harley 2253, *The Flemish Insurrection* (1302) and *The Execution of Sir Simon Fraser* (1306),[18] adopt a similar minstrel tone of address. The first takes the side of the weavers of Bruges against their French masters, while the second celebrates the death of a captured Scot. They are the beginnings of nationalistic propaganda, and show detailed knowledge of the events they describe. Both are in complex stanza forms, based on the alexandrine but heavily influenced by the native alliterative line. It is difficult to identify the authors of such pieces: perhaps it was someone like Roger (or Robert) Baston, a Carmelite friar whom Edward II took to Scotland, according to a fifteenth-century story,[19] to celebrate his expected victories there, but who was captured by the Scots at Bannockburn (1314) and made to sing to another tune. But the story may be a fanciful one, and in any case MS ascriptions to Baston, whether authentic or not, suggest that he wrote or was thought to have written Latin verse.[20] We have to look a little later for definite evidence as to authorship in such cases, and we may digress for a moment to speak of Laurence Minot, who composed a series of eleven poems on Edward III's Scottish and French campaigns of 1333–52, poems preserved in unique copies in another interesting MS miscellany, Cotton Galba E.ix. Minot is the first true national propagandist, violent, abusive, narrowly prejudiced, with a repellent glee, very appropriate to the genre, in gloating over the downfall of the enemy, and a knack for catching the coarse and raucous tone of the soldiery:

Rughfute riueling, now kindels þi care,
Berebag with þi boste, þi biging es bare....[21]

(*riueling* : rawhide boot [term of abuse for Scots], *berebag* : bag-carrier,
*biging* : dwelling)

Minot is important as a poet who cared enough about his work to prepare it
for 'publication' by revision and by adding rubrics to each poem to provide
historical continuity—and yet who was not a cleric. He seems to have come from
a Yorkshire family of landed gentry, perhaps a younger son who became a soldier
of fortune;[22] he is certainly not a minstrel. He is also important for his extensive
use of alliterative verse: five poems are in a stanza of 6 alliterative lines, with
heavy alliteration (normally *aa/aa* often *aa/xx* or *xx/aa*) and regular rhythm,
based on a monorhymed quatrain with a varied couplet refrain linked by concatenation (the repetition of the last words of one line in the first part of the
next); while four others are in 8-line stanzas of the non-native four-stress line,
but again with heavy alliteration (as in *Pearl*). Alliterative verse was obviously
not confined to the West in the fourteenth century.

It did, however, have particular strength there, and Harley 2253 has a group
of satirical and complaint poems which exhibit that strength. *The Song of the
Husbandman*, in 8-line and 4-line stanzas with alternate rhyme (*abab*, etc.),
linked by concatenation, is composed throughout in the alliterative long line,
with heavy alliteration (normally *aa/aa*, even *aaa/aa*, sometimes *aa/bb*) and a
tendency to regular rising rhythm:

Þus me pileþ þe pore and pykeþ ful clene,
    þe ryche me raymeþ wiþ-outen eny ryht;
ar londes & ar leodes liggeþ fol lene,
    Þorh biddyng of baylyfs such harm hem haþ hiht.[23]

(*raymeþ* : rob, *ar* : their, *leodes* : people, *hiht* : befallen)

It is written in the first person and speaks for all peasant farmers against bailiffs,
haywards, woodwards, and in general against the oppressions and extortions
of a system which seems designed to drive its basic producers into beggary. It is
specific and detailed, and comes from someone who knows the plight of the
bondman; it is different from the usual generalised complaint, in Latin, against
the abuses of society, and develops no religious counter-argument of apocalypse
or *contemptus mundi*. To speak of it as the 'voice of the people' is an exaggeration
of romantic populism, but it clearly speaks for and to the people: the distinction
is an important one for our view of poetry as the product of learned tradition.
There is enough evidence of the mendicants' sympathy towards the poor and
oppressed, particularly in the thirteenth century (see above, p. 96) to attribute
it to a friar, or to one of the humbler clerics who were their successors in the

123

fourteenth century. Langland is the great inheritor, of course, and *The Song of the Husbandman* is an ancestor of *Piers Plowman*, as well as *Winner and Waster*.

Other 'protest' poems in Harley 2253 have a different flavour. *The Satire on the Consistory Courts* is in a complex 18-line stanza, based on the alliterative long line with tail-rhyme grouping. A poor peasant describes his appearance on a charge of immorality before the diocesan court (the kind for which Chaucer's Summoner worked); he is rude, abusive and contemptuous, and disgusted at the verdict (he has to marry the woman). *The Satire on the Retinues of the Great* is in monorhymed quatrains of the alliterative long line. Alliteration is heavy, and, as in all this rhymed alliterative poetry, falls regularly on all four stresses, as distinct from the traditional pattern, *aa/ax*. This presumably has to do with the purely ornamental function and consequent increasing elaboration of alliteration in the rhymed, end-stopped line, as has the frequent tendency to patterns such as *aa/bb*: both developments indicate that alliteration is no longer structurally essential as a device for linking half-lines. The poem adopts a minstrel tone ('Of rybaudʒ y ryme ant rede o mi rolle'—in my roll), and is a fiercely scornful and colloquial attack on the arrogant and profligate followers of the great, especially mounted attendants. *On the Follies of Fashion* is in a loosely alliterative monorhymed quatrain, with bob and wheel to make a 7-line stanza. All these poems have popular appeal, but they exploit a rich and varied vocabulary in a sophisticated way, with some parody of conventional poetic phrasing[24] and a great deal of calculated rudeness, and are the work of alienated and irreverent clerics, the product of a goliardic tradition for which we found sporadic evidence in the friars' miscellanies. They have something of the freedom and vivacity of true satire—it is over-simple to assume that the clerical tradition can produce only 'complaint'[25]—and in one poem, *The Man in the Moon*, the bitter social consciousness of the *Husbandman* escapes into whimsy. The man in the moon, with his traditional bundle of thornwood, is a peasant caught cutting sticks from the lord's hedge; he has given a pledge to the bailiff as an admission of guilt, but seemingly fled the manor; the poet plans to get the bailiff drunk and recover the pledge.[26]

In tone, these poems are somewhat different from the Anglo-Norman pieces in the same MS.[27] *L'Ordre de bel ayse* is more reminiscent of *Cokaygne* than of the fierce abusiveness of the *Satire against Consistory Courts*, while the *Song against the King's Taxes*, though it complains of the suffering of the 'simple gent', does so as if from a distance, addressing itself to the king and begging him to be rid of false advisers. The outlaw's song of *Trailbaston* is interesting for different reasons. It is a complaint against a law introduced by Edward I in 1304 to deal with disturbers of the peace and 'comune contekours'.[28] The poet declares that the law will be used to imprison anyone who is maliciously slandered, and will drive good men, like himself, to be outlaws and live in the greenwood of 'Beauregard'. The association of this poem with the possible origins of the Robin Hood legend is evident, and there is a more particular association with the *Tale of Gamelyn*, an English romance of the early fourteenth century (see below, p. 144).

Perhaps the nearest to a 'popular' political poem in the Harley MS is *Thomas of Erceldoune's Prophecy.* The genre of political prophecy, in which various predictions are made, shrouded in mystification and with animal-symbols instead of names, was widely disseminated after Geoffrey of Monmouth's *Prophecies of Merlin.* The Harley *Prophecy* represents a debased form, in which the prediction of a future event, in this instance the ending of the Scottish wars, is made conditional on the fulfilment of certain impossibilities—mixed with cynical certainties:

> When wyt & wille werres togedere ...
> When ryþt ant wrong ascenteþ to-gedere....[29]

In form it is rough-cast, partly loose alliterative verse, partly prose, and looks like a genuine popular product. Such stray remnants were often attached to Thomas of Erceldoune, a Scotsman who had a historical existence in the thirteenth century and a reputation as a prophet and a rhymer.[30] The fifteenth-century Thornton MS includes a long prophecy, attributed to him, of the whole course of the war between England and Scotland, given to him by an elfin queen after she has abducted him—part of this story is echoed in the famous ballad of *Thomas the Rhymer.* It may all seem nonsense, and perhaps the Fool's prophecy in *King Lear* (III. ii. 91) anticipates modern feeling on the matter, but these prophecies were taken seriously by historians and scholars, even acted on by kings and princes.[31] Poets with social and political themes like Langland and the author of *Winner and Waster* were also influenced, particularly by the apocalyptic prophecies, while their popular manner, specious air of mystery and scornful sarcasm gave them a currency in the looser, popular alliterative tradition right down through the two 'Scottish Prophecies' and *Thomas à-Beket Prophecies*[32] to Waldegrave's print of Erceldoune's 'Whole Prophecy' (1603), which includes non-rhyming alliterative verse of authentic Langlandian cadence.[33]

Harley 2253 includes other non-courtly material, such as the *Proverbs of Hendyng* and the Pseudo-Daniel on dream-interpretation, and some homiletic pieces (a verse-sermon on mortality and the transience of life, a dialogue of Body and Soul, a simple verse-'drama' of the Harrowing of Hell), but it would be wrong to divert attention further from its particular splendours, the love-poems and religious poems. The former comprise the only substantial body of English secular love-poetry before Chaucer: without them, our knowledge would be confined to two cryptic love-songs, a fly-leaf fragment of popular dance-song with refrain (*carole*), some casually preserved jottings of strange poignant individuality, and a single semi-popularised version of the *Chanson d'aventure.*[34] There is no evidence of a tradition of courtly love-lyric, and the sophistication of these fourteen poems in Harley 2253[35] is therefore all the more unexpected. They employ a variety of verse and stanza forms, some of them quite complicated: most are in 8-, 10- or 12-line stanzas, predominantly tail-rhyme (*aab*, etc. or *aaab*, etc.), mixed sometimes with alternate-rhyming or *ballade* (*abba*) quatrains, and based on three- and four-stress lines with heavy alliteration;[36] one, *Annot and John* (No. 3 in Brook, *The Harley Lyrics*), is in the long alliterative line (often 5-stave, *aaa/aa*) in 10-line stanzas consisting of a monorhymed octave and a

125

couplet; two (Nos 24 and 25 in Brook), well-separated from the rest in the MS, are in the septenary/alexandrine monorhymed quatrain without alliteration. In addition to this metrical variety and sophistication there is also, in nearly all the poems, a deliberate attempt to cultivate a richer and more esoteric vocabulary, just as there is in the poems of the *Gawain*-MS, drawing on French and Scandinavian sources, on archaic and dialectal native sources apparently closely related to alliterative traditions, even on Welsh.[37] Finally, the poems are well-supplied with the characteristic images and sentiments of courtly lyric. Spring sharpens the anguish of unfulfilled longing:

> When þe nyhtegale singes þe wodes waxen grene;
> lef ant gras ant blosme springes in Aueryl, y wene,
> ant loue is to myn herte gon wiþ one spere so kene,
> nyht ant day my blod hit drynkes; myn hert deþ me tene.
>
> (Brook, 25. 1–4)

The lover wakes and sighs, is pale and full of care, doomed to an early death:

> Heo me wol to deþe bryng
> longe er my day
>
> (9. 21–2)

unless his lady will play the physician:

> a suete cos of þy mouþ mihte be my leche.
>
> (25. 12)

Love is secret and full of pain, the lover bound, chained, wounded, so that his lady is, by a favourite oxymoron, his beloved enemy:

> Ycham hire frend ant heo my fo.
>
> (9. 46)

The grace of God, paradise here and now, is to be in her arms:

> He myhte sayen þat Crist him seȝe
> Þat myhte nyhtes neh hyre leȝe,
> heuene he heuede here.
>
> (7. 82–4)

(*seȝe* : regarded favourably, *heuede* : had)

Two poems are particularly elegant, even precious, in their development: *Annot and John* is a litany of praise, drawing on ever more *recherché* comparisons with jewels, flowers, birds, spices, romance-heroes and heroines to characterise the lady (whose name is enclosed in a cryptogram) in obvious imitation of the catalogues of images for the Virgin:

> Muge he is ant mondrake þourh miht of þe mone,
> trewe triacle ytold wiþ tonges in trone;

such licoris mai leche from Lyne to Lone;
such sucre mon secheþ þat saneþ men sone. (3. 31–4)

(*Muge*: nutmeg, *triacle*: remedy, *ytold*: reckoned, *leche*: heal,
*saneþ*: cures)

*Blowe Northerne Wynd* uses a snatch of popular song as its refrain, counterpointed against an elaborate anthology of courtly themes, including a little inset allegory of the God of Love and his 'knyhtes' Sighing, Sorrow and Thought, presumably derived from the new allegorical poetry of the *Roman de la Rose* tradition.

The ultimate source of such courtly love-lyric is in the poetry of the Provençal troubadours, and a direct connection is not impossible,[38] since there were close political and economic ties between England and the South of France; Henry III's Queen, Eleanor, was the daughter of the Count of Provence. Even if the influence was exerted largely through the medium of Anglo-Norman, certain verse-forms seem to be direct borrowings from Provençal. French poetry also played a part, both the courtly tradition of the named *trouvères* and also the less exclusive tradition of the anonymous pieces: there is a *pastourelle*, a *débat* and a beautiful *reverdie*, or spring-song, all of them very familiar forms in the French poetry of the twelfth and thirteenth centuries,[39] and one trilingual macaronic is suggestive of student days in Paris:

Scripsi hec carmina in tabulis;
mon ostel est en mi la vile de Paris;
may y sugge namore, so wel me is;
ʒef hi deʒe for loue of hire, duel hit ys. (19. 17–20)

(I have written this song on my tablets; my lodging is in the middle of Paris. *sugge*: say, *hi*: I, *duel*: sad thing)

The goliardic Latin tradition is another important thread in this complex background, though not its characteristically frank eroticism: the nearest is a playful naughtiness:

Ich wolde ich were a þrestelcok
a bountyng oþer a lauercok,
    swete bryd!
Bituene hire curtel ant hire smok
y wolde ben hyd. (9. 51–5)

The fact that three of the poems come from the Welsh border[40] might suggest some link with the *cywyddan*, which also employed systematic alliteration; the exuberance, catalogue-structure and intimate knowledge of Welsh legend of *Annot and John* bring it closer to Dafydd ap Gwilym (c. 1325–80) than does its preciosity to the *trobar clus*.[41]

None of these traditions is irrelevant to the Harley love-lyrics, but the accumulation of such a formidable array of 'sources' may give a false impression, for these poems, though they affect much fashionable surface ornament, are not truly courtly. Generally speaking, they lack the theorising, abstraction, analysis and paradox of courtly Provençal and French lyric, the cult of pseudo-logic, of extremes of argument and sensibility. Instead, they are fundamentally simple and direct, much more like the anonymous semi-courtly love-poetry of thirteenth-century France, often given to homely and rustic imagery—the lover 'wery so water in wore' or the discarded lover falling off 'ase fen of fote'[42]—and it is the association, often faintly bizarre, between this homeliness and the courtly decoration that gives the lyrics part of their unique attractiveness. The poets have the wit often to echo the audacious conceits and 'metaphysical' language[43] of courtly tradition—

> He þat reste him on þe rode
> þat leflich lyf honoure!
>
> (14. 20–1)

(*leflich lyf*: lovely woman)

but often too the 'right' sentiments emerge in strangely bucolic language. Instead of the transcendental idealisation of the lady, we get—

> Wymmon war ant wys,
> of prude hue bereþ þe pris,
> burde on of þe best.
>
> (5. 34–6)

Instead of the willing self-abasement and humility of the lover,

> Wiþ longyng y am lad,
> on molde y waxe mad,
> a maide marreþ me.
>
> (5. 1–3)

(*lad*: afflicted, *molde*: earth)

The explanation of these incongruities is not far to seek: the poets were acquainted with the literary forms, images and sentiments of courtly lyric, but had no contact with a society which could sustain or nourish such composition. As far as literary decoration goes, they are accomplished enough, if perhaps a little *passé* in their cultivation of motifs like the inventory-description of the lady, but when it comes to poetic structures of argument which are genuinely complicated,[44] or to forms of sentiment, such as the extravagant idolatry of the lady or the extravagant self-abasement of the lover, which are only truly meaningful in their allusion, paradoxical or otherwise, to a sophisticated real milieu, they can only make sense in simpler terms. Their lack of real sophistication is also shown in the mixing of genres: *De Clerico et Puella* (No. 24) is full of courtly sentiment from the lover ('My deþ y loue, my lyf ich hate . . .') but the maiden replies in brisk, colloquial terms and sketches in a social setting which is nearer to that of *pastourelle* or even popular ballad (e.g. *Clerk Saunders*):

> Be stille, þou fol, y calle þe riht; cost þou neuer blynne?
> Þou art wayted day ant nyht wiþ fader ant al my kynne.
> Be þou in mi bour ytake, lete þey for no synne
> me to holde ant þe to slon, þe deþ so þou maht wynne!    (24. 17–20)

> (*cost* : canst, *blynne* : cease, *wayted* : spied on, *lete* : hesitate, *slon* : slay)

Yet the two are of equal rank as distinct from the *chevalier* and shepherdess of traditional *pastourelle*. The substitution of poet-'clerk' for poet-*chevalier* reminds us again what kind of poet we are dealing with, namely a class of clerical *jongleurs*, imitators of courtly tradition who could not always, fortunately, keep up the pretence. There is a temptation to fragment the Harley lyrics into more and less sophisticated groups, according to the presence of the more highly wrought alliterative style and to the presumption of western provenance. The two are not inter-dependent: the two poems in septenary/alexandrine quatrain are from the East Midlands, but on the other hand so is at least one in the alliterative style (No. 12). There is enough evidence, however, to postulate the existence of a 'school' of Western poets, perhaps members of an ecclesiastical household, who cultivated an alliterative and self-consciously 'poetic' style in an attempt to match what they knew of French, Anglo-Norman and Latin love-lyric, perhaps even of Provençal and Welsh too.

A similar kind of division might be made for the religious lyrics in the MS. Some are in the tradition of Franciscan 'love-song', with the effectively simple vocabulary of the thirteenth-century lyrics: indeed some of them are copies, often by memorial or oral transmission, of poems already well-known in the friars' miscellanies.[45] The metres are simple, dominated by the 6-line tail-rhyme stanza and by a 10-line stanza in which the former is combined with an alternate-rhyming quatrain,[46] and the background expectation is of musical delivery or pulpit use, but with personal meditation gradually emerging as the major function. The subjects are the Passion of Christ and the Compassion of the Virgin, developed at first as a direct stimulus to penitence, but softened to a more personalised and affective meditation in such poems as the two inspired by the Bernardine *Iesu dulcis memoria*. One, 'Suete Iesu, king of blysse', is expanded from three stanzas that first appear in Digby 86, an example perhaps of the 'literary' work that went on in the compilation of Harley 2253; the other is a long meditation on the same theme, 'Iesu, suete is þe loue of þe'—

> Ihesu my god, ihesu my kyng,
> þou axist me noon oþir þing,
> but trewe loue & herte ȝernyng,
> And loue teeris with swete mornyng[47]

129

which appears in similarly expanded form in the Harley MS—there is a shorter version in a late fourteenth-century MS which seems to go back to a more authentic original. Such copying, revision and expansion is a good index to the function of these poems, and of most English religious lyrics. They are essentially anonymous, public and practical; their materials are the commonplaces of scriptural and patristic writing and the liturgy, not individual experience; their object is to persuade, cajole and intimidate men into particular acts of meditation, love and penitence, not to explore personality or to strike poses: 'The lyrics are not illustrations of the spiritual man at prayer, but of the natural man ... being persuaded and coaxed by the imaginative resources of poetry into a religious disposition.'[48] A poem, once written down, is common property, available to any scribe or compiler to improve upon, expand or revise, and the better-known poems crop up in widely different versions in a variety of contexts.[49]

A further striking characteristic of the Harley religious lyrics, already antici-pated in the friars' miscellanies, is the infusion of secular love-themes. One meditation on the Passion begins with the traditional association of spring and the pangs of unfulfilled desire:

> When y se blosmes springe
>     ant here foules song,
> a suete loue-longynge
>     myn herte þourhout stong.                    (18. 1–4)

A whole stanza of complaint and celebration follows before the trap is sprung:

> When y miselue stonde
>     ant wiþ myn eȝen seo
> Þurled fot ant honde
>     wiþ grete nayles þreo.                        (18. 11–14)

(þurled : pierced)

This of course is a well-established Franciscan technique: it exploits the popu-larity of secular love-song, redirects a strong poetic impulse to religious ends, appeals to the love of paradox, punning and surprise, and is firmly grounded in the Bernardine belief in the propriety and potential spiritual usefulness of human emotion. Another poem, on the Five Joys of the Virgin, begins as a *pastourelle*, with no hint of its prospective theme:

> Ase y me rod þis ender day
> by grene wode to seche play,
> mid herte y þohte al on a may,
>     suetest of alle þinge.                        (27. 1–4)

(þis ender : the other, may : maiden)

Another poem to the Virgin echoes the *reverdie* in an autumn-opening,

> Nou skrinkeþ rose ant lylie-flour                            (23. 1)

and after developing the ensuing theme of transience, appears to contradict it by beginning again, on a personal note, as a secular *pastourelle*:

> From Petresbourh in o morewenyng,
> as y me wende o my pley3yng....                            (23. 11–12)

The image of the Virgin as physician, which is the central theme of the poem,

> from Catenas into Dyuelyn
> nis þer no leche so fyn                                     (23. 34–5)

> (from Caithness to Dublin ...)

is deeply contaminated by the transfer of the same image to secular love-poems.[50] 'I syke when y singe' develops its meditation on the details of the Passion in a similar vein, echoing throughout the thin plaintiveness, emphasised by the short three-stress line, of traditional love-complaint, but deflecting it ironically to a theme of deeper anguish, where the spear is real not metaphorical:

> Þe spere al to is herte
>    ant þourh is sydes gon.
> Ofte when y syke,
>    wiþ care y am þourhsoht....                 (22. 49–52)

> (*is*: his, *syke*: sigh, *þourhsoht*: pierced)

These poets are well aware of the potential for emotional manoeuvre that they gain by this exploitation of secular love-themes. The most explicit demonstration of this awareness is a religious 'parody' of a secular love-poem in which the pain of unfulfilled longing for a woman's love is systematically contrasted with the certainty of Christ's love. Secular parodies of religious poems are, of course, common, especially among goliardic poets, but here the existence of other attempts at a religious version[51] suggests that the secular is the original. The stanza-form is unique, an 8-line stanza, $a^4b^3a^4b^3bb^5c^7c^5$, the last two lines used as a refrain, and including the first intentional pentameters in English.

Apart from the poems on the Passion and the Virgin, some of which develop penitential as well as affective themes, there are a number of purely penitential lyrics in the Harley MS, meditations on death, old age and the transience of life. One, 'Wynter wakeneþ al my care', uses a winter-opening to announce the theme of transience, and echoes much thirteenth-century writing on the subject.[52] Another is the famous punning quatrain on 'earth',

Erþe toc of erþe erþe wyþ woh;
erþe oþer erþe to þe erþe droh;
erþe leyde erþe in erþene þroh.
Þo heuede erþe of erþe erþe ynoh.                    (Brook, *Harley Lyrics*, No. 1)

(*droh* : added, *þroh* : grave)

which appears to be the source of a great variety of similar pieces, in Anglo-Norman and Latin as well as English.[53] None is as sharp and pithy as the Harley text, where the punning not only startles, bewilders and enlightens but also conveys a vicious and bitter contempt for the world. Perhaps the most interesting of these penitential poems from a literary point of view, however, are the two that appear in the MS among the alliterative love-lyrics and political poems (Nos 2 and 13). All the other religious poems use the simpler language of the Franciscan poets, but these two are ambitious to experiment with alliterative techniques and to extend the range of vocabulary in the same way as the other alliterative pieces. The first is a homily, 'Middelerd for mon wes mad', using the four-stress line with regular alliteration in an unusual 11-line stanza; the second imitates Maximian's elegy,[54] using a 12-line tail-rhyme stanza of four- and three-stress alliterative lines, alternating with a similar 5-line stanza. Metrical and stylistic ambition is not altogether attended with success, and the first poem is often merely obscure, but the precious style of *Pearl* is clearly already in the making.

### Collections of religious verse

The richness and range of the Harley MS, essentially an anthology, provides a contrasting background for some simpler collections, in which the occurrence of English verse is determined by more severely practical considerations. B.M. MS Add. 46919 (formerly Phillipps 8336) for instance, an extensive collection of Anglo-Norman treatises and religious verse, includes a final quire of English verse, mainly translations of well-known Latin hymns, antiphons and responses. The scribe names himself as author, William Herebert, a Franciscan friar (d. 1333) and continuator, therefore, of well-established thirteenth-century traditions. The poems were presumably intended for private devotion[55] as well as pulpit use.[56] The translations are close, the verse correct, if awkward, the metres traditional,[57] and the spelling unusually eccentric, as if Herebert were more at home with Anglo-Norman. The poems have an additional interest in providing the earliest true examples of the carol (i.e. short poem with repeated refrain) in English, and an important foundation for Robbins's argument that the carol, which becomes so widespread in the fifteenth century, has its origins as a literary form in the Latin processional hymn with choric refrain, rather than in the secular ring-dance.[58] It is conceivable that the Herebert carols, like the more sophisticated later vernacular carols, which occur beside

Latin hymns and antiphons in liturgical MSS with music, were used for 'congregational singing'.[59]

Other MSS are more obviously preachers' handbooks, such as the collection of sermon notes and outlines made by Bishop Sheppey of Rochester,[60] where the place of the English verses in the Latin sermon is sometimes explicitly indicated. The poems, most of which have a liturgical origin, would be recited, or sung by the preacher to enliven and punctuate his discourse at strategic points. Franciscans were particularly active in the production of these manuals, often systematically arranged for reference under alphabetical headings, and in the later fourteenth century the habit of using English verses in sermons receives explicit recognition in the alphabetical sermon handbook (1372) of the Franciscan John Grimestone.[61] English notes and verses are scattered throughout: some are set directly beside Latin hymns and other verses of which they are translations, most probably by Grimestone himself; other poems are or become familiar anthology pieces, so that the MS as a whole is a good guide to the state of the simpler English religious lyric in its day. Most of the poems centre on the Passion, rather than on the Virgin or on themes of mortality, and must be drawn from the simpler tradition of devout lay meditation, in which the importance of the Passion was central.[62] The lyrics were designed for devotional practice, and composed in English verse as being easier to memorise for laymen who had no books. Some are simple, phrases or motifs taken up from well-known Latin meditative treatises or from the liturgy and developed briefly for their emotional effectiveness: such are the abrupt description of Christ's body, *Candet nudatum pectus* ('Wit was his nakede brest'), the call to contemplate Christ on the cross, *Respice in faciem Christi* ('Loke man to iesu crist/hi-neiled an þo rode'), Christ's own call to man, *Homo vide quid pro te patior* ('Senful man, be-þing & se/ Quat peine i þole for loue of þe') or to passers-by at the crucifixion, *O vos omnes qui transitis per viam* ('Ʒe þat pasen be þe weyʒe,/Abidet a litel stounde').[63] If these are for meditative purposes, they are for beginners only; their primary aim is to create an almost physical impact of shock and shame, rather than a response of loving devotion, to apply an immediate styptic to temptation:

> Þenc, man, er þu do þi sinne,
> Wath i þolede for man-kinne.          (Brown, *XIVth Century*, No. 3)

Such pieces would have fitted well into sermons, and there are others which, in their development of dramatic moments or situations from the Passion story, such as Christ's anguish in Gethsemane or the appeal of the Virgin to the Jews or at the Cross, with no mention of penitential or meditative function, quite clearly demand their sermon-context. The most characteristic pieces in the Grimestone MS, however, are those which draw on the strain of simple and personal devotion so sweetly dwelt upon by the Franciscan popularisers. Christ is often the speaker, whether from the cradle (Nativity poems, with their touching pathos, appear here in numbers for the first time) or the Cross, and his appeal is 'Ler to louen as i loue þe'. Touches of gentility are provided by occasional courtly ('Mi loue is falle up-on a may') and knightly allusion[64] ('I am iesu, þat cum to fith/With-outen seld & spere') and *chanson d'aventure* openings, as in the Harley lyrics, and there is an echo here and there of more sophisticated meditative writing, of the paradox of Jesu compelled and slain by love:

> Loue me brouthte,
> & loue me wrouthte,
> Man, to be þi fere.
> Loue me fedde,
> & loue me ledde,
> & loue me lettet here.

(Brown, *XIVth Century*, No. 66)

The stanza here is a derivative of the old septenary couplet, equipped with double medial rhyme: most of the other poems are in the alternative rhyming quatrain similarly derived from the old long line or in the short couplet. The simplicity of metrical form is striking, and matches well with the simple practical functions of the verse, whether one thinks of it in a meditative or homiletic context. The language is the direct product of the needs of the form, without pretence or adventitious ornament. It has in fact the virtues of good prose, in an age when poetic theory demanded as great a distinction as possible between verse and prose.

Grimestone's collection includes a number of pieces with an even more direct relation to simple lay devotional practice, what can loosely be called prayers in verse. Some are very short and simple, suitable for anyone to learn and say without prayer-book at church or on other appropriate occasions: these occur widely in commonplace-books and in treatises of popular instruction; they are particularly important as part of the half-conscious heritage of vernacular religious poets. Others are more extended, and begin to appear later in the century appended to Books of Hours and in private prayer-books.[65] The origins of both can be traced back to the early fourteenth century, when conscientious churchmen began the attempt to provide material for lay devotion during the Divine Office, which of course would be largely unintelligible to the lay congregation. Metrical treatises on the manner of hearing mass offered simple outlines of the main events of the Office, and gave metrical English versions of the most important prayers, tŏ be learnt by heart—

> Þo robryk is gode um while to loke,
> Þo praiers to con with-outen boke,[66]

as well as suggesting themes for private prayer during the priest's own devotions:

> When þo preste praies in priuete,
> tyme of prayere is þen to þe.

(29–30)

We may think that the design was as much to occupy wandering minds and prevent 'jangling' as to stimulate devotion, but there can be no doubt that this recommended practice gave great stimulus to the provision of suitable prayers and meditations, to be learnt and said over *sotto voce* at appropriate times in the service and eventually extending into the wider realms of extra-liturgical poetry.

Another liturgical source for religious verse of this simple and practical kind was provided by the *Prymer*, which can be described as a popular prayer-book based on the more readily comprehensible and unvarying parts of the Divine Office, the later accretions to it in fact, such as the Hours of the Blessed Virgin Mary, the Seven Penitential Psalms, and the Office for the Dead. These prayer-books were used in church, to help in following the service (though of course they would not form any part of the service), and were also used in private devotion. Some include, as part of the Office of the B.V.M., verses on the Hours of the Cross, a theme for meditation in which the stages of the Passion are related to the canonical Hours: this became a favourite subject for independent composition,[67] and clearly the popularity of the *Prymer* also stimulated the composition of the several poems based on the lessons from Job which form part of the *Dirige* in the Office for the Dead[68] as well as versions of the Seven Penitential Psalms. One quite elaborate version of the latter, with an 8-line stanza of translation and commentary to each psalm-verse, is that attributed in one MS to 'Richarde Maydenstoon', a Carmelite friar, author of Latin verses, sermons and treatises, and well-known as John of Gaunt's confessor. A version such as his has grown far beyond its liturgical origin and is evidently intended for the private use of an educated layman, as part of the preparation for confession[69] or of the act of penance itself. As a poem, it has occasional vigour, particularly in association with the alliteration which is a prominent feature of style.

With a writer like Maydenstoon we are on the edge of conscious poetic impulse, as we are with William of Shoreham (c. 1320), an Austin canon of West Kent who composed lengthy didactic verse expositions of the Seven Sacraments, the Ten Commandments, the Seven Deadly Sins, the Five Joys of the Virgin—in fact a comprehensive account of the essentials of Christian doctrine—presumably for the private edification of one of the more educated of his parishioners. A Hymn to the Virgin in the same unique MS[70] may be by the same writer, despite a rubric referring to 'Grosseteyte': it proceeds by a catalogue of types (dove of Noah, bush of Sinai, etc.) suggestive of the more ambitious Marian poems of the fifteenth century. Nevertheless, even when we have named poets and individual ambitions like this, the poets themselves, like all the unnamed verse-makers, are more a medium through which a store of instruction and devotional sentiment is transmitted than independent authors. The writer who changes this, who is memorable as an originator and who, through the force of his personality as well as his writings, shifted the direction and raised the level of English devotional verse, is Richard Rolle (d. 1349). Rolle was educated at Oxford, but spent most of his life as a hermit in Yorkshire, where he wrote a number of mystical and semi-mystical Latin treatises, commentaries and poems, with a strong autobiographical element. His history is that of a writer of great imaginative power seeking for subjects within the established devotional genres which would answer his need to communicate his own mystical experiences and the fervour of his devotion to the Holy Name of Jesus. The fame of his sanctity gathered to him a number of women disciples, and it was for these women recluses that he began to write in English, towards the end of his life, a series of prose meditations and epistles as guides to the contemplative life. His impact was tremendous, not only in England, and there are over 400 MSS of his authentic Latin and English works. Rolle's Latin prose is characterised by heavy alliteration, especially in the *Melum Contemplativum*, frequent assonance, and strong if irregular rhythmical patterning. Precedent for such prose can be found far back in Latin tradition, though Rolle does not use the systematic rhythms of the *cursus*, and his extremes of style are his own.[71] He may also have been influenced by the highly wrought alliterative prose of the *Wooing*-group and of *A Talkyng of the Love of God* (see above p. 83). Turning to English prose, he sought, like Ælfric and the writers of the *Katherine*-group, an equivalent rhetoric and, like them, found it in his own adaptation of the rhythmical, alliterative tradition. Perhaps the most perfect example of his controlled lyrical prose is the short piece, 'Gastly Gladnesse', inserted among his poems: 'Gastly gladnes in Jhesu, and joy in hert, with swetnes in sawle of þe savor of heven in hope, es helth intil hele. . . .'[72]

Rolle's attitude to verse was not unambiguous. 'Song' for him was, like 'heat' (*Incendium Amoris*, 'The Fire of Love', is his most important Latin prose work) and 'sweetness', a manifestation of the inward fervour of mystical devotion, an upswelling of the spirit expressed above all through repetition of the Psalms: 'Sange es a gret gladnes of thoght of lastand thinge and endeles ioy, brestand in voyce of lovynge'.[73] He is cautious to distinguish spiritual and fleshly song:

> Þe saule es anely comforted in lovyng and lufyng of God, and til þe dede com es syngand gastly til Jhesu, and in Jhesu, and Jhesu, noght bodyly cryand wyth mouth—of þat maner of syngyng speke I noght, for þat sang hase bath gude and ill.[74]

On the other hand, a passage in the *Incendium Amoris* suggests that he might experiment with verse as a medium for the expression of the divine inward 'song', or that his disciples might,[75] and the extant poems are perhaps the result. Some are incorporated into the English prose epistles, a Meditation on the Passion and a Song of Love-longing to Jesus (these are the themes of all Rolle's poetry) in the *Ego Dormio* and another *cantus amoris* in *The Form of Living*. They are introduced with a touch of condescension ('Þou may in þi langyng syng þis in þi hert'),[76] as if they are concessions to a simpler and frailer form of devotion. Nevertheless, they communicate something of the insistent and overwhelming power of Rolle's devotion, the longing for Jesus which floods into the verse through a rhapsodical and incantatory use of alliteration and rhyme. These poems, though loosely constructed, tend to fall into the septenary/alexandrine monorhymed quatrain, which Rolle may have imitated from his own early Latin poem, the *Canticum Amoris*, but which we have seen widespread in English poetry too. Within it he uses heavy, irregular medial rhyme and alliteration, sometimes being drawn, like other English poets before him, into the stress-patterns of alliterative verse. The independent lyrics are more formally constructed: the long-line quatrain is metrically more regular and medial rhyme and alliteration systematised. One may question the effectiveness of this sometimes, as in the transformation of lines like these from the *Ego Dormio*,

My sange es in syhtyng, my lyfe es in langynge,
Til I þe se, my keyng, so fayre in þi schynyng,
So fayre in þi fayrehede

as they appear in the poem 'Jhesu God sonn',

My sang es in syghyng, whil I dwel in þis way.
My lyfe es in langyng, þat byndes me, nyght and day,
Til I come til my kyng, þat I won with hym may,
And se his fayre schynyng, and lyfe þat lastes ay.[77]

But on the whole one thinks of Rolle's lyric writing as a composite and indivisible body rather than as a series of separate poems. They are woven together by a tissue of echoes and re-echoes,[78] linked in turn to the Latin and English prose works and to certain key documents in Rolle's devotional background like the *Iesu dulcis memoria*, so that a line like

For luf es stalworth as þe dede, luf es hard as hell,

startling enough in itself, gains a dimension of depth through varied reiteration. The poem from which it is quoted here, 'Luf es lyf',[79] based primarily on passages from the *Incendium Amoris*, is a magnificent outburst, perhaps Rolle's major poem, but the impact of all his poetry is cumulative.

Rolle's importance to English verse is that he opened it up to kinds of devotional and mystical meditation which had long been the preserve of Latin or of certain esoteric kinds of English prose. His influence was exerted not only on specialised meditative writing but as a leaven on other religious writing too. It is strong in poems associated with Rolle's name, though not under authentic Rolle rubrics, in the two most important MSS of his English lyrics, C.U.L. Dd. v. 64 (III) and Longleat 29. The former includes 'My trewest tresowre' (*XIV*.79), a poem on the Passion which exceeds Rolle in the controlled violence of its language and in the clarity of its structure, where the remembrance of Christ the Redeemer at the beginning of each stanza ('hope of my hele . . . salue of my sare') is systematically counterpointed against the uncompromising recital of his sufferings ('Whan þai schot in þi syght bath slauer & slyme') in the remainder. The poem is written in alternate-rhyming quatrains of regular alliterative verse, worth contrasting with Rolle's authenticated poems, where six- and seven-stress lines predominate and where alliteration, though often heavy, is irregular.

Longleat 29 includes 'Ihesu þat hast me dere I-boght' (*XIV*.91), a meditation on the Passion which is explicitly annotated for private devotional use in this MS. The poem is in fact a skilful patchwork of lines and groups of lines from a much longer work, the English verse translation of John of Howden's *Philomena*, a Latin mystical poem of the thirteenth century and an important influence in the fourteenth-century English mystical tradition. This translation,[80] a considerable achievement in itself, exists in only one MS, the shorter version in ten: as an act of plunder it was clearly very successful and served its more modest devotional purposes well. The heights of the *Philomena* are not attempted, but the poet communicates effectively the central conceit of the heart scored by a written memorial of Christ's sufferings and wounded by the arrows of his love:

> Ihesu, ȝite write in myne herte
> How bloode oute of þi wondis sterte;
> And wiþ þat bloode write þow so ofte
> Myne harde herte tile hit be softe....
> Let now loue his bowe benden
> And loue arowis to myne herte senden.[81]

Another poem, 'Crist makiþ to man a fair present' (*XIV*.90), which occurs in conjunction with English prose works by Rolle in two MSS, conveys more of the intrinsic mystical quality of the *Philomena*, especially the paradox of love slain by love, or of night's triumph over day (a reference to the eclipse at the Crucifixion, and a subtler demonstration, therefore, of the power of love than the more usual 'Ihesu þe nyght turnes to þe day'):

> Þe lord of loue loue haþ now slawe—
> Whane loue is strong it haþ no lawe....
> Loue haþ schewid his greet myȝt,
> For loue haþ maad of day þe nyȝt;
> Loue haþ slawe þe kyng of ryȝt,
> And loue haþ endid þe strong fiȝt.          (13–14, 33–6)

Poems like these are the finest fruits of the Rolle tradition, finer perhaps than anything Rolle himself wrote in verse.

Rolle's work was systematically exploited, adapted and imitated by devotional writers and compilers in the fifteenth century. His name was a promise of spiritual fervour and theological respectability, and much undistinguished verse was attributed to him and accepted uncritically by collectors like Thornton.[82] The practical application of his work is well illustrated in an important early fifteenth-century collection, B.M. MS Add. 37049. This MS, which has become widely known because of its uniquely close application of text to instructional picture and vice versa, uses many scraps of Rolle's prose and verse in its didactic programme, as well as original material, and material from other sources.[83] There is also much rhymed paraphrase of passages from Rolle's prose epistles, suggestive of cruder mnemonic use. The MS is of Carthusian origin and is presumably intended for the instruction of the novitiate. The establishment of the vernacular within the monastic strongholds could hardly require ampler demonstration. Finally, one of the more bizarre episodes in the history of the Rolle canon is the attribution to him in some MSS of *The Prick of Conscience*, a didactic verse-treatise of vast length (nearly 10,000 lines) and tediously competent execution, which was no doubt assigned to Rolle in order to cleanse it from heretical taint after it had been interpolated in some versions with Lollard material.[84] Its claim on our attention, a brief one, is that it occurs in more MSS (114) than any other Middle English poem. Such are the frustrations of a scrupulously historical enquiry: fortunately the second poem in terms of MS frequency is *The Canterbury Tales*.[85]

Mention of *The Prick of Conscience* provides occasion to record, in a cursory way, the continued production, throughout the fourteenth century, of a mass of didactic and homiletic verse, not always entirely different in purpose but certainly distinct in quality from the devotional verse we have been looking at. The *South English Legendary* continues to be expanded, both the *sanctorale* and the *temporale*, and there are many unaffiliated legends of saints designed likewise for recitation to a more or less popular audience. The development, towards the end of the century, of the *Northern Homily Cycle*, which includes a Legendary as well as verse-sermons (with illustrative tales) based on the Gospel-readings for every Sunday and every important feast-day of the liturgical year, marks a shift perhaps towards private lay reading—

> Here may men luke, who likes to lere,
> Of liues and dedis of saintes sere,
> And in olde times how it bifell
> Als men in inglis tung mai tell.
> Out of latyn þus er þai draune,
> Omong laud men forto be knaune.[86]

though the tone of address is not noticeably more sophisticated. The *Northern Passion*, a long independent poem which is associated with the cycle in the same way as the *Southern Passion* with the *South English Legendary*,[87] is from earlier in the century, a lively and colourful retelling of the Passion narrative, competing with the romances on their own level and designed for recitation or pulpit delivery to an unsophisticated audience. It may be contrasted with the late fourteenth-century *Stanzaic Life of Christ*, from Chester, a work of insipid monastic propriety designed primarily for reading.[88] Apart from these pieces, and from the continued production of narrowly practical works such as a versification of the Benedictine Rule (for women), there is also a great increase in biblical verse paraphrase, including a metrical version of the whole of the Old Testament and some particular attention to the apocryphal gospels of the Infancy and of Nicodemus.[89] It is historically proper to recognise the existence of this massive reservoir of verse, for the evidence it gives both of the continued dominance of verse as a medium of religious instruction and of the increase in private lay reading, and also for its importance in nourishing some more notable kinds of verse-making, as in the play cycles. Beyond that, these works have little intrinsic literary interest, though they are often remarkably competent in their handling of the short couplet, which is now the staple verse-form for such pieces.

## The Vernon MS

All forms of religious writing are represented, at the end of the century, in the monumental collection known as the Vernon MS (Bodley Eng. poet. a.1). This impressive book, which measures 22 by 15½ inches and weighs 48¾ lbs, is closely associated with an equally massive volume, the Simeon MS (B. M. MS Add. 22283), and with a third, Add. 37787, which once belonged to John Northwood, who entered Bordesley Abbey, in Worcestershire, as a novice in 1386.[90] It is tempting to associate all three MSS with Bordesley, a distinction for this small house which would be comparable with and no doubt related to its being honoured with the gift of Guy of Warwick's astonishing library in 1305.[91] The compiler of the Vernon MS, whoever he was, clearly intended to provide a comprehensive library of religious reading for every use, a complete *Salus animae* or 'Sowlehele', as he calls it. He includes the whole of both the *South English Legendary* and the *Northern Homily Cycle*; a shorter miscellaneous legendary based on the *Golden Legend*; an A-text of *Piers Plowman*, and another unrhymed alliterative poem, *Joseph of Arimathie*, as well as the stanzaic alliterative *Susannah* (these three poems will be treated in the next chapter); two pious 'romances', *Robert of Sicily* and *The King of Tars*; *The Prick of Conscience*; three versions, one in prose and two in verse, of the *Mirror of St Edmund*, a widely-known treatise of religious instruction ultimately derived from the *Speculum Religiosorum* of St Edmund of Abingdon (see above, p. 101); the *Ancren Riwle*, *A Talkyng of the Love of God*, and works, also in prose, by Rolle and Hilton; and a mass of other religious writing, all in English.[92] The existence of such a compilation is evidence in itself of the efficiency of the networks of MS dissemination in the fourteenth century. The compiler includes much material designed originally for popular or pulpit presentation, such as the *Miracles of Our Lady* ('Lordus, ȝif ȝe wol lusten to me'),[93] with their appeal to the most degraded taste for pious titillation, but the general direction of the collection seems to be towards reading aloud within a more confined circle—'priue carpyng' (Horstmann, XXXV. 272)—or towards private reading and meditation.[94] One version of the *Mirror of St Edmund*, for instance, is certainly addressed to a listening audience

> Þen mowe ȝe heere in þis ryme
> How a mon schal spende his tyme  (XXXII. 19–20)

whilst another is presented as a 'book' for reading, not exclusively by laymen, on feast-days:

> Þis may be ʒor halyday werk,
> Hit wol avayle boþe lewed and clerk. (XXXV. 29–30)

Reading such verse, and not only reading it but composing (e.g. I. 33) and transcribing it, was a beneficial exercise, and at the very least could be recommended as a way of occupying the mind and keeping it from sinful thoughts. The provision of reading matter on such a scale can be compared with the enormous expansion of the liturgical services, the *Opus Dei*, in monasteries: little time was left for sinful thoughts.

Guiding principles are hard to find for a collection so comprehensively envisaged, when availability—'I-writen I fynde a good stori' (XXXIV. 1)—might be the only criterion for inclusion, but certain trends are discernible. The volume, for one thing, as distinct from the earlier friars' collections, is almost exclusively in English, and with the friars, too, has gone a certain generosity and *debonnaireté* of attitude. A chill monastic propriety has set in, and the contents are exclusively religious and didactic, without a hint of secular relief. Even the lament over the transient joys of the world, the *Ubi sunt*, so hauntingly evoked in Friar Thomas's *Luue-Ron*, is here, in a comparable context (XXXIX. 141), brusquely dismissed. There is as yet no sign of the repressive orthodoxy of post-Lollard times, but certain fifteenth-century developments are well under way. Marian devotion, of a characteristically pompous and hieratic kind, is beginning to overwhelm the simpler and more affective devotion to Jesus of Franciscan tradition. There is much Marian invocation and salutation, heavy and repetitive, including a poem which offers an *Ave* for each part of the Virgin's body (XXV), in grotesque parody of the catalogue-description prescribed by rhetoricians for *descriptio feminae*. A version of the expanded 'Ihesu swete is þe loue of þe' from Harley 2253 (see above, p. 129) redirects devotion by interpolating stanzas of Marian invocation at regular intervals (XL). These are not new trends, of course, rather they are trends newly admitted into English verse from Latin meditative tradition. The same is true of a more technically extravagant kind of meditation on the Passion, as in a poem on the 'Charter of Christ', which develops the idea of Christ's body as a written charter or testament to his legatees, the parchment being his own skin,

> Strayte I-streynet on þe Rode,
> Streyned to druye on Rode-tre,
> As parchemyn oweþ for to be, (LIV. 78–80)

the ink the Jews' spittle, the pen the scourges, the letters his 5460 wounds. Such ingenuity is a very characteristic form of medieval 'wit', the resolutely literal pressing of every implication of a single *allegoria* rather than the search for imaginatively appropriate metaphor.[95]

Certain kinds of intellectual sophistication (and also pretension) are also more apparent in the Vernon MS than in earlier collections. The compiler shows a special fondness for dialogue-poems—of a Good Man and the Devil, of Jesus and the Jews, of a Christian and a Jew, and others, in addition to the usual Body and Soul debate—which could be regarded as a more thoughtful attempt to dramatise didactic teaching in a lively and succinct way. *The Dispute between a Good Man and the Devil* (XXXVII) has a low but deadly effectiveness as a piece of teaching, and shows some artistic consciousness too in its allocation of different metrical forms to the two speakers—though it is difficult to know why long-line couplets are appropriate to the good man and short couplets to the devil. *The Disputation between Mary and the Cross* is interesting for two reasons: it elaborates the symbolism of the Passion in the same extravagantly literal way as the 'Charter' poem, as when the Cross speaks,

> Rosted aȝeyn þe sonne,
> On me lay þe lomb of loue;
> I was plater, his bodi aboue (LII. 161–3)

(though at the end it explains, in a curiously naïve way, that the prosopopeia is only a fiction); and it is written in a complex 13-line stanza, directly imitative, as to rhyme-scheme, of the alliterative *Susannah* which stands next in the MS. Such metrical experimentation is rare outside Harley 2253, and rare in the Vernon MS, which is mostly content with standard forms, short couplet, long-line couplet or monorhymed quatrain, and tail-rhyme, apart from a favourite 8-line stanza, $^4 abababab$. Alliteration is frequent in the *Disputation*, as well as in one or two other poems in the MS (e.g. XXVIII, XLV), and exerts a particularly strong influence on a final group of poems, mostly peculiar to Vernon and its sisters, known as the Vernon refrain-poems.[96] These are written in imitation of French ballade-stanza, in 8- or 12-line stanzas, usually $^4abab(abab)bcbc$, with repeated or varied refrain at the end of each stanza. Alliteration is quite heavy, especially for effect at the opening of a poem: it often fades, just as the striking phrases of the opening often fade to monochromatic platitudes. A *chanson d'aventure* opening in 'Make Amends' (Brown, *XIVth Century*, 117) is mere prettification, and an extraordinary variation on the same opening in 'Mercy passes all things',

> Bi west, under a wylde wode-syde,
> In a launde þer I was lente,
> Wlanke deor on grounde gunne glyde,
> And lyouns Raumping uppon bente (95. 1–4)

with its bizarre heraldic wilderness, in the end involves the poet in more problems of explanation than it is worth. Some of the poems are simple, others are complex and abstract, with touches of both irony and pretentiousness. 'Maiden Mary and her Fleur-de-Lys' is intellectually sophisticated in a quite new way—

> A studi steer þer stod ful steere
> For steeres-men þat bi stremes gun stray (112. 49–50)

> (*studi* : steady, *steer* : star, *steere* : strong)

heavily alliterative, with a vocabulary inheriting much of the preciousness of Harley 2253 and *Pearl*. 'This world fares as a fantasy' (106) uses a different kind of language, close to that of the fifteenth-century aureate style ('Material Mortualite', line 93): it is based on Ecclesiastes, and preaches a peculiarly nerveless but certainly scholarly resignation. Poems on the earthquake of 1382 (113) and on the death of Edward III (Horstmann, LV. 19) have something of Langland's social and political concern, something of his range and variety of material, without his passion or poetry. A dominant strain in the poems is the pseudo-classical, pseudo-Christian materialistic wisdom of Cato's *Distichs* and the *Proverbs of Philosophers* (texts of both are in Vernon), that wisdom to which devotion is an afterthought (116), which preaches a mercantile view of salvation (100, 101), a flaccid and premature resignation (105), a paralytic moral quietism (109, 118), and whose general message is that Christian policy is the most successful policy (if you give away your money, your executors cannot mishandle it, 116). It is an extraordinary collection of poems, not without subtlety, ambition and sophistication, and, though often pretentious, certainly possessed of genuine if bookish learning; but the moral quality of its appeal to a comfortable bourgeoisie is as gross as it is astute, the very material of Chaucer's satire in the *Manciple's Tale* or *Summoner's Tale*.

## *The Auchinleck MS and the romances*

It may seem, from what I have said, that the fourteenth century, outside the alliterative and courtly traditions, and apart from exceptional productions like MS Harley 2253, was dominated by the continued massive output of religious and didactic verse. This would not be a false impression, at least so far as the extant records are concerned, but it ignores the romances, between forty and fifty of which are produced during the century. These may constitute less of an exception than might be expected, since the characteristic tone of many English popular romances is pious, didactic and exemplary and their characteristic provenance is in MSS of miscellaneous religious material. If medieval romance exists as the expression of chivalric idealism, as it does in its continental and élite forms and in certain late fourteenth-century courtly English poems of the alliterative and Chaucerian traditions, then these English romances have little claim to a share in the title.[97] They suppress or debase any manifestations of chivalric idealism, the most their heroes lay claim to being a kind of pragmatic piety.

Generalisations are difficult, and some warnings have already been recorded (above, p. 113) about the dangers of treating such an amorphous group of poems as a genre; nevertheless some generalisations need to be attempted. In terms of content, the romances draw on a variety of source-materials. Whereas most English romances of the thirteenth century[98] are derived directly from Anglo-Norman originals, the majority of fourteenth-century romances are derived,

143

at one or two removes, from French. The only ones based on Anglo-Norman are the didactic romance of friendship, *Amis and Amiloun*, and *Ipomadoun*, a close paraphrase of a thirteenth-century poem by Hue de Rotelande which, exceptionally, preserves much of the courtly, ironic and sophisticated tone of its original. Where English romances are not traceable to French or Anglo-Norman sources they are usually composites of stock incident, even when they have a smattering of local and historical allusion, like *Athelston*. Perhaps the one true exception is *The Tale of Gamelyn*, an early analogue for the Robin Hood story (and for *As You Like It*), which tells a tale of land law and inheritance, romanticised but essentially rooted in actuality. Its metrical form and MS descent are alike exceptional: it is written in the old septenary/alexandrine couplet, which had long been discarded by professional romances in favour of more fashionable forms; and its survival (in more MSS—twenty-six—than any other English romance) is due solely to its adoption by some scribes of *The Canterbury Tales* as a tale for Chaucer's Cook. In choosing it for such a purpose they perhaps give evidence of the disdain with which it might have been treated by the more fashion-conscious compilers, for it appears in none of the professional collections.

*Sir Degrevaunt*, for which again no source is known, constitutes perhaps another exception: its hero is not only a Knight of the Round Table and companion of Perceval and Gawain but also a Yorkshire country landowner with estates and gamekeepers, who replies to a bullying neighbour's encroachment with a letter demanding compensation. He later falls back into more conventional chivalric attitudes, but the opening is authentic to a local and litigious gentry. The metrical form is again unusual, a 16-line tail-rhyme stanza, the elements of which are thought to derive from the alliterative half-line (it is found also in *Sir Perceval* and *The Avowing of Arthur*) and so is the MS situation, for *Degrevaunt* is the only one of these romances (apart from the special case of *Gamelyn*) found in a Chaucerian MS (C.U.L. Ff. i. 6).

In subject-matter, the romances draw on the familiar cycles: the matter of France, the source of nine of the dreariest and most contemptible pieces, all from the Otuel and Firumbras cycles except for the fragmentary semi-alliterative *Song of Roland*; the matter of Britain, the Arthurian romances *(Arthur, Le Morte Arthur, Sir Perceval of Galles, Sir Tristrem, The Avowing of Arthur, Ywain and Gawain, Lybeaus Desconus)*; and the matter of Antiquity (two versions of the Troy story, one short and crude, *The Seege of Troye*, the other long and quite respectable, the *Laud Troy-book*). There is also a large group of romances *(Sir Isumbras, Sir Eglamour, Torrent of Portyngale*, two versions of *Octavian, Sir Tryamowre, The King of Tars, Le Bone Florence, Emare)* based on legends of the Constance-type (like Chaucer's *Man of Law's Tale*), which give ample scope for pious, sentimental and sensational incident, and a further group of what are called, or claim to be called 'Breton *lais*'. These are short tales of Celtic 'faerie', imbued by their twelfth-century literary progenitor, Marie de France, with great delicacy and subtlety of sentiment, but rather more briskly handled in English. Some are derived from known *(Sir Launfal* and its analogues, *Lai le Freine)* or presumed

*(Sir Orfeo)* French originals; of these, *Orfeo* has been admired for its evocation of the supernatural, especially of the faerie hunt—

> He miȝt se him bisides
> (Oft in hot under-tides)
> Þe king o fairy wiþ his rout
> Com to hunt him al about
> Wiþ dim cri & bloweing.... (281–5)

and of the Celtic otherworld, though one suspects that any literary effectiveness the poem has is the accidental triumph of content over form, for it is a banal production. *Sir Degare* is a pseudo-Breton *lai*, skilfully assembled from stock components, while *Sir Gowther* and *The Erl of Tolous*, the former an exemplary story of the crudest sort, the latter a quite respectable little domestic drama, simply call themselves 'Breton *lais*' to be fashionable.

There are other odd remnants in this rag-bag, such as the pious exemplary tales of *Sir Amadas*, *Sir Cleges* and *Robert of Sicily*, and the quasi-historical *Titus and Vespasian*, based on legends of the destruction of Jerusalem in AD 73 and full of the basest crusading fervour. It is noteworthy that the two last-named, which are remotest from any concept of 'romance', occur in more MSS (ten and thirteen respectively) than any other of the romances except *Gamelyn*. It may seem that the concept itself is not worth preserving, when so little definition is provided by the subject-matter, and when the poems blur off into contiguous forms on every side, into versified history in *Arthur*, a wretched mangling of Geoffrey of Monmouth, into something close to the rhetoricated epic of Lydgate in the *Laud Troy-book*, into exemplum and moral tale in *Isumbras*,[99] *The King of Tars*, *Amadas* and others. From this point of view the only possible definition is 'narrative designed for entertainment'. Yet from other points of view these romances have a remarkable homogeneity, which may be defined in terms both of their social context and of their formal and stylistic 'grammar'.

For the former, the Auchinleck MS (National Library of Scotland MS 19.2.1, about 1330) provides us with a point of reference. This famous MS, a miscellany of religious and didactic material with a strong London connection, contains fifteen romances (they occupy 244 of its 332 leaves), including texts of nearly all those discussed in Chapter 4, and many others, amongst them the first of the tail-rhyme romances. It has been convincingly argued[100] that the MS is the production of a commercial scriptorium, in fact a bookshop, which prepared books for sale to the growing London bourgeoisie, just as lay ateliers were at this time coming into existence for the illumination of more expensive religious MSS for secular patrons of the upper classes. The volume has been carefully prepared by a general 'editor', who has supervised the work of his translators and scribes, both probably working in the same premises. For example, *Guy of Warwick* has been neatly tailored into three consecutive romances of more manageable bulk, including a potboiler dealing with his son *Reinbrun* which has been deftly disentangled from the Anglo-Norman original; and finally, to make sure that no aspect of the work's popularity should remain unexploited, a straight-forward treatise of basic religious instruction is tagged to the story to masquerade as the *Speculum Guy de Warewyke*. This kind of basically competent hack professionalism is the literary context of the Middle English romances. The 'minstrel' can be forgotten, as a composer if not as a performer: no doubt popular entertainers, of whom there were many kinds, often had deboshed forms of romance in their repertoire, but these by their very nature would be unlikely to survive in written form (though it has been suggested that Lincoln's Inn MS 150, which contains only romances and a fragment of *Piers Plowman*, is a minstrel-book).[101] The audience for which these professional translators and composers catered was a general one, but an important element in it can be identified in a new semi-articulate but increasingly literate audience on the borders of social respectability, an aspirant bourgeoisie, who demanded fashionable romance in English, on the model of the French, as a mark of their status and the status of the English language. It is for this audience, with its piety, its appetite for violent and sensational incident, its lack of interest in sensibility or psychological analysis, that the romancers purveyed. The Auchinleck MS is only the first of a large number of similar MSS[102] which, in combining these romances with religious and didactic material, aimed to provide a suitable library of innocuous, entertaining and improving reading for a household or its members. The sense of social homogeneity remains strong even if one admits that such MSS would often come the way of more sophisticated readers—court officials, members of the higher civil service, the better class of merchant and guildsman, even men like Chaucer (who certainly had access to a MS something like the Auchinleck)[103] —and even if one admits too that certain romances, like *Ipomadoun*, *Degrevaunt* and the stanzaic *Le Morte Arthur*, appeal to more gentle tastes.

Within this social context, then, the English romances, though highly derivative, set their stamp on their borrowed material in a readily discernible way. There is, for instance, little interest in *fine amour*. Chrétien's subtle dialectic of love in *Yvain* is all omitted or vastly simplified in the English of *Ywain and Gawain*, which is on the whole a remarkably skilful adaptation of its original. Ywain is made much less abjectly submissive before his lady (1149) than he is in Chrétien (1975), while Chrétien's description of the lady's fashionably free flirtation with the knights of Arthur's court and his ridicule of those who are naïve enough to take this sort of amorous attention as a sign of love (2454–65) is reduced to two lines as wholesome as porridge (1433–4). The translator of *Gui de Warewic*, recognising that his audience will have trouble accepting the aloof disdain of Felice, gives her this explanation when her maid reproaches her for her cruelty in withholding her love from so noble and stricken a wooer:

Oft þou hast y-herd in speche
Þat we no schal no man biseche,
Ac men schul biseche wimen
In the feirest maner þat þai can.          (621–4)

This is the sort of naïve recital of 'correct' notions of social behaviour that one associates with the uninformed but anxious. The English redactor of *Li Biaus Descouneus* of Renaut de Beaujeu alters the whole story by his treatment of the lady of the Ile d'Or. In Renaud, she is an irresistibly desirable woman, and all the adventures of the hero centre on his love for her. In the English *Lybeaus Desconus* she is a sorceress who traps the hero into a liaison by her magical wiles. 'Alas he ne hadde y-be chast!' (1414, ed. EETS 261) comments the author, and writes of his departure from her castle as a fortunate escape from a tricky situation. Women have their part to play in English romance, but they are generally treated as potentially explosive objects, best left alone or handled gingerly. The English hero has little time for dalliance, and after his declarations of undying affection will hasten off, muttering vaguely of fights toward.

As for fighting, it would not be true to say that there is more fighting in English romance than their French and Anglo-Norman originals—this would be diffi-cult—but fighting looms larger in the characteristically abridged story-pattern. Excision of courtly material in *Lybeaus* makes of it little more than a prolonged succession of unrelated fights. Where there is no fighting, or where some favourite act of violence is lacking, the translator will make good the omission, as Thomas Chestre (the only name we have among all these romancers, though it means little)[104] does by adding a tournament and a giant-fight in *Sir Launfal* or the author of the English *Beves* by inserting a wholly gratuitous dragon-fight. Odds are lengthened, the numbers of the dead multiplied, the element of crude violence increased. The hero is more belligerent, more self-assured, and more completely infallible. Lip-service is paid to the chivalric code, but only where it serves to glorify the hero. A characteristic change in *Lybeaus* makes the hero dismount voluntarily to continue the fight on foot with his unhorsed enemy (336), where in the French he does so only when his own horse is killed. The popular debasement of chivalry into a form of spectacular quixotic bravado is well illustrated in two English versions of the same French romance, one *The Sowdone of Babylone*, more thoroughgoing in its adaptation of the material to popular taste, the other, the earlier *Ferumbras*, more faithful to its original. The audience of the *Sowdone* could stomach no reproach to the valour of their traditional heroes, nor could they accept the portion of chivalry meted out to the Saracens. Therefore the *Sowdone* omits all mention of the terror which the Saracen Ferumbras's challenge struck into the hearts of the assembled *douseperes* (*Ferumbras* 138). It moderates the contempt of Ferumbras for the disguised Oliver who comes to take up the challenge, and leaves out the Saracen's humi-liating proposal of a mock-joust. The chivalry of Ferumbras in offering to heal Oliver's wound (*Ferumbras* 511) is replaced by the added detail of Oliver's chivalry in helping his enemy to lace his helmet (*Sowdone* 1159). Another typical change is in Charlemagne's rebuke to Roland for refusing an order: in *Ferumbras* (166) he strikes him with his glove, in the *Sowdone* (1092) he punches him in the mouth and makes his nose spurt with blood.

Other types of change display the same adaptation of material to a lower social class. Descriptions of feasts, castles and other aspects of aristocratic life are reduced to the barest conventionalities, while limited understanding debases the complex texture of courtly manners to a few stereotyped gestures against a vaguely splendid background. Frequent extrusions of raw realism into this conventional idealisation give to the English romances their characteristic blend of the fantastic and the matter-of-fact, a feature also of their treatment of the supernatural.

The formal identity of the English romances is still more striking. Apart from the few exceptions already mentioned, and one or two others in unusual stanza forms (e.g. *Tristrem*, the Southern *Octavian*, *Le Morte Arthur*), all are written either in the short couplet or in tail-rhyme (usually $aa^4b^3cc^4b^3dd^4b^3ee^4b^3$), the latter in particular forming a strongly marked group—though not so strongly marked that they can be assigned *in toto* to a single regional 'school'.[105] Within these metrical forms there is an equally marked community of incident and situation. Stock motifs—the disguised hero, the false steward, the accused wife, the credulous husband, the giant or dragon-fight—recur from romance to romance. Sheer multiplicity of incident is often the dominant structural feature, especially in the patchwork miscellanies of stock episodes, such as *Sir Eglamour*, which are England's main original contribution to the development of romance. Episodes, stanzas, even lines, are strung loosely together in a manner merely consecutive, with little attempt to shape or develop a central story-line. Narrative transitions are casual and abrupt, and there is rarely any shift of focus to suit the needs of the story. Repetition of favourite incidents is often of the most meretricious kind: there are no less than five giant-fights in *Torrent*, while the translator of *Guy of Warwick*, struck by an episode in the original where Herhaud loses his sword and fights with his bare hands, duplicates it detail by detail with reference to Guy (5251–378). Titillation is the aim rather than any deep engagement of response, as if the composer could never be sure of his audience's attention unless he could satisfy an insatiable appetite for extravagance and novelty. Thus, Sir Degare not only marries his mother and fights against his father but also, for good measure, fights against his grandfather as well. The admission implicit from the start is that the romances set out to do no more than occupy an idle hour or two, and the romancer trims his tale so close to the most obvious tastes of his audience that there is little room for conscientious development of narrative. The romances are rarely dull but often trivial in a bright, bitty way. There is about all but the best of them a reluctance to attack or engage an audience, a sharp professionalism conscious only of popular rating.

Apart from these types and techniques of narrative, the English romances share a large body of conventional stylistic devices and conventional idiom. Beginnings and endings are stereotyped on the pattern of the religious benediction. Narrative transitions are indicated by set formulae. Comments on the action, prayers for the hero, curses on the villain, are inserted at every point. Similar devices are found in all literature which has to do with the conventions of oral delivery (which persist of course even when private reading grows common). Battles are described in set terms and amplified from an extensive conventional apparatus itself of French and Anglo-Norman origin. Emotions such as grief, joy, love and anger are expressed according to rigidly stylised formulae: it is rarely, for instance, that the romancer will attempt to convey sorrow without some brief but sufficient mention of swooning, hair-tearing and hand-wringing. Descriptive realism is hypostatised under set forms and set similes, especially in such recurrent features as personal description:

> Also whyt so lylye-flour,
> Red as rose off here colour,
> As bryȝt as blosme on brere. (*Athelston*, 70–2)

This formulaic element in the English romances, which is most marked in the tail-rhyme group, should be distinguished from the mass of verse-fillers and rhyming tags—asseverations, references to authority, inclusive phrases—which are the common property of all Middle English poets. These can properly be regarded as a form of verse-articulation, especially suitable for spoken verse, and of minimal artistic importance. Genuine formulae, on the other hand, can exist as a sort of stylised verbal equivalence, where a certain series of phrases, rigorously formalised in content, are the recognised stimulus, through their traditional associations, for a certain poetic response, a form of descriptive shorthand. Tags are not meant to be noticed, but formulae are, and it is the mark of the inferior romancer that he reduces conventional formulae to the level of tags. Most of the romancers, unfortunately, are inferior in this respect as they are in others.

# 6    Alliterative poetry

The title of this chapter should not be taken as suggesting that there is a body of poetry in Middle English which, on the basis of its metrical characteristics, can be completely isolated either socially or regionally or in terms of subject-matter. In fact, it will be the concern, in the discussion of certain individual poems, to restore them to the larger context in medieval writing from which they have often been artificially divorced by over-emphasis on their allegiance to an alliterative 'school'. On the other hand, the existence of an alliterative 'school', comprising a central 'classical' corpus of poems closely related in formal and stylistic character and with a definitely West Midland and North-Western regional bias, can hardly be denied. It therefore seems sensible to regard these poems as the nucleus of the chapter, the remainder as a penumbra shading off on every side into other forms of writing.

It has been the argument of earlier chapters that a tradition of alliterative writing, of which both Old English poetry and Old English alliterative prose were particular literary manifestations, remained in existence throughout the early Middle English period. In its most basic form it may have been no more than a penchant for two-stress alliterative phrases deriving from the most funda-mental rhythmic and dynamic characteristics of the language itself; but both in this and in somewhat more developed forms it existed as a continuum, a set of flexible and unformulated procedures on which literate verse-makers could draw (see above, pp. 74–85). We saw evidence of such use in the twelfth and early thirteenth centuries, not only in verse but in prose, and evidence too of fertile connections between the two. The traditions of alliterative prose continued unabated into the fourteenth century, especially in Rolle, and should never be neglected as a potential source of enrichment for the traditions of alliterative verse, but the characteristic development of the later thirteenth century in alliterative verse, the addition of rhyme, seems to drive a wedge between the two traditions (the use of rhyme in Rolle's alliterative prose is not comparable, since it is based largely on the irregular repetition of like inflexions, the Latin device of *similiter desinens*),[1] just as it is distinct, in its recognition of the line-unit, from the earlier application of rhyme to the half-line. Alliterative verse is quite widely used in the friars' miscellanies of the later thirteenth century, in the early fourteenth-century Harley 2253, in the poems of Minot and of Rolle's followers, but it is almost invariably associated with rhyme, whether in monorhymed quatrains, longer monorhymed stanzas or *laisses*, or more complex composite stanzas.

The effect of rhyme on alliterative verse is quite fundamental, as we saw as long ago as the Old English *Riming Poem*. It makes alliteration a superfluous ornament, instead of a structural device linking otherwise independent half-lines, with the consequent tendency either towards irregularity and lapse of alliteration or towards emphasis and excess of alliteration to compensate for loss of function; it demands a more regularly metrical alternation of stressed and unstressed syllables, since rhyme is based on the expectation of an isochronous recurrence of terminations; and it draws the weight of the line towards the last, rhyme-bearing stress, which can less easily in such a situation be a non-alliterating stress, as it is in traditional alliterative verse. The most obvious consequence of all this is the regular appearance of enriched *(aa/aa, aaa/aa)* and defective *(aa/bb, aa/xx, xx/aa)* patterns of alliteration in rhymed alliterative verse, as contrasted with the equally regular and structurally functional *aa/ax* (variants *ax/ax, xa/ax*) of traditional unrhymed alliterative verse.

The influence of the alliterative tradition is strong also in 'metrical'[2] rhymed verse, in two ways. One is the tendency of many poets to use alliteration, irregular but often heavy, as an additional ornament within non-native but established couplet and stanzaic forms. We have seen this in some poems of Harley 2253, including well-defined examples among the secular and religious lyrics, and we have seen it further in Minot, in Maydenstoon's version of the Psalms, in Rolle, in the Vernon MS, and elsewhere (see above, pp. 132, 142). In the Vernon MS, we suggested, alliteration was quite consciously used, in the refrain-poems, as an attention-catching device at the beginning of poems. The practice of some metrical romances is comparable: many, particularly those of late fourteenth-century northern provenance, use alliteration generously (*Ipomadoun, Rowlande and Ottuell, The Sege of Melayne,* and other tail-rhyme romances, *Le Morte Arthur*), and there seems a clear example in the *Laud Troy-book* of alliteration being used to whip up flagging interest at a key transition in the narrative.[3] This self-conscious use of alliteration, in the Vernon MS and in some later romances, may be seen as one of the direct consequences of the alliterative revival.

Another way in which alliterative tradition exerts its influence on metrical rhymed verse is the marked tendency of the loose septenary/alexandrine long line of the thirteenth century, of mixed Latin and Anglo-Norman descent, to be invaded by the cadences of the native four-stress line, with or without alliteration. We have seen this invasion, at various degrees of advancement, in poems from Jesus MS 29 and Harley 2253, in the *South English Legendary*, in poems by Rolle, in *Gamelyn* (see above, pp. 96, 122), and we can see it further in a poem from the Auchinleck MS called *The Simonie* or *On the Evil Times of Edward II*. This traditional piece of estates satire, which attacks the corruption of the times by passing in review all ranks of society in the accepted manner, with apocalyptic warnings, already partly fulfilled, of dearth and disorder as the visitations of

God's wrath, is interesting as a forerunner of *Piers Plowman*.[4] It uses the septe-nary/alexandrine monorhymed quatrain with a bob and sixth line rhyming together, but is deeply infiltrated by the rhythms of the native four-stress line, with sporadic alliteration.

One other hybrid needs to be mentioned, namely the rhymed alliterative half-line. The early development of the short couplet in English is often asso-ciated with the break-up of the alliterative line and the addition of rhyme at caesura and line-end. Some doubt was cast on this theory in the discussion above (p. 79) of Laȝamon and other early alliterative or partly alliterative poems, and it was dismissed in favour of the Anglo-Norman hexasyllabic couplet in the case of *King Horn*. On the other hand, it is not at all unlikely that short couplets of the *Horn* type were affected by two-stress half-line patterning, in just the same way that the metrical long line couplet was affected by the full alliterative line. Further evidence of such influence exists in the English tail-rhyme pieces in Langtoft's Chronicle (above, p. 122) and, more systematically developed, in the group of tail-rhyme romances associated with *Sir Degrevaunt*.[5]

### The alliterative revival

Everything, then, argues for the continued strength, throughout the thirteenth and fourteenth centuries, of alliterative tradition, in its various forms, and the continued process of adaptation to and fusion with other forms that it undergoes. The only apparent casualty in this development, and one very much to be expected, is the traditional unrhymed alliterative line itself. From the century 1250–1350, that is, the years following the latest examples of unrhymed allite-rative verse from the early Middle English period (Laȝamon's *Brut*, the *Bestiary*), only a few debased and dubious remnants survive. *Thomas of Erceldoune's Prophecy*, in Harley 2253, qualifies more because it lacks rhyme—and indeed any other mark of poetic identity—than because it is recognisably alliterative, though its descendants, the political *Prophecies* of the fourteenth, fifteenth and sixteenth centuries, are important evidence, as we have seen (p. 125 above), of the per-sistence of a loose, popular and partly oral alliterative tradition. A fragment of unrhymed alliterative verse quoted in Rolle's *Ego Dormio* has a more authentic ring:

> Alle perisches and passes þat we with eghe see;
> It wanes into wrechednes, þe welth of þis worlde.
> Robes and ritches rotes in dike,
> Prowde payntyng slakes into sorow.[6]

Even so, all the lines except one (the third quoted above) conform to the new alliterative patterns of rhymed alliterative verse (*aa/aa, aa/bb, aa/xx*). If we had no evidence from after 1350, we might presume that the old alliterative verse had been superseded, except in a few forms barely on the fringes of literate verse-making, and that its rhythmical and formal characteristics had been either rejected or totally absorbed into rhymed verse.

All this makes the sudden flowering or 'revival' of unrhymed alliterative verse in the second half of the century a most puzzling phenomenon. It begins with two poems that can be dated early in the period, *William of Palerne* and *Winner and Waster*, and continues on for nearly a century, with a gradual recession northwards. Within its orbit, a preliminary distinction can be made between two main groups of poems, though other distinctions will have to cut across them:[7] one can be called the *Piers Plowman* group, consisting of poems in the political, didactic and complaint tradition (*Piers Plowman* itself, of course, transcends such a grouping) and characterised by a pragmatic and 'unpoetic' handling of alliterative verse (*Richard the Redeles/Mum and Sothsegger, Pierce the Ploughman's Crede, The Crowned King, Death and Life*); the other, the *Gawain*-group, consisting of the poems of the *Gawain*-MS, the historical epics (the *Alexander*-poems, *The Destruction of Troy*, the *Morte Arthure, The Siege of Jerusalem*) and two other poems (*The Parlement of the Thre Ages, St Erkenwald*), characterised by regularity of metrical observance and by a sophisticated, consistent and self-conscious alliterative poetic—what I have called the 'classical' corpus. A few poems, like *Joseph of Arimathie* and *Chevelere Assigne*, hang on the fringes, and there are some significant scraps, like the *Satire on Blacksmiths* and the *Prophecies*.

To account for the sudden emergence of this poetry, some theory seems to be called for. It is usually assumed that the unrhymed alliterative line was kept alive, deep-frozen, in oral tradition and floated out quite deliberately into literary respectability by a school of western poets. Hints towards a consciousness of such ancestry have been taken from the lines in *Gawain*,

> If ȝe wyl lysten þis laye bot on littel quile,
> I schal telle hit as tit, as I in toun herde,
>                    with tonge;
> As hit is stad & stoken
> In stori stif & stronge,
> With lel letteres loken,
> In londe so hatȝ ben longe.                    (30–6, ed. EETS 210)

(*as tit* : straightway, *stad & stoken* : set down and fixed, *lel* : true)

which have been associated with similar lines in the prologue to *The Destruction of Troy* :

> To ken all the crafte how þe case felle,
> By lokyng of letturs þat lefte were of olde.                    (25–6, ed. EETS 39, 56)

The interpretation seems strained in the first instance, where the reference could as well be a conventional one to an authoritative tradition and a well-controlled poetic language, and mistaken in the second, where 'lokyng of letturs'

153

means 'the study of writings'.[8] A similar passage in *William of Palerne* has been seized on to suggest that the poet is apologising for employing a metrical form that has hitherto been considered 'low':

> But þouȝh þe metur be nouȝt mad　.　at eche mannes paye,
> Wite him nouȝt þat it wrouȝt　.　he wold haue do beter....
> (5524–5, ed. EETS, ES 1)

However, the apology seems to be part of the usual *topos* of modesty, with *metur* as an alliterating synonym for 'poetry'. On the whole, it seems too much to expect that we should get any help from internal evidence: self-conscious comment on metre or indeed on any aspect of poetic technique is, as we have seen, very rare in Middle English poetry. The trouble with assumptions about oral tradition is that, in the nature of things, no other evidence is likely to be forthcoming.

In the absence of such evidence, wild and patriotic speculation has supplied theories of direct continuity from Old English, of a native heroic spirit and native verse-form which go underground after the Conquest among the poetic *maquis* of the western marches, to reappear triumphantly as the Anglo-Norman usurpation is overthrown. It has even been supposed that the great baronial families of the West deliberately encouraged the cultivation of such verse as a patriotic and English counterblast to the dominance of a hated French-speaking court.[9] There is no need to disentangle in detail the improbabilities of such simple answers. They ignore the actual historical situation of the mid-fourteenth century and the late growth of linguistic 'national' consciousness as well as the fact that there is no 'heroic spirit' in Middle English alliterative verse which is incapable of being derived from Latin and Anglo-Norman writing, and no significant resemblance of style between Old English and Middle English alliterative verse—though every compound and every alliterative formula has been pressed into service to prove continuity.

Yet continuity of a kind there must have been, and it is not entirely explicable in terms of the extant written documents. For all the weight we have put behind the hypothesis of an alliterative 'continuum' from which writers of prose and verse could draw whatever was relevant to their needs, two things remain difficult to explain, and they may be related. One is the extraordinarily unanimous reversion to regular *aa/ax* patterns of alliteration, when all the tendencies of alliterative verse with rhyme and of metrical rhymed verse with alliteration have been towards the enrichment (especially *aa* in the *b*-line) or breakdown of such patterns; the other is the rejection of rhyme itself, for which the scraps of rhymeless verse we have noticed provide only a pathetic precedent. Alliterative prose can be cited as a model, but it is as difficult to believe that the alliterative poets disentangled a regular, systematic and traditionally authentic versification from the looser rhythms of prose as to believe that they did it by stringing together accidentally regular alliterative lines from the detritus of the septenary/

alexandrine tradition. In addition to these metrical features, there are certain kinds of poetic language, particularly synonyms for the staple noun 'man' (*burne, freke, gome, hapel*, etc.) which are cultivated by the 'classical' poets, both for their practical usefulness in providing alliterating words and, since they are usually words of high alliterative 'rank' (i.e. they rarely appear in non-alliterating positions), as a form of conscious poetic elevation. Some of these words are archaic and many are exclusive to alliterative verse:[10] combined with a strongly marked formulaic phraseology, which is also often archaic and exclusive, they constitute further proof of continuity

At this point, if we are not to fall back into quicksands of oral tradition (the objection to which, it must be understood, is not merely that it declares the subject inaccessible to rational argument but also that it does not fit the facts, for oral tradition in a literate society is inevitably 'low' and inevitably makes wretched what it touches), it is probably necessary to invoke again the fragmentary state of our knowledge of much Middle English poetry. Most of these alliterative poems exist in unique copies: only *Piers Plowman* and *The Siege of Jerusalem* exist in more than two, and these have the sanction of religious or pseudo-religious subject-matter. Take away a handful of MSS, therefore, and there would be no alliterative revival to be explained. If we transfer this situation to the late thirteenth and early fourteenth centuries, the period for which records fail us, and reckon with the added uncertainties of an earlier date, the disadvantaged status of English, and, by presumption, a predominantly secular subject-matter, it will not seem impossible that a tradition, perhaps tenuous and probably unfashionable with scribes, of unrhymed alliterative writing has been lost.

We may assume that it was a primarily Western tradition: there is evidence, as we have seen, of widespread acquaintance with alliterative writing, particularly in the North-East (Minot, Rolle), but the concentration of tradition was always stronger in the West. For the poems of the revival a West Midland of North-Western provenance is generally proven on the basis of dialect forms, though there has been some tendency to ignore contradictory evidence, and the assignation of the *Morte Arthure* to Lincolnshire[11] is a reminder that non-Western dialect forms are not necessarily to be dismissed as scribal. There are also significant links with other parts of the country: the author of *Winner and Waster* seems to be a Western man and he affects a distaste for the metropolis,

Dare neuer no westren wy, while this werlde lasteth,
Send his sone southewarde to see ne to here[12]

but his poem is metropolitan, not at all provincial, in outlook. *Piers Plowman*, again, is initially set among the Malvern Hills, but this loyal gesture to the poet's own youth and upbringing is a mere dream of reality beside the solid London milieu of the poem as a whole, the reality of the dream. *St Erkenwald* celebrates a London saint with a wealth of local reference that would be meaningless if the audience's knowledge were confined to Lancashire. In other words, the revival had its base in the West, and most of the poems were written there, but neither poets nor appreciative audiences were confined to the West. The comment of Chaucer's Parson is not without dramatic ambiguity—

> But trusteth wel, I am a Southren man,
> I kan nat geeste 'rum, ram, ruf', by lettre          (*Parson's Prologue*, 42–3)

but it certainly suggests that alliterative verse was primarily associated with the outlandish regions beyond the Home Counties; nevertheless, Chaucer does know about alliterative verse and pays it the compliment of skilful imitation in two well-known battle-passages.[13]

I have continued to use the term 'revival' despite the presumption of a lost written tradition, because it seems that some movement towards revitalisation if not resurrection did take place in mid-century. This movement can best be understood in relation to aristocratic patronage. Such patronage would explain the widespread dissemination of alliterative verse described in the previous paragraph, as well as its ability to draw on a metropolitan richness of source-materials, since the nobility had estates all over the country and travelled remorselessly with their train of courtiers, officials, clerks (and would-be alliterative poets); it would explain also the sophisticated range of social and courtly reference (particularly in a poem like *Sir Gawain and the Green Knight*), for which, as we have seen, there is no real precedent even in a MS like Harley 2253. External evidence of such patronage is not as forthcoming as one would wish or expect, but *William of Palerne* is dedicated to Humphrey de Bohun, Earl of Hereford, titular head (he was an invalid) of one of the greatest Western families, and the *Destruction of Troy* has a reference to 'the nome of the knight þat causet it to be made' in the list of contents in the MS (ed. EETS, 39, 56, p. lxx), though unfortunately the corresponding lines in the text are missing. The milieu of the *Gawain*-poet has traditionally been associated with the household of John of Gaunt,[14] albeit without concrete evidence. From internal evidence, we may assume that the opening address of *Alexander A*, not so much to those who like hearing about fighting, as in the professional romances, but to those who might actually do some fighting themselves, 'thinken to doo deedes of armes',[15] argues for an audience among the members of a noble household, while the author of *The Wars of Alexander* makes it very clear that his poem is intended for after-dinner reading to a well-bred audience. The prologue is unusually precise on this point, and the poem is systematically divided for delivery, with the breaks frequently indicated in the text, into 'fitts' or *passus*. A major transitional passage at line 3468 would have come about halfway through the original poem (the ending is lost), at the obvious structural break in the narrative, after the death of Darius, and may indicate a recital spread over two evenings:

> Now will I tary for a time  .  & tempire my wittis.
>
>                                                   (3466, ed. EETS, ES 47)

There is no need to assume that these allusions are structural relics, for the situation, with a cleric such as a chaplain reading his own work before the noble household to which he is attached, is entirely probable. It may be that we should not think too exclusively in terms of 'aristocratic' patronage: there are poems that we might prefer to associate with the lower but still 'gentle' ranks of the provincial gentry, a group of patrons, perhaps, like those for whom there is documentation in East Anglia in the early fifteenth century.[16]

If we ask what might have prompted these nobles and gentlemen to offer the prestige of their patronage to alliterative verse, the answer might be a simple one, namely, that Anglo-Norman verse, which hitherto absorbed nearly all courtly and aristocratic patronage, was now, about 1350, in a state of rapid decline. Alliterative verse would have offered itself as a ready substitute, suitable, like the alexandrine in *laisses*, for long and ambitious poems, and untainted by the hack professionalism and didactic opportunism of more current English forms, such as tail-rhyme, short couplet and the rough septenary/alexandrine long line. It probably had an archaic flavour, just as Laȝamon's *Brut* did even in its own day, but this may not have been altogether, or at all, a disqualification. The element of archaism may be a partial explanation of the tenuous scribal tradition: scribes with the antiquarian patience of Caligula A.ix (of the *Brut*) must have been rare.[17] It may be relevant that an unexpectedly large proportion of alliterative poems survive only in late and very bad texts.

## Early poems of the revival

The early poems of the revival, if it is the product of change and choice and not accident, ought to provide crucial evidence. *William of Palerne* is less helpful than might be expected. Though Humphrey de Bohun (d. 1361) commissioned the translation,

> Preiȝes for þat gode lord . þat gart þis do make,
> Þe hende erl of hereford . humfray de boune ...
> he let make þis mater . in þis maner speche,
> for hem þat knowe no frensche . ne neuer underston
>
> (5529–33; cf. 164–8)

he intended it not for himself, but for those who knew no French. This is aristocratic 'patronage' of a kind, but of a condescending and remote kind, and it would indeed be something of a paradox if Humphrey, whose patronage elsewhere extended to the most sumptuous illuminated MSS, had any closer relation with a poem so banal. Probably the commission was a casual one, to some insistent household clerk; perhaps it was intended for the kitchen staff.[18] The poem comes nearer to the popular romances in choice of subject (one of the fashionable twelfth-century French romances), in treatment and in tone, than any other alliterative poem. It is not by any means an incompetent paraphrase, and it has the characteristic thin fluency of English romance, with some fancy and touches of feeling. The peculiarity of the poem is that, although it observes the basic alliterative metric (three-quarters of the lines are *aa/ax*), it has none of the distinctive stylistic features of fourteenth-century alliterative poetry, neither in diction, phraseology nor in handling of syntax. One may conclude that the poet had only limited access to the tradition or simply that he was a poor poet; it seems very doubtful that he was deliberately modifying the tradition for more general consumption. Nevertheless, though the poem had no apparent influence, it is important as a record of the recognition in mid-century that the alliterative form was suitable for fashionable literary purposes.

With *Winner and Waster* we are on firmer ground. The prologue, despite many conventional features, reads like a declaration of intent, and the poem like a showpiece. The opening reference to the Trojan descent of Britain (1–4), with its sense of history, of a 'many-storied antiquity', becomes something of a signature of alliterative poetry: it is imitated as a framing device in *Gawain* and the *Morte Arthure* and alluded to in the *Destruction, Parlement* and *St Erkenwald*.[19] *Winner and Waster* itself may be the source of such references, or Laȝamon (though there is no definite evidence of a knowledge of the *Brut* amongst alliterative poets), or, most probably, Geoffrey of Monmouth himself, whose work, being in Latin, would have had a currency among educated writers that no vernacular poem could match. No such references appear in Chaucer: for him, as for contemporary French poets, Geoffrey of Monmouth, indeed the whole Arthurian tradition, would have appeared very old-fashioned. His only allusions to Arthurian story (e.g. in the tales of the Wife of Bath, the Squire and the Nun's Priest) are either contemptuous, playful or deliberately archaic. Chaucer would have had the same attitude to another weighty matter alluded to in the *Winner and Waster* prologue, the invocation of cryptic prophecy as warning of apocalypse, again ultimately derived from Geoffrey of Monmouth:

When wawes waxen schall wilde, and walles bene doun,
And hares appon herthe-stones schall hurcle in hire fourme ...
Thene dredfull domesdaye it draweth neghe aftir.           (13–17)

(*wawes* : waves, *hurcle* : crouch, *fourme* : form [hare's nest] )

We have already (p. 125 above) seen evidence of a specifically alliterative tradition of political prophecy: this is one of its more literary manifestations, and has a significance far beyond itself in that it is echoed in *Piers Plowman* (B.vi.328). It is one of a number of close links between *Winner and Waster* and *Piers Plowman* which enable us to say not only that Langland may have known the earlier poem,[20] but that it may indeed, with its wealth of vivid and satiric social detail, have provided him with a primary model and source of inspiration.

Finally, in this prologue there is a striking contrast drawn between old 'makers' and new-fangled entertainers:

Whylome were lordes in londe þat loued in thaire hertis
To here makers of myrthes, þat matirs couthe fynde,
Wyse wordes with-inn, þat writen were neuer
Ne redde in no romance þat euer renke herde.
Bot now a childe appon chere, with-owtten chyn-wedys,
Þat neuer wroghte thurgh witt three wordes to-gedire,
Fro he can jangle als a jaye, and japes can telle,
He schall be leuede and louede and lett of a while
Wele more þan þe man that makes hym-seluen.                    (20–8)

(*renke* : man, *appon chere* : in appearance, *Fro* : from the time that,
*lett of* : esteemed)

This comes perhaps a little too pat if we are looking for evidence of conscious inheritance of an old and respected poetic tradition, and certainly the situation is not as simple as it seems, for the prologue echoes here a conventional strain of complaint as old as *Deor*. Nevertheless, there is enough force in the repeated contrast of those who 'make' poetry (and an example, perhaps, in Laȝamon, who had as patron a 'lorde in londe'), as against the inferior breed of minstrel-performers, to carry conviction and suggest that it is not merely conventional.

The body of the poem is a debate between Winner and Waster, whose powers are allegorically drawn up as for battle before Edward III and the Black Prince, and who represent in effect the opposed economic principles of retrenchment and expansionism, or, more crudely, making money and spending it. The debate is conducted at an intelligent level, by a man who knows what he is talking about, both as a social observer and a satirist, and both sides make good points. The presentation of the King and the Black Prince, who act as arbiters and peace-makers, is particularly clever: both were conspicuous and notorious 'wasters', but the poet manages to suggest an admirable side to their extravagance. The poem is full of spectacular effects, from the enriched detail of the landscape-setting,

The throstills full throly they threped to-gedire;
Hipped up heghwalles fro heselis till othyre;
Bernacles with thayre billes one barkes þay roungen;
Þe jay janglede one heghe, jarmede the foles.                 (37–40)

(*throly* : keenly, *threped* : argued, *heghwalles* : woodpeckers, *bernacles* : wild
geese, *jarmede* : warbled)

to the brilliant and fictitious heraldic blazonry of Waster's army of merchants, friars and lawyers. Nor is it merely a brilliance of setting and spectacle, for the same wit and observation and characteristically alliterative concretion of detail are bedded deep in the texture of the debate, in Waster's description of Winner's house, for instance,

> The bemys benden at the rofe, siche bakone there hynges,
> Stuffed are sterlynges undere stelen bowndes $\qquad$ (251–2)

or in Winner's horrified account of Waster's feasts:

> Tartes of ten ynche, þat tenys myn hert
> To see þe borde ouer-brade with blasande disches,
> Als it were a rayled rode with rynges and stones. $\qquad$ (341–3)

> (*tenys* : grieves, *rayled* : adorned)

The poem is a *tour de force* of rich and controlled skills, in which traditions of social complaint, satire and debate, partly derived from Latin writing, perhaps through the medium of vernacular political and satirical verse like that of Harley 2253, are confidently adapted to more self-conscious poetic purposes and techniques. If I call it a showpiece, this is not meant to suggest that it is a deliberate advertisement of the potential of alliterative verse, but that this, judging from its known and presumed influence in both branches of alliterative poetry, may well have been how it struck contemporary writers.

### The techniques of alliterative verse

Alliterative verse, particularly that of the 'classical' school, has a strongly marked stylistic character, to which some allusion has already been made, and which must now be analysed in more detail. Technically, the development of the alliterative line in Middle English, in relation to its ancestor in Old English, is towards a strengthening of the pause at the end of the line and a weakening of the strong medial caesura. The two half-lines are drawn closer together, the second being made subordinate to the first, and, though the hemistich remains the basic unit, the long line becomes a more close-knit whole. In Old English, alliteration served the structural function of linking the freely-running half-lines in couples; in Middle English, the half-lines are bound together by natural rhythm in a strongly end-stopped line and alliteration is no longer structurally indispensable.[21] It tends either to be weakened, as in poems of the *Piers Plowman* group, where there is less conscious poeticism, and often dropped altogether in some marginal and incoherent examples of the genre like *Joseph of Arimathie* and *Chevelere Assigne*; or to be exaggerated and enriched, to compensate for loss of function, particularly in the *a*-line in the 'classical' poems. Whereas half the *a*-lines in Old English have one alliterating stave only, in Middle English nearly all have two, some three, and a few four. This involves the placing of alliteration on naturally unstressed syllables, and a further licence is the occurrence of alliteration on words which, though capable of stress, do not bear stress, being less important rhetorically or syntactically than another (non-alliterating) word in the half-line, as in the following examples from *Gawain*:

| | |
|---|---|
| Ly₃tly lépe₃ he hym tó | (328) |
| Gauan gripped to his áx | (421) |
| He dos hir fórth at þe dóre | (1308) |

The stress-pattern of the line, with its strong tendency towards a more regular rising rhythm, is dominant in determining scansion, and there is no basis for the assumption, often made in metrical studies of Middle English alliterative verse, that the number of stresses will correspond to the number of alliterating words, that a three-stave *a*-line, for instance, is necessarily an 'extended' metrical form. On the other hand, three-stress *a*-lines do seem to be admitted by some poets as a deliberate metrical variant, on the same principle that Dryden introduces alexandrines among his heroic couplets.

Other tendencies towards enriched alliteration include the running-on of the same alliterating letter through successive lines (a particular feature of *Morte Arthure*), the extended range of alliterating consonant-groups (*sn*, *sm*, *sl*, *sw*, *gr*, *cl*, *str*, as well as *st*, *sp*, *sc*, which usually alliterate as groups in Old English), and the reduction of vocalic alliteration, except where it is supported by the stronger aspirate alliteration.

The abandonment of the stichic, or run-on, system of Old English verse is associated with the virtual elimination of the compounding and variation which supported it stylistically. Syntax becomes more fluent, and the subordination of the *b*-line within the end-stopped long line means that it is frequently tautologous:

> Þan fettes hee a forcer freelich ischape,
> Þat wraught was of ivory wonderly faire;
> Sevin sterres, þat stounde, stoutlich imaked
> Hee showes forthe scheenely shynand bright. (*Alex. A* 628–31)

(*forcer*: casket [containing instruments for astrological prognostication])

Formulaic phrases are still prominent, and sometimes deliberately used for their archaic flavour—

> Stifest under stel-gere on stedes to ryde (*Gawain* 260)

but the most notable kind of formulaic usage, and one that any reader of alliterative poetry soon has ringing in his head, is the systematic employment of certain syntactical 'moulds', formal types of structure within the half-line which answer, at many levels of competence, the demands of a difficult verse-form.[22]

Certain developments in vocabulary, characteristic of alliterative verse, can also be associated, at least initially, with the verse-form. One is the enormous extension of vocabulary: alliterative poets use archaic and dialectal words, rare technical terms, and a vast range of French and Norse borrowings not normally current. Synonyms, some of them specifically 'poetic' and confined to alliterative verse, are multiplied, particularly for constantly recurring concepts, and words are often assigned unusual grammatical functions (as in the frequent absolute use of the adjective), or pressed well beyond their usual semantic range, producing, in extreme cases, that eccentric tumble of scrupulously alliterating words familiar to readers of these poems, and more familiar still in the later Scots alliterative poems. A large range of generally idealising epithets and adverbs are regularly employed: *clene*, for instance, occurs five times in 20 lines in the first part of the description of the Green Knight in *Gawain*, not once with specific meaning, and with some adverbs this non-specifying character is even more obvious:

Now schal we semlych se sleȝteȝ of þewes (916)

& þenne he meued to his mete þat menskly hym keped (1312)

To unlace þis bor lufly bigynneȝ (1606)

(*sleȝteȝ of þewes* : skilful display of good manners, *keped* : awaited, *unlace* : cut up)

Such words are virtually untranslatable. Many may be regarded as meaningful, at least in a poem like *Gawain*, in contributing to a general atmosphere of ideally courteous behaviour, just as the other features of diction become part of a cultivated art of poetry, but the characteristic pressures of the alliterative verse-form compel as well as encourage them.

## *The* Morte Arthure

The richness of diction in the *Morte Arthure*, to take now a specific example, and perhaps the most flamboyant of all, is astonishing. Alliterative patterns, far from imposing a series of constraints and exigencies, provide here rather an opportunity for the display of an unparalleled bravado. For Arthur's progress through Europe, a non-alliterative poet might have used verbs of motion like *wende* and *yede* and found poetic interest elsewhere; the alliterative poet concentrates on the verbs (and it seems pointless to remind ourselves that he had to), releasing the dynamism of the language and giving to the journey a resistless abandon:

Nowe bownes the bolde kynge with his beste knyghtes,
Gers trome and trusse, and trynes forth aftyre;
Turnys thorowe Tuskayne, taries bot littille,
Lyghte noghte in Lumbarddye bot whene the lyghte failede;
Merkes ouer the mowntaynes fulle mervaylous wayes,
Ayres thurghe Almaygne evyne at the gayneste;

Ferkes evynne into Flawndresche with hys ferse knyghttes.

(3591–7, ed. EETS 8)

(*Gers trome and trusse* : prepares his army and packs up)

There is a flourish in the handling of specialised subjects like feasts (176) and nautical affairs (740, 3601, 3652), a flaunting of technical terms, often desperately difficult in Thornton's spelling (the only MS is in one of his fifteenth-century collections), but, though often precious and obscure, the language is never bookish, like the aureate language of the fifteenth century. Violence, of course, is a perquisite of the alliterative style, as Chaucer recognised, and the battle-descriptions of *Morte Arthure* are thunderous:

> By that swyftely one swarthe the swett es by-leuede,
> Swerdez swangene in two, sweltand knyghtez
> Lyes wyde opyne welterande one walopande stedez;
> Wondes of wale men, werkande sydys,
> Facez feteled un-faire in filtered lakes,
> Alle craysed for-trodyne with trappede stedez.    (2145–50)

(*swett* : life, *sweltand* : dying, *wale* : noble, *feteled* : changed, *craysed* : bruised)

But it is a common mistake to think that these are the only effects the style is capable of. Eclectic sophistication is equally the mark of the *Morte Arthure*, a luscious and luxuriant receptivity to exotic borrowings, sometimes wildly playful,

> On a jamby stede fulle jolyly graythide    (373)

> He feyede his fysnamye with his foule hondez    (1114)

(*graythide* : equipped, *feyede* : wiped)

sometimes plain and serious,

> To ansuere the alyenes wyth austerene wordes.    (306)

Only again in Shakespeare's time, one would think, was the language so hospitable. Even with less exotic words there is a spirit of adventure abroad in the new extensions of meaning and new juxtapositions which is often marvellously effective:

> Planttez theme in the pathe with powere arrayede,
> To pyke up the presoners fro oure pryse knyghttez.    (1635–6)

Sometimes it is difficult to tell how apt an alliterative usage may have been:

163

Sir Clegis clynges in, and clekes another. (1865)

It is no accident that 'cheualers' on 'chalke-whytte stedez' are generally 'choppede' through (e.g. 2116) and it is unfortunate for the giant that he shares a palatal initial with so few portions of the anatomy:

Ewyne into inmette the gyaunt he hyttez,
Iust to the genitales, and jaggede thame in sondre. (1122–3)

(*inmette* : intestines)

On the whole the language is powerful and rich enough to carry such super-fluities.

It is in descriptive passages, however, that this solidity and density of language come into their own. There is no description in alliterative poetry—and description is its *forte*—quite like that of *Morte Arthure*, the giant of St Michael's Mount for instance:

His frount and his forheuede, alle was it ouer,
As the felle of a froske, and fraknede it semede,
Huke-nebbyde as a hawke, and a hore berde,
And herede to the hole eyghne with hyngande browes;
Harske as a hunde-fisch, hardly who so lukez...
Flatt-mowthede as a fluke, with fleryande lyppys,
And the flesche in his fortethe fowly as a bere. (1080–9)

(*froske* : frog, *fraknede* : freckled, *fluke* : flatfish)

Alliteration, with its insistent demand for heavily-stressed and therefore sub-stantive words, encourages this kind of concretion, and it is characteristic of alliterative verse to resolve an event or scene into its various simultaneous and particular aspects,[23] and so to profit by the cumulative tendency of independent line and half-line units:

Mynsteris and masondewes they malle to the erthe,
Chirches and chapelles chalke-whitte blawnchede.
Stone stepelles fulle styffe in the strete ligges,
Chawmbyrs with chymnes, and many cheefe inns,
Paysede and pelid downe playsterede walles. (3038–42)

(*masondewes* : churches [*maisons-dieu*], *malle* : strike, *Paysede* : crushed, *pelid* : threw)

But the poet of *Morte Arthure* obeys a more urgent demand than this, for his powers of vivid concretion of detail are engaged everywhere. Two warriors,

164

introduced to provide victims for Gawain and Bors, are momentarily ablaze in our consciousness, the one 'alle in fyne golde . . . in flawmande wedes' (1364–5), the other 'alle of pourpour, palyde with syluer' (1375). Descriptions of nature, an old device for narrative punctuation in epic poetry, are invested here with a gusto and a loving luxury of detail which only *Gawain* can match—the riverside wood near the giant's mount (920), or the new-mown field where Gawain's men graze their horses:

> Mawene and une-made, maynoyrede bott lyttylle,
> In swathes sweppene downe, fulle of swete floures.　　　　　(2507–8)

If this were all, one might praise *Morte Arthure* for the vigour and excitement of its language and leave it at that. But the rhetorical and syntactical skills of the poem are no less impressive, and demonstrate, incidentally, that the poet, like other alliterative poets, had access to learned traditions of rhetorical figuration. Descriptive passages may be constructed on simple lines, but the poet has the power of attending to the flow of the paragraph when he needs to, as in this passage from the Prologue:

> ʒe that liste has to lyth, or luffes for to here
> Off elders of alde tyme and of theire awke dedys,
> How they were lele in theire lawe, and louede God Almyghty,
> Herkynes me heyndly and holdys ʒow stylle,
> And I salle telle ʒow a tale, þat trewe es and nobylle,
> Off the ryealle renkys of the rownnde table,
> That chefe ware of cheualrye and cheftans nobylle,
> Bathe ware in thire werkes and wyse mene of armes,
> Doughty in theire doyngs and dredde ay schame,
> Kynde men and courtays, and couthe of courte thewes,
> How they whanne wyth were wyrchippis many,
> Sloughe Lucyus þe lythyre, that lorde was of Rome,
> And conqueryd that kyngryke thorowe craftys of armes.　　　　(12–24)

(*awke*: extraordinary, *couthe of* : familiar with, *thewes*: customs, *whanne wyth were* : won with war, *lythyre* : wicked)

Close analysis would reveal here the cunning interplay of balance and parallelism within half-line and line, the unerring control over the evolution of a long and complex sentence, the strength and elasticity of the whole. We would normally associate this kind of articulateness with Chaucer or the best prose. Alliterative verse may often degenerate into a helter-skelter of sound and hammering fury, but here one would hardly want a word changed.

Though from many points of view the *Morte Arthure* can be seen as above all a stylistic *tour de force*, and though the overwhelming impact of the narrative is one of profusion, richness and vigour, it is also a pondered telling of the story.

Freely expanded from some derivative of Geoffrey of Monmouth and Wace, it deals only with Arthur's European campaign and final fall, and treats it from the traditionally militaristic and nationalistic point of view, as an epic, not a romance.[24] The narrative is skilfully adapted to a tragic interpretation of Arthur's career, particularly by the placing of two prophetic dreams. The first precedes and is related to the fight against the giant of St Michael's Mount, Arthur's greatest single achievement, and one which he takes upon himself with a certain warrior-like pride, hiding his mission from his knights,

> For I wille seke this seynte by my selfe one. (937)

But no fault is seen in this, for he is fighting to defend his people, in truly heroic spirit. But the second dream, which comes when Arthur has embarked on wars of wanton aggression and conquest, brings in explicitly the revenge of time and Fortune, using the Nine Worthy as an exemplum of the transitoriness of glory and criticising Arthur in severely moralistic terms:

> Thow has schedde myche blode, and schalkes distroyede,
> Sakeles, in cirquytrie, in sere kynges landis. (3398–9)

> (*Sakeles* : guiltless, *cirquytrie* : pride)

This is as much a criticism of Arthur for being human as for being a conqueror, and we should recognise that there is no easy answer accepted in *Morte Arthure* to the opposed demands of glory and virtue. The tension is present in the attitude to the Nine, exempla of transience, but also immortals whom Arthur is to join. Arthur, whose lament over Gawain gives utterance to a sense of guilt which reminds us of a similar moment in *Beowulf*,

> He es sakles supprysede for syne of myne one (3986)

is the focus of this conflict between heroic and moralistic values, and in him it is expressed with profound poignancy.

*Other historical poems*

None of the other historical and quasi-historical poems of the revival quite matches the *Morte Arthure*. *The Destruction of Troy*, over 14,000 lines, is a competent and fluent paraphrase of the *Historia Destructionis Troiae* of Guido della Colonna (1287), one of the great source-books, with Geoffrey of Monmouth, of the Middle Ages. The poet follows Guido conscientiously through his endless battles and catalogues, omitting only a few learned digressions and mythological explanations. He expands little, though he has, like other alliterative poets, a taste for storms at sea, for which alliterative verse provides a ready vehicle, and which he turns into little rhetorical *tours de force*.[25] His handling of metre and alliteration is scrupulously and monotonously regular, and he mostly cultivates an unemphatic syntax: he is fond of using sequences of half-line units for abbreviated rapid narration, partly in imitation of the Latin devices *asyndeton* or *membrum orationis*:

> Þai kairen to þe cordis, knitten up þe saile,
> Atyrit the tacle, tokyn þere herte;
> Kachyn on kyndly, & þaire course held;
> Euyn turnit to Troy, taried no lenger;
> Past into port, proude of þere lyues;
> Lepyn up to þe lond, leuyn þere ship.              (2012–17)

(*kairen to*: go to work on, *Kachyn on*: pressed on)

His language is varied and versatile, tame beside *Morte Arthure*, but not beside most other Middle English poetry. Long before the end, however, the poem succumbs to its fatal facility and becomes a display of merely mechanical skills: the translation of Briseida's reply to Diomedes, 'Amoris tui oblaciones ad presens nec repudio nec admitto' (*Historia*, p. 164),

> Nauther list me my luff lelly the graunt,
> Ne I refuse the not fully þi frendship to voide              (8084–5)

makes one long for the simple prosaic statement of Chaucer's Criseyde—'I say nat therfore that I wol yow love,/N'y say nat nay.'[26]

The fragments known as *Alexander A* and *B* are similar in their comparatively plain and unemphatic handling of the alliterative style, though it must be stressed that such terms are relative, since the whole 'classical' school shares a common poetic. It is this that makes attributions of common authorship so plausible and yet so suspect (as well as pointless) for the poets not only draw on a common vocabulary and stock of stylistic devices but also imitate each other. There seems no good reason, therefore, for regarding *Alexander A* and *B* as fragments of one poem. The first tells of the battles of Philip of Macedon and Alexander's birth and boyhood and breaks off incomplete; the second deals only with Alexander's correspondence with Dindimus, king of the Brahmins (based on the *Collatio Alexandri et Dindimi*, one of the most interesting of the many medieval interpolations in the Alexander-legend), and is quite self-contained. Both poems draw on the Latin prose *Historia de Preliis*, though they use different recensions, and *Alexander A* adds much material from Orosius. Of their provenance, as for most alliterative poems, we know nothing: *A* survives only in a sixteenth-century MS, presumably the work of an antiquarian, and *B* is copied into a sumptuously illuminated late fourteenth-century MS of the French *Roman d'Alexandre* with a note saying that it is there to fill a hiatus in the French. There is in fact no hiatus, since the French is based on a different recension, and in any case the note is in

167

the wrong place. Clearly the scribe wanted to bring in a text of the well-known *Collatio Alexandri et Dindimi*, and the readiness with which he was able to do so tells us something of the MS situation in a medieval scriptorium. As for authorship, we may presume that the choice of a Latin prose text as source—as with other poems of the revival—indicates clerical authorship, a presumption strengthened for *Alexander A* by the further supplementation of the *Historia* from another Latin history, and by the deliberate insertion of a formal catalogue-description of Olympias, Alexander's mother (177–99), based directly on rhetorical models.

The author of *The Wars of Alexander* (sometimes called *Alexander C*), a more or less complete version of the *Historia de Preliis*, is a most conscious and sophisticated stylist, the 'poets' poet' of the revival. To the powerful syntactical articulation of the *Morte Arthure* he adds a fineness and delicacy of touch, and an obvious delight in matching the verbal intricacies of his Latin original, particularly in the formal rhetoric of the epistles which occupy a large part of the narrative (e.g. 4232–3, 4244–6); and where the diction of the *Morte* overwhelms us sometimes with an outrageous and intemperate delight, the verbal splendours of the *Wars* have deeper imaginative roots and a subtler effectiveness. Traditional opportunities for alliterative furore, such as the siege of Tyre (1361–448), are not neglected, and the brilliant display of ornate diction in the account of the arraying of Jerusalem to receive Alexander (1513–72) is perhaps unmatched in alliterative poetry. The wealth and extravagance of language, for which Alexander's adventures in the East provide further ample occasion, the expert vituperation of Darius' caricature of Alexander,

> Ane amlaʒe, ane asaleny   .   ane ape of all othire,
> A wirling, a wayryngle   .   a wawil-eʒid shrewe          (1705–6)

> (*amlaze*: imbecile, *asaleny*: little ass, *wirling*: dwarf, *wayryngle*: scallywag, *wawil-* : wall-)

the systematic concretion of the alliterative style, are all to be relished, but one remembers best, perhaps, those touches of vivid visualising imagination which make the story something more than a vehicle for pyrotechnic display: the moment in the death of Darius, for instance, when the Latin *semivivus* is expanded into four lines, culminating

> At ilk blast of his breth   .   þe blode fra him glidis          (3233)

or the magical bird that comes to Philip as an omen:

> Þen come þar-in a litill brid   .   into his arme floʒe,
> And þar hurkils & hydis   .   as scho were hand-tame;
> Fast scho flekirs about his fete   .   & fleʒtirs aboute,
> And þar it nestild in a noke   .   as it a nest were.          (503–6)

The poet, in fact, is trying to solve stylistically problems of imaginative control

168

which lie much deeper, for the great defect of the *Wars*, in relation to the *Morte Arthure*, is its failure to 'comprehend' the narrative. It is not difficult to understand this failure: the Alexander-legend, with its many accretions, was by now confused and incoherent in its basic moral and philosophical positions. The poet makes some attempt to shape a stronger pattern of destinal portent and the inevitable transience of human glory, but the most he manages is a commonplace tragedy of Fortune: the confusion of his materials and his own stylistic ingenuity, which elevates the particular without respect to the general, in the end defeat him.

The *Siege of Jerusalem* has a simpler story to tell, and manages it with gruesome effectiveness. The poem is itself a cunning interweaving of materials from Latin chronicles and legendaries,[27] whilst in style, being the latest of this group of 'historical' poems, it is imitative of all. Something of the close-knit quality of the alliterative school can be appreciated in tracing its borrowings from the *Destruction of Troy*, *Winner and Waster*, the *Parlement* and the *Gawain*-poet. The brilliance of its technique is undeniable, and the poet, through his style, gives an actuality to events which is far removed from the senseless fantasies and marvels of the rhymed *Titus and Vespasian*. If that actuality is often of a morbid and brutal kind, from the early description of Titus' disfigurement,

> Þe lyppe lyþ on a lumpe  .  lyuered on þe cheke;
> So a canker unclene  .  hit cloched to gedres  (29–30, ed. EETS 188)

(*lyuered* : clotted, *cloched* : clutched)

to the detail of siege-warfare and disembowelled elephants,

> Girdiþ out þe guttes  .  with grounden speres.
> Roppis rispen forþ ...  (566–7)

(*Roppis* : entrails, *rispen* : erupt)

and the famine and cannibalism among the besieged Jews,

> 'Entre þer þou cam out!'—& etyþ a schoulder  (1084)

the sources may be held responsible. But the poet's failure is that he embellishes without establishing any imaginative control of his own, and that an accomplished brutality of the visualising imagination is in the end put at the service of a crude and narrow vindictiveness. The *Siege* is a model of decadent poetic.

## The Gawain-*poems*

At the heart of the alliterative revival stand the poems of the *Gawain*-MS (B.M.

169

Cotton Nero A.x.4), *Pearl, Patience, Cleanness* and *Sir Gawain and the Green Knight*. Without them, the 'classical' revival would be a baroque episode; with them, it becomes one of the most important events in the history of English poetry. Nothing is known of the authorship of these poems, though it has become habitual to attribute them to the same poet. They have much in common, not only in stylistic mannerism, but also in use of imagery, particularly that of the pearl, and in profounder habits of thought. Perhaps the strongest argument for common authorship is the merely empirical one that poets so good do not usually come in twos and threes. The MS tells us nothing, only that the poems were thought worth copying with unusual care and worth decorating with simple pictures—a rare enough occurrence in vernacular MSS at this date (c. 1400).

*Cleanness* and *Patience* are homiletic poems: both begin with a text from the Beatitudes, and both recommend a virtue by portraying how God treats its opposite. *Cleanness* is often called *Purity* by modern editors and critics, in an attempt to evade a homely association that the poet is himself not at all reluctant to evoke. Indeed he begins with his own comment on how an 'urþly haþel' might regard one of his men who came to table

> Wyth rent cokrez at þe kne, and his clutte traschez,
> And his tabarde totorne, and his totez oute,[28]

(*cokrez* : stockings, *clutte* : patched, *totez* : elbows)

passes from this to the parable of the Wedding Feast (Matthew 22), and so to the theme of God's hatred of uncleanness. This theme is embodied in three main exemplary stories from the Old Testament, the Flood, the destruction of Sodom, and the fall of Belshazzar, illustrating God's punishment of three kinds of *fylþe*—sexual promiscuity, sodomy, and sacrilege (Belshazzar's use of the Jewish sacred vessels). The last may seem out of place, but the image of the 'vessel', pure or defiled, as a symbol of man has the power of associating Belshazzar's sacrilegious act with sexual uncleanness,[29] which is further evoked in the suggestion of orgy and sexual licence in Belshazzar's feast. Each episode has prefatory material: to the first is prefixed an account of God's treatment of Lucifer and Adam, to show how disobedience is punished 'al in mesure and meþe' (247) where uncleanness arouses, quite literally, God's anger, 'malys mercyles' (250). The story of Sodom is preceded by an account of God's visitation to Abraham, and the story of Belshazzar by an account of the beginning of the Jewish captivity under Nebuchadnezzar. These can be seen as further forms of contrast, but they seem fairly loosely integrated in the design.[30] In fact, one remembers the parts more than the whole, and above all the poet's gift for dramatic realisation and visualisation. The great descriptive set-pieces of the poem, such as the Flood, the overwhelming of Sodom, the Dead Sea into which Sodom sinks (a lurid passage taken from Mandeville's *Travels*), the sacred vessels, may display a kind of concretion different only in degree of power and precision from that of the *Wars* and the *Morte Arthure*; and a simile like that of sieved meal smoking for the fall of the angels,

Bot as smylt mele under smal sive smokez forþikke,
So fro heven to helle þat hatel schor laste                    (226–7)

may seem more aesthetically pleasing than dramatically powerful; but the poet's true uniqueness is in the way his imagination annexes every episode and projects it with breathtaking dramatic and human reality, the sad partings of friends and lovers at the Flood, for instance (399), or the comedy of Sarah's embarrassment before God (667). It is here that the poet's imaginative daring sometimes begins to undermine the Old Testament stories: it is not homiletically appropriate, for instance, that God should be brought down to earth so completely, and likewise the rendering of the story of Lot is so humane, his polite request to the marauding Sodomites to stop pestering his silk-haired angel-guests so plausible, that his offer of his daughters,

Hit arn ronk, hit arn rype, and redy to manne                    (869)

seems momentarily ridiculous. The poet encourages us to read in a way that is appropriate neither to homily nor to Old Testament. He is ambitious, with a well-developed literary consciousness that allows him a daring religious application of Jean de Meun's advice to lovers on how to please their ladies (1057), and an even more daring declaration by God of the unlimited play he gave to natural sexuality:

And dyȝt drwry þerinne, doole alþerswettest,
And þe play of paramorez I portrayed myselven . . .
At a stylle stollen steven unstered wyth syȝt,
Luf-lowe hem bytwene lasched so hote,
Þat alle þe meschefez on mold moȝt hit not sleke.                    (699–708)

(*steven* : tryst, *unstered* : undirected, *lowe* : flame)

The language here, with its evocation of *fine amour*, hints at complex relations of human and divine which are hardly realisable within the homiletic format.

To say that the poet of *Cleanness* got carried away would be false only if it implied that there was regret on our part at such transport, but certainly *Patience*, on its smaller scale, is a much more effective poem. The story of Jonah, through which the poet displays God's imperturbable patience contrasted with man's childish petulance and bad temper,[31] offers full play to the poet's brilliant dramatic gifts. The comedy of Jonah's evasions is exploited without prejudice to any of the story's moral and typological significance, and the language of dramatic realisation can now begin to suggest, in its own way, levels of hitherto unapprehended meaning. The famous simile of Jonah's entry at the whale's mouth, for instance,

As mote in at a munster dor, so mukel wern his chawleȝ                    (268)

is unforgettable as a visual image, but it also reminds us that Jonah's three-day sojourn in the whale's belly, as a figure of Christ's entombment, is a figure also of man's entry into the Invisible Church of the resurrection.

*Pearl* has no place in this chapter except in relation to the other poems of the *Gawain*-MS, for it is not written in alliterative verse. It uses a 12-line stanza, [4]*abababababbcbc*, of a kind not uncommon in the fourteenth century,[32] and a four-stress 'metrical' line with often heavy alliteration. The stanzas are grouped in fives by the varied repetition of an end-line refrain (not a mere technical device, for the refrains and the form of the repetitions are subtly related to the poem's intellectual and imaginative progress), and further linked by the systematic use of concatenation. There are 101 stanzas in all, exactly the same number as in *Gawain*, and the last line echoes the first, as in *Gawain* and *Patience*, as if to complete a circle.[33] The language is both precious and energetic, rich and precise, closer to the Harley tradition than to the revival, and far more controlled than either. Technically, it is one of the great masterpieces of English poetry.

It takes the form of a vision, in which the dreamer, lamenting the loss of his 'pearl' (an infant daughter), is transported to a heavenly landscape and there, across the river of death, is instructed by his daughter, now a Bride of Christ, in the ethics of grief and salvation. The poem ends with the vision of the Heavenly City of the Apocalypse, the dreamer's attempt to swim the river, awakening and resignation to God's will. *Pearl* takes a dramatic fiction for its basic structure[34] and invests this with unmistakable human poignancy, but its ambitions lie far beyond either elegy or conventional consolation. Essentially, it records a vision of superior and consoling truth, superimposing a transcendental view of human existence upon a temporal one, through a variety of metaphorical and dramatic techniques of persuasion. The central image of the pearl, for instance, is taken through a complex series of metamorphoses, beginning as a precious possession (and the father 'a joyleȝ juelere', 252), absorbing the pearl-image of the parable of the kingdom of heaven (Matthew 13:46) and ending as the very symbol of bridehood and communion with the Lamb. The immutability of the pearl is effectively contrasted by the pearl-maiden with the fading loveliness of the rose,

> For þat þou lesteȝ watȝ bot a rose
> Þat flowred and fayled as kynde hit gef.
> Now þurȝ kynde of þe kyste þat hyt con close
> To a perle of prys hit is put in pref. (269–72)

(*kyste* : chest, *put in pref* : proved to be)

and this in turn is reminiscent of a whole series of contrasts[35] between the luxuriant garden where the dreamer first proclaims his loss, with its remorselessly cyclic processes of ripening and decay, 'dung and death', including the dreamer's own earth-fast notion of death and burial ('That corpse you planted last year in your garden,/Has it begun to sprout?'),

> So semly a sede moȝt fayly not,

> Þat spryngande spyceȝ up ne sponne
> Of þat precios perle wythouten spotte (34–6)

and the unearthly paradisal landscape of the vision, all incorruptibly crystalline and metallic,

> As bornyst syluer þe lef on slydeȝ,
> Þat þike con trylle on uch a tynde. (77–8)

(*tynde* : branch)

Equally effective is the use made of the dramatic situation, first to draw us in to the dreamer's grief and make us emotionally aware of the need for solace, and then systematically to peg back every 'natural' human expectation. The dreamer's delight in finding his pearl is frustrated in his amazement at her tone of voice, which is that of Beatrice to Dante: she reproves him like a stern school-mistress for his incorrigibly worldly habits of mind ('Now haf I fonde hyt, I schal ma feste,/And wony wyth hyt in schyr wod-schaweȝ', 283–4), and when he turns to more general questions about her status in heaven and the justice of making one so young a queen in heaven—

> Bot a quene! Hit is to dere a date (492)

she preaches to him with decisive authority through the parable of the Labourers in the Vineyard (Matthew 20). Every speech and gesture is made to bring a divine scale of values—in which earth-bound views of existence, time and reward, however touching ('God forbede we be now wroþe,/We meten so selden by stok oþer ston', 379–80), are transcended—within the bounds of imaginative comprehension, not by contradiction and contempt, but by sublimation, meta-morphosis and paradox. Every word and image is under the same kind of con-trol—the unearthly glimmering of the vision of the procession, for instance, is conveyed through the simplest reminder of everyday experience,

> Ryȝt as þe maynful mone con rys
> Er þenne þe day-glem dryue al doun,
> So sodanly on a wonder wyse
> I watȝ war of a prosessyoun (1093–6)

so that we can say of this poem what Panofsky says of Jan van Eyck: 'No residue remained of either objectivity without significance or significance without disguise.'[36]

Sir Gawain and the Green Knight is not a better poem than Pearl, though it is more generally preferred, since it is not overtly didactic. Like Pearl, it is marked by a consummate control of every rhetorical and stylistic skill, every imaginative resource, and by the purposiveness with which these are all turned to a single end.[37] Technically, it marks a most important advance: the poet uses the traditional unrhymed alliterative line, but he varies the effect and avoids the monotonous hammering to which the line is prone in extended narrative by introducing a bob and wheel, of short metrical rhymed lines ($a^1baba^3$) at irregular intervals, creating a loose 'stanza' (varying from 12 lines to 37) comparable to the *laisse*.[38] The narrative flow is thus effectively punctuated, and the bob and wheel, in its turn, exploited in a variety of ways—for ironic comment, summary anticipation and recapitulation and particularly, since it is free from the pressures towards amplification and tautology, for abbreviated rapid narration.

The structure of the poem as a whole reflects the same care. The plot—in which Gawain fulfils the first public challenge, that of the beheading game, only to discover that his performance is to be assessed on the basis of another challenge, that of the bedroom temptations, which he thought was merely private—is a marvellous and ruthless machine for reducing the paragon of romance-heroes to hysterical self-accusation and sour self-contempt. The poem is a romance, and draws on many of the conventional motifs of the genre, but breaks with tradition in that the hero fails, and that not in a superhuman quest like that of the Grail, but in a simple matter of keeping his word and not playing false. The dénouement, in which Gawain finds out what has been happening to him, that he has been caught out, in fact, is a great tragi-comic scene of self-recognition. One's delight in the machinery of the plot is not dependent on suspense, and is fed at every turn by planned symmetries, as of the three temptations and the three hunts, and paradoxical contrasts, as of the pentangle and the girdle. In the pursuit of his game the poet shows himself a great master not only of descriptive writing—this we are used to in alliterative poetry—but of dramatic writing too. Every gesture is made to tell ('he droȝ doun his cote', 335; 'his ax he strokes', 416), every tone of voice is precisely evoked, whether it is the brusque contempt of the Green Knight ('"Wher is", he sayd,/"Þe gouernour of þis gyng?"' 224–5), the impatience of Arthur ('"Haþel, by heuen þyn askyng is nys",' 323), or the restrained politeness and diplomacy of Gawain's acceptance speech (343–60). In the temptation scenes, with their subtle interplay of seductive challenge and courteous parry, alliterative verse finally comes of age, graduating to that most difficult of dramatic forms, the comedy of manners.

*Gawain* is the first poem since *The Owl and the Nightingale* that can truly be said to tempt interpretation, and few have resisted. Some of the interpretation has been naïve, the invocation of vegetation-myths, for instance, or the allocation of any profound significance to Morgan la Fay (2446); some has been perhaps over-sophisticated, like the attempt to see irony in the portrayal of the Arthurian court, or the unravelling of hidden psychological complexities in Gawain's two confessions.[39] There has been some straining, too, to plot the nature of Gawain's dilemma in terms more narrowly precisian than the poet suggests, as if he had not made it clear, through the symbolism of Gawain's device of the pentangle, the 'endeles knot' (630), that failing, he fails in everything. On the other hand, the poet certainly leaves us with a question, whether Gawain is right to condemn himself so unreservedly, or whether Arthur's court (and the

Green Knight) is right in treating it as a very understandable lapse, considering. In that 'considering' is the hinge of the poem, for the best of men is inevitably drawn down by lesser frailties and in the end hangs on to life like grim death. It is a comic vision, generous in a measured way towards man in his predicament, but cool, precise, without warmth or tolerance.

The imaginative depths and recreative powers of the poem are not to be found so much in its moral patterning, which has perhaps received overmuch attention in our moralistic age, as in its inexhaustible resources of language. It is not merely that the poet conveys physical sensation—the biting cold of a winter journey, the furred and silken luxury of a warm hearth, the joy of the hunt—and physical action with unprecedented vigour and energy, though this is an element in the poem's intensity; nor that he embodies the sophistications of courtly life—feasting, hunting, exquisite dalliance—in language of unparalleled richness and brilliance of texture; it is also that through the language of his descriptions he suggests a larger dimension of human experience than is allowed for by pentangular virtues, shape-changing, magic girdles, and the rest of the apparatus of romance. It is a dimension in which the joys of life are confounded in transience,

> And þus ȝirneȝ þe ȝere in ȝisterdayeȝ mony;  (529)

in which the proud folly of building a code of social and courteous behaviour on a narrow base of ascetic monastic morality[40] is at last cruelly exposed; in which the external world of nature, so far from being a reflex of human aspiration and contentment, is imperturbably alien; and in which the most elegant grace of life and spirit only bring a man in the end to the moment when he lies awake in his warm bed, listening to the wind blow and the cock crow and waiting for the cold dawn, comfortless:

> Now neȝeȝ þe nwȝere & þe nyȝt passeȝ,
> Þe day dryueȝ to þe derk, as dryȝtyn biddeȝ;
> Bot wylde wedereȝ of þe worlde wakned þeroute,
> Clowdes kesten kenly þe colde to þe erþe,
> Wyth nyȝe in-noghe of þe norþe, þe naked to tene;
> Þe snawe snitered ful snart, þat snayped þe wylde;
> Þe werbelande wynde wapped fro þe hyȝe
> & drof uche dale ful of dryftes ful grete.
> Þe leude lystened ful wele, þat leȝ in his bedde,
> Þaȝ he lokeȝ his liddeȝ, ful lyttel he slepes;
> Bi uch kok þat crue he knwe wel þe steuen.  (1998–2008)

(*nyȝe* : bitterness, *tene* : torment, *snayped* : stung with cold, *wapped* : blew, *leude* : man, *steuen* : time)

Saints and romance-heroes do not live in this kind of world or have this kind of

175

problem, and, in rejecting both, the poet releases man into a world where he is, for the first time, truly alone.

### 'Classical' poetry: conclusion

Two poems complete the tale of the classical revival, *The Parlement of the Thre Ages* and *St Erkenwald*. Both have been associated with other poems, the *Parlement* with *Winner and Waster* and *St Erkenwald* with the *Gawain*-poems, on the usual flimsy grounds,[41] and perhaps neglected on that account. Both are splendid small-scale pieces, the former a morality-pageant, beginning in unrivalled exuberance with a brilliant springtime poaching scene (1–103) and ending, after a token debate of Ʒouthe, Medill Elde and Elde, with an encyclopaedic roll-call of the Nine Worthy and other exemplars of mortality (265–654), the latter a dramatic and powerful retelling of a miracle at St Paul's, densely evocative in its language, full of awe, mystery and sadness.[42]

I have suggested already that the classical poems of the revival, the product of a primarily regional school, annexed areas of patronage left vacant by the recession of Anglo-Norman, and that the choice of form was an attempt at elevation of status. The extent of this elevation should not be exaggerated, for we are after all dealing with a provincial patronage, however much it was enriched by aristocratic mobility. Indeed, there is a kind of ostentatious knowledgeableness about even the most sophisticated poems which suggests social aspiration: there is nothing in metropolitan court-poetry to correspond with the elaborately self-conscious correctness of the hunting and feasting scenes in *Gawain*. No doubt there are varieties of social expectation in the poems, but in one other point they exhibit a remarkable concurrence, and that is in the well-developed historical and moral consciousness that they display. This is not a matter of alliterative mystique nor of 'Englishness'[43]—in fact it is the character of much Anglo-Norman writing—but of books and learned traditions. These poets choose Latin prose texts where other English writers use Anglo-Norman and French poems (witness the difference between *Kyng Alisaunder*, the work of a gifted poet, and the alliterative Alexander-poems), and they sometimes manipulate a variety of Latin source-materials in a way that suggests access to libraries. Such libraries, such writers, and such habits of thought and traditions of historiography, are found above all in monasteries, and the nature of these poems would support the contention advanced earlier (p. 157), that the alliterative tradition, unlike the bulk of the best verse of 1250–1350, which was dominated by the influence of the friars and secular clergy and their special concerns, was a monastic tradition. For the close contacts of the large monastic houses with the nobility and the gentry, and for the generous accommodation that a monastery offered to vernacular and even secular poetry, we have only to refer to the example of Lydgate. It would not be necessary to suppose that all these poets were monks, indeed it seems unlikely, but clerics of the kind we have postulated as the authors of the poems would many of them have received their education in monastic schools.

Piers Plowman

If William Langland received his early education at a Western monastery, as seems probable,[44] there would be no mystery in his choice of the alliterative verse-form nor, in view of his subsequent move to London, in the modifications wrought in his practice of the style by his access to the broader traditions of the alliterative 'continuum', to vernacular prose as well as the alliterative tendencies of much rhymed verse. We must also reckon with the fact that he was not writing for a provincial and aristocratic audience but, based in London, for the widest possible audience, both clerical and lay.[45] Whether by accident of circumstance or design, he lacks, therefore, many of the classical mannerisms of diction, syntax and phraseology. His style has its own kinds of energy and particularity, but he is no conscious stylist, like the *Gawain*-poet: he is a missionary, a prophet, a voice crying in the wilderness, and niceties of language as well as versification give way to the urgency of communicating his vision.

Langland was a cleric in minor orders, married, without benefice, who eked out a living in London as a jobbing cleric, saying prayers for hire, one of the vast army of half-trained scholars who hung on the fringes of the ecclesiastical establishment and provided, as I have suggested before, one of the richest breeding grounds for writers of all kinds. The first version of *Piers Plowman*, the A-text, was written in the 1360s, and was begun, perhaps under the influence of *Winner and Waster*, as a topical narrative dream-allegory of the corrupt social condition of England (Prologue and Passus I–V)[46] and a vision of the reform of that condition, first through the action of Conscience and Reason at the King's court and then under the guidance of Piers Plowman (VI–VIII), a representative of Christian virtue in its apostolic simplicity. It becomes clear, however, during the ploughing of the half-acre, a concrete allegory of economic and social reform, that the good life, and the salvation that depends on it, are not to be won by external sanctions, and the first part of the poem, the *Visio*, ends with Piers's impatient tearing of the Pardon sent from Truth, which he sees as only a hollow answer to man's predicament. Salvation depends on a change of direction in the inner spiritual life, and the search for the good life, for Dowel, is interiorised in the *Vita de Dowel*, which follows. The dreamer becomes immersed in the problems of the speculative intellect as they are presented to him by a series of personifications, Thought, Wit, Study, Clergy and Scripture (IX–XI), and finding no end, 'in wandering mazes lost', finally rejects learning and falls back on the simple ideal of the honest ploughman (XII). The disintegration of the poem at this point is no doubt an honest record of spiritual crisis, and of the failure of even the most eager devotion to compass intellectually the mysteries of the faith. The second version of the poem, the B-text, was being written about 1378. It represents a radical revision, with much added material, of the Prologue and Passus I–XI of A, with a further nine passus added, altogether trebling the length of the poem. Langland takes us again through the thickets of intellectual speculation, but this time emerges with a more humble and comprehensive account, from a character called Imaginatif, of the validity of learning.

Much else of teaching on patience, poverty and humility is absorbed (XI–XVII) as the poem sweeps with ever greater certainty to its crowning vision of Charity in the person of Christ crucified and triumphant at the Harrowing of Hell (XVIII). Typically, in the last two passus of the poem (XIX–XX), Langland returns to the world, portraying the founding of the Church according to Christ's teaching, and then, back in fourteenth-century England, the gradual decay of the institution from within and insidious corruption from without (especially from the friars). The poem ends, full circle, with the dreamer going out once more in search of Piers Plowman, of the true inward bases of faith. The C-text, written during the 1380s, is a further revision of B, complete except for the last two passus. It is not so radical a reworking, and it has been castigated as the work of an old man, more narrowly doctrinaire and cautious. Certainly the poet here has a more austere sense of the perilous urgency of his task, and he discards some poetry of great imaginative splendour which he sees as impurely related to his task, but on the other hand he adds much new material, including the apology for his own life (C.vi. 1–108) and a passage on poverty (C.x. 71–161), which shows no decline in poetic power.[47]

*Piers Plowman* has been associated with many different kinds of writing, with sermons, with the literature of satire and social criticism, with scriptural exegesis, with mystical writings, with French didactic allegory, with apocalyptic and other theological writings,[48] in addition to the Bible and liturgy, which provide its constant sources of inspiration. None of these, however, provide a framework adequate to describe the poem. Certain broad outlines can be traced in its design: the *Visio*, for instance, deals with man in the world, in society, and with the right use of temporal goods, while the *Vita* deals chiefly with the inner spiritual life,[49] though neither category is exclusive, and Langland's notion of the inner life is always that of the Christian in society, never that of the mystic.[50] And again, certain key transitions stand out with brilliant clarity: the movement from outer to inner, for instance, as it reflects Christ's advice to the young man, of 'accommodation', contrasted with the desire for perfection ('Si vis perfectus esse . . .', Matthew 19: 16–22), or the Feast of Patience (B.xiii) when the dreamer first enacts the virtues he has learnt about, or the marvellous moment (B.xvi. 90) when the allegorical elucidation of the Tree of Charity suddenly gives way to the historical Annunciation, when Charity invades Time. But within these broad outlines, the structure of the poem is associative and idiosyncratic, the very sequence of materials often difficult to understand, its handling of dream and allegory shifting, inconsistent, opportunistic; what appears to be its main ordering structure, the triad of Dowel, Dobet and Dobest, turns out to be a façade, and the central theophanic character, Piers Plowman, a mystery; characters emerge, disappear, re-emerge, problems are taken up and dropped unsolved. By any standards but its own it is near to artistic breakdown.

Yet long acquaintance with the poem does not confirm the impression that it is a thing of parts only. On the contrary, it comes to have in one's mind, as a poem, or rather three poems, the strength and inevitability of an organic growth. This is partly because it *is* an organic growth, recording a deep and prolonged search for spiritual illumination and certainty, a purposive ordering of the contents of his mind, on Langland's own part. He obeys no rules but those of his own imagination,[51] and key passages and transitions are as likely to leave us bewildered (the Pardon episode, B. vii) as enlightened. Like Blake, he is mad in the sublunar sense, but his madness makes other poets' sanity look like time-serving.[52] The impression of structural integrity in the poem, in other words, is a reflection of Langland's own singular integrity as a man and a poet. All his poetry is informed by the same honesty, passion, indignation and pity: he returns again and again, with harrowing compassion, to the contemplation of misery and poverty:

> Ac pore peple, thi prisoneres  .  lorde, in the put of myschief,
> Conforte tho creatures  .  that moche care suffren
> Thorw derth, thorw drouth  .  alle her dayes here,
> Wo in wynter tymes  .  for wantyng of clothes,
> And in somer tyme selde  .  soupen to the fulle;
> Comforte thi careful  .  Cryst, in thi ryche.                    (B. xiv. 174–9)

(*ryche* : kingdom)

He accepts no easy answers, and grants no visions of grace till they have been dearly won. Friars, as the most vicious of all institutionalised parasites, he pursues with a dogged, almost obsessive insistence, but the same insistence makes his recurrent concern with more ambiguous groups, like beggars and minstrels,[53] a course of training for the awakened and uncomplacent conscience.

The sense throughout the three texts is one of continuous intellectual and spiritual growth, openness and receptivity, just as within each text there is a dynamic principle at work by which more and more is revealed to the dreamer as he grows in capacity to understand. The truths of the faith are expounded forcefully enough by Holy Church in Passus I, but the dreamer (and Langland) must learn them anew out of the need from within, and the poem therefore dedicates itself to giving a life more pressing and more dramatic to those truths, 'rendering imaginable what before was only intelligible'.[54] As a dramatic poem, a process of continuous but halting discovery, its procedures are ruminative[55] rather than dialectic, and Langland has no grand design, no scholastic principle of organisation. He was not a professional scholar[56] and tough and complex passages of exposition (such as the Tree of Charity, B. xvi) rub shoulders with the simplest kind of homiletic commonplace, but as a theologian he had tremendous intellectual energy, which often enables him to leap great divides that his scholastic contemporaries hesitated over, and an intellectual open-mindedness which enables him to entertain if not to endorse the most advanced speculation—one reason why he could be so radically misread by revolutionaries like John Ball in the fourteenth century and by Protestants in the sixteenth.

In *Pearl*, I talked about a transcendental order being superimposed upon a temporal one: there is never any doubt which is which, or how the one acts as a vehicle for the other. In *Piers Plowman*, a similar poem, similarly engaged in a programme of spiritual education, the two orders are inextricably mingled, so that the one *is* the other. The spiritual world is made concrete, the everyday world is spiritualised, dream is reality, reality is a dream within the dream (B.xi.4). This fusion of the literal and the allegorical, this surrealistic[57] levelling of all experience onto one plane of reality, is present in Langland's handling of dreamer, narrative, characters, space and time, and makes orthodox academic discussion of his 'allegory' almost impossible. It is present above all in his language. We have noted the concretion of alliterative language before, sometimes as bravado, a resource of self-regarding poeticism, sometimes as a mark of poetic energy or as a significant pointer to other levels of meaning. In Langland it is the very mode of vision. This is the way, for instance, he describes the origin in God's love of the Incarnation:

> For heuene myȝte nouȝte holden it  .  it was so heuy of hym-self,
> Tyl it hadde of the erthe  .  yeten his fylle,
> And whan it haued of this folde  .  flesshe and blode taken,
> Was neuere leef upon lynde  .  liȝter ther-after,
> And portatyf and persant  .  as the poynt of a nedle,
> That myȝte non armure it lette  .  ne none heiȝ walles.      (B. i. 151–6)

or the effects of the Crucifixion:

> The sonne for sorwe ther-of  .  les syȝte for a tyme
> Aboute mydday whan most liȝte is  .  and mele tyme of seintes;
> Feddest with thi fresche blod  .  owre forfadres in derknesse,
>     *Populus qui ambulabat in tenebris, vidit lucem magnam*;
> And thorw the liȝte that lepe oute of the  .  Lucifer was blent,
> And blewe alle thi blissed  .  in-to the blisse of paradise.
>
> (B. v. 499–503)

or on a smaller scale, the well-fed theology of the high table:

> Thus thei dryuele at her deyse  .  the deite to knowe,
> And gnawen god with the gorge  .  whan her gutte is fulle.
>
> (B. x. 56–7)

It is worth watching, in such passages, how every aspect of meaning—and some of the allusion is not at all obvious, as Bennett's notes show[58]—is animated and fused into a unique imaginative whole. Spiritual vision absorbs, sanctifies and is sanctified by a world of homely objects, just as Langland's similes for love both absorb and are enriched by human pathos and comedy:

> For thouȝ ȝe be trewe of ȝowre tonge  .  and trewliche wynne,
> And as chaste as a childe  .  that in cherche wepeth,
> But if ȝe louen lelliche  .  and lene the poure,

Such good as god ȝow sent  .  godelich parteth,
Ȝe ne haue na more meryte  .  in masse ne in houres,
Than Malkyn of hire maydenhode  .  that no man desireth.

(B. i. 177–82)

The concretion and energy of language, whatever it may derive from the alliterative form, is thus the substance of Langland's integrated vision. The literal is
invaded and possessed by the spiritual, the spiritual endorsed through the literal,
in a profound realism. 'The particular, the individual, the concrete, the fleshed,
the incarnate, is everywhere with the strength of reality and the irreducibility
of reality itself. Here is vision truly made flesh.'[59]


## The Piers Plowman group

Langland's vein of political commentary and satire and something of his more
pedestrian manner are taken up in two poems which are now usually yoked
together under the title *Mum and Sothsegger* (ed. EETS 199). The first, which
Skeat called *Richard the Redeles* and attributed to Langland himself, deals with
the events of 1398–9: it uses the heraldic animal symbolism, beast-fables and
name-punning of the prophecy tradition, and attacks Richard for relying on
favourites and flattering advisers, for countenancing bribery, intimidation and
extortion and—as familiar satirical themes take hold—for encouraging young
men to wear fantastic clothes and stay up late. The author mentions Bristol,
has a firm grasp of events, especially the Shrewsbury Parliament of 1398 (iv. 20–
93), and expects his poem to be noticed; he may have been a cleric in the civil
service.[60] He is garrulous, pedantic, and has a bustling way with the reader:

'What is þis to mene, man?' maiste þou axe...
A! Hicke Heuyheed! hard is þi nolle.

(iii. 62, 66)

On the whole, though he knows Langland well, he seems closer to the traditions
of Latin prophecy and political verse, such as Gower's *Cronica Tripertita* (which
deals with the same material in the same way). The second poem was discovered
by chance in 1928: it deals with the early reign of Henry IV, framing its commentary in terms of a conflict between Mum (the wise man who keeps tactful
silence, the time-server) and Sothsegger (the truth-teller). The poet spends a
long time looking for someone who will advise him about Mum (in patent imitation of the search for Dowel), visiting universities, friars, a mayor's banquet,
but finding Mum master everywhere. He falls asleep, and in a dream, wandering
through a charming pastoral landscape,[61] whose well-regulated bounty seems a
rebuke to the corruption of human society, he meets an old gardener who explains
some of the principles of bee-keeping, especially how to keep down drones, going
on to the obvious analogy with the commonwealth. The poet, waking, ends with
a forthright attack on political and social corruption, particularly the misuse

181

of litigation. The point of view is not elevated: the poet is really complaining about how the lack of a strong king (Genghiz Khan is suggested as a model, 1414) enfeebles the law and prevents small landowners, franklins and burgesses going about their business of 'winning' (there is not even grudging respect for 'wasting'). Imitation of Langland is close, both structurally and verbally, but often feeble and emasculated (e.g. 703), and the style in general is plain, with some quite untraditional syntactical characteristics (e.g. 570–5). Langland, it may be said, provides some verbal and structural tricks, but the essential tradition is that of Latin venality satire.

*The Crowned King* (ed. EETS 54) owes a similar debt to Langland, and has some of his muscularity of phrase, but Langland would have been ashamed to own it, for this short piece is straightforward propaganda for Henry V's French war (1415). In the poet's dream, the King, requesting a subsidy for the war from parliament, is addressed by a clerk who exhorts him to good governance, in the *regimen principum* tradition (below, p. 236). Pious prologue and epilogue complete a clerical *imprimatur* for Henry's action such as the King himself would have much appreciated. Langland's influence is much more authentically represented in a Wycliffite poem of the 1390s, *Pierce the Ploughmans Crede* (ed. EETS 30), an uncompromising attack on the friars. The poet, in search of someone to teach him the Creed, goes to each of the four orders of friars in turn, but they are only interested in advancing the claims of their own orders. The poet savages them with relish, for their lechery—

> Wiþ sterne staues and stronge . þey ouer lond strakeþ
> Þider as her lemmans liggeþ . and lurkeþ in townes,
> Grey grete-hedede quenes . wiþ gold by þe eiзen          (82–4)

and greed,

> A greet cherl & a grym . growen as a tonne,
> Wiþ a face as fat . as a full bledder,
> Blowen bretfull of breþ . & as a bagge hongeð
> On boþen his chekes, & his chyn . wiþ a chol lollede,
> As greet as a gos eye . growen all of grece;
> Þat all wagged his fleche . as a quyk myre          (221–6)

(*chol* : jowl, *eye* : egg)

and in the end gives them up in contempt. He meets a poor ploughman and his wife,

> Barfote on þe bare iis . þat þe blod folwede          (436)

and listens to a more direct, serious and homiletic diatribe against the friars—and learns his Creed. The little vignette of the ploughman, and his children,

And alle þey songen o songe  .  þat sorwe was to heren;
Þey crieden alle o cry  .  a carefull note.
Þe sely man siȝede sore, & seide  .  'children, beþ stille!'      (440–2)

with its enclosed tableau-like quality and slightly overwrought pathos, shows how easy it was to echo Langland's social compassion and yet to lack the deep and tenacious concern for the condition of humanity which gives such compelling imaginative power in him. Comparison with Langland, to be fair, dwarfs the best of these poems, even *Death and Life*, a poem of some conscious art. Composed in the early fifteenth century, and preserved only in a corrupt late text,[62] it reflects the influence not so much, as is usual, of the Langland of the *Visio* as of the apocalyptic visionary of B. xviii and xx. In it, the dreamer witnesses the confrontation and debate of Lady Life and Lady Death: both are vividly portrayed, more in the manner of pageant-allegory than Langland's passionate moral awareness usually allows (the portrait of Lady Life is in fact drawn from Alain de Lille's *De Planctu Naturae*), whilst the debate has an undisguised morality-play simplicity to which the characteristic alliterative concretion of phrase adds little.[63] 'When Eue fell to the fruite with fingars white' (272), for instance, recalls Langland's 'Tho Adam and Eve eten apples unrosted' (B. v. 612), but exchanges a significant little evocation of man's natural paradisal state for an irrelevant and perhaps even inappropriately class-oriented detail. The poem comes to its climax when Death, reproached for marring all man's joy, boasts of her power, even over Christ:

And with þat shee cast of her crowne, & kneeled downe low.      (348)

In the hush of awareness that follows, the dramatic Langlandian reversal and shift of level is completed: Life prays, and then unfolds, with some dramatic power and much indebtedness to Langland, the story of Christ's victory over Death—'But Death, how didst thou then?' (380). As an attempt at the sublime, the poem tries to do too much too quickly: it relies for its greatest power on its vicarious imaginative place in Langland's poem. To be a gloss on B. xviii, however, is no unworthy fate.

*Other alliterative poems*

There are a few unrhymed alliterative and semi-alliterative poems from the period which have little to do with the revival, even its modified Langlandian form. Alliteration and metre are so irregular in *Joseph of Arimathie* and *Chevelere Assigne* that their only formal identity comes to be their lack of rhyme. They are more the derelicts of the old alliterative continuum than the products of the revival. *Chevelere Assigne* is based on a version of the Swan-Knight legend which had acquired wide currency through being attached as ancestral material to the historical cycle of Godfrey of Bouillon, hero of the First Crusade. The English poem makes no mention of the association, presents the legend as complete in itself, in bald and prosaic language, without the fashionable romance-accretions, and tends to restore to it some of the vigour and violence of the original folk-tale. It is firmly in the tradition of popular romance, even to its touches of piety. *Joseph of Arimathie*, drawn from the early part of the French *Graal* and dealing with Joseph's adventures in the city of Sarras, is simple hagiography, full of miracles and marvels, and very suitable for inclusion in the Vernon MS. As in *Chevalere*, recognisable alliterative lines are the exceptional ones, though metre and alliteration become markedly more regular, just as the language is suddenly infused with energy, in the battle scenes (489–517). The half-line syntactical moulds and alliterative phrases stayed firmer in this conventional and obviously appropriate context, as we saw in Laʒamon, and as we can see too in *The Song of Roland*. This fragment, the only version in English of the *Chanson de Roland*, is really an alliterative poem in rhymed couplets, and though both alliteration and rhyme are loose and irregular, the general banality is redeemed by the residual vigour of the alliterative tradition in battle scenes and some other set descriptive pieces (e.g. 305, 336).

Such pieces as these would probably have come into existence, as the natural products of the alliterative continuum, without reference to the revival which, as I have argued (whilst trying to give a particular place to *Piers Plowman*), is regional, aristocratic, self-conscious, learned and high-style. Some other minor unrhymed alliterative pieces may likewise be associated with the general alliterative tradition, such as the Prophecies, which we have mentioned (p. 125 above), the *ABC of Aristotle* (alphabetical instructions on behaviour),[64] and some burlesque pieces,[65] including the brilliant *Satire on Blacksmiths*,[66] which echoes the noise of the smithy in a virtuoso display of onomatopoeic clangour, of which alliterative verse is at once the vehicle and the victim: there are even some joke-compounds (blacksmiths are *clopemerys* and *brenwaterys*). The use of alliterative verse, outside the region of the revival, for popular and burlesque pieces does not prove that its status in the South and East was necessarily low—there was a wide and respectable audience for *Piers Plowman*—but it was probably felt to be unfashionable, especially after Chaucer, and *Piers Plowman* itself would have been read for its matter, not as a 'poem'. At the same time, the native rhythmical four-stress line, the basic strength of the alliterative continuum, retains its fundamental character unimpaired. It appears with sporadic, occasionally heavy alliteration, in *Friar Daw's Reply* (c. 1420) to the Lollard pamphlet known as *Jack Upland* (a vigorous invective against the friars) and again in *Upland's Rejoinder* (c. 1450), whilst the presence of occasional alliterative lines in the prose of the original *Jack Upland*[67] shows how close the connection remained with semi-alliterative prose. The cadences and phrases of the native four-stress line flood back into the verse of Chaucer's successors, playing havoc with his finely turned but exotic pentameters, and accounting for much of the metrical confusion of the fifteenth century; and they continue to exert an influence, though more and more isolated for genre purposes, in Skelton, Wyatt and Spenser.

*Stanzaic alliterative poems*

Meanwhile, in the north, another group of poems, in rhymed stanzas, manifest the continued existence of alliterative tradition as a vehicle for sophisticated and high-style poetic. These poems may be divided into two groups, a North Midland and Northern group before 1400 or soon after, in a bob and wheel stanza, $ababababab^4c^1ddd^3c^2$ (*Summer Sunday, Susannah, The Quatrefoil of Love,* two St John poems), and a Scottish group of the mid to late fifteenth century, with the bob eliminated, $ababababc^4ddd^3c^2$ [68] (*Golagros and Gawane, Rauf Coilȝear, The Buke of the Howlat,* with *The Awntyrs off Arthure,* c. 1400, Northern, as transitional). The indication this grouping gives of recession northwards is probably not misleading, and it repeats a similar movement in the unrhymed poetry of the revival. Both schools represent attempts to create an effective poetic out of the alliterative tradition, both doomed to succumb to the encroachments of metropolitan fashion. On the other hand, the stanzaic poems are not a by-product of the revival, nor have they such a close-knit stylistic identity and cultural provenance: their lineage is in fact separate, since they alliterate systematically *aa/aa* (as must be the tendency always in rhymed alliterative verse) and go back directly to the poems of Harley 2253.

Of the English group, *Susannah* (formerly called *The Pistill of Susan*)[69] is the most attractive, a simple, romantic and dramatic retelling of the story of Susannah and the Elders from the apocryphal Chapter 13 of Daniel. There is no attempt to draw out the well-known typological significance of Susannah and her garden, nor to make a homily of it (cf. *Cleanness* and *Patience*), and the poet seems content with a tale of virtue triumphant. The language has some of the authentically alliterative concretion and vigour, and the description of the garden, one of the few passages the author amplifies, is a charming catalogue of trees, fruits, birds and spices, very much in the manner of *Annot and John* (above, p. 126). *Summer Sunday,* a vision of Fortune's wheel and the mortality of kings, is technically much more advanced. Alliteration is very heavy, extending to five and sometimes six staves in the line, and the ornate vocabulary and use of devices like concatenation associate this poem closely with *The Awntyrs off Arthure* and Awdelay's *Three Dead Kings,* as does the strange spectral quality of its opening hunting scene. *The Quatrefoil of Love* (ed. EETS 195) is quite different in character, being written in a plain style—as plain, at least, as this stanza allows—with light and irregular alliteration; the repetition of the first line at the end, as in the *Gawain*-poet, is one of the few evidences of conscious sophistication. On a May morning, the poet overhears a maid complaining that she has found no true love; a turtledove exhorts her to seek the four-leaf clover (a device for associating Mary with the Trinity), sign of the true divine love, which is then expounded in a complete and remarkably economical account of Fall, Redemption and Judgment. Maid and turtledove are quite forgotten, and the signification of the quatrefoil, which does little more than provide code-names for the persons of the Trinity and Mary ('fyrste lefe', 'seconde lefe', etc.) comes to

185

seem trumped-up. The two St John poems, the Thornton *St John the Evangelist* (ed. EETS 26) and the Wheatley *St John the Baptist* (ed. EETS 155), are both written in a variant stanza in which a tail-rhyme sestet of alliterative half-lines replaces the bob and wheel. Both adopt the apostrophic form (also used by Lydgate in the *Legend of St Giles*) for heightened effect, and the poems are evidently related. The Thornton poem uses full *aa/aa* alliteration and the lines alliterate systematically in pairs (a unique feature); in the Wheatley poem *aa/bb* is used as a regular alternative form of alliteration. Both are plain in style, and provide good examples of how a complex metrical technique can go hand in hand with a total poverty of verbal invention. They might have provided models for the use of alliterative stanzas in the play cycles, which we shall deal with later, in Chapter 8.

The second group is much more interesting, particularly *The Awntyrs off Arthure*. The title is misleading, for the two adventures concern Gawain. In the first, the court is out hunting in Inglewood Forest (in Cumberland) near the Tarn Wadling when Gawain and Guenevere are separated from the rest in a sinister midday storm. A fearful wraith from hell appears to them, Guenevere's mother, who warns Guenevere of the fate that awaits lechery and pride and Gawain against Arthur's overweening ambition and aggression, foretelling the fall of the Round Table:

> In riche Arthures halle / The barne playes at þe balle,
> Þat outray shalle you alle/Fulle derfely þat day.                    (309–12)

In the second, Galeron of Galway challenges Gawain to combat to recover the lands he has lost to him. They fight, Galeron acknowledges defeat and offers homage, which Gawain courteously sets aside by restoring the lands. The poem thus offers two related comments on Arthur, the first setting a profound sense of spectral doom[70] against the splendours of the court, the second contrasting Gawain's courtesy and prowess with Arthur's sometimes hollow and ruthless ambition. The links with *Gawain*, with its similarly sinister evocation of the eschatological imperative behind the courtly rituals, and with the theme of hubris in the *Morte Arthure*, are obvious, and there are further verbal associations with the latter which suggest imitation.[71] The two parts of the poem can be related thematically, but the second looks to have been grafted on to the first. The language is less vigorous, more conventional, and the poet, though he retains concatenation between stanzas, drops the concatenation between lines 8 and 9 of the stanza which is used so effectively in the first part.

The *Awntyrs* is notable for its vivid representation of courtly life and its genuinely courtly tone, in its accounts of hunting, feasting, dress and knightly combat. The same is true of *Golagros and Gawane*, another poem which questions Arthur's militaristic values.[72] It consists again of two episodes, both drawn from Chrétien's *Perceval*, the most important of which tells of Arthur's wanton aggression in attempting to secure homage from Golagros, whose castle he happens to pass. Gawane is pitched against Golagros to decide the issue and their strenuous combat occupies much of the poem. In the end Gawane is victor but Golagros scorns to ask mercy and Gawane, embarrassed, agrees to pretend that Golagros has won and be captured. Golagros is so impressed by this act of faith and courtesy that he agrees to pay homage, from which Arthur, after accepting his hospitality, releases him as he rides away. The poem thus turns out to be a competition in *gentilesse*,

It hynderis neuer for to be heyndly of speche                                    (358)

but the poet has a firm hand on the political implications (e.g. 282, 287). The language, as in the *Awntyrs*, is rich and forceful, prone to ornament and with the strongly idealising flavour of much poetry of the revival. If the poems have a fault, it is in the metrical form itself, where the spring and elasticity of the alliterative line is constantly hobbled by the precise conclusiveness of rhyme.

*Rauf Coilȝear*, written, like *Golagros*, in the latter part of the fifteenth century, takes up the theme of courtesy from a different angle, recounting Charlemagne's adventures when he is lost in the mountains in bad weather and has to take lodging, incognito, with a charcoal-burner. He is taught here, with shoves and clips on the ear, a few lessons in natural courtesy, particularly the importance of knowing how to receive hospitality as well as give it, and of not refusing, out of lordliness, the privileges of a guest. After this, with Ralph's return visit to Paris, where he is suitably awed and eventually knighted, the poem deteriorates into the complacent burlesque usual in other treatments of the theme of king encountering commoner.[73] The *Buke of the Howlat*, finally, is an ornamental and occasionally aureate poem, written about 1446 by Richard Holland, secretary to Archibald Douglas, Earl of Moray, and dedicated to the Countess. It is framed in imitation of the *Parlement of Foules* as a bird-allegory, using an old fable in which the Owl, ashamed of his ugliness and unpopularity, begs Pope Peacock and Emperor Eagle to call a council to do something about it. All the birds, clerical and secular, come to the great council, and the poet takes the opportunity to introduce an elaborate account of the Douglas arms ('O Dowglass, O Dowglass,/Tender and trewe!' 402–3) and the deeds they record (387–637). At the council, Nature decrees that each bird should give the Owl a feather to beautify him, but he grows so proud, 'So pomposs, impertinat, and reprovable' (924), that she takes them back. The appropriate moral is drawn, though the serious political meaning, which has reference both to those ambitious men who seek to advance by borrowing other men's feathers and to wider harmonies of church and government at stake in the conciliar struggles of the 1430s and 1440s,[74] lies deeper within the witty structure of the poem.

Alliterative poetry thus retains a vigorous life in Scotland well into the fifteenth century and we shall see, in dealing with Dunbar, Douglas and Lindsay, that its history does not end there. In England, as an independent poetic form, it was spent, and Caxton reflects fashionable taste in printing no example of it, not even *Piers Plowman*, and in his unusually systematic editorial elimination of alliterative vocabulary in that book of Malory's *Morte d'Arthur* which is based on the *Morte Arthure*.[75] Yet in Lancashire and Cheshire, and perhaps other parts of the north and west, the old traditions died hard: *Gawain* was still being read and imitated,[76] the *Destruction of Troy* copied and prized as an heirloom, the alliterative poems which went into the Percy Folio still being circulated.[77] And even if, for the future, there were only the eccentric interests of antiquarians, the polemic interests of the readers of Crowley's print of *Piers Plowman* (1550), the popular dissipation of the form and the ridicule of Shakespeare ('Whereat, with blade, with bloody blameful blade . . .'), the tradition died with at least something more than a whimper in the brave *Scottish Field*,[78] written by a gentle-man ('by Iesu'!) of Baguley, in Cheshire, in honour of the Stanleys' exploits at Flodden (1513), a poem in decent enough alliterative verse, unrhymed, evoking once more some of the old splendours.

# 7    Court poetry

The complex relationships of English and Anglo-Norman as literary languages during the Middle English period up to about 1350 have already been discussed (p. 88 above), and some demur entered against too strict a segregation or social hierarchy of roles. One constant factor in the relationship, however, is the exclusion of English poetry from royal and aristocratic patronage. The admission of alliterative poetry to the patronage of the provincial aristocracy and gentry after 1350 provided an important part of the cultural context for the last chapter; the admission of English poetry to the King's court and its associated metropolitan milieu is the starting-point for this chapter.

The title of this chapter, 'Court poetry', implies a relationship between social environment and literary production such as I have tried to maintain throughout, but it must be admitted that the growing complexity of the literary situation makes this relationship not always easy to define. The 'court' is itself an amorphous social organisation, and the dependence of individual poets upon its stimulus very varied. It will often be the case, therefore, that 'courtly poetry', that is, poetry expressive of the values associated with court society, may seem a better term than 'court poetry' since it does not insist on a direct social relationship. It may seem, furthermore, that 'courtly poetry', so defined, is insufficiently distinguished from some of the alliterative poetry discussed in the previous chapter, which had all the sophistication associated with courtly and aristocratic society. However, it is worth arguing for a distinction between the royal court and provincial households in a comparatively backward country like England, and worth insisting on the significance of Chaucer's role as an innovator, on the development of that role as being essentially related to his position at court, and on the influence of Chaucer in all the poetry discussed in this chapter. It is interesting, too, to remark in passing that the theme of nearly all this poetry is love, the courtly subject *par excellence*, whilst among the alliterative poems, despite a range of allusion that shows the poets (especially the *Gawain*-poet) thoroughly conversant with its ideals and language, there is not one that takes love as its subject.

The change-over from a predominantly French-speaking court to a predominantly English-speaking one was remarkably swift once it started: at the beginning of Chaucer's writing career, about 1370, it must have seemed a daring innovation for a poet with ambitions to the highest kind of recognition to write in English; by the time of his death in 1400 English was firmly established as the language of court poetry. Chaucer's poetry, in its bulk and quality, is the main evidence for this change, the main product of it, and perhaps even its major precipitant. It is hardly thinkable that Chaucer wrote no early poetry in French, of an ephemeral kind, for limited circulation. The circumstances of manuscript transmission and survival in the fifteenth century, which preserve one MS of Gower's *Mirour de l'Omme*, in French, against fifty-one of the English *Confessio Amantis*[1], would help to explain its loss. Such conjecture apart, the firmness of Chaucer's decision to write in English, signalled by the two translations from French, the *Romaunt of the Rose* and the *ABC* poem to the Virgin, which are thought to be his earliest works, is remarkable and almost inexplicable. Gower had no such certainty: his first poem, the *Mirour de l'Omme*, written perhaps with the *haute bourgeoisie*, the rich lawyers and wool merchants of London, in mind, is in French;[2] he does not attempt an English poem until the *Confessio Amantis*, in the late 1380s, when Chaucer has blazed a wide trail; whilst late in life, whatever date we assign to the original composition of the *Cinkante Balades* and the *Traitié pour essampler les amantz marietz*, Gower saw fit to dedicate them to Henry IV, 'Por desporter vo noble Court roial'.

The tenacity of French, in fact, eventually and inevitably to be rejected as it was, needs some stressing,[3] since it makes the unswerving dedication of Chaucer to English all the more remarkable. Though the royal court, the nobility and the *haute bourgeoisie* were certainly bilingual in the fourteenth century, it seems to have been a general assumption that anything formally committed to writing would be in French. Henry of Lancaster, for instance, the loyal fighting companion of Edward III and father of the Blanche whom Chaucer commemorated in the *Book of the Duchess*, wrote in 1354 a devotional treatise in Anglo-Norman called *Le Livre de Seyntz Medicines*, where, in making a conventional apology for the crudity of his style, he explains that, 'si le franceis ne soit pas bon, jeo doie estre escusee, pur ceo qe jeo sui engleis et n'ai pas moelt hauntee le franceis',[4] which indicates that French, though the natural language to write in, was not his first language. Froissart, whose native language was French, maintained himself as a poet and secretary in the household of Philippa, Edward III's queen, until 1369. Yet by 1395 the same poet and chronicler, delivering a book of his verses to Richard II, finds it worthy of note that the King looked in his book 'and read it in many places, for he could speak and read French very well'.[5] Perhaps Froissart was out of touch with conditions at the English court after his long absence, but his remark surely indicates a shift of emphasis in the relation of the two languages. As far as writing is concerned, one distinction that might be made is that French was reserved for business and official communication and record, English more used for private and personal matters: so Thomas of Woodstock, Richard II's uncle, wrote a short military treatise in French, but addressed his petition to Richard from Calais, where he was later murdered, in English.[6] On the other hand, the evidence of some personal letters in the possession of Lady Alice de Bryene at the very end of the century suggests that French was still the familiar language of upper-class society.[7] Any distinctions that we make between the two languages, whether written or spoken, are liable to be upset, and perhaps the most we can say is that, within a bilingual situation, the pre-eminence shifted from French to English during the reign of Richard II. After the Deposition, the decline of French accelerated: Henry IV was the first king to conduct government business in English, and Henry V the first who preferred to, and made a point of doing so. Perhaps the last bastion may be said to have fallen when the London Brewers' Company declared in 1422 that they would henceforth keep their records in English, in emulation of Henry V.[8]

## Chaucer at court

Chaucer's part in raising the status of English so that it could compete as a literary language with French was a vital one, and his position at court was the only vantage-point from which such influence could have been exerted. The history of Chaucer's career as a member of the royal household, as an ambassadorial secretary and as a civil servant is well-documented. From the first record of the young page in the household of the Countess of Ulster (1357), we can trace him through his various diplomatic missions to France and Italy, his enrolment among the esquires of the royal household (1368), his association, through his wife, with John of Gaunt (whose mistress, Katharine Swynford, was the sister of Chaucer's wife Philippa), his appointment as Controller of Customs in the port of London (1374–86) and as Clerk of the King's Works (1389–91), to a comfortable last decade as a royal pensioner. The richness of the documentation, the regularity of the payments of his various stipends and allowances, the intrinsic importance of the jobs that he did, all prove that he was a man of some importance in the court, certainly no mere hanger-on. His disappearance from the records and loss of office during the eclipse of Richard (1387–9) after the temporary success of the Lords Appellant suggest that he was closely identified with the king's own household, at least at that time. The rapidity, a few days after the Deposition on 30 September 1399, with which Chaucer penned an envoy to Henry IV (from whom he had already received marks of favour) to attach to his *Complaint to his Purse*,

> O conquerour of Brutes Albyon,
> Which that by lyne and free eleccion
> Been verray kyng, this song to yow I sende.[9]

suggests the growing alienation from Richard which most Englishmen felt during the last years of his reign, as well as the concern of an old man to secure his pension.

Chaucer evidently received royal patronage on a generous scale, but it is difficult to know exactly how this was related to his literary activities, if at all.

191

The major appointments were arduous professional jobs, not sinecures granted as a concealed form of literary patronage. He was valued, as far as the documents tell us, for his workaday skills as a secretary and accountant, not for his poetry. As for the poems themselves they offer little evidence of direct royal patronage. The Prologue to the *Legend of Good Women* (1386), which maintains the playful fiction that the legends are a penance imposed on Chaucer by the god of love for speaking ill of women in the *Romaunt of the Rose* and *Troilus and Criseyde*, is directed to Queen Anne, 'at Eltham or at Sheene' (F.497), and is clearly addressed to a court audience. The balade *Lak of Stedfastnesse* has an envoy addressed to Richard,

> O prince, desyre to be honourable,
> Cherish thy folk and hate extorcioun                    (22–3)

but princes do not usually offer their patronage in order to receive this kind of advice. The rest is speculation; and even the assumption that Chaucer was accustomed to read his poetry to the assembled court is based, we should remember, on the interpretation of a frontispiece to a *Troilus* MS (Corpus Christi College Cambridge 61) which has a by no means unambiguous relation to Chaucer's poem.[10] This piece of evidence is usually supplemented by reference to the intimacy and wit of Chaucer's address in a poem like the *Troilus* (e.g. ii.30), as if the immediate circle of the king's court were the only place where such qualities would be prized, and as if a great poet did not create his audience as well as the taste by which he is appreciated. Another supplementary form of evidence is drawn from the practice of other poets and households, such as Froissart's story of how he read his 30,000-line romance of *Méliador* to Gaston, Count of Foix, on successive nights after supper for ten weeks in the winter of 1388–9.[11] The picture we have in our minds of Chaucer reading his poetry aloud to a listening audience—to which we should add his practice of having his works copied by 'Adam, his oune scriveyn', for circulation among his friends (and sale?):

> Adam scriveyn, if ever it thee befalle
> Boece or Troylus for to wryten newe,
> Under thy long lokkes thou most have the scalle,
> But after my makyng thou wryte more trewe—

is no doubt a true one, but we should not identify the audience too readily with Richard's immediate entourage.

Indeed it is a matter for doubt whether Richard, whom we innocently tend to associate with any literary activity at court, was any sort of literary patron, though the general atmosphere of munificence and extravagance that he cultivated was no doubt stimulating. According to Gower's story Richard suggested a new poem (the *Confessio Amantis*) to him when he met him one day on the Thames,

Som newe thing I scholde boke,
That he himself it mihte loke
After the forme of my writynge.[12]

But this is the merest gossip, and the patron Gower actually sought out was Henry of Derby (Henry IV), to whom he dedicates the poem, and whose cause he later espoused vehemently in the *Cronica Tripertita*. Evidence for Richard's literary tastes is usually drawn from the contents of his library: a Memoranda Roll for 1384–5 lists Arthurian and Grail romances, *chansons de geste*, the *Roman de la Rose*, and other romances, all in French of course.[13] The evidence of such lists, however, as of all wills and inventories, is extremely difficult to evaluate. Many of these books were inherited, and some can be identified with those that came into Edward III's hands in 1358 on the death of his mother, Queen Isabel: what can these tell us of Richard's tastes? Again, such lists are always valuations of capital assets, and books may be recorded, just as they were often collected, because of their valuable bindings and illuminations, not because of their contents. The books that we are most interested in finding evidence of, that is, books in English, very rarely appear in lists and wills before the fifteenth century, perhaps for the very reason that they were designed for use and reading, not ornament and investment, and therefore never achieved the kind of status that legal documents are alone concerned with. What we know definitely of Richard's artistic tastes and commissions suggests that he was fascinated by delicacies, whether of miniature painting, embroidery, cooking or hygiene (he is credited with the introduction of the handkerchief), and books may well have fallen for him into the class of *objets de luxe*. Some books that he commissioned do survive: the only one that provides any sort of access to his interests is a book of Divinations, a *Libellus Geomancie*, which includes a treatise on physiognomy and a philosophy of dreams.[14] Perhaps Richard shared an interest in science and pseudo-science with Chaucer and Gower.[15]

It is just as difficult to know what the aristocracy contributed directly to the court culture which nourished Chaucer. Henry of Lancaster's *Livre* is alone sufficient to dispel the myth of the English nobles as 'growling and factious backwoodsmen',[16] but evidence of their literary tastes is not as easy to come by as evidence of their literacy. Occasional wills and the inventory of Thomas of Woodstock (by a legal accident, the only major inventories of the period, those of Burley, Woodstock and Scrope, are of the books of declared traitors) show that the nobility sometimes collected books on quite a large scale, but they are all in French and are evidence only of possession, as we have said, not of use. One of the few who can be proved to have profited by his education is Edward, second Duke of York (the Aumerle of Shakespeare's *Richard II*), who quotes from the Prologue to the *Legend of Good Women* in his translation (1406) of a French book of hunting.[17] The lines are garbled, but none the less valuable for that as evidence of actual reading and use of Chaucer. Gaunt, like the rest, is something of an enigma. He was a patron of Chaucer in early years and if we knew more of the library at the Savoy Palace (destroyed in 1381), where he kept a royal state, we might have more evidence of where Chaucer did his early reading. That *The Book of the Duchess* commemorates the death of Gaunt's first wife Blanche is not usually questioned: the grant of a pension by Gaunt to Chaucer in 1374 may be associated with the poem, though it has none of the character of commissioned funerary work. Thereafter Gaunt drops out of Chaucer's life. Of his son, the future Henry IV, we know more, and it may help to set Richard in perspective to recall that Henry Bolingbroke, whose usurpation Shakespeare represents as the triumph of the ruthless man of action over the artist of cultivated taste, was not only renowned for his prowess in tournament and for his extravagant personal tastes but was also a man of extensive formal education and considerable interest in learning.[18] Richard's characteristic innovations at the palace of Eltham were a spicery and a saucery: Henry added a room with large windows in which he could keep his books.[19] He bequeathed these interests to his sons, providing for their education with systematic care, and the reason that Henry V and his brother John, Duke of Bedford, both of them reputable patrons of letters and the arts, and above all his youngest brother Humphrey, Duke of Gloucester, the only patron of English letters in the Middle Ages who can bear any comparison with the great continental patrons, have a reputation inferior to Richard's is simply that they have no Chaucer to cause them to be remembered.

*The Chaucer circle*

For Chaucer's real sources of nourishment, for his audience, his circle, we have to look beneath the surface glitter of the royal court, to the multitude of household knights and officials, foreign office diplomats and civil servants who constitute 'the court' in its wider sense, that is, the national administration. It is here that we find men of similar background to himself, men for whom learning is equally a necessity of their professional lives, and whom the dynamic social mobility of the age—evidenced by the rise of men like William of Wykeham to the chancellorship (1367) and Michael de la Pole to the earldom of Suffolk (1385) from humble bourgeois origins, and already beginning to give way to a growing social stratification—has elevated to the very centres of political and intellectual activity. One group stands out, the so-called 'Lollard Knights': Sir Lewis Clifford, Sir Richard Sturry, Sir Thomas Latimer, Sir William Nevill, Sir John Clanvowe, Sir John Montagu and Sir John Cheyne.[20] The names of these seven are constantly linked in the records, and often with Chaucer. Four were Knights of the Chamber, close household servants of the King, and all had some experience of foreign courts, like Chaucer, through diplomatic and other missions. Montagu was a poet, with a reputation in France, where he was praised by Christine de Pisan (his poems, presumably in French, are lost); as Earl of Salisbury (1397–1400) and Richard's last faithful lieutenant he commissioned a French metrical history of the Deposition.[21] Clifford was a close friend of the French poets Deschamps and Otes de Granson, 'flour of hem that make in Fraunce',[22] and it was he who brought back from France Deschamps's poem in praise of Chaucer, 'Grant translateur' of the *Roman de la Rose*, which Chaucer answered allusively with extensive borrowing from Deschamps in the Prologue to the *Legend of Good Women*:

> And I come after, glenyng here and there,
> And am ful glad yf I may fynde an ere
> Of any goodly word that ye han left
> $\qquad$ (F. 75–7)

as well as playful echoes of his ballades of the Flower and the Leaf.[23] Clifford may have been godfather to Chaucer's son Lewis, for whom Chaucer wrote his *Treatise on the Astrolabe*, and it was to Clifford's son-in-law Sir Philip de la Vache, closely connected with this whole group, that Chaucer addressed his fine Boethian poem *Truth*.[24] Sturry was at the French court with Chaucer in 1377 and was an old friend of Froissart. Clanvowe was one of the witnesses to Chaucer's release from the charge of raping Cecily Champaigne in 1380;[25] more important, he composed the first 'Chaucerian' poem, *The Cuckoo and the Nightingale*, an elegant and accomplished love-debate with direct allusion to the *Knight's Tale*,[26] and also a homiletic treatise, *The Two Ways*, in which some neglect of sacerdotal privilege can be detected, though it is hardly Wycliffite.

A close-knit group of friends like this, with common intellectual and literary interests, exciting political and foreign contacts, a whiff of danger, are the real life of a poet, and furthermore they all lived at a time when what later became known as Lollardy was passing through its first phase, offering generous accommodation to speculation and scepticism as well as to personal anti-sacerdotal devotion. Lollardy was later to be found seditious and (therefore) heretical, and persecuted with the terror of *De Heretico Comburendo* (1401), a touch of fear from which the intellectual life of the fifteenth century never truly recovered, but meanwhile there was a moment of freedom. The importance of this freedom to Chaucer's kind of poetry (as well as Langland's) is incalculable.[27] And what is Chaucer's Parson but the Wycliffite ideal of the poor priest, purified of all spite?[28]

Chaucer's circle was not of course confined to the Lollard Knights. He also knew men like Sir Simon Burley, Richard's tutor as a boy and later one of the Knights of the Chamber, the inventory of whose library, compiled after his execution in 1388, is one of the very few that records a book in English, 'i livre de Englys del Forster et del Sengler';[29] and like Henry Scogan, later tutor to the sons of Henry IV, to whom he addressed a marvellous little occasional poem (with a begging envoy) of mock outrage at his repudiation of love:

> Hastow not seyd, in blaspheme of the goddes...
> That, for thy lady sawgh nat thy distresse,
> Therfore thow yave hir up at Michelmesse?...
> Now certes, frend, I dreede of thyn unhap,
> Lest for thy gilt the wreche of Love procede

> On alle hem that ben hoor and rounde of shap,
> That ben so lykly folk in love to spede[30]

and who himself composed a sober *Moral Balade* for his princely charges, full
of the memory of his 'mayster Chaucer . . . noble poete of Bretayne . . . that in
his langage was so curious'.[31] On a slightly lower social level, but still part of
'the court', there were government and city officials like Thomas Hoccleve, a
clerk in the office of the Privy Seal, who comforted Chaucer's last years with the
affection and earnest admiration of a true literary disciple, and Thomas Usk,
secretary to John of Northampton, Mayor of London 1381–3, also put to death
by the Lords Appellant in 1388, perhaps for his part in encouraging a Ricardian
faction among the citizenry. He wrote a long allegorical treatise in heightened
lyrical prose, *The Testament of Love* (1386–7), touched with Lollardy, which
draws on the same French reading as Chaucer as well as on Chaucer himself,
whom he calls Love's 'trewe servaunt, the noble philosophical poete in Englissh'.[32]
Among the citizenry too, the *haute bourgeoisie*, with whom 'the court' was closely
linked in every way (Sir John Montagu, for instance, married the daughter of
Adam Frainceys, a rich draper), and with whom Chaucer in his various offices
would have had particular opportunity to be acquainted, there were men who
loved books and poetry. The institution of the *Pui*, patronised by the Mayor
of London, seems to have been a kind of bourgeois Eisteddfodd to which burgesses brought poems in praise of loyal love and virtuous ladies: Gower's *Balades*
and *Traitié* would have suited very well.[33] It remains something of a mystery,
as does 'Adam, þe marchal, of Stretford-atte-bowe', who emerges briefly from
the shadows to proclaim his authorship of five prophetic *Dreams* (ed. EETS 69)
about Edward II. More substantial are the alderman of 1312 who wished his
sons to stay at school until they could compose reasonably good verses (in Latin,
presumably), or the two grocers of the 1390s whose stocks, inventoried after they
were bankrupt, contained four *libros de romaunc* as well as books in English.[34]

Beyond court and city there is also the importance of London, especially to
a poet of Chaucer's tastes, as a great intellectual centre,[35] less high-powered
than Oxford but more varied and more accessible to the layman. His dedication
of *Troilus* to Ralph Strode, a lawyer of eminence and a logician of international
repute, reminds us that Chaucer may well have received part of his education
at the Inns of Court; one of the less implausible speculations that have accrued
to the enigmatic *House of Fame* is that it was designed for performance at the
Christmas Revels of the Inner Temple.[36] Chaucer's extensive use, in the translation of Boethius and in the *Man of Law's Tale*, of the writings of Nicholas
Trivet, the typical scholar-encyclopaedist of the mid-fourteenth century, takes
on an extra dimension of local and historical reality if we remember that Trivet
was for a time Lector in the Dominican priory in London, while Chaucer's
mention of the scholar-theologian Thomas Bradwardine in the *Nun's Priest's
Tale* (VII. 3242) takes us back to St Paul's, where Bradwardine was chancellor
1337–48 and where Chaucer is presumed to have received, at the Almonry
School, his early education.[37] The school library at St Paul's was an excellent

one, and one of its important provisions was that scholars were allowed to borrow books from the library after they had left school. It contained many of the classical authors, for example Virgil, Ovid and Statius, that Chaucer is thought to have known, as well as the kind of miscellanies, *florilegia* and reference-books from which Chaucer derived his wide and scattered learning. Perhaps, therefore, we should think of London, with 'the court' in the widest sense as part of it, as Chaucer's literary milieu, and add finally to our picture of that milieu his long acquaintance with 'Moral Gower', co-dedicatee of the *Troilus*, and his tantalising proximity to Langland, with whom he must have crossed paths in the city for thirty years, and of whose work he shows at least some knowledge.[38]

## Chaucer: language, techniques and literary background

I have called Chaucer's decision to write in English inexplicable. Such it is, in the terms in which the decisions of a writer like Gower can be explained. Like many of Chaucer's decisions, it is a bold innovation masquerading as a natural and inevitable development and it is the extraordinary daring and incalculable opportunism of Chaucer's innovations that will be stressed in the following pages, since it is the aspect of his writing that most challenges the historian of poetry and one often obscured in accounts of Chaucer as a medieval poet or as a great poet, with all their predictable ambitions.

In choosing the English language, Chaucer chose a medium of much more limited range, especially of conceptual reference, than French or, of course, than Latin. He bequeathed to his successors an instrument of considerable resource and versatility, contributing thus to the enrichment of the language in general as well as to the rise in status which made that enrichment appropriate. The process is similar to that by which Dante established Italian as a status vernacular, the *volgare illustre*, against a background in which French (or Provençal) was similarly dominant as the international vernacular of court culture, and though Chaucer speaks of no deliberate intent and it is unlikely that he took Dante as a model, he is yet the first English poet to have a share in the classical concept of 'the poet', the first to show a concern for the correct transmission of his language and metre (a concern amply justified in the event) and the first to express awareness of the inadequacies of the English language as a medium for poetry:

> And eke to me it ys a gret penaunce,
> Syth rym in Englissh hath such skarsete,
> To folowe word by word the curiosite
> Of Graunson....[39]

Chaucer's contemporaries and successors speak of his language as 'curious' (much-studied), elaborate and highly wrought, and the tradition that he adorned and refined the language from its previous obscurity was soon established:

197

Noble Galfride, poete of Breteyne,
Amonge oure englisch þat made first to reyne
Þe gold dewe-dropis of rethorik so fyne,
Oure rude langage only t'enlwmyne.[40]

There is an element of conventionality in such praise, of course: his disciples speak of his achievement of an eloquent and ornate style, just as they speak of his sententiousness, because these are the virtues dictated by the critical vocabulary of the time as fitting to a great poet.[41] In the same way later ages, with a critical vocabulary no more infallibly attuned to 'permanent' values, will speak of his humour and realism, or of his cultivation of ambiguity, irony and paradox. Each age selects for special emphasis those qualities in a great poet which are most valued in its own culture. Yet those qualities are doubtless there. The difficulty for us, in assessing exactly what Chaucer contributed to the language of poetry, is that the way back to him is worn so smooth, through his own pre-eminence and influence as well as through the historical accident of his being a London poet and therefore at the sources of modern Standard English,[42] that we can hardly believe that his language was ever rich and strange. The opening of the General Prologue to the *Canterbury Tales*, for instance, is so smooth and so familiar,

Whan that Aprill with his shoures soote
The droghte of March hath perced to the roote,
And bathed every veyne in swich licour
Of which vertu engendred is the flour;
Whan Zephirus eek with his sweete breeth
Inspired hath in every holt and heeth
The tendre croppes, and the yonge sonne
Hath in the Ram his halve cours yronne...

that we may miss the correct 'register' of the language, which is markedly scientific and philosophical (*licour*, *engendred* and *inspired* are all technical words),[43] just as we may miss the effect that must have been created for contemporary readers by the use here of words that had rarely or never been used in poetry before. Dictionaries on historical principles are a help, of course, in analysing a particular passage like this, though a painful enough remedy for the losses wrought by time, the loss, above all, of a sense of the *quality*, the degree of formality, say, or of elevation, colloquialism or technicality, of Chaucer's language. The list of words first introduced by Chaucer from French, Latin and Italian is impressively long,[44] but it is overweighted by *ad hoc* forms used only once and by citations from the translation of Boethius, where technical problems almost overwhelm Chaucer, and gives only an arid account of Chaucer's creative achievement. For lexical innovation plays only a small part in the creation of a poetic language, which is virtually the task Chaucer set himself, and if it bulks large in the admiration of his followers for his 'gold dewe-dropis' and in their practice, in the cultivation of 'aureate' terms, then that bears witness to their difficulty in isolating the more intangible features of syntax and rhetoric as well as their poverty in imitation. The newness and richness of Chaucer's language can only be truly savoured by those who have been prepared for it by the plain diet of early fourteenth-century romance and religious poetry. Only then can one be fully sensible of the extent to which something like the opening of the *Parlement of Foules*,

> The lyf so short, the craft so long to lerne,
> Th'assay so hard, so sharp the conquerynge,
> The dredful joye, alwey that slit so yerne:
> Al this mene I by Love...

with its consummate ease and sophisticated urbanity, inaugurates a new age.

There is a natural inclination to look for the sources of Chaucer's poetic language in the work of his English predecessors, but the few brave investigations that have been made have turned up nothing but rubble. The one poetic tradition that comes near to matching his sophistication, that of alliterative poetry, was unfashionable in London and, except in its less highly-wrought Langlandian form, probably not widely known or fully intelligible. There was also a sophisticated clerical vernacular, as practised in the Harley lyrics, though it was always prone to fall back into rusticity. Apart from these there was the plain and sufficient language of the religious lyrics, which Chaucer never imitates, choosing instead the loftier idiom of Latin and Italian in the *ABC* poem (where he much augments his original in Deguileville) and the Marian invocations of the *Prioress's Tale* and the *Second Nun's Tale*; and there were the endless *chevilles* of the romances, which Chaucer satirises with merciless relish in *Sir Thopas*. The only debt, in fact, which Chaucer can be proved to owe to earlier English poetry[45] is one which he thought worth paying in withering scorn. Of course he takes over many conventional phrases, collocations and tags from these poems,[46] and turns them to effective use in the later poems in creating the illusion of conversational idiom, but they are no more than the rawest of raw material, and in the earlier poems in octosyllabic couplet often function quite innocently as padding. The attempt to see in *Sir Thopas* the root stock of Chaucer's poetic style, to see in the poverty of his poetic inheritance and the incapacity of English for a serious high style comparable with Dante's the explanation of Chaucer's persistent deflection into ironic and dramatic modes,[47] seems a perverse application of Auerbach's techniques. It ignores the fact that Chaucer did develop a number of high styles, the augmented hieratic style of the Marian poems,

> O mooder Mayde! O mayde Mooder free!
> O bussh unbrent, brennynge in Moyses sighte,
> That ravyshedest doun fro the Deitee,
> Thurgh thyn humblesse, the Goost that in th'alighte.

> (*CT*, VII. 467–70)

199

the courtly ceremony of the balade in the Prologue to the *Legend of Good Women*,

> Hyd, Absolon, thy gilte tresses clere;
> Ester, ley thou thy meknesse al adown;
> Hyd, Jonathas, al thy frendly manere;
> Penalopee and Marcia Catoun,
> Make of youre wifhod no comparysoun (F. 249–53)

as well as the rhetorical grandeur of the ending of *Troilus*:

> Lo here, of payens corsed olde rites,
> Lo here, what alle hire goddes may availle;
> Lo here, thise wrecched worldes appetites;
> Lo here, the fyn and guerdoun for travaille
> Of Jove, Appollo, of Mars, of swich rascaille! (V. 1849–53)

These styles provided the major Chaucerian models for imitation in the fifteenth century,[48] and they are not all of them deflated by the pressure of ironic contexts. Chaucer's low style mimetic mode, which we are bound to regard as his most memorable stylistic achievement, should not spoil our palate for his other varieties of style, nor should we underestimate the degree of artifice that went to its making.[49] The naturalness of what Coleridge called Chaucer's 'neutral' style (*Biographia Literaria*, Chapters XIX–XX), the apparent ease of the speaking voice, is the last triumph of art.

Chaucer's stylistic development is in part the history of his growing mastery of a more complex and ambitious syntax, metre and rhetoric than any English poet had previously attempted. His syntax, or at least that part of it concerned with the extended verse-paragraph, is from the start a French syntax, and Chaucer was long reluctant to abandon, even in his translations from Latin and Italian,[50] the props that French first provided him with. The extent of his debt in poetry is nowhere so great as in his prose translation of Boethius, where he follows Jean de Meun's French translation with dogged fidelity, falling into all kinds of crabbed and awkward literalness when he discards it, but French poetry certainly provided the models of a flexible and sustained verse-syntax which Chaucer needed before he could begin to restore to it the native colour and idiom which to us seem so natural. The techniques of adaptation are first practised in *The Romaunt of the Rose*, where Chaucer, translating at times very closely,[51] achieves smoothness of syntax and purity of rhyme at the cost of some padding. *The Book of the Duchess* is again marked by a certain thinness and diffuseness,[52] and only the charm of Chaucer's manner dissipates the longueurs. Some of this thin fluency is endemic in the octosyllabic couplet which, based on French[53] but lacking the compactness and precision of French, tends to prattle. In *The House of Fame*, in which Chaucer seems to parody many aspects of his own poetic development to that date, there is an occasional sense that Chaucer is allowing the form, which he calls 'lyght and lewed' (1096) to run into doggerel (509 ff) and self-parodying excess:

Telle me this now feythfully,
Have y not preved thus symply,
Withoute any subtilite
Of speche, or gret prolixite
Of termes of philosophie,
Of figures of poetrie,
Or colours of rethorike?                                    (853–9)

Having exhausted, and more, the potential of the short couplet, Chaucer abandoned it for ever and invented the English pentameter—and if this statement seems stark it may fairly be admitted that it is an over-simplification, since Chaucer had probably already experimented with the pentameter (as in the *ABC*, where he adapts the octosyllabics of Deguileville), but maybe its starkness is necessary to emphasise the boldness of Chaucer's initiative. The model was there, and had long been, in French, and needed only to be adapted to English accentual patterns, but the abruptness of the break with native rhythmical traditions,[54] in which pentameters had only previously occurred as freaks or accidents, is a quite startling example of Chaucer's technical daring.

Chaucer's pentameter is a true one, that is, a predominantly (but not invariably) decasyllabic line with five metrical stresses evenly distributed in 'iambic' rhythm, with reversal of stress not uncommon at the beginning of the line (and occasional after the caesura), and of course much variation, in accordance with the usual laws of poetic rhythm, in the playing off of rhetorical and syntactical stress against the basic metrical pattern. In the pentameter Chaucer found a freedom of manoeuvre which he first explored in a variety of 7-, 8- and 9-line stanza forms. Among the minor poems there are several which may record the stages of experimentation, and a piece like *Anelida and Arcite*, which never comes to fruition as a poem, is important as a proving ground for technical innovation. Shakespeare had Marlowe, Dryden his beloved Waller and Denham, but Chaucer had no one to do his donkey-work for him. The achievement of final control over the new form and its associated syntactical and rhetorical artifice is announced in the opening lines of *The Parlement of Foules*, already quoted. The 7-line stanza which Chaucer uses here, known as rhyme royal,[55] is adopted by Chaucer as his staple form for more formal and serious poems, such as *Troilus and Criseyde* and, within the *Canterbury Tales*, for those of the Man of Law, the Clerk, the Prioress and the Second Nun. The distinction of genre is consistent: there is no need to assume that these tales are early because they are not in couplet.

The pentameter couplet, presumably derived from the stanzaic line on the analogy of other couplet forms, is Chaucer's last and greatest technical achievement, and may be seen as a further attempt to extend the range and flexibility of the verse-paragraph beyond the more formal confines of the stanza. The Prologue to the *Legend of Good Women* may not have been the first venture into couplet (the *Knight's Tale*, in some form, is earlier) but again the opening has all the air of a demonstration of supple mastery, as Chaucer eases his audience imperceptibly away from shore:

> A thousand tymes have I herd men telle
> That ther ys joy in hevene and peyne in helle,
> And I acorde wel that it ys so;
> But, natheles, yet wot I wel also
> That ther nis noon dwellyng in this contree,
> That eyther hath in hevene or helle ybe....

The high drama of syntax is reserved for the opening of the General Prologue to the *Canterbury Tales*, where Chaucer, aware, like Milton, of the pregnancy of the moment for himself and posterity, maintains the paragraph flow with arrogant and unfaltering poise for a full 18 lines. Lydgate's desperate floundering after the same control[56] is a mark of recognition of Chaucer's achievement. With this mastery, Chaucer can now afford to open his poetry fully to the rhythms and cadences of ordinary speech and conversational idiom:

> And if he have noght seyd hem, leve brother,
> In o book, he hath seyd hem in another
>
> (*Man of Law's Tale*, Introduction, II. 51–2)

> But now, sire, lat me se, what I shal seyn?
> A ha! by God, I have my tale ageyn
>
> (*Wife of Bath's Prologue*, III. 585–6)

> 'Why so?' quod I, 'why wiltow lette me
> Moore of my tale than another man
> Syn that it is the beste rym I kan?'          (*Sir Thopas*, VII. 926–8)

Perfect ease and naturalness is plucked out of perfect artifice.

On a more formal level, Chaucer's handling of the self-conscious stylistic devices of the rhetorical tradition follows a similar development. He is not the first English poet to show an awareness of the tradition, but he is the first to float English poetry into its mainstream. The rhetorical tradition of the medieval Latin arts of poetry,[57] inherited from classical oratory, meant a good many things to medieval poets. It meant, in the broadest sense, the recognition of poetry as a species of eloquent discourse, a learnt and laborious art, not a mode of spontaneous self-expression: Chaucer would have shared this notion of poetry with most poets up to the Romantic period. It meant also the government of discourse according to established rules, both in the disposition of its parts, the methods of development or amplification, and the more detailed kinds of stylistic figuration and metaphor. There are many crudities in the medieval arts of poetry—many of them are mere pedagogic text-books—but the concepts according to which they are framed are of fundamental importance to all medieval poets. Analysis of Chaucer's debt to the rhetorical tradition has come far since Manly first drew attention to it and propounded the Romantic theory that Chaucer's achievement was to discard rhetoric.[58] There is now some recognition that the art which conceals art is no less hard-won, and that Chaucer's jokes at the expense of rhetoric, in the *Nun's Priest's Tale*, for instance (*CT*, VIII. 3347), which is on one level a full-scale parody of the pretensions of rhetoric, or in such sly asides as

> The dayes honour, and the hevenes ye,
> The nyghtes foo—al this clepe I the sonne                    (*Troilus*, ii. 904–5)

do not represent Chaucer's 'attitude' to rhetoric. At the opposite extreme, it may be admitted that the case for Chaucer's own direct knowledge of the arts of rhetoric has been overplayed.[59] This, however, does not strengthen the arguments for naturalistic style or organic form. Laurent de Premierfait, translator of Boccaccio's *De Casibus Illustrium Virorum*, recognises that eloquence may be learnt in various ways, by example and practice as well as by precept,[60] and Chaucer had in his reading of French and Italian a wealth of models for artificiality of discourse. We do not need to suppose that the line in the *Parlement*, 'Th'assay so hard, so sharp the conquerynge', was constructed after a consultation of Geoffrey of Vinsauf or Matthew of Vendôme on chiasmus. The figured artificiality of cadence was imbibed from French, as we may see by comparing another similar example,

> Wepinge to laughe, and singe in compleynyng

with its original in Granson,

> Rire plourant et en plaingnant chanter.[61]

These were the tunes that Chaucer learnt as he learnt what poetry was.

Chaucer's reading is as original, extensive and varied as his many technical innovations. He is the first English poet to absorb completely the *Roman de la Rose*, the first to use the newly fashionable French poetry of Machaut, Froissart and Deschamps, the first to use the great Italians, Dante (he has a rival here in the poet of *Pearl*), Petrarch and Boccaccio. He is far more adventurous than Gower, who is in most ways a man of superior learning. Chaucer's Latin is inferior to Gower's: his knowledge of the classical poets is limited, and probably largely derived from intermediate sources. In fact it is unlikely that Chaucer could handle classical poetry *in extenso* without a crib. Like Shakespeare, however, Chaucer made a little go a long way and like him he absorbed into the very body of his imagination and drew again and again on certain works which quickened his responses. The *Roman de la Rose*, Boethius's *Consolation of Philosophy*, Boccaccio's *Filostrato* and *Teseida*[62] are as much part of Chaucer's experience as experience itself. Even late in life, Chaucer still draws his first kindling warmth for the Pardoner and the Wife of Bath from the *Roman*. Like Shakespeare again, Chaucer has a power of imaginative penetration through which he can make anything he borrows inviolably his own. Sometimes he can take traditional material from the dreariest sources, as from a preachers' handbook by John of Wales, and by a shift of perspective, a new context, he can detach it from its antique moorings and push it out into the full stream of his drama.[63] The merest nudge is sufficient. On a larger scale, his recasting of Boccaccio's *Filostrato* in the *Troilus*, of his *Teseida* in the *Knight's Tale*, and of Petrarch's tale of Griselda in the *Clerk's Tale* makes them, despite many passages of close translation and a generally close adherence to the main story-line, into totally different and totally 'Chaucerian' poems.

### Chaucer as a narrative poet

To attempt some definition of this term 'Chaucerian' is to recognise that Chaucer is still out of our reach, despite the many assurances we have had that he is no different in his aims from other medieval writers.[64] He is the first English poet to provoke in us a deep interest in his personality, his 'real' nature and opinions: we search the portraits,[65] as we search those of Shakespeare, for evidence of the man, and equally fruitlessly, for no poet so systematically eludes us and defies discovery. Through consistent use of irony and of a fictionalised narrative *persona* he grants autonomy to his fiction, and with it to poetry and art, detaching it from authorial privilege and pressure as well as from exemplary function. The reluctance to commit poetry to an external moral function, or to an extrinsic function of any kind, is perhaps symbolised in his reluctance to end poems in any conclusive way. Many of his poems are unfinished or have jocular mock-endings: he writes conclusions to the two major poems (if we include the *Retractation*) but they are of such conventional and ruthless piety that they serve to make Chaucer's peace with the world rather than his poem.

It is through fiction, for he is above all a narrative poet, that Chaucer achieves the withdrawal, the evasion of authorial responsibility, which seems necessary to the fullest development of his freedom as a poet. If there is one group of poems that may be said to be neglected at the present time (though they were much admired and very influential in the fifteenth century), it is the minor poems or 'lyrics',[66] and the reason is perhaps that, though themselves the finest products of the rhetorician's art and sufficient, any one of them, to make the reputation of a lesser poet, they lack this freedom. Chaucer is either too much with us, in the unfamiliar role of moral guardian, or he is not there at all: in either case, the light and shade, the infinite recession of moral judgments into aesthetic perceptions, the feel for life, is missing.

From the first, it is this freedom to explore the world and to communicate something of the richness of a poet's and not a moralist's perception of it that he seeks. Even *The Book of the Duchess*, the first major poem and the only one with an 'occasion', is loosened from the stereotypes of elegy and consolation, as well as from those of the French *dits amoreux* to which Chaucer is so profoundly indebted, by the way Chaucer fictionalises the whole process.[67] The dreamer, groping his way forward, not only involves us in the comedy of his own misunderstandings but also, through the subtle prying open of perception that those misunderstandings involve, draws out the man in black to a more total and therefore consoling view of his loss. *The House of Fame*, attempting a more radical questioning of orthodox poetic procedures, is almost a poem about the impossibility of writing a poem, full of brave promises and false starts, endlessly about to be. The materials of what might have been several immortal poems are strewn about in comic confusion: is this it? the narrator seems to say, in his periodic and anxious spurts of energy. The mockery of every fit subject, of the poet's fear, bewilderment and undying hope, of the Eagle, whose earnest attempts to knock some sense into the narrator meet only hilarious frustration, is crowned in the poem's insolent incompleteness. *The Parlement of Foules*, though it retains a bewildered dreamer-narrator who seems the merest victim of circumstance ('Affrycan, my gide,/Me hente, and shof in at the gates wide'), contrives poetic autonomy in a different way, by setting different views of love and its part in human life—the relation of ungovernable instinct to a morally ordered universe, of sexual to procreative love, of courtly to domestic love—layer upon layer, in successive scenes. Chaucer's withdrawal from commitment, 'I wok, and othere bokes tok me to' (695), is in fact a very positive kind of commitment, since his reluctance to allow himself to be dominated by any one view is determined by his vigorous sense of the many possibilities open to a more generous understanding.

All these poems use or abuse the techniques of French love-vision, though the *Parlement* is enriched by Chaucer's first glimpse of Boccaccio's spectacular epic, the *Teseida*. Chaucer attempted one more vision-poem in the French manner, the Prologue to the *Legend of Good Women*, where he combines a guileless surface narrative and a traditionally witless narrator with a running series of subtle and playful comments on the complexities of the poetic art.[68] There is a sense that Chaucer is hovering on the brink again here, after the lofty and ambitious flights of the *Knight's Tale* and *Troilus*, and the delicacy of his hesitations is underlined if anything by the extensive revisions to which he subjected the Prologue. Some ends are tidied up, some contours reshaped, but the total strategy of the revision is as elusive as the original poem. The Prologue has a more pedestrian function as preparation for the series of 'legends' that follow, of women faithful and unfortunate in love, where Chaucer seems to be experimenting in the handling of shorter verse narrative. The subject proved a monotonous one and Chaucer learnt little from the experiment,[69] except that he needed a much more flexible framework if he wanted to continue with it.

The *Knight's Tale* and *Troilus* are Chaucer's major single poems, the ones on which he lavished most care and where his ambitions are highest. Both are freely translated and adapted from Boccaccio, who offered Chaucer new and brilliant models of autonomous narrative, the first, the *Teseida*, an imitation of classical epic, the second, *Il Filostrato*, a sophisticated contemporary love-story based on an episode from the siege of Troy. In the *Knight's Tale*, which as originally composed was not part of the *Canterbury Tales*, Chaucer offers his only large-scale attempt at a fully committed serious poem. By reinterpreting Boccaccio's

205

gods and goddesses as planetary deities and influences, and therefore aspects of Fortune, he gives a Boethian perspective to the tragic story, a perspective in which the arbitrary suffering to which man is exposed is at last reconciled with the view of benevolent universal government expounded by Theseus. This, at least, seems to have been Chaucer's design. It is not, however, exactly the poem's effect. The poetry of suffering, complaint and terror, the cruel vision of Mars, the cry of thwarted life,

> What is this world? what asketh men to have?
> Now with his love, now in his colde grave
> Allone, withouten any compaignye. (2777–9)

are more powerful than the poetry of reconciliation, more lasting:

> What governance is in this prescience,
> That giltelees tormenteth innocence? (1313–14)

Chaucer's sense of life is stronger than his sense of ritual, and the many surface irregularities and jarring incongruities of tone in the poem prove that he was incapable of tuning a narrative to a single over-riding purpose.

In *Troilus* he turns this apparent limitation into his greatest source of strength. Again he restores a Boethian perspective to Boccaccio's poem by adding many comments on Fortune and mutability and interpolating a long monologue by Troilus on freewill and predestination, but this perspective is one of several, not the meaning of the poem. The rain which keeps Criseyde in Pandarus' house on the fateful night is associated with the motions of the stars on high in their courses,

> But O Fortune, executrice of wyrdes,
> O influences of thise hevenes hye! (iii. 617–18)

but the effect of the passage is comic not tragic, for Chaucer has already shown the real decisions being taken—by human beings. Chaucer offers to his person-ages, especially Criseyde and Pandarus, an unprecedented quality of dramatic life, freedom and actuality which throughout books II and III is quite uncon-strained by any commitment to the idea that the way they behave proves a point, offers an example. Criseyde is not shaped to prove that women are fickle, nor Troilus to prove that love is blind, and the passionate desire that all of us, even Chaucer in the end, feel to draw out the infinite complexities of the poem into a 'statement' about life is earnest only of the profound revolution that the poem, with its inextricable joy and sadness, enacts in our thoughts and feelings. Chaucer secures the freedom of the poem in a variety of ways: by a full exploitation of dramatic modes, especially dialogue; by subtle manipulative shifts of emphasis and angle which keep alive the audience's sense of continuous living process; by techniques of layered and multi-levelled narration;[70] by the persistent dimension of comedy and irony which is contributed by Pandarus, Chaucer's own unrivalled creation; and by the use of a narrator who is charged with a bewildering variety of idiosyncrasy. The strains set up by the adaptation of Boccaccio's comparatively simple narrative are occasionally exposed, as at the beginning of book IV, but even these strains Chaucer absorbs into the structure of the poem by turning them into a hidden commentary on its artifice.

In the *Canterbury Tales* Chaucer sets aside the potential embarrassments of authorial narrative, as well as the singular triumph he won from the challenge in *Troilus*, by adopting a framework which claims to eliminate authorial responsibility and direction. The claim is an illusory one, of course, as he makes clear in some playful comments on realistic reportage in the General Prologue (725–46) and elsewhere, but all art is illusion, and the illusion of freedom is very important to Chaucer in an age which assigned an exemplary function to all kinds of narrative, even fabliau. Chaucer declares this freedom from the start, in the General Prologue, where every major portrait creates not only a character but also a context of values in which that character is to be appreciated and savoured.[71] Chaucer supplies a variety of kinds of moral and ironic commentary, but allows no simple moral arbitrement, and even portraits like those of the Parson and the Plowman give the sense of being framed according to their own not the author's values. In the tales themselves, set in the rich independent drama of the pilgrimage links, Chaucer revels in his freedom to explore the possibilities of autonomous narrative. It is not that he seems much concerned to develop very fully the relation of tale to pilgrim: some, such as those of the Wife of Bath and Pardoner, who both have extended 'autobiographical' prologues of a confessional kind, are obviously more apt than others to their teller, and have some function as extended dramatic self-revelation, but most are only generally appropriate. The 'dramatic principle' in the. *Canterbury Tales* has been much overworked:[72] having secured his freedom, Chaucer was most unlikely to compromise it by committing himself to a consistent dramatic ethic. What he wanted from the frame was a rich choice of different kinds of narrative and the indirection of authorial relation, the mask of anonymity, which alone gave him room for manoeuvre. The existence of the *Canterbury Tales* as a series of fragments, with many signs of fluctuation and partial revision, may bear further witness to his reluctance to commit himself to a total structure: arguments for the 'unity' of the *Canterbury Tales* based on the resolution of problems that Chaucer left unsolved may ignore the fact that the work's incompleteness is part of its meaning. At the same time, Chaucer makes us aware of some subtle relationships within the structure, as between the Wife of Bath and the Pardoner, between the Knight and the Monk,[73] between the *Merchant's Tale* and the *Franklin's Tale*, the gratuitous moral squalor of the one finding its complement in the equally gratuitous optimism of the other, or between the *Knight's Tale* and the *Miller's Tale*, where the latter suggests, among a good many other verbal, structural and thematic parodies of the *Knight's Tale*, that a man ('What is this world? What asketh men to have?') gets exactly what he deserves.

Chaucer deals in familiar genres of narrative in the *Canterbury Tales*—romance, fabliau, beast-fable, saint's life, pious exemplum—and sometimes he gives us little more than accomplished examples of the genre. But in his more developed work he extends each genre so as to catch up more and more of the richness, subtlety and irony of his vision.[74] Fabliau, defined in the *Shipman's Tale*, and lavishly enriched in the *Miller's Tale* and *Reeve's Tale*, is exploded in the *Merchant's Tale*, where the physical and emotional realities of fabliau innuendo are exposed with a disgust and cynicism so brutal and virulent as to be in themselves the objects of the mind's exercise. No one would be so foolhardy as to offer a 'moral' for the *Merchant's Tale*, and Chaucer deals in a similarly devastating way with the impertinent moralities of beast-fable in the *Manciple's Tale* and the *Nun's Priest's Tale*. Not all his handling of narrative is ironic, however. After some egregious parody of traditional romance in *Sir Thopas* and the *Squire's Tale*, he develops the romantic story of the *Franklin's Tale* with a delicacy and humanity which persuade us, if only evanescently, that virtue might be infectious. And if the *Man of Law's Tale* and the *Prioress's Tale* can perhaps best be regarded as exercises in certain modes of popular and sentimental religiosity (Chaucer is safe, of course, from the imputation that he himself was taken in), the *Clerk's Tale*, one of the most perplexing and powerful of all Chaucer's narratives, verges on suggesting that Griselda's self-martyrdom is a vindication and not a violation of her humanity. It would be no exaggeration to say that Chaucer uses narrative in the *Canterbury Tales* in ways that criticism has hardly yet begun to be able to describe.

*John Gower*

Chaucer's eminence obscures Gower's excellence, with the result that the latter has been most unjustly neglected, at least in modern times. In his own day his reputation stood high: testimony as varied as the translation of the *Confessio Amantis* into Portuguese and Spanish[75] and of the *Traitié pour essampler les amantz marietz* into English[76] is probably less important than the existence of forty-nine complete MSS of the *Confessio* (three times as many as the *Troilus*, a much shorter poem, and more than any other English poem except the *Prick of Conscience*, the *Canterbury Tales* and *Piers Plowman*), some of them elegantly illuminated—a mark of status very rarely accorded to Chaucer. On the other hand, he exerted little influence in the fifteenth century, was not much imitated, and seems to have been more respected than read, a misfortune which we may both understand, for he is exceedingly well-mannered and has a sense of decorum which can sometimes be misread as monotony, and deplore: the example of his purity and integrity of style and of the ease of his versification, which quite matches that of Chaucer within the simpler confines of the octosyllabic couplet, might have been more salutary for a lesser breed of writers than Chaucer's extravagant and inimitable singularity. His name is constantly linked with that of Chaucer and later with that of Lydgate, but the references to Gower become increasingly formal and peremptory, and Shakespeare hauls him on stage as narrator in

*Pericles* (he used Gower's story of Apollonius of Tyre as one of his sources) with more than a touch of condescension.

Gower acted out his life on a more obscure stage than Chaucer. He lived as a private gentleman, in Kent rather than London, probably much of his life in semi-retirement and the last part of it as an invalid. He had an interest in the law and in the speculative purchase of land, but held no office and received patronage only late in life from the future Henry IV. His story of how Richard II, in that hour of glory on the Thames, made the suggestion that led to the *Confessio* (Prologue, 34–85), should not be taken as evidence of more than a casual contact. Gower excised the reference in a later recension of the *Confessio* and confirmed the dedication to Henry of Lancaster, who rewarded him with a ceremonial collar. In all the growing vituperation of Richard and praise of Henry that shapes successive revisions of the *Confessio*, the *Vox Clamantis* and the *Cronica Tripertita*, there is no sense that Gower is acting as a hired man, a Lancastrian propagandist: he said what he believed, described what he saw—what most men saw, in fact—and Henry was grateful. 'Court poet', as I have intimated, is a term that fits Chaucer only loosely and partially; it fits Gower even less well, unless we make an exception for the *Cinkante Balades*. But of the qualities that go to the making of 'courtly poetry', sophistication and delicacy of sensibility, *gentillesse* and courtesy, whether we associate it with the royal court or not, he has all that is essential.

Chaucer's tribute to 'moral Gower' in the dedication to *Troilus* is not inapt for a poet who at that time (c. 1386) was renowned for the lengthy moral treatise in Anglo-Norman known as the *Mirour de l'Omme* and for the violent diatribe in Latin on the ills of contemporary society, the *Vox Clamantis*, to which he later added a spectacular allegorical account of the Peasants' Revolt. The *Confessio Amantis*, Gower's only major English poem, was not yet written. Chaucer's comment, however, hints prophetically at another reason for the obscuring of its later fame, namely, the insistence of Gower's moral concerns. Gower, writing perhaps under the immediate inspiration of Chaucer, for whom he declares his admiration,[77] and particularly of the *Legend of Good Women*, which is similar in providing a 'frame' for exemplary stories and in its extensive use of Ovid, begins his poem with a promise of variety and relaxation:

> I wolde go the middel weie
> And wryte a bok betwen the tweie,
> Somwhat of lust, somwhat of lore. . . .
> And for that fewe men endite
> In oure englissh, I thenke make
> A bok for Engelondes sake.           (Prol., 17–24)

(Since the 'fewe men' included Chaucer, the statement may appear odd to us, but it may be an accurate reflection of contemporary attitudes.) But Gower cannot descend from the pulpit so readily, and he first recapitulates familiar moral themes of human and social corruption in a long Prologue. The opening of book I appears to effect the long-awaited shift to more entertaining subjects:

> Forthi the Stile of my writinges
> Fro this day forth I thenke change
> And speke of thing is noght so strange...
> And that is love...
>
> (i. 8–15)

and we are soon embarked on the Lover's Confession, a seemingly playful variation on the theme of the 'religion of love', in which, as in a penitential manual, the lover confesses his sins against Love to Genius, the Priest of Venus, and, after listening to strings of exemplary stories relating to each of the Seven Deadly Sins (these 133 inset narratives constitute something over half the total of 33,444 lines), receives absolution. It soon becomes clear that Gower is not playing with any sophisticated amorous pseudo-morality, but is using love, because it is the focus of man's life, the area where his moral being is most vulnerable, and because of its intrinsic interest, as the point of reference for laying out a scheme of traditional and rational morality. Like man in general, the lover must eschew the deadly sins, including lechery, for 'fyn lovynge' is only the crown of fine living. The fruition of love is the control over blind passion, passion of 'Kinde', whose potential 'goodness' Gower nowhere denies, through the exercise of reason—

> It sit a man be weie of kinde
> To love, bot it is noght kinde
> A man for love his wit to lese
>
> (vii. 4297–9)

and the goal of love is marriage:

> Bot thilke love is wel at ese,
> Which set is upon mariage.
>
> (iv. 1476–7)

Gower is thus able to identify Lechery with Adultery, or *Gallica peccata* as he calls it in the *Vox Clamantis* (vii. 157–68), and the consistency of his conclusions was recognised by the several scribes who added the *Traitié pour essampler les amantz marietz* to MSS of the *Confessio*, with its Latin tag:

> Ordo maritorum caput est et finis amorum:
> Hec est nuptorum carnis quasi regula morum.

The Priest of Venus in all this fulfils a role more priest-like than venereal, and he is put in the peculiar situation, in book V, where the lover's innocent question about Vulcan and Venus prompts a long digression on Idolatry, of condemning his own mistress. Venus herself, in her address to the lover at the end of the poem, speaks the language of reason.[78] Gower is not at all reluctant to expose the inconsistencies and ambiguities of his fiction, nor to devote book VII to an ency-

clopaedic digression on Education, for in his conscious designs all fictions serve
and are validated by external truth.

If this were all, we might think that Gower deserved to be unread. His great
claim as a poet is that in the frame of the *Confessio* and in the inset narratives he
responds to human situations with a warmth and range of imaginative sympathy
which enables him to 'realise', in a way more compelling than any prescription,
the gentleness, courtesy, nobility and generosity of spirit that lie at the heart of
'fyn lovynge' and, with that, of fine living.[79] The portrait of the lover, on one
level, is full of dry and rueful comedy. Pressed by Genius for confession of sins of
sloth in love, such as unpunctuality, he replies that he never gets a chance to be
late for an appointment, because his lady never gives him one (iv. 271), and as
for sins of boasting (i. 2434), he only wishes he had something to boast about.
Like Pandarus, he 'hops alway behind'. Comedy is touched with pathos in the
several passages where he recalls his service to his lady, sitting with her as she
does her embroidery, playing with her dogs, helping her onto horseback, dancing,
leading her on his arm to church, little offices of exquisite pain:

> Thanne is noght al mi weie in vein,
> Somdiel I mai the betre fare,
> Whan I, that mai noght fiele hir bare,
> Mai lede hire clothed in myn arm. (iv. 1138–41)

The urgency of unfulfilled love is dissolved in the wistful evocation of sentiment,
and passion emasculated in the cultivation of a refinement of feeling which is,
as a purification of the will, its own reward. At the end of the poem, in an epilogue
which moves near to the realities of age and death, the superannuated lover is
retired from the service of love, as Cupid gropes his way towards him to pluck
out the 'fyri Lancegay' (viii. 2798), and Venus, with the reminder,

> Remembre wel hou thou art old, (viii. 2439)

recommends to him a 'beau retret' and pensions him off with a black necklace
inscribed *Por reposer*.

The tenderness of Gower's writing in the frame-narrative is something unexpected from a seasoned moralist, but it is in the exemplary stories that his
imagination as a poet finds its fullest freedom. He takes these narratives far
beyond their prescriptive or exemplary function, into a world where virtuous
conduct is seen to spring from fineness and unconstrained decency of feeling,
not from obedience to law, and where Vice is cast out and despised as intrinsically base and ignoble. With many of the stories from Ovid, what Gower does,
essentially, is to stake them out in a world of consistent moral values and civilised
feelings: through this means he makes sense, in human terms, even of a story so
inhuman as that of Tereus (v. 5551). A pious anecdote like that of Constantine,
who refuses the barbaric cure for his leprosy suggested by his physicians (a bath
of infants' blood), becomes in Gower's handling (ii. 3187) a moving exploration

of the inward sources of compassion. Chaucer has a favourite line, 'Pitee renneth soone in gentil herte', which he plays with in a variety of ironic and unironic contexts; Gower, with a quite un-Chaucerian directness, goes simply to the heart of the matter and shows its truth in action. Not all Gower's narratives, it will be seen, concern love, and neither lover nor confessor hesitate to remind us of this inconsistency, but it is the love stories that call forth his warmest imaginative response. To the situation of the traditional plaintiff of love, the woman betrayed, forsaken or violated, Thisbe, Phillis, Ceix, Lucrece (iii. 1331, iv. 731, 2927, vii. 4593), he gives a pathos more poignant because what is lost is so movingly evoked; to the story of Jason and Medea (v. 3247) he gives something of the freedom that Chaucer secured for *Troilus*, by refusing, in the same way as Chaucer, to be bound by stereotyped interpretations of human behaviour; and to Canacee's incestuous love, in one of the most touching of his narratives (iii. 143), he gives a sympathy as generous and spontaneous as it is just. Not all his subject-matter is responsive in the same way: some of the starker classical stories, as of Orestes (iii. 1885) and Hercules (ii. 2145), are beyond him, and he makes a nonsensical allusion to *Troilus* (vii. 7597), but we feel at the end that Gower, whatever role as moralist or guardian of the nation's conscience he cast himself for, understood in his poetry the 'civilisation of the heart'.

### Fifteenth-century courtly tradition

The death of Chaucer in 1400, and of Richard II in the same year, make a convenient period for histories of literature, and one fitting to the presentation of the fifteenth century as a lifeless interval before the Renaissance. The fifteenth century, however, is no more autonomous than any other, and I have chosen to stress, therefore, the strength and continuity of the traditions that Chaucer established by now taking the story of 'court poetry' up to the third quarter of the fifteenth century. Chaucer's influence is not confined to court poetry, of course, nor does it end there: his poetry went on being read and printed, and indeed enjoyed an Indian summer in the years following the publication of Thynne's collected edition of Chaucer and Chaucerian poetry in 1532. Nevertheless, the courtly Chaucerian tradition, embodied as it is in a remarkably homogeneous body of poetry (nearly all in rhyme royal and ballade stanza) and affected only by some modest infusions of French and Burgundian influence, ceases to be strictly definable, in both England and Scotland, towards the end of the century, as it is merged in other and more powerful influences from the continent. These more complex patterns of development will be dealt with in their proper place at the end of the next chapter.

'Court poetry' has been understood in the discussion so far to include both the poetry produced in and for a court environment (accepting the term 'court' in the broadest sense) and also poetry reflecting the values and sensibilities of that environment (i.e. 'courtly poetry'). The two are often the same, but the sense of a possible distinction is more necessary than ever in the fifteenth century, when the relationship of court poetry to court culture is often speculative, the poetry itself largely anonymous,[80] and its popularity among the provincial gentry and the urban middle classes well-documented. There is no need to assume that court poetry lives on in a kind of limbo, divorced from court culture. There were royal and aristocratic patrons of letters in the fifteenth century with better taste and education than Richard II, and courts just as brilliant and diverse as his court, notably perhaps the quasi-royal household of Humphrey, Duke of Gloucester, in the 1420s and 1430s, the court of Margaret of Anjou in the years after she became Henry VI's Queen in 1446, and the court of Edward IV in the 1470s. The last two had strong continental associations. In the nature of things, however, the patronage of a man like Gloucester is documented for poems that cannot be called 'courtly', such as Lydgate's *Fall of Princes*, whilst the courtly poetry of love, whatever its associations with court culture, remains, as coterie-verse, largely anonymous. Furthermore, the kind of manuscript in which this poetry is disseminated proves only how wide was its appeal outside the immediate confines of the courts. Much of the minor courtly poetry of Chaucer and Lydgate, and others, is preserved in the miscellanies and anthologies of John Shirley, who ran a flourishing commercial scriptorium and bookselling business in London (c. 1420–50).[81] His activities were not confined to copying and selling books, for he also ran the equivalent of a lending library, loaning books out to customers and providing, in his loquacious headings to poems, something very close to a publisher's 'blurb'. His clientele was varied, and he has a wide range of court gossip to retail, some of it from below stairs. His knowledge of Lydgate seems especially detailed, and his many marginal jokes at Lydgate's expense ('Be stille daun Iohan. Suche is youre fortune', when the monk complains, *in persona*, of his lack of success in love) suggest a quite close association: he acted, in effect, as Lydgate's literary agent in London. His MSS and their derivatives provided source-materials for collectors until well into the sixteenth century. Similar collections of 'Chauceriana' were being made by other copyists throughout the fifteenth century, sometimes at the behest of wealthy individuals, more often as a speculative commercial venture. The frequency of 'fascicular' MSS indicates how booksellers would keep separate quires of poems, ready copied, in stock, to be bound up to the tastes of particular customers. Some MSS, such as C.U.L. MS Gg. iv.27 and Bodley MS Fairfax 16,[82] contain only courtly and quasi-courtly poetry, and may represent the tastes of book-owners not far from the court circle itself; others are more varied and miscellaneous, and find their way usually into the possession of the well-to-do provincial gentry. C.U.L. MS Ff.i.6 is particularly interesting as a collection of courtly poems (by Chaucer, Lydgate, Hoccleve and Roos) and fashionable lyrics, which seems to have been copied partly by the ladies of a Derbyshire family and their neighbours, partly by itinerant scribes.[83] What is 'court poetry' by provenance becomes 'courtly poetry' by dissemination, in turn providing models for provincial composition.

The Chaucer of this tradition is primarily the Chaucer of the love-visions, the *Troilus* (sometimes excerpted for its inset 'lyric' poems), the lyrics and, among the *Canterbury Tales*, the *Knight's Tale* and the *Franklin's Tale*, in other words the

213

poet of love. Whether or not he was the only begetter of the tradition in English (his quotation of a scrap of love-poetry, the original of which has now been discovered,[84] in the *Complaynt d'Amours*, 24–5, suggests that there was already an embryonic tradition of courtly love-complaint), he was certainly so regarded. His love-poetry is inherited in simplified form, purged of ambiguity, and distilled further in the alembic of Lydgate's imagination, to give the thin, disembodied and motionless fervour which is characteristic of the fifteenth-century courtly tradition. Lydgate is here, as elsewhere, of fundamental importance as Chaucer's literary executor and the mediator of his influence to his successors.[85] The fact that Lydgate was a monk is of some importance here: though his life was by no means narrowly confined to the cloister, nor the cloister itself a narrow vocation, yet his role as a courtly poet was inevitably ambiguous, as Shirley perhaps recognises in his teasing comments, and it is a natural consequence that the poetry of love should appear in Lydgate strained pure of all sensuality and elevated into a form of 'service' and suffering barely distinguishable from general moral discipline.[86] His shorter love-poems are mostly complaints of loyal, enduring and unrequited love and eulogies of the lover's mistress. Like most courtly love-poems they are occasional poems of which the occasion has been lost, though Shirley gives a clue to Lydgate's role in one of his rubrics: 'Loo here begynneþe a balade whiche þat Lydegate wrote at þe request of a squyer þat serued in loves court'.[87] Lydgate was the professional craftsman who supplied the complaints and epistles of love's service, suitably void—and in this much to Lydgate's taste—of individual reference or concrete detail (*The Floure of Curtesy*, for instance, manages a 112-line praise of the lover's mistress entirely assembled from impersonal and abstract 'topics' or commonplaces). The service of love was a game, but a game that was actually played, and we deprive these poems of their essential roots if we treat them solely as literary exercises.

Lydgate's more ambitious courtly poems, *The Complaint of the Black Knight* and *The Temple of Glass*,[88] provide narrative settings for love-complaint and doctrinal analysis of sentiment. They are Lydgate's longest original poems (the bulk of his output is translation) and amongst his best. The *Black Knight*, drawing heavily on Chaucer, provides a garden-setting for the lover's complaint which is a comprehensive anthology of landscape and seasonal motifs, and typical of Lydgate in the way it is detached from its traditional allegorical resonances and elaborated as an independent piece of rhetorical bravura writing. The complaint itself is similar, an eloquent display of the rituals of courtly sentiment, the kernel of whose inspiration is often the impulse to elaborate rhetorical figuration and cadencing given by favourite lines in Chaucer:

> The thoght oppressed with inward sighes sore,
> The peynful lyve, the body langwysshing.... (218–19)

> Lo, her the fyne of loveres seruise.
> Lo, how that Love can his seruantis quyte.... (400–1)

*The Temple of Glass* has more of a story: set in the temple of Love, where lovers cry upon Venus for grace (the catalogue of lovers gives full scope for Lydgate's encyclopaedic habit of mind), it treats, through a series of complaints and supplications, the plight of the lover whose lady is already married. Lydgate does little to develop the drama of the situation,[89] his main interest in the theme being the opportunity it gives, especially through Venus' speeches, for the expression of the highest and most attenuated ideal of the service of love, unrequited and unrequitable, as a form of moral purification, a voluntary secular martyrdom. The narrative is really a frame for a series of eloquent love-poems and orations, as Lydgate makes clear in setting the couplets of the frame against the rhyme royal of the inset speeches. There are webs of personal and topical allusion in the poem, the significance of which is not now certainly recoverable, and major variants in the text[90] which suggest that at some time the poem was adapted for a different 'occasion'.

The occasions of love-poems are, as I have suggested, necessarily obscured from us, since the 'game of love', not merely through literary convention, is a secret one. Despite this, Lydgate appears here as a genuinely courtly poet and an important contributor to the courtly tradition. In most of the poems for which we have evidence of occasion and patronage he appears in a different light. The vast commissions which he executed for Henry V (the *Troy-book*, 1412–20, and probably *The Life of Our Lady*),[91] for the Earl of Salisbury (*The Pilgrimage of the Life of Man*, 1426–8), and Humphrey of Gloucester (*The Fall of Princes*, 1431–8), are not the work of a 'court poet' but that of a professional man of letters employed for the advancement of piety, learning and the English language. The same is largely true of the many lesser commissions he received from royal, aristocratic, clerical and bourgeois patrons. Even during the late 1420s, when Lydgate was closer to court circles than at any other time, and seems to have been part of the royal entourage both in England and France, his work is more that of Lancastrian propagandist and laureate, with all the narrow rigidity of role that that implies, than of court poet. He wrote a verse *Title and Pedigree of Henry VI* (1427) to publicise the young King's claim to the throne of France, and a series of poems to celebrate the King's coronation (1429) and triumphal entry into London, whilst among the *Mummings* there are three intended for presentation at court, where Lydgate seems to have acted for a time as an organiser of ceremonies. This is court-poetry of a kind, indeed, but hardly courtly.

Hoccleve's title as a 'court poet' is even more insecure. As a clerk in the office of the Privy Seal he had some access to court circles, and an early poem, *The Letter of Cupid* (1402), has some currency in the 'Chaucerian' manuscripts. It is a freely abridged version of *L'Epistre du Dieu d'Amours* of Christine de Pisan and shows Hoccleve imitating Chaucer at least in keeping up with fashions in contemporary French court culture. Christine's poem is a defence of women by the god of Love against the slanders of men; it is delicately and ironically serious, half earnest, half game, as befits a courtly contribution to the contemporary debate inspired by the *Roman de la Rose*. Hoccleve's treatment is altogether broader, ridiculously exaggerated and openly sarcastic where Christine had been playfully provocative and ironic, the effect being to turn Christine's arguments back upon herself.[92] It is a lively and talented piece, not at all un-suitable to the kind of court milieu that enjoyed Chaucer's *Envoy to Scogan*. Hoccleve's contacts with the court later in life seem to have been tenuous, and his main debt to Chaucer lies outside the courtly tradition. He dedicated his longest poem, *The Regement of Princes*, to Prince Henry (later Henry V) and canvasses Gloucester tentatively as a possible patron for his other long poem, the *Series*, but such claims represent no more than the optimism of an aspiring writer on the outer fringes of court patronage. They went unheeded, for Hoccleve received no advancement from his humble clerkship, not even for his venomous attacks on the Lollards (e.g. *To Sir John Oldcastle*, 1415), which he might have judged well-pleasing to the ruthless orthodoxy of Henry V. The closest Hoccleve came to court seems to have been in the witty begging-poems that he addressed to the Lord Chancellor and the unseasonable Somer, later Chancellor of the Exche-quer. Other poets, like George Ashby, Clerk to the Signet in the reign of Henry VI, had positions 'at court' (in the Civil Service) superior to Hoccleve's, but have little more to do with courtly tradition.

It would be wrong to think of the early Lancastrian courts as being inimical to the development of courtly poetry. Busy politicians like Henry IV and his son may have had little time for traditional divertissements, and the tastes of Henry V himself may have run, or been thought to have run, more to solid and worthwhile edification,[93] but there were always ladies to be amused, and clever and ambitious men with time on their hands. Nevertheless, the climate was not encouraging, and it may be thought a satisfying irony that the two best courtly poets of the period, the best indeed of the century, were both Lancastrian pri-soners. King James I of Scotland was captured as a boy on his way to France (1406) and kept at the English court as a political pawn. He fell in love with Joan Beaufort, daughter of the Earl of Somerset and niece of the powerful Bishop of Winchester (later Cardinal Beaufort), in 1422, and negotiations for his release, hastened by this happy chance, were completed with his marriage in 1424. It has never been denied that the events of the poem known as *The Kingis Quair* are based on James's history, and it is now generally accepted that he himself was the author.[94] If so, he was as noble a poet as he was a king. The *Quair* is a stylised allegorical reenactment of the events of his life, in which the lover, through his passion and 'Gude Hope', disciplined and guided by wisdom and love of virtue, attains to good Fortune, and the recognition that Fortune's power is contingent upon man's wisdom:

> Fortune is most and strangest euermore
> Quhare leste foreknawing or intelligence
> Is in the man.... (1038–40)

(*strangest* : strongest, *Quhare* : Where)

The poem is traditionally constructed, with dream-journeys to the palaces of Venus and Minerva and to the beautiful earthly garden where Fortune holds

216

sway. There is the same high moral tone as in *The Temple of Glass*, which is an important model for the *Quair*, but there is also an awareness of the complexities and delights of love and life which Lydgate never had. James's profounder debt is to Chaucer, and his poem can be seen as an answer to the questions posed in the *Parlement of Foules* and, more specifically, as a palinode to the *Knight's Tale*. The episode in which the lover catches his first sight of his lady from his prison window (211 ff) is introduced as a deliberate reminiscence of the *Knight's Tale*: the difference is that James has evidence to bring that sorrow is not always the latter end of joy and that the fruits of Boethian wisdom are not always sour grapes. His blend of the personal, the courtly (his Venus and Minerva speak like true goddesses) and the gravely meditative is uniquely attractive.

Charles of Orleans, who was an English prisoner from 1415, when he was captured at Agincourt, until 1440, is more of an innovator, not unexpectedly, since he was also a French courtly poet of distinction. His confinement was not arduous and he was not cut off from aristocratic society. It is inherently likely that he acquired a good command of English during his long exile (his younger brother, Jean d'Angoulême, also a captive, had a copy of Chaucer made for his own use)[95] and, in the absence of evidence to the contrary, the sequence of English ballades, roundels and narrative interludes which appears in MS Harley 682 and of which about half are close translations of Charles's French poems (or *vice versa*: the English may well be the originals) is usually ascribed to Charles himself.[96] The sequence is in three parts. The first begins with a declaration of allegiance to Love and follows the progress of his love for 'Lady Beauty' in a long series of ballades, ending with her death, his grief and renunciation of love (1–3070). The second is a book of 'Jubilee', a banquet of song and dance in which he celebrates his retirement from Love's service in roundels and caroles (3071–4637). The third part begins with a vision of Venus, who persuades the poet to re-enter her service; after a brilliant comic dialogue with Venus, the poet wakes and meets his new lady in an elegantly courtly pastoral interlude; the remaining ballades describe the varying, mostly sad fortunes of his second love, and the final parting (4638–6531). The language and phraseology show Chaucer's influence, but the complex, often unidiomatic syntax and the use of non-Chaucerian tags and vocabulary set Charles apart as 'neo-French'. Long before Wyatt, he introduces the intimate, passionate speaking voice into English courtly lyric (not necessarily raising the question of the relation of the poems to his 'life'), at the same time laying it under the strictest formal controls of rhetorical artifice and allowing a mischievous irony to flicker among the hot sighs and tears. Often he anticipates the Elizabethans in his cadences—

Syn hit is so we nedis must depart                           (5660)

as also in his development of conventional erotic themes (the exchange of hearts, the dialogue of the lover with his heart, the chess-game) and in the playfully conceited quality of his imagery.

A sequence of ballades, complaints and other love-poems in MS Fairfax 16 have a connection with some English poems (not in Harley 682) in the MSS of Charles's French poetry and they are all generally attributed to the Earl (later Duke) of Suffolk,[97] who was Charles's 'gaoler' from 1432 to 1436 and who visited him at Blois in 1444. Suffolk was himself a prisoner in France at one time, has some French poems attributed to him by Shirley in Trinity College, Cambridge, MS R.3.20, and it seems a reasonable assumption that he and Charles vied with each other in the composition of poetry in both English and French. The Fairfax poems are amongst the most characteristic products of the fifteenth-century English courtly tradition, effortless, transparent, lachrymose, monotonous, with little of Charles's brilliance, variety and wit. Chaucerian cadences are often echoed—

> The tyme so long, the payn ay more and more                    (XV. 1)

and there is some elaborately legalistic phrasing, as in a formal 'bill' or petition:

> Besechyth mekly in ryght lowly wyse,
> Now in hys nede your suget and seruaunt,
> That for as myche as he in your seruyse
> Hath of long tyme always bene attendaunt,
> Plese yt unto your goodnes for to graunt
> The sayed besecher sumwhat of coumfort....          (XIII. 1–6)

Many are cast as epistles, with a directness of address which can be touchingly effective:

> And yf ye lyst haue knowlech of my qwert
> I am in hele, god thankyd mot he be,
> As of body, but treuly not in hert,
> Nor nought shal be to tyme I may you se....
> I wryte to yow no more, for lak of space....
> Go lytill byll, and say thou were wyth me
> Of verey trouth, as thou canst wele remembre,
> At myn upryst, the fyft day of decembre.          (XIV)[98]

Two longer poems have as their subjects a Parliament of Love (XX) and the worship of the daisy (XIX)—a reference perhaps to Suffolk's liaison with Margaret (*marguerite*, daisy) of Anjou. The latter poem delivers an amusing and patronising reproof to Lydgate for speaking ill of women: Suffolk had a connection with Bury and his wife was Alice, daughter of Chaucer's son Thomas, at whose house in Ewelme Lydgate was a favoured visitor.[99]

Poems like these give us a tantalising if unsubstantiated insight into a truly courtly milieu.[100] For many of the love-poems of the period, even the longer allegorical narratives, we have no evidence at all of milieu. *The Flower and the Leaf*, for instance, the most charming of all the 'Chaucerian' love-visions, and the last to be expelled from the canon (1870), is first found in Speght's 1598 print of Chaucer, though it must belong to the fifteenth century. Its delicate use of a courtly pastoral 'game' in which members of the court declare their adherence to the orders of the Flower and the Leaf as part of the May festivities,[101] with a wealth of rich processional and symbolic motif, suggests courtly provenance, while the interpretation of the contrasted orders in terms of a lightly-stressed opposition of loyal love and fickle flirtation is a characteristic touch of fifteenth-century sobriety, none the less amusing and acceptable in a court context. The *Assembly of Ladies* has less of this courtly poise: the poem's leaden subject is the presentation of bills of love-complaint by ladies at the court of Lady Loyalty, and on the whole it is more interesting for its picture of the bustle and business of court life and household government than for its 'allegory', though there are touches of suggestiveness in the latter.[102] Both these poems maintain the fiction of a lady narrator, and the latter is almost entirely peopled by ladies, as is the vivacious fantasy of *The Isle of Ladies*,[103] and we may assume that in this respect they reflect the characteristic composition and tastes of a court audience.

More is known of Sir Richard Roos (c. 1410–82), the gifted translator of Alain Chartier's *La Belle Dame sans Merci*, whose career as soldier, diplomat and courtier gives us perhaps the classic picture of the knightly poet.[104] Chartier's poem, which had a sensational *éclat* in the fifteenth century for its undeviatingly ruthless portrayal of the cruel mistress, and gave the initiative for a whole series of replies, defences and counter-attacks, a new 'game' in fact, is a hard and brilliant exercise in the dialectic of love. The exquisite extremes of courtly sensibility are presented with subtle, muted delicacy, with an abstract intensity of feeling, 'all breathing human passion far above', in which the lovers are frozen for ever in the ritual postures of beseeching and cold disdain. Roos adds a brief narrative frame, but otherwise paraphrases Chartier faithfully; touches of colloquialism and flippancy occasionally jar, but his great achievement is not to misrepresent his original. English may be truly said to have come of age when it can match French, even in the hands of a minor poet, in subtlety and refinement.

Roos's poem is an important example of the continuing influence of contemporary French poetry in the English courtly tradition, where the frequent use of French phrases, song-titles and mottoes,[105] as well as the English provenance of important MSS of French poetry,[106] show that French was still a living language at court. The French poetry of the Burgundian courts was also influential: there is an English translation, *The Eye and the Heart*,[107] of the *Débat du Coeur et de l'Oeil* of Michault Taillevent, which brings into English poetry the characteristic extravagance and ostentation of dress, tournament and courtly ceremonial which we associate with Burgundian culture.[108] The love of decoration in poems like *The Flower and the Leaf* and *The Assembly of Ladies*, costumes in high fashion, symbolic colours and blazonry, may echo similar influences, as does the extravagant verbal artifice of the 'Balade coulourd and reuersid' in B.M. MS Arundel 26,[109] in which each line can be read backwards without loss of sense or rhyme, a rare example of English aspiring to the imbecile ingenuity of the Burgundian *rhétoriqueurs*. Native sources of enrichment include the encyclopaedias and Latin arts of poetry, which are riotously plundered for the descriptive passages of another Fairfax poem, *How a Lover praiseth his Lady*,[110] sometimes with startling effectiveness—

> Whos lyppys wyth chyld ben by maydenhede
> Swol and engreyned wyth rosys rede (346–7)

and, less successfully, the practice of aureation. Aureate language, that is, ornamental and above all a Latinate diction, was much cultivated in the fifteenth century, particularly under Lydgate's influence. At its best, it contributes to the flamboyance and heightened colour which is the character of much fifteenth-century art; at its worst, it results simply in floods of pompous verbiage, and there are not a few examples of the latter among later fifteenth-century courtly lyrics.[111]

The courtly tradition as a whole, however, is not notable for its variety. There are some charming and witty love-fantasies, like *The Lover's Mass* and *A Parliament of Birds (The Birds' Praise of Love)*,[112] a good deal of grimly playful 'doctrine' of love, like *The Ten Commandments of Love* (Robbins, *Secular Lyrics*, No. 177), and some reflection of the courtly anti-masque of love in satirical and insulting poems, praises *per contrarium*, exercises in abuse ('Hir comly body shape as a foot-bal') and straightforward obscenity.[113] But the staple for the shorter poems is the complaint or the love-epistle, and it is these poems, with their monotony and superficiality of theme and diction, which most challenge our understanding of court poetry. They need, more than any other poetry, their social context in the courtly 'game of love'[114] in order to be appreciated, their relationship to the excitements, snares and intrigues of court society, the dialogues and games, the covert allusions, the cults and ceremonies of 'the olde daunce':

> Who koude telle you the forme of daunces
> So unkouthe, and swiche fresshe contenaunces,
> Swich subtil lookyng and dissymulynges
> For drede of jalouse mennes aperceyvynges?
>
> (*Squire's Tale, CT.* V. 283–6)

Perhaps nowhere are we more sharply aware of the loss of this context than in the 'game'-poems, like *Ragman's Roll* and *The Chance of the Dice*,[115] where every line, we must imagine, is replete with allusions that the most laborious historical enquiry could never recover. Many of the shorter poems are set to music or designed for singing—not always those that we might consider the most singable, but also some of the aureate lyrics—and again the work of imaginative recreation is all to be done: such poems have little meaning if not sung 'in a room with many ladies present. The whole scene comes before us . . . we are having a little music after supper.'[116] The language is stilted and colourless, the themes commonplace, not because the poems are conventional literary exercises, but because they are part of a larger social activity which alone gives them valency: 'Until the conventions of courtly love are seen to arise out of the need to express the real character of courtly existence, it is difficult to take the poetry of courtly love as completely seriously as it deserves to be taken.'[117]

It is important to realise how much these poems are intended to be *used* rather than read as we read them. They are no one's property and the whole notion of authorship is in a way irrelevant.[118] Poems are borrowed and their allusions to date and circumstance changed so as to fit a new occasion.[119] Verses are incorporated into love-letters, as in the charming valentine of Margery Brews to John Paston III, the language of which echoes, in the most touchingly 'real' situation, the 'conventional' commonplaces of courtly complaint,[120] while the 'Verses by a Lady' that occur among the Paston papers[121] look like material for similar exploitation. Ascriptions to particular noble lords or ladies that we occasionally find in the MSS[122] probably do no more than record a particular dignity once assigned to a piece from the general repertoire. Famous repositories of 'love-talk', like *Troilus* and *The Temple of Glass*, are plundered to provide the materials of new wooing-poems and love-epistles;[123] stanzas from the common stock are interlaced and reworked; simple pieces, including popular songs, are adapted for more ostentatious purposes; famous opening stanzas and striking first lines are pressed into service again and again to launch new poems—

O thoughtfull herte, plunged in distresse...
My whofull herte plonged yn heuynesse...
O wofull hert profound in gret duresse...[124]

and everywhere there are the same tissues of commonplace phrases, varied and permutated, the shorthand as much as the language of love.

These points are perhaps nowhere better made than in an analysis of the early Tudor song-books and poetical miscellanies. In the former we have at last the full musical context which draws to itself and 'explains' every variety of medieval lyric,[125] while in the Devonshire MS (B.M. Add. 17492), a court album of the 1530s, we have not only some fully developed examples of cannibalisation, in a group of poems made up entirely of stanzas and lines extracted from Chaucer, Hoccleve and Roos,[126] but also, recreated for us, the very world of secrecy and intrigue, of longing and disappointment, of pain, imprisonment, even (for 'Pastime in the Queen's Chamber' could be mortal peril) of death, in which these poems have their life. There is as yet no break with the medieval tradition, and Wyatt, for all his laboured innovations elsewhere, appears here as very much the inheritor. The presence of directly copied Chaucerian material in the Devonshire MS is thought to reflect the influence of Thynne's collected Chaucer of 1532.[127] Perhaps it would be appropriate to close this chapter with mention of a poem, also probably inspired by a loving reading of that volume, which both pays tribute to the past vitality of the medieval courtly tradition and at the same time signals its approaching demise. *The Court of Love* (printed by Skeat in *Chaucerian and Other Pieces*) is a most elegant poem, touching eloquently on all the familiar themes of the love-vision. Yet it is written in a deliberately archaic imitation of Chaucer's language, not the language as naturally inherited, and the irony which plays around the poem is not any longer directed at the lover or at love but at this kind of poem. Without being a pastiche, and with a great delight still in the old manners, it indicates that Chaucerian court poetry can no longer be taken entirely seriously.

# 8    The close of the Middle Ages

*The fifteenth century*

The two previous chapters have carried the discussion of the traditions of alliterative poetry and court poetry well beyond 1400, and as a consequence the
fifteenth century has already been plundered of some of its best poetry. It is a
loss that the century can ill sustain, for it is not, except in Scotland, rich in good
poetry, and its most interesting innovations may well be thought to be in prose
and drama. It is not easy, and perhaps not profitable, to enter into explanations
as to the comparative poverty of the age in poetry, whether such explanations
have to do with civil disturbance and military setback, with religious repression
and persecution, or with the possibly enervating influence of a poet so un-
approachably excellent as Chaucer. History and literary history are often
adequate to explain why poetry is written, or why certain kinds are written,
but they cannot explain poetic excellence, or the lack of it. We should recall,
too, that it is a comparative poverty of which we speak, a judgment coloured by
the proximity of the golden age of English poetry in the late fourteenth century
and by the shadow of the great Elizabethans. In such a period, poetry is bound
to seem, if not to be, in decline, and we may be apt to ignore or undervalue its
substantial, unspectacular achievements. Perhaps we should think of the
fifteenth century as a shallow trough rather than an abyss in the history of
English poetry.

The most significant facts about fifteenth-century poetry, from any point of
view that is susceptible of historical analysis, are the great expansion in the
production and copying of verse, and the increase in the number of roles it
fulfils. English is now, for the first time, unquestionably the dominant literary
language, and English verse takes over many of the roles previously assigned to
Anglo-Norman and even Latin. We have already seen English verse annexing
areas of courtly and upper-class patronage left vacant by the decline of Anglo-
Norman; it advances also into realms of history, government, learning, philosophy and science that would previously have seemed more appropriate to
Latin. Translation is the characteristic activity of the fifteenth century,[1] as if
English, coming late to the scene, had to absorb into itself a mass of learning and
learned writing before it could move forward. Much of this process of absorption
and translation takes place in verse: there are treatises, for instance, on horti-

culture, warfare and economic policy which we may think would have been better done in prose. There seems no particular reason for the choice of verse, except that the language leans heavily on Chaucer for its newly acquired literary prestige, and writers tend to follow him, therefore, even when their matter defies art. Lydgate, in the devoutness of his imitation of Chaucer and the wide range of his own influence, strengthens this tendency. Distinctions of genre and audience are thus difficult to maintain: there are, for instance, translations of the encyclopaedic moral treatise, the *Secreta Secretorum*, of Deguileville's *Pelerinages*, and of Aegidio Colonna's *De Regimine Principum*, in both verse and prose,[2] while Chaucer's decision to translate Boethius into prose is reversed by his follower and imitator, John Walton. On the other hand, it should be made clear that the increased prestige of English verse, by which it begins to approach the intellectual and literary sophistication not only of French and Latin but also of the long-established and specialised traditions of native contemplative prose, is associated only with 'Chaucerian' or Lydgatian verse. There is still a world of difference between the prose of Nicholas Love's translation of the *Meditationes Vitae Christi* (1410) and the run-of-the-mill verse of the Vernon MS and its successors. A change, furthermore, is detectable as the century wears on, an increasingly marked shift towards prose for all literary purposes, religious and secular. Caxton's massive output of prose translations, made under the influence of Burgundian taste, is decisive in confirming this shift, which enables us to recognise, in the verse of the first three-quarters of the century, part of the process by which the status of English was consolidated and the language brought up to date, a process which may seem old-fashioned in the context of European literary tradition (both the Latin and French sources of Lydgate's *Fall of Princes*, for example, are in prose), but which was none the less necessary. The shift to prose also enables us to appreciate the embarrassment of late fifteenth- and early sixteenth-century poets, who found their role both as teachers and entertainers usurped by prose, and who were as yet insufficiently sophisticated or touched by the Renaissance to evolve alternative and more specialised roles.

The century as a whole, though, as I have said, is marked by the great increase in the amount and kinds of verse produced, and this expansion is to be associated with important changes in publication, production and consumption. The fifteenth century sees a vast increase in the reading public, which now includes not only those who used to read French but also more and more of those who previously had no access at all to books. The spread of education, not all of it exclusively clerical,[3] is one of the phenomena of the age, and its effects on poetry are to increase the number and extend the social range of those who wish to read and possess copies of established poets like Chaucer and Lydgate, and also to press poetry into new secular roles, in which the manners of courtly poetry are adapted to more sober and mediocre tastes. Characteristic evidence for the latter is provided by the versified books of 'nurture' or etiquette, including Lydgate's *Stans Puer ad Mensam*,[4] which become frequent in the fifteenth century and which presumably cater for the newly aspirant, and also by a large range of moralistic, didactic and informational verse.[5] It is not that all this teaching had previously been unavailable or unnecessary:[6] the new taste is that which asks for it to be made available in Chaucerian rhyme royal or ballade stanza, as in Lydgate's *Dietary* or *Pageant of Knowledge*, or Peter Idley's *Instructions to his Son*. As for the broader-based readership of established poets, it is well-evidenced in the very varied provenance and wide dissemination of the MSS, which range from luxurious patrons' copies designed for the aristocracy and perhaps produced, like some MSS of Lydgate's *Troy-book*, in a well-equipped monastic scriptorium;[7] through more modest yet still handsome books like the MS of Lydgate's *Troy* and *Thebes* which seems to have been a prized possession of the Knevet family in Norfolk;[8] down to workaday editions produced at a venture by scribes like Shirley and sold or lent out to London merchants or country gentry, like those which eventually found their way into the hands of Roger Thorney, a rich London mercer of the late fifteenth century.[9] Lydgate himself is such a voluminous and versatile writer that a MS like Harley 2251, almost entirely devoted to his own poetry,[10] could alone serve the purpose of a speculative publisher who wanted a 'catch-all' miscellany or anthology. There are a growing number of commercial scriptoria, and more scribes available to take on individual commissions, like the William Ebesham who copied books for Sir John Paston, including a 'Grete Booke' which seems to have been a variant of a bestselling miscellany adapted to the tastes of the individual customer.[11] In addition there are gentleman-amateur collectors like Robert Thornton, who produced literary miscellanies of varied content for his own interest and that of his family,[12] and also a growing fashion for commonplace-books, in which city officials like William Gregory (Mayor of London 1451) and Richard Hill (c. 1530)[13] would copy or have copied all kinds of things which took their fancy, from prognostications, recipes and medical hints to fashionable courtly poems and devotional pieces. Not all of these developments are new, of course: it is the scale on which they are practised that distinguishes the fifteenth century.

Book-ownership, too, is much more widespread: the great collectors, like Humphrey of Gloucester and John Tiptoft, Earl of Worcester, have many more books than have ever before been in the possession of a layman, of much greater variety and quality, including classical and humanistic Latin texts brought direct from Italy,[14] whilst lesser collectors, like John Carpenter, town clerk of London, and Sir John Paston, who was not much more, after all, than a country gentleman, have libraries which only the most exceptional fourteenth-century collections can match.[15] Carpenter's library is an old-fashioned one, such as Gower might have been at home in, but Paston's includes a remarkably large proportion of Chaucer and Chaucerian poetry. Likewise, although it is not always easy to distinguish readership and book-ownership from patronage, what knowledge we have suggests that poetry was being commissioned by and written for a much wider variety of patrons. Lydgate, for instance, wrote for royal and aristocratic patrons, like Henry V and Henry VI, Humphrey of Gloucester, and the Earls of Salisbury and Warwick, and for noble ladies like the Countesses of Shrewsbury, Warwick, Suffolk and Stafford; but he also wrote for government servants like Thomas Chaucer, for provincial gentlewomen like Lady Sibille

Boys,[16] and for John Carpenter, for the London guilds, and for 'a werþy citeseyn of London'.[17] Finally, we should remark on the new kinds of poet who begin to appear in the fifteenth century. Up to now, poets have been clerics or hacks, sometimes both, with perhaps only Chaucer and Gower as real exceptions. The fifteenth century is strong still in both clerics and hacks, but a new breed is emerging, again reflecting the broader social range of poetry—civil servants, in the mould of Chaucer, like Hoccleve, Ashby and perhaps Adam Moleyns; country gentlemen, members of the 'professionally educated gentility',[18] in the mould of Gower, like John Quixley, the Yorkshire gentleman who translated the nineteen ballades of Gower's *Traitié pour essampler les amantz marietz*,[19] Gilbert Banester, Peter Idley and Humfrey Newton, whose commonplace-book, the Capesthorne MS (now Bodleian MS Lat. misc. c. 66) includes poems of his own composition in both alliterative and courtly style;[20] and also London merchants like Henry Lovelich, as well as genuine amateur eccentrics like Metham, Ripley, Norton and John Crophill, village doctor of Wix in Essex, who has a poem in the genre of 'The Ale-Wife and her Gossips' in his medical notebook.[21]

It is important not to neglect, in all this, the false emphasis that may be given by a merely fortuitous weight of evidence. In other words, one reason why there is more poetry in the fifteenth century is that the technology of reproduction and dissemination is more advanced, and another is that the century is more recent, so that more both of poetry and documentation survives. Such base and inescapable realities affect, though they cannot seriously undermine, our view of the fifteenth century as an age of expansion and inflation in poetry. But they do have one further and paradoxical consequence: that the age which sees English poetry advanced to the pedestal prepared for it by Chaucer is also the one which for the first time begins to reveal, in any significant quantity, the sub-literature of popular and semi-popular secular verse. Hitherto there have been only dubious scraps and fragments: now the greater frequency of written copies and the improved chances of survival mean that a popular and predominantly oral verse begins to be preserved, so that the age of Lydgate is also the age of the first recorded ballads.

## John Lydgate

The fifteenth century, whatever else, can guarantee bulk, and in this as in all things Lydgate is its representative and its formative influence. As a professional man of letters over a period of some fifty years, ubiquitous monk of Bury, court-poet, official 'orator', laureate in all but name, he responded to every call, commission and occasion, whether for an epithalamion or an epic, a love-poem or a *memento mori*, an exposition of the Mass or a treatise for laundresses. His prestige was high, and his reputation in the fifteenth century sometimes threatened to eclipse Chaucer's, as in fact may have been Lydgate's intention, despite his adulation of his master, since his literary career often looks like a pompously inflated version of Chaucer's, 'fortifying' and improving *The House of Fame* in

*The Temple of Glass*, *Troilus* in the *Troy-book*, the *Knight's Tale* in *The Siege of Thebes* and the *Monk's Tale* in *The Fall of Princes*. Lydgate's version of Chaucer is the fifteenth century's version, simplified in content, more grandiose in style, brought into conformity with what was expected of a high style poetic (see above, p. 198). This is not to suggest that the comic Chaucer was not widely read and enjoyed: there is evidence that he was, in the very number of manuscripts of the *Canterbury Tales* that were copied, and in the existence of a lively and pungent 'Canterbury prologue' to the *Tale of Beryn* (ed. EETS, ES 105), a poem in the old septenary/alexandrine couplet of *Gamelyn* which is inserted as a second tale for the Merchant in one MS of the *Canterbury Tales*. Even Lydgate attempts, not altogether unsuccessfully, an imitation of Chaucer's comedy in the Canterbury prologue to his own *Siege of Thebes* and in his *Mumming at Hertford*, and has some satirical genre-pieces such as *Against Millers and Bakers* and the *Ballade of Jak Hare*.[22] However, as I have suggested, the conventional language of literary praise allowed no expression to such appreciation, and Chaucer's comedy, where it was imitated, was coarsened and encapsulated according to rhetorical decorum as 'low' style.

It is sententiousness and rhetoric, therefore, for which Chaucer is praised and largely imitated. Lydgate refers frequently to the simpler moral function of poetry, the poet's responsibility to teach virtue through examples and allegory—

Ther cheeff labour is vicis to repreve
With a maner couert symylitude[23]

and Lydgate selects for special commendation, among the *Canterbury Tales*, those of the Clerk and the Monk and the *Tale of Melibeus*.[24] The distortions involved here—for no amount of 'historical' understanding can see them as anything else—are repeated in Lydgate's view of Chaucer's style, which leads him to praise him for his ornate rhetoric (even the reference to his 'gaye style' in *The Floure of Curtesy*, 240, probably means 'showy') and to turn again and again for models to those passages in Chaucer which conform to a cruder taste for grandiloquence, like the *Swich fyn* and *Lo here* stanzas of the *Troilus* epilogue, passages which we may think of as uncharacteristic, even unworthy, of Chaucer.

Lydgate's version of Chaucer is consistently distorted in this way. Taking over Chaucer's poetic vocabulary, he fortifies it (in Dryden's phrase, again) with new borrowings and usages for which the English language was necessarily grateful but which cannot, in their undigested state, enhance the attraction of his own style. These innovations, all of them designed to inflate and heighten the language of poetry, are not accurately described as 'aureation', a term which has been too freely used of fifteenth-century poetic style and which should be reserved for the Latinate transformations of Lydgate's florid religious poetry (see below, p. 234). Lydgate's usual practice, which is cruelly exemplified in these lines from the opening of *The Churl and the Bird* (ed. in EETS 192),

Problemys, liknessis and figures
Which previd been fructuous of sentence,

227

> And han auctoritees groundid on scriptures
> Bi resemblaunces of notable apparence,
> With moralites concludyng in prudence....

is more truly derived from Latin and French epistolary style, with their endless ostentation, abstraction, evasion and qualification. The manner of the language is inseparable from the manner of the syntax, where again Lydgate, profiting, as he thought, from the model of Chaucer, attempts a complexity of construction which is quite beyond his poetic powers. The opening of the Prologue to *The Siege of Thebes*, for instance, attempts a sentence like that of the opening of Chaucer's General Prologue, but collapses again and again and finally expires unconsummated. Defective in such radical ways, Lydgate can seldom be confidently quoted at length, even when there are legitimate grounds for admiration: words and sentences slip away from him, blurred and out of focus, just as eloquence gives way to grandiloquence, sonority to bombast, and moral seriousness to maudlin platitude.

Lydgate's metre is perhaps the most striking demonstration both of his incalculable debt to Chaucer and of his incapacity to render worthy repayment. Lydgate takes over Chaucer's major metrical forms—rhyme royal, the pentameter couplet, the ballade stanza and the octosyllabic couplet—and transmits them, the pentameter forms, at least, in crippled and mutilated form to his followers. The awkwardness of Lydgate's verse is notorious, and particularly the prevalence of 'broken-backed' lines (lines defective of an unstressed syllable at the caesura) which no textual surgery can mend. The fairest way to illustrate Lydgate's practice is to quote him at his best, as in this carefully and formally composed passage from the *Troy-book* (ed. EETS, ES 97, 103, 106, 126), where I have marked the caesura in the broken-backed or 'Lydgate lines':

> For she of cher/pale was and grene,
> And he of colour liche to ashes dede;
> And fro hir face was goon/al þe rede,
> And in his chekis deuoided was þe blod,
> So wofully atwene hem two it stood.
> For she ne myȝt/nat a worde speke
> And he was redy with deth/to be wreke
> Up-on hym silfe, his nakid swerd be-side;
> And she ful ofte gan to grounde glide
> Out of his armys, as she fel a-swowne,
> And he hym silf/gan in teris drowne;
> She was as stille and dowmb as any ston,
> He had a mouþe, but wordis had he non.[25]
> Þe weri spirit flikered in hir breste,
> And of deth/stood vnder arreste.          (*Troy-book*, iii. 4166–80)

Historical explanations in terms of the decline of final sonant -*e*, which is of course important in Chaucer's versification, do not work, since Lydgate uses final -*e* more or less as Chaucer does and also since there are other contemporary poets who write regular metre within the same context of change. Nor can much blame be laid at the door of corrupt texts. The conclusion seems inescapable that Lydgate intended to write as he wrote, that he recognised certain metrical variants in Chaucer, variants that Chaucer himself, with his inimitable sense of the verse-paragraph, could bend against the regular flow, and that he erected these variants into 'types'.[26] Working as he did, line by line, Lydgate was able to treat each line as potentially broken-backed or 'headless' (lacking the initial unstressed syllable), so that emphatic variants occur without the rhetorical or syntactical justification that a well-tuned ear would recognise as necessary. His metre, therefore, is not confused but excruciatingly rigid, and those who imitate him closely, like Benedict Burgh and Hawes, can hardly improve matters. Lydgate's practice, which is systematic and explicable, should be distinguished from a more general 'prosodic vertigo' which Saintsbury[27] is not mistaken in recognising in the fifteenth century, a confusion which we can attribute to the reassertion of older four-stress patterns within the artificially poised Chaucerian pentameter,[28] as in the opening lines of Ashby's *A Prisoner's Reflections* (ed. EETS, ES 76):

> At the ende of Somer, when wynter began
> And trees, herbes and flowres dyd fade,
> Blosteryng and blowyng the gret wyndes than
> Threw doune the frutes with whyche they were lade.

This confusion is eventually introduced into Chaucer himself, whose couplets begin to be read by sixteenth-century poets like Gascoigne and Spenser as rough four-stress 'riding-rhyme'. Increasingly corrupt texts, such as Chaucer feared (*Troilus*, v. 1796), made such reading difficult to correct until the manuscripts were rediscovered in the eighteenth century. It should be added, finally, so that the century shall not suffer a general discredit, that there are some poets in the fifteenth century, like Quixley and Metham, whose metre admits of no historical or other rational explanation: Quixley, for whom the term 'gentleman amateur' has a sinister truth, seems unaware of the principle of stress in English versification, while Metham, purporting to write in rhyme royal, pays as little attention to the number of stresses or syllables in the line as to the number of lines in the stanza.

Lydgate, as I have said, saw his role as the systematic consolidation of Chaucer's achievement in establishing a high-style poetic for English. As far as language is concerned, it is perhaps the work of Lydgate and his followers, their great influence in settling the form of poetic language, that makes Chaucer so 'English', that makes the journey back to him so simple for us. In other respects they misrepresent Chaucer: unresponsive to his innovations in narrative and poetic structure, they reassert traditional habits of thought, especially the simpler moralistic habits, thus enclosing Chaucer in a capsule of medieval commonplace. Lydgate above all reverts continually to well-established moral, didactic and encyclopaedic functions for poetry, working in the manner more of a pedantic scholar accumulating his 'examples' from the familiar store-houses, a Holcot, a Trivet or a Whethamstede,[29] than of a Chaucer. He does not lack learning, but it is thin, much thinner than Gower's, and even more old-fashioned.

It is very striking that Lydgate and other fifteenth-century poets, though they have before them the model of Chaucer using and translating the best and most recent French and Italian poets, prefer to return to older traditions,[30] sometimes to the stalest kind of medieval hack-work, for their major translations, as Lydgate returns, for instance, to the Latin prose of Guido della Colonna for his *Troy-book*, where Chaucer had used Boccaccio's Italian. No doubt Lydgate saw this as a step forward, since Guido was more authoritative and comprehensive, and certainly he is very conscious of the new dignity he is imparting to English by his translation, which Henry authorised, as he says,

> By-cause he wolde that to hyʒe and lowe
> The noble story openly wer knowe
> In oure tonge, aboute in euery age,
> And y-writen as wel in oure langage
> As in latyn and in frensche it is.                    (Prologue, 111–15)

Beyond this, and his repeated assertion, presumably for the benefit of his royal patron, that the work will provide an example of antique chivalry, there is little sense of motive or shaping energy in this vast 30,000-line poem. Lydgate, unlike Chaucer, who absorbs and recreates where he borrows, follows Guido closely, taking every description, digression, apostrophe, exclamation and lament through all the familiar rhetorical processes of amplification, as if this alone were a sufficient fulfilment of poetic ambition. There are touches of individuality and power in some of the seasonal passages, where he draws, characteristically, on the encyclopaedic tradition of the *Secreta Secretorum* rather than on Chaucer, and in book IV the laments for Troy and its heroes have occasionally a faded grandeur and threadbare sense of the mutability of things. But the poem, where it lacks these sources of inspiration, relapses into an encyclopaedia of classical history and mythology or a storehouse of moral examples. *The Siege of Thebes* is shorter, less ambitious, less inflated, and handles its story with admirable frankness as a theme for asserting some sound if unoriginal truths, adumbrated in the *Troy-book*, concerning war and peace, the virtues of wise government and the dangers of divided rule. It is freely translated from some version of the French prose *Roman de Edipus*, and it is clear that Lydgate, working with a vernacular and unostentatious source such as this, and without a patron to put him on his mettle, wrote with greater ease and honesty and much less straining after effect.

In *The Fall of Princes*, Lydgate, writing now at the behest of his greatest patron, Humphrey of Gloucester, reassumes his most magniloquent manner. The amplification to which Boccaccio's *De Casibus Illustrium Virorum* had already been subjected in the French prose version of Laurent de Premierfait, which is Lydgate's direct source, is here further extended, so that the careful design of Boccaccio's work, where substantial narratives of major victims of Fortune alternate with group-scenes of lesser complainants and interludes involving the narrator, is now quite obscured, in the swollen dimensions of the whole, which runs to over 36,000 lines. Lydgate has no sense of governing poetic structure but that of the encyclopaedia: the ordering is chronological, but it could as well, in Lydgate's version, be alphabetical, and indeed the medieval attitude to history would not be ill-represented in such an arrangement. Even in local matters of style, the catalogue, the accumulation of images or examples, is what dominates, as if certain stimuli tripped off a torrent of associated responses, the disgorgement of which constituted poetic amplification. Such unthought processes of accumulation represent Lydgate at his worst: they can also show him at his best, for when the subject is one which responds well to the techniques of medieval encyclopaedism—the arbitrariness of Fortune, the transitoriness of human life, the immutability of Fate—there is no poet who can steep it more richly in the familiar wisdom of example or who can, under the stricter formal control of the stanza, turn to better effect the weighty cadences of traditional rhetoric:

> God hath a thousand handis to chastise,
> A thousand dartis off punycioun,
> A thousand bowes maad in vnkouth wise,
> A thousand arblastis bent in his dongoun,
> Ordeyned echon for castigacioun;
> But where he fynt meeknesse and repentaunce,
> Mercy is maistresse off his ordynaunce. (i. 1331–7)

Such passages clearly represented the fundamental appeal of the *Fall* to its age: they were accepted quite frankly as independent pieces of sententious writing and often, like the eloquent Envoy on Rome (which is still flawed by some desperate lapses of the most basic kind of poetic attention), copied as separate poems, just as Wynkyn de Worde, rather than print the whole poem, made from it a collection of sententious sayings or *Proverbs of Lydgate*.[31]

Humphrey of Gloucester would not have despised this quality in Lydgate nor in his poem, nor would any thinking man of the age: indeed, Humphrey gave Lydgate direct encouragement to interpret his commission in this vein by instructing him to add Envoys to each chapter in Boccaccio, expounding the 'moralitee' in formal terms. Yet Humphrey's patronage can also be seen in a more generous light as an attempt to introduce into English, through the agency of the major poet of the time, something of the dignity and repute of continental classical learning, of which Boccaccio was not an inadequate representative. At one point he even offered Lydgate a copy of the famous *Declamatio* of Lucretia by the Italian humanist Coluccio Salutati as a model of the latest kind of Latinity, so that he might include it in his translation.[32] His hopes were not realised, for Lydgate's habits of mind were too profoundly medieval to respond to novelty. He translates Coluccio dutifully but unenthusiastically, and throughout his treatment of the *De Casibus* he obscures Boccaccio's emergent philosophy of tragedy, and suppresses or dilutes any expression of strong opinion about political matters, or any suggestion of tragic meaningfulness in the fate of pagan heroes, or any larger 'humanistic' sense of the function of poetry.[33] As always, in the face of innovation, he reasserts or relapses into the medieval, the commonplace, the traditional. Here is his strength, and *The Fall of Princes* is worth some attention as an example of the medieval mind at its characteristic work.

These three translations, all of which occur in numerous MSS, are and were clearly thought to be Lydgate's major contribution to the Chaucerian tradition, as it was understood. Two other long translations were less highly regarded, and appear only in one or two very late MSS: both are versions in octosyllabic couplet of fourteenth-century French poems in the didactic and encyclopaedic tradition of Jean de Meun, *The Pilgrimage of the Life of Man* from Deguileville's *Pelerinage de la Vie Humaine*, and *Reason and Sensuality* from *Les Echecs Amoureux*. Lydgate's authorship is only flimsily attested for either, and he would not suffer from being relieved of the *Pilgrimage*, a degraded piece of hack-work, written to order for the Earl of Salisbury (1426–8) and perhaps farmed out to an apprentice. *Reason and Sensuality*, even at 7,000 lines only a fragment of its vast original, is an unexceptionably pleasing poem, a nostalgic return to some familiar landscapes, the forest of Diana and the Garden of Delight, with the moral meanings not too ponderously underlined. The tale of Lydgate's other translations is long and not particularly distinguished. Some were simply done to order, like the translation of *The Title and Pedigree of Henry VI*, a piece of dynastic propaganda, which he made at the request of the Earl of Warwick in France in 1427. A few years earlier, he had written *Guy of Warwick* for Warwick's daughter Margaret, Countess of Shrewsbury, to celebrate her family's putative ancestor; with a characteristic respect for the seriousness and dignity of his subject, Lydgate chose to versify part of the Latin history in which Guy was now enshrined rather than the original ancestral romance. Not all such commissions were mere routine: the one that he received from John Carpenter to complete his translation of the *Danse Macabre*, based on the French verses inscribed in the cloister of the Church of the Holy Innocents in Paris, so that it could be similarly used near St Paul's, inspired one of his most powerful pieces. The severe control exerted by the limited wall-space and the compactness of the French original curbed Lydgate's natural verbosity, whilst his penchant for the catalogue, for persistent reiteration and accumulation, can here, in the procession of death's victims, itself be made structurally significant. Other translations Lydgate seems to have taken on himself for practice, like his version of *Isopes Fabules*, an early work, which may show him learning the techniques of rhetorical amplification; or simply to demonstrate what can be done with the high style, like the *Fabula duorum Mercatorum*, a slight fable on which is erected a quite remarkable rhetorical superstructure, as if Lydgate had missed the point of Chaucer's commentary on moralised fable in the *Nun's Priest's Tale*. *The Churl and the Bird* is simpler, but, like the *Fabula*, it is drawn from the *Disciplina Clericalis*, a school-book of fables and exempla, and it is very revealing to find Lydgate going back for his imaginative sustenance to basic school-texts like this and the Æsopic fables, accepting without question their simple philosophy of literature, which Chaucer had mocked in the tales of the Nun's Priest and the Manciple, and concentrating exclusively on stylistic gloss. In this, as in all respects, Lydgate is the complete medieval rhetorician.

Translation shades off into commissioned and occasional work of all kinds, didactic, informational, practical and political, historically rather than intrinsically interesting, but salutary in reminding us how rapidly Lydgate absorbed every form of discourse to the Chaucerian manner. There are, among these poems, rules of diet and health (the *Dietary*—which occurs in more MSS than any other Lydgate poem), rules of behaviour *(Stans Puer ad Mensam)*, monastic charters (the *Cartae Versificatae*), a 'souvenir programme' for a royal occasion (the *Triumphal Entry of King Henry VI into London*), verses to accompany painted cloth hangings in a citizen's house *(Bycorne and Chychevache)* or in the hall of a craft-guild *(The Legend of St George)*. There are also satirical pieces directed against women, recurring to themes developed with heavy playfulness in the *Troy-book* and *Fall*, *Mummings* for court and city, and a large group of moralistic refrain-poems, presumably in the same tradition as the Vernon MS (p. 142, above), which exercise themselves in the multiplication of illustrations for moral commonplaces—*Everything to his Semblable, The World is Variable, A Wicked Tunge will sey amys*—in a manner of breathless vacuity. With their random and allusive modes of association and gnomic syntax they are often near to being unintelligible. But Lydgate retains the capacity to surprise us, even in these unlikely contexts: *The Debate of the Horse, Goose and Sheep* is a political animal-fable with a good deal of pith and point; *Horns Away*, where we might have expected a conventional diatribe on women's headdresses, turns into a serious and fervent reflection on human and divine beauty; while *As a Mydsomer Rose*, elaborating quietly the mutability of human life in the image of the rose, is suddenly lifted to a new dimension by the memory of the other Rose that crowns the martyrs' wounds:

> Ther bloody suffraunce was no somyr roose.
> It was the Roose of the bloody feeld,
> Roose of Iericho that greuh in Beedlem.[34]

In these last two poems it is devotional fervour that breaks through the mechanisation of poetic habit. Not all of Lydgate's more specifically religious poetry, to which we now turn, is inspired by the same fervour, nor would it be appropriate if it were. Much of this poetry is again translation, and some of it is of a straightforward practical nature. There are verse-prayers that follow well-established fourteenth-century traditions, a verse *Kalendare* that has the most direct relation to the day-to-day realities of monastic life, poems on the Passion which usually have a simple hortatory function, often in relation to a crucifix or other visible manifestation of Christ's suffering, and a translation of the Paternoster and exposition of the Mass which differ from comparable fourteenth-

century poems only in their more sophisticated literary flavour. This sophistication is clearly related to the class of patron for whom Lydgate is writing:
*The Virtues of the Mass* is for the Countess of Suffolk (formerly Alice Chaucer,
daughter of Thomas), *The Fifteen Joys of Our Lady* for the Countess of Warwick,
the *Invocation to St Anne* for the Countess of Stafford, while *A Valentine to her that
excelleth all*, a Marian poem, dedicated to Queen Katherine, has a well-main-
tained literary and 'Chaucerian' air, rather like the pleasantly diversified
Passion-meditation *A Seying of the Nightingale*.[35] The sophisticated language of
these poems should not, however, disguise from us the essential simplicity of their
didactic function. They are quite different from Lydgate's more florid and
ambitious religious poetry, as it is evidenced in the translations of Latin hymns,
sequences and antiphons and in the invocatory Marian poems, where his
audience is likely to be a narrower circle of the higher clergy, and one furthermore with a taste for fine writing. Abbot Whethamstede of St Alban's, a great
lover of flowery language, *(florida verborum venustas)*, comes to mind,[36] as does
Edmund Lacy, Dean of the Royal Chapel at Windsor from 1414–17 and later
Bishop of Exeter, with whom Lydgate has direct connections.[37] Henry V took
an interest in both Lacy and Lydgate, and it is probable, especially in the light
of his patronage of the *Troy-book* and presumed patronage of *The Life of Our Lady*,
and in the light too of his well-known piety and dedication to the English language, that he was directly influential in encouraging Lydgate, as the most
promising poet of his day, to develop a high style in liturgical composition in
which English could match Latin. It is with this kind of background that we
should associate the remarkable exhibitionism of Lydgate's *Exposition of the
Paternoster*, a *tour de force* of rhetorical display, his rhapsodic elaboration on the
themes of exultation in his 'translation' of the sequence *Letabundus*, and above all
the development in his version of the *Te Deum* (ed. in EETS, ES 107) of a kind of
Latinised English which represents aureation in its extreme form:

> *Te chorus* glorious of apostolate,
> Memorial make, modulacioun,
> The laudable nombre of the prophetys astate
> Evir Ioyng gaudent in Iubilacioun,
> Te letabilem laudat in laudacioun,
> *Te martirum candidatus exercitus*
> Principium polorum in al pausacioun
> *Te laudat omnis spiritus.*                                                    (25–32)

There is nothing lovely about such exhibitions, though they do demonstrate a
buoyancy and vigour which Lydgate is often thought to lack. In the Marian
poems, where Latin presses just as closely on the English, the control is greater,
perhaps because Lydgate was less willing to submit this more sensitive area of his
devotion to literary experiment, or perhaps because the influence of Chaucerian
models, in the Prologue to the tales of the Prioress and the Second Nun, and in the
*ABC* poem to the Virgin, exerted a restraining influence. His versions of the

antiphon *Ave Regina Celorum*, with their invocatory *Ave*-structure and accumulation of 'types' for the Virgin from the rich repertoire of biblical sources, were influential in establishing the main literary modes of Marian praise and celebration in the fifteenth century. The best of these poems, however, is the *Ballade at the Reverence of Our Lady*, where Lydgate adds systematic alliteration to his heavily Latinate version of a passage from the *Anticlaudianus* of Alain de Lille:

> Paradys of plesaunce, gladsom to all good,
> Benygne braunchelet of the pigment-tre,
> Vinarye envermailyd, refrescher of oure food,
> Lycour aȝens langour that pallid may not be,
> Blisful bawm-blossum, bydyng in bounte,
> Thi mantel of mercy on oure myschef spred,
> Or woo awak us, wrappe us undyr thi weed.[38]

The technique here is subtler than in the *Te Deum* or *Letabundus*, where the intention seemed to be to overwhelm both resistance and understanding and create a kind of linguistic hypnosis. Here the defiance of both sensuous 'truth' and rational association in the accumulation of types is carefully controlled syntactically, so that the mind is driven back on the only kind of truth that is relevant, an illuminated conceptual truth. The difference is one that could be paralleled in fifteenth-century painting.

Such achievement is rare in Lydgate. Luxuriance of language and metaphor easily passes over into mere flamboyant display, and it was the latter, unfortunately, that lent itself most readily to imitation. Lydgate's influence in another sphere of religious poetry, the saint's legend, was equally powerful and little more fortunate. He wrote a number of shorter saints' lives, some of them rhetorically elaborate and experimental in form, like those of *St Austyn, Dan Joos* and *St Giles*, the last of which uses an invocatory structure (see above, p. 186), but his main influence was exerted through his massive epic treatment of the lives of the patron saints of his own monastery and of nearby St Alban's, works again in which he was self-consciously expanding and improving on his Chaucerian model in the *Man of Law's Tale*. The *Life of St Edmund and St Fremund* has some strong passages of narrative dealing with the martyrdom of the East Anglian king by the Danes, but the mass of surrounding amplification is lifeless; the *Life of St Albon and St Amphabell*, the text of which is inflated with some inept early sixteenth-century additions, has nothing to recommend it. Amplification is here so mechanical that the siege of Albon in his house, a significantly doom-laden moment in the narrative, is introduced with a traditional spring-description (ii. 856–69). At such moments one despairs of Lydgate, and deplores the stimulus he gave to so much bad writing. But he returns to console us, in the *Testament*, a carefully constructed poem which uses the 'facts' of a pseudo-autobiography to enforce some telling lessons in penitential meditation and devotion, and above all in *The Life of Our Lady*, which survives in over forty MSS. Not unflawed, this is yet Lydgate's best long poem, one of the few in which he

235

THE CLOSE OF THE MIDDLE AGES

was moved to assemble and organise a variety of literary sources, and one in which he was able to do so because the material of his poem was so intimately familiar to him. He makes of it, not a life in the usual sense, but a compendium of Mariolatry, a rhapsodic meditation on a series of episodes from the life of the Virgin, interspersed with invocation, celebration and exposition of dogma. Narrative, so uncongenial to Lydgate on the whole, is discarded, for the poem's sequence has more to do with the celebration of the liturgical feasts to which no doubt it is directly related. There is no sense in this poem that Lydgate is working at a task, or that the processes of verse-making have been smoothed to a mechanical amplification. The language is rich when it needs to be rich, in the splendours of apostrophe and invocation, but happiest when Lydgate moves among traditional imagery of star and rose, daystar and night, with a familiar certainty of touch:

> O fayre rose, O Rose of Iericho,
> That hast this day god and man also
> In Bedlem borne aȝen the gray morowe
> The nyght to voyde of al our olde sorowe.[39]

## The formal poetic tradition

Discussion of the formal poetic tradition of the fifteenth century, which is largely, it should be made clear, Lydgatian rather than Chaucerian, must revert for a moment to Hoccleve, who, working in the first quarter of the century, is not influenced by Lydgate. From his precarious foothold in the office of the Privy Seal, and perhaps with some encouragement from Chaucer, whom he may have known,[40] Hoccleve seems to have had ambitions for court recognition and advancement. His *Letter of Cupid* (see above, p. 215) anticipates a court or courtly audience, and elsewhere he claims the privilege of congratulating Henry V on his efforts against the Lollards, in his *Balades to Henry V and the Knights of the Garter* and *Balade after King Richard II's bones were brought to Westminster*, with which we may compare the virulent *Address to Sir John Oldcastle*. He dedicates *The Regement of Princes* to Henry, as Prince of Wales, but whether this means much more than the optimistic canvassing of Gloucester as patron in the *Complaint* series it is hard to say, in view of the apparent unsuccess of Hoccleve's life. He certainly lacks anything like Lydgate's access to court patronage, and even his begging poems, not at all unwitty as light comic performances (though lacking the linguistic and metaphorical complexity of Lydgate's *Letter to Gloucester*), have a pathetic edge to them in that they are addressed, not to potential patrons, but to the government officials responsible for the payment of his annuity. Apart from these occasional pieces and some respectable routine religious verse, including a Marian prayer, *Mother of God*, long attributed to Chaucer, Hoccleve's main poetic activity was, like Lydgate's, in the field of translation. *The Regement of Princes* is freely conflated from Aegidio Colonna's

*De Regimine Principum*, the *Secreta Secretorum*, and other well-known Latin compilations, the tendency of which was to suggest that princes should follow virtue and eschew vice. To the exemplary stories which frequently illustrate these unexceptionable propositions, Hoccleve gives a pungent liveliness (notably in the story of John of Canace, 4180–354), but for the most part, lacking Lydgate's range, gravity and taste for the high style, he is content to let the morality speak fairly soberly for itself. The multiplication of copies of the *Regement* (there are over forty MSS) is a sign that people wanted an English version of this well-known 'Mirror for Princes' material, not that they wanted a poem by Hoccleve, who had little influence or fame in the fifteenth century. Such was the function of verse translation.

Hoccleve's more individual poetic gift emerges in the 2000-line quasi-auto-biographical prologue to the *Regement*, cast in the form of a dialogue with a Beggar. Hoccleve complains bitterly of the disappointments of his life, his 24 years in the office of the Privy Seal, his failing eyesight, the problems of getting paid, the tyranny of jacks-in-office, his failure to get the benefice he deserved, the poverty that awaits him in old age; he also reflects sharply on some more general abuses of the age, such as sartorial excess, simony, child-marriages, heresy and the ill-treatment of old soldiers; the Beggar offers consoling truths concerning the virtues of poverty and the fickleness of Fortune. There are ways in which this extraordinary display can be related to well-established traditions of confessional literature, in the *Romance of the Rose*, Chaucer and Gower, and we can certainly admire the way Hoccleve has woven old truths out of apparently new experience without assuming that the experience has to be autobiographically true. The unique quality here should be identified as a dramatic one, a control over the exchange of dialogue so that it seems to proceed naturally from the responses of the participants, and a gift for colloquial idiom in which Hoccleve appears the true inheritor of Chaucer's well-bred low vernacular.

The *Complaint* series is an attempt to make a longish poem out of nothing, perhaps in a late bid for poetic recognition (parts of the work appear elsewhere, and the whole series in a MS dedicated to the Countess of Westmoreland). It consists of a series of routine moralistic translations, two of them, the *Tale of Jereslaus's Wife* and the *Tale of Jonathas*, amplified from the *Gesta Romanorum*, the other, *How to Learn to Die*, from a chapter in the *Horologium Sapientiae*. They are associated in a peculiar way, presented as themselves the evidence of Hoccleve's regained sanity and poetic competence after the experiences of mental breakdown and loss of memory described in the prefatory *Complaint*. This *Complaint*, though it has behind it a long tradition of complaint and consolation literature, and a specific debt to Isidore's *De lamentatione animae dolentis*,[41] still manages to communicate an ineradicable sense of personal reality, where we recognise that what Hoccleve is doing is to take over Chaucer's habit of talking ironically about himself as a technique and precedent for talking truly about himself. The *Complaint* is followed by the *Dialogue with a Friend*, who arrives to see how he is getting on and knocks on the door,

> And cryed alowde 'Howe, Hoccleve, arte thow here?
> Open thy dore, me thinkethe it full yore
> Sythen I the se. What, man, for goddes ore
> Come out! for this quartar I not the sy,
> By owght I wot'. And out to hym cam I.　　　　　　　(3–7)

The dialogue that follows, in which 'the Friend' jokes and cajoles Hoccleve into confidence and reconcilement, is done with great verve and skill. The quality of immediacy, which looks so well beside Lydgate's bookishness, is almost enough to make us believe Hoccleve's own account of how he writes poetry:

> Freend, I nat medle of matires grete. . . .
> If I lightly nat cacche may th'effect
> Of thyng in which laboure I me purpose,
> Adieu my studie, anoon my book I close.
> By stirtes whan þat a fressh lust me takith
> Wole I me bisye now and now a lyte.
> But whan þat my lust dullith and asslakith
> I stynte wole and no lenger wryte.　　　　　　　(498–508)

Again it is essentially a dramatic gift that Hoccleve displays here, a gift for vivid, ready and revealing colloquial exchange, with little sense of the author's inter-position. Perhaps one of the successes of Hoccleve's other 'autobiographical' poem, the *Male Regle*, is again dramatic, this time a solo performance in which Hoccleve acts the fool in order to win laughter and perhaps the long-delayed payment of his annuity. It is in fact a begging-poem, framed as a penitential confession,[42] in which Hoccleve describes the waste he has made of his life, going to taverns, kissing girls (but never 'the deede'—'Whan þat men speke of it in my presence,/For shame I wexe as reed as is the gleede', 156–9), wasting his afternoons on the Thames, where the particular attraction was the obsequious-ness of the boatmen—

> Othir than 'maistir' callid was I neuere. . .
> Me thoghte I was y-maad a man for euere:
> So tikelid me þat nyce reverence
> Þat it me made larger of despense　　　　　　　(201–5)

and promises amendment now that he has learnt his lesson. He will now be a good investment. Hoccleve lacks the care and stamina (as he well knows) of a major poet, but even so there are few minor poets who can touch the heart, the conscience and the funnybone all at once, as he does.

Hoccleve's success as a poet is almost independent of the translating activities which are his main 'occasions' for writing poetry. John Walton, canon of Ose-ney, near Oxford, has a sterner sense of vocation, and devotes himself with scru-pulous care to the translation of Boethius (1410; ed. EETS 170) commissioned by Elizabeth Berkeley, daughter of Trevisa's patron Lord Berkeley, for whom

Walton probably did a prose translation of *Vegetius De Re Militari* (Elizabeth married the Earl of Warwick, and it was their daughter who commissioned Lydgate's *Guy of Warwick*). Walton is a most skilful versifier: his metre, like Hoccleve's, is careful and regular, and he knows well how to manage the stanza so as to violate neither metre nor sense,

> And wordes eke als neigh as may be broght
> Where lawe of metir is noght resistent. (St. 3)

He shows good sense in switching from ballade to rhyme royal (which has one rhyme fewer) for books IV and V, with their more complex programme of philosophical exposition. Walton has learnt many of his basic techniques from Chaucer's poetry, and he makes systematic use also of Chaucer's prose translation of Boethius, to which his own is in most respects superior. It is interesting also to compare Walton's lucid handling of the predestination debate (e.g. stanzas 854–7) with Chaucer's fumbling in *Troilus* (iv. 1016–43).

It may seem an over-simplification to attribute the corruption of this sensible and unostentatious verse-tradition to the intervention of Lydgate's influence, but the conclusion seems inescapable with Benedict Burgh, a follower of Lydgate and East Anglian cleric of some eminence. He has a translation of the *Disticha Catonis*, a school-text and source of much of the pragmatic wisdom ('Yiff place to hym, that excedith thy myht', 1109)[43] of the Middle Ages and after, which he did for a member of the East Anglian Bourchier family in a shrewd and metrically regular middle style. But he also came under the influence of Lydgate, to whom he wrote a verse *Letter* of ludicrous pomposity, and when he was asked to complete the translation of the *Secreta Secretorum* which Lydgate left unfinished at his death he did so in Lydgate's high style, even to the extent of imitating Lydgate's confused syntax and broken-backed lines. George Ashby, Clerk to the Signet, was similarly influenced: his main work is a translation of the *Dicta Philosophorum*, a favourite collection of moral saws similar to those in the *Secreta*, and he wrote also *The Active Policy of a Prince*, in the *Regement* tradition, for Edward, Prince of Wales, and *A Prisoner's Reflections*, where he applies the consolations of *Fall of Princes* literature to his own fallen state. Ashby is not unintelligent, and some of his reflections on government in the *Active Policy* show clear and uncluttered thinking,[44] but he is bedevilled by the muse, under the influence of which he can only throw out a fog of Lydgatian abstraction:

> A feire speker with swete mansuetude
> Refreynethe grete noyes & displeasance,
> Where rigorous speche, vengeable & rude,
> Subvertithe al polletique ordenance. (*Dicta*, 1177–80)

John Metham is another writer whose admiration for Lydgate, if it persuaded him to try his hand at poetry, proved his undoing. His romance of *Amoryus and Cleopes* (ed. EETS 132), dedicated in 1449 to Sir Miles Stapleton, one of the group of East Anglian patrons with whom Lydgate, Burgh and Bokenham are associated, is promisingly curious in its excursions into astrology, pagan religious practice and necromancy (Metham also wrote treatises on palmistry and physiognomy), but its metre is indescribable and its patches of Lydgatian ornament wholly adventitious. *The Assembly of Gods* (ed. EETS, ES 69) shares with Lydgate (to whom it was once ascribed) a taste for the friars' versions of classical mythology, and contains also a full-blown *psychomachia*, perhaps related to morality-plays, which make it an important document in the history of late medieval allegory;[45] its misfortune is to be in verse, for its metre is a nightmare version of Lydgate's.

A different kind of pretentiousness marks two strange and strangely neglected professional translations of Latin treatises, *Palladius on Husbondrie (De Re Rustica)* and *Knyghthode and Bataile (Vegetius De Re Militari)*, both probably by the same Robert Parker, who was early in the household of Humphrey of Gloucester and later a King's clerk and priest in Calais.[46] The translation of Palladius was made about 1440 as part of Humphrey's campaign to dignify and enrich English letters, for the purpose of which he encouraged, at various times, Lydgate, Ashby, Norton and Capgrave. He took a keen interest in this particular translation, correcting it in draft section by section:

> And lo my lord in honde hath Feueryeer;
> Wul he correcte? Ey what haue y to done?
> He wul doon as a lord.... (iii. 1211–13)

The poet says that Humphrey, whom he addresses with an egregious, almost comic, awed reverence—

> Serenous prince! or thus: O prmcis flour!
> Or thus: O prince in pees and duc in werre!
> Or nay: O Goddis knyght and Cristis tour!
> Or ellis thus: O londis lif and sterre
> Of light!...
> Or y noot what, excedyng so nature ...
> But God, me semeth, best thou mayst resemble. (i. 1186–94)

was particularly concerned about metre, and certainly metrical regularity has been achieved, if at the cost of natural stress, idiom and sometimes sense. The most licentious enjambement ('Ronk lond a fote and half, a valey twey/Feet deep is at the best', ii. 169–70) and contorted word-order ('The lupyne is no wedyng on to spende', ii. 59) combine to suggest that the author, quite regardless of native speech rhythms, set out to reshape English verse on the model of Latin metrical and syntactic patterns; his transliterations of technical words ('At Janyueer ablaqueacioun/The vynys axe in placis temporate./Italiens excodicacioun/Hit calle', ii. 1–4) evince a similar regard for Latinity. None of this is unintentional incompetence, as the poet shows in the increasingly ambitious ballade envoys that he adds to each book (perhaps, like Lydgate, at Gloucester's instigation, as parades of rhetoric), replete with single, double and triple internal rhyme and single and double *rime brisée*, ending with a stanza that reads the same down as across (xiii. 71–8).[47] With all this, the translation has great vigour, power of compression, and a vein of irrepressible whimsy, as when he comments on the uselessness of goose-dung as fertiliser:

> Fy on you, gees; fy on your tail for shame!
> Your dounge is nought, turn out your taille of game.
>
> (i. 531–2, EETS ed. only)

If Parker was learning his craft in the Palladius he shows himself to have profited in his translation of the treatise on war by Vegetius which he presented to Lord Beaumont to dedicate to the King in 1458. Verse and style have the same basic character, abounding in inversions, neologisms and self-consciously Latinate constructions ('Forthi comynge a foo, vitaile thee', 1134), and there is the same scrupulous attention to metre, including a warning to the scribe, reminiscent of Chaucer's, 'that neither he take of ner multiplye' (3028), but the poet allows himself much more freedom to introduce new material. He makes of the work, in fact, both a glorification of martial chivalry (quite different from the un-emotional pragmatism of the original),

> Here is the day of conflict vncerteyn,
> Here is to se deth, lif, honour & shame.
> Glade vs, o Lord, this day & make vs fayn,
> And make vs of this grete ernest a game! (1706–9)

and also a piece of open Lancastrian propaganda against the rebellious Yorkists:

> What is this oost, aduerse, rebelliouns
> Presumptuous, periurious, mischevous,
> Heresious with circumcelliouns?...
> Her lord is Lucifer, the kyng of pride. (2014–19)

A totally imaginary sea-battle between Lancastrians and Yorkists is done with tremendous vigour, and everywhere there is the same inexhaustible pugnacity and panache:

> Lepe o thi foo, loke if he dar abide;
> Wil he nat fle, wounde him, mak woundis wide,
> Hew of his honde, his legge, his thegh, his armys;
> It is the Turk; though he be sleyn, noon harm is. (372–5)

The extravagance, abandonment and stylistic furore, the obsession with verse-technique, as well as the sense that these qualities are being paraded self-cons-

241

ciously, half-humorously, before us, make Parker something of a minor Dunbar.

Other poets working within the formal verse-tradition are content to accept the dignity it imparts to their simpler practical and didactic purposes. *The Libel of English Policy* (1436), probably by Adam Moleyns,[48] a high-ranking civil servant and churchman, sometime Clerk to the Council, is a knowledgeable and well-argued statement of economic and naval policy, while *Peter Idley's Instructions to his Son* (c. 1450),[49] written by an esquire of Oxfordshire who eventually followed in Chaucer's footsteps by being appointed Controller of the King's Works (1456–62), is a compendium of moral and spiritual counsel, and a good example of both practical verse and practical verse-making, borrowing freely as it does from Mannyng and Lydgate. A similar 'levelling' of the Chaucerian style to practical purposes can be seen in courtesy-books like *The Babees Book* (ed. EETS 32), written to give instruction in etiquette to squires and *henxmen*, 'yonge Babees, whom bloode Royalle ... Hath enourmyd' (15–17), in service at the court of a great lord, or *The Book of Curtesye* printed by Caxton (ed. EETS, ES 3), written for the young son of a well-educated man, who praises Gower, Chaucer, Lydgate and, interestingly, Hoccleve at length (323–413). Such poems signal both the new social dignity of English and also the pragmatic levelling of the poetic style which had helped to win that dignity.[50] Finally, the general penetration of verse, characteristic of the fifteenth century, into every possible area of 'literary' activity is extravagantly demonstrated in the alchemical treatises which royal interest encouraged at this time, the *Ordinal of Alchemy* (1477), in pentameter couplet, by Thomas Norton of Bristol, and the *Compend of Alchemy* (1471), in rhyme royal, by George Ripley, canon of Bridlington, which begins its Preface[51] with a grotesque flourish of Lydgatian aureation but thereafter disintegrates under the weight of technical language.

In this formal non-courtly tradition, in which we could trace Lydgate's influence further in medical pieces, dedications, pageant poems, civic welcomes and occasional poems of other kinds,[52] the one poem that has any claim as a poem is *The Court of Sapience*. This long didactic and encyclopaedic work treats Sapience first in terms of the spiritual Wisdom which encouraged the Son to reconcile the Four Daughters of God by offering himself to atone for man's transgression, and second in terms of the mundane wisdom which man gains from the knowledge of God's creation and from study. Book I is thus devoted mainly to the Debate of the Four Daughters, an eloquent display of rhetorical set speeches rather different from the lively altercation in *Piers Plowman* (B. XVIII) and superior to the treatment of the same theme in Lydgate's *Life of Our Lady* (book II). The eloquence has an occasional touch of grandeur:

> Fowre thowsand yere and more ys suffysaunt
> For to punysshe olde Adam for a tast,
> And well awey, hell ys exuberaunt
> Wyth hys ospryng and owre reame standeth wast.[53]

The second book is an undisguised encyclopaedia of the names and properties of precious stones, rivers, fish, flowers, trees, birds and animals, and of the content of the main subjects of academic study, including Grammar ('And whyche ys nowne, whyche verbe and whiche pronown', 1817) and Dialectic ('Whiche ys quatkyn, what hys proporcioun/What thyng he ys and hys diuisioun', 1854–9). The treatment is crisp, intelligent and well-informed, and provides a salutary reminder, not at all dispiriting, that the fifteenth century was healthily unconstrained in its sense of what was 'fit' for poetry. The pleasing picture of students at work,

> Many a babe of souerayn heuynly chere,
> Desyrous all in konnyng to habound,
> Abowte Dame Gramer sate, to haue theyr ground.　　　　　(1839–41)

and of their interest in their studies,

> Wyth sophyms strong straunge matyers they dyscus,
> And fast they cry oft: 'Tu es asinus'.　　　　　(1868–9)

suggest that the poem might have been by a university teacher or perhaps, as Spindler suggests (p. 105), by the master responsible for *The Babees Book*. The versification is impeccable, and the poet acknowledges only Gower and Chaucer as 'erthely goddes two' (50), with no mention of Lydgate; Hawes' attribution of the poem to Lydgate is unacceptable on many counts.


*Religious poetry*

The formal verse-tradition is characterised basically by the use of certain kinds of metre, namely the pentameter in couplet, rhyme royal and ballade stanza (a distinction of status observed by Caxton in nearly all the English poetry he printed),[54] by the styles associated with those metres, and by the reverential acknowledgment accorded to Chaucer or Lydgate. Much of the religious poetry of the fifteenth century could be seen as belonging to the same tradition, though the immediate debts are to Lydgate, again the century's paradigm, rather than to Chaucer. Nevertheless, the continuity of older and simpler forms should be recognised, as well as the influence of other traditions than the Chaucerian towards a more heightened literary presentation. There are in fact a range of styles available to fifteenth-century religious poets, appropriate to different functions and to the different needs of a much expanded audience. At the most basic level, there continue to be put forth simple expositions of doctrine, for the use and instruction of the lower laity and clergy, like the verses on the Creed and Ten Commandments in Lambeth MS 853 (ed. EETS 24) or the *Instructions for Parish Priests* (ed. EETS 31) compiled by John Myrc, canon of Lilleshall in Shropshire, which works on a level of low expectation (priests are not to administer baptism when drunk, 623) and which is dominated by the need to give fundamental instruction in the Ten Commandments and Seven Deadly Sins for them 'Þat haue no bokes of here owne,/And oþer þat beth of mene lore' (2036–7). Short mnemonic pieces, prayers and hymns, of a kind long familiar in the fourteenth century, continue to be copied in the *Fasciculus Morum*[55] and in sermon notebooks like Harley MS 7322 (ed. EETS 15). Many of these pieces are copies or versions of older poems, as is often the case with other fifteenth-century texts: the famous thirteenth-century macaronic 'Of on þat is so fayr and briȝt' (see above, p. 100), for instance, is adapted as a carol,[56] and other poems are constantly being reworked, like the *Erthe upon Erthe* poems (EETS 141), or fitted to new fashions by the addition of a burden or a *chanson d'aventure* opening (e.g. Brown, *XVth Century*, Nos 1, 7), or simply copied, with more or less random variation. This is another useful reminder of the continuity of tradition, and of the difficulty of relating consumption closely to composition, as opposed to production. The existence of many different kinds of poem within the same MS, which is characteristic of fifteenth-century collections and miscellanies, likewise serves to remind us how difficult it is to correlate subject, form and function, except at the extreme ends of the social scale. Thus the instructional pieces mentioned above (though they could be matched with instructional pieces on the same subjects in a higher style, as we have seen in Lydgate) are clearly intended for an uneducated audience, and so are the lively verse-sermons in Lambeth 853 (ed. EETS 24) called *Þe Deuelis Perlament*, 'þerof is red in tyme of ȝeere/On þe first sunday of clene lent' (491–2), and *The Mirror of the Periods of Man's Life*, a morality play in the form of a sermon ('Now haue ȝe herde...' 633). But the simple prayers that are offered for rising and going to bed, or to be said, in accordance with long-recommended practice, at esoteric points in the divine service,[57] could be useful to all classes. Sometimes changes are simply responses to the new literary situation: thus the version of the Seven Penitential Psalms by friar Thomas Brampton (1414),[58] identical in context with that of Maydenstoon, is equipped with seasonal introduction and refrain, and is in four-stress ballade rather than alternate-rhyming stanza. What we can distinguish, as the property of an educated audience, is the *Prayer of the Holy Name* (Brown, *XVth Century*, No. 125), simple as is its function, in rhyme royal.

Metrical form, with these provisos, is valuable in determining class use and function, and the level of literary expectation. The simpler pieces described above use forms well-established in the fourteenth century, such as the short couplet and alternate-rhyming four-stress quatrain and octave. Pentameter rhyme royal and ballade stanza is the distinguishing feature of the high style, as it is found in the 'aureate' collections such as Add. 20059 and Arundel 285,[59] while there is a middle style, not untouched by aureation and its associated alliteration, which is dominated by the four-stress ballade stanza or by more complex stanzas based thereon, often with the use of refrain (the repetition of the last integral line of the stanza, sometimes with variation: to be distinguished from the independent and unvarying 'burden'). The ambitions of this middle style should not be underestimated, in view of the difficult rhyme-scheme of the ballade stanza, particularly when it is equipped with refrain, which effectively

determines rhymes for the whole poem.[60] The greater formality of verse-struc-
ture has its counterpart in the systematic methods of thematic construction,
enumerative, acrostic and alphabetic, which are now more widely practised.
As to function, it can be assumed that the dominant purpose of these pieces,
apart from those that cater for simple instruction and celebration, is to assist
penitential and devotional meditation at every level, to exhort, console, inform,
inspire and afflict. So Myrc, in his book of sermons, the *Liber Festivalis*, or *Festial*
(ed. EETS, ES 96), quotes, in his sermon on the Assumption, a poem on the
Seven Joys of the Virgin (pp. 232–3) to be said 'wyth mynd and deuocyon',
while on a higher level the traditions of Rolle are still strong. Though there is
little new composition, the copying, reworking, versifying and imitating of his
meditative writing is important in the fifteenth century, as in Thornton's Lincoln
MS, which contains, amongst much prose, prayers and devotions to Jesus,
including poems by Rolle, or in Lambeth 853, where there is a copy of a well-
known meditation on the sweetness of Jesus and a version of 'Loue is liif þat
lastiþ ay'.[61] In the same meditative tradition there is a fine translation of Pecham's
*Philomena*, edited as *The Nightingale* (EETS, ES 80). MS Arundel 285 was presumably intended for the use of a religious house, and includes specific instructions for devotional practice—'Heir endis þe exercicioun for Setterday' (Brown,
*XVth Century*, No. 94) or 'Heir followis ane deuoit orisoun To be said in the honour
of þe sevin wordis that our saluiour spak apoun þe croce' (No. 96). At the same
time, we can recognise both a more ruthless didactic colouring that is given to
devotion[62] and also, in the frequent use of dialogue and in the more sophisticated
development of narrative frames, movements towards drama and realism which
give evidence of some degree of 'literary' expectation, and one more interesting
than the taste which is satisfied by bastardised Anglo-Latin.

Marian poetry is perhaps the most interesting in the fifteenth century for the
examination of these developments. Much of it is of a routine nature, translations,
more or less elaborate, of the favourite hymns and antiphons, *Ave*-poems, celebrations of the Five Joys of the Virgin and, perhaps more characteristic of this
inflated century, of the Seven Heavenly Joys. Formal liturgical structures like
these, purged of personal devotion or the need for emotional articulacy, offer
the fullest opportunity for the display of aureate technique:

> All haile! whose solempne glorious concepcioun
> Full of glorie and hye ioye tryumphaunte,
> Bothe celestyall & terrestriall gif laude with Iubilacioun
> Of new ioy & gladnesse with solace incessaunte.
>
> (Brown, *XVth Century*, 12. 8–11)

There is also a modified aureate style, associated with a heavily alliterative four-
stress line, as in this poem on the Coronation of the Virgin,

> Undir a park ful prudently pyght,
> A perillous path men passyd by,

> There herd I a melody of myght,
> Scandaunt on skalys, above the sky.... (39. 1–4)

From the literary point of view, however, the most interesting poems are those relating to the Compassion of the Virgin, where the tendencies towards drama, dialogue and realism characteristic of the century are most effectively exploited: examples are the magnificent Marian lament, *Filius Regis Mortuus Est* (No. 6), introduced as the poet, wandering through a wilderness, finds 'a solempne cite' and a maiden 'at þe citeys ende' sobbing:

> 'The kyngis sone,' sche saide, 'is dede'.[63]

and *Quia Amore Langueo*, the Virgin's Complaint of love for Man, famous for its evocative opening,

> In a tabernacle of a tour,
> As y stood musynge on þe moone,
> A crowned queene, moost of honour,
> Me þouȝte y siȝ sittinge in trone. (EETS 15, p. 148)

The most powerful emotional development is of the Pietà, as where the Virgin compares her state to that of other mothers:

> O woman, woman, wel is the,
> Thy childis cap þu dose vpon;
> Þu pykys his here, be-holdys his ble,
> Þu wost not wele when þu hast done.
> But euer, alas! I make my mone
> To se my sonnys hed as hit is here;
> I pyke owt thornys be on & on,
> For now liggus ded my dere son, dere. (7. 9–16)

Or, with more brutal physicality,[64] how mothers fondle the feet of their children as they dance them on the knee,

> But þe most fyngur of any hande
> Thorow my sonnys fete I may put here
> And pulle hit out sore bledand. (7. 45–7)

Another moving Pietà, *Who cannot weep come learn of me* (9), with its burden 'Sodenly afraide', is in an unusual 9-line stanza and can be seen as a companion piece to *Woefully Arrayed* (103), an appeal from the Cross.

Elsewhere we can see how the influence of Marian devotion gathers up other literary forms, as when Mary addresses the audience as if she were a minstrel, 'Listyns, lordyngus, to my tale' (10), or when the form and language of courtly love-lyric (47) and love-epistle (46) are taken over in addresses to the Virgin, even to the last cadence:

> Goe, lytyll byll, & doe me recommende
> Vn-to my lady with godely countynaunce.[65] (46. 1–2)

An important development, and one which shows the century in its least pompous light, is the adoption of the carol for Marian, as for other themes. The carol, the origin of which has already been discussed,[66] is a song-form, basically associated with music and often appearing with musical text in the MSS, and characterised by the repetition of a burden, by simplicity of form, and on the whole by themes of joy and celebration, particularly of the Nativity, whence the close connection with Christmas. It should be emphasised that the fifteenth-century religious carols, though (artfully and deceptively) simple in form and function, and of course universal in appeal, are not presumed to be of popular provenance. In details of form, carols vary: they may have burdens in Latin or in English; the stanza may be longer in some literary versions of carol; the themes may be doctrinal, or moral, or sad, as in the Nativity dialogue carols:

> When gabrell cnellyd before my face,
> And sayd 'heylle lady full of grace',
> He neuer told me nooþing of þis. (Brown, *XVth Century*, 1. 26–8)

or the famous Corpus Christi carol of the early sixteenth century, 'Lully, lulley; lully, lulley;/The fawcon hath born my mak away' (Greene, *Early English Carols*, No. 322). But the most numerous, characteristic and delightful are the carols of Annunciation, Nativity and Epiphany—'Make we myrth/For Crystes byrth,/ And syng we Yole tyl Candelmes' (Greene, *Early English Carols*, No. 8), 'Tyrle, tyrlo/So merylye the shepperdes began to blowe' (Greene, *Early English Carols*, No. 79: used in the Coventry Nativity play), 'Ther is no rose of swych vertu/As is the rose that bare Jhesu' (Greene, *Early English Carols*, No. 173). Associated with the carols in spirit of joyful celebration are the two finest short lyrics of the English Middle Ages, 'I syng of a myden þat is makeles' (Brown, *XVth Century*, No. 81) and 'Adam lay I-bowndyn' (No. 83), the first characterised by the subtle muta-tion of traditional Marian and Incarnation imagery, the second by a joyful little parody of dialectic.[67] Both, it should be noticed, are in the old long line.

The Passion is less important in a century dominated by Mariolatry, and is treated both less flamboyantly and with less feeling, perhaps partly because the focus of devotion has shifted to the pictures of the wounded Christ, the *imago pietatis*,[68] which the shorter poems on the Passion were often designed to accom-pany. There are amplifications of traditional Passion and Resurrection themes in the less extreme aureate style in Arundel 285 (Brown, *XVth Century*, Nos 91, 112), some development of numbered meditative themes such as the seven blood-sheddings (92) and the Seven Words from the Cross (96), and lengthy elaboration of the appeals from the Cross (see above, p. 133), *O vos omnes*, *Homo vide* and

247

*Popule Meus* (Brown, *XVth Century*, Nos 102–6). Significant is the development of the last theme in terms of a dialogue of Christ and man (107), which may be compared with the very long dialogue in William Lychefelde's *Complaint of God*.[69] These are essentially didactic poems, calling for moral reform rather than love, in a way characteristic of fifteenth-century treatments of the Passion (Woolf, *English Religious Lyric*, p. 183), and the more unexpected therefore is the moving power of *Brother, Abide*, a poem in rhyme royal from the end of the century, which takes the *O vos omnes* as the starting point of a long, detailed and powerful 'autobiography' of Christ, with care for close narrative and for intellectual articulation rare in the fifteenth century:

> Off tendure love, all this I dyd endure;
> Love dyde me lede, love dyde me thus constrayne;
> And, for my dede & grevouse adventure,
> More aske I nott but love for love a-gayne. (109. 190–3)

At the opposite extreme is the devotional fervour and mystical imagery of *Quia Amore Langueo* ('In the vaile of restles mynde', to be distinguished from the Marian poem with the same refrain), where Christ shows his hands and feet gloved and shod with blood and speaks in the language of the Song of Songs of the chamber in his side where his love may nest and of the apples that 'ben rype in my gardine' (EETS 15, p. 155).

The moralistic, monitory and penitential poems, in which the century, as might be expected, abounds, mostly move on Lydgate's low level of ambition and interest, content with Cato and the universal ministry of death as their fount of inspiration. A poem on the Seven Deadly Sins (Brown, *XVth Century*, 178) is different from the usual morality refrain-poems (e.g. 182, 186) in the kind of sharp colloquialism, reminiscent of Langland ('Auaricia is an horribill sore', line 73, 'Accidia is a sowkyng blayne', 85), it brings to its treatment of the sins as diseases, while *Reuertere*, another refrain-poem, makes a cunning allegory out of the *chanson d'aventure* opening so meaninglessly habitual elsewhere.[70] Attempts to dramatise presentation by the use of dialogue are not uncommon, while the message of mortality, 'This lyfe, I see, is but a cheyre feyre', comes over particularly strongly when spoken by a dead man:

> To-day I sat full ryall in a cheyere,
> Tyll sotell deth knokyd at my gate,
> And on-avysed he seyd to me, chek-mate!
> Lo! how sotell he maketh a devors—
> And wormys to fede, he hath here leyd my cors.
> Speke softe, ye folk, for I am leyd aslepe! (149. 10–15)

There is no excessive morbidity, such as is often associated with the late Middle Ages on the continent. One poem (163), indeed, speaks of death as the soul's friend, for it is 'ende off werdes wo', so 'Thynk þat þou ert ded alway,/qwyllis þat þou dwellis here' (lines 54, 61–2), while another (164) has death as 'the porte of peese, & resstfulnes/to them that stondeth in stormes of dysese'. We might put beside these the noble consolation of Hermit and Carthusian in Lydgate's *Danse Macabre*.

For all these poems, we know little of provenance or authorship. One or two secular names seem to emerge from the morality poems, 'R. Stokys' for one (181) and a 'Squire Halsham' for another (171), a cleverly constructed little piece twice plundered by Lydgate.[71] The vast majority of the others, and all the specifically religious pieces, must be by clerics, and some are associated with religious houses (5, 31, 154). The well-known hymn of Richard de Caistre (64), vicar of St Stephen's church at Norwich, shows how little it would help if we did know more of the authors, since his hymn is largely adapted from an earlier poem. James Ryman, the Franciscan rhymer of the late fifteenth century, might be important if his large output of carols (119 of the total of over 500) were less mediocre.

John Awdelay, however, is more interesting. Chantry priest to a Shropshire lord, he seems to have retired when sick to Haghmond Abbey where, his death being unexpectedly delayed, he wrote his poems (ed. EETS 184) about 1426:

> As I lay seke in my langure
> In an abbay here be west,
> Þis boke I made with gret dolour
> When I myȝt not slep ne haue no rest. (No. 18. 482–5)

He tells how he had a dream of God's coming vengeance, and hastened to do what he could to improve both clergy and laity, to provide a 'cownsel of conseans' or 'ladder of heuen' (18. 417–18). His claim,

> Fore al þat is nedful to bode and soule
> Here in þis boke þen may ȝe se (18. 14–15)

is strikingly reminiscent of the similar claim of the Vernon MS (see above, p. 140), which he may have used. Of the 55 poems in Awdelay's MS, the first 18 contain the basic doctrinal instruction, along with themes for more advanced meditation and prayer. Awdelay seems to use tail-rhyme and other simple metres for the basic course and his favourite 13-line stanza (four-stress ballade + $c^3ddd^4c^3$) for the others. The poem in this group that compels attention is No. 2, a long and sprawling anthology of reproof and instruction to the clergy, written in the same 13-line stanza but with the octave in the long line (e.g. 'Þai woldon þai wroȝton wysely þat schuld ham lede and lere', 69), deeply penetrated by alliteration and alliterative rhythms (e.g. 'ȝif þai foloyn his fare þai fallyn to foly', 81). The poem is in fact profoundly influenced by *Piers Plowman* (there was an A-text in the Vernon MS), with mention of 'Mede þe maydyn' (705) and constant echoes of cadence and phrasing, as this, of lords:

> Þaȝ ȝe be leders of þe lond, gete ȝou louyng,
> And cale þe clarge to ȝour counsel, þat beryn Cristis kay,

> And holdist vp hole cherche þe prinse of heuen to pay;
> Y dred lest dedle sun þis reme wyl dystry.　　　　　　　　　(237–40)

After the first group of 18 poems, which Awdelay seems at one time to have regarded as his completed work (and which may well be the only poems that are entirely his own composition), there follow celebrations and salutation-poems (19–27), carols on a wide variety of subjects (28–52), an exposition of the Paternoster (53), and then the extraordinary poem of *The Three Dead Kings* (54). This is in a 13-line stanza consisting of genuine alliterative lines (usually alliterating *aa/aa*) rhyming alternatively in the octave, with a 5-line wheel of loose alliterative three-stress lines rhyming *cdccd*. The *ab* and *cd* rhymes are themselves inter-connected by assonance, there is concatenation between octave and wheel, and furthermore the lines alliterate systematically in groups, *aabbccdd/ddeff*. Such pyrotechnics have only been seen before in the *Pearl* tradition and *The Awntyrs off Arthure*, and the poem seems to have a further link with the latter in its story, which, after an opening boar-hunt,

> An a byrchyn bonke þer bous arne bryȝt,
> I saw a brymlyche bore to a bay broȝt.
> Ronke rachis with rerde þai ronnon a-ryȝt,
> Of al hore row and hore rest lytil hom þoȝt　　　　　　　　　(1–4)

tells how three kings get caught in a mist and meet three grisly spectres, 'schadows unschene', who warn them of their mortality. There are also reminiscences of *Sir Gawain and the Green Knight*, and *The Three Dead Kings* is clearly a product of the northern rhyming alliterative school which Awdelay borrowed and which he moralises upon in his last poem (55), 'Here may ȝe here now hwat ȝe be'.

Saints' lives constitute the bulk of the remaining religious poetry of the fifteenth century, though there is little new composition in the popular style: continued copying of the older Southern and Northern Legendaries presumably catered for this audience. What gaps there were had to do with local saints, like St Robert of Knaresborough, whose legend is very respectably translated from the Latin sources in brisk short couplet (ed. EETS 228), or St Etheldreda of Ely, treated rather more ponderously, with much historical material from the monastic sources, by a writer who claims that he was on pilgrimage there.[72] *The Legend of the Blood of Hailes* is quite specifically directed at pilgrims to that famous shrine, having been translated for their sake ('Bot for latyn endytyng cumburus is/For dyuerce pylgrymes þat may not dwelle,/Rede owre þat here in ynglys es', 33–5), and ending with the suggestion that they should take confession before presuming to look on the Holy Blood—'A penytancere es all-way redy þare' (394). *The Legend of St Wolfade and Ruffyn*, addressed to pilgrims at Stone in Staffordshire, is even closer to the modern guide-book, and suggests that they will want to see the nearby tablet inscribed with the story of the shrine's foundation:

> And all that on this tabull redes, God grante them hys grace,

Throe the meyne of these marters in heuen to haue a place.     (381–2)

Confession and grace alike, of course, would cost money. Most of these poems would be by local amateurs, and they lack both the vigour and technical competence of the professionals of the Legendaries and international pilgrim-guides,[73] and when they attempt anything more than the simple four-stress couplet they fall into chaos, as does the legend of *St Dorothea*, written in the worst Lydgatian high style. One of the few interesting pieces (it is from before 1400) is the *St Cristine* written by William Paris, Squire to the Earl of Warwick and his sole companion on the Isle of Man when he was exiled there by Richard II. Paris can write verse (he uses four-stress ballade) and he has the authentic touch for his virgin-martyr:

She toke hire tonge vpe, where ite lay,
Ande euene sche caste it at Juliane eye.     (465–6)

Otherwise the energies of popular hagiography seem to be transferred to the sensational domestic legends and pious tales which circulated freely in the Middle Ages, of the son, for instance, who watches his father burn in hell for lechery,[74] or the daughter who kills her mother, has three children by her father, kills her father, is touched by a pang of remorse and dies saved, or *The Child of Bristowe*, the story of a son who tries to save his avaricious father from hell after his death, full of detail of money, borrowings and security, and done with traditional panache.

Some of these legends are infected by 'literary' ambition, but the main inheritors of Lydgate's inflated hagiographic style are known clerics of some standing, two of them from East Anglia. Osbern Bokenham, Austin friar of Stoke-Clare, wrote a series of *Legendys of Hooly Wummen*, 1443–7 (ed. EETS 206), many of them commissioned by members of the local nobility and Suffolk gentry,[75] in which he reminds us with considerable frequency of his knowledge of Chaucer and Lydgate, his mastery of rhetoric, his learning in astronomy and medicine, whilst at the same time telling us at equally considerable length that he knows nothing of such things. He has in fact all the rhetorician's gambits, which he is not willing to be thought lacking, but seems happiest and is at his best in the more homely style of the prologues and linking passages, in couplet, where he chats in a lively way about his busy life and commissions from customers. The lives themselves, in bumpy rhyme royal, are a little monotonous, as the procession of virgin-martyrs are variously scourged, mutilated, broken, roasted, grilled, tipped in boiling oil, all to no seeming effect. The exception is *St Elizabeth*, neither virgin nor martyr, famed for her life not her passion, whose story is told with an attention to domestic detail quite affecting. John Capgrave, Austin friar of Lynn, is a more important figure: he was Prior of his house, Provincial of his order 1453–7, and author of commentaries on the Bible dedicated to Humphrey of Gloucester, a Latin *Liber de Illustribus Henricis* dedicated to Henry VI and an English prose *Chronicle* dedicated to Edward IV. In later years he seems to have run a 'publishing house' for his own works from his head-quarters in Lynn.[76] He also wrote lives of *St Norbert* and *St Katharine* in rhyme royal. The former, yet unedited, is sober enough, as befits a work written for the abbot of a nearby house (West Dereham) in honour of his order's founder, but *St Katharine* (ed. EETS 100) is important as an example of embellished hagiography in the Lydgate tradition which yet constantly falls back on older traditions for its sources of poetic energy. Capgrave's pentameter is much affected by the cadences of four-stress verse, not so much those of alliterative verse as of the popular romances; some echoes of *Havelok*, written in Lincolnshire, are close enough to suggest direct influence. *The Life of St Werburge* by Henry Bradshaw, monk of Chester, printed by Pynson in 1521 (ed. EETS 88), may be mentioned here as a posthumous survival of the Lydgate tradition long made obsolete by Caxton's prose version of *The Golden Legend*. Bradshaw's poem is both devout and ambitious, drawing on a wealth of historical sources to fill out the narrative of a revered local saint. He has the techniques of Lydgatian amplification at his command, but no poet demonstrates more the viciousness of Lydgate's influence, in persuading a serious man that poetry was what he had to write, and that poetry consists in a due sprinkling of polysyllables and the fitting with rhyme of roughly equal portions of prose.

## Drama

The drama of the fifteenth century is exclusively in verse,[77] and some attention should be given to it here, without trespassing on the history of the drama. Of the mystery cycles it must be said that, though they contain some of what is good in the religious verse of the century, they contain more of what is bad, and that whatever interest these plays have from the point of view of theatre, social history or theology, little of that interest derives from any use of language that might be called effectively poetic. The local clerics, such as guild-chaplains and chantry-priests, who were presumably responsible for the writing of the plays, seem to have considered complexity and variety of metre and stanzaic form, often combined with alliteration, to be the distinguishing features of 'poetry', and the successive piecemeal revisions to which the four extant cycles[78] were subject manifest the increasing strength of this notion, which we may relate to general fifteenth-century taste as well as to the demands of civic prestige. Pentameter, as might be expected, is never used in these plays, nor is there much of the bastard Latinising which goes by the name of aureation, perhaps because most of the texts as we have them were copied in the mid-fifteenth century, before the style fully took hold. There is nothing in the York plays (except for the late fragment of the *Coronation of the Virgin*) quite so grotesque as the Civic Welcome offered to Henry VII in 1486,[79] which reflects the civic poetic ambitions of the day, though there is an introduction to the Chester *Fall of Lucifer* and other interpolated passages (VIII. 261, XIII. 1) which represent later aureate taste, and the non-cycle Norwich *Grocers' Play of the Fall* from the early sixteenth century is badly afflicted by the disease:

I have plantyd an orcheyard most congruent
For hym to kepe and to tylle, by contemplacion:
Let us make an adjutory of our formacion
To hys symylutude, lyke in plasmacion.                    (5–8)

The mystery plays generally suffer from a milder form of verbal inflation, their most characteristic quality being an insistent pedestrian bookishness which obscures sense, significance and dramatic impact alike in the stretching of the text over its rigid metrical frame and in the contortions, repetitions and padding induced by the tyrannies of rhyme and metre:

My witte is waste nowe in wede,
I walowe, I walke, nowe woo is me,
For laide nowe is þat lufsome in lede,
The Jewes hym nayled vntill a tree.
My doulfull herte is euere in drede,
To grounde nowe gone is all my glee,
I sporne þer I was wonte to spede,
Nowe helpe me God in persones three.          (York, XXXIX. 9–16)

All the mystery cycles owe a debt to the professional didactic writing of the fourteenth century, to the *Cursor Mundi*, the *Northern Passion*, the *Gospel of Nicodemus* or the *Stanzaic Life of Christ*,[80] and indeed in many ways the plays are nothing so much as a transmuted form of the extended *Temporale* sequences in the earlier Legendaries (see above, p. 104). Their method, however, in dealing with these practical, professional, unostentatious pieces of writing is to expand and inflate meaninglessly, not out of gratuitous ostentation nor out of feebleness of mind, but through rigid commitment to an inflated idea of poetry that is, in its effects, neither poetic nor dramatic. The *Gospel of Nicodemus* is little enough as poetry but has at least the fourteenth-century virtue of saying simply what is to be said: here is the treatment it receives in one of the most admired of the York plays:

Crist said: ilk man a mowth has fre
To weld at his awen will                            (*Nicodemus*, 221–2)

Cf. [Jesus:] Euery man has a mouthe, þat made is on molde,
In wele and in woo to welde at his will             (XXXIII. 301–2)

I have wele herd why yhe him hate                   (*Nicodemus*, 317)

Cf. But I haue herde al haly why in hertes ȝe hym hate.    (XXXIII. 326)

It is sometimes difficult to believe that the monotonous hammering of alliteration and rhythm, in the York and Towneley plays especially, was ever suited or even intended for dramatic presentation, and it may be that what we have in the unique MSS of these plays, which are both Registers or official civic records, are, so to speak, the 'Minutes' of the plays, suitably doctored, polished and clad in the garb of official poetic respectability.

It would not be entirely true to say that the cycles are at their best when they are at their least ambitious, but simplicity is a virtue one learns to prize in such compositions, and the sonorous empty rhetoric of the opening of the York plays,

> I am gracyus and grete, god withoutyn begynnyng,
> I am maker vnmade, all mighte es in me,
> I am lyfe and way vnto welth wynnyng,
> I am formaste and fyrste, als I byd sall it be.
> My blyssyng o ble sall be blendyng,
> And heldand fro harme to be hydande,
> My body in blys ay abydande
> Vnendande withoutyn any endyng

can be set beside the grave lucidity of its close,

> Nowe is fulfillid all my for-þoght
> For endid is all erthely thyng.
> All worldly wightis þat I haue wroght
> Aftir þer werkis haue nowe wonnyng.
> Thei þat wolde synne and sessid noght
> Of sorowes sere now schall þei syng,
> And þei þat mendid þame whils þei moght
> Schall belde and bide in my blissing

so as to make clear that the difference is one of success in achieving the expression appropriate to a genre, not one of contextual significance. Many of the best passages in the cycles draw on non-dramatic contexts for their effectiveness, not so much here the longer narrative sources, which tend to be absorbed into the prevailing poetic, as lyric sources such as the Marian lament, the Complaint of Christ (as in the Towneley *Resurrection*), the penitential lament of the old man (as in the Towneley *Noah*: 'And now I wax old,/Seke, sory, and cold,/As muk apon mold/I widder away', III. 60–3) and the warning of mortality (as in the Towneley *Lazarus*, 'Amende the, man, whils thou may', XXXI. 174, or the fine *Memento Mori* in the N-town *Death of Herod*).[81] One greets such interludes with relief, like arias in an otherwise incomprehensible opera.

The York cycle is the longest and most respectable of the four cycles, its weakness a strained monotony of diction and alliteration rather than disorder or incompetence. Twenty-two verse-forms are used, but the ambition displayed in the use of such a large variety of metres is not matched by a strong sense of dramatic propriety. Whatever linguistic energy is displayed tends towards the bombastic, the raucous and the scatological, and the pressure of poetic form often exposes the inadequacies of poetic language, as in the way simple biblical statements are stuffed out with padding: 'A man lyvis noght in mayne and mode/with brede allone' (XXII. 75–6). The contrast with the grace and economy of contemporary religious prose (which has no laurels to win) is illuminating. Perhaps the 'York Realist',[82] responsible for reworking eight of the plays in the Passion sequence and for interventions in others, should be exempted from some of these strictures. He has gifts for dramatic realism, for creating atmosphere and filling out the implications of an event, and he has enough linguistic sophistication to burlesque bombastic styles (e.g. XXX. 28, XXXI. 13, XXXIII. 409). He writes vigorously in a variety of rhymed alliterative stanzas, related to those of the Northern and Western alliterative schools (see above, p. 185), but is too easily drawn by his medium into the thrashing and ranting to which it is so well suited, an effect which, however apt to the first scenes of buffeting and abuse, palls by repetition.

The Towneley cycle would be, except for some dramatic skill in its handling of *Abraham and Isaac* and *The Flight into Egypt*, in large measure a lesser York cycle, from which it borrows five plays, if it were not for the work of the 'Wakefield master', who has rewritten six plays and made his mark on seven others. He writes, except in *The Killing of Abel*, in a 9-line stanza, consisting of a quatrain of verses of the alliterative type (but not always with alliteration), with internal rhyme, and a wheel of shorter lines. He handles this exacting form with violent vigour and panache, and his choice of subject consistently reflects an understanding of the propriety of this style to low, violent and wicked characters— Herod, Pilate, shepherds, torturers and demons. His stanza is open to the charge of lacking dramatic variety, but most objections are overwhelmed in the fury of his attack and the bewildering sophistication of his rhyming, joking, punning and wild humour, as in the shepherd's complaint of his wife:

> For, as euer red I pystyll / I haue oone to my fere,
> As sharp as a thystyll / as rugh as a brere;
> She is browyd lyke a brystyll / with a sowre loten chere;
> Had she oones wett hyr whystyll / she couth syng full clere
> Hyr pater noster.
> She is as greatt as a whall,
> She has a galon of gall:
> By hym that dyed for vs all,
> I wald I had ryn to I had lost hir.                    (XIII. 100–8)

He has a wide variety of reading in social complaint-poetry, satires against women and satires on clothing, which he uses in the Shepherds' plays and in the brilliant scene of Tutivillus and the demons inserted in the *Last Judgment*, and a gift for density of detail and for casual realism which allows him to differentiate such traditionally faceless groups as the shepherds and torturers and also to supply totally unexpected touches of authenticity such as the shepherds' comment on the noise of Mak's singing as they approach his cottage (XIII. 476).[83] These are his preoccupations, and it is sometimes very difficult to see how they relate to the professed didactic function of the cycle.

The Chester plays are modest in ambition and achievement and mostly use older and simpler verse-forms such as the alternate-rhyming or tail-rhyme 8-line stanza. They are more explicitly didactic, more eclectic in borrowing, more homely in incident and language (there is more evidence of popular dramatic traditions in the Chester plays than anywhere else). There is little sign of individual poetic activity in the text, except for some homely touches in the plays of Noah and the Shepherds, and striking passages are likely to be derived from other sources, as the *Sacrifice of Isaac*, for instance, must be a corrupt descendant of the non-cycle Brome *Abraham and Isaac*,[84] an unaffectedly sentimental treatment of the story with which we may also compare the unrelated non-cycle Northampton (or 'Dublin') play on the same subject. It is difficult to talk about the poetic character of such palimpsest-like texts, and perhaps nowhere more so than in the *Ludus Coventriae* or 'N-town' plays, where two major sequences, one on the childhood of Mary and one on the Passion, are grafted onto the cycle from pre-existing plays. The text we have is that of the compiler and shows many of the stages of accretion, just as it shows the elaborate attention to staging, spectacle, music, processions and 'devices' (like the one for the Incarnation, p. 107) which is even more prominent in this fixed-stage cycle than in the Northern processional cycles. There is much to admire in the *Ludus Coventriae*, not only the harsh and vivid satirical spirit of the *Trial of Joseph and Mary*,

> In Feyth I suppose þat þis woman slepte
> With-owtyn all coverte whyll þat it dede snowe
> And a flake þer of in to hyre mowthe crepte
> And þer of þe chylde in hyre wombe doth growe　　　　　(132/273–6)

but also the sophistication which can make the shepherds' formal *Hail*-poem (p. 149) into a prophecy of Redemption, or vary metres to suit character in the *Adoration of the Magi*, or see the aptness of the alliterative battle-style to Herod:

> Shewyth on ʒour shulderys scheldys and schaftys
> Shapyht amonge schel chownys ashyrlyng shray....　　　　　(170/30–31)

Of these poets it is possible to say that at least they know what poetry should do, even if they cannot do it. Of the learned compiler, if he is responsible for linking passages such as those spoken by Contemplacio in the Marian sequence, it can only be said that he manages to combine the worst of both Lydgate and the alliterative tradition. The only play that makes anything of the high style is the non-cycle Croxton *Play of the Sacrament* (c. 1465), a clever dramatisation of the peculiar legend of the torturing of the Host by the Jews. Alliteration, amplification and the semi-aureate four-stress ballade stanza are well handled in the boastful speeches of Christian merchant and Jew (81–196) and there is effective interpolated comic incident of a doctor and his servant.

The three Digby plays (ed. EETS, ES 70), also from the latter half of the century, are characterised by their laboured attempts at a Lydgatian elevation. They use forms of the ballade and rhyme royal stanza and waver between the pentameter and the four-stress line. Quite different are the two linked plays of the *Burial* and the *Resurrection*, long associated, quite arbitrarily, with the Digby plays.[85] They are in fact a liturgical play in two parts, an extended meditation on the Passion in the form of lamentations by Magdalene, Joseph of Arimathaea, Mary and Peter. The verse is in an older style, touched with grace from the start,

> A Soule that list to singe of loue
> Of Crist, that com till us so lawe,
> Rede this treyte, it may hymm moue,
> And may hym teche lightly with awe

and the 'play' thus introduced is so close to its narrative origins that the speech-prefixes are still occasionally included. The emotional core of the play is Mary's long lament (612–791), which is written quite formally, with refrains and careful figuring:

> Your face, most graciose to behold,
> To beholde so comly, euer I wold,
> I wold, I wold, still with you bee,
> Still with yow, to ly in mold,
> Who can not wepe, com lern at me!          (697–701)

The Macro plays (ed. EETS 262), earliest of the morality plays apart from fragments, are not interesting from the point of view of the historian of poetry, nor are any of the morality plays that follow. *The Castle of Perseverance* (c. 1420) disappears under the load of its own verbosity and the semi-alliterative 13-line stanza (as in the York plays) which it uses. Both *Wisdom* ('Mind, Will and Under-standing') and *Mankind*, from later in the century (c. 1470), make a distinction between ballade and tail-rhyme stanza, with the style appropriate to them, for good and bad characters respectively: in one of the plays indeed the distinction is commented on:

> [Mercy:] Mercy ys my name by denomynacyon.
>   I conseyue ȝe haue but a lytyll fauour in my communycacyon.
> [New Gyse:] Ey, ey! yowr body ys full of Englysch Laten.
>   I am aferde yt wyll brest.          (*Mankind*, 122–5)

Both are sophisticated pieces of writing, and *Mankind* is particularly skilful in catching the cadences of colloquial speech in the dialogue of the three ne'er-do-wells, New Gyse, Nowadays and Nought. This vivid dramatic language, which is effectively prose,

> Ey, Mankynde, Gode spede yow wyth yowr spade!
> I xall tell yow of a maryage:
> I wolde yowr mowth and hys ars þat þis made
> Wer maryede junctly together          (344–7)

257

is strangely contrasted with the 'poetry' of the good characters, which is used with no apparent intention of parody:

> O Mercy, my suavius solas and synguler recreatory,
> My predilecte spesyall, ʒe are worthy to hawe my lowe;
> For wythowte deserte and menys supplicatorie
> ʒe be compacient to my inexcusabyll reprowe.                    (871–4)

It was a long time before this idea of 'poetry' could be exorcised, and meanwhile the verse of the Tudor morality plays and interludes,[86] whatever historical and dramatic interest may attach to them, 'may wel be rym dogerel'. These plays use a wide variety of metres,[87] and some of them, such as *Hyckescorner* and Henry Medwall's *Fulgens and Lucrece*, attempt the same kind of prosodic distinction as the Macro plays between dignified and comic passages, using ballade and rhyme royal for the former, tail-rhyme and couplet for the latter (the School farces, *Ralph Roister Doister* and *Gammer Gurton's Needle*, are almost entirely in forms of couplet), while *Mundus et Infans* has some stanzas adapted to the ages of man (e.g. 135, 216); but the distinctions are not consistently preserved, and are in any case obscured by the doggerel metre of individual lines and the ubiquity of alliteration. John Heywood comes nearest to a real stylistic differentiation in *The Play of the Wether*, where the rhyme royal associated with Jupiter has some recognisable pentameters. How easy it was for Chaucer's delicate balance to be lost, whether through linguistic change or verbal alteration, is shown in Heywood's *The Pardoner and the Frere*, where he copies Chaucer line by line:

> Here is a mytten eke, as ye may se,
> He that his hande wyll put in this myttayn,
> He shall have encrease [Chaucer: multipliyng] of his grayn,
> That he hath sowne [sowen], be it wete or otys,
> So that he offer pens or els [elles] grotes.                    (128–32)

The learning, wit, sophistication and intelligence of these plays should not be underestimated, nor the historical and theological importance of the new Protestant biblical drama of Bale, but the kind of intelligence one would appreciate from the point of view of poetry, namely, to use prose, is not there.


*Romances and popular poetry*

Romance, which we have defined as secular narrative designed for entertainment, continues to be an important poetic form in the fifteenth century, expanding its social range both upward and downward. The older type of romance, written for a general audience by professional translators and hacks, goes on being copied and circulated: most extant texts of those discussed in Chapter 5

258

are from the fifteenth century and probably some, such as *Sir Torrent of Portyngale*, were actually composed after 1400. The history of these all-purpose entertainments does not end with Caxton and Malory, whose innovations in prose romance mostly captured a higher class of reader, and prints of *Sir Degare, Sir Eglamour, Sir Isumbras, Sir Tryamowre* and other romances were being made well into the sixteenth century, probably for audiences of increasingly debased taste. Before Caxton, however, romance can be seen reaching out to the reading élite, as it had begun to do before 1400 in romances like *Ipomadoun. Parthonope of Blois* (ed. EETS, ES 109), like most of these more ambitious pieces a translation from the French, would have appealed to the audience that enjoyed *The Isle of Ladies*, with its close reminiscences and sometimes direct copying[88] of Chaucer, its many amusing pseudo-Chaucerian interpolations, and its generally brisk and witty manner. *The Romans of Partenay* (ed. EETS 22) and *Generydes* (EETS 55, 70), both in rhyme royal (*Parthonope* is in short couplet), are no less ambitious, if a little dull, and *Generydes*, where the handling of the pentameter is extremely efficient and quite untouched by the 'Lydgatisms' of *Partenay*, can be illuminatingly compared with a definitely more popular version of the same story in the Helmingham MS.[89] It is difficult to know where to place Henry Lovelich (c. 1420), the London Skinner, who did two enormously long verse-translations of the *Holy Grail* and *Merlin*, in this socio-literary hierarchy: the safest assumption, perhaps, is that Lovelich wrote for no one's benefit but his own, since his work is very tedious and manages to reduce even the simple short couplet to doggerel. Yet he is patient enough in his handling of the sources and it is a matter of some interest that a rich merchant should have embarked on such a work at all.[90] His aspirant tastes are perhaps reflected in some of the more generally popular romances composed during this period, in *The Knight of Curtesy and the Fair Lady of Faguell*,[91] for instance, where the story of the lady who eats her lover's heart is treated with an unexpected delicacy of sentiment, and in *The Squyr of Lowe Degre*,[92] where there is a marked tendency to fill out the narrative with decorative catalogues of trees and birds and with quasi-courtly descriptions of feasts and high life, rather more convincingly done than in the majority of earlier popular romances, *Sir Degrevaunt* excepted. New versions and copies of older romances also follow this fashion: the fifteenth-century translation of *Guy of Warwick* (ed. EETS, ES 25–6), for instance, has a more self-consciously 'romantic' air and expands with much picturesque detail on the ceremony of Guy's dubbing (387–422), showing the interest in chivalric ritual and display which gathered strength as the practical function of knighthood disappeared.[93] On a somewhat lower level, the fifteenth-century copy of *The Seege of Troye* (ed. EETS 172) in MS Harley 525 shows a concern to erase forms of popular address and some of the more crass misunderstandings of the earlier texts, such as the association of Saturn, Mercury and Jupiter with Venus, 'Foure ladies of eluene land' (508), in the story of Paris and the apple, and makes several learned and poetic interpolations. A late version of *Sir Gowther*[94] (MS Royal 17.B.xliii) tries to moderate the violence and coarseness of its original for a more delicate-stomached audience, though there is little enough to be done with some passages:

> His modur fell a fowle unhappe,
> Apon a day bad hym þo pappe,
>   He snaffuld to hit soo [And he ariȝhte hire soo]
> He rofe þo hed fro þo brest; [He tare the oon side of hire brest]
> Scho fell backeward and cald a prest, [The lady cried after a prest]
>   To chambur fled hym froo.                      (127–32)

In the event, these aspirations were short-lived, destined to be absorbed into the fashion for prose romance brought over from Burgundian Flanders by Caxton, which offered a more secure guarantee of social prestige and exclusive readership. It is the lower popular tastes that begin to dominate romance and which annex it to other kinds of narrative entertainment. This process is under way in some fifteenth-century copies of earlier romances such as MS Harley 3810 of *Sir Orfeo*, where the degeneration of the poem during a century or so of popular circulation is clearly demonstrated,[95] but the most characteristic record of popularisation is the one that is conveyed in the kind of texts that would not previously have been preserved at all, often indeed in copies whose existence and survival, even at this late date, are themselves quite exceptional. The most important and enigmatic document of this kind is the Percy Folio MS,[96] a mid-seventeenth-century collection, made presumably by an antiquarian, which includes, amongst a good deal of later verse, copies of romances and other kinds of narrative poem, including ballads, which must have formed part of the repertoire of a popular entertainer at the end of the Middle Ages. These entertainers, from whom it is wise to withhold the term 'minstrel', which usually refers to instrumental musicians in medieval sources, had presumably always existed, though their activities, being sub-literate, would not often achieve written record. In the Percy Folio, their wares are laid before us, and for the most part they make a sorry spectacle.

*Sir Lambewell*, for instance, a version of the fourteenth-century translation from Marie de France's *Lanval* known as *Sir Landevale* (not to be confused with Chestre's *Sir Launfal*),[97] corrupts and coarsens an already popularised original, offering as early as line 5 readings so mangled in transmission as to be meaningless,

> With him he had many an heire

> Cf. He had with hym a meyné there                      (*Landevale*, 5)

and having Lambewell bid goodbye to his mysterious and all-powerful faery mistress in the tones of a rustic comedy:

> 'Farewell my hony, farwell my sweete!'
> 'Farewell, Sir Lambwell, till oft we meete!'                      (203–4)

> Cf. He toke hys leue, & went sone.                      (*Landevale*, 166)

The Percy Folio *Squyr* is 'a mangled and clumsily condensed version' (ed. Mead, p. xix) of its original, reducing 1132 lines to 170, obliterating all the charm and delicacy of the original and omitting so much of the plot that the action becomes almost unintelligible. The incoherence produced by the elimination of key elements and pointers in the narrative, the juxtaposition of unrelated incidents, the reintroduction of stock (or 'archetypal') motifs whether relevant or not, are all characteristic constituents of this kind of popular narrative. The random association of detail created by loss and corruption has a cryptic suggestiveness which sophisticated readers are all too apt to take seriously, and when it is combined with stereotyped forms of repetition (7–14) and with the lyric tendency of formally reiterated complaint (127–48) it may be seen that we have the makings of the ballad. *Eger and Grime* is another example, in the Huntingdon-Laing version a coherent narrative, 'effortlessly and unobtrusively noble in sentiment,'[98] with careful attention to the behaviour of the main characters. In the Percy Folio, incidents are strung together without articulation, the social background is universalised and stylised, archetypal motifs reintroduced, and sensational detail given obtrusive emphasis. One incident illustrates well the character of change: Eger, defeated in battle by Gray-Steel, is recovering from his wounds, and his revenge must be secretly undertaken by Grahame (Grime) in disguise. To convince everyone that he is fit, Eger is to appear at his window, in his robes, on nine successive days, reading 'Books of Romances' (708). In Percy the detailed and careful plan is hardly given any attention, but on the day of departure,

> Early on the other day
> theese 2 knights did them array:
> into a window Sir Egar yeede,
> bookes of Romans for to reede
> that all the court might him heare.
> The Knight was armed & on steere.

Perhaps the Percy passage has an additional instructiveness in the comic way it represents its hero reading his romances *aloud* to the bewildered auditors (as if no other form of reading could be imagined) before, supposedly, rushing down into the courtyard to complete his absurd and inexplicable charade. It is often suggested, though an incident like the one recounted above would seem to make it unlikely here, that texts like the Percy *Eger and Grime* are really older and simpler versions of stories worked over by later poets: 'The Percy manuscript contains the older and better version.'[99] One has the suspicion that 'better' here is a synonym for 'older', but whether being older makes a poem better is something that not everyone would agree on with the folk-lorists and myth-hunters.

The Percy Folio also has a number of Gawain-romances, *The Turke and Gowin*, *The Marriage of Sir Gawaine*, *The Grene Knight* and *The Carle of Carlile*, which combine with others, some related, preserved in miscellaneous ways, *Syre Gawene and the Carle of Carelyle* in MS Porkington 10, *The Weddynge of Sir Gawen and Dame*

*Ragnell* in MS Rawlinson C.86 and *The Jeaste of Sir Gawain* in a sixteenth-century transcript of an earlier print, to reveal another world of sub-literary activity. These romances preserve popular versions of stories elsewhere handled by sophisticated writers (as Chaucer's *Wife of Bath's Tale* relates to the *Marriage* and *Weddynge*) and are marked by the same crude tastes as the other Percy romances. They are mostly in a 6-line tail-rhyme stanza, often corrupted beyond recall. One in particular, *The Grene Knight*, is a good example of the worst that the popularisers were capable of. A version of *Sir Gawain and the Green Knight*, no less, it starts off with an 'explanation' of the plot (so much for the original author's peculiar skill in postponing such explanations until they are irrelevant) which tells us how Sir Bredbeddle, 'a man of Mickele might' that 'dwelled in the west countrye' (39) is sent by his mother-in-law Agostes ('shee cold transpose knights & swaine', 52) to win Gawain for her daughter, one of his secret admirers (or 'to proue Gawaines points 3', we are not quite sure which). The whole retelling of the story, the arrival of the green knight at court ('That was a Iolly sight to seene,/when horsse and armour was all greene,/& weapon that hee bare', 79–81), the stock comic byplay with the porter and Sir Kay, the journey through the wilderness ('Many furleys there saw hee/of wolues & wild beasts sikerlye;/on hunting hee tooke most heede', 283–5), is of consummate idiocy and banality, as good as *Sir Thopas* in its way, with every mystery revealed to us ('For that was the greene knight/that hee was lodged with that night', 340–1) and the exchange of winnings turned into a nonsensical agreement to share them. In some romances we can trace in more detail this process of degeneration. The *Weddynge*[100] is coarse enough, with obvious relish in its description of Gawain's bride-to-be:

> In the sholders she was a yard brode,
> Hangyng pappys to be an hors-lode. (241–2)

But Gawain behaves like a gentleman throughout, as does Arthur, in asking Gawain's permission before agreeing to the hag's plan, and there are some effective touches, as in the description of the transformed bride on the morning after when Arthur calls:

> She stod in her smok alle by that fyre,
> Her her was to her knees as red as gold wyre. (742–3)

In the Percy Folio, in ballad-verse (i.e. septenary couplet) as distinct from the usual tail-rhyme, is the *Marriage*, a crudely abbreviated version of the same story (which still finds time to drag in Sir Kay) of irredeemable banality. Rather closer in manner are two versions of another Gawain adventure, with the Carl,[101] the Percy copy being a reduction into couplets of the MS original. Here there is no delicacy of any kind, only more and more extravagant and nonsensical displays of quixotic 'courtesy' on Gawain's part, and the homely additions of the couplet version, as in describing the Carl,

> His fingars were like to teddar-stakes,
> And his hands like breads that wiues may bake          (185–6)

are only marginally cruder than the original romance.

We are moving, it will be seen, towards the ballad, and many of the ballads of the Percy Folio, such as *Sir Lionel*, *Sir Cawline*, *King Arthur and King Cornwall*, *King Arthur's Death* and *Guy and Colbrand*, as well as some from other sources, such as *Hind Horn* and *King Orfeo*, are no more than abbreviated popular versions of known romances or romance-traditions. The case of the Robin Hood ballads is not so straightforward: a number of these appear in the Percy Folio, but are less important than the two which appear in genuine fifteenth-century MSS, *Robin Hood and the Monk* and *Robin Hood and the Potter*, and one, *A Gest of Robyn Hode*, in an early sixteenth-century print.[102] These are the only attested medieval ballads, and their origins are interesting. A song of *Robyn and Gandeleyn* appears in the early fifteenth-century MS Sloane 2593: it is in ballad-verse, that is, the septenary couplet, emphatically divided and thus resistant to the traditional encroachment of alliterative rhythms, and with the additional advantage from the division that the rhyming-line can readily be reduced to the status of a 'filler' (or a burden) so that the writer can achieve the satisfaction of rhyme with the minimum of inconvenience. *Robyn and Gandeleyn* also has the beginnings of those forms of repetition, incremental and otherwise, so characteristic of the ballad,

> Wrennok schette a ful good schote,
> And he schet not to hye          (St. 13)

> Now xalt þu neuer ʒelpe, Wrennok,
> At ale ne et wyn...
> Now xalt þu neuer ʒelpe, Wrennok,
> At wyn ne at ale...          (St. 16–17)

as well as anticipations of familiar cadences:

> He hadde not þe der i-flawe,
> Ne half out of þe hyde....          (St. 6)

Like other pieces in Sloane 2593, *Robyn* has affiliations with popular song, suggesting that this therefore is one of the elements we have in the development of the ballad. On the other hand, though *Robyn* is not necessarily Robin Hood, and *Gandeleyn* is not Gamelyn, the combination is suggestive enough of the part that *The Tale of Gamelyn*, which it will be remembered (see above, p. 144) is in the old septenary/alexandrine couplet and which was widely circulated in the fifteenth century as Chaucer's *Cook's Tale*, played in the growth of the Robin Hood legend. *Gamelyn*, like the earlier romance of *Fouke Fitzwarine*, with which the Robin Hood legend has also been associated,[103] can be assigned an audience among the provincial gentry, but deductions about the social and literary origins of the legend should not influence too much our view of composition and circu-

lation in the fifteenth century.[104] The Robin Hood ballads, as they come down
to us, are clearly designed for reading by a popular entertainer, like the romance-
ballads above, and we may regard them as another example of professional
expertise in seizing on some widespread and obviously popular story-motifs.
They cultivate the 'yeoman' assiduously,

> God haffe mersey on Roben Hodys solle,
> And saffe all god yemanrey! *(Robin Hood and the Potter)*

and the *Gest*, a *rifacimento* of Robin Hood stories, begins with stout assertions of
yeoman virtue, of Robin's piety, and of the 'ideals' that he lays down for his
robber-troop (rather as Malory does for King Arthur's Knights). At the end of
the *Gest*, Robin Hood is reconciled with the King, a reminder of how profoundly
indebted the whole legend is to the motif of the meeting of King and Subject,
which we have already met in *Rauf Coilzear* (above, p. 187) and which appears
in many popular fifteenth-century poems, including *John the Reeve*, *The King and
the Barker*, *The King and the Hermit* and *King Edward and the Shepherd*.[105] Even the
ballad of *Adam Bell, Clim of the Clough, and William of Cloudesly*, a vigorous glorification of the bowman-gangster ('And all that with hand-bowe shoteth,/That
of heuen they may neuer mysse!'), ends with the hero, Cloudesly, entering the
King's service, while his son gets a job in the wine-cellar and his wife becomes the
royal nursery-governess. This is hardly 'yeoman minstrelsy', whatever that
means, and it should be recognised that such poems represent shrewd professional
assessment of popular taste, not popular production.

One would make a similar case for the subsequent development of the ballad,
including its absorption of elements from popular song, and certainly the
characteristic sixteenth-century production is that of professional rhymers, now
with access to cheap broadside forms of printing, writing on contemporary
historical events (i.e. conveying 'news'), or versifying historical incidents culled
from the chronicles, or reworking traditional romances and romance-motifs.
Perhaps some elements were incorporated from oral tradition in poems like
*The Battle of Otterburn* and *The Hunting of the Cheviot*, so lovingly recalled by
Sidney, but ballad-mongers, as I have suggested for the popular romancers,
knew very well how to incorporate old motifs, and antiquity of reference does not
signify archaic composition. It is not necessary to press this case to its conclusion
for all ballads in Child's collection, since the corpus he has created exists only in
terms of his own definitions. In particular, one should recognise that Percy
ballads like *Little Musgrave and Lady Barnard* and *Child Waters* and the other
Scots and border ballads, mainly collected in the eighteenth century, which
constitute over half Child's collection, are in a different class as poetry from the
banal English productions, and in a different category as literary phenomena,
needing the explanation which can only be given by the conditions of a particular border society.

There is, in addition to the ballads and versions of romance, a mass of 'popular'
verse in the fifteenth century, increasing as the modes of dissemination become
more freely available and as the chances of survival improve. Much of it is

contained in commonplace books such as Richard Hill's MS (Balliol 354) or the MS kept probably by an Oxford student (Gonville and Caius 383),[106] while the secular carols often sit comfortably side by side with religious carols in the song-books, such as MS Sloane 2593 and Bodley MS Eng. poet. e. 1. We should not associate these song-books too readily with 'minstrels', since the MSS themselves seem to come from religious houses, which is a reminder that the barriers we build between secular and religious, and which the ecclesiastical authorities of the Middle Ages would certainly have approved, are not barriers that existed in the day-to-day life of religious houses. Furthermore, to call these secular songs and carols 'popular' is to recognise only that they have universal appeal, that they deal with scenes from humble life, like the drinking songs and the songs of unwanted pregnancy and unwanted marriage,[107] and that they may incorporate elements from genuine folk-song. The term 'popular' should not tempt us to associate these songs with crude entertainers or with an exclusively lower-class audience. There is real need of a term 'popular' which would not be 'populist' in implication and which would not insinuate that coarseness of subject is inappropriate to more sophisticated levels of literary activity.

A similar point may be made about the 'popular' political verse of the period. A few scraps may survive, comparable with those from the years of the Peasants' Revolt, of genuine popular outcry, complaint and abuse, like the snatches of prophecy which may be associated with the popular alliterative tradition of prophecy (above, p. 125), or the rallying calls for freedom, or the coarse abuse that follows Suffolk.[108] Such pieces are usually identifiable by their brevity, metrical form and random provenance. But a great deal of other 'popular' political verse is professional propaganda, designed to appeal to the people and consisting, like Minot's poems and those of Harley 2253, of chauvinistic celebration of military victories, attacks on rebels, and abuse of political opponents. There was a high-style propaganda too, usually distinguished by Lydgatian metres and language (see above, p. 242), and the Wars of the Roses gave additional incentive to the production of such pieces, many of them having a close association with chronicles written for similar purposes.[109] These truly political poems should in turn be distinguished from the generalised 'complaints' against the corruption of the times, which continue in the fifteenth century at a variety of levels, from the philosophical mutability poems in the *Fall of Princes* tradition, like the *Lament of the Duchess of Gloucester* and the *Epitaph for the Duke of Gloucester*, and from the generally moralistic refrain-poems such as those of MS Digby 102, where the political events of the day are used as sober exempla.[110]

The search for a truly 'popular' poetry might end up with the charms, calendar calculations, prognostications and short gnomic verses which are scattered through fifteenth-century MSS, wherever they caught the fancy of a collector or owner of books.[111] Nonsense and burlesque poems, a complaint by a 'schoolboy', and the brilliant *Monologue of a Drunkard* are clearly of learned provenance,[112] and it was a sophisticated taste, anticipating Skelton's, that appreciated the comic *Tale of the Prioress and her Three Wooers*, the burlesque alliterative *Tournament of Tottenham*, or the whimsical *Tale of the Basyn* ('the

265

same that thei make water in'), all in the complex 9-line stanza of quatrain and wheel.[113] Of a like sophistication are the charming mock-sentiment of the monologue of *The Hunted Hare*, the heavily veiled obscenities of *Piers of Fullham*, or the obscene Riddles copied in a Cambridge medical treatise (CUL Dd. v. 76).[114] Perhaps the rough tales of *The Wright's Chaste Wife* (ed. EETS 12) and of *Jak and his Stepdame and of the Frere* (ed. EETS, ES 101, p. 120), both in tail-rhyme (their methods and style are not radically different from the crude edifying fables mentioned above, p. 251), have been lifted from popular sources for more discerning delectation. *The Nut Brown Maid*,[115] preserved in an early print and in Balliol MS 354, has no such affiliations: written in a 12-line stanza of deceptive simplicity, essentially based on ballad-metre with internal rhyme in the non-rhyming lines, it is a touching dialogue, with alternate stanzas given to the lover, who pretends he is to be banished ('Wherfore I too/The woode wyl goo/Alone a banysshed man'), and the maiden, who declares her readiness to follow him, even in disguise if necessary or if he has a hundred paramours waiting for him in the greenwood ('For in my mynde/Of all mankynde/I loue but you alone'), and demonstrating with exquisitely controlled sentimental extravagance a fidelity in woman's love which echoes the *Clerk's Tale* as it anticipates *Child Waters* and *As You Like It*.

## The Transition

The period in the history of English poetry between the introduction of printing into England (1476) and the publication of Tottel's *Songes and Sonettes* (1557) is one that has an ambiguous place in this volume, though a number of intrusions have already been made into it in the study of particular genres of writing. It is aptly called 'the Transition', since within it old habits and new influences coexist, not altogether happily, the former staled by repetition, the latter only half-assimilated, so that it is sometimes difficult to know which is the more painful to witness, the creeping-on of death or the pangs of birth. Both, at any rate, are long drawn out, and an end to the confusion, in which issues of politics, religion, society, education and the proper function of poetry are all involved, is not fully in sight until the 1570s.

Stephen Hawes, Groom of the Chamber to Henry VII, may at first sight seem untouched by any new ideas. His main poem, *The Pastime of Pleasure* (1506; ed. EETS 173), with its fulsome and frequently expressed admiration for Lydgate and imitation of his aureate language and rhetorical topics of amplification, draws on a number of medieval forms, the allegorised narrative of man's life (as in *The Pilgrimage of the Life of Man*), the love-vision (as in *The Temple of Glass*), the encyclopaedic allegory (*The Court of Sapience*) and the romance. The hero, Graunde Amour, after choosing the active life in preference to the contemplative, is prepared for a life of love and action by a long training in the Seven Liberal Arts (during which time he meets his beloved, La Bell Pucell, in the Tower of Music) and in Chivalry. Going out into the world he meets love's detractor in the person of the foul-mouthed Godfrey Gobelive, makes his avowal to love in the Temple of Venus, and then embarks on a series of fights against many-headed giants of vice, finally winning his lady. A long chapter of conclusions brings Graunde Amour to an avaricious middle age and a penitent death, following which there are several epitaphs on man's mortality, the mutability of earthly existence, the transience of Fame and the consolations of Eternity. With all the conventionality of his materials, however, Hawes is often strikingly original in the way he combines them, if not always successful, and he is evidently touched by new ideas. His view of chivalry, 'that hath be longe decayed' (2985), as the necessary service of the commonwealth ('And no quarell a knyght ought to take/But for a trouthe or for the comyns sake', 3373–4) rather than the self-validating life of a social élite is a serious one, and his emphasis on learning, in the form of an academic education, as an essential part of the knight's training is anticipatory of Tudor ideals of governorship.[116] A more pragmatic view of love and marriage is frankly declared, with a new role for Disdain ('A, quod dysdayne, knowe ye his substaunce?' 4585) and an acceptance of the dynamic social role of marriage for the aspirant bachelor ('she hath ynoughe in her possessyon/For you both, for you shall neuer lacke/Yf that ye ordre it by good reason', 1857–9). Wooing, beseeching and complaint give way to plans and settlements, 'And lex ecclesie dyde me to her wedde' (5324). Hawes is conscious also of the lofty mission of the poet, a theme to which he returns constantly, particularly in the account of Rhetoric in the Tower of Doctrine, echoing both Lydgate, on the power of poetry,

> Clokynge a trouthe with colour tenebrous
> For often under a fayre fayned fable
> A trouthe appereth gretely profytable    (712–14)

and Chaucer, in a plea against 'mysse metrynge by wronge impressyon' (5804).

Yet these new ideas are never fully absorbed or assimilated. Graunde Amour's learning is put to no use at all in his monster-slayings, which follow the most egregious popular traditions, while the two views of love are merely juxtaposed, quite incongruously, and the brave words about poetry and chivalry offer only a superficial disguise for Hawes's inert acceptance that both exist 'to eschewe ydlenes' (772, cf. 546, 572). Hawes in fact is a poet whose ambitions far outrun his capacity. He recognises the importance of contrast, of presenting the non-ideal view of love through a Pandarus or a Dinadan, but his descent into low style comedy for Godfrey is as crude and abrupt as anything in popular writing. He displays a devastating narrative incompetence, in the repetitious handling of the learning sequences and the giant-fights, in the endless recapitulations of 'the story so far', and in the extraordinary gaffe by which the 'I' narrates not only his brave and successful encounters with monsters of vice, but also his own death. Hawes's most serious defect, however, is his style, a labouring pentameter on the verge always of breakdown, and a contrast between the deliberate and factitious ornamentation of his aureate manner,

> Encensynge out the aromatyke fume
> Our langage rude to exyle and consume (923–4)

and the threadbare diction of his unmannered style sufficient to make the former appear tawdry and the latter drab. The best parts of his poem are those which lean heavily on Lydgate or on some unmistakable formal convention, description of seasons, gardens or architecture, some of the passages of love-complaint and dialogue, and the sober platitudes of the conclusion. Of Hawes's minor poems (ed. EETS 271), which display a remarkable homogeneity of style with the *Pastime*, *The Conversion of Swearers* is a straightforward verse sermon against swearing, and *A Joyful Meditation* a celebration of Henry VIII's coronation. The traditional topics of homily and eulogy, respectively, are not ineffectively exploited, and perhaps even more can be said for *The Comfort of Lovers*, where the pleading of the lover's suit is suggestively framed in an apparently topical political allegory. Hawes's tentative and stumbling movement towards the world of Spenser is here as elsewhere obscured by his radically defective poetic technique. Hawes's earliest poem, *The Example of Virtue*, can readily be seen as a preliminary sketch for the *Pastime*,[117] without the ambitious attempt to extend the role of chivalry, but with the same blending of the allegory of love and of life's pilgrimage. 'Blending' is perhaps too strong a word to describe Hawes's eclectic method, which recognises no conflict in the life of Virtue (an invitation from Lechery is received: 'Nay sayd dyscrecyon that may not be/No sayd I in no maner of wyse', 1156–7) and therefore no need to resolve conflict, and which is happy to have Jerome, Ambrose, Bede, Gregory and Cupid, 'the kynge of feruent loue' (1717), side by side as guests at the wedding of Virtue and Cleanness.

Alexander Barclay, monk and friar, whose patrons included both bishops and dukes, is in some ways a more interesting writer than Hawes, though his work is all translation. He shows some responsiveness to changing taste in using a fifteenth-century humanist source, Mantuan, for his *Life of St George* (ed. EETS 230), and he is the first to work in the newly fashionable tradition of pastoral in his five *Eclogues* (ed. EETS 175), based on Æneas Sylvius and Mantuan. On the other hand, Barclay is little interested in the more specifically humanist qualities of his originals, tending to suppress classical and mythological allusion in *St George* and replacing Mantuan's discourse on classical monsters with a sermon from St George to the inhabitants of the city (1254–330). In the *Eclogues* his most characteristic success is in the portrayal of homely life (I) and in the vivid impression he gives of life around the lower tables and kitchens of a court household (II, III), all of it richly expanded from Æneas Sylvius. The ambiguity of Barclay's position is nevertheless demonstrated here too, for Eclogue IV includes an original occasional poem on the death of Sir Edward Howard which has some importance in the history of pastoral elegy.[118] Barclay's other main work is *The Ship of Fools*,[119] based on a Latin translation of Sebastian Brant's German original, the famous and widely popular *Narrenschiff* (1494), a vigorously contemporary version of traditional satire on folly and the corruption of the times. Here the preacher's tone breaks through more stridently, revealing Barclay for what he is, a medieval preacher in a threadbare Renaissance disguise, with the characteristic vigour and taste for homely illustration of the type. His major virtues as a poet are the clarity of his syntax and the unconstrained vitality of his language when it is unaffected by 'poetic' considerations. He demonstrates the problem that the early sixteenth century faced in having a poetic diction which was increasingly divorced from living sources of speech, and which yet monopolised the high style.[120] Dramatists had attempted to evade the problem by recognising sharper and sharper distinctions of high and low styles, and Hawes in a similar way by opposing the gimcrack pretentiousness of his Lydgatian style against the raw obscenity of Godfrey Gobelive. It is to be a long time before the language of Tudor verse can reassume the flexibility of its prose, which Barclay himself demonstrates in his translation of Sallust, and the paralysis of diction is matched by an equal problem of versification, where the high style still aspires after the pentameter, while the low style frankly accepts the complete infiltration of four-stress patterns. This is the only rational explanation of Barclay's metre, where the increased pressure of rough four-stress rhythms and half-line phrasing becomes noticeable as satiric and homiletic themes take hold. Barclay recognises the appropriateness of rough verse to satire,

> But if I halt in meter or erre in eloquence
> Or be to large in langage I pray you blame nat me
> For my mater is so bad it wyll none other be  *(Ship,* i. 16)

but it would be over-generous to assume that such roughness is entirely deliberate, or does not reflect a general decay of the pentameter in which it accommodates alexandrines and fourteeners (septenaries) from the old long line, as in the passage above, as well as four-stress rhythms and, on occasions, unscannable prose.

No one exhibits these problems of language and versification more acutely than John Skelton, who, as priest, scholar and, like Hawes, tutor to Henry VII's sons, has great ambitions as a poet without much certainty of the role in which those ambitions can be fulfilled.[121] The role of the poet is in fact shifting, and Skelton is perhaps the last English poet of whom we do not think it an exceptional fact that he is a cleric. The function of the poet in relation to society, especially of a clerical poet in relation to a secular society, is no longer self-evident, and Skelton's poetry, like his life,[122] is an index to the dilemma. Nearly all his poetry is a parody of poetic activity, a sprawling annexe to *The House of Fame.* Beginning in a conventional way with a decorously aureate *Elegy on the Earl of Northumberland* (1489) in the heavy Lydgatian ballade, and with some skilful exercises in familiar lyrical modes, he soon begins to exert a kind of imaginative, linguistic and comic energy within the old forms which threatens to shatter their stability. *The Bowge of Court* has a conventional enough theme, a dream-allegory of court life and its follies and corruption, but Skelton's own presence within the poem and the sense he conveys of sinister and powerful realities behind the stereotyped personifications is enough to disturb the decorum of the genre. Some of his satirical power achieved expression within the form of the morality play in Skelton's *Magnificence*, where the psychomachia of man's life is given a broader political and secular context by the association of 'Magnificence', the hero, with kingship and of his enemies with the hypocrisy and corruption of court intrigue. The play is long and ambitious, rich in comic invention, and exploits to the full the metrical distinctions (as of rhyme royal and couplet) adumbrated in earlier morality plays, giving perhaps the clearest evidence from the whole period of the deliberate employment of the four-stress line, with balanced rhythm, that seems so much a product of confusion and decay with lesser writers. But Skelton's main answer to his own poetic dilemma was the invention of the Skeltonic, the wild rampage of two- and three-stress lines, rhyming to extinction, which offered no resistance to and no constraint on his characteristic energies. Whilst one can see why Skelton developed this form, and how he derived it from models such as the wheel of the 9-line alliterative stanza, it cannot be regarded as a uniformly happy solution to his problems. The satirical skills, which are very considerable, of *Colin Clout* and *Why Come Ye not to Court?* are dissipated in a flurry of snarling and spluttering abuse, where neither target nor method are fully identified and where the strongest influences at work seem to be the undiscriminating accumulative techniques of medieval anti-clerical satire. One is in fact more captured by the poems' own inventiveness and comic wit than by a conviction of their truth or relevance to the subject, and Skelton seems to recognise this as his strength in the other two main poems in Skeltonic, *The Tunning of Elinour Rumming*, a low-life exercise in 'The Ale-Wife and her Gossips' genre, a piece of wild grotesquerie, and *Philip Sparrow*, a lament for a girl's pet bird. The latter is mostly spoken by the girl, Jane Scrope, and parodies elegiac and other literary and liturgical forms, and with these hostages given to poetic pretension Skelton can develop his most winning vein of comedy and fantasy, touching on death, sorrow, love and beauty in glancing style, and making astute comment, through Jane and in his own 'Commendations', on rhetorical ornament and the English poetic tradition. The other poems in Skeltonic, such as *Against Garnesche* and *The Duke of Albany*, are occasional pieces of invective of little poetic interest, and the same might be said of one of Skelton's most ambitious poems, *Speak, Parrot*, in rhyme royal, where his solution to the problem of the poet's role and voice (and, in this perilous age, his continued good health) is to enclose what seems to be a political satire in a highly contrived hermetic style of cloaked allusion. Finally, there is *The Garland of Laurel*, in many ways Skelton's best poem, where he abandons all serious questions of the poet's role and simply glorifies himself as a poet. Skelton's vanity was prodigious, and he often celebrates the laurel crowns he had received from Oxford and Cambridge (a kind of honorary Ph.D.), but here, as he presents himself before the bar of Fame to receive the laurel from his poetic ancestors, his self-regard is attractively shot through with self-ridicule. The poem uses the creaking machinery of allegory, and is itself a brilliant display of the poetic achievement whose reward it fantasises, with some splendid imitation of fifteenth-century aureate style, constantly invaded by colloquialism and rapid dialogue and by Skelton's typically harebrained tirades and gutter virtuosity, and interrupted at one point by a series of graceful and saucy lyrical eulogies of the Countess of Surrey and her ladies. The poem is a pyrotechnic display, of great technical resource, which both illuminates and explodes late medieval poetic tradition in England.

Skelton's innovations are idiosyncratic, and he has little influence on sixteenth-century poetry. His classical learning, though more extensive than that of any previous English poet, is only superficially humanistic, and his essential habits of mind are medieval. The inertia of the English poetic tradition, in fact, in face of the profound changes that were taking place in attitudes to learning and literature (Erasmus is Skelton's younger contemporary), is quite remarkable, and the first half of the sixteenth-century is preoccupied with the working out of medieval traditions. Henry Parker, Lord Morley (1476–1556), for instance, gentleman usher in the court of Henry VIII, was still making translations of works like the *Somnium Scipionis* and Boccaccio's *De Claris Mulieribus* for the King and Princess Mary, though in verse he did a laborious couplet translation of the *Trionfi*, the work with which Petrarch began to make his reputation, in sixteenth-century England, as a vernacular poet, distinct from the Latin moralist of medieval fame.[123] Thomas Feilde's *Controversy between a Lover and a Jay*[124] is an anthology of motifs from medieval love-debate, not unattractive, with much Chaucerian allusion. *The Castell of Pleasure* (1518; ed. EETS 179) of William Nevill, a son of the aristocratic Latimer family, is a last relic of the Lydgate-Hawes allegorical love-vision tradition, tired, outworn and metrically chaotic. It was one of the works printed by Robert Copland, who brought out a good deal of the miscellaneous English writing of the period, as well as reprints of medieval romances and didactic works,[125] and whose attitudes to poetry and life are communicated in a prologue he offers to a new translation (1532) by William Walter of Boccaccio's *Guiscardo and Ghismonda* (the same tale, from the same Latin source, as Banester nearly a century earlier: see above, p. 230) and *Titus Gisippus* (ed. EETS 205):

> The wretched lyfe of osyosyte
> Engendreth slouth pouerte and payne
> It is nouryce of voluptuosyte...
> Ergo good besynesse is gate of vertue.　　　　　　　　　　(8–10, 28)

At the same time, in his own writing, such as the old-fashioned 'estates satire' of *The Hye Way to the Spyttel Hous* and *Jyl of Braintfords Testament*,[126] and especially in some of his other prologues on the book trade and the hard lot of the publisher, Copland displays the kind of vigour that it is the misfortune of the sixteenth century to have divorced from the high style. Vigour and coarseness seem to be inseparable in the estates satire tradition, as we see it further in the 'Ship of Fools' satire of *Cock Lorells Bote* and the anti-feminist verse of the period, like

*The Schole-House of Women.*[127] Even a comparatively sophisticated writer and court 'wit' like John Heywood, whose *Dialogue containing Proverbs, Epigrams* and political allegory of *The Spider and the Fly*[128] show some originality of a sub-humanist kind, lacks vigour except where he resorts to the low style ('A byg breecht man fearyng a deere yere to cum,/Bestowde in his breeche a cheese hard by his bum', Epigram 600). One of the most important developments of the later sixteenth century is the breaking of the bondage of the decorum of styles in popular dramatic writing and the 'mixing' of styles in Shakespeare.

Meanwhile, it is the dissemination of medieval poetry in successive reprintings that provides stimulus for some of the most characteristic sixteenth-century poetry. Thynne's 1532 Chaucer provoked a number of imitations, as we have seen (p. 221 above), and the late 1530s saw a poetic miscellany, *The Court of Venus*,[129] which anticipates Tottel by 20 years and includes an allegorical Chaucerian prologue to 'The Court of Venus', designed to introduce the sequence of 'bills' or love-complaints which follow, some of them by Wyatt. It also includes a strange anti-Papist *Pilgrim's Tale*, directly influenced by Thynne's Chaucer, which demonstrates, in a confused medley of anti-clerical, apocalyptic and prophetic materials, how Chaucer, or at least a sixteenth-century version of Chaucer, was made an instrument of Reformation propaganda.[130] The print of Lydgate's *Fall of Princes* in 1554 was probably even more influential. It prompted George Cavendish (d. 1562) to include in his *Life of Wolsey* a series of *Metrical Visions*[131] in which characters from his history come forward and lament in the style of the *Fall* 'What it is to trust to Fortunes mutabylitie' (56). Cavendish imitates Lydgate's metre and syntax closely, copies phrases and lines, and lifts one whole stanza verbatim (246–52), a demonstration of the authority of the poetic tradition which we can only view with the more bewilderment when we contrast it with the supple and energetic prose of the *Life*. Barclay's writing presented the same paradox, and we may recall further that Heywood and Morley were writing at the same time as Berners, the translator of Froissart, and Bale at the same time as the great biblical translators Tyndale and Coverdale. But much more important than the *Metrical Visions* is the influence of the 1554 print on *The Mirror for Magistrates*, that fundamental Elizabethan document,[132] which was designed first of all (1555) as a Tudor sequel to the *Fall of Princes*. Various writers contributed, most of them state officials and civil servants of various kinds, and the work grew by accretion in successive reprints, developing from the laboured Lydgatian imitations of William Baldwin and George Ferrers, with their traditionally loose metrics, to the ingenious and obscure 'conceited' style of John Dolman and the sophisticated histrionics of Thomas Sackville, Earl of Dorset, who contributed an *Induction* in 1563. Sackville is one of the few poets of the period who writes in a way to inspire confidence:

> And small fowles flocking, in theyr song did rewe
> The winters wrath, wherwith eche thing defaste
> In woful wise bewayld the sommer past.　　　　　　　(12–14)

Much of the Induction has a suspicion of pastiche, as if neither the allegorical vision (of a Dantesque Inferno) nor the tone of unrelieved lamentation were being taken entirely seriously, but Sackville, like the poet of *The Court of Love*, is in full stylistic control, whether fully serious or not, and is unfailingly musical. The reader no longer feels that he is extracting sense and metre from a wilderness of possibilities.

Early sixteenth-century lyric, as has been suggested (above, p. 221), is medieval in most essentials of form and subject. Much of our knowledge of medieval lyric, in fact, is derived from sixteenth-century collections, particularly Richard Hill's commonplace-book (Balliol MS 354), which includes one of the very best of the carols,[133] and from the Tudor song-books,[134] where we find that most evocative of lyric cries:

> Westron wynde when wyll thow blow
> The smalle rayne downe can rayne
> Cryst yf my love wer in my armys
> And I yn my bed Agayne.[135]

The song-books follow fifteenth-century tradition in including both secular and religious lyrics, and enlarge upon it in including both simple and ornate forms of both, anything indeed that can be fitted to music. It is important to recognise that these song-books are repertoires of texts for singing, not collections of poems: their common meeting-ground is song, and they violate in their association every kind of poetic or literary category. Words and poems, in this tradition, as also in the tradition of the courtly miscellany like the Devonshire MS (see above, p. 221), have a kind of anonymous existence, and mention of 'authors', like the attribution of 'Pastyme with good companye' and 'Alas what shall I do for love' to Henry VIII in B.M. MS Add. 31922, may in reality be to 'composers', since it is in the music that the distinction and individuality reside. Poetry gains from this more relaxed role, particularly if we recall the pressures to which it is subject in the more formal literary tradition, and the songs, including the love-lyrics attributed to sixteenth-century poets[136] such as Wyatt, have an unforced grace whose only defect (and it is one that they have only in the false context, divorced from song and social assembly, of modern editions) is their monotonous plangency. Even John Heywood has some songs, like 'All a grene wyllow is my garland' and 'Be merye, frendes', which charm by their effortlessness, while William Cornish, a choirmaster of the Chapel Royal, to whom several songs and carols are attributed, wrote a *Treatise bitwene Trowth and Enformacion* in rhyme royal[137] which is as lumbering and awkward as his songs are light and easy. Wyatt's position in this world of courtly song-making is ambiguous. No one can be sure that the association of large numbers of lyrics with his name is anything more than a convenience, a posthumous canon which served to endorse his reputation as the first of the courtly makers. The new points of growth in Wyatt are to be found outside the medieval anonymity of song, in his experimentation with metrical form, in his knottily personal and idiosyncratic structures of narrative and argumentation in poems like 'They fle from me that sometyme did me seke',[138] and in his new approach to Petrar-

273

chan models in a sonnet like 'Who so list to hounte I know where is an hynde' (VII), where the process of absorption and recreation, rather than imitation, is what we expect of an active poetic imagination. More important still, in the *Satires*, loosely imitative of Horace, Wyatt addresses himself to Skelton's problem, that of re-founding 'the right to moral satire in the conditions of a Christian world',[139] and at the same time to the more profound problem of restoring poetry to the world of living language and serious intellectual activity, the world of Erasmus and More rather than Hawes and Skelton. A long process of adaptation and recovery is still to be gone through, in particular the acquisition of familiarity with classical (as opposed to humanist or sub-humanist) materials, in the translations of Phaer, Golding and Turberville, the reforging of the penta-meter in Surrey's translations from the *Æneid*, and the establishment of a corpus of the new poetry in Tottel. In this process Chaucer and other medieval poets are not lost sight of—Googe, Churchyard, Gascoigne and of course Spenser are all 'Chaucerians'—and 'it is hard to distinguish the last medieval writers from the earliest medievalists, the survival from the revival',[140] but somewhere in this process the history of medieval English poetry can be said to come to an end.

## Scots poetry

Scots poetry deserves more than a postlude, for in consistency and quality it far surpasses the English poetry discussed in this chapter, and indeed, in the work of Henryson, Dunbar and Douglas, begins to claim comparison with Chaucer and the *Gawain*-poet. Its place in a history of English poetry is not unambiguous: the language itself, 'Inglis', was a form of Northern English spoken in the Lowlands of Scotland which only began to produce a distinctively 'Scots' literature when it began to speak of Scottish themes. This early phase is initiated and fully represented in the *Bruce* (1375; ed. STS, I. 31–2) of John Barbour, Archdeacon of Aberdeen and a royal exchequer clerk, a 13550-line poem in short couplet celebrating the winning of independence under Robert the Bruce. It is a stirring poem, both a memorial and a call to action after the less glorious reign of David II (1329–71), and its celebration of independence and freedom—'A! fredome is a noble thing!' (i. 225)—is only less splendid than the words of the Declaration of Arbroath (1320), in which the Scottish nation first truly recognised itself: 'For so long as one hundred of us shall be left alive, we shall never in any degree submit to the domination of the English. For it is not for glory, riches or honour that we fight, but for Freedom alone, which no good man surrenders but with his life.'[141] Barbour's language is vigorous, often colloquial, never ostentatiously poetic, and his poem is conceived as a loosely constructed chronicle romance:

> Lordingis, quha likis for till her,
> The romanys now begynnys her. (i. 445–6)

In form and spirit he often reminds one of Laȝamon (Barbour also wrote a lost *Brut*), but he is superior to Laȝamon in the care with which he develops Bruce as a model of political and military leadership, a blend of nobility and canniness similar to Shakespeare's Henry V, as he goes about his troops, for instance, on the eve of Bannockburn—'Ay as he met thame in the way,/He welcummyt thame with gladsum fair,/Spekand gud wordis heir and thair' (xi. 255–7).

This phase of Scots poetry, when its identity is asserted in its celebration of national themes, is further represented in the short-couplet *Original Chronicle of Scotland* of Andrew Wyntoun, Prior of Lochleven until 1422, and at its most magnificent in Hary's *Wallace* (c. 1478; ed. STS, IV. 4–5). This is a much more sophisticated poem than Barbour's ('Blind Harry', the poet's usual soubriquet, gives an altogether false impression of bardic simplicity), and echoes both Chaucer and Lydgate in its handling of pentameter couplet, its use of seasonal-astronomical transitions ('Zepherus ek with his suet vapour,' ix. 133) and other forms of ornamentation. It is also carefully constructed, deliberately reshaping history so as to glorify Scotland's greatest national hero, and moving with a fine sense of climax to its account of Wallace's martyrdom, where his grim resignation—'Maist payn I feill at I bid her our lang' (xii. 1368)—and his contemptuous dismissal of the English clerk who is sent to preach repentance of all his wrongdoings and killings,

> Than Wallace smyld a litill at his langage.
> 'I grant', he said, 'part Inglismen I slew,
> In my quarell me thocht nocht halff enew'. (xii. 1384–6)

has something of Icelandic saga. Hary's treatment of his subject is more literary and romanticized than Barbour's, but he is animated by the same fierce spirit of independence and hatred of the English:

> Our ald Ennemys cummyn of Saxonys blud,
> That neuyr ȝeit to Scotland wald do gud. (i. 7–8)

> Full fals thai war and euir ȝeit has beyn. (viii. 143)

In conception, form and detail the *Wallace* is immeasurably superior to Lydgate's *Troy-book*, to which, presumably, it is indebted.

Such works as these, which are Scots by assertion, are easily distinguished from the poems in the Scottish dialect which are mere offshoots of the English tradition, the massive *Legendary*, for instance, wrongly attributed to Barbour, the popular romances such as *Sir Tristrem*, *Eger and Grime* and *Roswall and Lillian* which happen to have been composed across the border or to have survived in Scottish copies, and the general mass of religious and didactic verse, such as *Ratis Raving*. Some of this writing may be dialectal translation or copying as much as composition.[142] The *Kingis Quair*, likewise, has no particular place in a history of Scots poetry, in the strict sense in which that term is defined here, nor the lengthy versions of the *Buik of Alexander*, one attributed to Barbour, the other by Sir Gilbert Hay, nor the faded courtly glamour of *Lancelot of the Laik*, translated from the French prose *Lancelot* with some infusions of seasonal punctuation from Lydgate's *Troy-book*. It is when we come to the late fifteenth and early sixteenth centuries that we enter the second and more truly independent phase of Scots poetry, the one which gives it such an ambiguous place in this volume, when its identity resides not in the patriotic assertions of individual poets but in a total cultural independence. It is often called court poetry, and certainly Dunbar was a court man (it seems absurd to call him a 'courtier') and Douglas and Lindsay both held important positions at court, but a new definition of court poetry would be needed to cover the obscenities, the bitterness and animal high spirits of much of Dunbar. The influence of James IV (1488–1513) is likewise often regarded as important to the flourishing of Scots poetry in this period, and, though Henryson had nothing to do with the court and Lindsay came later, it may be that the personality of the King, vigorous, bustling, magpie-like in his interests, full of glamour yet devoid of pomp and self-reverence, had something to do with the encouragement of poetry. One might suggest also that the expansion of the Scottish educational system in the fifteenth century—all these poets are men of learning—may have been still more influential.[143] But one should recognise a larger context for these poets, a phase in the history of a small nation (like that of Iceland) when social hierarchies were absorbed in a ferocious national self-consciousness, when a cat might look at a king, and when poetry, profiting from a prevailing democratisation of impulse, could draw freely on vigorous native resources of language as well as feed on the neighbouring English and French cultures without loss of independence. It is this independence, as well as their extensive debt to the northern alliterative tradition, that makes the term 'Scottish Chaucerians' so inapposite for these poets. They are respectful towards Chaucer, and Lydgate too, and they are indebted to them for their major verse-forms (rhyme royal, pentameter couplet, ballade stanza and its derivatives) and some characteristic modes of aureation and rhetorical ornamentation. But they take only what they want from Chaucer, absorb and renew what they take, and live in his light rather than under his shadow.

Of the three great Scots poets of this golden age, which spans almost exactly the drab age of the Transition in England, the most immediately attractive to the modern reader is always likely to be Robert Henryson (fl. 1490), 'scolmaister of Dumfermling'.[144] Henryson absorbs into his poetry a good deal of learning, in law, medicine, music and allegorised classical mythology as well as in other fields; he is scrupulously attentive to detail; and he is an artist of great technical expertness and resource, admirable not so much in *tours de force* like the majestic *Prayer for the Pest*, with its stanzas of triple internal rhyme, as in the systematic conciseness of his style, in which every word is weighed. None of these preoccupations intrudes, however, upon the honesty, humanity and compassion which are Henryson's most important gifts as a poet. If such terms seem inappropriate to *The Testament of Cresseid*, a sequel to *Troilus and Criseyde* which is designed to correct both Chaucer's morality and his poetics (a palinode, like the *Kingis Quair*), it is perhaps worth commenting that the fearful machine which Henryson has constructed to destroy Cresseid by punishing her with leprosy is not in fact the instrument of her repentance. She has to pay the world in its own coin, but her progress through misery is untouched by self-knowledge until she meets Troilus, in a scene of overwhelming yet totally unsentimental poignancy. Only then does she say 'Nane but my self as now I will accuse' (574), illumination having been bestowed not by punishment and suffering but by the recognition of what Troilus' love was and is, and redemption won by a renewal of truth and faith in human love. The relation of the *Testament* to the greatest English poem of the Middle Ages has perhaps distracted attention from Henryson's own most important work, the *Morall Fabillis*, a series of retellings of fables from Æsop and the medieval beast-epic of Reynard which Henryson makes the vehicle for a commentary on human nature and society both harrowing and zestfully comic. All is rooted in the traditional verities of God's order (explicitly in *The Preiching of the Swallow*, 1622–712), just as the poem is rooted in traditional shell–kernel aesthetic (15–18), with a *Moralitas* appended to each Fable; and the cry of the oppressed sheep, 'Lord God, quhy sleipis thow sa lang' (1295), is answered only in the consolation of 'Sen that we ar opprest/In to this eirth, grant us in hevin gude rest' (1319–20). Nevertheless, Henryson does not undervalue human life; he recognises its dignity as well as its pathos, and his animals have a rare humanity. Henryson's other poems, less vigorously enlivened by this sense of human comedy and tragedy, are still marked by the same fineness of finish: the *pastourelle* of *Robene and Makyne*, the richly learned moral allegory of *Orpheus and Eurydice*, and a series of moralistic poems which favour the debate form and the point of view of reconciled old age—'The more of age the nerar hevynnis blis' *(The Prais of Aige)*. *Sum Practysis of Medecyne*, a series of burlesque prescriptions, is an example of the kind of alliterative tirade, usually obscene and often impenetrable, for which all the Scots seem to have had a weakness.

The poetry of William Dunbar (fl. 1500) is wider in range, thinner in substance and more brilliant in technical accomplishment than Henryson's. All his poems, from the demonic pageantry of *The Dance of the Sevin Deidly Synnis* and the wild abandonment of abuse in *The Flyting of Dunbar and Kennedie* to the concussive grandeur of *On the Resurrection of Christ* ('Done is a battell on the dragon blak,/Our campioun Chryst confountet hes his force'), can be seen as displays of verbal energy[145] and unparalleled technical virtuosity in familiar medieval genres. It is difficult to perceive any core of poetic intention in Dunbar's work and he may appear most characteristically engaged in the occasional pieces he wrote for a lively court *(The Wowing of the King, Of a Dance in the Quenis Chalmer)* or in the moralistic poems that often turn to a contemplation of his own inadequately rewarded state *(Meditatioun in Wyntir, Of the Warldis Instabilitie)* or in the technical and verbal trickery of twisted refrains *(Ane his Awin Ennemy)* and hypnotically repeated internal rhymes *(Ane Ballat of Our Lady)*. Yet there is more to Dunbar than this, more than a virtuoso Lydgate.[146] His poetry, in its sensuous vigour and verbal luxuriance, embodies a real dichotomy of spirit, between the splendours of life and its roots in filth and obscenity, or, if one may adopt the allegorical language of the morality-poem of *King Hart*, attributed to Douglas, between the turreted and pinnacled castle of 'King Hart' (74) and the brackish moat that laps its walls,

> Blak, stinkand, sowr, and salt as is the sey,
> That on the wallis wiskit, gre be gre,
> Boldning to ryis the castell to confound. (76–8)

In *The Goldyn Targe*, *The Thrissil and the Rois* and *The Merle and the Nychtingaill*, poems where allegory is the merest gesture, Dunbar uses his 'anamalit termes celicall' (*Goldyn Targe*, 257) to reach out to a vision of nature in which sun ('the goldyn candill matutyne', 4) and sky, leaf and flower, are arrested in motion and mutability and hypostatized in crystalline splendour:

> The cristall air, the sapher firmament,
> The ruby skyes of the orient,
> Kest beriall bemes on emerant bewis grene;
> The rosy garth, depaynt and redolent,
> With purpur, azure, gold, and goulis gent
> Arayed was, by dame Flora the quene. (37–42)

It is not mere verbal panache, for Dunbar's sense of colour-values, under this unearthly light,

> The purpur hevyn, our scailit in silvir sloppis,
> Ourgilt the treis, branchis, lef, and barkis (26–7)

is strangely subtle. At the opposite pole is a *chanson d'aventure*, 'In secreit place', where love-talk degenerates into comically nauseous baby-talk ('My belly huddrun, my swete hurle bawsy,/My huny gukkis, my slawsy gawsy', 38–9), and above all *The Tretis of the Tua Mariit Wemen and the Wedo*. This poem, in unrhymed alliterative verse (the only one, amongst all these Scots poets, though all use heavy alliteration quite frequently), rejoices in contrasting the elaborate courtly ceremony of its 'Midsummer evin' opening, its 'thre gay ladeis' in 'ane grene arbeir', and the grossness of their talk about their husbands. The form, the *chanson à mal mariée*, is traditional, the debt to Chaucer's Wife of Bath and Merchant's Tale obvious, the vein of sexual disgust one frequently tapped in the Middle Ages, but Dunbar's frenetic energy takes his poem well beyond the familiar pale of comic decorum.

Gavin Douglas (d. 1522) gave up poetry after Flodden (1513) to concentrate on state affairs, eventually becoming Bishop of Dunkeld. If *King Hart* is not his, then his only important poem apart from the Virgil is *The Palice of Honour*, a veritable encyclopaedia of themes from medieval allegory and love-vision, as if Douglas were gathering a last bouquet before the flowers faded. It shows a

powerful poetic imagination, not least in its capacity to hold in suspension the
traditional pageantry of processions and personifications, the richest aureation
of language, and touches of vivid personal realism like the dreamer's fear of
being metamorphosed by Venus:

> That oft I wald my hand behald to se
> Gif it alterit, and oft my visage graip. (743–4)

Douglas's great achievement, however, is the translation of the *Æneid*. His
attitude to his work, though he has respect for his text and rebukes Chaucer and
Caxton for their inaccuracy, is not noticeably touched by the Renaissance: he
praises Virgil, as is customary, for his rhetoric, his 'scharp sugurate sang' (I, Prol.
29) and 'polyst termys redymyte' (34), and for his 'sentence', for 'under the
clowdis of dyrk poecy/Hyd lyis thar mony notabill history' (193–4), and takes
the opportunity in the Prologue to book IV to moralise further on 'lufe inordinat'
in the case of Dido. The triumph of his poem is a triumph of diction, and one in
which he reflects the central strength of the Scots tradition, especially as opposed
to English poetry of the period, that is, its capacity to absorb both literary and
colloquial elements into a coherent poetic language of both vigour and beauty.
Douglas approaches Virgil without affectation or striving after elevation; his
language is proper and rich and when he expands on his source he expands,
as one might say, in the spirit of his original, as in his account of the storm that
drives Æneas ashore,

> A blastrand bub out from the north brayng
> Gan our the forschip in the baksaill dyng[147]

or of Dido running wild through Carthage:

> Scho wyskis wild throu the town of Cartage,
> Syk wyse as quhen thir nunnys of Bachus
> Ruschis and relis our bankis, brays and bus.[148]

Douglas also offers, in his Prologues, amongst other splendours, three passages
of seasons and landscape description, of winter (VII), of May (XII) and of a
summer night (XIII), which are quite incomparable in medieval or indeed in
any other poetry, in their precision of evocative detail ('The wynd maid waif
the red wed on the dyke', VII. 59), their sense of space and perspective, of light
and shade,

> The lyght begouth to quynchyng owt and faill,
> The day to dyrkyn, declyne and devaill;
> The gummys rysis, doun fallis the donk rym,
> Baith heir and thar scuggis and schaddois dym.
> Upgois the bak with hir pelit ledderyn flycht... (XIII. 29–33)

of the busy life of field and labourer ('Puyr lauboraris and bissy husband men/ Went wait and wery draglit in the fen', VII. 75–6), all invigorated and made personal by Douglas's own presence within the scene.

Sir David Lindsay (d. 1555), an important figure in the court of James V, is the least of these poets, yet not disgraced in their company, for he is, like all of them, honest and decisive in all his poetic choices. He has a stronger consciousness of the political, moral and didactic responsibilities of the poet, and of the reforming power of poetry, and is less of a stylist: the *Dialogue betuix Experience and ane Courteour*, better known as *The Monarche*, is a racy exposition of world history from Fall to Doomsday, contrasting the antique empires with the Spiritual Monarchy of Christ; his *Dreme*, beginning with a winter stroll ('with dowbyll schone, & myttanis on my handis', 72) on the seashore ('The see was furth; the sand wes smoith & dryye', 115), develops into a vision of hell, heaven, earth and the sad state of Scotland, designed as a 'Mirror for Princes', with 'Ihone the comoun weill' (931), a favourite character of Lindsay's, making a first appearance and a powerful complaint; *The Testament and Complaynt of the Papyngo* records the advice given by a dying pet parrot to kings, nobles and clergy, ending, with savage aptness, with the dead parrot being torn to pieces by her executors. Lindsay never misses an opportunity to press home a lesson on his young king, to whom he acted as a father in his childhood, as he describes in his *Complaynt*, nor to enforce his Reformation sympathies. He has his lighter moments, however. The vitality of *Ane Satyre of the Thre Estaitis*, certainly the best of all the morality plays, if a little too long, derives as much from its irresistibly comic ribaldry as from its fierce anti-clericalism; there is a very funny *Justing* between two doctors; and finally, *Squyer Meldrum* is a poem with no ambition but to please, to give romance to reality (Meldrum was a contemporary historical personage who fought, as the poem describes, against the English in France) and reality to romance. It has its moments of frank comedy ('Ʒit, quhen his schankis wer schorne in sunder,/Upon his kneis he wrocht greit wounder', 1349–50), frank sensuality (940 ff), and arrant fantasy, including the damsel in distress of all romantic dreams ('SpuilƷeit, naikit as scho was borne./ Twa men of weir wer hir beforne', 109–10), but it is superbly narrated and sounds the end of medieval romance like a clarion-call.

These four major poets are surrounded by a host of lesser luminaries and anonymous poets, the work of all of them amply represented in the great sixteenth-century MS collections of Scots poetry, the Bannatyne MS (1568; ed. STS II. 22–3, 26, III. 5), the Maitland Folio (c. 1580; ed. STS II. 7, 20) and the Maitland Quarto (1586; ed. STS II. 9). Their work shows the strength in depth of the Scots tradition, ranging freely from the carnival horseplay and burlesque of *Colkelbie Sow* (Bann. CCCCI), *Christis Kirk on the Grene* (Bann. CLXIV) and *Peblis to the Play* (Mait. Folio XLIX), to the most precious kinds of courtly and religious poetry, aureate, metrically sophisticated and ornamented with every device of rhetoric (e.g. 'O hicht of hicht and licht of licht most cleir', Bann. XXII, and 'Flour of all fairheid', Bann. CCLXXIII). Even after Lindsay there are poets like Alexander Scott, Alexander Montgomerie and Alexander

Hume in whom the traditions are still alive. It is a brief life, however, and the Bannatyne and other MSS have already a retrospective air. Perhaps the Reformation of 1560 brought a change. Perhaps, on the other hand, one can look too hard for patterns of change and evolution. As C. S. Lewis puts it (*English Literature in the Sixteenth Century*, p. 113), 'We ask too often why cultures perish and too seldom why they survive; as though their conservation were the normal and obvious fact and their death the abnormality for which special causes must be found. It is not so.'

# 9  Conclusion

A retrospective view over the centuries we have traversed reveals two distinct periods during which English poetry may be said to be truly comparable in achievement with the best continental traditions. The first of these 'golden ages' is the period in the eighth and ninth centuries when Anglo-Saxon monastic culture was passing through its first and most generous phase and when most of the extant Old English poetry is presumed to have been written. This golden age was the product of the grafting of rich continental Latin and Christian traditions on to a strong native stock; it came to an end with the decay of learning of which Alfred speaks. The conditions of the monastic revival of the tenth century were not favourable to any more than a sporadic re-invigoration, though that revival made the earlier poetry accessible to us. The second golden age is the fourteenth century, and is similar to the first in that it is another period during which English poetry becomes fully receptive to and capable of absorbing continental influences. The particular precipitant here is the reassumption by the English language, after a long period of subordination, of the central role as the language of poetry. The range of poetry produced can be related to other factors of social, religious and intellectual history, and some poems, such as *Piers Plowman*, can be seen as essentially related to native inheritance, but it is the return of English poetry to the centres of social prestige that provides the conditions for Chaucer, Gower and the provincial alliterative poets.

Between these two ages there is a confused pattern of change, decline and adaptation, with occasional bold erratics like the *Brut* and *The Owl and the Nightingale*, which suggest as much as anything the extent to which our elucidation of patterns is determined by the accidents of manuscript survival. But even with such reservations, it has to be admitted that the long period between the writing down of the Anglo-Saxon poetic codices and the first intimation of new growth in MS Harley 2253 is one of comparative paucity in English poetry. This has nothing to do, it should be emphasised, with the state of English intellectual life, which was as vigorous in the tenth and eleventh centuries as in the eighth and ninth (if in somewhat different ways), and which in the twelfth and thirteenth centuries can lay fair claim to an essential, even at times a central place in the European tradition. However, much of this intellectual life was not in any case accessible to vernacular poetry, and English poetry was further excluded from the courtly and aristocratic centres of social patronage. It remains, therefore, a mainly clerical tradition, with the occasional liberties that such a tradition allows, but dominated by didactic concerns. As far as English poetry is concerned, these concerns, given the generally if not totally subordinate social function of English, are predominantly to do with the vernacularisation of religious teaching, and the great mass of verse produced during the thirteenth and fourteenth centuries, and still bulking large in the fifteenth, is the verse of instruction, piety and devotion. Much of it is on a low level, socially, intellectually and artistically. Apart from this there is a literature of entertainment, in the romances, which again exists on a low level until it is enriched by the rise of status of English in the fourteenth century.

The fifteenth century is perhaps the most complex for the historian of poetry and the most difficult to summarise in any useful way. The range of poetic activity is for the first time complete, with every kind of function for poetry represented at every social level, whilst the production of poetry is expanded and the chances of survival improved. With such a mass of evidence, and in the absence of a great writer who focusses in himself the movements of the age, it is difficult to elicit clearly defined patterns. It might be called a century of consolidation, in which English poetry, after the first splendours of exploration in the fourteenth century, absorbs into itself the accumulated stock of learned and literary traditions hitherto available only in Latin or French. This is bound to be a pedestrian exercise, dominated by translation. The paradox for English poetry, however, is that it finds itself poised to receive its full European inheritance at the very moment when the traditions of that inheritance are devitalised and exhausted. Poetry is overtaken by prose, in the continental mode introduced by Caxton; it is overtaken by the Renaissance with its new concepts of style and the poet's role; and it is overtaken by the Reformation, which throws into disrepute its traditionally most serious subject-matter. It may be the delayed action of these influences in Scotland that allows there a flourishing of poetry in the medieval tradition in the late fifteenth and early sixteenth centuries. In England, with tendencies towards inflation already established in the style of the century's most influential poet, Lydgate, poetry is deprived of its middle ground by prose, thus sharpening the distinction between the low vernacular style and the artifically inflated high style, and the latter, already partly moribund, is in its turn deprived of its essential central roles by the changes in attitude towards poetry and its function associated with the Renaissance and the Reformation. A poet like Skelton is the victim of these dilemmas. What we are witnessing, in fact, is a shift in the role of poetry from a social form to an art-form. For the medieval poet, poetry is an aspect of the general intellectual tradition, a form of discourse not essentially different in kind from other forms of discourse, except in its capacity to give pleasure. This is now changing: poetry, when it is not relegated to base functions, is now becoming the property of a reading élite and the product of a particular kind of elevated being, the Poet. It is difficult to imagine an *Apology for Poetry* in the English Middle Ages, or to imagine the kind of attack on poetry as a form that produced the *Apology*. Nevertheless it is the tenacity of the medieval tradition that is remarkable in the early sixteenth century, and it is partly out of the debris of the old that the new is created, in Wyatt, in the *Mirror for Magistrates*, and in Spenser.

# Appendix 1 Technical terms, mainly metrical

ACCENTUAL VERSE  see METRE

AFFECTIVE  a term used in the discussion of devotional and other spiritual writing to describe that kind of writing which makes a deliberate appeal to the emotions.

ALEXANDRINE  in French versification, a line of 12 syllables; in English, a line of 6 stresses developed in imitation of the French line but with less syllabic regularity. See SEPTENARY

ALLITERATIVE VERSE  a type of verse based on a line consisting of two half-lines, independent in Old English (see p. 15), progressively less so in Middle English (see p. 77), each of two stresses. The stresses are arranged in rhythmical rather than metrical (i.e. with regular distribution of stressed and unstressed syllables: see METRE) patterns. The syllable that carries the first stress of the *b*-line (i.e. the second half-line) and at least one of the two stressed syllables of the *a*-line (the first half-line) alliterate together. The pattern of alliteration in a line is conventionally indicated by the use of *a* for an alliterating and *x* for a non-alliterating stressed syllable, thus: *aa/ax*, *ax/ax*, etc.

AMPLIFICATION  in the classical arts of rhetoric and the medieval arts of poetry, the technical name given to the various devices for expanding on a given subject-matter (e.g. description, digression, exclamation, APOSTROPHE, etc.)

ANACRUSIS  that part of a line of (alliterative) verse which precedes the first stressed syllable.

ANTIPHON  a verse or series of verses in the church liturgy, usually one with alternate parts for two choirs or parts of a choir (the original form and sense of 'anthem').

APOSIOPESIS  a breaking-off in mid-sentence for the sake of effect: a recognised device of classical rhetoric.

APOSTROPHE  rhetorical address, usually exclamatory in form, to a person not present, or to an abstract or inanimate object.

ARS POETICA  (Lat.) a consciously designed and accepted art of poetry.

ASYNDETON  the Greek name for a rhetorical figure which consists in omitting conjunctions.

AUREATE  lit. 'golden', a term used in the fifteenth century to describe the

284

heavily Latinate vocabulary admired in English poetry; often used more loosely to describe elevated diction of any kind.

BALLAD METRE or COMMON METRE    a quatrain of alternately four- and three-stress lines, rhyming alternately, $a^4b^3c^4b^3$ or $a^4b^3a^4b^3$ (i.e. a SEPTENARY couplet with or without medial rhyme).

BALLADE or BALADE    a type of poem developed in France in the early fourteenth century consisting normally of 3 stanzas and an ENVOY. The last lines of each stanza and of the envoy are the same (sometimes with variation) and constitute a REFRAIN. The systematic tendency in the ballade towards one kind of stanza, an 8-line stanza rhyming *abbaabba*, leads to the identification of this form as the *ballade-stanza*. The characteristic rhyming pattern (which of course needs only a 4-line sequence to identify itself) is often called *ballade-rhyme*.

BERNARDINE    influenced by or associated with St Bernard of Clairvaux, particularly with reference to the type of passionate or AFFECTIVE devotion inspired by his Sermons on the Song of Songs.

BOB    a short line (usually only 2 or 3 syllables, single stress) linking the longer alliterative lines of a composite stanza with the shorter lines of the WHEEL.

BURDEN    the repetition, usually unvaried, of a line or sequence of lines which are independent of the main structure of a poem, as in the CAROL; a chorus. See REFRAIN (2).

CAESURA    the pause (real or imaginary) at or near the middle of a long line of verse.

CAROL    a short poem with repeated REFRAIN or BURDEN.

CHANSON D'AVENTURE    (Fr.) a type of poem developed in France in the twelfth century which treats of unexpected love-meetings, usually in a pastoral setting. The opening is characteristic, touching on the spring season and the occasion of the poet going forth 'on adventure'.

CHANSON DE GESTE    (Fr.) 'a song of heroic action', the name given to the French poems of the eleventh to thirteenth centuries dealing with epic themes, usually associated with Charlemagne.

CHEVILLE    (Fr.) a TAG.

CHIASMUS    reversal of syntactic order in the two parallel elements of a balanced sentence or line of verse (e.g. p. 203).

COMMON METRE    see BALLAD METRE.

COMPLAINT    (1) a poem protesting against the state of society; (2) a poem complaining of unrequited love.

CONCATENATION    the repetition of the last words of one line in the first part of the next, or of the last line of a stanza in the first line of the next.

CURSUS    the systematisation of rhythmical structure, particularly of sentence-closure, in Latin prose.

ENCOMIUM    praise of a formal (literary) kind (*adj.* ENCOMIASTIC).

ENJAMBEMENT    the running-on of the sense of a line of verse to the next line without pause or 'end-stopping'.

ENVOY    the concluding lines of a BALLADE or other poem, often containing the author's direction of his poem to its recipient.

EXEGESIS   the practice of biblical interpretation and commentary.

EXEMPLUM   a short story with a moral, as used in a sermon to exemplify a particular point.

FABLIAU   a type of comic narrative which reports low sexual intrigue, usually in a bourgeois setting, with a degree of obscenity and surface realism.

FASCICULE   (1) one of the parts of a MS made up in the first place separately as a gathering or QUIRE; (2) one of the parts of a book as it is published in instalments.

FITT   a section of a poem, as marked in the MS, usually thought to be that part of the poem that might conveniently be recited at one sitting without pause, or a relic of such practice.

FLORILEGIUM   (Lat.) an anthology of prized passages ('flowers') of wisdom, eloquence or poetry.

FORMULA   a conventional phrase which forms an accepted part of a conscious ARS POETICA, distinct in artistic significance and effect from a TAG.

FOURTEENER   a name given to the sixteenth century line of 14 syllables (or 7 stresses) derived from the SEPTENARY (or from relineation of BALLAD METRE).

GNOMIC   briefly expressive of fundamental moral platitudes or axioms.

GOLIARDIC   to do with or resembling the Latin poetry of the goliards (OF, 'gluttons'), irreverent and sophisticated clerical poets of the twelfth century.

HAGIOGRAPHY   the writing of saints' lives.

HEMISTICH   half-line.

HEXAMERAL   to do with the *hexameron* (also *hexaemeron*), or Six Days of Creation described in Genesis; or, more generally, with the story of Creation.

HEXASYLLABIC   having 6 syllables.

HISPERICAN   a style among Anglo-Latin writers of the Anglo-Saxon period imitative of or resembling that of the *Hisperica Famina* (see p. 13), and characterised by a cult of the difficult and obscure in language, syntax and rhetoric.

HOMILETIC   to do with homilies (i.e. sermons).

HYPERMETRIC   of a line having more syllables or stresses than the prevailing metrical pattern.

IAMBIC   a term derived from Latin prosody and conventionally used in English prosody to describe a pattern based on 'rising' rhythm, i.e. one in which an unstressed syllable precedes a stressed syllable: $x/x/$, etc. It is the normal rhythm of English verse.

JONGLEUR   (Fr.) a professional poet or minstrel of northern France in the twelfth to fourteenth centuries. The term is commonly used to refer to a lower class of minstrel than the TROUVÈRE, but it is not easy to justify this distinction (as for instance by defining the *jongleur* as itinerant and the *trouvère* as permanently attached to a particular court) in historical terms.

KENNING   in OE poetry, a nominal poetic compound with a metaphoric element.

LAISSE   (Fr.) in French verse, and especially in the CHANSON DE GESTE, a sequence of lines linked by rhyme or assonance: the number of lines in the sequence varies, but is rarely below 15 or above 30. The *laisse* constitutes a narrative unit.

LECTIONARY   (n.) a book of readings from the Scriptures for use in the divine service; (adj.) pertaining to such readings, or to the *lectiones* which were a customary part of the monastic curriculum also on more informal occasions.

LEGENDARY   a collection of saints' lives, usually arranged as a SANCTORALE.

LINGUA FRANCA   (Lat.) a language understood by a number of linguistic groups some or all of whom have a different primary language.

'LONG LINE'   the line derived from the SEPTENARY/ALEXANDRINE in thirteenth-century English poetry; often called the 'old long line', and so distinguished from the ALLITERATIVE long line.

MACARONIC   verse composed in two or more languages, with close relation and usually syntactical connection, within line or stanza, of the different languages.

MATIÈRE and SENS   (Fr.) terms originally derived from Chrétien de Troyes (*san* and *matiere*, *Le Chevalier de la Charrete*, line 26) and used in modern criticism to refer to the subject matter or given material (*matière*) of a story in so far as it is distinct from the interpretation or meaning (*sens*) given to it by the individual writer.

MEMBRUM ORATIONIS   (Lat.) the repetition of a co-ordinating conjunction in a sequence of co-ordinate clauses.

METRE   the arrangement of language in lines of verse based on fixed rhythmical patterns regularly repeated. In English verse the principle of organisation is stress or accent: stress determines the metrical pattern of a line, and the presence, number and distribution of unstressed syllables is less important. Such verse may be called ACCENTUAL. However, most English verse, influenced by French practice, recognises a degree of regularity in the distribution of unstressed as well as stressed syllables. Such verse may be called SYLLABIC, though it should be emphasised that the principle of organisation is still stress. The balancing of natural speech-stress against the metrical stress-pattern produces RHYTHM, which may in particular contexts of actual heard sound be close to or widely variant from the basic metrical pattern.

MIMETIC   imitative of real life, representative of reality: adj. from *mimesis* (Gk., 'imitation'), the word used by Aristotle to describe the fundamental process of dramatic representation.

MNEMONIC   designed to aid the memory.

MONORHYMED   having a single rhyme.

MUMMING   a dramatic performance put on by 'mummers' or mime actors as an interlude at a feast or festival. The actors may sometimes have been given lines to speak, but mostly the text was spoken by the poet or master of ceremonies.

OCTAVE   an 8-line stanza or sequence of lines.

OCTOSYLLABIC   having 8 syllables.

OCTOSYLLABIC COUPLET   a term derived from French versification, used to describe the four-stress or 'SHORT' COUPLET in so far as it is partly influenced by the more regularly SYLLABIC French form.

ORAL-FORMULAIC COMPOSITION   poetic composition by improvisation, practised by illiterate singers, and based on the extensive use and repetition of fixed phrases or FORMULAE.

PALINODE   the reversing of a statement, whether literally, in terms of the order of words, or metaphorically, in terms of its meaning.

PASSUS   (Lat.) literally, 'a step': a section of a poem, i.e. a stage in its development, often perhaps to be thought of, like a FITT, in terms of oral delivery.

PASTOURELLE   a type of poem of French origin, in which a knight and shepherdess meet in a pastoral setting. The form can accommodate other kinds of meeting and event, not always to do with love.

PATRISTIC   to do with the writings of the Fathers (authoritative writers and biblical commentators) of the Christian Church, especially Latin writings collected in the *Patrologia Latina* ('Latin Writings of the Fathers'), ed. J. P. Migne, 221 vols, Paris, 1844–64.

PENTAMETER   in strict terms, in reference to Latin quantitative verse, a line of five feet; conventionally used in reference to English verse to describe a line of five stresses, with regular alternation of stressed and unstressed syllables and a predominantly IAMBIC or rising movement, viz. $x/x/x/x/x/$.

PERSONA   (Lat.) the poetic first person or 'I' conceived of as a dramatic character distinguishable from the poet.

PROSOPOPEIA   the practice of representing absent persons, animals or inanimate objects as speakers.

QUANTITY   syllabic length (whether determined by vowel length or other criteria) as used to provide the organising principle of QUANTITATIVE metre.

QUATRAIN   a stanza of four lines.

QUIRE   a gathering of pages or 'little book' (whence *Kingis Quair*).

REFRAIN   (1) the repetition, often with variation, of the integral last line of a stanza, as in the BALLADE; (2) the repetition, usually unvaried, of a line or sequence of lines which are independent of the main structure of a poem, as in the CAROL. The term 'chorus' or BURDEN is preferable for the latter, though there is no consistency of usage.

'REGISTER'   that quality in language which reflects the social level or context of its use.

RESPONSE   (1) a verse or series of verses in the Church liturgy, said or sung after the lesson, with alternate parts for priest and choir or for choir and congregation (cf. ANTIPHON); (2) the 'response' (opposed to 'versicle') in such a sequence.

REVERDIE   (Fr.) a song to celebrate the return of spring.

RHYME ROYAL   the 7-line stanza, $^{5}ababbcc$, first used by Chaucer (see p. 201).

RHYTHM   see METRE.

RIFACIMENTO   (It.) a re-working.

RIME BRISÉE   (Fr.) a rhyme sequence based on internal segments of successive (not neccessarily consecutive) lines, e.g. the first half of a line rhyming with the first half of the next line.

RIME COUÉE   (Fr.) TAIL-RHYME

ROUNDEL (Fr. *rondel, rondeau*) a lyric of fixed form on two rhymes, in which the opening line or lines are repeated at the middle and end of the poem. The basic form is of 10 lines, *abbabRabbR*, where *R represents* the repetition of the first line only.

RUBRIC the heading given to a poem (or a picture) in a MS: it often takes the place of a title.

RUNIC pertaining to an early Germanic alphabet of *runes*, letters of angular character suitable for incising in wood or stone.

SANCTORALE (Lat.) a calendar of saints' days and saints' lives.

SCHRIFTSPRACHE (Gm.) a written or literary language, a language (such as late West Saxon) which has become stabilised in written form so as to be resistant to the processes of change in the spoken language.

SCOP the name given in Anglo-Saxon poetry to the professional poet or singer of heroic tradition.

SENS see MATIÈRE.

SEPTENARY an English imitation of the Latin *septenarius* (a line of 7 feet), essentially a line of 7 stresses (and, more strictly, 15 syllables) with IAMBIC movement. Separating at its natural CAESURA, it produces COMMON METRE. Associated with the ALEXANDRINE, it produces the characteristic loose LONG LINE of Middle English, the SEPTENARY/ALEXANDRINE.

SEQUENCE a composition in verse or rhythmical prose said or sung at a fixed point in the Church liturgy.

SHORT COUPLET see OCTOSYLLABIC COUPLET.

SKALDIC to do with the poetry of the *skalds* or professional poets of the Old Icelandic tradition.

STANZA a regularly repeated structure of rhymed lines.

STAVE in ALLITERATIVE VERSE, a stress-bearing and alliterating syllable.

STICHIC of a type of verse in which individual lines or half-lines are run on freely into verse-paragraphs of varying length: opposite to STROPHIC or stanzaic verse.

STROPHIC arranged in STANZAS.

SYLLABIC see METRE.

TAG a conventional phrase deprived of significance through thoughtless repetition; cf. FORMULA.

TAIL-RHYME (trans. from Fr. RIME COUÉE) a structure of rhymed lines based on the repetition of a rhyme after the interval of at least two rhyming lines, e.g. *aabaab*. It is usually thought to be of Latin origin: see *PMLA* 22 (1907), 371–420. The commonest tail-rhyme STANZA in Middle English is $aa^4b^3cc^4b^3$, but forms with only two rhymes are common, as are 12-line multiples with a single tail-rhyme. Another form is based on 4-line sequences, *aaabcccb*, etc. The 'tail' is commonly shorter than the other lines of the stanza (whence the name) but not always so. A particular form of tail-rhyme is that based on alliterative half-lines of varying stress-pattern (see pp. 144, 152).

TEMPORALE (Lat.) a calendar of the festivals of the Church year.

TOPOS (Gk., pl. *topoi*) a conventional poetic motif with a strong formal element, as described in E. R. Curtius, *European Literature and the Latin Middle Ages* (1948; English trans. by W. R. Trask, 1953).

TROUVÈRE  (Fr.) a professional court poet or minstrel of northern France in the twelfth to fourteenth centuries; cf. JONGLEUR.

TYPOLOGY  that form of biblical exegesis which is concerned with the allegorical interpretation of the Old Testament as a prefiguration of the New, of its characters as 'types' of Christ.

VARIATION  the practice in OE poetry of amplifying a sentence by working variations upon its elements in the form of appositional constructions, often separated from their antecedents.

WHEEL  a sequence of short lines used to conclude a composite stanza (usually one based on the alliterative line). The wheel may have alternate rhyme or TAIL-RHYME and may consist of ACCENTUAL lines of three stresses or RHYTHMICAL lines (presumed to be derived from the alliterative half-line) basically of two stresses. See BOB.

# Appendix 2   Chronological Table

This Chronological Table lists (1) important historical events for the period covered, mainly in England; (2) date or approximate date of writing or completion of poems in English, with some reference to other works in English, and to important works in other languages composed either in England or abroad; (3) the most important MSS of poetry. As to the latter, those MSS which consist entirely or mainly of texts of single long poems which are extant in many copies (e.g. *Canterbury Tales*, *Confessio Amantis*, *Piers Plowman*) and which are mentioned elsewhere in the Table are not separately listed. In other words, the MSS mentioned are mainly anthologies or miscellanies: nevertheless, very few important MSS of poetry from before 1400 have to be omitted on these grounds. The dates given for MSS in the Table are nearly always approximate, and their exact place in the Table often arbitrary; where this might be misleading, the broader dating is given in the conventional way (XIV in, XIV ex, XIV $\frac{2}{4}$, etc., i.e. beginning, end, second quarter, etc., of the fourteenth century). The Index (s.v. Manuscripts) gives cross-references to the text.

| | |
|---|---|
| 410 | Withdrawal of Roman legions. |
| 429 | First visit of Germanus, Bishop of Auxerre: establishes monachism within British Church. |
| 449 | First visits of 'Saxon' adventurers at invitation of Kentish King Vortigern. |
| c. 500 | Battle of Mons Badonicus (not identified): British victory over Saxons, followed by some re-migration of Saxons to continent. |
| 577 | Defeat of British at Dyrham, near Bath. |
| 597 | Landing of Augustine in Kent. |
| 615 | Defeat of British at Chester by Æthelfrith, King of Northumbria. |
| 616–32 | Edwin King in Northumbria: period of Northumbrian supremacy. |
| 627 | Conversion of Edwin, during Paulinus' mission to Northumbria. |
| 633–41 | Oswald King in Northumbria. |
| 634 | Aidan founds Lindisfarne with monks from Iona. |
| 641 | Penda King of Mercia defeats and kills Oswald. |
| 663 | Synod of Whitby: assertion of Roman Church over Irish. |
| 664 | Cuthbert becomes Prior of Lindisfarne (d. 687). |
| 669 | Arrival of Archbishop Theodore and Abbot Hadrian at Canterbury. |
| 680 | Death of Hild, Abbess of Whitby, during whose abbacy Caedmon was active. |

689   Death of Benedict Biscop, founder of Wearmouth–Jarrow monasteries.

        c. 700–50   Assumed date of composition for earliest scriptural poems, e.g. *Genesis*.

709   Death of Aldhelm, Abbot of Malmesbury and Bishop of Sherborne.

716   Æthelbald becomes King of Mercia: period of Mercian supremacy.

c. 720   Lindisfarne Gospels.

722   Boniface (Winfrith) consecrated Bishop to the Germans (d. 754).

731   Bede completes *Historia Ecclesiastica*.

735   Death of Bede.

        c. 750   *Beowulf*.

757–96   Offa King in Mercia.

        c. 775–825   Cynewulf active: *The Fates of the Apostles, Christ II, Elene, Juliana*.

        c. 775–825   The 'Cynewulfian' poems: *The Dream of the Rood, The Phoenix, Christ I and III, Guthlac*; also *Exodus, Andreas*.

782   Alcuin leaves York for court of Charlemagne.

793   Lindisfarne plundered by Norwegian raiders.

800   Charlemagne crowned Emperor in Rome.

        c. 800–50   Assumed date of composition for later religious poems, e.g. *The Wanderer, The Seafarer*.

825   Egbert of Wessex defeats Beornwulf of Mercia at Ellendun, near Swindon, and establishes West Saxon supremacy.

835   First Danish raiders in Sheppey.

850   Danes first take winter quarters in England.

865   Invasion of England by Danish host.

871   Succession of Alfred in Wessex.

877   Partition of Mercia.

878   Battle of Edington, near Bristol: Alfred's decisive victory over Danes, who now concentrate on East Anglia and East.

886   Alfred recognised as overlord of all England not under Danish rule; treaty with Danes.

        892–9   Alfredian translations of *Cura Pastoralis*, Orosius, Bede, Boethius.

899   Death of Alfred: succession of Edward the Elder.

920   Edward secures submission of all N. England.

        c. 925   *Genesis B*; *Judith* ($IX\frac{1}{2}$).

937   Battle of Brunanburh: Athelstan's victory over Northern alliance of Scots and Norsemen makes him first true King of England.

        937   Chronicle poem of Brunanburh.

940   Establishment by Edmund of Dunstan as Abbot of Glastonbury.

959–75   Reign of Edgar: free from invasion: revival of monasticism and culture.

960   Dunstan made Archbishop of Canterbury.

963   Oswald made Bishop of Worcester and Æthelwold Bishop of Winchester.

975   Council of Winchester: Regularis Concordia: monastic rule.

        975   Chronicle poems on death of Edgar

        c. 975–1000   Exeter Cathedral Library MS. The 'Exeter Book'. Rich collection of mainly religious verse, including *Christ, Juliana, The Phoenix, Widsith, Deor, The Wanderer, The Seafarer*, etc.

c. 975–1000   Vercelli (N. Italy) Cathedral Library MS. The 'Vercelli Book'. *Andreas, The Fates of the Apostles, Dream of the Rood, Elene,* prose homilies.

980   Norse raids begin again.

991   Great raids on South and East coasts: practice begins of 'buying off' invaders.

991   Battle of Maldon.

994   Danes, under Swein, join the raids.

c. 1000   Bodley MS Junius XI (SC 5123). The 'Caedmon MS'. Scriptural poems: *Genesis, Exodus, Daniel, Christ and Satan.*

c. 1000   B. M. MS Cotton Vitellius A.XV. The 'Beowulf MS'. *Beowulf, Judith,* prose works.

1002   Massacre of Danes ordered by Æthelred.

1003   First of a series of raids/invasions by Swein and followers.

1005   Ælfric becomes Abbot of Eynsham.

1012   Murder of Archbishop Ælfeah before Danish army at Greenwich.

1013   Swein's invasion: acclaimed King in North and East but d. 1014.

1014   *Sermo Lupi ad Anglos* of Archbishop Wulfstan of York.

1016   Death of Æthelred: Edmund his son defeated at Battle of Ashingdon (Essex) by Swein's son Cnut: establishment of Anglo-Danish kingdom.

1027   Cnut's journey to Rome for coronation of Emperor Conrad.

1028   Cnut forces Norway into temporary submission.

1035   Death of Cnut: collapse of empire.

1036   Murder of Alfred the Ætheling, instigated by Godwine.

1036   Chronicle poem on Alfred.

1042   Edward elected King by popular acclamation.

1047   Harold Hardrada, last of the Vikings, succeeds Magnus as King of Norway.

1051–2   Duke William entertained by Edward.

c. 1060   Corpus Christi Cambridge MS 201. Worcester, XI¾. Liturgical poems among prose homilies and legal documents.

c. 1060   Bodley MS Junius 121 (SC 5232). Worcester, XI¾. Liturgical poems in a vernacular version of the Divine Office.

1066   Accession of Harold Godwinson; killed at Hastings; Norman conquest of England under William I.

1070   Lanfranc made Archbishop of Canterbury: Normanisation of English Church.

1077   Pope Gregory VII (Hildebrand) absolves Emperor Henry IV at Canossa.

c. 1080   *Chanson de Roland* (Fr.).

1087   Accession of William II.

1095   Death of Wulfstan, Bishop of Worcester since 1062, last Anglo-Saxon Bishop.

1096–9   First Crusade: capture of Jerusalem.

1100   Accession of Henry I.

1112   Bernard arrives at Cîteaux: beginnings of monastic revival.

1132   Rievaulx: first great Cistercian foundation in England.

1135   Accession of Stephen.

1138   Geoffrey of Monmouth's *Historia Regum Britanniae* (Lat.).

c. 1139   Gaimar's AN *Estoire des Engleis.*

1139–53   Civil war of Stephen and Matilda.

1147–9  Second Crusade.
1152  Marriage of future Henry II to Eleanor of Aquitaine.
1154  Accession of Henry II.
      1154  Last entries in Peterborough copy of *Anglo-Saxon Chronicle*.
      1155  Wace dedicates AN *Roman de Brut* to Eleanor.
      1165  Benoit de Ste Maure's *Roman de Troie* (Fr.).
      c. 1165  AN *Tristan* of Thomas.
1170  Murder of Becket.
      c. 1175  *Proverbs of Alfred* (XII$\frac{3}{4}$).
      c. 1180  Marie de France active at English court.
      c. 1180  Chrétien de Troyes active at court of Champagne.
      c. 1180  AN *Horn* of 'Maistre Thomas'.
      c. 1180  *Poema Morale*, or *Moral Ode* (XII ex).
      c. 1185  AN *Ipomedon* of Hue de Rotelande.
1189  Accession of Richard I.
1189–92  Third Crusade: capture of Acre.
      c. 1190  Beroul's AN *Tristan*.
1199  Accession of John.
      c. 1200  *Owl and Nightingale* (XII ex).
      c. 1200  *Orrmulum* (XIII in).
      c. 1200  Worcester Cathedral Library MS 174. XIII in. Worcester
            fragments; *Soul's Address to Body*.
1202  d. Alain de Lille.
1204  Loss of Normandy: division of Angevin kingdom.
1209  Albigensian Crusade launched in S. France by Pope Innocent III.
1210  England laid under interdict by Innocent III.
      c. 1210  Geoffrey of Vinsauf's *Poetria Nova* (Lat.).
1215  Magna Carta.
1215  Fourth Lateran Council: annual confession obligatory.
1216  Accession of Henry III.
      c. 1220  Laȝamon's *Brut* (XIII$\frac{1}{4}$).
1221  Arrival of Dominican friars in England.
1224  Arrival of Franciscan friars in England.
      c. 1225  *Katherine*-group of prose texts from WM (XIII$\frac{1}{2}$).
      c. 1225  *Roman de Renart* (XIII$\frac{1}{2}$,Fr.).
1226–70  Louis IX King of France.
1227  End of Henry III's minority.
      c. 1230  *Bestiary*; *Genesis and Exodus* (XIII$\frac{2}{4}$).
      c. 1230  Development of French prose 'Vulgate Cycle' of Arthurian
            romances.
      c. 1235  *Roman de la Rose* (Fr.) begun by Guillaume de Lorris.
      c. 1240  AN *Gui de Warewic*.
      c. 1250  *Jacob and Joseph*.
1253  d. Robert Grosseteste.
1258  Provisions of Oxford, designed to limit royal power. First official use of
      English since Conquest.
      c. 1260  B. M. MS Cotton Caligula A. ix. XIII$\frac{3}{4}$. Earlier version of
            Laȝamon's *Brut*, *Owl and Nightingale*; homiletic poems, poems
            on death and doomsday.

c. 1260    C. U. L. MS Gg.iv.27 (2). XIII$\frac{3}{4}$. *King Horn, Floris and Blaunche-flur, Assumption of Our Lady* (imp.).

1264   Battle of Lewes: victory for Simon de Montfort.
1264–6   Barons' war against Henry III.

c. 1270    Jesus Oxford MS 29. XIII$\frac{3}{4}$. Franciscan miscellany of AN and English with some Latin. Later text of *Owl and Nightingale; Poema Morale, Proverbs of Alfred, Luve-Ron*, poems on death, doomsday and mortality, verse-sermons. Sister-volume to Calig. A.ix.

c. 1270    Trinity Cambridge MS 323 (B.14.39). XIII$\frac{3}{4}$. Dominican miscellany of Latin, AN and English. *Proverbs of Alfred* (frag.), *Judas*, homiletic poems, macaronic songs, etc.

1272   Accession of Edward I.
1274   d. Aquinas.

c. 1275    Bodley MS Digby 86 (SC 1687). Dominican miscellany of Latin, AN and English, with wide variety of AN and English poems. *Proverbs of Hendyng, Thrush and Nightingale, Fox and Wolf, Dame Sirith*, homiletic and devotional poems.

c. 1275    B. M. MS Cotton Otho C.xiii. Later version of Laȝamon's *Brut*.

c. 1275    Jean de Meun's continuation of the *Roman de la Rose*.

c. 1280    Franciscan *Meditationes Vitae Christi* (Lat.).

c. 1280    *Legenda Aurea* (Lat.) of Dominican Jacobus de Voragine.

c. 1280    Beginning of *South English Legendary*.

c. 1290    Early romances: *Havelok, Guy of Warwick, Beves of Hamtoun, Richard Coeur de Lion, Arthour and Merlin, Kyng Alisaunder* (XIII ex).

c. 1290    B. M. MS Harley 913. XIII ex. Franciscan miscellany from Kildare in Ireland. *Land of Cokaygne*, Latin and English satirical poems.

c. 1290    Bodley MS Digby 2 (SC 1603). XIII ex. Franciscan miscellany. Short English poems among Latin treatises.

1296–1306   Edward I's Scottish campaigns.

c. 1300    Bodley MS Laud Misc. 108 (SC 1486). Early version of *South English Legendary*. Also (2) *King Horn, Havelok*, c. 1310. (3) *Summer Sunday*, three saints' lives, XV in.

c. 1300    Robert of Gloucester's Chronicle.

c. 1300    *Cursor Mundi*.

1303    Robert Mannyng begins *Handlyng Synne*.

1305   New Pope installed at Avignon.
1307   Accession of Edward II.
1308   d. Duns Scotus.
1314   English defeat at Bannockburn.
1321   d. Dante.
1324   William of Ockham leaves Oxford.

c. 1325    B. M. MS Add. 46919. AN treatises and religious verse, with addition of English translations of Latin hymns, etc., by Franciscan William Herebert.

1327   Deposition and murder of Edward II; accession of Edward III.

    c. 1330   Nat. Lib. Scotland MS 19.2.1. The Auchinleck MS (London). Important collection of romances, religious and didactic poems. Unique texts of *Lai le Freine, Roland and Vernagu, Otuel, Sir Tristrem, Horn Childe*. Earliest texts of *King of Tars, Amis and Amiloun, Sir Degare, Guy of Warwick* (and *Reinbrun*), *Beves, Arthour and Merlin, Kyng Alisaunder, Orfeo, Richard Coeur de Lion* (some imp.). Also *Floris and Blauncheflur*.

    c. 1330   B. M. MS Harley 2253. Herefordshire. Rich (friars'?) miscellany of English verse, AN verse and prose, with a few Latin prose pieces. In English, political and satirical poems, love poems, religious poems, especially - in genre of passion-lyric. Also *King Horn, Proverbs of Hendyng*, etc.

    c. 1330   Deguileville's *Pélerinage de la Vie Humaine* (Fr.).

    1333–52   Poems of Laurence Minot.

1337   Beginning of Hundred Years' War.

    1338   Boccaccio's *Filostrato* (It.).

    1338   Mannyng completes his trans. Chronicle.

c. 1343   b. Chaucer.

1346   English victory at Crécy.

1348–9   Black Death.

1349   d. Richard Rolle.

    c. 1350   *Tale of Gamelyn* (XIV med).

    c. 1350   *William of Palerne*.

1351   First Statute of Labourers.

    1352–3   *Winner and Waster*: beginning of alliterative revival.

    1354   Henry of Lancaster's *Livre de Seyntz Medecines* (AN).

1356   English victory at Poitiers.

1356–7   Fitzralph's sermons at St Paul's Cross against friars.

1357   First record of Chaucer: page to Countess of Ulster.

    c. 1358   Boccaccio's *De casibus* (Lat.).

1360   Treaty of Bretigny.

    c. 1360   *Prick of Conscience* (XIV$\frac{3}{4}$).

    c. 1360   Alliterative Alexander fragments (XIV$\frac{3}{4}$).

    c. 1362   *Piers Plowman*, A-text.

1369   d. Queen Philippa. Froissart leaves English court. War with France renewed.

    c. 1370   Chaucer, *Book of the Duchess*.

    1372   Nat. Lib. Scotland MS 18.7.21. Preachers' handbook compiled by Franciscan John Grimestone, with meditative and devotional verses in English.

    c. 1374–8   Gower, *Mirour de l'Omme* (AN).

1374   d. Petrarch.

1374–86   Chaucer at the Customs.

1375   d. Boccaccio.

    1375   Barbour's *Bruce*.

    c. 1375   Northern Homily Cycle (XIV$\frac{2}{2}$).

1376   Death of Black Prince.

1377   Accession of Richard II.

1377   d. Machaut.

    c. 1377   *Piers Plowman*, B-text.

1378   Beginning of Papal Schism.
           1378   First record of York plays.
           c. 1380   Chaucer, *House of Fame*.
1381   Peasants' Revolt.
1382   Official condemnation of Wycliff's opinions. Richard's marriage to Anne of Bohemia.
           c. 1382   Chaucer, *Parlement of Foules*.
           c. 1382–5   Chaucer, *Troilus and Criseyde*.
           c. 1385   Gower's *Vox Clamantis* (Lat.).
           c. 1385   Clanvowe's *Cuckoo and Nightingale*.
1385   Deschamps's tribute to Chaucer.
           c. 1385–6   Chaucer, *Legend of Good Women*.
1386   Council of Regency.
           c. 1386   Gower begins *Confessio Amantis*.
           c. 1387   Trevisa's prose translation of Higden.
           c. 1387   Chaucer begins *Canterbury Tales*.
1388   Merciless Parliament. Execution of Thomas Usk.
1389   Richard resumes full royal power.
1389–91   Chaucer Clerk of King's Works.
1389–1418   Christine de Pisan at French court.
           c. 1390   *Piers Plowman*, C-text.
           c. 1390   *Parlement of Thre Ages, St Erkenwald*.
           c. 1390   B. M. MS Cotton Nero A.x (4). NWM, XIV ex. *Sir Gawain and the Green Knight, Pearl, Patience, Cleanness*.
           c. 1390   Bodley MS Eng. poet. a.1 (SC 3938). The Vernon MS.XIV ex. Massive collection of English religious and didactic verse and prose, including *South English Legendary, Northern Homily Cycle, Piers Plowman* (A), pious romances, treatises, dialogues, etc.
           c. 1390   B. M. MS Add. 22283. The Simeon MS. XIV ex. Sister-volume to Vernon.
           c. 1390   C. U. L. MS Dd.v.64 (III). Northern, XIV ex. The most important collection of Rolle lyrics.
           c. 1390   B. M. MS Egerton 2862. XIV ex. Romances only: *Beves, Richard, Seege of Troye, Eglamour, Degare, Floris and Blauncheflur, Amis and Amiloun*.
           c. 1395   Purvey's second version of the Wycliffite Bible in English.
           c. 1395   Lollard *Pierce the Ploughman's Crede*.
           1398   Trevisa's prose translation of Bartholomew's Encyclopaedia.
1399   Deposition of Richard II; accession of Henry IV.
           c. 1399–1406   *Mum and Sothsegger (Richard the Redeles)*.
1400   d. Chaucer.
           c. 1400   *Morte Arthure; Destruction of Troy*.
           c. 1400   Northern rhymed alliterative poems: *Awntyrs off Arthure, Susannah*, etc.
           c. 1400   B. M. MS Cotton Galba E.ix. Miscellany of romances (e.g. unique text of *Ywain and Gawain*) and religious and didactic poems (e.g. *Gospel of Nicodemus, Prick of Conscience*); also poems of Minot.
           c. 1400   Lincoln's Inn MS Hale 150. Copies of *Arthour and Merlin*,

*Lybeaus Desconus, Kyng Alisaunder, Seege of Troye*; also *Piers Plowman* (frag.). Often regarded as a popular entertainer's book.

c. 1400    Laud *Troy-book* (XV in).

c. 1400    B. M. MS Add. 37049. XV in. Carthusian manual of instruction with much didactic and devotional verse.

c. 1400    Gonville and Caius Cambridge MS 175. XV in. *Richard, Beves, Isumbras*, three religious pieces, and the unique copy of *Athelston*.

1401    First statute of burning against Lollard heretics.

     1402    Hoccleve's *Letter of Cupid*.

1403    Battle of Shrewsbury.

1408    d. Gower.

     1410    Walton's trans. of Boethius.

     c. 1410    *Death and Life*; *Tale of Beryn* (XV in).

     c. 1412    Hoccleve's *Regement of Princes*.

     1412–20    Lydgate's *Troy-book*.

1413    Accession of Henry V.

1414    Oldcastle's Lollard insurrection.

1415    Battle of Agincourt.

     1415    Important record of York play cycle.

     1415    *The Crowned King*.

1415–40    Charles d'Orléans prisoner in England.

     1416    Lydgate's *Life of Our Lady*.

1417    End of Papal Schism.

1419–67    Philip the Good Duke of Burgundy: golden age of Burgundian culture in Netherlands.

     1420    Treaty of Troyes.

     c. 1420    Wyntoun's *Original Chronicle of Scotland*; *Castle of Perseverance*.

     c. 1420    *Wars of Alexander*; *Siege of Jerusalem* (XV in); *Plowman's Tale*; *Jack Upland* (XV in).

     1421–2    Lydgate's *Siege of Thebes*.

1422    Accession of Henry VI, 9 months old.

     c. 1425    *Kingis Quair*.

     c. 1425    Henry Lovelich active (XV$\frac{1}{2}$).

     c. 1425–50    John Shirley active in publishing and book-production. His MSS include much Chaucer and Lydgate, often in unique copies, and also courtly and religious verse by other writers, as well as miscellaneous material. His own MSS include B. M. MS Add. 16165, B. M. MS Harley 7333 (important text of Canterbury Tales), Trinity Cambridge MS R.3.20 (600). Later copies, derived from Shirley MSS, include B. M. MS Harley 2251, Add. 34360, Trinity Cambridge MS R.3.19 (599) and R.3.21 (601), all XV ex. B. M. MS Add. 29729 is a copy by John Stowe (XVI med) of a Shirley MS.

     c. 1426    John Awdelay writes down his poems.

     1426–8    Lydgate's *Pilgrimage of the Life of Man*.

1427–30    Lydgate active at court as laureate and propagandist.

     c. 1430    Development of Wakefield play cycle.

     c. 1430    C.U.L. MS Gg.iv.27. Important early collection of Chaucer's poetry, including major poems; also Lydgate's *Temple of Glass*.

c. 1430    Lambeth Palace MS 853. Collection of homiletic, instructional and devotional verse.

1431  Joan of Arc burnt.

b. Villon.

1431–8  Lydgate, *Fall of Princes*.

c. 1433  Lydgate, *St Edmund*.

1435  Death of Bedford, regent in France.

Humphrey of Gloucester's first gift of books to Oxford.

1436  *Libel of English Policy*.

1439  Lydgate, *St Albon*.

c. 1440  Trans. of Palladius (by Parker?).

c. 1440  Devlopment of N-town play cycle.

c. 1440  *Parthonope of Blois, Partenay, Generydes* (XV$\frac{2}{4}$).

c. 1440  B.M. MS Harley 2255. Lydgate anthology, probably from Bury St Edmunds.

c. 1440  Robert Thornton's MSS (XV med): Lincoln Cathedral MS 91 (A.5.2.). Romances (*Erl of Tolous, Isumbras, Octavian, Eglamour, Degrevaunt, Awntyrs off Arthure*, and unique texts of *Percyvelle of Galles* and *Morte Arthure*), didactic and devotional pieces, much of Yorkshire origin.

B.M. MS Add. 31042. Unique texts of *Winner and Waster, Rowlande and Ottuell, Sege of Melayne*. Also *Parlement of Thre Ages, Siege of Jerusalem, Quatrefoil of Love, Richard Coeur de Lion*, and much miscellaneous religious and didactic poetry.

1441  Founding of King's College Cambridge by Henry VI.

1443–7  Bokenham's *Legendys of Hooly Wummen*.

1445  Henry VI m. Margaret of Anjou.

c. 1446  Capgrave's *Life of St Katharine*.

c. 1446  Richard Holland's *Buke of the Howlate*.

1447  d. Humphrey of Gloucester.

1449  d. Lydgate.

1449  Metham's *Amoryus and Cleopes*.

1450  Cade's rebellion; death of Suffolk.

1450  Bible first printed, at Mainz.

c. 1450  Idley's *Instructions to his Son*.

c. 1450  Benedict Burgh completes Lydgate's *Secrees of the old Philisoffres*.

c. 1450  Sir Richard Roos's *La Belle Dame Sans Merci* (XV med.).

c. 1450  *The Squyr of Lowe Degre* (XV med).

c. 1450  B.M. MS Cotton Caligula A.ii. Important miscellany of romances (unique texts of *Launfal, Emare, Chevalere Assigne* and the Southern *Octavian*), pious tales, religious and didactic poems, with some Lydgate.

c. 1450  Bodley MS Fairfax 16 (SC 3896). Important anthology of courtly poetry, including minor poems of Chaucer and Lydgate and the poems attributed to Suffolk.

c. 1450  B.M. MS Sloane 2593. Song-book: carols.

c. 1450  Chetham Manchester MS 8009. XV med. Unique texts of *Torrent of Portyngale* and *Ipomadoun*.

1453 Turks take Constantinople.

   End of Hundred Years' War.

1455 First battle of Wars of Roses at St Albans.

   c. 1456 Gilbert Hay's *Buik of Alexander*.

    1457 Nat. Lib. Naples MS XIII.B.29. Romances (*Beves, Lybeaus Desconus, Isumbras*), a saint's life, and Chaucer's *Clerk's Tale*.

    1458 Trans. of Vegetius (by Parker?).

   c. 1460 Benedict Burgh's translation of Cato's *Distichs*.

   c. 1460 *Golagros and Gawain, Rauf Coilʒear* (XV¾).

   c. 1460 *Court of Sapience* (XV¾).

   c. 1460 (with additions) Lambeth Palace MS 306. *Lybeaus Desconus*, pious tales, historical, religious and didactic poems.

   c. 1460 C.U.L. MS Ff.ii.38. XV¾. Important miscellany of saints' lives, pious tales, religious and instructional poems of all kinds, ending with ten romances (including unique text of *Le Bone Florence*).

   c. 1460 C.U.L. MS Ff.i.6. XV¾, North Midlands. The 'Findern anthology'. A household commonplace-book, with courtly poems by Chaucer (*Parlement*) and others (*Cuckoo and Nightingale, La Belle Dame*), and sub-courtly poems; also *Degrevaunt*.

   c. 1460 Nat. Lib. Wales (Aberystwyth) MS Porkington 10. XV¾. Miscellany of religious, instructional and practical pieces. Also songs and unique text of *Sir Gawain and the Carl of Carlile*.

1461 Battle of Towton. Henry VI deposed; Edward IV proclaimed king.

1466 Henry VI imprisoned in Tower.

1470 Henry VI reinstated by Warwick.

   c. 1470 Morality plays: *Wisdom, Mankind*.

   c. 1470 (with additions to c. 1520) B.M. MS Add. 5665. 'Ritson's MS'. Song-book, with music: repertoire of a West-country choir.

   c. 1470 B.M. MS Egerton 1995. XV¾. William Gregory the Skinner's commonplace-book. *Seven Sages of Rome*, historical and instructional poems, treatises on etiquette, hunting and health.

1471 Henry VI deposed and murdered; Edward IV restored.

1474 Treaty with Burgundy.

   c. 1475 *Lancelot of the Laik*.

   c. 1475 *Flower and the Leaf*; *Assembly of Ladies*.

1476 Introduction of printing into England by Caxton.

    1478 Caxton's first print of *The Canterbury Tales*.

   c. 1478 Hary's *Wallace*.

   c. 1480 Bodley MS Eng. poet.e.1 (SC 29734). Song-book: carols.

1483 Edward IV dies; Gloucester acts as Protector for Edward V; then succeeds as Richard III.

1485 Battle of Bosworth Field; accession of Henry VII.

    1485 Caxton's Malory.

1488–1513 James IV King of Scotland.

    1489 Skelton's *Elegy on the Duke of Northumberland*.

   c. 1490 *fl.* Henryson.

   c. 1490 Bodley MS Ashmole 61 (SC 6922). XVex. Late copies of five romances, also many moral and religious poems.

1492 Columbus lands in West Indies.
    1492 Carols of James Ryman.
1497 Cabot lands in N. America..
    c. 1497 Medwall's *Fulgens and Lucrece.*
1498 Erasmus at Oxford.
    1499 Skelton's *Bowge of Court.*
    c. 1500 *A Gest of Robyn Hode.*
    c. 1500 B.M. MS Harley 2252. Unique texts of stanzaic *Morte Arthur* and shorter *Ipomydon.* Belonged to early sixteenth-century London mercer, John Colyns, who copied in poems by Skelton, etc.
    c. 1500 B.M. MS Add. 5464. The 'Fayrfax MS'. Early Tudor song-book, with music.
    c. 1500 Bodley MS Rawlinson C.86 (SC 11951). XVI in. Unique texts of *Landeval* and the *Wedding of Sir Gawain.* Much secular and religious verse, and extracts from Chaucer, Gower and Lydgate.
    c. 1501 Douglas, *Palice of Honour.*
    1506 Hawes, *Pastime of Pleasure.*
    1508 Dunbar's *Goldyn Targe* and *Tua Mariit Wemen.*
1509 Accession of Henry VIII.
    1509 Barclay's *Ship of Fools.*
    c. 1510 Douglas, trans. of *Æneid.*
1513 Battle of Flodden.
    1513 Macchiavelli, *The Prince* (It.).
    c. 1513 Bradshaw's *Life of St Werburge.*
    c. 1515 Barclay's *Eclogues.*
    c. 1515 B.M. MS Add. 31922. 'Henry VIII's MS'. Early Tudor song-book, with music.
    1516 Erasmus, Greek New Testament.
    1516 More's *Utopia* (Lat.).
    1516 Ariosto's *Orlando Furioso* (It.).
    c. 1516 Skelton's *Magnificence.*
1517 Luther's Wittenberg theses.
    1518 Nevill's *Castell of Pleasure.*
    c. 1520 B.M. MS Royal Appendix 58. Early Tudor song-book, with music.
    1521 Skelton's *Speak, Parrot.*
    1522 Skelton's *Colin Clout* and *Why Come Ye not to Court?*
    1523 Skelton's *Garland of Laurel.*
    1528 Castiglione, *The Courtier* (It.).
1529 Disgrace of Wolsey.
    1530 Lindsay's *Papyngo.*
    1530 Copland's *Hye Way to the Spyttel Hous.*
    c. 1530 Balliol Oxford MS 354. Richard Hill's Commonplace book. Important collection of medieval lyrics, also romances, doctrinal and moral poems.
    c. 1530–40 B.M. MS Add. 17492. The 'Devonshire MS'. Court 'album' of verses, including many poems by Wyatt.

1532    Thynne's collected Chaucer.

1532    Rabelais, *Pantagruel* (Fr.).

1533    Heywood's *Pardoner and Frere* and *Play of the Wether*.

1534   Act of Supremacy; execution of More.

1535    Coverdale's Bible.

c. 1535   *The Court of Love*.

1536–9  Dissolution of the monasteries.

1540   Execution of Thomas Cromwell.

1540    Lindsay's *Satyre of the Thre Estaitis*.

c. 1542   Surrey's trans. of *Æneid* I–II.

1543   Copernicus, *De Revolutionibus*.

1546    Heywood's first *Dialogue of Proverbs*.

1547   Accession of Edward VI.

1549   Cranmer's Book of Common Prayer.
Act of Uniformity.

1553   Accession of Mary.

c. 1553   Nicholas Udall's *Ralph Roister Doister*.

1554    *Mirror for Magistrates*.

c. 1555   Cavendish, *Metrical Visions*.

1557    Tottel's *Songes and Sonettes*.

# Notes

## Chapter 1  *Beowulf* and the Anglo-Saxon poetic tradition

1 Tacitus, *Germania*, cap. 2.
2 See F. Norman, 'The early Germanic Background of Old English Verse', in *Medieval Literature and Civilisation: Studies in Memory of G. N. Garmonsway*, ed. D. A. Pearsall and R. A. Waldron (1969), 3–27 (p. 24).
3 G. Shepherd, 'Scriptural Poetry', in *Continuations and Beginnings: Studies in Old English Literature*, ed. E. G. Stanley (1966), 1–36 (p. 3).
4 See R. Girvan, *Beowulf and the Seventh Century* (1935, rev. 1971), pp. 59–60.
5 Bede's *Ecclesiastical History of the English People*, ed. (with trans.) B. Colgrave and R. A. B. Mynors (Oxford, 1969), iv.24 (p. 417); *The Anglo-Saxon Minor Poems*, ed. E. V. K. Dobbie (*ASPR* VI), p. xcv. Bede himself offers only a Latin prose paraphrase, 'for it is not possible to translate verse, however well composed, literally from one language to another without some loss of beauty or dignity' (p. 417).
6 E. G. Stanley, 'The search for Anglo-Saxon paganism', *NQ* 11 (1964) and 12 (1965), *passim* (quot. from 11.249).
7 K. Sisam, *Studies in the History of Old English Literature* (Oxford, 1953), pp. 116–18.
8 Sisam (*Studies*, p. 98) comments on the number of gross errors in the text which would surely have been corrected by a careful reader who understood what he was reading.
9 See W. F. Bolton, 'Pre-Conquest Anglo-Latin: perspectives and prospects', *CL* 23 (1971), 151–66.
10 Sisam, *Studies*, p. 66.
11 *Beowulf* (ed. F. Klaeber, New York, 1922; 3rd ed., 1941; frequently revised), 1063–8: cf. 867–74.

12 See F. M. Stenton, *Anglo-Saxon England* (1943; 3rd ed., Oxford, 1971), pp. 79, 299, 384, 423; *English Historical Documents*, ed. Dorothy Whitelock (1955), pp. 26–7, 55–8, 373, 379, 780; Dorothy Whitelock, *The Audience of Beowulf* (1951), pp. 13–19, 86 ff.
13 See C. E. Wright, *The Cultivation of Saga in Anglo-Saxon England* (Edinburgh, 1939). Wright thinks of the originals as short prose sagas.
14 See the description in Chapter 100 of *Njal's Saga*.
15 See J. F. Kenney, *Sources for the Early History of Ireland: Ecclesiastical* (Columbia U.P., 1929; repr. 1966), p. 3.
16 See K. Jackson, *Language and History in Early Britain* (Edinburgh, 1953), pp. 229–46.
17 King Ethelbert of Kent, at whose court Augustine first arrived, had a Christian Frankish princess as queen (Bede, *Ecc. History*, i.25), and although Bede says specifically that the British never preached to the Anglo-Saxons (i.22) there must have been some contact; see also Bede's account of Augustine's meeting with the leaders of the British Church (ii.2).
18 C. M. Bowra, *Heroic Poetry* (1952), p. 435.
19 Lines 35–6: text from *ASPR* VI.
20 See W. P. Lehmann, *The Development of Germanic Verse Form* (Austin, Texas, 1956), p. 33.
21 See *The Oldest English Texts*, ed. H. Sweet (EETS 83, 1885), p. 179; R. W. Chambers, *Beowulf: an Introduction* (Cambridge, 1971; 3rd ed. 1959), p. 316.
22 See Margaret Schlauch, *Medieval English Poetry and its Social Foundations* (Warsaw, 1956), pp. 10–14.

23 E. Auerbach, *Mimesis: the Representation of Reality in Western Literature* (first pub. in German, 1946; trans. W. Trask 1953; Anchor Books, New York, 1957), p. 36.

24 Bowra, *Heroic Poetry*, p. 48.

25 W. P. Ker, *The Dark Ages* (1904; Mentor Books, 1958), pp. 163–4.

26 For some extreme examples of this kind of interpretation, see L. E. Nicholson's *Anthology of Beowulf Criticism* (Notre Dame, Ind., 1963). Other allegorists make more modest claims, e.g. M. W. Bloomfield in *Traditio* 7 (1949–51), 410–15, and R. E. Kaske in *SP* 55 (1958), 423–56.

27 John Scot Erigena, *Expositiones super hierarchiae caelesten S. Dionysii*, quoted in B. F. Huppe, *Doctrine and Poetry: Augustine's Influence on Old English Poetry* (New York, 1959), p. 54.

28 See Whitelock, *Audience of Beowulf*, pp. 4–11.

29 Whitelock, *Audience of Beowulf*, p. 97. There is of course an element of contrast, quite explicit in the treatment of Heremod (915).

30 *Beowulf* 572–3, 1552–6.

31 See Bede, *Ecc. History*, iii. 30, iv. 27; *Life of St Cuthbert*, cap. IX.

32 See C. Donahue, '*Beowulf* and Christian tradition', *Traditio* 21 (1965), 55–116.

33 Bede, *Ecc. History*, i.34, ii.2. Likewise, St Augustine prefers pagan fables to Manichean philosophy: 'Verses and poems can provide real food for thought' (*Confessions*, iii.6, trans. R. S. Pine-Coffin, Penguin, 1961).

34 Whitelock, *Documents*, pp. 753–4; and see L. D. Benson, 'The Pagan Coloring of *Beowulf*', in *Old English Poetry: Fifteen Essays*, ed. R. P. Creed (Providence, R. I., 1967), pp. 193–214.

35 Benson, 'Pagan Coloring'. Sisam suggests (*Studies*, pp. 288–90) that some of the story-materials of the poem may also have been transmitted through such contacts, as with the Frisians: Hygelac's grave at the mouth of the Rhine was well known to continental travellers.

36 See, e.g., Rosemary Cramp, '*Beowulf* and archaeology', *Med. Archaeology*, 1 (1957), 57–77; Hilda Ellis Davidson, 'Archaeology and *Beowulf*', in *Beowulf and its Analogues*, trans. G. N. Garmonsway, Jacqueline Simpson (1968), pp. 350–60.

37 Bede, *Ecc. History*, i.30, ii.15; Stenton, *Anglo-Saxon England*, p. 128; Whitelock, *Documents*, p. 363 (for the laws of Wihtred, King of Kent, in 695).

38 See W. Whallon, *Formula, Character and Context* (Cambridge, Mass., 1969), p. 125.

39 See J. R. R. Tolkien, '*Beowulf*: the monsters and the critics', *PBA* 22 (1936), 245–95.

40 *Beowulf*, ed. cit., p. lxvii.

41 *Wordhord onleac* (*Beowulf* 259); cf. *wordhord onwreah*, in *Vainglory* (in the Exeter Book), line 3.

42 See A. G. Brodeur, *The Art of Beowulf* (Berkeley, Calif., 1959), p. 18. The term kenning is also extended to certain uncompounded periphrases.

43 *Beowulf*, 1208, 10, 1965.

44 Snorra Sturlusonar, *Edda*, ed. G. Jónsson (Reykjavik, 1949), pp. 117, 143. For some examples of analysis of Norse kennings, see Margaret Ashdown, *English and Norse Documents Relating to the Reign of Ethelred the Unready* (Cambridge, 1930), Appendix IV. Alcuin's *Dialogue*, and the Icelandic *Alvíssmál* both provide what Ker calls a kind of 'dictionary of poetical synonyms and periphrases' (*Dark Ages*, pp. 62, 178).

45 See Kenney, *Sources*, pp. 255–8; M. Winterbottom, 'On the *Hisperica Famina*', in *Celtica* 8 (1968), 126–39; M. Herren, 'Hisperic Latin: "luxuriant culture-fungus of decay"', *Traditio* 30 (1974), 411–19.

46 Whitelock, *Documents*, p. 505.

47 See W. Levison, *England and the Continent in the Eighth Century* (Oxford, 1946), pp. 138–9, 290–4.

48 'indicates a main stress, a secondary stress, × one or more unstressed syllables. Quantity is observed in Anglo-Saxon poetry to the extent that stresses normally fall on long syllables, but quantity is subordinate to stress as a determinant principle of versification. The following example is the one used by W. P. Lehmann, *Germanic Verse Form*, p. 38.

49 By J. C. Pope, *The Rhythm of Beowulf* (New Haven, 1942).

50 See Marjorie Daunt, 'Old English verse and English speech rhythm', *TPS* (1946), 56–72.

51 A. J. Bliss, 'The Appreciation of Old English Metre', in *English and Medieval Studies presented to J. R. R. Tolkien*, ed. N. Davis and C. L. Wrenn (1962), pp. 27–40 (p. 29).

52 See J. B. Bessinger, 'The Sutton Hoo Harp Replica and Old English Musical Verse', in *Old English Poetry*, ed. Creed, pp. 3–26.

53 F. P. Magoun, 'The oral-formulaic character of Anglo-Saxon narrative poetry', *Speculum* 28 (1953), 446–67. For a general appraisal of the theory, see R. F. Lawrence, 'Formulaic Theory and English Alliterative Poetry', in *Essays on Style and Language*, ed. R. Fowler (1966), pp. 166–83.

54 A. B. Lord, *The Singer of Tales* (Harvard

*Stud. in Comp. Lit.* 24, Cambridge, Mass., 1964), p. 4.

55 *Beowulf*, 529, 631, 957, etc.; 371, 456, 1321; 2862, 3076.

56 See J. J. Campbell, 'Learned rhetoric in Old English poetry', *MP* 63 (1965–6), 189–201; L. D. Benson, 'The literary character of Anglo-Saxon formulaic poetry', *PMLA* 81 (1966), 334–41; S. B. Greenfield, 'The canons of Old English criticism', *ELH* 34 (1967), 141–55. It may be argued, as Magoun does in *Speculum* 30 (1955), 49–63, that Bede's Caedmon is a clear example of an oral singer. But Caedmon does not compose extempore (except in the 'miracle' of the *Hymn*, which Bede treats distinctly as a miracle): he learns his facts, goes away and absorbs them, *quasi mundum animal ruminando*, 'like some clean animal chewing the cud' (*Ecc. History*, iv.24), composes and then recites. Composition without writing, as Sisam points out (*Structure of Beowulf*, p. 3), is not at all the same as oral improvisation.

57 Lord, *Singer of Tales*, pp. 54, 131.

58 Lord, *Singer of Tales*, pp. 198, 200.

59 R. P. Creed, 'The making of an Anglo-Saxon poem', *ELH* 26 (1959), 445–54.

60 *Beowulf*, 90, cf. *Æneid*, i.742; *Beowulf* 1999–2151, cf. *Æneid*, ii,iii. For a rather extravagant comparison of the two poems, see T. B. Haber, *A Comparative Study of the Beowulf and the Æneid* (Princeton, 1931). Even the influence of Statius has been suggested: R. J. Schrader, 'Beowulf's obsequies and the Roman epic', *CL* 24 (1972), 237–59.

61 By Ekkehard I of St Gall (d. 973): it deals with the same Walter legend as the O. E. *Waldere*. See K. Sisam, *The Structure of Beowulf* (Oxford, 1965), pp. 63–4.

62 See J. W. Rankin, 'A study of the kennings in Anglo-Saxon poetry', *JEGP* 8 (1909), 357–422, 9 (1910), 49–84; A. Keiser, *The Influence of Christianity on the Vocabulary of Old English Poetry*, Univ. of Illinois Stud. in Lang. and Lit., Vol. 5 (1919), Nos. 1/2.

63 See W. F. Bolton, *A History of Anglo-Latin Literature 597–1066*, vol. 1: 597–740 (Princeton, 1967), p. 225.

64 Kenney, *Sources*, pp. 1–2.

65 *Gesta Pontificum*, ed. N.E.S.A. Hamilton (Rolls Series 52, 1870), p. 336. The 'Book of Alfred', which Wm. claims as his source, is not extant. Elsewhere, we are told that Alfred knew and admired Aldhelm's English poems (Stenton, p. 182).

66 See R. Derolez, 'Anglo-Saxon Literature: "Attic" or "Asiatic"? Old English Poetry and its Latin Background', repr. in

*Essential Articles for the Study of Old English Poetry*, ed. J. B. Bessinger and S. J. Kahrl (Hamden, Conn., 1968), pp. 46–62 (p. 52).

67 *Anglo-Saxon Minor Poems (ASPR* VI), p. 107.

68 *Ibid.*, p. 57.

69 Asser's *Life of King Alfred*, Chaps 22–3, 75–6: in Whitelock, *Documents*, pp. 266–7.

70 See Derolez, *passim*; Campbell, 'Learned Rhetoric'.

71 Kenney, *Sources*, pp. 225–35, etc., Nora K. Chadwick, 'The Celtic Background of Early Anglo-Saxon England', in *Celt and Saxon: Studies in the Early British Border*, ed. Nora K. Chadwick (Cambridge, 1963), pp. 323–52.

72 See Huppé, *Doctrine and Poetry*, p. 4.

73 See M. L. W. Laistner, *Thought and Letters in Western Europe AD 500–900* (1931), p. 29.

74 Bede, *Ecc. History*, iv. 1, 2.

75 See Bolton, *Anglo-Latin Literature*, p. 97.

76 See R. B. Hepple, 'Early Northumbrian libraries', *Arch. Æliana*, 3rd series, 14 (1917), 92–106; Levison, *England and the Continent*, pp. 144–8.

77 *Oldest English Texts*, ed. H. Sweet (EETS 83, 1885), esp. pp. 7–11.

78 See M. L. W. Laistner, 'The Library of the Venerable Bede' in *Bede: his Life, Times and Writings*, ed. A. Hamilton Thompson (1932), pp. 241–2; A. Campbell, 'Some linguistic features of early Anglo-Latin verse and its use of classical models', *TPS* (1953), 1–20; cf. E. F. Jacob, 'Some aspects of classical influence in medieval England', *Vorträge der Bibliothek Warburg* 9 (1930–1), 1–27, esp. 4–9.

79 See R. B. Hepple, 'The monastery school at Jarrow', *History* 7 (1922), 92–102.

80 Levison, *England and the Continent*, p. 28. See Bede's Letter to Archbishop Egbert, in Whitelock, *Documents*, pp. 740–2.

81 Whitelock, *Documents*, p. 699, and see p. 83.

82 See Bede, *Ecc. History*, iii.18, iv.19, v.7, 19; Stenton, *Anglo-Saxon England*, pp. 91–2; Chadwick, in *Celt and Saxon*, p. 332; C. Albertson, *Anglo-Saxon Saints and Heroes* (Fordham U. P., 1967), pp. 18–22.

83 Translation in *The Literature of Medieval England*, ed. D. W. Robertson (New York, 1970), p. 98. The original is in *Albini Epistolae*, ed. E. L. Dummler: *Monumenta Germaniae Historica, Epistolae*, IV (Berlin 1895), letter 124, p. 183.

84 2 Corinthians 6:15. See Robertson, *loc. cit.*, and Ker, *Dark Ages*, p. 25; also R. Levine, 'Ingeld and Christ: a medieval problem', *Viator* 2 (1971), 105–28.

85 Whitelock, *Documents*, p. 766.

86 Sisam, *Structure of Beowulf*, p. 62.
87 P. Dronke, *The Medieval Lyric* (1968), p. 27; for the further references to Carolingian practice, see pp. 27, 91–2.
88 *Ibid.*, p. 27.
89 Sisam, *Structure of Beowulf*, pp. 67–71. The loss of all earlier copies is presumed to be due to the destruction of the monasteries by the Norsemen and Danes in the ninth century; an indication of the extent of this destruction is given by the fact that most extant MSS of Anglo-Latin are of continental provenance (Levison, p. 146).
90 B. Colgrave (ed.), *The Earliest Life of St.*

*Gregory the Great* (Lawrence, Kansas, 1968), p. 13.
91 Chadwick, in *Celt and Saxon*, p. 334.
92 Sisam, *Studies*, pp. 119–39.
93 Whitelock, *Documents*, p. 788.
94 Stenton, *Anglo-Saxon England*, pp. 270–1.
95 See W. Oakeshott, *Classical Inspiration in Medieval Art* (1959), pp. 34–6.
96 See Oakeshott, *Classical Inspiration*, pp. 32–4; T. D. Kendrick, *Anglo-Saxon Art to A.D. 900* (1938), p. 128; F. Saxl, 'The Ruthwell Cross', in *England and the Mediterranean Tradition* (Oxford, 1945), p. 18.

## Chapter 2    Anglo-Saxon religious poems

1 G. Shepherd, 'Scriptural Poetry', in *Continuations and Beginnings: Studies in Old English Literature*, ed. E. G. Stanley (1966), 1–36 (p. 24).
2 R. Willard, '*Andreas* and *The Fates of the Apostles*', *MP* 62 (1964–5), 45–51 (p. 46).
3 *Beowulf* (ed. F. Klaeber, New York, 1922; 3rd ed., 1941; frequently revised), p. ci.
4 See Sisam, *Studies in the History of Old English Literature*, (Oxford, 1953), p. 7.
5 *ASPR* VI, p. 106; see p. xcv. All quotations from Old English verse in this chapter are from the relevant volume of *ASPR*.
6 Bede, *Ecclesiastical History of the English People*, ed. (with trans.) B. Colgrave and R. A. B. Mynors (Oxford, 1969), iv.24 (p. 417).
7 Huppé's interpretation of the *Hymn* (*Doctrine and Poetry: Augustine's Influence on Old English Poetry* (New York, 1959), pp. 109–15) as embodying a subtle allusion to the Trinity, in *meotodes meahte, Modgepanc* (Wisdom) and *weorc wuldorfæder*, and a fine distinction between creation *in principio* (*or onstealde*) and creation in time (*ærest sceop*), seems to presuppose a genuine miracle. It is odd that Bede's Latin translation misses all the points noted by Huppé.
8 *Life of St Cuthbert*, Chap. 17, in *Two Lives of St. Cuthbert*, ed. B. Colgrave (Cambridge, 1940), p. 215.
9 O. J. Kuhnmuench, *Early Christian Latin Poets* (Chicago, 1929), p. 82.
10 *Praefatio* 23–8, in *Pat. Lat.* 19:59.
11 See H. D. Meritt, *Old English Glosses: a Collection*, MLA General Series XVI (New York, 1945).
12 *Carmen* i.17–26, in *Pat. Lat.* 19:553.
13 *Pat. Lat.* 19: 346–79, e.g. lines 65, 141, 168.

14 *Pat. Lat.* 19:386. For some examples from Aldhelm, see W. F. Bolton, *A History of Anglo-Latin Literature* (Princeton, 1967), p. 73.
15 Lines 759–62, in *Pat. Lat.* 59:1064.
16 See J. D. A. Ogilvy, *Books known to Anglo-Latin Writers from Aldhelm to Alcuin* (*670–804*), Medieval Academy of America, Studies and Documents, No. 2 (Cambridge, Mass., 1936). Ogilvy's evidence may be supplemented from the authorities listed above, in note 78 to Chap. 1.
17 P. de Labriolle, *Histoire de la littérature latine chrétienne*, 3rd ed., rev. G. Bardy (Paris, 1947), pp. 750–1: the English translation by H. Wilson, *History and Literature of Christianity from Tertullian to Boethius* (1924), was reissued in 1968 (see pp. 488–9).
18 This is not to imply equality; but English was not always inferior, and some Old English poems have a more learned cultural background than a Latin work like the Whitby *Life of St Gregory*. See B. Colgrave, 'The Earliest Life of St. Gregory', in *Celt and Saxon: Studies in the Early British Border*, ed. Nora K. Chadwick (Cambridge, 1963), pp. 119–37.
19 See Huppé's illuminating discussion of the poem in *Doctrine and Poetry*, Chap. V.
20 See F. M. Stenton, *Anglo-Saxon England* (1943; 3rd ed. Oxford 1971), p. 175; Dorothy Whitelock (ed.), *English Historical Documents* (1955), p. 90.
21 See Stenton, *Anglo-Saxon England*, pp. 271, 444.
22 See M. J. Capek, in *Neoph.* 55 (1971), 89–96.
23 See Rosemary Woolf, 'The Devil in Old English Poetry', *RES*, n.s. 4 (1953), 1–12.
24 Though there is no certain evidence of a

25 Compare 364–8 with Avitus, ii.89–90; 403–5 with Avitus, ii.108–9.

26 *Pat. Lat.* 59:334.

27 See J. M. Evans, '*Genesis B* and its background', *RES*, n.s. 14 (1963), 1–16, 113–23.

28 See Huppé, *Doctrine and Poetry*, pp. 218–23.

29 See J. E. Cross and S. I. Tucker, 'Allegorical Tradition and the Old English *Exodus*', *Neoph.* 44 (1960), 122–7; J. W. Earl, 'Christian Tradition in the Old English *Exodus*', *NM* 71 (1970). 541–70.

30 See A. G. Brodeur, 'A Study of Diction and Style in Three Anglo-Saxon Narrative Poems', in *Nordica et Anglia: Studies in Honor of Stefán Einarsson* (The Hague, 1968), 97–114 (p. 111).

31 J. F. Kenney, *Sources for the Early History of Ireland: Ecclesiastical* (Columbia U.P., 1929; repr. 1966), p. 254.

32 See Alison Jones, in *MÆ* 35 (1966), 95–102.

33 Cf. 273–7. The repetition has produced theories of composite structure, but the poet is doing no more than follow the sequence of events in the Vulgate: see R. T. Farrell, 'The unity of the Old English *Daniel*', *RES*, n.s. 18 (1967), 117–35.

34 See Huppé, *Doctrine and Poetry*, pp. 227–31.

35 See Shepherd, 'Scriptural Poetry', in *Continuations and Beginnings*, p. 33.

36 Bede, *Ecc. History*, ii.13 (ed. cit., p. 183).

37 *Ibid.*, iii.1 (p. 215).

38 *Life of Bishop Wilfrid*, ed. B. Colgrave (Cambridge, 1927), cap. XIX (p. 41).

39 Whitelock, *Documents*, p. 747.

40 *The Web of Words* (Albany, N. Y., 1970), pp. 136–48.

41 Huppé, *Web of Words*, pp. 146–7.

42 See Shepherd, 'Scriptural Poetry', in *Continuations and Beginnings*, p. 12.

43 See E. G. Stanley, in *Continuations and Beginnings*, p. 111 (but cf. Brodeur, in *Einarsson Studies*, p. 101). For a similar example of incompetent borrowing, see *Andreas and The Fates of the Apostles*, ed. K. R. Brooks (Oxford, 1961), p. xxv.

44 See e.g. 700, 934, 1214, 1603, 1718.

45 Sisam, 'Cynewulf and his Poetry', in *Studies*, p. 13.

46 See *Juliana*, ed. Rosemary Woolf (Methuen's O. E. Library, 1955), p. 16.

47 See R. B. Burlin, *The Old English 'Advent': a Typological Commentary*, Yale Studies in English, Vol. 168 (New Haven, 1968), p. 3.

48 See *The Advent Lyrics of the Exeter Book*, ed. J. J. Campbell (Princeton, 1959), p. 35.

49 See D. A. Pearsall, *John Lydgate* (1970), pp. 263–4, 272–3.

50 Bede, *Ecc. History*, iii.2; and see W. O. Stevens, *The Cross in the Life and Literature of the Anglo-Saxons*, Yale Studies in English, Vol. 23 (New Haven, 1904), p. 82.

51 See J. A. Burrow, 'An approach to *The Dream of the Rood*', *Neoph.* 43 (1959), 123–33.

52 Text and translation from the Missal, Good Friday. For further resemblances to Tatwine's *De Cruce Christi*, see J. V. Fleming, '*The Dream of the Rood* and Anglo-Saxon monasticism', *Traditio* 22 (1966), 43–72 (p. 67), and W. F. Bolton, in *Archiv* 200 (1963), 344–6; and for possible connections with the cult of the cross in works such as Hraban Maur's *De laudibus sanctae crucis*, see Barbara Raw, '*The Dream of the Rood* and Christian art', *MÆ* 39 (1970), 239–56.

53 Rosemary Woolf, 'Doctrinal influences in *The Dream of the Rood*', *MÆ* 27 (1958), 137–53 (p. 138). Cf. the scrupulous subtlety of Langland's handling of the Incarnation, *Piers Plowman*, C.XXI. 20–5.

54 See Huppé, *Web of Words*, p. 10.

55 *Ibid.*, p. 36.

56 *Carmen de ave phoenice*, 33–4: text from Appendix I, p. 89, in *The Phoenix*, ed. N. F. Blake (Manchester, 1964).

57 See J. E. Cross, 'The Conception of the Old English *Phoenix*', in *Old English Poetry: Fifteen Essays*, ed. R. P. Creed (Providence, R. I., 1967), pp. 129–52.

58 J. C. Pope, 'Dramatic Voices in *The Wanderer* and *The Seafarer*', in *Medieval and Linguistic Studies in Honor of F. P. Magoun (Franciplegius)*, ed. J. B. Bessinger and R. P. Creed (New York, 1965), pp. 164–93 (p. 172).

59 The essential thematic relationship of these poems to the more conventionally homiletic pieces in the Exeter Book is stressed in the excellent introduction to *The Wanderer*, ed. T. P. Dunning and A. J. Bliss (Methuen's O. E. Library, 1969), p. 79.

60 Like those whom the *Anglo-Saxon Chronicle* describes arriving at the court of Alfred in 891. See Dorothy Whitelock, 'The Interpretation of *The Seafarer*', in *Early Cultures of North-West Europe: H. M. Chadwick Memorial Studies*, ed. C. Fox and B. Dickins (Cambridge, 1950), pp. 261–72.

61 See Pope, 'Dramatic Voices', p. 176; *The Seafarer*, ed. Ida L. Gordon (1960), Introduction, pp. 6–8.

62 *The Seafarer*, ed. Gordon, p. 16. For extended analysis of a genre of 'penitential poetry' in early Welsh and Irish and Old English,

see P. L. Henry, *The Early English and Celtic Lyric* (London, 1966).

63 IV. 8, in *Two Lives of St. Cuthbert*, ed. Colgrave, p. 123.

64 See Ida L. Gordon, 'Traditional themes in *The Wanderer* and *The Seafarer*', *RES*, n.s. 5 (1954), 1–13 (p. 8).

65 See above, p. 19.

66 See P. Dronke, *The Medieval Lyric* (1968), pp. 91–3; also *Poetic Individuality in the Middle Ages* (Oxford, 1970), p. 27.

67 See K. Malone, 'Two English *Frauenlieder*',

*CL* 14 (1962), 106–17.

68 *Early Irish Lyrics*, ed. G. Murphy (Oxford, 1956).

69 R. E. Kaske, 'A poem of the Cross in the Exeter Book', *Traditio* 23 (1967), 41–72.

70 M. J. Swanton, '*The Wife's Lament* and *The Husband's Message*: a reconsideration', *Anglia* 82 (1964), 269–90.

71 W. F. Bolton, '*The Wife's Lament* and *The Husband's Message*: a reconsideration revisited', *Archiv* 205 (1968–9), 337–51.

## Chapter 3   Late Old English poetry and the transition

1 *King Alfred's West-Saxon Version of Gregory's Pastoral Care*, ed. H. Sweet (EETS 45, 1871), p. 3.

2 F. M. Stenton, *Anglo-Saxon England* (1943; 3rd ed. Oxford, 1971), pp. 436, 226–8, 348–9, 427.

3 T. D. Kendrick, *Anglo-Saxon Art to A.D. 900* (1938), p. 215.

4 D. Knowles, *The Monastic Order in England* (Cambridge, 1940), pp. 32–6, 695.

5 K. Sisam, *Studies in the History of Old English Literature* (Oxford, 1953), p. 98: see above, chapter I, note 8.

6 *The Old English Version of the Heptateuch, Ælfric's Treatise on the Old and New Testament and his Preface to Genesis*, ed. S. J. Crawford (EETS 160, 1922), pp. 76–7.

7 *Byrhtferth's Manual*, ed. S. J. Crawford (EETS 177, 1929), p. 132. See C. Hart, 'Byrhtferth and his Manual', *MÆ* 41 (1972), 95–109.

8 See above, pp. 32, 38.

9 L. Whitbread, 'Old English and Old High German: a note on *Judgment Day II*', *SP* 60 (1963), 514–24.

10 L. Whitbread. 'The Old English poem *Judgment Day II* and its Latin source', *PQ* 45 (1966), 635–56.

11 Margaret Ashdown, *English and Norse Documents Relating to the Reign of Ethelred the Unready* (1930), pp. 8, 75, 243.

12 *English Historical Documents*, ed. Dorothy Whitelock (1955), p. 843.

13 See A. Campbell, 'The Old English Epic Style', in *English and Medieval Studies presented to J. R. R. Tolkien*, ed. N. Davis and C. L. Wrenn (1962), pp. 13–26.

14 N. F. Blake, '*The Battle of Maldon*', *Neoph.* 49 (1965), 332–45 (p. 338).

15 As will be seen from a comparison of Boethius, bk II, m. 8, III. m. 9, IV. m. 6, with Alfred's metres 11, 20, 29 (in *ASPR* V)

16 E.g. *Thureth, Aldhelm*, in *ASPR* VI, which contains texts of most of the Old English poems mentioned in this chapter.

17 See *The Poetical Dialogues of Solomon and Saturn*, ed. R. J. Menner, MLA Monograph Series, XIII (New York, 1941), pp. 38–9.

18 For Ælfric, see *The Homilies of the Anglo-Saxon Church*, ed. B. Thorpe (2 vols, 1844–6), i. 114; Menner, *Poetical Dialogues*, p. 139. For Alfred, see F. Anne Payne, *King Alfred and Boethius* (Madison, Wisc., 1968).

19 Sisam, *Studies*, p. 48.

20 In the conventional classification, MSS C and D. The other major versions of the Chronicle are A, the Parker Chronicle, a Canterbury MS of Winchester origin; B, a relation of C, which ends at 977 (the others go up to or beyond the Conquest); and E, the Peterborough Chronicle. The first four 'classical' poems all appear in ABC, the first two in D as well. None are represented in E, which might suggest that 'classical' verse had no repute outside Southern and West Mercian areas, though cf. p. 70 below.

21 Whitelock, *Documents*, p. 208.

22 See above, p. 16.

23 See O. Funke, 'Studien zur alliterierenden und rhythmisierenden Prosa in der alteren altenglischen Homiletik', *Anglia* 80 (1962), 9–36; Frances R. Lipp, 'Ælfric's Old English prose style', *SP* 66 (1969), 689–718. Ælfric is also influenced by the example of the heightened prose of Latin, though he does not imitate its methods: see Dorothy Bethurum, 'The Form of Ælfric's *Lives of the Saints*', *SP* 29 (1932), 515–33. Ælfric's prose is placed firmly in the tradition of the plainer verse by S. M. Kuhn, 'Was Ælfric a poet?' *PQ* 52 (1973), 643–62.

24 See especially *Homilies of Ælfric: a Supplementary Collection*, ed. J. C. Pope (EETS 259–60, 1967–8), Introduction,

pp. 105ff—the whole section on 'Rhythmical prose'.

25 *Ælfric's Lives of the Saints*, ed. W. W. Skeat (EETS 76, 82, 1881–5, and 94, 114, 1890–1900).

26 P. Clemoes, 'Liturgical influence on punctuation in late Old English and early Middle English MSS', Occasional Papers of the Department of Anglo-Saxon, Cambridge, No. 1, 1952.

27 *Homilies of Ælfric*, ed. Pope, Introd., p. 135.

28 Homily V, St Sebastian, 148–51, i.126.

29 Homily XXIX, St Denis, 220–5, ii.182.

30 See above, p. 39.

31 Lines 301–6, in *Angelsächsische Homilien und Heiligenleben*, ed. B. Assmann (Kassel, 1889; repr. with supplementary introduction by P. Clemoes, Darmstadt, 1964), p. 111.

32 See especially A. McIntosh, 'Wulfstan's Prose', *PBA* 35 (1949), 109–42.

33 *Sermo Lupi ad Anglos*, ed. Dorothy Whitelock (Methuen's O. E. Library, 1939), lines 55–62; cf. lines 102–4 in Homily V, 'Secundum Marcum', p. 140 in *The Homilies of Wulfstan*, ed. Dorothy Bethurum (Oxford, 1957).

34 See above, p. 65 and note 20.

35 Text from *Two of the Saxon Chronicles Parallel*, ed. J. Earle, rev. C. Plummer (2 vols, Oxford, 1892–9), i. 119–21. *ASPR* VI prints only the 1036 poem from this group.

36 Lines 1–14, Earle–Plummer, p. 158.

37 Lines 1–9, Earle–Plummer, pp. 220–1. The lineation and punctuation of Earle–Plummer is followed in all these quotations.

38 See J. W. Rankin, 'Rhythm and rime before the Norman Conquest', *PMLA* 36 (1921), 401–28 (p. 421).

39 Occasionally in a more deliberate way, e.g. *Elene*.

40 The *Riming Poem* is well-known as a *locus desperatus* for translation: sense, like everything else, is sacrificed to rhyme. No claims are made for the translations offered here. They may be the more inaccurate for attempting to make sense.

41 More generous views are expressed by Ruth P. M. Lehmann, 'The Old English *Riming Poem*: interpretation, text, and translation', *JEGP* 69 (1970), 437–49; O. D. Macrae-Gibson, 'The literary structure of *The Riming Poem*', *NM* 74(1973), 62–84.

42 W. P. Ker, *The Dark Ages* (1904; Mentor books, New York, 1958), p. 130.

43 See above, pp. 6, 55.

44 Bodley 343, Corpus Christi (Cambridge) 303, Cotton Vespasian D.xiv, Cambridge University Library Ii.1.33, Cotton

Faustina A.ix, Hatton (Bodley) 116: see *Homilies of Ælfric*, ed. Pope, Introd., pp. 14–93.

45 As in Vespasian D. xiv, at least two pieces in which were composed in the twelfth century: see N. R. Ker, *Catalogue of Manuscripts containing Anglo-Saxon* (Oxford, 1957), pp. 275–6. On the other hand, the annals at Christ Church in Caligula A. xv (which ignore the Conquest) are in English only till 1109, thenceforth in Latin (Ker, p. 175).

46 Not to be confused with the earlier Wulfstan, Archbishop of York.

47 See *Homilies*, ed. Pope, pp. 185–8; *Homilies of Wulfstan*, ed. Bethurum, pp. 104–6; Ker, *Catalogue*, p. xlix.

48 Ker points out that, by the thirteenth century, in most centres of learning, MSS in Old English were regarded as lumber (*Catalogue*, p. xlix). Nevertheless, A. F. Cameron, 'Middle English in Old English Manuscripts', in *Chaucer and Middle English Studies in Honour of R. H. Robbins*, ed. Beryl Rowland (1974), pp. 218–29, gives a list of 44 such MSS, with annotation ranging from titles and rubrics to glosses.

49 As does S. J. Crawford, 'The Worcester Marks and Glosses', *Anglia* 52 (1928), 1–25.

50 Ker, *Catalogue*, pp. 320, 368; J. P. Oakden, *Alliterative Poetry in Middle English*, 2 vols, Vol. I: *The Dialectal and Metrical Survey*, Vol. II: *A Survey of the Traditions* (Manchester, 1930–5; repr. Archon books, 1968), i. 136–7.

51 J. L. Rosier, 'Instructions for Christians', *Anglia* 82 (1964), 4–22.

52 It is interesting that the early marginalia in this MS include two short metrical pieces in French (Ker, *Catalogue*, p. 23), a suggestion perhaps of the coexistence of the two traditions, at least in monasteries.

53 Lines 15–19: text from *Selections from Early Middle English*, ed. J Hall, 2 vols (Oxford, 1920), p. 1. The piece has some of the petulance of the 'patriotic' entries in the Chronicle.

54 Such as Oakden provides, *passim*. The usefulness of Oakden's book is much limited by this mechanical approach, but it is the only survey of the whole body of alliterative writing in Middle English. Oakden points out, incidentally, that *The Grave* is related to *The Soul's Address* (ii.4), though it would be hard to determine in which direction the borrowing has taken place. For the relation of *The Grave* to *The Soul's Address*, see Louise Dudley, '*The Grave*', *MP* 11 (1913–14), 429–42.

55 N. F. Blake, in 'Rhythmical Alliteration', *MP* 67 (1969), 118–24, comes to similar conclusions.

56 Lines 150–3: text from Hall, *Selections*, p. 23. Hall prints the Jesus copy; texts of all the MSS and a full study of the poem are provided by O. S. Arngart, *The Proverbs of Alfred*, 2 vols, Vol. I: *A Study of the Texts*, Vol. II: *The Texts* (Lund, 1942–55).

57 Arngart, *Proverbs*, ii. 6–7.

58 Arngart, *Proverbs*, ii. 28, 32, 37.

59 Arngart, *Proverbs*, i. 76.

60 Lines 368–74: text from Hall, *Selections*, p. 187.

61 M. Dominica Legge, *Anglo-Norman Literature and its Background* (Oxford, 1963). pp. 22–3.

62 *Laȝamon* is the historical form, which descends as *Laweman* (used by some scholars) in later spelling. There is no reason for *Layamon*, the usual modern form, except the convenience of printers.

63 Lines 20070ff in *Laȝamon's Brut*, ed. F. Madden, 3 vols (1847); text from *Selections from Laȝamon's Brut*, ed. G. L. Brook Oxford, 1963), 2301–25, with indication in square brackets of passages omitted from the Otho MS. Madden's text (32241 short lines) is not yet replaced by that of G. L. Brook and R. F. Leslie, of which vol. I (EETS 250, 1963), containing long lines 1–8020, has appeared.

64 See the last line but two in the quotation above.

65 See above, pp. 78–9 and further Legge, *Anglo-Norman Literature*, pp. 35, 77. The coexistence of alliterative long line and couplet is not at all unlike the coexistence of alexandrines (in *laisses*) and octosyllabics in Anglo-Norman. It may also be compared, as an attempt to break up the monotonous hammering of end-stopped alliterative lines, with the use of 'bob and wheel' in *Sir Gawain and the Green Knight* (see below, p. 174).

66 First text (Cotton Vespasian D. xiv) from *Early English Homilies*, ed. Rubie D.–N. Warner (EETS 152, 1917), p. 12; second (Lambeth 487) from *Old English Homilies*, 1st Series, ed. R. Morris (EETS 29, 34, 1868), p. 109. The semi-colon in the latter represents the *punctus elevatus* of the MS.

67 The other three prose lyrics in the *Wooing*-group are *On Lofsong of ure Lefdi*, *On Lofsong of ure Louerde* and *Þe Wohunge of ure Lauerd*: a fifth, *On God Ureisun of ure Lefdi*, is in rhyme (see below, p. 96). The *Katherine*-group includes three saints' lives (Juliana, Katherine, Margaret), and three treatises in plainer prose, *Ancrene Wisse*, *Hali Meiðhad* and *Sawles Warde*.

68 See R. M. Wilson, *Early Middle English Literature* (1939, 2nd ed. 1951), pp. 125–6.

69 *Þe Wohunge of ure Lauerd*, 1–10, ed. W. Meredith Thompson (EETS 241, 1958), p. 20.

70 *Wohunge of ure Lauerd*, 541–6.

71 See two articles by Margery Morgan, 'A Talkyng of the Love of God' *RES*, n.s. 3 (1952), 97–116, and 'A treatise in cadence', *MLR* 47 (1952), 156–64.

72 *Seinte Marherete*, ed. Frances M. Mack (EETS 193, 1934), p. 5, line 11.

73 *Seinte Marherete*, p. 25, lines 27–34.

74 N. B. Lambeth MS 487, above, and see Dorothy Bethurum, 'The connection of the Katherine Group with Old English prose', *JEGP* 34 (1935), 553–64.

75 See the reference to 'old English' in *Marherete*, p. 53, line 31; also *Sawles Warde*, ed. R. M. Wilson (Leeds, 1939), p. xxi.

76 See below, pp. 121ff.

## Chapter 4 Poetry in the early Middle English period

1 See G. T. Shepherd, 'Early Middle English Literature', in the Sphere *History of Literature in the English Language*, Vol. I: *The Middle Ages*, ed. W. F. Bolton (1970), pp. 67–106 (pp. 67–8).

2 H. J. Chaytor, *From Script to Print: an Introduction to Medieval Literature* (Cambridge, 1945), Chap. III, 'Language and Nationality'; V. H. Galbraith, 'Nationality and language in medieval England', *TRHS* 23 (1941), 113–28.

3 Rosalind Wadsworth, 'William Longespée', *Neoph.* 56 (1972), 269–72.

4 *Laud (Peterborough) Chronicle*, s.a. 1087 (*Two of the Saxon Chronicles Parallel*, ed. J. Earle, rev. C. Plummer, 2 vols, Oxford, 1892–9, p. 224). For the Chronicler's indignation, see his account of the attempt to introduce Norman customs at Glastonbury, s.a. 1083 (Earle–Plummer, p. 215).

5 See M. Dominica Legge, 'Anglo-Norman and the historian', *History* 26 (1941), 163–75; 'The French Language and the English Cloister', *Medieval Studies Presented to Rose Graham* (Oxford, 1950),

pp. 146–62; also the two books mentioned below.

6 M. Dominica Legge, *Anglo-Norman Literature and its Background* (Oxford, 1963), p. 204.

7 M. Dominica Legge, *Anglo-Norman in the Cloisters* (Edinburgh, 1950), p. 1.

8 Legge, *Anglo-Norman Literature*, p. 291.

9 Legge, 'Anglo-Norman and the Historian', p. 164; F. M. Stenton, *Anglo-Saxon England* (1943; 3rd ed. Oxford, 1971), p. 419.

10 R. W. Chambers, *On the Continuity of English Prose from Alfred to More and his School* (an extract from the Introduction to Nicholas Harpsfield's *Life of More*, EETS 191A, 1932); R. M. Wilson, *Early Middle English Literature* (1939; 2nd ed. 1951), and 'English and French in England 1100–1300', *History* 28 (1943), 37–60.

11 Legge, *Anglo-Norman in the Cloisters*, p. 48; *Anglo-Norman Literature*, p. 5.

12 Legge, 'Anglo-Norman and the Historian', p. 167.

13 Legge, *Anglo-Norman Literature*, p. 240.

14 See above, p. 75.

15 Legge, *Anglo-Norman Literature*, p. 41.

16 *Ibid.*, p. 63.

17 35, 142 (Trinity MS): text from J. Hall, ed., *Selections from Early Middle English*, 2 vols (Oxford, 1920), pp. 33, 39.

18 See above, p. 81.

19 Legge, *Anglo-Norman in the Cloisters*, pp. 31–5; *Anglo-Norman Literature*, pp. 134–8.

20 See above, p. 78. Fitzwilliam McClean 123 found its way in the fourteenth century to a convent at Nuneaton: see Betty Hill, in *NQ* 12(1965), 87–90.

21 The *Poema Morale*, for instance, contrasted with the lyrics of the *Wohunge*-grout.

22 E.g. Walter Map's *Dialogus inter Aquam et Vinum*, in *Latin Poems of Walter Mapes*, ed. T. Wright (Camden Society, 1841), pp. 87–92. See H. Walther, *Das Streitgedicht in der lateinischen Literatur des Mittelalters*, Quellen und Untersuchungen zur lateinischen Philologie des Mittelalters, V.2 (1920).

23 'Le petyt ple entre le Iuuencel e le Veylard', as it is called in Jesus 29. See Legge, *Anglo-Norman Literature*, pp. 200–1.

24 Lines 95–6, in the edition of E. G. Stanley (Nelson's Medieval and Renaissance Library, 1960).

25 For the friars' miscellanies and the friars as composers, see H. Pfander, *The Popular Sermon of the medieval friar in England* (New York, 1937); *The Early English Carols*, ed. R. L. Greene (Oxford, 1935),

pp. cxi–viii; R. H. Robbins, 'The authors of the Middle English religious lyrics', *JEGP* 39 (1940), 230–38, and 'The earliest carols and the Franciscans', *MLN* 53 (1938), 239–45, and also his introduction to *Secular Lyrics of the XIVth and XVth Centuries* (Oxford, 1952; 2nd ed., 1955), pp. xvii–xviii.

26 A. G. Little, *Studies in Early Franciscan History* (Manchester, 1917), p. 99.

27 Convenient lists of contents in N. R. Ker's Introduction to the facsimile of the MSS of *The Owl and the Nightingale* (EETS 251, 1963), pp. ix–xi.

28 See Betty Hill, 'The history of Jesus College Oxford MS 29', *MÆ* 32(1963), 203–13.

29 The English contents of Jesus 29 are printed *seriatim* in *An Old English Miscellany*, ed. R. Morris (EETS 49, 1872). These two poems appear on pp. 162 and 168, the latter called *Death*; the title above is from *English Lyrics of the XIIIth Century*, ed. C. Brown (Oxford, 1932), where the poems are Nos 28 and 29. See also Pfander, *The Popular Sermon*, pp. 27–9.

30 Brown, *XIIIth Century*, pp. 188–91; Rosemary Woolf, *The English Religious Lyric in the Middle Ages* (Oxford, 1968), pp. 94–7.

31 Lines 49–56; text from Morris, *Miscellany*, p. 171, but with the lineation of Brown, *XIIIth Century*, lines 25–8.

32 Morris, *Miscellany* p. 101; cf. Brown, *XIIIth Century*, No. 71 and notes, and No. 11.

33 Brown, *XIIIth Century*, p. 173.

34 Legge, *Anglo-Norman Literature*, pp. 35, 77, 160, 273. Another debt to Anglo-Norman is in the admission of extended rhyme, over 4 lines, in poems predominantly in couplets (e.g. *The Passion of Our Lord*).

35 *Doomsday*, 1–2, in Morris, *Miscellany*, p. 163.

36 Morris, *Miscellany*, p. 89. Friars, in these early days, are often associated with attacks on corruption and oppression: see Pfander, *The Popular Sermon*, pp. 14–15.

37 Morris, *Miscellany*, p. 90. For the 'invasion' of the four-stress line, compare *On God Ureisun of Ure Lefdi* (Brown, *XIIIth Century*, No. 3), which appears in the same MS, Cotton Nero A. xiv, as the prose lyrics of the *Wohunge*-group.

38 Morris, *Miscellany*, p. 157; Brown, *XIIIth Century*, No. 10 ('Death's Wither-Clench'), prints the text from the Maidstone MS, where it is accompanied by music.

39 The two poems are in Morris, *Miscellany*,

pp. 37 and 187. On these and other
'verse-sermons', see Pfander, pp. 20–51.

40 Lines 65–72: text from *Early Middle
English Texts*, ed. B. Dickins and R. M.
Wilson (1951), p. 105 (and see note to
line 72, *cleo*, p. 218). Cf. Morris, *Miscellany*,
p. 93, and Brown, *XIIIth Century*, No. 43.

41 Line 34: text from Dickins and Wilson,
*Texts*, p. 72.

42 Lines 13–16: text from Brown, *XIIIth
Century*, No. 53. Brown reads it as septenary,
since he refers to another similar poem
on the love of Jesus as being 'in the same
measure' (p. 209): 'Lufe es thoght
wyth grete desyre, of a fayre louing;/Lufe
I lyken till a fyre, þat sloken may na
thyng;/Lufe us clenses of oure syn, lufe
us bote sall bryng;/Lufe þe keynges hert
may wyn, lufe of ioy may syng.' It is
impossible to agree with him, (or with
Rosemary Woolf, *English Religious Lyric*,
p. 171).

43 For the contents, see *Catalogi Codicum
Manuscriptorum Bibliothecae Bodleianae*,
Pars IX, *Codices Digbeiani*, ed. G. D.
Macray (Oxford, 1883), cols. 91–7.
For further information, see B.D.H.
Miller, 'The early history of Bodleian
MS. Digby 86', *Annuale Mediaevale*
4 (1963), 23–56.

44 Brown, *XIIIth Century*, p. 204.

45 Lines 265, 268–9: text from Brown,
*XIIIth Century*, No. 51.

46 See the introductory note to the excerpt in
*Early Middle English Verse and Prose*,
ed. J. A. W. Bennett and G. V. Smithers
(Oxford, 1966), p. 65. The apparatus
throughout this collection is extremely
valuable.

47 Lines 243–6: text from Bennett and
Smithers, *Verse and Prose*, p. 75.

48 As do two articles by S. Bercovitch, in
*JEGP* 65 (1966), 287–94, and N. von
Kreisler, in *JEGP* 69 (1970), 650–8.

49 Bennett and Smithers, *Verse and Prose*,
pp. 77–80; R. Axton, 'Popular modes
in the earliest plays', in *Medieval Drama*
(Stratford-upon-Avon Studies 16),
ed. N. Denny (1973), pp. 13–39
(pp. 16–19), and the same author's
*European Drama of the Middle Ages* (1974),
Chap. I.

50 Brown, *XIIIth Century*, pp. 184–6; M.R.
James, *The Western MSS in the Library
of Trinity College Cambridge: a Descriptive
Catalogue*, 4 vols (Cambridge, 1900–4),
i. 438–47.

51 Brown, *XIIIth Century*, Nos 22, 15, 16, 17.
The latter had the status of Latin hymns:
No. 17 appears also in a learned Latin MS
(Woolf, *English Religious Lyric*, p. 126).

52 Brown, *XIIIth Century*, Nos 21, 25.

53 Brown, *XIIIth Century*, No. 66.

54 Line 104: text in Bennett and Smithers,
*Verse and Prose*, p. 142.

55 The first is printed in *Reliquiae Antiquae*,
ed. T. Wright and J. O. Halliwell (2 vols,
1841–3), ii. 174; the remainder in
*The Political Songs of England*, ed. T.
Wright (Camden Society, 1839), pp.
195, 210, 224. The MS also includes a
number of the usual 'verse-sermons':
all the English poems are printed in
W. Heuser, *Die Kildare-Gedichte* (Bonner
Beiträge zur Anglistik, 14, 1904).

56 Brown, *XIIIth Century*, Nos 7 and 8. The
latter is short and extraordinary enough
to quote in full: 'Foweles in þe frith,/þe
fisses in þe flod,/And i mon waxe wod./
Mulch sorw I walke with/for beste of bon
and blod.'

57 Brown, *XIIIth Century*, No. 63.

58 Corpus Christi College, Cambridge, MS
59. See C. Brown, 'A 13th century MS
from Llanthony Priory', *Speculum* 3 (1928),
587–95.

59 A similar attempt to provide a set of
verse sermons on the Sunday Gospels is
made in the *Miroir* of Robert of Greatham
(Legge, *Anglo-Norman Literature*, p. 213):
the difference—and it is suggestive of one
of the general differences between English
and Anglo-Norman—is that Robert is
chaplain to a noble family.

60 The standard edition is by R. M. White
and R. Holt (Oxford, 1878). There are
extracts in Hall, *Selections*, Dickins and
Wilson, *Texts*, and Bennett and Smithers,
*Verse and Prose*.

61 Elsham Priory in North Lincolnshire is
one possible home; Bridlington is
suggested by J. C. Dickinson, *The
Origin of the Austin Canons* (1950), p. 228.

62 G. T. Shepherd, 'Early Middle English
Literature', in the Sphere *History*, p. 102.

63 Lines 1–4, ed. O. Arngart (Lund Studies
in English 36, 1968). See also Legge,
*Anglo-Norman Literature*, p. 180.

64 The standard edition is that of A. S.
Napier (Oxford, 1916). Quotation here is
from the extracts in Dickins and Wilson,
*Texts*.

65 This is the MS edited by C. Horstmann,
*The Early South-English Legendary* (EETS
87, 1887). The later edition, *The South
English Legendary*, by Charlotte
d'Evelyn and Anna J. Mill (EETS 235–6,
244, 1956–9), is based principally on
Corpus Christi College, Cambridge, MS
145, with some material from Harley
2277.

66 See Minnie E. Wells, 'The structural

development of the *South English Legendary*', *JEGP* 41 (1942), 320–44; *The Southern Passion*, ed. Beatrice D. Brown (EETS 169, 1927), Introduction, pp. xciii–cx. But cf. M. Görlach, *The Textual Tradition of the South English Legendary*, Leeds Texts and Monographs, n.s. 6 (Leeds, 1974), pp. 46–50. Görlach suggests that the original version of the Legendary was written for nuns.

67  See Beverly Boyd, 'A new approach to the *South English Legendary*', *PQ* 47 (1968), 494–8.

68  Ed. D'Evelyn and Mill, p. 26, lines 47–8, and p. 362, line 123.

69  *Ibid.*, p. 288, lines 267–8. See R. M. Wilson, *The Lost Literature of Medieval England* (1952; 2nd ed., 1970), p. 99.

70  Ed. D'Evelyn and Mill, pp. 287, 291.

71  E.g. the opening of St Wulfstan (p. 9), or St Swithun (p. 274).

72  St Peter, p. 260, line 392.

73  Not in D'Evelyn and Mill, but separately edited by Beatrice D. Brown (EETS 169, 1927), with a valuable introduction.

74  Lines 1349, 1524, 1583. See Beatrice Brown's introduction, pp. lxxviii–xcii, and for 'deictic' techniques, Pamela Gradon, *Form and Style in Early English Literature* (1971), pp. 297–331, esp. p. 308.

75  Ed. J. M. Cowper (EETS 60, 1875). It is attributed, surely wrongly. to Robert Mannyng of Brunne (see below, p. 108).

76  Lines 267–8, from Cotton Vespasian A.iii, in *Cursor Mundi* ed. R. Morris (EETS 57, 59, 62, 66, 68, 99, 101, 1874–93). Morris prints 4 MSS parallel, of 10 known.

77  E.g. at lines 2315, 3409, 5495, 6451.

78  The passage is printed in *Fourteenth Century Verse and Prose*, ed. K. Sisam (Oxford, 1921), pp. 148–9.

79  See Ruth Crosby, 'Robert Mannyng of Brunne: a new biography', *PMLA* 57 (1942), 15–28.

80  Line 10804: ed. F. J. Furnivall (EETS 119, 123, 1901–3).

81  D. W. Robertson, 'The cultural tradition of *Handlyng Synne*', *Speculum* 22(1947), 162–85 (p. 169).

82  See above, p. 80.

83  Lines 6–7 in Brook (EETS 250). For editions, see above, p. 80; reference and quotation here is from Madden unless otherwise indicated.

84  See above, p. 81.

85  See J. S. P. Tatlock, *The Legendary History of Britain* (Berkeley and Los Angeles, 1950); R. H. Fletcher, *The Arthurian Material in the Chronicles* (Boston, 1906; 2nd ed., New York, 1966).

86  The Caligula MS of Laȝamon's prologue says Queen Eleanor, but it is hard to understand why no Wace-scribe mentions this.

87  *Le Roman de Brut de Wace*, ed. I. Arnold (SATF, 1938–40), 10767–72; *Laȝamon's Brut*, ed. F. Madden, 3 vols (1847), 24957–64.

88  E.g. the story of Uther and Ygerne: see *Middle English Romances*, ed. A. C. Gibbs (York Medieval Texts, 1966), Introduction, pp. 16–18.

89  See E. G. Stanley, 'Laȝamon's antiquarian sentiments', *MÆ* 38 (1969), 23–37; also T. A. Stroud, 'Scribal editing in Lawman's *Brut*', *JEGP* 51 (1952), 42–8, and W. J. Keith, 'Laȝamon's *Brut*: the literary differences between the two texts', *MÆ* 29 (1960), 161–72. Both the latter think of the Otho scribe as an intelligent improver.

90  An outburst against the Normans, with their *niðcraften* (ed. Brook, 3547), is quite out of place: Wace's tone (3769–70) is perfectly neutral.

91  Ed. Brook, 1135–55, 1660–70, 1704–18.

92  In the analysis that follows, quotation is from G. L. Brook's *Selections from Laȝamon's Brut* (Oxford, 1963), with cross-reference to Madden: these are lines 2326–8 (Madden 20,120–5).

93  This reference is only in the Otho prologue, but it gains authority from the fact that the MSS are now presumed to be of approximately the same date: see E. G. Stanley, in *NQ* 15 (1968), 85–8.

94  Tatlock (*Legendary History*, pp. 515–30) derives it from his residence in Ireland.

95  J. S. P. Tatlock, 'Laȝamon's Poetic Style and its Relations', *Manly Anniversary Studies* (Chicago, 1923), pp. 3–11.

96  This point is made by H. Pilch, *Laȝamon's Brut: eine literarische Studie*, Anglistische Forschungen 91 (Heidelberg, 1960), p. 117.

97  Even the 'seasonal headpiece' (24,195): see *Kyng Alisaunder*, ed. G. V. Smithers, Vol. II (EETS 237, 1957), Introduction, p. 31.

98  Fletcher, *Arthurian Material in the Chronicles*, pp. 143–4.

99  See R. M. Wilson, *Lost Literature of Medieval England*, pp. 50–4, 113–15.

100  Legge, *Anglo-Norman Literature*, p. 144.

101  Gradon, *Form and Style in Early English Literature*, p. 269.

102  This is the usual method; attempts at a formal classification, by length and verse-form respectively, have been made by D. Mehl, *The Middle English Romances of the 13th and 14th Centuries* (1968; first published in German, 1967), and D.

Pearsall, 'The development of Middle English romance', *MS* 27 (1965), 91–116.

103 See below, p. 146. Romance-writers also, of course, imitate minstrel habits of address.

104 K. Brunner, 'Middle English Metrical Romances and their Audience', in *Studies in Medieval Literature in Honour of A. C. Baugh*, ed. MacE. Leach (Philadelphia, 1961), pp. 219–26 (pp. 220–2).

105 E.g. in the twin episodes of Horn's return to rid his betrothed Rymenhild of unwelcome suitors (1051–210, 1407–92: ed. J. R. Lumby, EETS 14, 1866; re-ed. G. H. McKnight, 1901).

106 W. H. French, *Essays on King Horn* (Ithaca, N. Y., 1940), pp. 1–19.

107 Legge, *Anglo-Norman Literature*, p. 133.

108 See above, p. 104.

109 See especially the opening description of the wise, just and firm rule of King Athelwold.

110 See, e.g. *Guy* (Auchinleck version, ed. J. Zupitza, EETS, ES 42, 49, 59, 1883–91), 621, compared with *Gui de Warewic* (ed. A. Ewert, CFMA 74–5, 1933), 582; 1206, cf. 1119, 6711, cf. 6805; stanzas 248, 271 (in the continuation), cf. 11003; 3997, cf. 3989; 4789, cf. 4904; 5251–378, cf. 5385. There are some warnings, however, against easy assumptions concerning the relative interests of Anglo-Norman and English writers, in the comments by the editors (p. 13) on the recently-discovered *Fragments of an Early Fourteenth-century Guy of Warwick*, ed. M. Mills and D. Huws, Medium Ævum Monographs, n.s. 4 (Oxford, 1974).

111 See Smithers's Introduction to *Kyng Alisaunder*, pp. 58–60.

112 *Ibid.*, pp. 35–9.

113 Lines 21–4, ed. K. Brunner, *Wiener Beiträge zur englischen Philologie* 42 (Vienna, 1913).

114 Lines 19–26, ed. E. Kölbing, *Altenglische Bibliothek* 4 (Leipzig, 1890).

115 Legge, *Anglo-Norman in the Cloisters*, p. 125.

116 See the Introduction by W. Aldis Wright to his edition of the *Chronicle* (Rolls series, 1887), pp. xxxiii–xxxvii.

117 Lines 7542–7, ed. Wright.

118 Line 6: ed. F. J. Furnivall (Rolls series, 1887).

119 16709–12. Mannyng, however, uses Wace's *Brut* for British history (see 55–70) instead of the first part of Langtoft, adapting his metre to match his source (four-stress couplets for Wace, long couplets for Langtoft). Furnivall's edition is of the first part.

120 There are Lincolnshire allusions in one of the most finely turned of the Harley lyrics: see below, p. 129.

121 Legge, *Anglo-Norman Literature*, pp. 177, 212.

## Chapter 5 Some fourteenth-century books and writers

1 E. Auerbach, 'The Knight sets forth', Chap. 6 in *Mimesis: the Representation of Reality in Western Literature*, trans. W. R. Trask (New York, 1957; first published in German, 1946).

2 *Middle English Romances*, ed. A. C. Gibbs (York Medieval Texts, 1966), Introduction.

3 Rosemary Woolf, *English Religious Lyric in the Middle Ages* (Oxford, 1968), p. 1.

4 As in Chaucer, *Troilus and Criseyde*, V. 1793–8.

5 *English Lyrics of the XIIIth Century*, ed. C. Brown (Oxford, 1932), Introduction, p. xxxviii.

6 For information on the provenance and date of the MS, and a complete list of contents, see the Introduction by N. R. Ker to the facsimile edition (EETS 255, 1965).

7 For a list of items common with Digby 86, see Brown, *XIIIth Century*, p. xxxvii.

8 Brown, *XIIIth Century*, No. 72, p. 131: this is the refrain. For the pun, cf. the French *Song of the Peace with England*, in *Political Songs of England*, ed. T. Wright (Camden Society, 1839), p. 65.

9 Wright, *Political Songs*, pp. 14, 46, 56, 63, 121, 160, 206, 231, 400.

10 The question, however, is a complex one: see E. K. Chambers, *The Medieval Stage*, 2 vols (Oxford, 1903), Vol. 1, 39–77, and G. R. Owst, *Literature and Pulpit in Medieval England* (Cambridge, 1933), pp. 10–16, 214–26. One complication is the temptation to use continental evidence to eke out evidence from England.

11 R. L. Greene, *Early English Carols* (Oxford, 1935), p. xciii.

12 R. M. Wilson, *The Lost Literature of Medieval England* (1952; 2nd ed., 1970), pp. 200–1.

13 *Chronicle of Pierre de Langtoft*, ed. T. Wright (Rolls Series, 1866–8), i. 234–64, 364; see also Wright, *Political Songs*, pp. 273–323; Wilson, *Lost Literature*, pp. 201–6. Mannyng (see above, p. 117) adds to these originals, but the additions are his own, in a more pedestrian, non-alliterative style.

14 Langtoft, *Chronicle*, ed. Wright, ii. 264.

15 In Harley 2253: ed. Isabel S. T. Aspin, *Anglo-Norman Political Songs*, Anglo-Norman Texts XI (1953), pp. 24–35.

16 Aspin, *Anglo-Norman Political Songs*, p. 15.

17 A. G. Little, *The Grey Friars in Oxford* (Oxford, 1892), pp. 32–3.

18 These and other 'political' poems from Harley 2253 are printed in *Historical Poems of the XIVth and XVth Centuries*, ed. R. H. Robbins (New York, 1959).

19 In the *Scotichronicon*: see Robbins, *Historical Poems*, p. xl.

20 Wright, *Political Songs*, pp. 262, 388–9; also *Political Poems and Songs*, ed. T. Wright (Rolls Series, 1859–61), i. 53.

21 Poem II. 19–20, in *Poems of Laurence Minot*, ed. J. Hall (3rd ed., Oxford, 1914), p. 5. Cf. Robbins, *Historical Poems*, p. 31.

22 Hall, *Minot*, Introduction, p. xii. See also D. C. Stedman, *The War Ballads of Laurence Minot* (Dublin, 1917), pp. xi–xii, xiv–xxii.

23 Lines 25–8, in Robbins, *Historical Poems*, p. 8.

24 E.g. *Consistory Courts*, 60, 'uncomely under calle', recalling the many phrases of the *brightest under bys* type (see *Early Middle English Verse and Prose*, ed. J. A. W. Bennett and G. V. Smithers (Oxford, 1966), p. 320).

25 J. Peter, *Complaint and Satire in Early English Literature* (Oxford, 1956), p. 54.

26 See V. J. Scattergood, *Politics and Poetry in the Fifteenth Century* (1971), pp. 352–3.

27 In Aspin, *Anglo-Norman Political Songs*. One English poem, on the *Death of Edward I*, is a translation from an Anglo-Norman original in another MS; they are little different, though the English (81–2) omits one reference to Aristotle and Virgil (75–6: both in Aspin, pp. 79–92).

28 Langtoft, *Chronicle*, p. 360.

29 Lines 5, 14, in Robbins, *Historical Poems*, No. 8. On the subject in general, see R. Taylor, *The Political Prophecy in England* (New York, 1911).

30 *The Romance and Prophecies of Thomas of Erceldoune*, ed. J. A. H. Murray (EETS 61, 1875), Introduction, p. xvii.

31 Murray, *Thomas of Erceldoune*, pp. xvii–xxx; Robbins, *Historical Poems*, p. xlv. John of Bridlington dedicated his long series of Latin prophecies (in Wright, *Political Poems*, i. 123–215) to Humphrey de Bohun (c. 1370).

32 The first two are printed by Robbins, *Historical Poems*, Nos 44 and 45; the last by J. R. Lumby (EETS 42, 1870). These poems are more numerous in MS than any other alliterative poems apart from *Piers Plowman*.

33 Murray, *Thomas of Erceldoune*, p. xxxvii.

34 'Mirie it is while sumer ilast' and 'Foweles in the frith' (see above, p. 101); 'Icham of Irlaunde' (in *Fourteenth Century Verse and Prose*, ed. K. Sisam (Oxford, 1921) p. 166); Pieces Q and R in Bennett and Smithers, *Verse and Prose*, p. 128; 'Nou sprinkes þe sprai', in Sisam, *Fourteenth Century Verse and Prose*, p. 163.

35 The lyrics in the MS are conveniently assembled in *The Harley Lyrics*, ed. G. L. Brook (Manchester, 1948). All the English poems are printed in *Altenglische Dichtungen des MS. Harl. 2253*, ed. K. Böddeker (Berlin, 1878).

36 For some statistics, see Merle Fifield, '13th century lyrics and the alliterative tradition', *JEGP* 62 (1963), 111–18.

37 See notes in Brook, *Harley Lyrics*, and Bennett and Smithers, *Verse and Prose*, *passim*.

38 See H. J. Chaytor, *The Troubadours and England* (Cambridge, 1923). J. Audiau, *Les Troubadours et l'Angleterre* (Paris, 1927) is less cautious, and R. S. Briffault, *The Troubadours* (Bloomington, Ind., 1965), pp. 38, 40, 237–8, quite extravagant.

39 A. Jeanroy, *Les Origines de la poésie lyrique en France au Moyen Age* (3rd ed., Paris, 1925).

40 Brook, *Harley Lyrics*, Nos 3, 7, 14: see Bennett and Smithers, *Verse and Prose*, p. 322. A. T. E. Matonis, recognising the bilingualism that existed along the Anglo-Welsh border, argues, in *MP* 70 (1972–3), 91–108, for extensive influence of Celtic (i.e. Welsh and Irish) poetry in the Harley Ms, not only in the love-lyrics but in all those that use complex formal devices of stanza, rhyme, alliteration and concatenation: the analysis in this article of the language and form of the English poems is unfortunately not always accurate.

41 The cult of the obscure among the troubadours. For Dafydd, see J. P. Clancy,

*Medieval Welsh Lyrics* (1965), and for poetic structure, especially p. 10.

42  4.32, 14.76: *wore*: troubled pool, *fen*: mud.

43  P. Dronke, *Medieval Latin and the Rise of European Love-Lyric*, vol. I (Oxford, 1965), pp. 117–25.

44  E.g. Bernart de Ventadorn, 'Lo tems vai e ven e vire', No. 23 in *Introduction á l'Étude de l'ancien Provençal*, ed. F. R. Hamlin, P. T. Ricketts and J. Hathaway (Geneva, 1967). This poem is not untypical.

45  Brook, *Harley Lyrics*, Nos 15, 18, 20, 22, 26. See above, p. 98.

46  This stanza first appears in a poem in Trinity 323: Brown, *XIIIth Century*, No. 24. It is also the stanza of several of the Harley love-lyrics.

47  Lines 29–32 in the better, later text printed in *Religious Lyrics of the XIVth Century*, ed. C. Brown (Oxford, 1924; 2nd ed., rev. G. V. Smithers, 1957), No. 89. For the Harley text, see Böddeker, *Altenglische Dichtungen*, pp. 198–205.

48  Woolf, *English Religious Lyric*, p. 14.

49  A stanza of 'Suete Iesu, king of blysse', for instance, appears in the margin of some Anglo-Norman civic records at Wilton (Brown, *XIVth Century*, p. 245).

50  As in *Annot and John*, quoted above, p. 126. For a useful analysis of No. 23, see S. Manning, *Wisdom and Number* (Lincoln, Neb., 1962), pp. 100–5.

51  Brown, *XIIIth Century*, pp. 235–7. The poems are Nos 31–2 in Brook, *Harley Lyrics*. See the note by Betty Hill in *NQ* 19 (1972), 46–7.

52  Cf. 17. 6–7 and Thomas of Hales's *Luue-Ron*, 73; 17. 15 and *Three Sorrowful Tidings* (Brown, *XIIIth Century*, Nos 11–12).

53  See *Erthe upon Erthe*, ed. Hilda M. R. Murray (EETS 141, 1911).

54  See above, p. 99. This poem is to be distinguished from the corrupt and bowdlerised text of the Digby *Maximian* which also appears in Harley (Böddeker, *Altenglishe Dichtungen*, pp. 244–53).

55  Robbins calls them 'closet hymns' (*Secular Lyrics of the XIVth and XVth Centuries*, p. xxi). F. E. Patterson (*The Middle English Penitential Lyric*, New York, 1911, p. 22) thinks of them as intended for devotional purposes. Herebert's own rubric—'Qui usum huius quaterni habuerit, oret pro anima dicti fratris'—is not entirely unambiguous.

56  This is proven: see H. Gneuss, 'William Hereberts Übersetzungen', *Anglia* 78 (1960), 169–92. Carleton Brown, who printed 14 of the 19 poems in *Religious Lyrics of the XIVth century*, Nos 12–25, assumed that they were introduced into sermons (p. xiv). The existence of Nicholas Bozon's *Contes Moralisés*, a favourite source of sermon exempla, elsewhere in the MS would argue that it is in part a preacher's handbook.

57  Viz. the old long line and its stanzaic derivatives (e.g. alternate rhyming quatrains, $a^4b^3a^4b^3$ or $a^4b^3c^4b^3$, based on the long line with medial rhyme), the short couplet and tail-rhyme.

58  R. H. Robbins, 'Middle English carols as processional hymns', *SP* 56 (1959), 559–82; 'Friar Herebert and the carol', *Anglia* 75 (1957), 194–8. For the opposite view, see R. L. Greene, *Early English Carols* (Oxford, 1935), Introduction, e.g. p. xcii, and the same author's *Selection of English Carols* (Oxford, 1962), p. 44.

59  See a note on Herebert by A. G. Little in *EHR* 49 (1934), p. 302.

60  Merton College, Oxford, MS 248. See Brown, *XIVth Century*, Nos 35–41.

61  Advocates' Library, Edinburgh, MS 18.7.21. See H. G. Pfander, 'The medieval friars and some alphabetical reference-books for sermons', *MÆ* 3 (1934), 19–29; Brown, *XIVth Century*, Nos 55–76; E. Wilson, *A Descriptive Index of the English Lyrics in John of Grimestone's Preaching Book* (Medium Ævum Monographs, n.s. 2, 1973).

62  Woolf, *English Religious Lyric*, pp. 27, 85.

63  Brown, *XIVth Century*, Nos 1, 2, 70, 74 (not all are from Grimestone, but Grimestone has examples of all). See Woolf, *English Religious Lyric*, Chap. II, *passim*.

64  Brown, *XIVth Century*, Nos 75, 73, 63.

65  See R. H. Robbins, 'Popular prayers in Middle English verse', *MP* 36 (1939), 337–50; 'Private prayers in Middle English verse', *SP* 36 (1939), 466–75. For the latter, see Brown, *XIVth Century*, Nos 122–4.

66  Lines 624–5, in *The Lay Folks' Mass Book*, ed. T. F. Simmons, EETS 71 (1879), printed from B. M. MS Royal 17.B.xvii.

67  See pp. 15–30, 82–7, 347 in *The Prymer or Lay Folks' Prayer Book*, ed. H. Littlehales, EETS 105, 109, (1895–7); Brown, *XIVth Century*, Nos 30, 34, 55.

68  These include the fine piece known as 'Pety Job', in *Twenty-six Political and other Poems*, ed. J. Kail, EETS 124 (1904), p. 120.

69  See line 123: *The Wheatley Manuscript*, ed. Mabel Day, EETS 155 (1921), p. 24.

70 B. M. MS Add. 17376. See *The Poems of William of Shoreham*, ed. M. Konrath, EETS, ES 86 (1902), p. 127; Brown, *XIVth Century*, No. 32.

71 'He is likely to have derived from the medieval stylistic traditions . . . no more than a general sense of sanction in using ornaments in his prose' (Hope Emily Allen, *Writings ascribed to Richard Rolle and Materials for his Biography*, MLA Monograph series III, 1927, p. 80).

72 *English Writings of Richard Rolle*, ed. Hope Emily Allen (Oxford, 1931), p. 51.

73 From the *English Psalter*, in *English Writings*, p. 6.

74 From *The Form of Living*, in *English Writings*, p. 106. See also Patterson, *Penitential Lyric*, pp. 17–18.

75 Allen, *Writings*, pp. 303–6.

76 From *The Form of Living*, in *English Writings*, p. 107.

77 *English Writings*, pp. 70, 42.

78 Well illustrated by the cross-references in the modernised texts of F. M. M. Comper, *The Life and Lyrics of Richard Rolle* (1928), pp. 228–71.

79 *English Writings*, p. 45; cf. pp. 74, 111, and Woolf, *Religious Lyric*, p. 171.

80 Known as *Meditations on the Life and Passion of Christ* in the edition of Charlotte d'Evelyn (EETS 158, 1921). For comment on this edition see Woolf, *Religious Lyric*, p. 161.

81 Lines 49–52, 109–10. For parallels with the *Meditations*, see the edition of d'Evelyn pp. 61–3.

82 The tradition is carried on in *Yorkshire Writers, Richard Rolle of Hampole*, ed. C. Horstmann, 2 vols (1895–6), which nevertheless remains the only edition of much of this writing.

83 See Allen, *Writings*, pp. 306–11; Comper *Richard Rolle*, pp. 315–18; and for further notes on the MS, T. W. Ross, 'Five 15th-century "Emblem" verses from B. M. Addit. MS 37049', *Speculum* 32 (1957), 274–82.

84 Allen, *Writings*, p. 395.

85 See the table, Preservation of Texts, in C. Brown and R. H. Robbins, *The Index of Middle English Verse* (New York, 1943), p. 737.

86 Lines 1–6 of the *Incipit* to the *North English Legendary*, in *Altenglische Legenden, Neue Folge*, ed. C. Horstmann (Heilbronn, 1881), p. 3. For further references to reading, see pp. 8 (line 279), 11 (line 6), 14 (line 251), 15 (line 363), etc.

87 See above, p. 105. The *Northern Passion* is

88 See the Introduction to the edition by Frances A. Foster (EETS 166, 1926), pp. xvii–xix.

89 There are convenient accounts of these works in the second volume of the revision of J. E. Wells, *A Manual of the Writings in Middle English*, ed. J. Burke Severs (Connecticut Academy of Arts and Sciences, 1970), pp. 382, 391–4, 447–9, 460.

90 See K. Sajavaara, 'The relationship of the Vernon and Simeon manuscripts', *NM* 68 (1967), 428–39.

91 Madeleine Blaess, 'L'abbaye de Bordesley et les livres de Guy de Beauchamp', *Romania* 78 (1957), 511–18.

92 See Mary S. Serjeantson, 'The Index of the Vernon manuscript', *MLR* 32 (1937), 222–61.

93 *Minor Poems of the Vernon MS*, ed. C. Horstmann and F. J. Furnivall (EETS 98, 117, 1892–1901), XXIX. 1.

94 See A. I. Doyle, 'The Shaping of the Vernon and Simeon Manuscripts', in *Chaucer and Middle English Studies in Honour of R. H. Robbins*, ed. Beryl Rowland (1974), pp. 328–41. The presence of a number of pictures in the MS argues further for private use and inspection.

95 See Woolf, *Religious Lyric*, p. 53.

96 In Brown, *XIVth Century*, nos 95–120, as well as Horstmann.

97 In a general survey, John Stevens, *Medieval Romance* (1973), only seven of the fourteenth-century romances are mentioned, and those only briefly. See also above, p. 120, and for editions of the romances mentioned here the items cited in note 102, p. 313.

98 I refer to the earlier 'wave' of romances discussed in Chapter 4: some may have been written a little after 1300.

99 Laurel Braswell's study of the relationship between *Isumbras* and the legend of St Eustace, in *MS* 27 (1965), 128–51, illustrates well the close affinities of hagiography and 'secular' romance.

100 By L. H. Loomis, 'The Auchinleck Manuscript and a possible London bookshop of 1330–1340', *PMLA* 57 (1942), 595–627.

101 *Kyng Alisaunder*, ed. G. V. Smithers (EETS 227, 237, 1952–7), Introduction, p. 12; see also W. E. Holland, 'Formulaic diction and the descent of a Middle English romance', *Speculum* 48 (1973), 89–109. S. T. Knight argues for oral transmission in *Sir Launfal* in *MÆ* 38

(1969), 164–9. See also above, p. 113.

102 E.g. B. M. MS Add. 31042 (Thornton), B. M. MS Cotton Caligula A.ii, Cotton Galba E.ix, Bodley MS Ashmole 61, C. U. L. MS Ff.ii.38, Gonville and Caius College, Cambridge, MS 175, Advocates' Library, Edinburgh, MS 19.3.1., Lambeth Palace MS 306, Lincoln Cathedral MS 91 (Thornton), Chetham (Manchester) MS 8009, Royal Library, Naples, MS XIII.B.29. No attempt is made here at an analysis of the detailed patterns of provenance and audience that these MSS present. Enough has been said of the Auchinleck MS to give an indication of the general picture, and to make possible the brief generic analysis of the social and stylistic identity of the form that follows. For general comment on the romance MSS see D. Mehl, *Middle English Romances*, pp. 257–62, and K. Brunner, 'The Middle English Metrical Romances and their Audience', in *Studies in Medieval Literature in Honor of A. C. Baugh*, ed. M. Leach (Philadelphia, 1961), pp. 219–27; and see Appendix 2.

103 See the articles cited by Loomis, 'The Auchinleck Manuscript', p. 601.

104 It has become customary to attribute the 'Southern' *Octavian* and *Lybeaus Desconus* to Chestre as well as *Sir Launfal*: see M. Mills, in *MÆ* 31 (1962), 88–109.

105 The argument of A. McI. Trounce, in a series of articles in *MÆ* 1–3 (1932–4).

## Chapter 6   Alliterative poetry

1 E.g. the opening of *Ego Dormio*: 'Mykel lufe he schewes, þat never es irk to lufe, bot ay standand, sittand, gangand, or wirkand, es ay his lufe thynkand, and oftsyth þarof es dremande' (*English Writings of Richard Rolle*, ed. Hope Emily Allen, (Oxford, 1931), p. 61).

2 I use this term to describe verse constructed according to foreign metrical models, with a more or less regular alternation of stressed and unstressed syllables, as opposed to the rhythmical type-structure of native alliterative verse (see above, p. 16).

3 Lines 3243–56 (ed. EETS 121–2). See further the comments in my article on 'The development of Middle English romance', *MS* 27 (1965), 91–116.

4 Elizabeth Salter, '*Piers Plowman* and *The Simonie*', *Archiv* 203 (1967), 241–54. The Auchinleck text is printed in T. Wright, ed., *Political Songs of England* (Camden Society, 1839), pp. 323–45.

5 See above, p. 144, and, for further discussion of the metre of these poems, the editions by L. F. Casson of *Degrevaunt* (EETS 221, 1949), pp. xxxi–xli, and by M. Mills of *Lybeaus Desconus* (EETS 261, 1969), pp. 20–2.

6 *English Writings*, p. 64.

7 There is much information, and many dubious statistics, in the general book on the subject, J. P. Oakden, *Alliterative Poetry in Middle English*, 2 vols (Manchester, 1930–5).

8 The lines are in fact loosely translated from Guido's own prologue: *Historia Destructionis Troiae*, ed. N. E. Griffin (Cambridge, Mass., 1936), p. 3.

9 J. R. Hulbert, 'A hypothesis concerning the alliterative revival', *MP* 28 (1931), 405–22. For criticism, see Elizabeth Salter, 'The alliterative revival', *MP* 64 (1966–7), 146–50, 233–7.

10 But perhaps not as exclusive as once was thought: for some, it is a matter of being excluded *from* Chaucerian verse. On the subject generally, see Marie Borroff, *Sir Gawain: a Stylistic and Metrical Study* (New Haven and London, 1962).

11 A. McIntosh, 'The Textual Transmission of the Alliterative *Morte Arthure*', in *English and Medieval Studies Presented to J. R. R. Tolkien*, ed. N. Davis and C. L. Wrenn (1962), pp. 231–40.

12 Lines 8–9: ed. I. Gollancz, *Select Early English Poems*, III (2nd ed., 1930).

13 *Knight's Tale*, *CT* I. 2602–16; *Legend of Good Women*, 635–49 (Legend of Cleopatra). Chaucer is cited throughout from the 2nd edition of F. N. Robinson, *The Works of Geoffrey Chaucer* (Cambridge, Mass., 1957).

14 Salter, 'The alliterative revival', and the references on p. 233.

15 Line 5, ed. in *The Gests of King Alexander of Macedon*, ed. F. P. Magoun (Cambridge, Mass., 1929).

16 S. Moore, 'Patrons of letters in Norfolk and Suffolk', *PMLA* 27 (1912), 188–207; 28 (1913), 79–105, esp. pp. 103–5.

17 The fact that some later recensions of Robert of Gloucester's *Chronicle* use a good written text of Laȝamon (see above, p. 117) is evidence that this tenuous scribal tradition may have been monastic.

18 T. Turville-Petre, 'Humphrey de Bohun and *William of Palerne*', *NM* 75 (1974), 250–2, remarks that Humphrey spent most

of his time in Essex, and suggests that the poem was written for members of his household established in the South West Midlands.

19 It is interesting to observe that the Mortimer family, earls of March, one of the most powerful Western households (whom we have already seen associated with Harley 2253), made a special point of enlarging on their descent from Arthur and Brutus. See Mary E. Giffin, 'Cadwalader, Arthur, and Brutus in the Wigmore Manuscript', *Speculum* 16 (1941), 109–20.

20 S. S. Hussey, 'Langland's reading of alliterative poetry', *MLR* 60 (1965), 163–70.

21 It remains, however, aesthetically important and is not submitted to the kinds of licence we have seen to be characteristic of rhymed alliterative poetry (p. 151, above); in particular, the authentic character of the *b*-line (*ax*) is, in all the 'classical' poems, scrupulously preserved.

22 R. A. Waldron, 'Oral-formulaic technique and Middle English alliterative poetry', *Speculum* 32 (1957), 792–804. The assumptions about oral-formulaic usage need to be discarded (see above, p. 17), but Waldron's analysis stands perfectly well without them.

23 See L. D. Benson, *Art and Tradition in Sir Gawain and the Green Knight* (New Brunswick, N. J., 1965), pp. 151–8, 173–80.

24 See W. Matthews, *The Tragedy of Arthur* (Berkeley, 1960); *Morte Arthure* (selections) ed. J. Finlayson (York Medieval Texts, 1967), Introduction.

25 E.g. 1938, 3686, 4625, 12487 (the scribe sometimes signals them as set-pieces: 'A Tempast on þe See', etc.). Cf. *Siege of Jerusalem* 53, *Patience* 893, and see N. Jacobs, 'Alliterative storms: a topos in Middle English', *Speculum* 47 (1972), 695–719.

26 *Troilus and Criseyde*, v. 1002–3. The poet of the *Destruction* has been thought to indicate a knowledge of Chaucer's poem in line 8054. If this were true, it would argue an extraordinary self-sufficiency in alliterative poetry in its resistance to the first contacts with the new tradition of Chaucer.

27 There is a debt also to the thirteenth-century *Bible en françois* of Roger d'Argenteuil: see Phyllis Moe, 'The French source of the alliterative *Siege of Jerusalem*', *MÆ* 39 (1970), 147–54.

28 Lines 40–1: *Purity*, ed. R. J. Menner (New Haven, 1920).

29 See Charlotte C. Morse, 'The image of the vessel in *Cleanness*', *UTQ* 40 (1970–1), 202–16.

30 Cf. the account of the poem's structure in A. C. Spearing, *The Gawain-Poet* (Cambridge, 1970), pp. 41–55.

31 Ordelle G. Hill, 'The audience of Patience', *MP* 66 (1968), 103–9, suggests that it is addressed, as an exemplum of the reluctant preacher, to a clerical audience. The poem is edited by J. J. Anderson (Manchester, 1969).

32 We have seen examples in the Vernon refrain-poems (p. 142 above). See also p. 87 in the standard edition by E. V. Gordon (Oxford, 1953).

33 For this 'structural circularity' see J. A. Burrow, *Ricardian Poetry* (1971), pp. 64–6, and for an interesting parallel in the *dúnadh* of Celtic poetry see P. L. Henry, 'A Celtic-English prosodic feature', *Zeitschrift für Celtische Philologie* 29 (1962), 91–9. There are further comments on the structure of *Pearl* in I. Bishop, *Pearl in its Setting* (Oxford, 1968), 27–33. 'Numerical composition' in medieval poetry, including Dante, is treated by E. R. Curtius, *European Literature and the Latin Middle Ages* (trans. W. R. Trask, New York, 1953), pp. 501–9. For the *Pearl*-poet's knowledge of Dante, see P. M. Kean, *The Pearl: an Interpretation* (1967), pp. 120–32.

34 E. V. Gordon (ed. *Pearl*, p. xiv) is doubtful about a purely fictitious 'I' in such a poem. Bishop argues strongly (*Pearl in its Setting*, pp. 5–9) that the poem is based on autobiographical fact, and represents the author's own meditative experience and spiritual progress. This view of the poem is certainly truer to the experience of reading it than that which treats it as purely allegorical. For further discussion, see A. C. Spearing, *The Gawain-Poet*, pp. 96–170.

35 Kean (*The Pearl: an Interpretation*, pp. 53–85) argues that these images work by transformation, not contrast, and cites examples of flower and garden symbolism from patristic sources to prove that they relate to the theme of regeneration. The effect, however, within the poem, is one of contrast.

36 E. R. Panofsky, *Early Netherlandish Painting* (Cambridge, Mass., 1953), p. 180.

37 'And that discourse, which at every point has its hand on the main purpose, may well be said to come from the workshop of the rhetorician' (Dante, *Convivio*, III. iv. 26).

38 Laȝamon, it has been argued (above,

p. 81), was attempting a similar kind of variation in line-grouping. Other poems (*Cleanness, Patience, Erkenwald, Wars of Alexander, Siege of Jerusalem*) show a more or less consistent tendency to group lines in quatrains, obviously under the influence of the old monorhymed quatrain. For earlier use of the bob and wheel, see above pp. 121, 124.

39 J. A. Burrow, *A Reading of Sir Gawain and the Green Knight* (1965), is not free from such faults, but it remains the best guide to the poem. Cf. also Spearing, *The Gawain-Poet*, pp. 171–236.

40 Spearing, *The Gawain-Poet*, p. 201; D. R. Howard, *The Three Temptations* (Princeton, 1966), p. 223 *et passim*.

41 *St Erkenwald* is rejected from the *Gawain-canon* with unexpected firmness by L. D. Benson in *JEGP* 64 (1965), 393–405.

42 For a stimulating account of *Erkenwald*, see T. McAlindon, 'Hagiography into art: a study of *St Erkenwald*', *SP* 67 (1970), 472–94.

43 Cf. G. T. Shepherd, 'The nature of alliterative poetry in late medieval England', *PBA* 56 (1970), 57–76.

44 There are accounts of Langland's life in E. T. Donaldson, *Piers Plowman: the C-text and its Poet* (New Haven, 1949), pp. 199–226, and in G. Kane, *Piers Plowman: the Evidence for Authorship* (1965). The latter seems to have closed the question of multiple authorship.

45 See J. A. Burrow, 'The audience of *Piers Plowman*', *Anglia* 75 (1957), 373–84.

46 Though the poem is conventionally divided into passūs (*pl.*) it would not appear to be designed for oral delivery.

47 An excellent account of the C-text is given by Donaldson, *Piers Plowman: the C-text and its Poet*. References are to the edition by W. W. Skeat of all three texts (Oxford, 1886).

48 See, respectively, e.g. G. R. Owst, *Literature and Pulpit in Medieval England* (Cambridge, 1933), and A. C. Spearing, 'The Art of Preaching in *Piers Plowman*', in his *Criticism and Medieval Poetry* (2nd ed., 1972), pp. 107–34; J. A. Yunck, *The Lineage of Lady Meed* (Notre Dame, Ind., 1963); D. W. Robertson and B. F. Huppe, *Piers Plowman and Scriptural Tradition* (Princeton, 1951); Elizabeth Salter, *Piers Plowman: an Introduction* (Oxford, 1962), pp. 81–90; Dorothy L. Owen, *Piers Plowman: a Comparison with some Earlier and Contemporary French Allegories* (1912); M. W. Bloomfield, *Piers Plowman as a Fourteenth-Century*

*Apocalypse* (New Brunswick, N. J., 1962).

49 See T. P. Dunning, *Piers Plowman: an Interpretation of the A-Text* (1937), and 'The structure of the B-text of *Piers Plowman*', *RES*, n.s. 7 (1956), 225–37; N. Coghill, 'The pardon of Piers Plowman', *PBA* 30 (1944), 303–57.

50 See P. M. Kean, 'Justice, Kingship and the Good Life in the second part of *Piers Plowman*', in *Piers Plowman: Critical Approaches*, ed. S. S. Hussey (1969), pp. 76–110.

51 See J. Lawlor, 'The imaginative unity of *Piers Plowman*', *RES*, n.s. 8 (1957), 113–26, and *Piers Plowman: an Essay in Criticism* (1962).

52 For hypocrisy and formalism as major themes of attack in Langland, see J. A. Burrow 'Words, Works and Will: Theme and Structure in *Piers Plowman*', in *Critical Approaches*, ed. Hussey, pp. 111–24.

53 Donaldson, *Piers Plowman: the C-text and its Poet*, pp. 130–55.

54 C. S. Lewis, *The Allegory of Love* (Oxford, 1936), p. 160.

55 N. Coghill, 'The character of Piers Plowman', *MÆ* 2 (1933), 108–35 (p. 128).

56 Greta Hort, *Piers Plowman and Contemporary Religious Thought* (n.d.), pp. 56–9.

57 The term is Charles Muscatine's—*Poetry and Crisis in the Age of Chaucer* (Notre Dame, Ind., 1972), pp. 88, 106. See also Lawlor, *Piers Plowman*, pp. 254–65, and J. A. Burrow, 'The action of Langland's Second Vision', *EC* 15 (1965), 247–68.

58 *Prologue and Passus I–VII of the B text*, ed. J. A. W. Bennett (Oxford, 1972), pp. 113–14, 183–6.

59 C. S. Singleton, of Dante, in *Dante Studies*, I (Harvard U. P., 1954), p. 13, quoted by P. Cali, *Allegory and Vision in Dante and Langland* (Cork U. P., 1971), p. 186. For a fine account of 'Langland's kind of poetry', see N. Coghill, 'God's wenches and the light that spoke', in *English and Medieval Studies presented to J. R. R. Tolkien*, ed. Davis and Wrenn, pp. 200–18.

60 N. Denholm-Young, *The Country Gentry in the Fourteenth Century* (Oxford, 1969), p. 38, refers to the practice by which retired civil servants might enter monasteries as 'corrodars' or pensioners; see also T. F. Tout, 'The English Civil Service in the fourteenth century', *BJRL* 3 (1916), 185–214. For the way in which detailed information of events in London might easily reach the provinces, see the letter written by a member of Richard II's entourage, describing his reconciliation with the City of London, 1392, which

ended up at Llanthony Priory (Helen Suggett, in *EHR* 62, 1947, 209–13).

61 Something of an alliterative *topos*: Cf. the openings of *Winner and Waster* and the *Parlement*, and *Destruction of Troy*, 326–48, with its original in Guido's *Historia* (ed. Griffin), p. 14. There are some interesting manipulations of point of view, e.g. 885, 889. As an allegory of good government, the passage in *Mum* recalls the frescoes of Ambrogio Lorenzetti at Siena and anticipates familiar scenes in Shakespeare's history-plays (e.g. *Richard II*, III. iv).

62 In the famous Percy Folio, discovered by Bishop Percy in 1769 at a house in Shifnal, Shropshire, being used by maids to light the fire. The edition used here is that of I. Gollancz (*Select Early English Poems*, V, 1930); there is a useful introduction in the earlier edition by J. H. Hanford and J. M. Steadman, *SP* 15 (1918), 223–94.

63 But cf. D. V. Harrington, 'The personifications in *Death and Liffe*', *NM* 68 (1967), 35–47.

64 Various versions are printed in *The Babees Book*, ed. F. J. Furnivall (EETS 32), pp. 9–12, and *Queene Elizabethes Achademy*, ed. Furnivall (EETS, ES 8), pp. 65–7.

65 Printed in *Reliquiae Antiquae*, ed. T. Wright and J. O. Halliwell (2 vols, 1841–3), i. 81, 84, 85, 291: only the second is unrhymed.

66 In K. Sisam, ed., *Fourteenth Century Verse and Prose* (Oxford, 1921), p. 169.

67 All three pamphlets are edited by P. L. Heyworth (Oxford, 1968).

68 The stress-count refers to rhythmical stress (i.e. as for alliterative verse) not metrical; the wheel, unlike the metrical wheel of *Gawain*, is based on alliterative half-line equivalents and is often ambiguous rhythmically.

69 The *Pistill* and the four poems of the second group are all in the misnamed *Scottish Alliterative Poems*, ed. F. J. Amours (STS, I, 27, 38). A more recent edition of *Susannah* is that of Alice Miskimin (Yale U.P., 1969), and of the *Awntyrs* that of R. J. Gates (Philadelphia, 1969). *Summer Sunday* is in *Historical Poems of the XIVth and XVth Centuries*, ed. R. H. Robbins (New York, 1959), No. 38, where it is supposedly a lament for Edward II: it is shown to be of early fifteenth-century provenance in an article by T. Turville-Petre, '"Summer Sunday", "De Tribus Regibus Mortuis", and "The Awntyrs off Arthure": three poems in the thirteen-line stanza', *RES*, n.s. 25 (1974), 1–14, an article important

for its discussion of this whole group of rhymed alliterative poems. The extensive influence of alliterative form in other fifteenth-century poetry, as in Awdelay and the York plays, is dealt with in Chapter 8, pp. 249, 255 below.

70 Other *Gawain*-poems, *The Marriage of Sir Gawaine*, *The Weddynge of Sir Gawen and Dame Ragnell* and *The Avowing of King Arthur*, associate the Tarn Wadling with spectral phenomena: see Ralph Hanna III, '*The Awntyrs off Arthure*: an interpretation', *MLQ* 31 (1970), 275–97. See also *The Three Dead Kings*, a poem closely associated in form and technique with the *Awntyrs*: a Western copy of a Northern text, it was included by Awdelay among his collected poems, and is discussed below, p. 250.

71 Such resemblances were the basis for the attribution of many of these poems in the late nineteenth century to 'Huchown of the Awle Ryale', a poet mentioned in Wyntoun's Chronicle as author of 'the gret Gest off Arthure,/And the Awntyre off Gawane,/The Pystyll als off Swete Swsane' (Amours, *Scottish Alliterative Poems*, p. lii). The proliferating theories were scotched by H. N. MacCracken in *PMLA* 25 (1910), 507–34: there surely was a Scottish poet called Huchown (dim. of Hugh), presumably a palace chaplain, but the only poem with which his name can plausibly be linked is *Susannah*.

72 W. Matthews, *The Tragedy of Arthur* (Berkeley, 1960), sees political allusion in this poem, as well as the *Awntyrs*, to relations between Scotland and England (e.g. p. 166).

73 E.g. *John the Reeve* in the Percy Folio, *King Edward and the Shepherd* in *Middle English Metrical Romances*, ed. W. H. French and C. B. Hale (New York, 1930), and *The King and the Hermit* in C. H. Hartshorne, *Ancient Metrical Tales* (1829).

74 See M. P. McDiarmid, 'Richard Holland's *Buke of the Howlat*: an interpretation', *MAE* 38 (1969), 277–90.

75 See N. F. Blake, *Caxton and his World* (1969), pp. 183–7, and 'Caxton and courtly style', *E & S* 21 (1968) 29–45.

76 See R. H. Robbins, 'A *Gawain* epigone', *MLN* 58 (1943), 361–6, and 'The poems of Humfrey Newton, Esquire, 1466–1536', *PMLA* 65 (1950), 249–81.

77 See C. A. Luttrell, 'Three North-west Midland manuscripts', *Neoph.* 42 (1958), 38–50, esp. pp. 48–50.

78 Ed. J. P. Oakden, Chetham Society Miscellanies 94 (1935). Another version appears in the Percy Folio.

## Chapter 7  Court poetry

1 The difference of language is admittedly only one of several factors that need to be taken into account here: see J. H. Fisher, *John Gower: Moral Philosopher and Friend of Chaucer* (New York, 1964), p. 92.

2 If I seem to use Anglo-Norman and French as interchangeable synonyms, the reason is that their relationship in the fourteenth century is rather complex. Anglo-Norman, with its insular forms, grammatical licences and generally hybrid character, is still the language of law, government and business, as well as Chaucer's Prioress ('For Frenssh of Parys was to hire unknowe'), but there was a movement among more sophisticated writers, including Gower, to purify the language and make it approximate more closely to continental French.

3 See Helen Suggett, 'The use of French in England in the later Middle Ages', *TRHS* 28 (1946), 61–83.

4 *Le Livre de Seyntz Medicines*, ed. E. J. Arnould (Oxford, 1940), p. 239.

5 *Chronicles*, translated by Lord Berners, ed. G. C. Macaulay (1895), p. 430.

6 G. Mathew, *The Court of Richard II* (1968), p. 110.

7 Edith Rickert, *Chaucer's World*, ed. Clair C. Olson and M. M. Crow (New York, 1948), p. 141.

8 K. B. McFarlane, *Lancastrian Kings and Lollard Knights* (Oxford, 1972), p. 119.

9 *Complaint of Chaucer to his Purse*, 22–4, in *The Works of Geoffrey Chaucer*, ed. F. N. Robinson (2nd ed., Cambridge, Mass., 1957), p. 540. All quotations from Chaucer here are from this edition.

10 Such a frontispiece reflects only the tastes of the manuscript's editor and of the illuminator. It is, at the least, highly stylised, and Patricia Kean is properly cautious in entitling it 'The Poet Reading to an Audience' on her frontispieces to the two volumes of *Chaucer and the Making of English Poetry* (1972): even then, the book from which he is 'reading' is not very obvious in the picture. There is some unguarded speculation in Margaret Galway, 'The *Troilus* Frontispiece', *MLR* 44 (1949), 161–77, and in A. Brusendorff, *The Chaucer Tradition* (London and Copenhagen, 1925), pp. 19–23.

11 In *Le Dit dou Florin*: see *Meliador*, ed. A. Longnon (SATF 36), Introduction, p. iii.

12 *Confessio Amantis* (ed. EETS, ES 81–2), Prologue (unrevised version), 51–3. Gower's increasing disillusion with Richard led him to excise the passage in 1393.

13 Edith Rickert, 'King Richard II's books', *Library*, 4th series, 13 (1932–3), 144–7.

14 Mathew, *Court of Richard II*, p. 40.

15 For the extent of their interest, see W. C. Curry, *Chaucer and the Medieval Sciences* (New York, 1926; 2nd ed., 1960), and G. G. Fox, *The Medieval Sciences in the Works of John Gower* (Princeton, 1931).

16 K. B. McFarlane, *The Nobility of Later Medieval England* (Oxford, 1973), p. 161. For the education of the nobility, see pp. 41–7, 228–47: McFarlane draws heavily on fifteenth-century evidence.

17 *The Master of Game*, ed. W. A. and F. Baillie-Grohman (1904), pp. 3–4.

18 K. B. McFarlane, *Lancastrian Kings*, pp. 22–3, 116–17; *Nobility of Later Medieval England*, p. 244.

19 Mathew, *Court of Richard II*, pp. 32–3.

20 McFarlane, *Lancastrian Kings*, pp. 139–226.

21 Ed. and trans. by J. Webb, *Archaeologia* 20 (1824), 1–423.

22 Chaucer, *Complaint of Venus*, 82. This poem is a translation of ballades by Granson. See H. Braddy, *Chaucer and the French Poet Graunson* (Baton Rouge, 1947).

23 See G. L. Kittredge, 'Chaucer and some of his friends', *MP* 1 (1903–4), 1–18; J. L. Lowes, 'The Prologue to the *Legend of Good Women* as related to the French *Marguerite* poems and the *Filostrato*', *PMLA* 19 (1904), 593–683; *The Floure and the Leafe*, ed. D. A. Pearsall (Nelson's Medieval and Renaissance Library, 1962), pp. 22–6.

24 Edith Rickert, 'Thou Vache', *MP* 11 (1913–14), 209–25.

25 For some discussion of this controversial episode, see *Chaucer Life-Records*, ed. M. M. Crow and Clair C. Olson (Oxford, 1966), pp. 343–7.

26 Lines 1–2 quote *Knight's Tale*, I. 1785–6. Clanvowe's works are edited and discussed by V. J. Scattergood in *EPS* 9 (1965), 47–83, 10 (1967), 33–56, and *Anglia* 82 (1964), 137–49.

27 See R. S. Loomis, 'Was Chaucer a Free Thinker?' in *Studies in Medieval Literature in Honor of A. C. Baugh*, ed. M. Leach (Philadelphia, 1961), pp. 21–44.

28 The Host refers to the Parson as 'a Lollere' in the cancelled Epilogue to the

*Man of Law's Tale*, II. 1173.

29 M. V. Clarke, *Fourteenth Century Studies* (Oxford, 1937), p. 120.

30 *Lenvoy de Chaucer a Scogan*, 15, 18–19, 29–32.

31 *A Moral Balade*, 65–6, 126, printed in *Chaucerian and other Pieces*, ed. W. W. Skeat (Oxford, 1897), pp. 237–44.

32 III.iv.249, in *Chaucerian and other Pieces*, p. 123. Usk also borrows from Langland.

33 Fisher, *John Gower*, pp. 78–88.

34 Sylvia L. Thrupp, *The Merchant Class of Medieval London* (Ann Arbor, 1948, repr. 1962), pp. 160, 162.

35 See the excellent chapter in D. W. Robertson, *Chaucer's London* (New York, 1968), pp. 179–222.

36 R. J. Schoeck, 'A legal reading of Chaucer's *Hous of Fame*', *UTQ* 23 (1953), 185–92.

37 Edith Rickert, 'Chaucer at school', *MP* 29 (1931–2), 257–74.

38 J. A. W. Bennett, 'Chaucer's Contemporary', in *Piers Plowman: Critical Approaches*, ed. S. S. Hussey (1969), pp. 310–24; Jill Mann, *Chaucer and Medieval Estates Satire* (Cambridge, 1973), pp. 208–12.

39 *Complaint of Venus*, 79–82: Chaucer touches the statement with characteristic irony by incorporating it in a 10-line stanza on only two rhymes, impeccably handled. For further evidence of his poetic self-consciousness, see *Troilus*, v. 1786–99; *Legend of Good Women*, Prologue 1–88; *House of Fame*, 1091–100, 1876–82; *Man of Law's Tale*, Introduction, *CT* II. 45–89; and see R. O. Payne, *The Key of Remembrance: a Study of Chaucer's Poetics* (New Haven, 1963), pp. 60–90.

40 Lydgate, *Troy-Book* (ed. EETS, ES 97, 103, 106, 126), ii. 4697–700. For further comments by Lydgate, see D. Pearsall, *John Lydgate* (1970), pp. 63–5 and notes; for Hoccleve, *Regement of Princes* (ed. EETS, ES 72), 1958, 2077, 4978. See also Caroline F. E. Spurgeon, *500 Years of Chaucer Criticism and Allusion*, Vol. I (Cambridge, 1925), pp. 15 ff.

41 P. M. Kean tries to show, not altogether unsuccessfully, that their language is more carefully chosen than I suggest here: *Chaucer and the Making of English Poetry*, Vol. II, pp. 216–37.

42 The difficulty of reading *Sir Gawain*, by contrast, is partly that it represents a dialectal *cul de sac*, but even with Gower, a London poet, the proportion of his French borrowings which survive in

modern English is much lower than with Chaucer: see J. Mersand, *Chaucer's Romance Vocabulary* (New York, 1937), pp. 44–7. In a sense Chaucer's was the gamble that came off. He is also assisted, incidentally, for the modern reader, by the long-established habit of printing his text without obsolete letters (*p. 3*).

43 See Rosemond Tuve, *Seasons and Months: Studies in a Tradition of Middle English Poetry* (Paris, 1933), pp. 52–8.

44 Mersand, *Chaucer's Romance Vocabulary*, counts 1180 (p. 53): see pp. 159–73.

45 L. H. Loomis, 'Chaucer and the Auchinleck MS', *Essays and Studies in Honor of Carleton Brown* (New York, 1940), pp. 111–28; 'Chaucer and the Breton Lays of the Auchinleck MS', *SP* 38 (1941), 14–33.

46 D. S. Brewer, 'The Relationship of Chaucer to the English and European Traditions', in *Chaucer and Chaucerians*, ed. D. S. Brewer (1966), pp. 1–38.

47 J. A. Burrow, *Ricardian Poetry* (1971), pp. 12–23.

48 See, e.g. Pearsall, *John Lydgate*, pp. 52–5; V. L. Rubel, *Poetic Diction in the English Renaissance* (Modern Language Association of America, Revolving Fund Series XII, New York, 1941), pp. 14–30.

49 C. Muscatine gives a brilliant account of Chaucer's development of his 'mixed' style in *Chaucer and the French Tradition* (Berkeley, 1957), still the best critical study of Chaucer.

50 Chaucer used a French translation of Petrarch's Latin for the *Clerk's Tale*, and a French intermediary for Boccaccio's Italian in *Troilus*: see R. A. Pratt, 'Chaucer and *Le Roman de Troyle et de Criseida*', *SP* 53 (1956), 509–39. His Ovid is often the medieval French *Ovide Moralisé*.

51 Original and translation are printed side by side in R. Sutherland, *The Romaunt of the Rose and Le Roman de la Rose* (Oxford, 1967).

52 For some analysis of the poem's diffuseness, especially in relation to the custom of oral delivery, see A. C. Spearing, *Criticism and Medieval Poetry* (1964), Chap. I.

53 Chaucer is not uninfluenced by the native (or naturalised) short couplet, but his techniques, especially in the development and control of the verse-paragraph, are quite different, and the differences are nowhere more clearly exemplified than in the passages chosen from the romances and Chaucer by P. M. Kean (*Chaucer*

and the Making of English Poetry, Vol. I,
pp. 6–10) for comparison.

54 There is no basis for the view, expressed
by J. G. Southworth (Verses of Cadence,
Oxford, 1954) and others, that Chaucer's
pentameter is really a form of the native
four-stress line. See M. L. Samuels,
'Chaucerian Final "-e"', NQ 19 (1972),
445–8.

55 The form is from French, the name
ultimately from a tenuous connection
with the French chant royal, fortified by a
further association with the royal
authorship of the Kingis Quair, in the
same 7-line stanza: see H. N. MacCracken,
in MLN 24 (1909), 31–2.

56 See English Verse between Chaucer and
Surrey, ed. E. P. Hammond (Durham,
N. C., 1927), pp. 120–3; Pearsall,
John Lydgate, p. 59.

57 Les Arts poétiques du XII^e et du XIII^e siècle,
ed. E. Faral (Paris, 1923).

58 J. M. Manly, 'Chaucer and the
rhetoricians', PBA 12 (1926), 95–113.
There is a simple but full account of the
teaching of the rhetoricians in Janette
Richardson, 'Blameth nat me': a Study of
Imagery in Chaucer's Fabliaux (The Hague,
1970), pp. 18–54, and sensitive analysis of
Chaucer's debt to the tradition in Dorothy
Everett, 'Chaucer's "Art Poetical"', in
her Essays on Middle English Literature,
ed. Patricia Kean (1955), pp. 149–74,
and in R. O. Payne, Key of Remembrance.

59 See J. J. Murphy, 'A new look at Chaucer
and the rhetoricians', RES, n.s. 15 (1964),
1–20.

60 See Lydgate's Fall of Princes, ed. H.
Bergen, Vol. IV (EETS, ES 124, 1927),
p. 268; and cf. Gervais de Melkley, Ars
Versificaria, in Faral, Les Arts poétiques,
p. 328.

61 Complaint of Venus, 28; Granson is quoted
from Braddy, Chaucer and Graunson, p. 62.

62 R. A. Pratt, in 'Chaucer's use of the
Teseida', PMLA 62 (1947), 598–621,
examines Chaucer's successive returns to
the Teseida in Anelida, the Parlement,
Troilus, the Legend of Good Women
Prologue, the Franklin's Tale, as well as
his full-scale rehandling of the poem in the
Knight's Tale.

63 For John of Wales, see R. A. Pratt,
'Chaucer and the hand that fed him',
Speculum 41 (1966), 619–42. The Wife of
Bath's Prologue is particularly rich in such
metamorphosis. For some similar practice,
see R. Hazelton, 'Chaucer and Cato',
Speculum 35 (1960), 357–80.

64 I refer, of course, to the attempt by

D. W. Robertson, in his monumental
Preface to Chaucer (Princeton, 1962)
and other works, to read Chaucer's
poems as more or less covert allegories of
Augustinian doctrine. Robertson's
work cannot be ignored: many of the
disciples he has carried in his wake have
perhaps mistaken the ark of the covenant
for a band-waggon.

65 For which see Brusendorff, The Chaucer
Tradition, pp. 13–27.

66 These deficiencies begin to be repaired in
the sensitive and erudite analysis of
J. Norton-Smith, Geoffrey Chaucer (1974),
pp. 16–34, 213–25.

67 J. Wimsatt, in his excellent book, Chaucer
and the French Love-Poets (Chapel Hill,
N. C., 1968), argues for a debt even in the
fictionalising process.

68 Payne, Key of Remembrance, pp. 91–111.

69 R. W. Frank, however, in Chaucer and the
Legend of Good Women (Cambridge, Mass.,
1972), sees the legends as being closely
and effectively related to Chaucer's
development of independent narrative,
'narrative without reference to the
conventions or moralizings ordinarily
appealed to' (p. 19).

70 See e.g. R. M. Jordan, Chaucer and the
Shape of Creation (Cambridge, Mass.,
1967), pp. 64–75.

71 Mann, Chaucer and Medieval Estates
Satire, pp. 188–202.

72 In G. L. Kittredge, Chaucer and his
Poetry (Cambridge, Mass., 1915), and
R. M. Lumiansky, Of Sondry Folk: the
Dramatic Principle in the Canterbury Tales
(Austin, 1955).

73 R. E. Kaske, 'The Knight's interruption of
the Monk's Tale', ELH 24 (1957), 249–68.

74 I have dealt with this subject at more
length in 'The Canterbury Tales',
Sphere History of Literature in the English
Language, Vol. I, The Middle Ages, ed.
W. F. Bolton (1970), pp. 163–94.

75 Complete Works of John Gower, ed. G. C.
Macaulay, 4 vols (Oxford, 1899–1902),
Introduction, pp. vii, clxvii. This is the
standard edition of Gower. The
authoritative biographical and critical
work is J. H. Fisher, John Gower; Moral
Philosopher and Friend of Chaucer (New York,
1964).

76 H. N. MacCracken, 'Quixley's Ballades
Royal (?1402)', Yorkshire Archaeological
Journal, 20 (1909), 33–50.

77 Confessio, viii. 2941–57. The excision of
this passage in later recensions of the
Confessio has encouraged speculation
about a possible quarrel or breach of

relations between Gower and Chaucer: see Fisher, *John Gower*, pp. 27–36, 119.

78 J. A. W. Bennett, 'Gower's "Honeste Love"', in *Patterns of Love and Courtesy: Essays in Memory of C. S. Lewis*, ed. J. Lawlor (1966), pp. 107–21 (p. 119).

79 I have tried to talk about this in 'Gower's narrative art', *PMLA* 81 (1966), 475–84.

80 Most of it was ascribed to Chaucer or Lydgate in the fifteenth and sixteenth centuries. Scholarly investigation has stripped them of much of it (the Lydgate canon is still insecurely established, and the canon of Chaucer's lyrics often doubtful), thus adding to an already large corpus of anonymous poetry. Ethel Seaton in her book *Sir Richard Roos: Lancastrian Poet* (1961), has claimed nearly all of it, as well as some genuine Chaucer, for Roos, translator of *La Belle Dame Sans Merci*: the book is valuable for its evocation of fifteenth-century court-culture and for its individual insights as well as for Dr Seaton's unrivalled knowledge of fifteenth-century poetry and poetic MSS, but it should be said at once that her attribution of over 400 poems to Roos, on the basis of double acrostic anagrams for which there is no precedent and no evidence, is quite preposterous. She has destroyed even the reasonable case that might be made, on reasonable grounds, for Roos.

81 For Shirley, and the other Chaucerian MSS mentioned here, see Brusendorff, *The Chaucer Tradition*; Eleanor P. Hammond, *Chaucer: a Bibliographical Manual* (New York, 1908), pp. 326–49; also her *English Verse between Chaucer and Surrey*, pp. 191–7, and articles in *Anglia* 28 (1905), 1–28, and 30 (1907), 320–48; Pearsall, *John Lydgate* (1970), pp. 72–82.

82 The former contains some important and authoritative texts of Chaucer, including the only copy of the revised Prologue to the *Legend of Good Women*; it looks like the first attempt to collect 'Chaucer's Works', a kind of First Folio.

83 R. H. Robbins, 'The Findern Anthology', *PMLA* 69 (1954), 610–42. Compare also 'The Poems of Humfrey Newton, Esquire, 1466–1536', edited by R. H. Robbins in *PMLA* 65 (1950), 249–81.

84 E. G. Stanley, in *NM* 60 (1959), 287–8.

85 This is one of the themes of Pearsall, *John Lydgate*, where I deal with Lydgate in detail.

86 This of course was a recurrent tendency in medieval love-poetry: see Wimsatt, *Chaucer and the French Love-Poets*, e.g.

pp. 38–9.

87 *Minor Poems of Lydgate*, ed. H. N. MacCracken: Part II, Secular Poems (EETS 192, 1934), p. 379.

88 These two poems are included in *John Lydgate: Poems*, ed. J. Norton-Smith, (Oxford, 1966), where the former is entitled *A Complaynt of a Loveres Lyfe*.

89 Cf. C. S. Lewis, *The Allegory of Love* (Oxford, 1936), p. 241.

90 J. Norton-Smith, 'Lydgate's changes in the *Temple of Glas*', *MÆ* 27 (1958), 166–72.

91 New evidence for a date 1416 makes Henry's patronage, which is attested in 11 of 42 MSS, more of a likelihood: see J. Parr, 'The astronomical date of Lydgate's *Life of Our Lady*', *PQ* 50 (1971), 120–5.

92 See J. V. Fleming, 'Hoccleve's "Letter of Cupid" and the "Quarrel" over the *Roman de la Rose*', *MÆ* 40 (1971), 21–40.

93 He did have a copy of *Troilus and Criseyde* made for him when Prince of Wales, the beautiful Campsall MS (*Troilus and Criseyde*, ed. R. K. Root, Princeton, 1926, p. lii), now in the Pierpont Morgan Library, New York.

94 For recent discussion, and full references, see the editions by J. Norton-Smith (Oxford, 1971), from which quotation here is made, and by M. P. McDiarmid (1973).

95 See M. M. Crow, 'John of Angoulême and his Chaucer Manuscript', *Speculum* 17 (1942), 86–99; also P. Strohm, 'Jean of Angoulême: a fifteenth-century reader of Chaucer', *NM* 72 (1971), 69–76.

96 For discussion, see the edition of the English Poems by R. Steele (EETS 215, 220, 1941–6). Hammond (*English Verse between Chaucer and Surrey*, p. 214) does not accept this view.

97 Originally by H. N. MacCracken, who edits the poems, 'An English friend of Charles of Orléans', *PMLA* 26 (1911), 142–80. See also Hammond, *English Verse between Chaucer and Surrey*, pp. 198–201, and *Secular Lyrics of the XIVth and XVth Centuries*, ed. R. H. Robbins (Oxford, 1952; 2nd ed., 1955), pp. 282–6. There is not, to be candid, a shred of evidence that either Charles or Suffolk wrote poetry in English.

98 Cf. 'And yf it please yowe to here of my welefare, I am not in good heele of body ner of herte, nor schall be tyll I here from yowe': Margery Brews's valentine to John Paston III (1477),

in *The Paston Letters*, ed. J. Gairdner,
3 vols (1900), no. 783 (ii. 170).

99 As we see from his ballade *On the
Departing of Thomas Chaucer* (ed. Norton-
Smith, p. 4).

100 Allusions to date and occasion in
these (e.g. XIV. 21, XVIII, XX.
5, 104) and other poems (e.g. the
*Compleynt* added to some MSS of *The
Temple of Glass*, lines 248, 259, 585;
Robbins, *Secular Lyrics*, No. 198, lines
52–3) give us glimpses of lost circumstance.

101 Referred to in the Prologue to the
*Legend of Good Women* (F. 72, 188–96);
see the Introduction, pp. 22–9, to my
edition of *The Floure and the Leafe* and *The
Assembly of Ladies* (Nelson's Medieval and
Renaissance Library, 1962).

102 See J. Stephens, 'The Questioning of Love
in *The Assembly of Ladies*', *RES*, n.s.
24 (1973), 129–40.

103 Ed. Jane B. Sherzer (Berlin, 1903).
Also in the *English Poets* of Alexander
Chalmers, Vol. I (1810), p. 378, entitled
'Chaucer's Dream'; this volume is the
last resting-ground of many 'Chaucerian'
pieces.

104 See Chapter II of Ethel Seaton, *Sir
Richard Roos*.

105 E.g. *To my Soverain Lady* and *A Goodly
Balade*, both in *Chaucerian and other
Pieces*, ed. Skeat (an important collection
of Chaucer apocrypha); *The Flower and
the Leaf* and *The Assembly of Ladies*; and
Robbins, *Secular Lyrics*, No. 172 (No. 157
occurs, weirdly spelt, in a Burgundian
*chansonnier*, and No. 207 declares itself
translated from French).

106 E.g. B. M. MS Royal 19.A.iii, which
includes both *La Belle Dame* and the
*Débat du Coeur et de l'Oeil* (below).

107 Ed. E. P. Hammond, *Anglia* 34 (1911),
235–65.

108 See J. Huizinga, *The Waning of the Middle
Ages* (1924; Anchor Books, New York,
1954), esp. Chaps IX, XIX and XX.

109 Printed by MacCracken with the Fairfax
poems, *PMLA* 26, p. 179.

110 Ed. E. P. Hammond, *MP* 21 (1923–4),
379–95.

111 E.g. Robbins, *Secular Lyrics*, Nos 130, 178,
190, 198, 207. *The Craft of Lovers*, a
dialogue between a lover and his lady
(Chalmers, *English Poets*, p. 558), is
surely a parody ('My name is trew loue
of carnal desidery,/Of mans copulacion
the very exemplary') of such language: see
A. K. Moore, in *Neoph.* 35 (1951),
231–8.

112 Ed. E. P. Hammond, *JEGP* 7 (1907–8),

95–109, the former also in *English Verse
between Chaucer and Surrey*, pp. 210–13.

113 E.g. the Ballade *Against Women Unconstant*,
in Robinson's Chaucer (p. 540); Lydgate's
*Servant of Cupid Forsaken* (*Minor Poems*,
p. 427), *Beware of Doublenesse* (p. 438),
and *Ballade per Antiphrasim* (p. 432);
*A Ballad Pleasant* and *O Mossie Quince* in
Chalmers, *English Poets*, pp. 563–4, and in
*Cambridge Middle English Lyrics*, ed. H. A.
Person (Seattle, 1953), Nos 48–9;
Robbins, *Secular Lyrics*, Nos 208–12,
*Medieval English Love-Lyrics*, ed. T.
Stemmler (Tubingen, 1970), pp. 90–3,
104–5. *The Hood of Green*, indisputably
filthy, is in an authoritative Lydgate MS
(Pearsall, *Lydgate*, p. 77). Much of this
material is in Trinity College, Cambridge,
MS R. 3.19, a sixteenth-century sub-
courtly miscellany.

114 See the excellent chapter in J. Stevens,
*Music and Poetry in the Early Tudor Court*
(1961), pp. 154–202.

115 Ed. W. C. Hazlitt, *Remains of the Early
Popular Poetry of England* (1864–6),
i. 69–78; E. P. Hammond, in *Englische
Studien* 59 (1925), 5–16.

116 C. S. Lewis, *English Literature in the
Sixteenth Century* (Oxford, 1954), p. 230.

117 R. Southall, 'The Devonshire Manuscript
collection of early Tudor poetry 1532–41',
*RES*, n.s. 15 (1964), 142–50 (p. 150).

118 Cf. the comments on Wyatt by H. A.
Mason, *Humanism and Poetry in the Early
Tudor Period* (1959), pp. 167–78.

119 A poem in rhyme royal (Fairfax poems,
ed. MacCracken, no. XIV) is so adapted,
and also 'renewed' in ballade stanza by the
addition of extra lines (ed. EETS 15,
p. 68).

120 See above, p. 325. Of the verses in the
letter, the first couplet looks to be
borrowed, the rest Margery's own
composition.

121 No. 870, *Paston Letters*, ed. Gairdner,
iii. 302.

122 E.g. 'ffinis quod Quene Elyzabeth' at the
end of a love-poem in MS Rawlinson
C.86, f. 55v (Seaton, *Sir Richard Roos*, p.
430), or 'Explicet Amor per ducem
Eboracensis nuper factus' in Robbins,
*Secular Lyrics*, No. 205.

123 For the use of *The Temple of Glass* in
B. M. MS Sloane 1212, see *Lydgate:
Poems*, ed. Norton-Smith, p. 143, and
Seaton, *Sir Richard Roos*, p. 376; for the
copying of extracts from *Troilus*, see
R. H. Robbins, 'The Lyrics', in
*Companion to Chaucer Studies*, ed. Beryl
Rowland (Toronto, 1968), pp. 313–31

(pp. 315–16), and for its use in C.U.L.
MS Ff.i.6 see Robbins, 'The Findern
Anthology', *PMLA* 69, p. 616.

124 First lines from Lydgate's *Life of Our
Lady*, the 'Findern' poems, No. L (ed.
Robbins, p. 638), and Fairfax No. VII
(ed. MacCracken, p. 160). Cf. also the
relation of Nos 130 and 205 in Robbins,
*Secular Lyrics*.

125 Stevens, *Music and Poetry in the Early
Tudor Court*.

126 Ethel Seaton, 'The Devonshire Manuscript
and its medieval fragments', *RES*,
n.s. 7 (1956), 55–6.

127 R. Harrier, 'A printed source for the
Devonshire Manuscript', *RES*, n.s.
11 (1960), 54.

## Chapter 8   The close of the Middle Ages

1 See D. Fox, 'Chaucer's Influence in
Fifteenth-century Poetry', in *Companion to
Chaucer Studies*, ed. Beryl Rowland (Toronto
and Oxford, 1968), pp. 385–402
(p. 399); also P. M. Kean, *Chaucer and the
Making of English Poetry*, 2 vols (1972),
ii. 212–15.

2 See D. Pearsall, *John Lydgate* (1970),
pp. 70–1.

3 H. S. Bennett, *Chaucer and the Fifteenth
Century* (Oxford, 1947), p. 100. For the
spread of education generally, see J. W.
Adamson, 'The extent of literacy in
England in the 15th and 16th centuries',
*Library*, 4th Series, 10 (1929–30),
163–93; C. L. Kingsford, *Prejudice and
Promise in XVth Century England* (Oxford,
1925), pp. 34–43; A. F. Leach, *The
Schools of Medieval England* (1915), pp.
235–76; and especially N. Orme,
*English Schools in the Middle Ages* (1973),
Chap. 7.

4 In *Minor Poems*, ed. H. N. MacCracken,
Vol. II (EETS 192, 1934). The title
('The Boy standing at the Table') is taken
from Latin treatises on the subject. There
is full discussion of Lydgate's poetry in
my book, referred to above, which will
not be repeated here.

5 See H. S. Bennett, *Chaucer and the Fifteenth
Century*, pp. 104–23, 156–60; 'The author
and his public in the 14th and 15th
centuries', *E & S* 23 (1937), 7–24;
'Caxton and his public', *RES* 19 (1943),
113–19; 'Science and information in
English writings of the 15th century',
*MLR* 39 (1944), 1–8; 'The production
and dissemination of vernacular MSS in
the Middle Ages', *Library*, 5th Series,
1 (1946–7), 167–78.

6 There was, for instance, a lower-class
vernacular literature of parental
instruction in the fourteenth century,
such as *The Good Wife taught her Daughter*
(ed. T. F. Mustanoja, Helsinki, 1948).

7 Pearsall, *John Lydgate*, p. 33.

8 D. Pearsall, 'Notes on the manuscript of
*Generydes*', *Library*, 5th Series, 16 (1961),
205–10.

9 G. Bone, 'Notes on Roger Thorney',
*Library*, 4th Series, 12 (1931–2), 284–306.

10 Pearsall, *John Lydgate*, p. 76.

11 C. F. Bühler, 'Sir John Paston's *Grete
Booke*, a fifteenth-century "best-seller"',
*MLN* 56 (1941), 345–51.

12 This is assuming that the scribe of B. M.
MS Add. 31042 and Lincoln Cathedral
MS 91 (A.5.2) is Robert Thornton of
East Newton in Yorkshire: see the
Introduction in the edition of the *Liber de
Diversis Medicinis* by Margaret S. Ogden
(EETS 207, 1938), pp. viii–xv.

13 B. M. MS Egerton 1995, associated with
Gregory (the Skinner), is discussed in
*The Historical Collections of a Citizen of
London*, ed. J. Gairdner, Camden Society,
n.s. 17 (1876), and by Bennett, *Chaucer
and the Fifteenth Century*, p. 164; Richard
Hill's Commonplace Book, Balliol MS
354, is edited by R. Dyboski (EETS, ES
101, 1908). The 'Findern Anthology'
(see above, p. 213) may be regarded as a
communal commonplace-book. See
further, *Secular Lyrics of the XIVth and XVth
Centuries*, ed. R. H. Robbins, (Oxford,
1952; 2nd ed., 1955), p. xxiv.

14 See K. H. Vickers, *Humphrey Duke of
Gloucester* (1907), Chaps IX, X, and
R. J. Mitchell, *John Tiptoft, 1427–1470*
(1938), pp. 150–71.

15 See T. Brewer, *Memoir of the Life and
Times of John Carpenter* (1856), p. 130,
and *The Paston Letters*, ed. J. Gairdner,
3 vols (1910), iii. 300–1; also Pearsall,
*John Lydgate*, pp. 72, 171.

16 There is a link here with the circle of
Bokenham's patrons among the provincial
nobility and landed gentry of East
Anglia: see below, p. 251.

17 Pearsall, *John Lydgate*, p. 180; and further,
pp. 70–7, 160–86.

18 A phrase used in M. H. Keen, *England in*

the Later Middle Ages (1973), p. 334.

19 Ed. H. N. MacCracken, in Yorkshire Archaeological Journal, 20 (1909), 33–50.

20 See R. H. Robbins, 'The poems of Humfrey Newton, Esquire, 1466–1536', PMLA 65 (1950), 249–81. Robbins refers to other little-known examples from the fifteenth century of this class of amateur poets, 'the country squire or town gentleman' (p. 279). See also above, pp. 188 and 213.

21 MS Harley 1735: see R. H. Robbins, 'John Crophill's ale-pots', RES, n.s. 20 (1969), 182–9.

22 The lively little satire on London called London Lickpenny (ed. Eleanor P. Hammond, English Verse between Chaucer and Surrey, Durham, N. C., 1927, p. 237) in rough four-stress ballade stanza is not, unfortunately, now accepted as Lydgate's.

23 Fall of Princes (ed. EETS, ES 121–4), iii. 3830–1. There is a brief list of standard Lydgate editions on p. 301 of my book, John Lydgate, and a complete list of Lydgate's poems in W. F. Schirmer, John Lydgate: a Study in the Culture of the XVth century (publ. in German, 1952; English translation by Ann E. Keep, 1961), pp. 264–73.

24 Fall of Princes, i. 346–50. Lydgate's taste in this matter is perfectly representative of the century: See D. S. Silvia, 'Some Fifteenth-Century Manuscripts of the Canterbury Tales', in Chaucer and Middle English Studies in Honour of R. H. Robbins, ed. Beryl Rowland (1974), pp. 328–41.

25 This effective line, characteristically structured as a formal rhetorical antithesis with chiasmus, is a favourite with Lydgate; he repeats it, with understandable economy, in Fall of Princes, i. 6931, Temple of Glass, Compleynt, 49, and varies it elsewhere (see Hammond, English Verse between Chaucer and Surrey, p. 444). The next line is a creditable imitation of Troilus, iv. 1221.

26 This is substantially the explanation put forward by Eleanor P. Hammond, in 'The 9-syllabled pentameter line in some post-Chaucerian manuscripts', MP 23 (1925–6), 129–52, and English Verse between Chaucer and Surrey, pp. 17–24, 83–6. See also Pearsall, John Lydgate, pp. 60–3.

27 History of English Prosody, 3 vols (1906), i. 218–34.

28 C. S. Lewis, in 'The 15th-century heroic line', E & S 24 (1938), 28–41, presents essentially this case, with some fanciful additions, but neglects the specialised

perversity of Lydgatian verse.

29 Beryl Smalley, English Friars and Antiquity in the Early 14th Century (Oxford, 1960); Pearsall, John Lydgate, pp. 37–45.

30 The verse translation (ed. EETS 205) of Boccaccio's tale of Guiscardo and Ghismonda from the Decameron made by Gilbert Banester, a Kentish gentleman (d. 1487), is based on a French version of the Latin translation of this single tale, selected for its tragic 'moralitee', by Leonardo Bruni in 1438.

31 Secular Lyrics, ed. Robbins, No. 107. See A. S. G. Edwards, 'Selections from Lydgate's Fall of Princes: a check-list', Library, 5th Series, 26 (1971), 337–42.

32 Eleanor P. Hammond, 'Lydgate and Coluccio Salutati', MP 25 (1927), 49–57.

33 The attribution of 'humanistic' interests to Lydgate in the studies of Schirmer (cited above, note 23) and A. Renoir (The Poetry of John Lydgate, 1967) is a piece of wishful as well as falsely evolutionary thinking.

34 Lines 112–14, in John Lydgate: Poems, ed. J. Norton-Smith (Oxford, 1966), p. 24 (see also p. 138).

35 Both these poems are in rhyme royal, which Lydgate treats with a degree of formal ornateness between that of couplet and ballade.

36 See E. F. Jacob, 'Florida verborum venustas', BJRL 17 (1933), 264–90; Pearsall, John Lydgate, pp. 44–5.

37 John Lydgate: Poems, ed. Norton-Smith, p. 195; Pearsall, John Lydgate, p. 31.

38 Lines 43–9 in the edition of Norton-Smith (where the poem is called Balade in Commendation of Our Lady), p. 26. See also p. 143, and Isabel Hyde, 'Lydgate's "Halff Chongyd Latyne": an illustration', MLN 70 (1955), 252–4.

39 Ed. J. Lauritis, R. Klinefelter and V. Gallagher, Duquesne Studies, Philological Series, No. 2 (Pittsburgh, 1961), iii. 1761–4.

40 The evidence is discussed in J. Mitchell, Thomas Hoccleve (Urbana, Ill., 1968), pp. 115–18. Hoccleve's poems are edited in EETS, ES 61, 72, 73.

41 See A. G. Rigg, 'Hoccleve's Complaint and Isidore of Seville', Speculum 45 (1970), 564–74.

42 The relation of the Male Regle to the tradition of the penitential lyric is discussed in an article by Eva M. Thornley, NM 68 (1967), 295–321. For an interesting discussion of Hoccleve's 'autobiographical' poems in relation to medieval attitudes towards madness,

see Penelope B. R. Doob, *Nebuchadnezzar's Children: Conventions of Madness in Middle English Literature* (New Haven and London, 1974), Ch. 5.

43 The *Disticha* are edited by M. Forster in *Archiv* 115 (1905), 298–323 and 116 (1906), 25–40. The *Letter to Lydgate* is in Hammond, *English Verse between Chaucer and Surrey*, p. 188, and the translation of *The Secrees of old Philisoffres* in EETS, ES 66.

44 For which he is commended by A. B. Ferguson, *The Indian Summer of English Chivalry* (Durham, N. C., 1960), pp. 135, 195. His poems are in EETS, ES 76.

45 See, e.g., Pamela Gradon, *Form and Style in Early English Literature* (1971), pp. 369–73.

46 *Palladius* is edited in EETS 52, 72, and also by M. Liddell (Berlin, 1896), *Knyghthode and Bataile* in EETS 201. See H. N. MacCracken, 'Vegetius in English', *Kittredge Anniversary Papers* (1913; New York, 1967), pp. 389–403.

47 The only apt comparison is the *Epitaph on the Duke of Bedford* analysed by J. M. Berdan (*Early Tudor Poetry*, New York, 1920, pp. 129–33), which has Latin side-notes drawing attention to its bewildering variety and complexity of Latin metres and rhetorical figures.

48 See the edition by Sir George Warner (Oxford, 1926), p. xl.

49 Ed. Charlotte d'Evelyn, MLA Monograph Series 6 (Boston, 1935).

50 Cf. also Lydgate's *Stans Puer ad Mensam*. Side by side with upper-class works like these there are verse etiquette books at lower social levels, including works of instruction for servants, such as the *Boke of Nurture* (also in EETS 32) of John Russell, Usher and Marshall of the Hall to Humphrey of Gloucester, and also poems of homely moral instruction such as *How the Good Wiif tauȝte hir douȝtir* and *How the Wise Man tauȝt his sonne* (ed. EETS, ES 8) and at much greater length, *Ratis Raving* (ed. STS III. 11). These works are in the non-formal metres such as the short couplet and the old long line, where *The Babees Book* and its affiliates are in rhyme royal. See further *The Good Wife taught her Daughter*, ed. T. F. Mustanoja (Helsinki, 1948), with useful introduction.

51 In *Theatrum Chemicum Britannicum*, ed. Elias Ashmole (1652; reprinted with Introduction by A. G. Debus, *Sources of Science*, No. 39, New York, 1967), p. 121. Ashmole prints both poems; there are extracts from Ripley in Hammond,

*English Verse between Chaucer and Surrey*, p. 252, and Norton's *Ordinal* is now edited by J. Reidy (EETS 272).

52 E.g. Nos 77, 79, 94, 104, 105, 120–3, in *Secular Lyrics*, ed. Robbins.

53 Lines 666–9: ed. R. Spindler (Leipzig, 1927). C. S. Lewis praises the poem extravagantly in *The Allegory of Love* (Oxford, 1936), pp. 262–4.

54 See N. F. Blake, *Caxton and his World* (1969), pp. 70–1.

55 E.g. No. 27 in *Religious Lyrics of the XVth Century*, ed. C. Brown (Oxford, 1939). See S. Wenzel, 'The English verses in the *Fasciculus Morum*', in *Chaucer and Middle English Studies in Honour of R. H. Robbins*, ed. Beryl Rowland (1974), pp. 230–48.

56 Brown, *XVth Century*, No. 17.

57 Brown, *XVth Century*, Nos 115, 127–9. See above, p. 134.

58 Ed. W. H. Black, Percy Society (1842). See above, p. 135.

59 E.g. Brown, *XVth Century*, Nos 12, 38, 51, 69, 91, 112; also, in other MSS, Nos 8, 13, 36.

60 *The Plowman's Tale* (ed. W. W. Skeat, *Chaucerian and Other Pieces*, Oxford, 1897, pp. 147–90), an early fifteenth-century Lollard piece which first appears with 'Canterbury Prologue' in Thynne's collected Chaucer of 1542 (see A. N. Wawn, 'The genesis of *The Plowman's Tale*', *YES* 2 (1972), 21–40), abandons its first refrain, begun at line 53, with these words: 'To accorde with this worde "fal"/ No more English can I find;/Shewe another now I shall,/For I have moche to say behind' (477–80). We might comment also on the stimulus given by ballade-rhyme to the use of semi-aureate vocabulary, where there were large groups of words ending, for instance, in *-able, -aunce, -cioun*.

61 Compare Thornton (ed. EETS 26), pp. 88, 107, and Nos 81, 86 in *Religious Lyrics of the XIVth Century*, ed. Carleton Brown (Oxford, 1924; 2nd ed., rev. G. V. Smithers, 1957); and Lambeth (ed. EETS 24), pp. 8, 22, and Nos 48, 84 in Brown, *XIVth Century*.

62 For this development, and others, see Rosemary Woolf, *English Religious Lyric in the Middle Ages* (Oxford, 1968).

63 This poem provides an interesting example of reworking: the Harley 3954 text (in EETS 15, p. 204) adapts the poem to a treatment of the Resurrection and the refrain, from line 96, as 'For resurrexit! non mortuus est!'

64 This characteristic fifteenth-century

development is demonstrated in extreme and 'hysterical' (Woolf, *English Religious Lyric*, p. 259) form in a long Pietà poem, *De Arte Lacrimandi* ('The Art of Weeping'), ed. R. M. Garrett, *Anglia* 32 (1909), 269–94.

65 There is much of this in the fifteenth as in other centuries: religious carols often take over burdens or themes from secular lyrics (e.g. R. L. Greene, *Early English Carols* (Oxford, 1935), Nos 261, 270), *The Nutbrown Maid* (see below, p. 266) provokes *The New Notbroune Mayd upon the Passion of Cryste* (in *Early Popular Poetry of England*, ed. W. Carew Hazlitt, 4 vols, 1864–6, iii. 1), while a stanza added at the beginning of a poem in Trinity College, Cambridge, MS R.3.19 (in *Cambridge Middle English Lyrics*, ed. H. A. Person, Seattle, 1953, p. 14) turns it from 'An Epistle to his Mistress' into 'An Orison of the Blessed Virgin'.

66 See above, p. 132. All the carols are edited by R. L. Greene, *Early English Carols* (Oxford, 1935), and he provides an excellent *Selection of English Carols* (Oxford, 1962) with more recent introduction and annotation.

67 The former, particularly, has been frequently analysed, as in S. Manning, *Wisdom and Number* (Lincoln, Neb., 1962), pp. 158–67; D. Gray, *Themes and Images in the Medieval English Religious Lyric* (1972), pp. 101–6; Sarah A. Weber, *Theology and Poetry in the Middle English Lyric* (Ohio State University, 1969), pp. 55–60.

68 Woolf, *English Religious Lyric*, pp. 183–6, 198–210, 389–91; Gray, *Themes and Images*, pp. 41–55. There is also the poem on *The Symbols of the Passion* (ed. EETS 46), which appeared in many MSS, usually with simple illustrations (Woolf, *English Religious Lyric*, p. 208).

69 Ed. E. Borgström, *Anglia* 34 (1911), 498–525. Cf. also the two complaints of Christ, the second in the form of a dialogue, in EETS 15, pp. 161, 169.

70 In EETS 24, p. 91. Cf. *Parce michi Domine* ('The Bird with Four Feathers'), No. 121 in *Religious Lyrics of the XIVth Century*, ed. Brown.

71 For an identification of Halsham, see Helen P. South, 'The question of Halsam', *PMLA* 50 (1935), 362–71 (she identifies in Harley 7333 another versifying esquire, Richard Sellyng, p. 371). For Stokys, see C. Brown, in *MLN* 54 (1939), 131–3.

72 Line 1113 in *Altenglische Legenden, Neue*

*Folge*, ed. C. Horstmann (Heilbronn, 1881), p. 307. All the pieces that follow in this paragraph are edited, rather haphazardly, in this volume or its companion, *Sammlung Altenglischer Legenden*, ed. C. Horstmann (Heilbronn, 1878).

73 Like *The Stacyons of Rome* (e.g. EETS 25) and *Stasyons of Jerusalem* (Horstmann, *Alt. Leg.*, p. 355), frequently copied. There is a lively poem of *The Pilgrims' Sea-Voyage* in EETS 25.

74 Called 'The Adulterous Falmouth Squire' in EETS 15, p. 96. These poems are in tail-rhyme and use popular romance techniques.

75 See S. Moore, 'Patrons of letters in Norfolk and Suffolk, c. 1450', *PMLA* 27 (1912), 188–207; 28 (1913), 79–106.

76 See P. J. Lucas, 'John Capgrave, O. S. A. (1393–1464), Scribe and "Publisher"', *Trans. Cambridge Bibl. Society*, 5 (1969), 1–35.

77 With the exception of a few lines in Medwall's *Nature* (c. 1495), there is no prose in drama until after 1580: see J. F. Macdonald, 'The use of prose in English drama before Shakespeare', *UTQ* 2 (1933), 465–81.

78 Viz. *York Plays* (ed. Lucy Toulmin Smith, Oxford, 1885), *Chester Plays* (ed. EETS, ES 62, 65), *Towneley Plays* (ed. EETS, ES 71), and *Ludus Coventriae* (ed. EETS, ES 120). NB also the two *Coventry Plays* (ed. EETS, ES 87) and *Non-Cycle Plays and Fragments* (ed. EETS, Supp. 1).

79 No. 123 in *Secular Lyrics*, ed. Robbins.

80 See *The Northern Passion*, ed. Frances A. Foster (EETS 147, 1916), pp. 81–101; *A Stanzaic Life of Christ*, ed. Frances A. Foster (EETS 166, 1926), pp. xxviii–xliii (also R. H. Wilson, in *SP* 28, 1931, 413–32; W. A. Craigie, '*The Gospel of Nicodemus* and the *York Mystery Plays*', in *An English Miscellany presented to Dr. Furnivall* (Oxford, 1901), pp. 52–61. *Nicodemus* is edited by C. Horstmann, in *Archiv* 53 (1874), 389–424.

81 See G. S. Taylor, 'The English "Planctus Mariae"', *MP* 4 (1906–7), 605–37, and 'The relation of the English Corpus Christi play to the Middle English religious lyric', *MP* 5 (1907–8), 1–38; also Woolf, *English Religious Lyric*, pp. 44, 205, 263–5, 318–19.

82 See J. W. Robinson, 'The art of the York Realist', *MP* 60 (1962–3), 241–51.

83 See further *The Wakefield Pageants in the Towneley Cycle*, ed. A. C. Cawley (Manchester, 1958), pp. xxvii–xxx,

and H. J. Diller, 'The craftsmanship of the Wakefield Master', *Anglia* 83 (1965), 271–88.

84 See J. Burke Severs, in *MP* 42 (1944–5), 137–51. The Abraham and Isaac story is one that lends itself readily to un-comic but effective dramatic treatment: this no doubt is why there are two good plays on the subject independently preserved.

85 See the note by D. C. Baker and J. L. Murphy in *RES*, n.s. 19 (1968), 290–3.

86 Convenient selections in *Specimens of the Pre-Shakesperean Drama*, ed. J. M. Manly, 2 vols (Boston, 1897), and *Chief Pre-Shakspearean Dramas*, ed. J. Q. Adams (Cambridge, Mass., 1924).

87 J. E. Bernard, *The Prosody of the Tudor Interlude* (New Haven, 1939).

88 E.g. 11128–45, cf. *Knight's Tale*, *CT*, I. 2600–18, 2636–7; see B. J. Whiting, 'A fifteenth-century Chaucerian: the translator of *Parthonope of Blois*', *MS* 7 (1945), 40–54.

89 See my article in *RES*, n.s. 12 (1961), 229–37, where I also associate the rhyme royal *Generydes* with the author of *The Assembly of Ladies*.

90 See R. W. Ackerman, 'Henry Lovelich's *Merlin*', *PMLA* 67 (1952), 473–84.

91 Ed. Elizabeth McCausland, *Smith College Studies in Modern Languages*, Vol. IV, No. 1 (1922).

92 Ed. W. E. Mead (Boston, 1904).

93 A. B. Ferguson, *The Indian Summer of English Chivalry*, pp. 13–17.

94 Ed. K. Breul (Oppeln, 1886).

95 See the edition of A. J. Bliss (Oxford, 1954; 2nd ed., 1966), p. xvi.

96 See above, p. 321. Its contents are edited by J. W. Hales and F. J. Furnivall, 3 vols (1867–8) with a supplementary volume of *obscenae*.

97 There is a text of *Landevale* on pp. 105–28 of *Sir Launfal*, ed. A. J. Bliss (Nelson's Medieval and Renaissance Library, 1960).

98 C. S. Lewis, *English Literature in the Sixteenth Century* (Oxford, 1954), p. 68. *Eger and Grime* is edited, in both versions, by J. R. Caldwell, *Harvard Studies in Comparative Literature*, 9 (Cambridge, Mass., 1933).

99 Mabel van Duzee, *A Medieval Romance of Friendship: Eger and Grime* (New York, 1963), p. 9.

100 Ed. Laura Sumner, *Smith College Studies in Modern Languages*, Vol. V, No. 4 (1924).

101 Both ed. A. Kurvinen, *Sir Gawain and the Carl of Carlisle* (Helsinki, 1951).

102 There is a convenient one-volume condensation of Child's collection, *English and Scottish Popular Ballads*, ed. Helen C. Sargent and G. L. Kittredge (Boston and New York, 1904). Some short Robin Hood plays of the fifteenth century are edited in Adams, *Chief Pre-Shakespearean Dramas*, pp. 345–9.

103 See J. C. Holt, 'The origins and audience of the ballads of Robin Hood', *Past and Present* 18 (1960), 89–110.

104 It has perhaps been confusion of the two questions that is partly responsible for the debate among historians about the Robin Hood ballads. R. H. Hilton, 'The origins of Robin Hood', *Past and Present* 14 (1958), 30–44, sees them in their origins as the literature of peasant discontent, Holt ('Origins and audience') as the literature of the gentry. M. Keen, *The Outlaws of Medieval Legend* (1961) and 'Robin Hood—peasant or gentleman?' *Past and Present* 19 (1961), 7–15, thinking more of fifteenth-century audiences, sees the bias against 'the establishment' as indicative of no specific audience, neither peasants nor knights.

105 The first in Percy, the next two in *Remains of the Early Popular Poetry of England*, ed. W. Carew Hazlitt, 4 vols (1864), i. 4–10, 12–34, the last in *Middle English Metrical Romances*, ed. W. H. French and C. B. Hale (New York, 1930), p. 950.

106 For these and other MSS, see the Notes on Manuscripts in R. L. Greene's *Selection of English Carols*, pp. 170–85, and cf. the Introduction to *Secular Lyrics*, ed. Robbins, pp. xxvi–xxx.

107 Robbins, *Secular Lyrics*, Nos 13, 29, 43.

108 For examples, see *Historical Poems of the XIVth and XVth Centuries*, ed. R. H. Robbins (Oxford, 1959), Nos 16–18, 24, 75, and, on the whole subject, V. J. Scattergood, *Politics and Poetry in the Fifteenth Century* (1971).

109 For the two kinds of propagandist poem, see Robbins, *Hist. Poems*, Nos 27–9, 31–2, 77–8, 82, 84, 87, 90–2; 30, 40, 70, 76, 79, 88–9, 93–4.

110 For these three groups, see Robbins, *Hist. Poems*, Nos 49–63; 42, 71–4; 13–15 (see also EETS 124, Nos I–XIV).

111 Robbins, *Secular Lyrics*, Nos 61–71, 75, 82–7.

112 Robbins, *Secular Lyrics*, Nos 113, 115–17.

113 In the edition of J. Prinz (Berlin, 1911), in *Middle English Metrical Romances*, ed. French and Hale, p. 990, and in Hazlitt, *Remains*, iii. 44–53, respectively.

331

114 Edited, respectively, in Robbins, *Secular Lyrics*, No. 119, in Hazlitt, *Remains*, ii. 2–15, and in Person, *Cambridge Middle English Lyrics*, p. 53.

115 In Hazlitt, *Remains*, ii. 272–94, and frequently in anthologies.

116 A. B. Ferguson, *The Indian Summer of English Chivalry*, pp. 66–8, 209–12.

117 See further W. Wells, 'Hawes and *The Court of Sapience*', *RES* 6 (1930), 284–94.

118 See R. J. Lyall, 'Tradition and innovation in Alexander Barclay's "Towre of Vertue and Honoure",' *RES*, n.s. 23 (1972), 1–18.

119 Ed. T. H. Jamieson, 2 vols (Edinburgh, 1874). There are extracts from Barclay, and other poets mentioned in this section, in Hammond, *English Verse between Chaucer and Surrey*.

120 There is discussion of poetic diction in this period in V. L. Rubel, *Poetic Diction in the English Renaissance* (MLA Revolving Fund Series, XII, New York, 1941).

121 A suggestive book by S. E. Fish, *John Skelton's Poetry* (Yale Studies in English, 157, New Haven, 1965), analyses Skelton's poetry as 'a verbal dramatization of the problem of moral action . . . of how to write' (p. 15).

122 The lives of a number of these transitional poets document the shifting of role, particularly the assumption by poets of a greater share of public responsibility: see A. J. Slavin, 'Humanists and government in early Tudor England', *Viator* 1 (1970), 307–25.

123 Chaucer's use of a Petrarch sonnet in *Troilus* i. 400–20 is exceptional: see R. Coogan, 'Petrarch's *Trionfi* and the English Renaissance', *SP* 67 (1970), 306–27. For Morley's translation, see *Lord Morley's Tryumphes of Fraunces Petrarcke*, ed. D. D. Carnicelli (Cambridge, Mass., 1971).

124 Modernised version in Edward Arber's *Dunbar Anthology* (1901), pp. 192–216.

125 F. C. Francis, *Robert Copland, Sixteenth Century Printer and Translator* (Glasgow, 1961).

126 The former in Hazlitt, *Early Popular Poetry*, iv. 17–72, the latter edited by F. J. Furnivall (1871).

127 The former edited by J. P. Edmond (1884), the latter in Hazlitt, *Early Popular Poetry*, iv. 105–46.

128 The first two in *John Heywood's Works and Miscellaneous Short Poems*, ed. B. A. Milligan, Illinois Studies in Lang. and Lit., 41 (Urbana, Ill., 1956), the last edited by

J. S. Farmer (1908).

129 Ed. R. A. Fraser (Durham, N. C., 1955).

130 See also A. N. Wawn, 'Chaucer, *The Plowman's Tale* and Reformation propaganda: the testimonies of Thomas Godfray and *I Playne Piers*', *BJRL* 56 (1973–4), 174–92.

131 In the edition of the *Life* by S. W. Singer, 2 vols (1825–7). See A. S. G. Edwards, 'Some borrowings by Cavendish from Lydgate's *Fall of Princes*', *NQ* 18 (1971), 207–9.

132 Ed. Lily B. Campbell (Cambridge, 1938), with *Parts Added* (1946).

133 The Corpus Christi carol, 'Lully, lulley', which is associated with events of Henry VIII's reign by R. L. Greene in *MÆ* 29 (1960), 10–21. See above, p. 247.

134 Fully discussed by J. Stevens, *Music and Poetry in the Early Tudor Court* (1961).

135 From B. M. MS Royal Appx 58, which is edited with B. M. MS Add. 31922 ('Henry VIII's MS') by E. Flügel, *Anglia* 12 (1889), 225–72.

136 There is little new writing of religious lyric, first because its functions are now supplied by short printed prose texts and subsequently because of the decline of affective meditation in Protestant tradition: see Rosemary Woolf, *English Religious Lyric*, pp. 358–64.

137 Ed. E. Flügel, *Anglia* 14 (1892), 466–71.

138 No. XXXVII in *Collected Poems of Sir Thomas Wyatt*, ed. K. Muir and Patricia Thomson (Liverpool, 1969).

139 H. A. Mason, *Humanism and Poetry in the Early Tudor Period* (1959), p. 90.

140 C. S. Lewis, *English Literature in the Sixteenth Century* (Oxford, 1954), p. 156.

141 Translated and quoted in K. Wittig, *The Scottish Tradition in Literature* (Edinburgh, 1958), p. 15.

142 The Scots version of *The Buke of the Sevyne Sagis* (c. 1500) in the Asloan MS (ed. STS II. 16) is independent of the widely copied English *Seven Sages of Rome* (ed. EETS 191), and should be further distinguished from the more elaborate Scots version by John Rolland, *The Sevin Seages* (ed. STS III. 3), published in 1578.

143 See J. MacQueen, *Robert Henryson* (Oxford, 1967), pp. 4–23.

144 Henryson is edited by H. Harvey Wood (Edinburgh, 1933), Dunbar by W. M. Mackenzie (1932), Douglas in STS III. 25, 27–8, 30 and IV. 3, Lindsay in STS III. 1–2, 6, 8.

145 E. Morgan, 'Dunbar and the language of poetry', *EC* 2 (1952), 138–58.

146 Dunbar's debt to Lydgate, like that of

many 'Chaucerians', is much more direct
and extensive than his debt to Chaucer:
see P. H. Nichols, 'Dunbar as a Scottish
Lydgatian', *PMLA* 46 (1931), 214–24.

147 I. iii. 15–16. Cf. *Æneid* i. 102–3:
'Aquilone procella/velum adversa ferit'
('A storm from the North struck full on
the sail').

148 IV. vi. 40–2. Cf. *Æneid*. iv. 300–2:
'totamque incensa per urbem/bacchatur,
qualis commotis excita sacris/Thyias'
('She raved enraged through all the city,
like a Thyiad excited by the sacred
rituals'). The 'nunnys of Bachus' are
from the gloss of Ascensius, 'sacerdos
Bacchi', for 'Thyias'.

# Index

351